BANKERS

EXPORT/IMPORT TRAFFIC MANAGEMENT and FORWARDING

Sixth Edition
Revised and Enlarged

Alfred Murr

M.B.A., Dr. Jur.
Formerly Lecturer in Transportation
at New York University, School of Commerce,
and The College of Insurance, New York.

CORNELL MARITIME PRESS, INC.
Centreville   Maryland

Library of Congress Cataloging in Publication Data

Murr, Alfred,   1898-
   Export/import traffic management and forwarding.

   Bibliography: p.
   Includes index.
   1.   Freight forwarders.   2.   Shipment of goods.
I.   Title.
HE5999.A3M8   1979   380.5'2   79-18987
ISBN 0—87033—261-9

Contents

Appendices

v

Acknowledgements

The author wishes to express his sincere thanks and deep appreciation to his many good friends in the shipping, transportation and banking fields for their valuable assistance and cooperation.

Particularly to Dr. Herbert B. Dorau, Chairman, Department of Public Utilities and Transportation, School of Commerce, New York University, New York, for the encouragement, guidance and assistance in the preparation of this volume; further to my associates of D. C. Andrews & Co., Inc., for aid and counsel so freely given; to the following banks for the privilege of reproducing appropriate financial tables and forms: The Chase Manhattan Bank, New York; The First National City Bank of New York, New York; Morgan Guaranty Trust Company of New York, New York; Irving Trust Company, New York.

To the New York Chamber of Commerce and Industry for the permission of quoting from their "Foreign Consular Regulations."

To the National Foreign Trade Council, Inc., for the privilege of quoting the "Revised American Foreign Trade Definitions— 1941" and complementary paragraphs.

To the International Chamber of Commerce for the privilege of quoting their "Uniform Customs and Practice for Commercial Documentary Credits" and the pertinent provisions, further to Atlantic Mutual Insurance Company, New York.

To the American Institute of Marine Underwriters; Flota Mercante Grancolombiana S. A., New York; Grace Line Inc., New York; Moore-McCormack Lines, Inc., New York; North Atlantic Continental Freight Conference; North Atlantic Mediterrean Freight Conference; Trans-Atlantic Associated Freight Conferences, New York; U.S. Department of Commerce, Washington, D.C.; U.S. Treasury Department, Washington, D.C.; United States Lines Co., New York, go the author's thanks for supplying miscellaneous forms and other information.

United States and Foreign Export/Import Forms are printed and obtainable from UNZ & CO., 190 Baldwin Avenue, Jersey City, N.J. 07306, and many commercial stationers.

For whatever errors of omission or commission appear in this book, the writer requests the reader's indulgence, and proposes corresponding notification for possible later correction.

Introduction

Early in 1947, the School of Commerce, Accounts and Finance at New York University published as the second in a series of studies in public utilities and transportation a pamphlet entitled THE FOREIGN FREIGHT FORWARDER which, in a concise manner, explained the essential functions and operations performed by and the facilities offered by the international forwarder.

World War II had then just come to an end, and we were beginning to pick up our disrupted lines of foreign trade. The war had brought about an increased recognition of the importance and extent of traffic, particularly in foreign transportation. We now understood what a vital role shipping had played. Shipping had served well as an important instrument of national policy but was to become an important factor in the conduct of our international affairs as we undertook definite commitments for the restoration of economic order and the maintenance of peace. The business community readied itself for the resumption and extension of foreign commerce.

The war had also another profound effect upon shipping. Soldiers and seamen released from service had gained a more intimate and comprehensive knowledge of the importance of ocean transportation and traffic management. Furthermore economic disruption caused by war required the assistance of the United States in furnishing relief and rehabilitation supplies such as provided by the Marshall Plan, loans, grants and practical aids through the ECA (Economic Cooperation Administration), MSA (Mutual Security Administration) and the Point IV Program. This led to an upsurge of interest and employment in all aspects of foreign trade. With it came an increasing demand for informed personnel. Vocational schools, colleges and universities became the natural centers for those who aspired to improve and extend their education in foreign commerce and to translate their knowledge into business practice.

Arduous as vocational education for foreign trade and shipping may seem, an even higher degree of skill, patience and effort is required from those who as professional foreign traffic managers act as intermediaries between seller, buyer and the ocean carrier. These specialists called "foreign freight forwarders," represent a small but nonetheless important segment of the huge mechanism of international traffic and transportation. They offer a highly specialized and competitive service to the foreign trader, exporter and importer alike, which will not only meet their needs, but will also keep international traffic flowing freely and at the lowest possible cost. Thus they contribute to and assist in the promotion and development of our domestic and foreign commerce.

This book is an attempt to explain in a comprehensive manner the diverse functions and varied services and the whole range of ocean traffic management which forwarders have developed over more than a century, a mechanism for keeping abreast of changing foreign and domestic governmental restrictions, rules and regulations applicable in different countries, ports and on different trade routes and by providing a complete documentation service to facilitate and coordinate the movement of goods in international commerce.

The preparation of this definitive book on the subject of Export/ Import Traffic Management and Forwarding was undertaken by Dr. Murr at my suggestion for three reasons: First, because the two editions of The Foreign Freight Forwarder were out of print, secondly because no book of value on the subject had appeared during the intervening ten years, and finally, because of constantly growing need for an up-to-date, comprehensive coverage of this important phase of international business.

For Dr. Murr this may well have been a labor of love which however, combines a wealth of practical and useful experience with a deep and persistent scholarly interest.

Herbert B. Dorau

New York University
School of Commerce
Dept. of Public Utilities
   and Transportation

CHAPTER I

History of Foreign Freight Forwarding

The history of foreign freight forwarding is intimately connected with the story of maritime enterprise, which, in turn, is portrayed in the commercial histories of the successive national leaders of world trade.

At the time of the supremacy of Venice, about the beginning of the thirteenth century, this state's considerable trade via the Alps to Germany and other European countries employed the services of a middleman, the so-called "Frachter," who was a combination carter and forwarding agent. His wagon transported the merchant and his goods and he was escorted by a troop of armed guards to protect life and property against highway robberies. He also arranged for the payment of local dues and tolls on the many border crossings and attended to the change of horses on the way stations. The merchandise was conveyed under a consignment note and was sold personally by the merchant at destination.

Three hundred years later, about 1600, the "Frachter" had become an independent operator who knew his way over the lands. He was familiar with the various trade routes and mercantile centers, had organized wagon trains, had set up transportation agencies and transit storage places, had issued bills of lading and had collected freight, duties, and merchandise values from the consignees. He was the international forwarding agent of the rich merchant princes, such as the famous "Fuggers," who were the bankers and suppliers of emperors, kings, and popes. His activities had also extended to the seaboards, where he had established himself as the freight broker of the large trading houses.

Not until the end of the 18th century, however, after the upheavals and wars due to religious, political and economic developments, was security on the roads in Europe reestablished for commerce to move freely without danger. The merchants settled in the trade centers and remained in their "Kontors," or business offices. Mercantile exchange switched again from a local, territorial basis to a national area, and required, to assure its unhampered flow, the services of a transportation specialist. He, through his steady contact with the various wagon carriers, could assist the merchant in finding new markets and supplies; thus, he contributed in great measure to the extension of trade.

This expediter of traffic, now called *spediteur*, undertook this service professionally for the payment of fees and had his counterparts or

1

correspondents all over Europe. The designation "spediteur" is derived from the Latin *expedire* and the Italian *spedire*.

With the advent of the railroad, the traffic expediter's economic position increased significantly. Wherever wagon carriers and forwarding agents had maintained a transportation route that proved the traffic needs and their rentability, the railroad followed suit. However, there was a multitude of small sovereign nations that dotted the map of Europe and they lacked interest in any technical, economic, or administrative cooperation.

Cars of one railroad were not permitted to cross over to neighboring lines, and similar restrictions applied in international commerce. Railroad tariffs and bills of lading were issued only for intrastate traffic. Here was an area where the business acumen of the foreign freight forwarder could find application. Placing his experience and thorough knowledge in matters of transportation at the disposal of the railroads and trade alike, he gradually removed all obstacles. He facilitated the growth of foreign trade by being instrumental in the creation of consolidated carload services for export and import. He arranged, also, for the issuance of through bills of lading and through rates in interstate and international commerce. His expert position in the trade community is accorded recognition by his being selected for advisory positions in groups such as chambers of commerce, official railroad councils, and governmental commissions on tariffs, the judiciary and commerce.

The geophysical and geopolitical features of Europe have always been an extraordinary stimulant to economic expansion and activity. The Rhine River, which flows from the Alps to the North Sea through a valley that stirs with dynamic forces of great significance, is an international waterway, with tributaries and attending canals which are shared by Austria, Switzerland, France, Germany, and the Netherlands. The Danube opens the way to the rich East. Conversely, these same features have contributed to a phenomenon called "particularism." Resembling an hereditary disease, it permeated almost every phase of social life and in equal degree the political structure of the country. The nineteenth century still disclosed a thousand independent states and possessions. Great strides were required to eliminate this sectionalism in communication and transportation. Paradoxically, this situation, which was replete with diversity in tariffs, rates, currencies, duties, and weights and measurements necessitated the acquisition of a high degree of comprehensive knowledge, which redounded to the forwarder's benefit.

By organizing local and national associations, staffed with full-time experts in the fields of law and economics, and supported by a well-edited trade journal, the international forwarder secured for his profession the cooperation and understanding of his clientele in commerce and industry. He successfully supported his groups' efforts to ally his interests with those of the growing shipping industry. By introducing universal practices and principles, they worked in common partnership on the gradual removal of the barriers which obstructed the modernization of the European tariff structure and transportation systems.

Therefore, it is not surprising, but nevertheless indicates the initiative, perseverance, and foresight of the forwarder that his relationship with government agencies is one of mutual respect, cooperation, and benefit.

Twice—in the middle, and towards the end of the nineteenth century, when the codification of the law of commerce developed—he was called upon to render counsel. Simultaneously he gained for himself a satisfactory legal standing on the statute books.

Awareness of modern economic processes brings him in close contact with buyers and sellers encircling the globe. Their confidence in him enhances his function and indispensability.

His dominant interest in international transportation, with its relationships affecting executive planning, production and distribution by management, found concrete expression through the establishment of The Institute of Transportation Study, as an affiliated college, at the University of Cologne in 1921. The idea for this undertaking was conceived in German forwarding circles. This group had recognized a definite need for a specialized educational institute devoted exclusively to extensive research in, and teaching of, all matters pertaining to transportation.

Progressing with the ever-expanding foreign trade and its ramifications in the technological, financial, and political field, the European foreign freight forwarder of the twentieth century proved equal to his task of safely guiding his clients through the maze of government regulations and promoting the exchange of goods in all parts of the world. He serves, also, as a model to his counterpart across the Atlantic, where a young national giant is starting to measure his strength in peaceful, but competitive, participation in world trade.

In the following chapters, it will be seen how the methods, procedures, and practices of European forwarders have been adapted by his American colleagues, although regulatory, managerial, historical, and economic reasons tended to modify this influence and retard his emancipation.

American foreign freight forwarding and its development over the last two hundred years is best visualized by a study of the United States shipping business, as illustrated by the history of the greatest port in the world, New York.

In colonial days, a few years before the American Revolution, New York was already a busy, sprawling town of twenty thousand people. Along the East River, where the shipping trade centered, was a vista composed of the masts of ships berthed at the wharves. The merchants' counting houses were located at Broad, Wall, Little Dock Street—now part of Water Street—, and those parts of Front Street's "made land" which had been reclaimed from the River.

America required for her needs from abroad wrought iron, metals, cordage, sailcloth, paint, clothing, dry goods, and Sheffield wares. In exchange she exported timber, flour, wheat, beans, oats, venison, furs, skins and similar products. Exporters and importers, then called *shipping and commission merchants*, were "jacks-of-all-trades," and combined the functions of the merchant proper and the broker. Some of them owned outright the ships that carried their goods; others were part owners. Either way, they did everything themselves, including the basic documentation necessary for overseas shipping.

Aftermaths of the Revolution included a period of trade expansion; the port was busy and its facilities were taxed to capacity. New York commanded the trade of half of New Jersey, most of Connecticut, part of Massachusetts, and the rich Hudson Valley. Frequently scheduled sailings to foreign ports were the main attraction of New York, which became the preeminent gateway of America's foreign commerce. In March, 1801, the newspaper *Commercial Advertiser* said, "Shipping of the port increases faster than we can build docks." The Hudson River had been pushed back, South and West Streets had been constructed along the East and North River waterfronts, new piers and wharves had been built.

Freight specialists, known as *ship brokers*, first appeared on the scene about 1815. A veteran marine insurance "hand" defined a ship broker as "one who acted for the shipowner and merchant, and cheated them both." A more objective description is found in a "philosophical" advertisement, announcing the establishment of a freight brokerage business as follows: "The owners of ships desire freights, and those who have freights search and advertise for ships; ——almost every trader engaged in extensive business is frequently in need of a commercial agent, as every one concerned in navigation wants the services of a ship broker."

Regular transatlantic services began with the packet lines whose frequent sailings attracted that era's principal United States export cargo, cotton from the South. From Europe, whose population had been pauperized by the Napoleonic Wars and urged by exaggerated stories of American prosperity, a wave of immigrants crowded into the westbound packets. The opening of the Erie Canal in 1825, which connected New York directly with Buffalo and the Great Lakes region, created new vistas for getting rich. A steady stream of canal boats carried imported supplies, manufactured goods, and settlers to the new frontier country in the Middle West. This pathway, then called "Clinton Ditch," greatly influenced the early growth of cities like Cleveland and Chicago. It started the promotion of rapid, long-distance transportation by forwarding merchants, the forerunner of later transportation and dispatch companies, and of today's domestic freight forwarders. They established themselves on all important transiting points on route; maintained their services over both roads and canals; attended to the storage, and redispatch of goods, and collections thereon; quoted through rates; and issued waybills. These forwarding merchants acted simultaneously as commission houses which dealt in one or more staple commodities, such as grain, lumber, or produce.

Meanwhile, a new influence was manifesting its potentialities in the Port of New York, as well as in all ship-building centers, and was threatening the absolute mastery of the sailing vessel on the high seas and coastal waters. This was the appearance of the newfangled "teakettles," the steamboats. Stimulated by the invention of the steam engine by James Watt, many men in the United States were ambitious to utilize this new locomotive force.

Oliver Evans, born in Delaware in 1755, was one of them. Until his death in 1819, he believed in steam engines hauling carriages on rails. Said he: "If the present generation shall adopt canals, the next may try the railway with horses, and the third generation use the steamcarriage." Another of these railroad prophets was John Stevens of Hoboken, a so-called fanatic. During the 1820's he obtained from New Jersey and Pennsylvania charters for the construction of railroads across the states. News of the first English railroads had come across the sea by word of mouth and in reports prepared by American experts like William Strickland, who had been sent to England to learn what he could about the new steam railways there. Bitter and continuous opposition by stagecoach and canal interests and complacency about or fear of the awesome "animal" could only temporarily delay the excitement, which a few years later brought a rush of railroad chartering in most of the settled regions.

In 1827, a group of progressive citizens incorporated the Baltimore & Ohio Railroad. In quick succession other companies were chartered and put into operation. However, their efficiency was limited because of the continued use of horsepower and sail.

It was not until 1830, that the South Carolina Railroad pulled its first train of cars by steam engine. This event crushed the last resistance and heralded the beginning of a new era which, by evolution and in a roundabout way, gave birth to that transportation industry we now call *international freight forwarding*.

In 1834, when the first railroad out of Boston got under way, a young man, William Frederick Harnden, took a job as conductor on the Boston & Worcester.

A short study of his career will show how his indomitable initiative and keen vision created a completely new conception of transportation service. Prior to Harnden, the concept of carriage and attendance of goods was that of purely mechanical operation; Harnden elevated it to a personalized, intellectual one, by modernizing the application of "Service."

After three years of sixteen-hour workdays as a conductor, he decided to seek less confining work in a more active business. While spending his vacation in New York, in 1837, he discussed his situation with James W. Hale, prominent owner of the Tontine Coffee House, at the Corner of Wall and Pearl Streets. This conversation produced the idea of establishing an individual, franchised "Express Service" between Boston and New York. Until then the railroads had entrusted the safekeeping and handling of parcels and packages to their conductors. It had become obvious that this combination of essential railroad duties and supplementary delivery traffic was too much for them.

Harnden approached the Superintendent of the Boston & Providence Railroad, which also controlled the New Jersey Steam Navigation Company, operating between New York City and Providence. He obtained an exclusive franchise with special rates and privileges for the transportation of a wooden crate, five feet wide, five feet high and six feet long, marked "Contents Unknown." He also secured from this railroad a contract for a regular "Express Package Service" on its Boston-New York run. In the *Boston Herald* of February 23, 1839, the following announcement appeared:

Boston & New York Express Car

Important to Merchants, Brokers, Booksellers and others—

W. F. Harnden, for the last five years conductor and passenger clerk for the Boston and Worcester Railroad Company, has made arrangements with the Providence Railroad and New York Steamboat Companies, to run a car through from Boston to New York, and vice versa, four times a week, commencing on Monday, 4th March. He will accompany a car himself, for the purpose of purchasing goods, collecting drafts, notes and bills. Orders of all kinds promptly attended to. He will take charge of all small packages of goods, bundles, etc., that may be entrusted to his care, and see them safely delivered, and attend to forwarding merchandise of all descriptions (except that proscribed by the Railroad Companies) if directed to his care. All packages, bundles etc., must be sent to office, No. 9 Court Street, Boston, or No. 1 Wall Street, New York.

Orders may be left at J. W. Clark & Co's, 6 City Hall; Colman's Pavilion, Tremont Street; E. C. Stowell, 7 Elm Street, Boston and at J. P. Smith & Co., 30 Wall Street, New York. Will leave Boston Mondays, Wednesdays, Thursdays and Saturdays, and New York the same days.

Boston, February 23, 1839.

The first two months showed little promise, because brokers and merchants found it difficult to accept the idea of paying a service fee for what had often been previously performed gratis by stagecoach drivers, steamboat captains, or the casual traveler. However, this resistance was gradually overcome, for the business world and press generally acclaimed the advantages offered by a reliable, regular, and prompt delivery operation.

Early in 1840 Harnden extended his services to Philadelphia. His first step into the foreign field came shortly thereafter. Meanwhile, the Cunard Line had established a regular run between Liverpool and Boston, resulting in the delivery of many packages destined for New York and Philadelphia. This induced Harnden to send his partner, Dexter Brigham, Jr. to England, in November, 1840, to establish a transatlantic express line and to organize a foreign exchange business. By 1842, Harnden & Company had established offices throughout Europe.

Recognizing the need for an increased labor supply if the "West" were to be developed, they interested themselves in mass immigration by securing cheap passage on a line of Boston packet boats, as well as on Hudson River and Erie Canal boats, and by facilitating the transfer of money through the sale of bills of exchange on their foreign offices. They became akin to a popular institution for all international matters pertaining to "money, material, and man." Of course, the establishment of Harnden's Express was quickly followed by other companies, operating in every direction. Some of these later grew to vast proportions, as illustrated by Adams, Wells Fargo, United States, and American Express, for this type of business was attractive because of the possibility that it could expand and handle heavier freight loads.

Characteristic of their operation were protected and expedited service in the dispatch and delivery of goods and personal attention of a specialized nature, such as preparation and execution of papers and collection and payment of monies. Critically analyzed, the service performed was only indirectly a transportation service.

Within a decade the express business, fed by the continuous expansion of American domestic and foreign commerce, was flourishing so well that other transportation agencies, such as regular freight forwarders and ship brokers, were entering or adopting this type of operation. Individual organizations now combined all the functions of the freight broker, transportation company, and express service. A new industry had arisen.

According to *Doggett's Business Directory, Part II*, 27 Forwarding and Transportation Merchants were listed for the Port of New York, alone, in 1846. They offered: (1) to give reduced rates on small packages, thus overcoming the minimum freight by combining many parcels and/or packages on one bill of lading; (2) to act as port representatives; (3) to provide through service to foreign inland destinations; (4) to quote through rates in connection with through service on rail, canal, road, and ocean service; (5) to render C. O. D.

service; (6) to issue express export or through bills of lading from and to interior points; (7) to issue express tariffs or rate sheets showing their through rates on parcels of different weights; and (8) to issue money orders and bills of exchange.

The centralization of indirect transportation within one organization must be regarded as an historical milestone in the functional development of the foreign freight forwarding business. It was conditioned by the economic expansion of our international and domestic commerce, and supported by the growing industrial and political advance. The influence of the mechanical and technological revolution was not confined to the urban centers of the East. The railroads had cut channels from the seaboard to the West, establishing a two-way flow of goods. New factories had arisen. The American population was becoming increasingly urban and its demand for material goods grew proportionately. This led to the importation of wares, beyond the bare necessities, from the Old World. Custom tariffs and import procedures were slight obstacles, for a new member in the family of transportation specialists, the custom house broker, handled these onerous details. Transportation and shipping had grown increasingly complex by the middle of the nineteenth century; it required greater skill, training, and thought. "Specialization" was necessary, and the functional evolution of this middleman between shipper, carrier, and consignee continued.

Although the introduction of "steam and ironclads" had accelerated the decline of American flag shipping, a further serious loss must be ascribed to the fortunes of the Civil War. Congress had directed that those ships that had deserted during the emergency by transferring to foreign flags, could not return to American registry. After the war the booming cargo trade had switched to the more reliable and faster steamboats, whose lower operating costs, when translated into cheaper freight and insurance rates, had dealt a deadly blow to the American clippers and the whole Merchant Marine. Moreover, while the vast prairies and cattle ranches had attracted the adventurous youth, mining and railroading diverted the interest of the country and channeled eastern capital away from foreign trade. Between 1860 and 1890 the railway milage had increased from 30,000 miles to 166,000 miles. Connecting the Union Pacific and Central Pacific, and completing the first transcontinental railroad, the last spike was driven on the central line to the Pacific in 1869. New railways were also being built in the East, short lines were combined into systems, and countless little towns and villages in far-scattered rural regions were linked to the great cities and with one another. The Industrial Revolution was in full swing, production was expanding, and commerce was flourishing.

The Port of New York was handling over 50% of the country's leading exports and imports. New steamship services were being established; these resulted from the increased production flowing from the Middle West. Competition of every type began to develop in the shipping trade. Speed records in transatlantic crossings were news highlights. Competition also became keen for the immigrant trade. Fares and freight rates were slashed. Other ports were vying for a larger share of the profitable overseas trade. Measures were devised to cope with these varied conditions and included the formation of Steamship Conferences, which were designed to regulate competitive practices with respect to fares and rates between members, and to present a solid front against outsiders. Sir Samual Cunard organized the first such conference in New York in 1868. The disappearance of the American flag on the high seas removed automatically any possible opposition to this obviously monopolistic tendency. Port competition was successfully countered by extensive harbor improvements, and by the construction of new railroad terminals, freight stations, and docking facilities. New York thus retained its superiority, despite railroad differentials granted to rival ports.

Gradual growth of the railroads, with attendant concentration in the structural organization of the forwarding industry, marked the period from 1840 to 1890. Forwarders began to realize that their original function—to offer transportation service—had lost much of its power and inducement. However, their expert knowledge of all matters pertaining to traffic, as well as their resourcefulness, rendered them equal to the new situation. They recognized the need and importance of traffic coordination and promptness in the dispatch of shipments. They reasoned that by proper application of railroad tariffs, a reduction of transportation costs could be attained, and would be accompanied by increase in the flow of goods, which would mutually benefit the buyer and seller, and themselves. Effecting this idea marked the beginning of the consolidated export carload service. Foreign freight forwarders at the seaboard set up inland offices, not only to reach the interior exporters more directly, but also to gain for these shippers a substantial saving resulting from the lower carload freight. Moreover, the exporters profited by faster delivery and avoided the risk of damage or loss incident to transfer of less-than-carload lots at rail transfer points. In the domestic field, the former transportation, dispatch, and fast-freight companies followed the pattern to become familiar carloading and distributing companies.

By then the foreign freight forwarder had assumed a triple role: as ship broker and international forwarder, he was an agent; an export carloader; and an indirect carrier with full liability to his clients, like railroads. G. W. Engelhardt, in *New York, the Metropolis*, aptly describes the freight brokerage and forwarding business at the beginning of the twentieth century as follows:

Where, as here in New York, so much foreign business is carried on, the forwarding and freight brokerage business assumes uncommon importance. About

35 or 40 houses figure here as freight brokers, and most of them are forwarders also. The business of the freight broker is to secure favorable rates for the shipper from the steamship lines direct and connecting. He looks to the transportation agency for compensation, and attends to all the formalities with which the shipper may be unfamiliar. His clientele consists largely of inland manufacturers seeking a market for their surplus output abroad.

But the forwarding branch of the business is the more important. Export and commission houses do their business largely through the forwarder. He takes full charge of goods, attends to hauling, etc., and sees that the goods reach destination. He maintains offices in London and in other cities overseas, and is sometimes the middleman for foreign railroads. Through him rates may be obtained to any city or town on the other side. A market replete with home-made goods is his harvest, for then the movement sets in to sell the factory surplus abroad.

No better formulation of the economic value of the foreign freight forwarding business could have been made. It clearly indicates to what extent this industry was contributing to the promotion and expansion of American foreign trade by offering its specialized services as a means of reaching an ever-growing number of potential overseas buyers.

At this time our foreign commerce became a decisive factor in the conduct of our foreign relations. The United States was emerging as a true world power and evidently wished to continue this policy, which was dictated by a heavy interest in the peace, order, and prosperity of the increasingly interdependent family of nations. It was also taking on the role of protector of backward and needy peoples. The Spanish-American War, the establishment of the Republic of Panama, and the construction of the Panama Canal were the results of this two-pronged drive, which had set out to attain this goal by effecting freedom of commercial intercourse and promotion of American trade and investments abroad. As a further consequence, relations with Great Britain and its Commonwealth began to improve and to grow closer.

America had started the twentieth century with new vigor, except in matters of maritime affairs concerned with our Merchant Marine. We carried a bare ten percent of our exports and imports which already involved billions of dollars.

With the advent of the First World War in 1914, the United States was rudely awakened; it now had to start to pay for fifty years of neglect and lack of foresight in the maintenance of an adequate Merchant Marine. Suddenly, foreign vessels, neutrals as well as belligerents, ceased bringing us the goods we needed, such as rubber, silk, minerals, coffee, tea, and sugar. Cotton and tobacco piled up in the warehouses and wharfs of the South; general cargo like machinery, agricultural implements, automobiles, and trucks congested the docks and warehouses in the Port of New York; freight rates jumped sky-high; increases amounting to a thousand percent were no exception. Government and country finally realized that without control of the "delivery wagon," one cannot effect deliveries in time of emergency.

Faced by this critical turn of events, Congress enacted the Shipping Act of September 17, 1916. Its twin purpose was to aid the Merchant Marine and to regulate port-to-port charges, services, and practices of ocean shipping, with the Shipping Board as the regulatory and administrative Federal agency. It must be emphasized, however, that the provisions of the Act were only partially the result of the emergency. From the outset they provided regulation that was to continue after war conditions had come to an end. The exercise of control was to be a permanent one.

Thirty years later the Supreme Court of the United States, in its famous decision of February 25, 1946, made the foreign freight forwarding business subject to this Act. This must be regarded as the "Magna Charta" of the foreign freight forwarding industry, for the legislation should ultimately prove a boon to the American foreign freight forwarder: the very statute that gives the government regulatory rights over the industry also grants the industry rights of self-government that were not otherwise obtainable.

A more detailed discussion of this very important piece of legislation will be found in the chapter on "Government Regulation of Foreign Freight Forwarding." Therefore, as far as the historical development of the American international forwarding business is concerned, it suffices to point out that the Act had an immediate and profound bearing on business methods and practices of the forwarding business. Congress thought these should preferably be self-corrected, for they appeared to hinder our foreign commerce. It is noteworthy that prior to World War I an extreme shortage of shipping space existed. Then forwarders booked with a number of steamship lines large blocks of space, which were peddled out at whatever price the traffic could bear. Freight was a purchasable commodity, bought from the ocean carrier and sold to the shipper like any other merchandise.

Not only forwarders, but anyone who hoped to turn over a profit through this marketing of space, engaged in this practice like futures on the Produce Exchange. Exporters complained with some justification that this sort of activity by forwarders was detrimental to the proper distribution of shipping facilities. The regulatory provisions of the statute definitely discouraged these practices, and by removing the incentive of quoting through— or inclusive rates, which were based on the original ocean freight plus profit, brought about the appearance of the so-called *handling* or *service fee*. Because of the great increase in available space due to overtonnage and the slackening volume of cargo offerings, this particular aspect lost its significance after World War I.

Port-war market conditions changed rapidly from a seller's to a buyer's market because of surplus inventory. Europe and Asia rapidly resumed production, particularly Germany and Japan, contrasting with World War II; so we encountered heavier competition than here-tofore in all foreign markets. Following the Bolshevik Revolution our trade with Russia reached a stalemate. It was obviously essential that we intensify our efforts to secure new business to overcome the slump in foreign commerce. With characteristic alertness and zeal, the forwarding industry extended its clientele worldwide, but focused particularly on our neighbors in Central and South America. These forwarders performed excellent spadework for our export trade.

The favorable experience gained by the European forwarders in soliciting consignee accounts was utilized by his American counter-part. The inception of the Good Neighbor Policy further strengthened our trade position in Latin America, and the American forwarder increased his business by establishing his own offices in the major cities or by periodic solicitations.

The improvements in our foreign commerce, after a decade of depression and panic, were partly ascribed to political change. Roose-velt's "New Deal" administration tackled the abysmal state of our economy with drastic legislative action. Introduction of the "Re-ciprocal Trade Policy" in 1934 and the enactment of the Merchant Marine Act of June 29, 1936, indicated a new positive approach to our maritime affairs. Congress recognized that national security and development necessitated maintenance of our domestic and foreign commerce and that the United States required an adequate American-owned merchant marine, and efficient supplementary facilities and auxiliary services. This generally implied cessation of the "laissez-faire" policy by the Federal government, but applied particularly to the foreign freight forwarding industry. This segment of the national transportation system had achieved adequate status to warrant the attention of Congress, whose objective was to extend direct assistance to and promote those who were performing essential services in the sphere of overseas shipping.

Government promotion and assistance are subject to controls where they relate to problems that involve the unhampered flow of our com-merce and the prosperity of a considerable segment of the American industry. Conversely, there are—and always will be—onerous ob-stacles to the free movement of goods; these impose complicated formalities on the clearance and entry of goods everywhere. World-wide restrictive trade policies, adopted in the 20's and 30's, increased their number and complexity.

It is noteworthy that the American foreign freight forwarding business had not realized by this period that its activities were so important to the proper functioning of our foreign trade. Analysis relating the industry to the politico-economic scene would have re-vealed the trend. A clash of interests—free enterprise vs. government control—was inevitable.

Immediately upon the inception of World War II, the forwarding industry was threatened with complete extinction because of the practice of foreign governments under lend-lease and other aid arrangements to concentrate forwarding activities within their own organizations. In achieving this by adding to their governmental buying missions corresponding transportation agencies, they deprived the forwarder of business opportunities and threatened the complete disruption of his organization, including his potential ability to play an important part in post-war rehabilitation.

Appealing to Congress for relief, the forwarders were sustained by the so-called *Bland Freight Forwarding Act* of March 14, 1942, codified as Section 217 of the Merchant Marine Act of 1936. This basic statute, named in honor of the late Judge Bland, a longtime friend and proponent of foreign freight forwarders, embraces foreign freight forwarding as a part of our merchant marine industry. It directed the then Maritime Commission, now called the Federal Maritime Board, to coordinate and preserve the freight forwarding aspects of our water-born foreign commerce; it emphasized that this development and preservation was also to be a post-war project, rather than one limited to the war emergency, and finally, instructed other Federal departments and agencies to cooperate with the Maritime Commission's compliance with the Act's provisions.

After the requested aid had been granted, it became clear that the government would capitalize on it. Accordingly, in August, 1942, the Maritime Commission displayed new interest in problems relevant to forwarding, and ordered the first forwarder investigation. The industry (in New York, alone, the number of forwarders had risen from approximately 40 in 1900, to nearly 400), manifested amazement and alarm, questioned the jurisdiction of the Commission, went to court—and lost its case. The Supreme Court, as mentioned previously, upheld the Commission in its decision of 1946.

As of June 1st, 1950, forwarders were required to register under General Order #72 with the Federal Maritime Commission. The post-war period with its tremendous changes in the economic development of U.S. export exemplified by Lend-Lease, E.C.A., relief and rehabilitation under the Marshall Plan, Point Four Program, etc., evolved a policy which made close cooperation between government and the forwarding industry not only imperative but demanded a stabilization of the forwarding profession through control and protection by the government. In this way, the forwarders could take the necessary steps to develop an affirmative program to demonstrate the importance of their functions in the over-all advancement of our merchant marine, foreign commerce and nation. Ten years later, recognizing these facts, the 87th Congress provided for licensing of independent ocean freight forwarders by enacting Public Law 87-254 on September 19th, 1961.

CHAPTER II

The Political and Economic Significance of Foreign Freight Forwarding

Despite increasing awareness of the significance of international trade, it still is not generally appreciated that flourishing trade among nations constitutes one of the major bedrocks of world peace. Intensive market research, plus improvements in transportation and communication, can bring to people in all trading countries a greater variety and abundance of commodities. Increased exchange of everyday goods both improves living standards and stimulates international trade.

Some nations are in the fortunate position of possessing enough resources and skills for self-sufficiency, while others must seek world markets where they can obtain essential items and can sell their surplus products. All nations may venture into every corner of the globe in search of profitable business—an activity that is basically an exchange of goods and services.

Substantial foreign trade is essential to continuous national prosperity, for such prosperity depends largely upon the effective employment of labor, agriculture, and all other factors of production. One major reason for America's extraordinary economic achievement is the extent of the market which permitted industrial mass production and which helped place this nation in its desirable position of a leading exporter.

Inseparable from the problems of international trade are those of our merchant marine. As a job producer, the merchant marine assures work to thousands of seamen, and to labor engaged in the large shipbuilding and maintenance industries. Exporters, however, are more immediately concerned with the assurance of equal freight rates and market opportunities along the world's trade routes, which are free of the potential handicaps that could confront them were they dependent on foreign shipping.

Unfortunately, the job-producing elements of extensive foreign trade and an expanded merchant marine are not yet sufficiently recognized. Every export, up to the point where the goods are loaded "on board," is viewed as a domestic transaction. Conversely, immediately upon discharge from the vessel, every import starts its "domestic journey." Nevertheless, raw material purchases in foreign countries and the process of manufacturing finished products and foodstuffs to be sold back to the foreign countries as exports, create a multitude of

14

job-producing transactions. Although ostensibly domestic, the involved functions reveal the inseparable relationship between domestic and foreign economies and demonstrate how foreign trade considerably buttresses domestic prosperity.

Import-export transactions may influence the livelihood of vast population segments. Railway and truck workers, longshoremen, ship personnel and seamen, bankers, insurance brokers, exporters, importers, forwarders, car-loaders, clerks, stenographers, warehousemen, farm hands—all may find their jobs dependent upon foreign trade in varying degree.

Disciplined political and economic thought is a requisite for the comprehension of the complex problems involved in foreign trade. Unfortunately, we discover short-sightedness and hostility among those who exert an influence over our foreign trade. This group fears unrestricted imports and competition because it refuses to recognize that free, reciprocal international commerce, with abandonment of unmerited trade discriminations, may help secure and promote worldwide political and economic peace. Prosperity is not one-sided, a situation involving "have and have not" nations has proved disastrous. To insure full domestic employment and access to all foreign markets, we must provide our customer countries opportunities to pay us for our products. However, this principle, although elementary, is not widely understood.

The general public lacks interest in this subject because it is unfamiliar with the basic concepts of international commerce. People's thinking is determined largely by their jobs and the atmosphere in which they work. The factory worker, immersed in his technical routine, often does not realize that the material he works with might have come from abroad, and were such imports lacking, he might be denied employment. The farmer thinks primarily of competition when he hears about international trade; he does not analyze that his standard of living is intertwined with the volume of agricultural exports. The housewife who buys rice, coffee, tea, cocoa, fruits, or manufactured goods is often too busy to consider the "story behind" her purchases.

Significantly, these are "The People," and their ballots exert a decisive influence on our foreign trade policy.

National prosperity and political security require that those who understand and who have the most direct interest in foreign trade, assume responsibility to educate the populace to the reciprocal relationship between domestic prosperity and international prosperity, and that opportunities for world peace may improve correlative with the unrestricted flow of goods among nations. Government, chambers of commerce, colleges, schools, business organizations, and unions should support this educational campaign, which will adequately explain foreign trade as a job-producer and will clarify how international commerce affects war and peace.

Domestic trade is not so comprehensive nor, to many, as interesting as international trade. The world market presents new conditions and problems every day. In this sphere we become acquainted with all nations—their people's habits and ways of doing business, which differ vastly from our own. Our knowledge of geography is refreshed and the field of languages reopened. These offer abundant possibilities to expand areas of interest. Foreign traders (broadly defined here as all those who by profession or occupation concern themselves with global thinking) thus may be molded by their work into combinations of far-visioned idealists and hard-boiled realists.

Much remains to be done. To overcome evident current indifference and neglect, much must be accomplished. Railroads, ocean carriers, and airlines are among the few industries serving foreign commerce which have gained recognition.

Foreign freight forwarders render indispensable services that merit increased public recognition and appreciation. Few vocations are as demanding as that of the international forwarding agent because of the perpetual need for intensive study. His operations and facilities require and offer an inexhaustible fount of knowledge. His valuable experience is gained through years of arduous work on an intricate and bewildering maze of exacting detail and documentary procedure. Additionally, his intensive training in all phases of world-wide trade, his acumen and determination in judging situations and seizing opportunities, and his devotion to those who utilize his services render him a meritorious figure in the service of international commerce. He fills a unique need. National progress in foreign trade depends considerably on the efficiency, economy, and discernment he evidences in performing his functions.

Efficient conduct of foreign trade depends upon the availability of ample and diversified transportation and shipping facilities, the provision of adequate and economical services, and on competent traffic management. Transportation and shipping costs often exert great influence on the pricing of merchandise, as well as on the trade methods and trade channels, international competition, and the technique of foreign trade to be employed. Selecting existing foreign markets, and the possible development of other overseas outlets, depends upon geographical location, which is a principal factor affecting the cost and character of service. Ocean freight rates and inland transportation charges by railroads, motor carriers, or water carriers, combined with speed, frequency, and service regularity, may seem remote, but are key factors conditioning foreign trade. Emphatically, the "landed" cost of the product on the foreign buyer's shelf is the determinant, for without proper consideration of the problems inherent in the marketing and distribution mechanism, high transportation costs might limit the geographical bounds within which the merchandise could be sold.

Savings in delivery costs and improved service arrangements

affect import-export volume. Less obviously, the price of a commodity, as expressed in the various forms of quotations, such as F. O. B., F. A. S., C. and F., or C. I. F. (see Appendix J), indicates the importance of service costs in foreign transportation. This quotation factor serves also, as a standard to meet competition successfully.

CHAPTER III

The Functional Position of the Foreign Freight Forwarder in International Commerce

Export shipments pass through various stages, including contact with the activities or services of the following enterprises: railroads or motor carriers, ocean carriers, steamship agents, ship brokers, freight brokers, customs brokers, insurance brokers or underwriters, truckmen, warehousemen, harbor railroads, federal, state, and municipal authorities, and foreign consulates. The foreign-freight forwarder embodies in his organization the essential combination of functions that utilize all required facilities and services in international traffic. He relieves the exporter of the multitudinous details involved in traffic and assists the importer with dispatch and economy.

The foreign freight forwarder is the indispensable link in international transportation and cannot be eliminated or replaced by any other traffic arrangement or scheme. The fact that some manufacturers, railroads, and steamship lines find it convenient or profitable to maintain foreign traffic departments does not and cannot reduce the fundamental necessity for, or impair the indispensability of, the commercial foreign freight forwarder's function. No sound basis exists for assuming that these specialized business functions can, except under most unusual circumstances, be eliminated and corresponding facilities and services provided through such devices as a manufacturer's export department, railroad foreign traffic department, or steamship forwarding division.

Examination of each of the aforementioned operations reveal that, as a whole, they lack the functional completeness characteristic of the commercial forwarder's organization.

Some exporters, and only a few manufacturers, are located at the principal ports of shipping. The origin and destination of goods largely determines the ports of clearance, such as New York, New Orleans, or San Francisco. Only large concerns can maintain an export department. The trend is to abandon these special offices and use the services of specialized organizations.

Experience gained during the post-war decade has demonstrated to manufacturers and merchants, upon reexamination of their competitive trade position, comparative costs and related facts, that their built-in traffic department is less efficient and more expensive than engaging the services of a first-class forwarder. Because he handles all classes of goods to world-wide markets, the forwarder has acquired a "know-how" that few private shipping departments can match.

Contrasting with the commercial forwarder's flexibility, the exporter or manufacturer has to maintain a shipping department adequate to handle traffic during his busiest periods. Consequently, he must absorb a fixed overhead, which adds a disproportionate "load" per unit shipment during his slack season. These unavoidable "peaks" and "valleys" in the flow of goods make a seller's forwarding department an expensive luxury.

The importer, or buyer, also benefits from the forwarder's service. This contrasts with the shipper's traffic department. Since it adheres to the company's general policy and usually thinks in terms of its own needs, it tends to render minimum attention to buyers' requirements. The forwarder is more aware of changing conditions than is the average manufacturer, and his training equips him to deal with circumstances requiring special efforts, because of imminent strikes, rate increases, expiry of letters of credit or import licenses, or other extraordinary conditions. Furthermore, since most importers deal with more than one manufacturer or exporter, the selection of a foreign freight forwarder is of prime importance. The forwarder, only, is willing and competent to render the personalized service pertaining to supervision and coordination that a buyer requires. The commercial forwarder, then, is an indispensable link between the buyer and his source of supply—the manufacturer or exporter.

The overwhelming majority of small or medium-sized exporters, located in the interior, have no alternative other than to rely on the commercial forwarder.

The railroad foreign freight departments, with minor exceptions, do not perform essential forwarding services, including foreign documentation, banking, financing, insurance and consolidations. Their functions are of limited local nature, such as tracing cargo placing railroad cars to pier, and supervising routing to seaboard. Issuance of the "Through Railroad Export Bill of Lading" is actually restricted to the Far East Trade moving from the United States West Coast and to a few bulk commodities, such as grain. Lacking the elements of service and rate competition, this document has proved to be impractical and disadvantageous to the development of international trade. In addition, the following considerations limit the use of the so-called "export through bill of lading":

1. Banks will not accept this bill of lading if payment is to be made by Letter of Credit, unless this bill of lading is specifically provided for in the credit instrument.

2. Consignments under this bill may be tied up at seaboard for a period of thirty or more days.

3. Transfer arrangements can often be more expeditiously obtained at lower cost by the commercial forwarder.

4. The liability clauses set forth in the bill of lading does not provide the exporter or importer with sufficient protection.

5. The ocean carrier (more so, if a foreign line) is not bound by contract to accept cargo forwarded via the through export bill of lading for a particular steamer.

6. Difficulties will arise in obtaining proper legalization by accredited foreign consulates.

The steamship forwarding departments are interested solely in their own traffic requirements. Their activities have been limited to single routine shipments moved via their own lines, and they are unable and unwilling to offer any of the qualified, diversified services to which the commercial foreign freight forwarding agent owes his unique position. Steamship lines must establish a tremendous forwarding department to carry the peak load of all combined forwarding business tendered to their lines, in order to satisfy the peculiar needs of the individual shipper. However, the uneven flow of shipments during the dead intervals between sailings, the routing instructions issued by buyers or sellers directing their consignments to specific carriers, and, the interest of the lines in furthering their friendly relations with the forwarding industry tend to remove any justification for the upkeep of separate forwarding departments. It is known that the cost factor, resulting from the 2:1 ratio of the number of small to large shipments, makes it prohibitive for any ocean carrier to perform an efficient forwarding service without the international forwarding house.

The multitude of various services the forwarder is required to perform both for the shipper and the foreign buyer will be discussed in later chapters. We shall list here only the most frequent, regular services in which the forwarder engages:

1. Advising exporters of shipping and market conditions;

2. Procuring sources of supply and confidential reports;

3. Translating foreign language correspondence;

4. Contacting the supplier for the account of the foreign buyer, and arranging for shipment on the order's date specified, or close thereto;

5. Arranging with the shipper for proper packing, marking, invoicing, and other procedures, to meet the requirements of the buyer and foreign governments;

6. Arranging for the most economical inland transportation to the most favorable port of exit;

7. Tracing the goods, if necessary, to assure steamer connection;

8. Arranging for transfer to steamer upon arrival at port of exit;

9. Consolidating shipments from different suppliers for one buyer, in order to be able to ship them on the same steamer;

10. Attending to customs clearance;

11. Arranging insurance coverage with either American underwriters or foreign insurance companies;

12. Arranging preparation of consular invoices to meet the customs regulations of country of destination;

13. Arranging and booking steamer space, and

14. Preparation of banking and collection papers.

Performing these operations would only burden the steamship lines' freight earnings. Moreover, in soliciting business the forwarder can provide a better information source to shippers than the ocean carriers themselves. This service on the part of the commercial forwarder covers not only the quoting of ocean freight rates and the arranging for space, but also provides exporters with needed information concerning sailing schedules and shipping regulations and practices. Importers seek counsel, too, regarding ocean freight rates, routing, and sailing schedules. Finally, the forwarder will protect the American ocean carrier against foreign competition.

This chapter has dealt, so far, with the forwarder's place within the international traffic mechanism. It seems advisable to discuss briefly various distinctions between the levels of the foreign freight forwarders from the viewpoints of location, special activities, and agency. Supplementing the well-known "port" forwarding agent, a good many firms in the interior are engaged in the foreign freight forwarding business. Some of these firms are located on the border. A second important distinction is the activities of the dispatching forwarder contrasted with those of the receiving forwarder. A "port" forwarder exercises both of these activities because he accepts goods from the interior of the greater port area and arranges for redelivery overseas.

There is a third distinction between the main forwarder and his sub-agent in the case of combined land and sea transportation. If the intermediate forwarder, executing through-transportation, was selected by the main forwarder, he acts as the main forwarder's sub-agent, and is responsible only to the main forwarder.

Lastly, we classify foreign freight forwarders according to their specialized activities in handling a certain commodity more or less exclusively. Forwarding concerns have won a distinguished reputation as specialists in the conduct of foreign forwarding business in wine, cotton, lumber, steel, automobiles, and other products.

The forwarder's economic position is determined by the parties who employ him. The shipper usually specifies a forwarder when the merchandise he is selling is quoted on a C. and F. (cost and freight) or C. I. F. (cost, insurance, and freight) basis, and the consignee usually employs or designates a forwarding agent when transportation costs beyond the factory or the port of shipment are for his account or risk. The cost of the forwarder's service is, of course, added to the charges of all transportation that enter into the "landed cost" of the goods.

While fees and charges can be placed on a ledger, there are, however, other intangibles such as loyalty, integrity, and constructive aid in promoting international business on which no price can be placed either by the forwarder or his customer, and which must be individually discovered to be appreciated. These intangibles, more than material qualifications, often determine the selection of a forwarder. Important points to be evaluated, which play a decisive part in the acquisition of patronage are:

Number of years in business, management experience, reputation among shippers and carriers, connections in other centers of commerce, educational or travel background, membership in trade associations, and ability and efficiency of personnel.

How can one obtain information about all these qualifications which complete the professional picture of the international forwarder? His activities are characterized by two distinct qualities—diversity of operation and expert business education. Any intelligent manufacturer or merchant can gather the necessary information by personal observation and by investigation through the usual channels. The facts elicited, plus his personal reaction to the character and abilities of the contact man with whom he deals, will soon reveal whether he has a loyal and intelligent ally who is ready to help him move his goods to the entire satisfaction of the ultimate customer. The well-established house will spare no effort in behalf of its client, either in correcting mistakes that have cropped up before the goods reached the seaport, or in making constructive suggestions to reduce future transit time and cost.

In conclusion, then, the foreign freight forwarder not only facilitates "free freight flow," but also is the irreplaceable link between the trading nations of the world, a most experienced coordinator of freight services, an ambassador of good will, and a specialized purveyor of first-class ability.

CHAPTER IV

Government Regulations Affecting Forwarders and Their Practices

The status of the foreign freight forwarder, regarded from a regulatory point of view, has been obscure until recently. Congress attempted to provide some degree of regulation by making forwarders subject to certain provisions of the 1916 Shipping Act, the details of which will be discussed later in this chapter. However, when the Maritime Commission endeavored to investigate the industry in 1942, it found that the vague language of the statute raised doubt as to this federal agency's power to regulate the forwarding business. The industry challenged the commission's jurisdiction in the courts; but until this litigation was settled by a Supreme Court decision in 1946, the industry enjoyed unrestricted freedom.

It is, therefore, relevant to investigate the development of federal controls and their exercise by governmental agencies, as applied to the forwarding industry.

Federal control derives from the famous *Munn vs. Illinois* decision of the United States Supreme Court in 1877. This decision referred to the regulation of grain-storage warehouses, then classified as a business affected with the public interest. The court, in sustaining the legislation of the State of Illinois to regulate, pointed out that "it has been customary in England from time immemorial, and in this country from its first colonization, to regulate ferries, common carriers, hackmen, bakers, millers, wharfingers, innkeepers, etc., and in so doing to fix a maximum of charge to be made for services rendered, accommodations furnished, and articles sold." Further, the court ruled that when private property is "affected with a public interest, it ceases to be *Juris Privati* only," and its owner must submit to public control for the common good.

In addition, the power "to regulate commerce with foreign nations, and among several States," is, under Article I, Section 8, of the Constitution of the United States, delegated to the federal government. This provision is known as the "Commerce Clause."

The United States Shipping Board, which was created upon the enactment of the Shipping Act of 1916, was delegated the power to regulate port-to-port traffic, including charges and services, and to prevent unreasonable freight-rate discrimination.

Originally, the Board consisted of five members, appointed by the President, with the advice and consent of the Senate. Besides its regulatory function, this administrative body was to encourage, develop, and create a naval auxiliary and naval reserve, and a merchant marine to meet the requirements of the commerce of the United States with its Territories and Possessions, and with foreign countries. The Merchant Marine Act of 1920, provided for a board of seven members, which was reduced in number to three members, in 1932, by the "Economy Act." One year later, the board was abolished and its activities were transferred to the Department of Commerce. Our entire economy was beset by the depression; our maritime industry had the least chance of survival without long-range assistance. Many solutions were proposed, but no definite action was forthcoming until a United States Senate Committee, chaired by Senator Hugo Black, now Mr. Justice Black, initiated a searching inquiry of the entire dismal situation.

Scandalous disclosures ensued. Limited governmental assistance—chiefly in the form of small subsides—was allocated to a few favored steamship lines. Despite the disproportionately high rates these lines received from the postal service, they disclaimed making a profit. There were other accusations, principally of favoritism by the United States Shipping Board in the disposal of government-owned ships and trade routes. The Shipping Acts of 1920, and 1928, were scrutinized, and determined deficient. The investigation revealed to the committee that rectification would require a completely new bill to provide the framework for a strong American Merchant Marine. Legislative action ensued, creating the five-member United States Maritime Commission, as provided by the Merchant Marine Act of 1936.

Whereas previous legislation had been confined to the two functions of aid and regulation, the 1936 policy made it mandatory, also, for the agency to promote the development, and encourage the maintenance, of an efficient, well-equipped merchant marine and auxiliary services. These auxiliary services were declared to be essential to the fulfillment of the task, as set by the statute.

This additional objective was to highlight the interdependence of the problems involving governmental assistance and essential control, with those involving the assurance of an unhindered flow of our foreign trade, and in which auxiliary services, such as the forwarding industry, participated.

This basic philosophy guided the Maritime Commission in all of its decisions until its functions, under President Truman's Reorganization Plan No. 21, of May 24, 1950, were transferred to the Federal Maritime Board and Maritime Administration, as units of the Department of Commerce. This measure was another attempt to solve administrative difficulties which arose in fulfilling the government's responsibilities in maritime affairs. It aimed to separate at the administrative level the function of regulation in the public interest from that of promotion of a strong maritime industry.

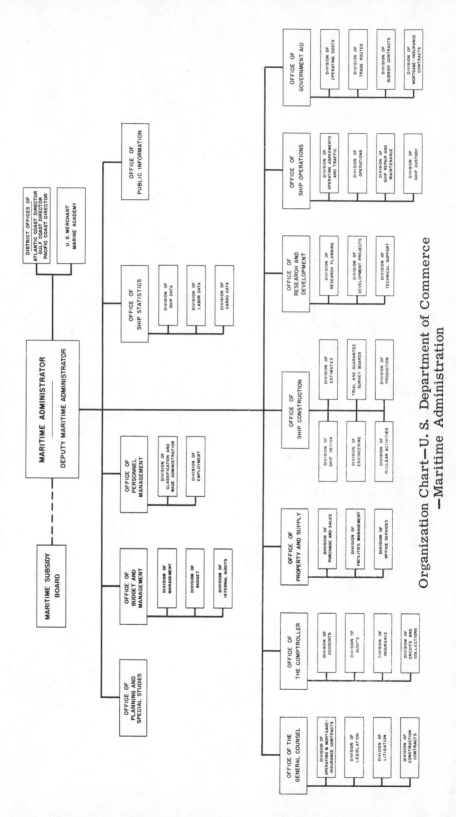

U.S. DEPARTMENT OF COMMERCE
MARITIME ADMINISTRATION

Organization Chart—U.S. Department of Commerce —Maritime Administration

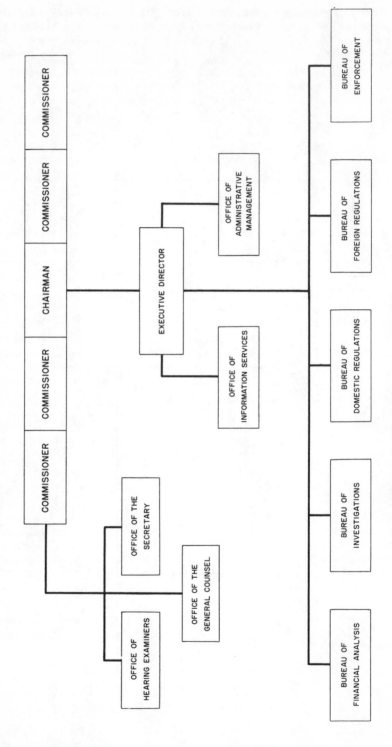

FEDERAL MARITIME COMMISSION

Organization Chart—Federal Maritime Commission

A second, equally important, goal was the creation of effective machinery for the formulation and coordination of our national transportation policy in general.

To attain these objectives, Plan No. 21 created the Maritime Administration, to be directed by an Administrator, and a Federal Maritime Board, to be composed of three members, including a Chairman, who was to act in a dual capacity as the Maritime Administrator and as Chairman of the Board. Each member was appointed by the President, with the advice and consent of the Senate, with one of the members designated as Chairman. The Board, with respect to its quasi-judicial and quasi-legislative functions, and the Chairman, with respect to those of his duties as relate to the regulatory functions, were independent of the Secretary of Commerce. In the performance of all their functions and duties, the Board and its Chairman, who, to repeat, also served ex-officio as Maritime Administrator, were guided by the general policies of the Secretary of Commerce.

The post World War II years, however, had brought out the fact that the newly created foreign merchant fleets, banded together in shipping conferences and heavily supported by diverse aids from their governments, created a threat to the growth of our own merchant marine, on one hand, and a need for increased and more comprehensive regulatory actions on the part of the Maritime Board, on the other.

Reorganization Plan #7 signed by President Kennedy on August 12th, 1961, took cognizance of these developments by declaring that existing organizational arrangements had not proved to be satisfactory and that the intermingling of regulatory and promotional functions had tended to dilute responsibility, and had led to serious inadequacies, particularly in the administration of regulatory functions.

The basic objective of the plan was to strengthen and revitalize the U.S. Merchant Marine by concentrating responsibility in completely separate agencies for the performance of regulatory functions, on one hand, and of promotional and operating functions, on the other.

With these objectives in mind. Reorganization Plan #7 abolished the Federal Maritime Board and created a Federal Maritime Commission as an independent agency, composed of 5 Commissioners, appointed by the President, by and with the consent of the Senate, one of the Commissioners being designated by the President to be Chairman, exercising regulatory jurisdiction. Nonregulatory functions, including the determination and award of subsidies and other promotional and operating activities, were concentrated in the head of the Department of Commerce who was best qualified to coordinate these activities with other transportation and related economic programs.

The regulatory functions of the Commission include jurisdiction over:

A. Common carriers by water in the domestic off-shore trades between the Continental United States and Alaska, Hawaii and the territories and possessions of the U.S.A. There are about 60 carriers in this trade in addition to about 75 non-shipowning or operating companies that hold themselves out as Common carriers in this trade and who utilize shipowning or operating companies to carry on the transportation by water.

B. Common carriers by water in the foreign trade of the U.S.A., comprising approximately 400 different carriers of which circa 35 are U.S. citizen operating companies, about 30 are U.S. non-shipowning companies and the balance are foreign flag lines.

C. Independent Ocean Freight Forwarders. This term, as defined in Public Law 87-254 of Sept. 19th, 1961, which legislative act will be discussed later, applies to a person carrying on the business of freight forwarding (the dispatching of shipments by ocean-going common carriers in the U.S. trade on behalf of others) for a consideration, who is not a shipper or consignee and who has no beneficial interest in the cargo for which he acts as forwarder.

D. Terminal Operators, persons who furnish wharfage, dockage, warehouse or other terminal facilities in connection with transportation by oceangoing common carriers. There are about 400 terminal operators subject to Federal Maritime Commission regulation.

The Maritime Administration established in the Department of Commerce by Reorganization Plan #21 of 1950 was continued by Reorganization Plan #7 of 1961 as a primary organization unit in the Department of Commerce, headed by a Maritime Administrator who is appointed by the President and responsible to the Secretary of Commerce through the Undersecretary of Commerce for Transportation for all matters which concern the fostering, development and maintenance of an American Merchant Marine sufficient to meet the needs of the national defense and of the domestic and foreign commerce of the U.S. The functions of the Maritime Administration which includes also the Maritime Subsidy Board, cover, therefore, the award of construction-differential and operating-differential subsidies to the American Merchant Marine, the construction, repair and operation of merchant ships, the maintenance of national defense reserve fleets of Government owned ships, the administration of subsidy programs and other aids to shipping.

Summarizing, the objective of Reorganization Plan #7 of 1961 was to vest in the Maritime Commission the power to review and regulate rates, services, practices, agreements, charges, classifications, and tariffs of common carriers by water, who are engaged in foreign commerce, and other persons subject to the shipping Act, 1916 (forwarders and terminal operators).

Note that the phrase, "control over rates, services, practices etc.," does not imply that the Commission fixes rates, and so forth. Unlike the Interstate Commerce Commission's power over land carrier, coastal and intercoastal ship lines, the Commission does not have such authority. The Commission's control over rates, services, charges, practices, etc., can only be exercised where the rates, etc., are discriminatory. In other words, the Commission can prevent a steamship line from charging one rate to one shipper, and a different rate to a second consignor; it can interfere with respect to the forwarding business as to practices contrary to the public interest, or detrimental to the unhampered flow of our foreign commerce. In executing its functions, the Commission is guided by the Declaration of Policy contained in the Title I of the 1936 Act.

Moreover the Federal Maritime Commission can regulate practices of ocean freight forwarders and terminal operators, license independent ocean freight forwarders who are found to be fit, willing and able to properly carry on the business of forwarding, and supervise their practices thereafter; also approve, disapprove, cancel or modify conference agreements between common carriers by water in the foreign and domestic off-shore trades of the United States; further approve or disapprove contract rate systems used by common carriers by water or conferences of such carriers in foreign commerce; make rules and regulations affecting shipping in the foreign trade to meet conditions unfavorable to shipping which result from foreign laws, rules or regulations or from competitive methods used by foreign flag carriers; also hear complaints of alleged violations of the various provisions of the Shipping Act and make decisions as to whether or not a violation has occurred, including the awarding of reparations for injuries in appropriate circumstances.

In contrast, the functions of the Maritime Administration are less authoritative, though broader. The Administration, in general, investigates maritime problems, determines certain requirements, recommends assistance, administers contracts, purchases or charters ships, maintains national defense reserve fleets, operates the U. S. Maritime Training Service, insures mortgages, regulates sales of ships to aliens and transfers to foreign registry.

It includes, also, the General Counsel's Office, the Maritime Subsidy Board, the Office of Planning and Special Studies, the Offices of Ship Constructing, of Ship Operations and Government Aid, the Offices of the Coast Directors and the United States Merchant Marine Academy.

It can well be reiterated that the fundamental objective of the Federal Maritime Commission in connection with the forwarding industry, regarded from a purely governmental aspect, is based on a twofold concept: negatively, regulation and control, and positively, responsibility for the promotion of the industry, as one of the essential services to our American Merchant Marine.

The jurisdiction of the Federal Maritime Commission over the foreign freight forwarding business does not extend to an allied activity in which the forwarder participates, such as custom's brokerage since the existence of controls by the Customs Service of the U.S. Treasury Department limits the need for control by the Maritime Commission.

However, the forwarding industry has been decidedly affected in its relationship with another government agency within the Department of Commerce, namely, the Office of International Trade. This office is charged with the control of all exports under general or validated licenses, as per the Export Control Act of 1949. Although the exercise of its jurisdiction is confined to only one of the many functions of forwarder activities, it burdens the forwarder. Failure on the part of the forwarder to perform the obligation of screening export shipments, in order to assure compliance with existent export controls, may lead to the suspension of the forwarder's right to conduct business for a period of weeks or months. The forwarder cannot exculpate himself because of carelessness, errors, or omissions either on his part or on that of the exporter.

Comprehensive export control enforcement was based on foreign policy considerations, known as "cold war" measures. Distinct from the government's export control of commodities in critically short supply, control was intended to channel strategic and essential material to friendly nations and to withhold exports to "Iron Curtain" countries. Here, too, the exercise of control rested on the principle that any violation would adversely affect the public interest. This motive is apparent in all legislation dealing with public affairs or foreign policy matters, and concerns the foreign freight forwarding industry, as an instrument of our foreign trade.

The inter-relationship of forwarding to transportation in foreign commerce was recognized in the Shipping Act of 1916. Under Sections I and 17, it required steamship lines, forwarders, and concerns engaged in providing wharfage, dock, warehouse, or other terminal facilities in the foreign trade to establish, and observe "just and reasonable regulations and practices relating to or connected with the receiving, handling, storing, or delivering of property," and granted the then Shipping Board powers to prescribe a just and reasonable regulation, or practice, for any found to be unjust and unreasonable.* This declaration of Congress made the forwarding business an essential adjunct of our maritime industry and defined its legal position within the framework of governmental legislation. Forwarding was recognized as a subject of regulation and promotion.

Although the objective of the Shipping Act was dual—regulation and promotion—and although the development functions of the Shipping Board and the Maritime Commission, respectively, for the next

*Section 1 reads: "The term 'other person subject to this act' means any person not included in the term 'common carrier by water,' carrying on the business of forwarding or furnishing wharfage, dock, warehouse, or other terminal facilities in connection with a common carrier by water."

Section 17 provides in relevant part: "Every such carrier and every other person subject to this act shall establish, observe, and enforce just and reasonable regulations and practices, relating to or connected with the receiving, handling, storing, or delivering of property. Whenever the board finds that any such regulation or practice is unjust or unreasonable it may determine, prescribe, and order enforced a just and reasonable regulation or practice."

three decades occupied more time and attention than the regulatory functions, the last two decades—since the end of World War II—have pushed this federal agency into the public limelight as an arbiter, and as a regulator in matters of competitive practices and rates between carriers, or carriers and shippers. The phrases "Conferences" and "Dual Rate System" had become a public or even an international issue. Decisions by the Federal Maritime Board and its successor, the Federal Maritime Commission had been appealed to the Courts. A widespread discontent with the agency's performance arose in the halls of Congress which brought about the passage of Public Law 87-346 of October 3rd, 1961, amending the 1916 Shipping Act, and thus legalizing the contract/non-contract (dual) rate system used in world-wide ocean liner operations. A following chapter, "Conferences," will present a detailed account of this subject. Here, it suffices to outline the salient features of the Shipping Act.

The statute prohibits common carriers by water in foreign commerce and in interstate commerce, on the high seas, or the Great Lakes, on regular routes from port to port, and also concerns engaged in business such as forwarding, from giving any undue or unreasonable preference or advantages to a particular person, locality, or description of traffic. It is unlawful to transport property at less than the regular rate by means of false billing, classification, weighing or weight reports, or by other unjust or unfair device, and to persuade or influence an insurance company or underwriter to discriminate against a competing carrier. It equally prohibits the disclosure to any persons other than shipper or consignee, except with their consent, any information regarding their cargoes that may be used to their detriment. The use of deferred rebates and of "fighting ships," is also declared unlawful.* It further forbids retaliation against shippers which have patronized other lines. Ocean carriers and other concerns, such as forwarders, must file with the Federal Maritime Commission a true copy, or memorandum, of every agreement regarding rates, privileges or advantages, the control of competition, the pooling of traffic, the control of sailings by the allotment of ports, or any other exclusive, or

---

* Section 14. "That no common carrier by water shall directly or indirectly—
First. Pay, or allow, or enter into any combination, agreements, or understanding, express or implied, to pay or allow, a deferred rebate to any shipper. The term "deferred rebate" in this Act means a return of any portion of the freight money by a carrier to any shipper as a consideration for the giving of all or any portion of his shipments to the same or any other carrier, or for any other purpose, the payment of which is deferred beyond the completion of the service for which it is paid, and is made only if, during both the period for which computed and the period of deferment, the shipper has complied with the terms of the rebate agreement or arrangement.
Second. Use a fighting ship either separately or in conjunction with any other carrier, through agreement or otherwise. The term "fighting ship" in this Act means vessel used in a particular trade by a carrier or group of carriers for the purpose of excluding, preventing, or reducing competition by driving another carrier out of said trade."

special arrangement. The Commission has the authority to "disapprove, cancel or modify any ocean conference agreement which it finds to be unfair as between carriers, exporters, importers, or ports, or between exporters from the United States and their foreign competitors, or to operate to the detriment of the commerce of the United States, or to be in violation of this Act." Any agreement approved, however, is automatically exempt from the prohibitions of the Anti-Trust Laws.

Before passage of Public Law 87-346, there was no statutory requirement that rates and tariffs by common carriers in foreign commerce be published or filed in advance. Private or contract carriers (tramps) are not covered by the Shipping Act of 1916; they are free to meet competitive conditions on short notice.

An order issued by the Shipping Board in 1934 required all common carriers by sea in our *outbound* (export) trade to file with the regulating authority. In 1935 schedules showing charges and rates for, or in connection with, transportation of property from and to the U.S.A. were required to be filed but only within 30 days from the date on which they became effective, which measure did not afford any long range protection on forward commitments so important to shipper's business. The new law of 1961 changed this to require that all new or initial rates, tariffs, and all increases in rates must be filed with the Federal Maritime Commission 30 days in advance of their effective date. The tariffs must be kept open to public inspection and copies of all tariffs must be furnished to any person at a reasonable charge. Upon showing of good cause, a new rate or an increase in rates, may become effective in less than 30 days.

So that carriers and merchants alike will at all times be in a competitive position, reductions of rates may be effected simultaneously with filing. A new carrier coming into a trade must file his tariff 30 days in advance, even though his rates may be lower than those of other carriers already in the trade. This measure is taken in order to reduce the impact on a stable rate structure which would be caused by the sudden intrusion of a cut-rate operator.*

The filing requirements apply to all cargoes except full shiploads of liquid bulk cargoes, other than chemicals and except dry cargo loaded and carried in bulk without mark or count. Since the law clearly stipulates that the rates and charges which are specified in the tariffs of the common carriers by water in foreign commerce must be *on file with the Commission,* duly published, and in effect at the time of assessment, the receipt of these rates and charges by the Commission is an essential ingredient of a filing with the authority and the mere placing of the rates etc. in the mail, is invalid because it does not constitute either "receipt" nor being on file.

As to violations of any stated provisions of the Act, severe penalties are imposed, ranging from five thousand dollars to twenty-five thou-

---

*Section 18b of Shipping Act 1916.

sand dollars for each offense. This helps assure fair and equal treatment of all shippers, large and small, by all ocean common carriers doing business in the United States, both American and foreign.

One of the aims of the shipping legislation, as embodied in the Statutes of 1916, 1920, 1928, and 1936, was to prohibit any discriminatory practices, by enforcing fair and equal treatment for, and among, all parties concerned. Therefore, it was inevitable that those persons who were performing auxiliary services in connection with overseas transportation would attract the attention of their "patron," the Maritime Commission, should complaints come forward.

With the outbreak of hostilities in Europe leading to World War II, shortages in shipping space raised new problems involving forwarders. Rationing and allocation of steamer space, in accordance with the essentiality of the cargo, and "the size of the individual forwarding enterprise," proved to be a difficult task. These conditions placed a premium on the forwarder's skill and gift of persuasion and he, if successful, like any reputable expert, charged accordingly "for services performed."

The consequent irritation of shippers in the United States, and foreign buyers abroad, taking exception to the various practices in connection with booking of space, billings, and other trade facets, led to complaints which induced the Maritime Commission to renew interest in the problems relating to the forwarding business. One of the complainants, The Port of New York Authority, charged absence of clearness and uniformity in the classification of service, lack of specification of charges for services, lack of professional responsibility and experience necessary to the efficient performance of forwarding functions, overcharging on ocean freight, "lump sum" billing, and padding of bills. Much of this was attributed to the "fog" which surrounded the industry, some of whose members "carried their offices in their hats."

Other objections were directed against the collection and use of shipper's funds, sixty to ninety days before they were remitted; the wide discrepancy in the charges assessed by forwarders at different ports; the differences in charges of the same forwarder for the same description of service at New York; and the issuance by the forwarder of a receipt which purported to be a bill of lading.

Possibly the irregularities complained of were exaggerated because of the misdeeds practiced by a comparative few. Strangely, the padding of bills might have been caused by foreign buyers on whose behalf the forwarder, as appointed shipping agent, acted under instructions, so that their profit based upon a percentage of cost could be increased in the resale of the goods to third parties. Possible causes were of minor interest to the Maritime Commission, compared to the fact that temptations to malpractice arising from keen competition, coupled with the lack of any regulation of the industry, would lead to injury of our foreign commerce.

Accordingly, beginning in 1942, the Commission sent to some 320 forwarders in the Port of New York a questionnaire regarding their practices and activities, which was fully answered. The ensuing hearing was adjourned to enable the Commission to obtain additional information by issuance of a second, more detailed and extensive questionnaire. Fully alarmed by now, the forwarding industry instituted court proceedings questioning the extent of the jurisdiction of the Commission over forwarders. This resulted in the Court of Appeals (*American Union Transport v. United States*, 55 F. Supp. 682) restraining the Commission and enjoining its order, based on Section 21 (requiring the filing of reports, records, and documents relating to persons subject to the 1916 Act), to pursue its investigation.

This ruling was immediately appealed to the Supreme Court, which reversed in favor of the Maritime Commission on February 25, 1946. In so doing, and speaking for five judges, with only three dissenting, Justice Rutledge said:

In several sections, for example, 15, 16, 17, 20 and 21 of the Shipping Act of 1916, other persons as well as common carriers by water either are made subject to affirmative duties or are prohibited from engaging in certain activities.

Section 15 requires filing of specified agreements or memoranda with the Commission and exempts from the operation of the antitrust laws arrangements made by carriers and 'other persons' among themselves or with one another which have been filed with and approved by the Commission. The Commission is given the power to disapprove, cancel or modify, among others, any agreement which it finds to be unjustly discriminatory or unfair as between carriers, shippers, exporters, importers or ports, or between United States exporters and their foreign competitors; or to operate to the detriment of the commerce of the United States; or to be in violation of the Act. Obviously agreements or understandings between forwarders or between forwarders and shippers or between forwarders and carriers may be discriminatory in such a way as to violate the provisions of § 15. Moreover, since forwarders arrange the terms of carriage for shippers with carriers, they may be the active agents who bring about the very types of agreement or arrangement the section contemplates, the Commission shall have power and opportunity to outlaw. Consequently, jurisdiction by the Commission over forwarders would seem essential to effectuate the policy of the Act and the absence of jurisdiction well might prevent giving full effect to that policy.

Section 16 forbids various forms of discrimination, as well as other practices, on the part of any common carrier by water 'or other person,' which an independent forwarder readily may commit or induce. It is suggested, however, that whatever discriminations might be practiced necessarily would be in pursuance of an agreement between a carrier and a forwarder who, it is well to point out again, acts as agent of the shipper; and that since Congress has given the Commission jurisdiction over the carriers, it is to be presumed that such jurisdiction was thought to be sufficient.

Whether or not the premise is correct, the conclusion does not follow. That the Commission may have jurisdiction over one of the two parties to a discriminatory agreement or arrangement hardly means that it shall not have jurisdiction over both. Indeed, unless the jurisdiction includes both, it may be ineffective as to the one covered; for the Commission then might lack the necessary means of obtaining or checking upon information (cf. § 21) necessary to ascertain the existence of a discrimination or to take other action commanded by the statute. Moreover, some of the practices forbidden appear to be peculiarly if not exclusively susceptible of commission or inducement by forwarders, brokers and shippers' agents, all specifically mentioned in the section.

The purpose of § 17, in relevant part, is to provide for the establishment, observance and enforcement of just and reasonable regulations and practices relating to or in connection with the receiving, handling, storing or delivering of property. By the nature of their business, independent forwarders are intimately connected with these various activities. Here again, unless the Commission has jurisdiction over them, it may not be able effectively to carry out the policy of the Act.

Section 20, which for the most part was copied from § 15 (11) of the Interstate Commerce Act, forbids the disclosure of confidential information by a common carrier by water or other person, when the information might be used to the detriment or prejudice of a shipper or consignee, or of a carrier, or might improperly disclose his business transactions to a competitor.

Finally, § 21, which is immediately involved in this case, requires the filing of reports, records and documents relating to the business of persons subject to the Act.

The intimate relationship of the forwarder to both shipper and carrier, essentially that of go-between, gives him not only unique sources of information, perhaps in its totality available to no one else, but also unique opportunity to engage in practices which the Act contemplates shall be subject to regulation, some of which we have emphasized in quoting the statutory provisions. The statute throughout is drawn in very broad terms. It forbids direct or indirect accomplishment of the outlawed acts. It broadly covers specific practices, including false billing, classification, weighing, and the manner of placing insurance, § 16, as well as general practices resulting in forbidden evils, §§ 15, 17, which forwarders, affiliated or independent, are favorably placed to bring about. It mentions forwarders specifically, not only in § 1, but elsewhere, e.g., §16, without suggestions of distinction between independent and affiliated operators. To include the latter but exclude the former would be incongruous, not only for want of any such explicit suggestion, but because inclusion of one without the other would create a statutory discrimination tending in time to force out the affiliated forwarder and with that achieved, to remove forwarding entirely from the reach of the regulatory plan. We do not believe that Congress had in mind such a self-defeating scheme. Almost as well might it have exempted all forwarders in the first place. Nor do we think the design of the Act was merely by indirection to forbid carriers of their affiliates to act as forwarders.

Although the decision of the Supreme Court was neither an unmixed blessing nor an unmitigated curse, it should have awakened the industry from its lethargy, and made it realize, by some vision, that only by candid, open, and courageous cooperation with the statutory agencies, as representatives of the public interest, could desired benefits be secured. This cooperation was essential to eliminate malpractices within the industry and to organize a cohesive unit of all forwarders, which would be capable of maintaining close contact with the Commission and with Congress.

This consideration should have been the most obvious and logical consequence to be drawn from the Supreme Court decision, particularly because only a few years prior, the enactment of The Bland Freight Forwarding Act, of March 14, 1942, had demonstrated the willingness of Congress "to coordinate the functions and facilities of public and private agencies engaged in the forwarding and similar services to waterborne foreign commerce of the United States for 1) the efficient prosecution of the war, 2) the maintenance and development of present and post-war trade, and 3) the preservation of forwarding facilities and services for the post-war restoration of foreign commerce." In addition, Congress directed and authorized "other Federal departments and agencies to cooperate with the then Maritime Commission by entering into and carrying out such agreements as may be necessary to effectuate the purpose of the Act."

This favorable expression of congressional intent was repeated by a similar statement of policy contained in the Merchant Ship Sales Act of 1946, although forwarding, as such, was only indirectly mentioned: "It is necessary for national security, and development and maintenance of the domestic and foreign commerce of the United States to have an efficient and adequate American-owned merchant marine—supplemented by efficient American-owned facilities . . . ., and other auxiliary services."

Incredibly, there was still no full comprehension on the part of the forwarding industry as to its legal position and the possible economic consequences resulting from Congressional legislation. Was this condition caused by lack of education and training in public affairs, deficiency in managerial abilities, disunity in purpose, indifference caused by want of good will, or passive resistance against, and dislike of, government interference? Being international forwarders, should they not have been stimulated to study transoceanic experiences, since their colleagues all over the world have flourished for decades by close, and mutually beneficial, relationship with their governments? Accustomed to rugged competition within their fraternity, and to continuous changes in international market conditions, were they not expected to fend the challenge?

Albeit, only feeble attempts had been made so far—and these only during the war emergency—to formulate a bold program, and to activate a sound policy of self-regulation and cooperation with a Congress, which was willing to listen and to assist.

In 1947, the hearings in the matter of the Port of New York Freight Forwarding Investigation were resumed in New York and Chicago, and concluded. The Maritime Commission, in its ruling of November 17, 1949, declared:

> The opinion of the Supreme Court in *U. S. v. American Union Transport, supra* leaves no doubt as to our power to prescribe reasonable regulations designed to remedy any unreasonable practices shown of record herein. In reviewing the regulatory scheme and policy of the Shipping Act, 1916, the court pointed out that forwarders are in a position to enter into agreements with carriers which may be contrary to the policy of section 15 of the Act, and to commit or induce discriminations forbidden by section 16. They are intimately connected with the receiving, handling, storing, and delivering of property, the practices as to which must be just and reasonable under section 17; and they have access to confidential shipping information, the disclosure of which is forbidden by section 20. See also *California v. United States*, 320 U. S. 577.
>
> We are of the opinion that any person carrying on the business of dispatching shipments by ocean going vessels in foreign commerce and domestic commerce with or between our territories and possessions, and of handling the formalities incident thereto, is a forwarder within the provisions of the Shipping Act, 1916.

This definition includes manufacturers, exporters, export traders, manufacturers' agents, resident buyers, and commission merchants if they do not ship in their own name and if they charge a fee for forwarding services. Merely because one offering a forwarding service is engaged in other businesses does not remove him from our jurisdiction. Such definition does not include the foregoing persons, however, if they ship in their own name even though a forwarding fee is charged directly or is concealed in the price of the goods. Admittedly, in the latter instance they might be competitive with regular forwarders, but that is not the test. The status applies to persons "carrying on the business" of forwarding. Persons who merely perform forwarding on their own behalf can not be regarded as carrying on a forwarding business. Moreover, a shipper who performs his own forwarding, though he passes the cost on to the buyer, needs no protection. The record demonstrates, however, that shippers who do not forward their own shipments but rely through choice or necessity upon professional forwarders, do need a measure of protection. This is true particularly in reference to shippers located far from ports through which their cargoes are shipped.

While it is evident that many of the irregularities complained of have been practiced by a comparative few, it is also evident that temptations arising from keen competition, coupled with the lack of any regulation of the industry, have caused many forwarders to engage in practices which are unjust and unreasonable and detrimental to commerce.

The most common abuses arise from the forwarders' methods of billing—the failure to specify clearly and state separately all service charges, and to segregate them from actual out-of-pocket costs for accessorial services. We are not convinced by the argument that segregation of charges would upset the foreign consignee, and thus prove injurious to our foreign trade. It would seem that the more logical reason why some forwarders do not segregate their charges is that since the business is highly competitive, the present method of billing affords more leeway in bidding. Certain service charges can be made to appear nominal while the profit is concealed in such items as trucking, insurance, and warehousing. This practice is unjust and unreasonable. Itemization of charges and exact disclosure of outlays for which reimbursement is sought, should be made either prior to the shipment, or thereafter in an appropriately detailed invoice.

During the course of the hearing and in briefs the suggestion was made that forwarders act as independent contractors. The only significance that can be attached to this claim is that once the charges are agreed upon, any ground for complaint as to the reasonableness thereof, either from the shipper or forwarder, is removed. In *U. S. v. American Union Transport, supra,* the court said (p. 443) : "By engaging in these many activities of the forwarding business, independent forwarders—and particularly the appellees[*]—act as *agents of the shipper."* (emphasis supplied). But for regulatory purposes, it is immaterial whether the forwarder acts as agent or independent contractor. What he does determines his status and the resultant obligations under regulatory statutes. *United States v. California,* 297 U. S. 175. Whether a forwarder is an agent or an independent contractor, he is in either case precluded by the equality provision of section 16 of the Shipping Act from unduly or unreasonably preferring, or discriminating against, any person for whom he performs forwarding service. *Contract Rates— Port of Redwood City,* 2 U. S. M. C. 727. It is realized of course that the services of forwarders are specialized and varied. However, the record indicates a possibility of discriminatory treatment resulting from the great variety of methods upon which charges are based.

The evidence shows instances of a forwarder who, at the same place but under a different name, transacts business as a shipper, simultaneously collecting brokerage under another name as a forwarder of his own shipments. Brokerage

[*] "The appellees were those respondents who contested the Commission's jurisdiction."

paid to a shipper on his own shipments constitutes a rebate in violation of section 16 of the Shipping Act—and this is true notwithstanding that the shipper may also be a forwarder and may purport to receive the brokerage money in his forwarder capacity. Similarly, a forwarder who has any beneficial interest in a shipment and accepts brokerage thereon, is equally guilty of accepting a rebate in violation of section 16.

One effective way of controlling abuses disclosed by the present record would be through legislation providing a system of licensing similar to that applied to custom brokers. In the absence of such legislation, it is essential that we require all forwarders to register with the Commission, since a program of regulation undertaken without means of identifying the members of the industry would be largely ineffective. The Port Authority, representatives of forwarders and shippers, and Commission counsel concede the necessity for registration with us of all forwarders. A requirement for registration will be a step in the right direction and will give us an opportunity to decide further as to the need for licensing legislation.

We find:

1. that there is need for the registration of all forwarders;

2. that it is an unreasonable practice in violation of section 17 of the Shipping Act, 1916, for a forwarder, in submitting invoices for services or reimbursement of advances in connection with the forwarding of any shipment for export: (a) to fail to disclose accurately and separately all amounts advanced or contracted for or on behalf of the shipper or consignee; or (b) to fail to itemize all service charges, unless such forwarder and shipper or consignee shall have agreed in advance as to the charges and method of billing and reference to said agreement is made in the statement presented;

3. that the issuance of a receipt for cargo by a forwarder, which purports to be a bill of lading, is an unreasonable practice in violation of section 17 of the Shipping Act, 1916.

Exceptions were filed to the report by one of the members of the Commission, and his dissenting view definitely indicated a more realistic grasp of the intricate problems involved, and also took cognizance of the unusual functional and economic position which the forwarder occupies as a link between seller and buyer.

Commissioner McKeough declared:

I concur in the majority's definition of forwarders, except for the blanket exclusion of common carriers.

The majority states that its definition of forwarders includes: "manufacturers, exporters, export traders, manufacturer's agents, resident buyers, and commission merchants if they do not ship in their own name and if they charge a fee for forwarding services."

Earlier in the body of the majority decision, the following finding, although not so labeled, appears: "Common carriers by water in some instances offer forwarder service, but they have not shown any desire for such business and charge rates which are generally below those of regular forwarders but which have not been shown to be non-compensatory. Charges are published in tariff form, some as minimum charges and others as specific itemized rates."

The question of carriers' "desire for such business" can hardly affect their legal status as long as they do "offer forwarder service." Nor can the fact that carriers charge rates for forwarding service "which are generally below those of regular forwarders" justify special treatment of common carriers, when offering forwarding services; to the contrary, the practice of certain steamship companies to perform forwarding services for the public at "cut-rates" may well be one of the reasons why "regular forwarders" find themselves pressed, as we have found, to hide service charges in lump sum billing or in the "padding" of bills for accessorial services.

I can see no grounds for exemption from regulation as forwarders in the fact that common carriers may not offer all the services customarily offered by forwarders, or that they offer forwarding services only as an unimportant "sideline." The same, after all, can be said of many of the businesses which the majority has decided to include in its definition.

Neither publication of some common carriers' forwarding charges in their tariffs, nor the definition of "other person subject to this Act" in Section 1 of the Shipping Act, 1916 ("any person not included in the term 'common carrier by water' carrying on the business of forwarding . . . in connection with a common carrier by water") justify exempting common carriers "carrying on the business of forwarding" from such standards as we determine should be established for, and followed by those "carrying on the business of forwarding."

Such exemption is as alien to the board regulatory policy of the 1916 Act and the intent of the framers, as if we were to exempt common carriers who also furnish wharfage, dock, or other terminal facilities from standards applied by us to independent or affiliated persons furnishing the same facilities. Congress, as is clear from the legislative history of the Act, wanted to make sure that certain of the provisions of the Act apply not only to actual transportation, but to certain accessorial services, as well. As these are frequently furnished by persons other than common carriers, Congress provided for a separate category of "other person subject to this Act." Now for us, however, to apply the provisions of the Act to "other persons," yet not to the common carriers themselves *when they perform the same functions*, would not only bring about a most incongruous result, but, in addition, would mean charging the Congress with setting up a "double standard" without any apparent justification or purpose whatsoever. I refuse to so charge the Congress.

Accordingly, finding it necessary to regulate the business of forwarding in connection with a common carrier by water for hire, we should regulate everybody carrying on this business, lest we lay ourselves open to the accusation of playing favorites.

I am unable to concur in the majority's findings "(3) that the issuance of a receipt for cargo by a forwarder, which purports to be a bill of lading, is an unreasonable practice in violation of section 17 of the Shipping Act, 1916."

This finding is unsupported, in the body of the majority's decision, by any argumentation, explanation, or discussion, and, therefore, appears arbitrary and capricious. The finding is believed to be based upon a single case, not referred to or discussed in the majority's decision. There is no indication that that particular complaint and the damage complained of would have been avoided had the document in question been identified as a cargo receipt rather than a bill of lading. Moreover, due to absence of definitions, indefiniteness in language, and lack of supporting discussion, the finding leaves it open to conjecture whether we condemn, as an unreasonable practice, the issuance of a real bill of lading by a forwarder, or the issuance of a cargo receipt which purports to be, and actually is, a bill of lading, or only the issuance of a receipt for cargo which purports to be, *but actually is not*, a bill of lading.

I concur with another finding made in the body of the majority's decision, but omitted, in my opinion erroneously, from its formal findings. Although Docket 621 is primarily an investigation into the practices of forwarders in their relations with shippers and consignees, and although it may be held, therefore, that matters involving the relations between forwarders and common carriers by water are extraneous to the issues, nevertheless, we found, and the majority reports, evidence of a forwarder who collected brokerage from a common carrier on shipments in which the forwarder had a financial interest as shipper.

The majority concludes that "Brokerage paid to a shipper on his own shipments constitutes a rebate in violation of the Shipping Act. . . . Similarly, a forwarder who has any beneficial interest in a shipment and accepts brokerage thereon, is equally guilty of accepting a rebate in violation of section 16."

I agree, but having determined that a certain practice constitutes a rebate in violation of Section 16, I believe that we should have included such determination among our formal findings as well as a prohibition of that practice among the proposed rules and regulations; or, if we find that we may not do so because the proceeding was one solely under Section 17 of the Act, the discussion of this matter falling under section 16 should have been omitted from our report entirely.

I am not at this time concurring in the proposed rules and regulations as we are inviting interested persons to submit to us their views on these proposed rules and regulations, which in no case will become effective except after 60 days from their publication in the Federal Register. Questions relating to the effectiveness of some of the proposed rules and regulations and to the practicability of others can be better resolved when the comments of interested persons will have been received.

On May 24, 1950, General Order 72, effective June 1, 1950, was issued and published in the Federal Register, reading as follows:

TITLE 46—SHIPPING

Chapter II—United States Maritime Commission

[General Order 72]

PART 244—BUSINESS PRACTICES OF FREIGHT FORWARDERS

On December 3, 1949, the Commission published in the FEDERAL REGISTER (14 F. R. 7275), pursuant to section 4 of the Administrative Procedure Act, a notice of proposed rule making, setting forth proposed rules for the regulation of freight forwarders. Comments thereon have been received and considered by the Commission. The proposed rules have been modified and shall take effect as hereinafter set forth.

AUTHORITY: §§ 244.1 to 244.15 issued under sec. 204, 49 Stat. 1987, as amended; 46 U. S. C. 1114. Interprets or applies 39 Stat. 734; 46 U. S. C. 816.

§ 244.1 *Definition.* A freight forwarder is any person engaged in the business of dispatching shipments on behalf of other persons, for a consideration, by oceangoing vessels in commerce from the United States, its territories or possessions to foreign countries, or between the United States and its territories or possessions, or between such territories and possessions; and of handling the formalities incident to such shipments. This definition includes independent freight forwarders, common carriers, manufacturers, exporters, export traders, manufacturers' agents, resident buyers, commission merchants, and other persons when they engage for and on behalf of any person other than themselves, in return for a consideration, money or otherwise, in the aforementioned activity.

§ 244.2 *Registration.* All persons who engage in the business of forwarding shall register with the Commission, such registration to be in addition to any registration under General Order 70. Registration shall be accomplished by executing and filing with the Commission Freight Forwarder Registration Form M. C.—21,* set out at § 244.14. Copies thereof will be furnished by the Commission upon request.

(a) *Existing firms.* All persons engaged in the business of freight forwarding on the effective date of this part shall register with the Commission within sixty days after such date.

(b) *New firms.* All persons who first engage in the business of freight forwarding after the effective date of this part shall register with the Commission before engaging in such business.

*Filed as part of the original document.

(c) *Extension of time.* For good cause shown, the Commission, upon written request of the registrant, may extend the time for registration.

§ 244.3 *Additional information.* Registrants shall submit such additional information as the Commission may request from time to time, and shall notify the Commission of any change in facts reported to it under this part, within ten days after such change occurs.

§ 244.4 *Information available to public.* Information set forth in Freight Forwarder Registration Form M. C.–21 shall be public information and available for public inspection at the offices of the Commission.

§ 244.5 *Registration numbers: Suspension and cancellation of registration.* (a) Each forwarder who has filed the required information will receive from the Commission a registration number which shall thereafter be set forth on the registrant's letterheads, invoices, advertising, and all other documents relating to his forwarding business. Use of these registration numbers in any manner other than to indicate the fact of registration with the Commission, is prohibited.

(b) A forwarder's registration may be suspended or cancelled after notice and hearing, if the Commission finds that the registrant has violated this part or the Shipping Act, 1916.

§ 244.6 *Registration lists.* The Commission will compile periodically, and make available to the public upon request, lists of all registrants with their respective registration numbers.

§ 244.7 *Billing practices.* All forwarders shall use invoices or other forms of billing which state separately and specifically, as to each shipment:

(a) The amount of ocean freight assessed by the carrier;

(b) The amount of consular fees paid to consular authorities;

(c) The amount of insurance premiums actually disbursed for insurance bought in the name of the shipper or consignee;

(d) The amount charged for each accessorial service performed in connection with the shipment;

(e) Other charges.

Provided, however, That forwarders who offer to the public at large to forward small shipments for uniform charges available to all and duly filed with the Commission, shall not be required to itemize the components of such uniform charges on shipments as to which the charges shall have been stated to the shipper at time of shipment, and accepted by the shipper by payment; but if such forwarders procure marine insurance to cover such shipments, they must state their total charge for such insurance, inclusive of premiums and placing fees, separately from the aforementioned uniform charge.

§ 244.8 *Consolidated shipments.* In the case of consolidated shipments, the invoice or other form of billing concerning each shipment shall state the minimum ocean freight and consular fees that would have been payable on each shipment if shipped separately, and the amounts actually charged for these items by the forwarder, on the shipment in question.

§244.9 *Special contracts.* All special agreements or contracts between forwarders and shippers or consignees shall, if in writing, or if confirmed in writing, be maintained in the files of the forwarder for a period of 12 months, for submission to the Commission upon request.

§ 244.10 *Nondiscriminating treatment required.* To the extent that special agreements or contracts are entered into by a forwarder with individual shippers or consignees, such forwarder shall not deny to other shippers or consignees similarly situated, and whose shipments are accepted by such forwarder, equal charges for forwarding and accessorial services to be rendered by the forwarder, in so far as such forwarding and accessorial services are similar to those performed for shippers or consignees holding special contracts; and such forwarder shall advise such other shippers or consignees as to the terms under which such special contracts or agreements are available.

§ 244.11 *Exceptions as to special contracts.* In the case of special contracts whereby the parties have agreed in advance as to the charges for services in connection with the forwarding of a shipment, the invoice or other form of billing shall refer to the agreement, in which event the charges need not be itemized.

§ 244.12 *Forwarders' receipts.* Forwarders' receipts for cargo shall be clearly identified as such and shall not be in form purporting to be ocean carriers' bills of lading.

§ 244.13 *Brokerage.* No forwarder, after the date on which he is required to register, shall accept brokerage from ocean carriers unless and until such forwarder has been assigned a registration number pursuant to these rules. Registration shall not entitle a forwarder to collect brokerage from a common carrier by water in cases where payment thereof would constitute a rebate—i. e., where the forwarder is a shipper or consignee or is the seller or purchaser of the shipment, or has any beneficial interest therein or where the forwarder directly or indirectly controls or is controlled by the shipper or consignee, or by any person having a beneficial interest in the shipment. A forwarder shall not share any part of the brokerage received from a common carrier by water with a shipper or consignee. No forwarder shall demand or accept brokerage during the period his registration number is under suspension or after his registration number has been cancelled pursuant to these rules.

§ 244.14 *Registration form.* Form M. C.-21* is hereby prescribed for registration under § 244.2.

§ 244.15 *Effective date.* Sections 244.1 to 244.14, both inclusive, shall become effective June 1, 1950.

By the Commission.
[SEAL]

                                            A. J. WILLIAMS,
                                                  Secretary.

May 18, 1950.
        [F. R. Doc. 50–4449; Filed, May 23, 1950; 10:20 a. m.]

Prior to Order 72, the Maritime Commission, in pursuance of the mandate received under the Bland Freight Forwarding Act, issued General Order 70 on May 26, 1949, declaring that the public interest requires the employment of private foreign freight forwarders in connection with the export of cargo for foreign relief and rehabilitation under the Foreign Assistance Act of 1948, and other similar statutes. Forwarders interested in handling this type of cargo had to register with the Commission, which submitted a corresponding list to provide selection, to all government agencies concerned with relief. Undoubtedly, this order was of great assistance to the forwarding business, because the overwhelming majority of our export trade was then government-financed and government-furnished. This order was already revised, one year later, on May 4, 1950, and stipulated that the services of private freight forwarders should be used, except where existing conditions made such use unreasonable or impracticable, whereas the original order listed as only exception the case of emergency. This revision reflected imminent threatening coolness in the relations between government and forwarding industry.

Therefore, it was no coup, in October, 1954, when the Federal Maritime Board announced a second, nationwide investigation into the business practices of foreign freight forwarders. Although the Board emphasized that the undertaking would not be of a punitive nature, it

---

* Filed as part of the original document.

was maintained that it was necessary to determine to what extent, if any, foreign freight forwarders were using business methods, or practices, which resulted in injustly discriminatory, or unduly prejudicial, treatment of shippers, consignees, carriers or others, and whether or not forwarders had entered into agreements, or cooperative working arrangements with others, or had taken concerted actions without obtaining approval pursuant to Section 15 of the Shipping Act, 1916. Formal notices were sent to about fifteen hundred forwarders, with hearings to follow.

Regarded by the Board as a logical additional step to aid the commerce and trade of the United States, the Board hoped the inquiry would establish standards which might help stabilize the forwarding industry, and assure fair and equitable treatment to forwarders and their clients. Among the practices to be scrutinized were the collection of ocean freight brokerage from shipping lines, by forwarders who also were acting for exporters and importers, and the splitting of brokerage commissions with shippers. The Board legitimately contended that sharing of brokerage fees with shippers, or the waiving or reduction of customary handling charges to exporters or importers because of receipt of brokerage, constituted a violation of the 1916 Shipping Act, since it resulted in "An Indirect Rebate."

In March, 1955, the Office of Investigation, U. S. General Accounting Office, published a *Report On The Use Of Private Export Freight Forwarders By Departments And Agencies Of The United States*, which was highly critical because it linked questionable forwarder practices to the payment of brokerage by subsidized American steamship lines. The report intimated that these practices might operate to increase indirectly Government expenditures, as well as freight charges.

In the Fall of 1955, Congress, through the House Merchant Marine Committee, followed suit by opening hearings as to the role of the foreign freight forwarder in handling government cargo, and whether the Bland Freight Forwarding Act of 1942 should be revised.*

Finally, Senator Yarborough, from the Senate Committee on Commerce, to whom Senate Bill No. 1368 was referred to, to amend the Shipping Act, 1916, in order to provide for licensing independent ocean freight forwarders, submitted a report on this bill to the Senate (87th Congress 1st Session) for approval on August 9th, 1961 and was passed on September 1st, 1961. Shortly thereafter, the House of Representatives on September 5th, 1961, concurred and on September 19th, 1961, President Kennedy signed it into law as Public Law 87-254, reading as follows:

* See Appendix H. Special report of the Hearings before the Sub-committee on Foreign Freight Forwarders and Brokers (N. Y. Freight Forwarders and Brokers Assoc.)

An Act

75 STAT. 522.

To amend the Shipping Act, 1916, to provide for licensing independent ocean freight forwarders, and for other purposes.

Be it enacted by the Senate and House of Representatives of the United States of America in Congress assembled, That the first section of the Shipping Act, 1916 (46 U.S.C. 801), is amended by adding at the end thereof the following new paragraphs:

"The term 'carrying on the business of forwarding' means the dispatching of shipments by any person on behalf of others, by ocean-going common carriers in commerce from the United States, its Territories, or possessions to foreign countries, or between the United States and its Territories or possessions, or between such Territories and possessions, and handling the formalities incident to such shipments.

"An 'independent ocean freight forwarder' is a person carrying on the business of forwarding for a consideration who is not a shipper or consignee or a seller or purchaser of shipments to foreign countries, nor has any beneficial interest therein, nor directly or indirectly controls or is controlled by such shipper or consignee or by any person having such a beneficial interest."

SEC. 2. The Shipping Act, 1916, is further amended by redesignating section 44 as section 45, and inserting immediately after section 43 the following new section:

"SEC. 44. (a) No person shall engage in carrying on the business of forwarding as defined in this Act unless such person holds a license issued by the Federal Maritime Commission to engage in such business: *Provided, however,* That a person whose primary business is the sale of merchandise may dispatch shipments of such merchandise without a license.

"(b) A forwarder's license shall be issued to any qualified applicant therefor if it is found by the Commission that the applicant is, or will be, an independent ocean freight forwarder as defined in this Act and is fit, willing, and able properly to carry on the business of forwarding and to conform to the provisions of this Act and the requirements, rules, and regulations of the Commission issued thereunder, and that the proposed forwarding business is, or will be, consistent with the national maritime policies declared in the Merchant Marine Act, 1936; otherwise such application shall be denied. Any independent ocean freight forwarder who, on the effective date of this Act, is carrying on the business of forwarding under a registration number issued by the Commission may continue such business for a period of one hundred and twenty days thereafter without a license, and if application for such license is made within such period, such forwarder may, under such regulations as the Commission shall prescribe, continue such business until otherwise ordered by the Commission.

"(c) The Commission shall prescribe reasonable rules and regulations to be observed by independent ocean freight forwarders and no such license shall be issued or remain in force unless such forwarder shall have furnished a bond or other security approved by the Commission in such form and amount as in the opinion of the Commission

Shipping Act,
1916, amendment.
Ocean freight
forwarders.
39 Stat. 728.
Definitions.

40 Stat. 903.
46 USC 842.

Licenses.

Issuance.

49 Stat. 1985.
46 USC 1245.

Conditions.

44

will insure financial responsibility and the supply of the services in accordance with contracts, agreements, or arrangements therefor.

"(d) Licenses shall be effective from the date specified therein, and shall remain in effect until suspended or terminated as herein provided. Any such license may, upon application of the holder thereof, in the discretion of the Commission, be amended or revoked, in whole or in part, or may upon complaint, or on the Commission's own initiative, after notice and hearing, be suspended or revoked for willful failure to comply with any provision of this Act, or with any lawful order, rule, or regulation of the Commission promulgated thereunder.

Compensation of licensees.

"(e) A common carrier by water may compensate a person carrying on the business of forwarding to the extent of the value rendered such carrier in connection with any shipment dispatched on behalf of others when, and only when, such person is licensed hereunder and has performed with respect to such shipment the solicitation and securing of the cargo for the ship or the booking of, or otherwise arranging for space for, such cargo, and at least two of the following services:

"(1) The coordination of the movement of the cargo to shipside;

"(2) The preparation and processing of the ocean bill of lading;

"(3) The preparation and processing of dock receipts or delivery orders;

"(4) The preparation and processing of consular documents or export declarations;

"(5) The payment of the ocean freight charges on such shipments:

Separate compensation.

Provided, however, That where a common carrier by water has paid, or has incurred an obligation to pay, either to an ocean freight broker or freight forwarder, separate compensation for the solicitation or securing of cargo for the ship or the booking of, or otherwise arranging for space for, such cargo, then such carrier shall not be obligated to pay additional compensation for any other forwarding services rendered on the same cargo. Before any such compensation is paid to or received by any person carrying on the business of forwarding, such person shall, if he is qualified under the provisions of this paragraph to receive such compensation, certify in writing to the common carrier by water by which the shipment was dispatched that he is licensed by the Federal Maritime Commission as an independent ocean freight forwarder and that he performed the above specified services with respect to such shipment. Such carrier shall be entitled to rely on such certification unless it knows that the certification is incorrect."

Approved September 19, 1961.

Thus, the independent ocean freight forwarding industry, one of the most complex and important segments of the economy of the United States, having forfeited the anticipated high standards through default became subject to specific regulatory control through licensing.

Three months later, the Federal Maritime Commission issued General Order 4 putting into effect as of December 22nd, 1961, regulations concerning licensing of independent ocean freight forwarders, therein outlining the scope and purpose of the law, the definitions of terms and practices involved, the requirements of licensing and procedural applications as well as rules concerning fitness of the applicants. These freight forwarder rules were slightly modified in the following seven years, and for this reason, a revised General Order 4 reissued in its entirety, on September 6, 1968. Meanwhile, additional minor amendments were published on September 24, 1969, October 2, 1969 and August 16, 1972. The substance of the Forwarder Law can be broken down into four main categories:

1. No brokerage commission or other compensation shall be paid by an oceangoing common carrier to any person other than a licensed independent ocean freight forwarder or bona fide ocean freight broker.

2. Any person who has any ownership connection with export cargo is precluded from being licensed.

3. Oceangoing common carriers or affiliates thereof are not precluded from being licensed.

4. Only a shipper or a licensee can perform freight forwarding services on export shipments.

Following is a summary of the most important rules of General Order 4 including amendments,* as in effect today:

1. A non-vessel operating common carrier by water, for the purpose of the rules, is deemed a shipper of cargo via the underlying oceangoing common carrier. Such non-vessel operating common carrier may perform forwarding services with respect to shipments moving on his own through export bill of lading.

2. A licensee who has reason to believe that a principal has not, with respect to a shipment to be handled by such licensee, complied with the law or has made any error or misrepresentation in, or omission from, any export declaration, bill of lading, affidavit, or other paper which the principal executes in connection with such shipment, shall advise his principal promptly of the suspected noncompliance, error, misrepresentation or omission, and shall decline to participate in such transaction involving such document until the matter is clarified.

3. No licensee shall withhold information relative to a forwarding transaction from his principal.

4. Each licensee shall promptly pay over to the oceangoing common carrier or other person when due all sums advanced by a principal for the payment of any and all charges, debts, or obligations in connection with the forwarding transaction, and shall promptly account to his principal for funds received in behalf of the principal for overpayments, adjustment of charges, reductions in rates, insurance refunds, insurance money paid to the forwarder as the result of claims, proceeds of C.O.D. shipments, drafts, letters of credit and any other sums due to such principal.

5. Every licensee shall use invoices or other forms of billing which state separately as to each shipment (1) the actual amount of ocean freight assessed by the oceangoing common carrier, (2) the actual amount of consular fees paid, (3) the premium cost of insurance arranged, (4) the charge for each accessorial service performed in connection with the shipment. All other charges or fees assessed by the licensee for arranging 1, 2, 3, and 4 above shall be itemized.

*See Appendix H/A

6. Each licensee shall maintain correctly and in orderly, systematic, convenient and readily available manner, and keep current, all records and books of account in connection with carrying on the business of forwarding. Such records shall be retained for a period of five years and shall include a copy of each document prepared, processed or obtained by the licensee.

7. Each licensee shall make available promptly all records and books of account in connection with carrying on the business of forwarding, for inspection or reproducing or other official use upon request of any authorized representative of the Commission.

8. No oceangoing common carrier shall pay to a licensee, and no licensee shall charge or receive from any such carrier, either directly or indirectly, any compensation or payment of any kind whatsoever, whether called "brokerage," "commission," "fee," or by any other name, in connection with any cargo or shipment wherein the licensee's name appears on the ocean bill of lading as shipper or as agent for an undisclosed principal.

9. No licensee shall render, or offer to render, any forwarding service free of charge or at a reduced freight forwarding fee in consideration of the licensee receiving compensation from oceangoing common carriers on the shipment, provided, however, that a licensee may perform freight forwarding services for recognized relief agencies or charitable organizations designated as such in the tariff of the oceangoing common carrier, free of charge, or at reduced fees.

10. No licensee shall share, directly or indirectly, any compensation or freight forwarding fee with a shipper, consignee, seller, purchaser, or their agents, affiliates or employees, nor with any person or persons advancing the purchase price of the merchandise or guaranteeing payment, therefore, nor with any person or persons having a beneficial interest in the shipment.

11. An oceangoing common carrier may compensate a licensee to the extent of the value rendered such carrier in connection with any shipment forwarded on behalf of others when, and only when, such carrier is in possession of a certification in the form prescribed in these rules.

12. A true copy of all existing special arrangements or contracts, including amendments, modifications and cancellations thereof, between a licensee and his principal shall be filed with the Commission within 30 days after the effective date of these rules, and, or oral, shall be confirmed in writing and a true copy shall be filed with the Commission within such time. All such future arrangements, contracts, amendments, modifications, or cancellations shall be filed within 10 days after they have been entered into.

13. No oceangoing common carrier, or agent thereof, may perform freight forwarder services without a license. Charges for such services shall be published in tariffs filed with the Commission.

14. Nothing in these rules shall be interpreted to prohibit a per-

son from performing freight forwarding services on his own behalf, or on behalf of a wholly owning parent company or a wholly owned subsidiary, or to require such a person to be licensed.

Concluding this chapter a few words may be added about the "special interest" legislation of the 89th Congress of 1966. The Department of Transportation, created under Public Law 89-670 of October 15th, 1966, within eight months after being proposed by President Johnson in March, 1966, does not include the Maritime Administration nor the Maritime Commission. The regulatory body, leaving these agencies within the Department of Commerce where "organized lobbies" representing special interests of both management and labor in the field of Transportation wanted them to stay. These lobbies included the ocean shipping industry and labor unions that benefit most from federal subsidies and grants. However, it is to be hoped that the advocates of a strong and effective transportation department may soon see the day that those forces who oppose the inclusion of "Maritime" in the Department will be "importuning Congress to include them."

CHAPTER V

Legal Status of the Foreign Freight Forwarder

Today, we distinguish two systems of law in the Western World: the Roman, or Civil Law, and the English, or Common Law. The former system, dating back to the Roman Empire, became the law of modern continental Europe, Scotland, and of all the Americas, except Canada and the United States. Evolving through the centuries, its rules and doctrines were compiled, digested, and codified, until at the turn of the twentieth century it had attained a certain stability. The second system originated in England in the thirteenth century and consisted of rules formulated by the decisions of the courts. Originally, these decisions were based on the habits and customs of the community, but these were eventually superseded by national rules and principles. It is also called "case law," in contrast to the rules and regulations established by legislation, or statutory law.

Law governing merchants' transactions or commercial practices, that is, the law concerning agency, bailments, insurance, brokerage, sureties, warehouses, and other services is called "law merchant" or mercantile law. It has now been mostly absorbed, by the common law, or crystallized by legislative enactments.

Admirality law applies to maritime affairs, such as relations between master and seaman, and other business transacted upon the high seas or navigable waterways, natural or artificial. Under Article III, Section 2, Number 1, of the Constitution of the United States, admiralty and maritime jurisdiction resides in the federal courts. There are no separate admirality courts. The text of jurisdiction depends on the locality and the subject matter involved. Therefore, federal district courts have original jurisdiction in practically all civil and/or criminal actions brought by, or against, foreign freight forwarders.

Among admirality counsel and others who, through practical experience, have gained knowledge of local usage, there is an opinion that a foreign freight forwarder is not an agent, but is a contractor limiting his liability by agreement. While this view is widely held, court decisions have definitely confirmed the author's standpoint, advocated for many years, that an international freight forwarder is an agent and, consequently, the affairs of his business should be treated under the Law of Agency.

The forwarder's diversified activities and functions challenges the application of uniform legal principles. He is a middleman, who assists directly in effecting a transfer of title to, and possession of, goods. He is a coordinator of freight services, who exercises traffic control by selecting suitable routes, securing favorable ocean, air, or railroad rates, and making effective use of transportation facilities. Primarily, he is an agent representative of shipper and consignee, placing at their disposal his expert knowledge of foreign trade, and his services in moving freight efficiently and rapidly.

Further difficulty in defining the international forwarder's legal position exists in that his elaborate and complicated business transactions partially parallel those of the domestic freight forwarder, whose status has been legally fixed by statutory law through an act of Congress regulating practices and rates. In part IV of the Interstate Commerce Act, section 402 (a) 5, as approved May 16, 1942, and amended November 12, 1943, the term "freight forwarder" is defined as "any person (individual, firm, partnership, corporation, company, association, or joint-stock association) which holds itself out to the general public to transport or provide transportation of property, or any class or classes of property, for compensation, in interstate commerce, and which, in the ordinary and usual course of its undertaking, (A) assembles and consolidates or provides for assembling and consolidating shipments of such property, and performs or provides for the performance of break-bulk and distributing operations with respect to such consolidated shipments, and (B) assumes responsibility for the transportation of such property from point of receipt to point of destination and (C) utilizes, for the whole or any part of the transportation of such shipments, the services of a carrier or carriers subject to Part I, II or III of this ACT."*

This definition, however, does not cover the foreign freight forwarder since it applies only to the domestic freight forwarder. The other definition as contained in Public Law 87-254 of September 19, 1961 also lacks, like the one issued by the Federal Maritime Commission in General Order 4 of September 6, 1968 plus its amendments of September 24, 1969, October 2, 1969 and August 16, 1972 (see Appendix H/A) factual and functional completeness.

Firstly, the persons who, as international traffic specialists, offer many valuable transportation facilities and whose services are engaged by a certain group of customers or principals, namely, consignor and consignee, are termed "foreign freight forwarders." This appelation doesn't indicate the scope of their actual functions or services. Secondly, this type of commercial "forwarder" does not transport, or forward, goods in the literal sense, but only assists in, or provides for, moving freight through carriers. Thirdly, the "forwarder's" compensation is derived from arranging transportation and services, and not from actually transporting goods. Finally, the main function of a carrier is the carriage of goods, a physical activity, whereas the "forwarder's" functions are directed to the solution of non-physical prob-

*An act of Congress regulating practices and rates of freight forwarders (part IV of the Interstate Commerce Act, section 402 (a) 5, November 12, 1943.)

lems, which arise in connection with satisfactorily arranging the actual transfer of goods.

In contrast with the domestic freight forwarder, as termed in the Interstate Commerce Act, part IV, the foreign freight forwarder does not enter into the functions, or assume the rights or obligations of a common carrier. He retains his actual, and legal, independence as *a shipping agent who professionally undertakes to provide and to arrange for, efficient and complete transportation of goods to foreign countries by means of common carriers for account of his principal, shipper or consignee, in his own name.*

Including the economic and functional position of the "international shipping agent," which is what the foreign freight forwarder should be called, this definition also does justice to his legal relations with the parties whom he represents and for whom he transacts business under delegated authority. Therefore, the law of agency should be applied, and we may classify the shipping agent as "a general agent" who is authorized by consignor, or consignee, to transact all of his affairs connected with forwarding his shipments to foreign countries."

Interesting to note is that the Supreme Court, in its famous decision of February 25, 1946, *United States v. American Union Transport,* 327 U. S. 437, said (p. 443) : "By engaging in these many activities of the forwarding business, independent forwarders—and particularly the appellees—act as agents of the shippers."

Of late, other courts have confirmed the applicability of the agency principle. On February 9, 1953, the U. S. Court of Appeals, Second Circuit, Docket 22549, Per Curiam, affirmed the dismissal of the Admirality suit of J. C. Penny Co. v. American Express Company. The lower court dismissed the libel on the ground that "the Express Company which handled details of shipment, procured overseas transportation by carrier, and paid all charges therefor, and which received reimbursement from owner of cargo and payment of fee for its services, was not carrier but was merely forwarding agent for owner and, as such was liable only for its own negligence."

In this case, "the forwarding agent of the cargo owner was not expected or authorized to secure a value bill of lading from the American Export Lines, and failure to secure such a bill of lading did not render the American Express Company secondary liable to the J. C. Penny Company for water damage to the cargo, while it was at sea."

On the other hand, the foreign freight forwarder, being engaged in specialized foreign trade work, must perform in line with shippers' instructions and cannot deviate from them, unless by consent. Otherwise, he will be held liable for damages arising from his errors or negligence, as shown in the case *Princess Pat, Ltd. v. Judson-Sheldon*

Division of National Carloading Corporation, decided on June 15, 1955 in the U. S. Court of Appeals, Seventh Circuit, on appeal from the U. S. District Court, Northern District of Illinois, Eastern Division. There, the exporter collected not only the fines and penalties assessed on a shipment, but also an amount representing the loss of his profit. In brief, the facts of the case were as follows:

Princess Pat, Ltd. hired the Judson-Sheldon Division of National Carloading Corporation to handle an export shipment of eighteen cases of its products to Brazil. The company's export manager secured space on a Delta Line ship leaving New Orleans and on Nov. 7, 1946, Judson-Sheldon accepted the cases and initialed a memorandum bill of lading. However, the cases were sent by pool car to New York, instead of to New Orleans, where subsequent shipment was made in two lots by two different ships. As a result of these and other errors, Princess Pat claimed that it sustained penalties amounting to $4,389.33, for non-compliance with Brazilian customs regulations and a loss of seven months marketing time.

In the lower court, a jury awarded Princess Pat, Ltd. $16,000 for penalties and loss of profits. The Court of Appeals refused to overthrow the jury verdict, since the president of the company had testified without cross-examination, or objection, that the billed price was $8,917.68, and the mark-up was two-thirds of the invoice, or $5,945.12, which for two three-month periods of lost sales would amount to $11,890.24. There was also evidence that the defendant had been informed that this was a special shipment; that the cases were an initial shipment to a new distributor; and that arrival was planned for the carnival season in Brazil.

The appointment of the forwarder as agent of shipper or consignee may be made by an informal appointment, or a verbal or written agreement. State laws, and the fourth section of the Statute of Frauds, determine the particular requirements. The appointments by estoppel, or ratification, are sporadic.

The international shipping agent's extent of powers regarding third parties, with whom he has to deal in his capacity as representative of his customer, is important. The sources of his authority are fourfold: (1) declared, (2) incidental, (3) customary, and (4) apparent. These sources are discussed in the following listing.

1. If the buyer, or consignee, in his instructions to the shipping agent, stipulates that payment of the seller's invoice may only be effected against delivery of merchandise to steamer pier, and further remittance of signed dock receipt to the shipping agent, he is not permitted to deviate from this instruction. When the agent indicates that he is bound to act under the aforementioned stipulation, the seller, as third party, must take notice of the agent's obligation.

2. If the shipper in the interior forwards a consignment sold on a Cost, Insurance Freight basis for reshipment overseas, without

furnishing the funds to pay the ocean freight, the shipping agent has the implied power to advance payment for the ocean carrier's bill.

3. As shipping agent, he has the authority to perform any act which, according to custom in the export trade, usually accompanies the transaction for which he is authorized. For instance, if the cargo has been booked for a certain sailing of ocean carrier A, and arrived too late at the port of exit and missed the vessel, the shipping agent may arrange for rebooking with carrier B, which offers immediate sailing opportunity, thus avoiding undue delay by waiting for the next sailing of steamship line A, with which the consignment was originally booked.

4. The shipping agent can, also, under certain circumstances, delegate his authority by appointing sub-agents, if this transfer is based on the implied and expressed consent of the customer, or principal. In case the goods are sold "free inland destination" in a foreign country, a correspondent agent at the port of destination may be engaged for the execution of the final delivery. Sub-agents may also be engaged where the acts involve only mechanical and clerical duties, in cases of unforseen emergency, or justified necessity, as well as in those instances when it is expected by the parties that sub-agents would be employed.

Duties Imposed on Agent by Law

The shipping agent, like any other agent, is subject to many duties imposed by law. The significant ones in this respect are loyalty, obedience, care and skill, accounting, information, and performance.

Loyalty. The agent is required to protect the interest of his customer, and has to abstain from every act that would be detrimental to his principal. Except where there is no conflict in interest, he cannot represent another party in a transaction which he is conducting for his principal.

Obedience. The agent must comply with his customer's directions and cannot deviate from them unless his principal has consented. In case the instructions are confusing, the agent should, if time permits, obtain clarification. Otherwise, he may follow a reasonable interpretation of the instructions without liability.

Care and skill. The shipping agent must exercise reasonable skill, care, or diligence, in the performance of duties. This is measured by the standard applicable in similar services. Being engaged in specialized foreign trade work, he requires a high degree of skill, which increases his burden of liability.

Accounting. The duty to account to his principal is an important one. The shipping agent often holds his customer's funds, from which he makes payments to shippers for merchandise delivered to him. He should keep such money separate from his own. Collections made by the shipping agent for account of the shipper should, also, be given due notice, and an accurate account of all receipts and expenses should be rendered.

Information. The shipping agent must inform his principal of all facts that tend to change the normal course of events in the business transaction. If, for instance, the cargo arrives at the dock in damaged condition, the principal is to be notified.

Performance. The agent must live up to the terms of his contract. He must stay within the scope of his authority. Any transgression will make the shipping agent liable.

DUTIES IMPOSED ON PRINCIPAL OR EMPLOYER

These duties on the part of the shipping agent, or foreign freight forwarder, correspond to certain obligations that are imposed upon the principal or employer (consignor or consignee).

Compensation. Same is implied when the performance of services reasonably and usually justify the expectation of being paid. The amount of the compensation is, in absence of an expressed agreement, determined by usage, or customary fees or rates.

Reimbursement. The customer, shipper, or consignee is under obligation to reimburse the shipping agent for all disbursements made or expenses incurred in pursuance or fulfillment of the principal's instructions. However, expenses incurred through misconduct or negligence on the part of the shipping agent cannot be recovered by him from his customer, but will have to be absorbed by him.

Indemnity. It is the customer's obligation to indemnify the shipping agent for any losses or damages suffered that occurred in execution of the given instructions or in the course of the transacted business when it was not the agent's fault.

Performance. The principal's duty is similar to that of the agent, inasmuch as he also has to comply with the terms of the agreement.

Of further interest and importance is the relation of the customer, shipper or consignee, to third parties. The former may become liable to third parties on actions in contract, or in tort, as a result of the acts of the agent; and the same situation exists with regard to the relation of the third party to the customer of the shipping agent. The principal is liable to third parties for all contracts lawfully entered into by the shipping agent in the principal's name, provided that the forwarding agent's transactions were within the scope of his authority, or subsequently ratified. The same principle applies also to statements made by the shipping agent while performing transactions within the scope of his authority.

Finally, we must mention the termination of the agent's relation to his principal. This may be (1) by operation of law. Such cases can be dispensed with summarily. They are death, insanity, or bankruptcy on the part of agent, or principal, unless the authority is coupled with an interest in the subject matter. And (2) termination of the agency relation by act of either principal or agent, with or without the approval of the other. Usually, the agency relation, which is created by mutual consent, will be similarly terminated. Agency may also be terminated upon the expiration of specified time, upon occurrence of a certain event, or upon accomplishment of the subject matter.

Inasmuch as the principal is the party that creates the agent's authority, he has the power, and usually the right, to revoke the agent's authority. Only in cases where the agency is coupled with an interest, the authority cannot be withdrawn by the principal. These conditions prevail if the agent has an interest in the authority, by having given a consideration, or if the agent has an interest in the subject matter. On the other hand, the agent may terminate the agency by renouncing the authority given him by the principal, in case of an agency at will, or because of wrongful demands or misconduct by the principal. When the agency relation has been terminated, the agent loses all his authority between the direct parties. However, a revocation by the principal necessitates notification to the agent. Third parties must also be advised of the termination of the agency based on revocation.

THE INTERMODAL CONCEPT

The advent of containerization in the export and import trade has brought about a variety of problems and changes concerning the carriage, handling and regulation of the freight movement involved. The traditional segmented handling of shipments from point of origin via rail, truck and ocean carrier to the final point of destination has been more or less replaced by containerized thru-movement of goods, called Intermodalism and the creation of the Combined Transport Operator called NVOCC (Non-Vessel Operating Common Carrier), and with it the necessity for the formalization of an officially coordinated interagency mechanism for the purpose of exchanging information and achieving consensus on intermodal problems of mutual interest, and, last but not least, to secure an agreement on international through-rates. Unfortunately, jurisdictional jealousy of the participating governmental agencies did not go, until now, beyond the creation of the Interagency Committee on Intermodal Cargo (ICIC), not a regulatory but only an advisory body, represented by the Federal Maritime Commission, Interstate Commerce Commission, Civil Aeronautics Board and Department of Transportation whose task is to consider all aspects of house to house freight rates, simplified documentation such as standardized forms of thru-bills of lading, cargo liability, tariff-filing procedure reforms and matters of commodity descriptions and codes, etc.

Although the Federal Maritime Commission and members of Congress introduced in 1973 and 1974 legislation to settle the present and future status of the Foreign Freight Forwarder as agent respectively intermodal carrier, no final decision has been reached by the middle of 1974. At the present, the NVOCC is recognized by the Federal Maritime Commission as common carrier who publishes his tariffs after having filed same with that authority.

CHAPTER VI

United States Export Control

(1) It is the policy of the United States both (A) to encourage trade with all countries with which we have diplomatic or trading relations, except those countries with which such trade has been determined by the President to be against the national interest, and (B) to restrict the export of goods and technology which would make a significant contribution to the military potential of any other nation or nations which would prove detrimental to the national security of the United States.

(2) It is the policy of the United States to use export controls (A) to the extent necessary to protect the domestic economy from the excessive drain of scarce materials and to reduce the serious inflationary impact of abnormal foreign demand, (B) to the extent necessary to further significantly the foreign policy of the United States and to fulfill its international responsibilities, and (C) to the extent necessary to exercise the necessary vigilance over exports from the standpoint of their significance to the national security of the United States.

(3) It is the policy of the United States (A) to formulate, reformulate, and apply any necessary controls to the maximum extent possible in cooperation with all nations with which the United States has defense treaty commitments, and (B) to formulate a unified trade control policy to be observed by all such nations.

(4) It is the policy of the United States to use its economic resources and trade potential to further the sound growth and stability of its economy as well as to further its national security and foreign policy objectives.

(5) It is the policy of the United States (A) to oppose restrictive trade practices or boycotts fostered or imposed by foreign countries against other countries friendly to the United States, and (B) to encourage and request domestic concerns engaged in the export of articles, materials, supplies, or information, to refuse to take any action, including the furnishing of information or the signing of agreements, which has the effect of furthering or supporting the restrictive trade practices or boycotts fostered or imposed by any foreign country against another country friendly to the United States.

(6) It is the policy of the United States that the desirability of subjecting, or continuing to subject, particular articles, materials, or supplies, including technical data or other information, to United States export controls should be subjected to review by and consultation with representatives of appropriate United States Government agencies and qualified experts from the private industry.

This declaration of policy, quoted from Section 3 of the Export Administration Act of 1969 as amended and extended by the Equal Export Opportunity Act of August 29, 1972, and the Export Administration Amendments of 1977, Public Law 95-52 of June 22, 1977 (H.R. 5840), provides the president with the authority to prohibit or curtail exports from the United States, its territories, and possessions, and authorizes him to delegate this authority to such departments, agencies, and officials of the government as he deems appropriate. The export control authority, which has been delegated to the Secretary of Commerce, is administered by the Office of Export Administration, Bureau of East-West Trade. The pertinent regulations are published in the Federal Register and in the U.S. Department of Commerce,"Export Administration Regulations" and their supplements, the "Export Administration Bulletins," which represent an authoritative and complete statement of export control provisions and which impose responsibilities on exporters, carriers and forwarding agents in connection with both United States export transactions generally and, specifically, with respect to the carriage, transporting or handling of export, as an integral part of export operations. The aforementioned export control provisions purpose is to constantly review the Commodity Control List, a listing by export control commodity number of all commodities for which the export licensing authority is exercised by the Office of Export Administration, Bureau of East-West Trade. Based on the Census Bureau Schedule B, Statistical Number Classification of Domestic and Foreign Commodities exported from the United States, with which all exporters and foreign freight forwarders are familiar, it is designed to facilitate determination of proper controls by exporters. It identifies, for each listed commodity or category, the destinations to which a validated export license is required, a formal document issued to an exporter by the Department of Commerce, based on his signed application. It authorizes exportation of commodities or technical data within the specific limitations of the document. Commodities may be exported under general license which is a broad authorization established by the Department of Commerce permitting certain exports of commodities and technical data under specified conditions without the necessity of applying for a license document. There are several different general licenses. The conditions for use of each general license are set forth in the Export Administration Regulations, part 371, and the regulations governing the export of technical data, including validated license requirements, in part 379.

Exempt from the rules and regulations of export control are ten groups of commodities and technical data, since they are controlled or licensed by other government departments, agencies, or commissions. They are:

1. Commodities for the official use of, or consumption by, the Armed Forces of the United States, and commodities for general consumption in occupied areas under their jurisdiction, when the transport facilities of the Armed Forces are used to carry such shipments.

2. Commodities exported by the Department of Defense pursuant to section 414 of the Mutual Security Act of 1954.

3. Arms, ammunition, implements of war, technical data relating thereto, and certain classified information, which are licensed by the Department of State.

4. U.S. 1-cent coins containing bronze (pennies), which are licensed by the Treasury Department.

5. Source material, "by-product material," special nuclear material, and facilities for the production or utilization of special nuclear materials, which are licensed by the Nuclear Regulatory Commission (except components for such facilities, which are licensed for export by the Bureau of East-West Trade). Related technical data are licensed by the Energy Research and Development Administration.

6. Vessels (other than vessels of war), which are licensed by the Maritime Administration, Department of Commerce. Vessels sold by the Maritime Administration for scrapping abroad also are controlled by the Bureau of East-West Trade.

7. Natural gas and electric energy, which are licensed by the Federal Power Commission.

8. Tobacco seed and plants, which are licensed by the Department of Agriculture.

9. Narcotics and dangerous drugs, which are licensed by the Department of Justice.

10. Endangered species of fish and wildlife, migratory birds, and bald and golden eagles or any part, product, egg or offspring thereof, or the dead body or parts thereof, whether or not incorporated into a finished product, which are licensed by the Department of Interior.

For export control purposes, all foreign destinations are divided into seven country groups, excluding Canada which is not included in any country group since exports to that country are normally not controlled: Group Q: Romania; Group S: Southern Rhodesia; Group T: All countries of the Western Hemisphere, excluding Canada and Cuba; Group W: Poland; Group Y: Albania, Bulgaria, Czechoslovakia, East Germany (German Democratic Republic and Soviet sector of Berlin), Estonia, Hungary, Latvia, Lithuania, Outer Mongolia, the People's Republic of China, and the U.S.S.R.; Group Z: North Korea, Communist-controlled areas of North Vietnam, South Vietnam, Cambodia and Cuba; and Group V: all other countries, excluding Canada.

As stated before, the Commodity Control List (CCL) is the key to determining whether a specific shipment is exportable under a validated or general license authorization, and each commodity on the CCL is identified in the first column by its "Export Control Commodity (ECC) Number." This number is composed of the first one to five digits of the seven-digit Schedule B commodity classification number applicable to the commodity and by italicized digits in parentheses indicating the sequence of that entry among all those entries that have the same preceding digit(s). This is followed by a code letter indicating the country groups for which a validated license is required. To determine whether a specific commodity requires a validated license, it is necessary to find first the Schedule B number under which it is classified. Then, using that number as the key, one has to locate the commodity on the CCL. As an example, the Schedule B number for Chlorendic Anhydride is 512.0290; the Export Control Commodity Number is, therefore, 512(7). The CCL indicates that for No. 512(7) chlorendic anhydride, a validated license is required for shipment to Country Groups Q, S, W, Y and Z, whereas exports to Country Groups T and V can be made under General License G-DEST.

TYPES OF EXPORT LICENSES

No special authorization is required by the Department of Commerce to engage in export-import trade. However, exports, except to Canada, may not be made unless authorized by either a general or a validated license.

A Validated License is a document authorizing the export of commodities within the special limitations set forth in that document. It is issued only upon the basis of a formal application made to the Department of Commerce, based on a specific transaction or group of transactions. No fee is charged to apply for or receive a validated export license.

A General License is a general authorization permitting the export of certain commodities and technical data without the necessity of applying for a license document. There are several different general licenses. Their symbols and uses are summarized in the Appendix.

FILING OF VALIDATED EXPORT LICENSE APPLICATIONS

Once it has been determined that a validated export license is required for a specific export, an application for license must be submitted to the Office of Export Administration, U.S. Department of Commerce, Washington, D.C. 20230. An application consists of a completed Form DIB-622P, Application for Export License, and Form DIB-623P, Application Processing Card, which forms are obtainable free of charge from either the U.S. Department of Commerce in Washington or any of its District Offices. The applicant for an export license must be subject to U.S. jurisdiction; if he is not, he should appoint an agent in the United States, such as a Foreign Freight Forwarder, to act as applicant in his behalf. Each item on the application form should be completed—all parties in interest; the commodity described in Commodity Control List terms; Export Commodity Control Number; Processing Number; a full description of the end use; and signature of the applicant and of the order party, if any. The applicant for a license should be that person who, as the principal party interested in the export transaction, has the responsibility to control the good's exportation and is, thus, the exporter. To this end, the applicant's identity and his role in the transaction, rather than the terms of sale is the Office of Export Administration's primary concern.

If the seller of the goods intends to burden the foreign buyer or importer with the responsibility of effecting exportation, or the latter's forwarding or purchasing agent in the United States, he should not apply for the export license or appear as exporter but, in such a case, the forwarding or purchasing agent should as applicant and exporter. This would be the case if the sale is made on a f.o.b. factory basis, although it is recognized that such terms of sale may relate only to price and not necessarily regarded inconsistent with the assumption by the seller of full responsibility for effecting the exportation. Export controls require the fullest disclosure of all interested parties, so that decisions on applications may be made with complete knowledge of all relevant facts. Candid disclosures also assure that the identity and the whereabouts of persons who know most about the transactions, may be easily ascertained in the event of inquiry. The applicant must fully disclose on the application for the license the names of all parties who are concerned with, or interested in the proposed exportation and who are participating on their own account. These include: the applicant as exporter, the ultimate consignee, the intermediate consignee, and the purchaser. If the application is filed for an account other than that of the applicant, the agent, as applicant, must disclose the name of the foreign principal for whose account the exportation is made. The true parties in interest, as known to the applicant, must be disclosed. The applicant for a license should be that person who, as the principal party in interest in the transaction of exportation, has the power and responsibility to determine and control the sending of the goods abroad and is thus in reality the exporter. The person located abroad who is the true party in interest in actually receiving the exportation for the designated end use, must be named as the "ultimate consignee." The bank, forwarding agent, or other intermediary (if any) who acts in a foreign country as an agent for the exporter, the purchaser, or the ultimate consignee for the purpose of effecting delivery of the goods, must be named on the application, if known. Insofar as legal liability for any violation of the export control law and regulations is concerned, every person who in any capacity participates in an exportation, knowing it to be unauthorized, may be held to account, whether or not he appears as the party on the application for the export license. As previously pointed out, an application for a validated license must be submitted on Form DIB-622P, Application for Export License, accompanied by Form DIB-623P, Application Processing Card. An application is incomplete and will be returned to the applicant unless accompanied by a processing card with both portions completely and correctly filled out.

Certain commodities and destinations, subject to the provisions of Part 375 of the Export Administration Regulations require that supporting documentation from the foreign importer be submitted with the application. Two of the most important supporting documents are the Import Certificate and the Consignee/Purchaser statement. The import certificate is required when the applicable ECC (Export Commodity Control) Number is followed by the code letter "A," the commodity proposed for export is valued at $2200 or more, and it is destined to any of the following countries: Austria, Belgium, Denmark, France, Greece, Hong Kong, Italy, Japan, Luxemburg, Netherland, Norway, Portugal, Turkey, United Kingdom, West Germany and West Berlin. In conjunction with the import certificate requirement, the exporter may also be asked to secure a delivery verification document from his foreign importer as evidence that the U.S. commodities have officially entered the approved country of destination. This procedure, known as the Import Certificate/Delivery Verification (IC/DV) Procedure, was established by the participating countries in a mutual effort to prevent the unauthorized diversion of strategic commodities. The second major supporting document is the Statement by Ultimate Consignee and Purchaser, Form DIB-629P which form must be submitted by the importer (ultimate consignee) resp. overseas buyer or purchaser, to the U.S. exporter or seller with whom the order has been placed and who in turn must attach this form to his export license application for export of a commodity valued at $2200 or more, to any destination except Country Group T, unless an import certificate or other similar document is required. The statement represents a certification by the importer to the Office of Export Administration regarding the nature of the transaction and the proposed disposition of the commodities to be imported. Switzerland and Jugoslavia provide their own form of documentation similar to the import certificate, the Swiss Blue Import Certificate, and the Jugoslav End Use Certificate. They are required will all license applications for those countries regardless of the value of the order.

In addition to individual export licenses, the Office of Export Administration provides certain simplified procedures under which one license application can cover a number of transactions. The most widely used are:

Project License: A single license covering the exportation of all goods, except complete aircraft, either assembled or knocked down, nuclear commodities and a number of specified articles, for a special, officially recognized project or program such as construction schemes, petroleum development programs, etc. abroad for a period of approximately 2 years from issuance of the license. A "project" is a new foreign operation, or the expansion of an existing one, for which the ordered material is required. A "program" is the maintenance, repair or operation, and production requirements, of goods for a foreign operation. (See Sec. 373.2 of Export Adm. Regulations.)

Periodic Requirements License (PRL): A single license authorizing the export to one or more named ultimate consignees, in a single country of ultimate destination in Country Groups T or V, of an estimated one year's requirements of commodities identified by the symbol "P" in the "Special Provisions List" column of the Commodity Control List. (Sec. 373.5)

Time Limit License (TL): A license covering shipments of unlimited quantities of goods to one or more ultimate consignees in a single country in Country Group T. Commodities identified by the symbol "R" in the "Special Provisions List" column of the Commodity Control List (CCL) are not eligible under the Time Limit License procedure. (Sec. 373.6)

Service Supply License (SL): A license that allows persons or firms in the United States or abroad to provide prompt service for equipment (a) exported from the United States, (b) produced abroad by a subsidiary, affiliate, or branch of a U.S. firm, or (c) produced abroad by a manufacturer who uses parts imported from the United States in the manufactured product. It permits the export of spare and replacement parts to consignees in Country Group T or V, and, under certain conditions, the export of replacement parts to consignees in Country Groups Q, W, and Y. (Sec. 373.7)

Technical Data License: The provisions governing exports of technical data (excluding classified data) set forth in Part 379 of the Export Administration Regulations. They relate to data exportable under General License GTDA and GTDR, as well as to data for which validated licenses are required. Special attention is called to the requirement in Sec. 379.4(e) for written assurances as to the disposition of certain data and the product manufactured therefrom.

LICENSING POLICIES FOR SPECIFIC AREAS

Most goods can move to destinations in the Free World under either General License G-DEST or General License GLV. General License G-DEST may also be used for most commodities destined to East European Countries and the People's Republic of China. Briefly, the policies applicable to the licensing of exports to various Country Groups are:

1. U.S. Possessions: No export authorization is required for shipments of goods or technical data intended for use or consumption by persons in Puerto Rico or U.S. territories, dependencies, and possessions. Such shipments are considered domestic shipments.

2. Canada: As a general rule, no goods or technical data require export licenses to Canada for consumption in Canada. Whenever a commodity or technical data do require a validated export license for Canada, that requirement is shown in the Export Administration Regulations.

3. Cuba (in Country Group Z): U.S. restrictions on trade with Cuba have been in effect since 1960 and are part of the U.S. Government's total effort, in conjunction with the policies of the Organization of American States, to isolate the present communist regime and to counter its threat to the Western Hemisphere. Under the terms of the embargo, exports to Cuba are kept to an absolute minimum consistent with humanitarian considerations. Goods meeting the provisions of certain general licenses, such as Gift and Baggage, may be sent to Cuba, as may publications, periodicals, and technical data exportable under General License GTDA. All other exports require validated export licenses, and applications therefore are generally rejected.

4. North Korea and the Communist-controlled area of Vietnam (Country Group Z): There is an embargo on commercial shipments to North Korea and the Communist-controlled area of Vietnam. However, personal baggage, publications, periodicals, and technical data exportable under General License GTDA, may be shipped to these areas.

5. East European Communist Countries and People's Republic of China (in Country Group Y): For the past several years the U.S. Government has consistently followed a policy of permitting some non-

strategic trade with the USSR and other East European Communist countries, and more recently with the People's Republic of China. Commodities that are essentially peaceful in nature are subject to General License G-DEST. Where a validated license is required, the proposed transaction is reviewed carefully to determine whether the transaction would contribute significantly to the military potential of the countries mentioned above in a way that would be detrimental to the U.S. national security.

6. Romania (in Country Group Q) and Poland (in Country Group W): Exports to Romania and Poland are also restricted for reasons of national security, but the restrictions are less severe than for exports to other Eastern European countries.

7. Southern Rhodesia (in Country Group S): In conformity with the United Nations Security Council's Resolutions of 1965, 1966 and 1968 condemning the refusal of the present regime in Southern Rhodesia to take steps to offer self-determination to the majority African population, the United States has imposed a near total embargo on with that country. Validated licenses are required for all exports except commodities or technical data meeting the provisions of certain general licenses, and documentary motion picture film and certain printed materials that may be shipped under General License G-DEST. Validated licenses are issued only for commodities or technical data specifically intended for particular medical, humanitarian, or educational uses.

8. Other countries (Country Group T and V): The Department of Commerce generally approves applications to export to T and V countries. Applications for T and V destinations are required primarily to assure that the commodity to be exported will not be diverted to an unauthorized or restricted destination. It should be noted, however, that in support of the United Nations Security Council's Resolutions of 1963 condemning the Republic of South Africa's apartheid policy, the United States prohibits exports to that country of arms, munitions, military equipment and materials, also material and machinery for their manufacture and maintenance. The Department of Commerce therefore generally rejects applications for related items under its jurisdiction when there is a likelihood of military end use. Otherwise, export controls to the Republic of South Africa are the same as for other destinations in these Country Groups.

ENFORCEMENT REGULATIONS

All the aforementioned complex provisions of the export control regulations require from exporters, carriers, and forwarding agents an adequate understanding with respect to the responsibilities involved and impose an onerous task on them in performing their operations. Violations of these regulations are subject to sanctions which may cause imposition of heavy fines, and suspension or denial of export privileges.

Handling the bulk of all export cargo, the foreign freight forwarder bears the brunt of these additional responsibilities in his daily work, and must exercise utmost vigilance in connection with the clearance of export shipments.

The pertinent regulations provide that the shipper's unauthenticated export declaration and export license will be submitted to the exporting carrier before the vessel, aircraft, or overland transport departs. The exporting carrier shall, in turn, present this declaration to the U.S. Customs Service. The exporting carrier is responsible for the completeness and accuracy of information on these export declarations regarding the name of the exporting carrier (and flag for shipments by vessel), foreign port of unloading, and bill of lading or air waybill number, and for filing the declarations with the U.S. Customs Service, within the prescribed time period. The exporter continues to be fully responsible for all statistical information on the declaration and for submitting these declarations to the carrier prior to departure. If the carrier is required to file a cargo manifest with the U.S. Customs Service, declarations must be submitted by the carrier to the U.S. Customs Service before the vessel, aircraft or overland transport departs. A copy of each export declaration covering a shipment under a Project License shall also be submitted by the exporter directly to the Office of Export Administration at the end of each month.

It should be stressed that a shipper's export declaration (Form 7525-V) must be executed and deposited with the exporting carrier regardless of whether the shipment is clearing under a validated or a general license. The export declaration must conform in all respects with the information in the export license, or with the provisions of a general license, and must correctly describe the commodities in terms of the Commodity Control List. In addition, if the commodity description on the license does not include as much detail as is required by the Bureau of the Census for statistical purposes, the Declaration must also meet Census requirements. The seven-digit Schedule number, rather than the Export Control Commodity Number, should be shown on the declaration. For validated license shipments the italicized digit(s) in parentheses from the Export Control Commodity Number on the Commodity Control List must be entered immediately below each Schedule B number. The exporter is responsible for signing the export declaration, but, as said before, he may appoint an agent, like his forwarder, to act in his behalf either on a case-by-case basis by signing the power of attorney in Item 18 of the export declaration form or on a continuing basis by a general power of attorney.

To help insure that U.S. exports go only to authorized destinations and do not find their way illegally to other destinations, a Destination Control Statement (see Sec. 386.6 of the Export Administration Regulations) is required on shipping documents. Under this requirement, practically all commercial shipments leaving the United States must show one of three statements, as appropriate, on the commercial invoice and bill of lading or air waybill. All three statements, as shown below, notify the carrier and all foreign parties (ultimate and intermediate consignees and purchaser) that the U.S. material has been licensed for export only to certain destinations and may not be diverted contrary to U.S. law.

The exceptions to the use of the destination control statement are shipments intended for consumption in Canada and shipment being made under certain general licenses.

The statements are as follows: No. 1 or 2 should be used for validated license shipments, and any of the three may be used for general license shipments.

Statement No. 1:

"These (commodities) (technical data) licensed by the United States for ultimate destination (name of country). Diversion contrary to U.S. law prohibited."

Statement No. 2:

"These (commodities) (technical data) licensed by the United States for ultimate destination (name of country) and for distribution or resale in (name of country/countries). Diversion contrary to U.S. law prohibited."

Statement No. 3:

"United States law prohibits disposition of these commodities to the Soviet Bloc, People's Republic of China, Laos, North Korea, North and South Vietnam, Cambodia, Cuba, or Southern Rhodesia, unless otherwise authorized by the United States."

In statements 1 and 2, enter in the blank country space the country of ultimate destination named on the export declaration and the validated license, if any.

In the last space in Statement 2, (a) for validated license shipments enter the countries shown on the license as approved for distribution or resale. If no such country is shown on the license, enter the word "none"; and (b) for general license shipments enter:

"any destination except Soviet Bloc, People's Republic of China, North Korea, North and South Vietnam, Cambodia, Laos, Cuba, or Southern Rhodesia, unless otherwise authorized by the United States."

If the export requires a validated license for Poland or Romania, include these countries in the last space. If the export does not require a validated license for a country in the prohibited list above, that country may be deleted.

Statement 3 permits distribution or resale to any country not specifically excepted. If the export does not require a validated license for an excepted country, that country may be deleted. If the export requires a validated license for Poland or Romania, all these countries to the prohibited destinations listed in this statement. For details, see Sec. 386.6 of the Export Administration Regulations.

The Department of Commerce maintains district offices in the principal cities of the United States and in Puerto Rico. When there is need for export control information, or assistance with an export shipment, district offices will help. They can: (a) Get priority action for processing an application for export license, if an emergency exists, (b) Extend the validity period of an export license, (c) Make other amendments to an export license, (d) Explain export control regulations, (e) Help with clearance of export shipments, (f) Assist with commodity classification problems, (g) Approve United States import certificates, and (h) Provide export control forms and printed informational material.

A table of General Licenses, District Offices of the U.S. Department of Commerce, sample forms for shipper's export declaration, validated export license application will be found in the Appendix.

CHAPTER VII

Freedom of the Seas

INTERNATIONAL PRINCIPLES

Intense clashes of interest, often ultimately expressed in wars, have marked the history of seafaring nations since antiquity. Demonstrating the interdependence of trade and politics, the basic causes of these conflicts are embodied in the rules of international law. Concrete illustration of this interdependence is provided by the simultaneous functioning of highly developed commercial nations as leading political powers on the international scene. Correlation in these areas existed with such regularity that an economic law could conceivably be formulated, relating the growth of nations in proportion to the developmental stage of its transportation means and facilities. Nations, despite these conflicts, have come to regard the freedom of the high seas as a right of commercial ships.

"Seapower" or "Command of the Seas" has always been so imperious, that it has been tolerated only when maintained and accepted as "Sea police" or "Freedom of the Seas." Nations would only respect "Seapower" conditionally—that is, if in return for "sea power"—an adequate and advantageous "sea police" was to be provided. When "Sovereignity of the Seas" is exploited by one interest or one nation to its own advantage without offering any service in return, the doctrine of the "Freedom of the Seas" challenges that of the "Command of the Seas." Mutually accepted principles are that no one institution, entity, or state should be allowed to dominate the oceans by force; and, in case of war, the rights of neutral nations to peaceful commerce should be respected.

Practically operated, this doctrine of neutrality obliged the nonparticipants in the conflict not to interfere in any way with the military operations of the belligerents, and not to disturb the non-military trade of the neutrals among themselves, or with enemy countries. "Sea police" embodied the concept of enforcing the "rules of the game" through "sea power."

Ancient history records Rome dominating the *Mare Nostrum* (Mediterranean); the City State of Venice controlling the Adriatic Sea; Genoa, the Ligurian Gulf; England, the Channel; Sweden, the Baltic Sea. At the end of the 15th Century, Pope Alexander VI, by the "Bull of Demarcation" divided the recently traversed Atlantic Ocean and the newly-discovered America between Spain and Portugal, the leading Catholic seapowers. England and Holland, the Protestant seapowers, challenged this papal partition with unrestricted sea warfare, which successfully asserted the "Freedom of the Seas" against this interference. The controversy between the concepts of "Freedom of the Seas" and "Command of the Seas" involves two conflcting doctrines: the first remains unchallenged in time of peace, unless as a preparatory step for the second, The Command of the Seas, in war.

American foreign policy, since the presidency of George Washington, has been based on the principle known as, "the doctrine of the freedom of the seas." This doctrine was implemented and extended by John Hay and, later, Theodore Roosevelt. John Hay originated the "Open Door" Policy, which kept the entire Orient accessible to American shipping and commerce. The war with Tripoli, the War of 1812, the Philippine Campaign, the Boxer Rebellion in China, Perry's opening entry into Japan, the War with Spain, and the Treaty with Panama were all fought, or negotiated, by American arms; and statesmen became imbued with the conviction that for national prosperity, domestic industrial development of its industries, and international understanding and peace no better device existed than the free intercourse of trade and commerce.

Reaffirmation of this policy, contained in the Atlantic Charter under Point 7, is stated thus: "Such a peace should enable all men to traverse the high seas and oceans without hindrance." The Atlantic Charter was signed by the President of the United States and the Prime Minister of the United Kingdom in August, 1941.

Some critics claim, perhaps justifiably, that lack of comprehension or considerations of expediency have sometimes permitted our foreign policy to appear vacillating and to have weakened our position in world opinion. However, our perpetuation of the concept of "freedom of the seas" is indubitably sound and constitutes the only practicable solution for the maintenance of order and security on the high seas in times of war and peace.

Two reasons account for the development and maintenance of a definite, special system of laws governing maritime or admiralty affairs: (1) Each state can reserve the right of complete jurisdiction over all ships only in its territorial waters, except by waivers provided in the form of international treaties (Treaties of Friendship, Commerce and Navigation); and (2) violators in admiralty matters are often beyond the reach of the plaintiff's court. Maritime law is a universal body of rules with worldwide principles of procedures and convenants, which are administered by specialized courts with powers directed against the instrument of commerce, namely the ship, regardless of its ownership, and binding the parties at interest without legal notification.

Today we recognize four basic freedoms governing the movements of vessels and the carriage of people and goods on the high seas:

1. The right to bring ships and cargo to places within the territories of all nations.

2. Equal treatment of vessels of all flags in stationing them, loading and unloading them in ports, harbors, and docks everywhere.

3. No discrimination in matters of pilotage, quarantine, duties on tonnage, and other charges affecting vessels everywhere.

4. Prohibition of the discriminatory flag treatment, as a result of which a nation's merchant marine would receive privileges not accorded to other flag vessels.

These principles were never completely adhered to by all seafaring nations, but their general observance was adequate to foster the progress of civilization and international trade.

DISCRIMINATIONS

Little in the record indicates conspicuous evidence of discrimination against American goods or ships by foreign countries. Individual instances of unfair treatment have existed and may manifest themselves intermittently. They have stemmed from the conflcting ambitions of nations at sea, which have led to hostile economic policies. The reason for these policies, as was treated previously in this chapter, is found in the unique relationship between shipping and politics. Certain discriminatory practices, nevertheless, were always recognized as proper; other deviations were, and still are, considered more or less unfair. Competing nations have usually either neglected to protest, or thought little of minor violations, because these measures were regarded as unintelligent and, contrary to achieving increased economic power, resulted only in proper retaliation.

Discriminatory practices usually emerge as actions of preferential treatment for national flag shipping versus foreign flag carriers. They operate in different ways. They may be disguised by the cloak of political expediency while, actually, they are of economic nature.

Some foreign governments insist upon the shipment of a large part, if not all, of their commerce in ships of their nationality, particularly when the cargo in question is government-bought, and respectively owned, in contrast to orders imported by regular traders. In this case, American vessels are not afforded an equitable competitive opportunity.

Currency and exchange regulations and, sometimes, preferential charges operate against shippers who would otherwise patronize United States flag vessels. One South American republic has practiced discrimination over a period of time by charging lower port and consular fees on goods carried by its own vessels, thus disadvantaging our ships.

Discriminatory, also, is the "variable" application of tonnage measurement. Legislation to determine registered tonnage as an international unit reverts a century, when the Moorsom ton of 100 cubic feet was adopted.

The closed-in-capacity of a vessel in tons of one hundred cubic feet was then, as now, termed gross tonnage. After deductions were made for officer and crew accommodations and navigational and propelling power spaces, the resultant figure was called net tonnage. As port dues and many other charges were based upon a vessel's net tonnage, the British Board of Trade sponsored a Merchant Shipping Act, in 1894, which gave their ships a lower net tonnage than comparable vessels of other countries.

This result was accomplished, first, by exempting from measurement certain closed-in spaces, such as shelter-decks, forecastles, bridges and poop, which was available and ordinarily used for cargo, by reason of so-called "tonnage openings"; and, second, by permitting a "Percentage Rule" for propelling power deductions, which were far greater than the actual volume of the spaces provided for the machinery.

With all other maritime nations having formulated national measurement rules for registry that were basically British, each in self-defense adopted this chicanery in their own measurement rules.

The Panama Canal Rules of Measurement, which were based on the relatively correct computation of the Suez Measurement Rules of 1874, were put into effect by the United States in 1914. However, some essential exceptions relating to public rooms led to additional efforts toward international uniformity of tonnage measurement rules. The rules laid down by the Oslo Convention in 1947 have been ratified so far by only a few countries. Until the Inter-governmental Maritime Consultative Organization, a United Nations Agency, renders final decision on these rules, discrimination in tonnage or other taxes will go on.

Governmental interest in the development of their respective national merchant marines has tended to transform competition among the fleets of different countries into a competition among governments. This interest is bifacial: it represents a definite threat to amicable relations, but it is also a means which may prove that it is possible to overcome the conflicting demands of various nations in the international carrying trade. A modus vivendi can be established, as in other fields, whereby the legitimate aspirations of any country can be reconciled through collaboration. The sole alternative to this course of action is chaos and cut-throat competition among the world's merchant marines. Prerequisite to success in international cooperation is the willingness of all participants to understand other's problems. In this respect, the United States, as a great trading nation, is certainly entitled to maintain a merchant marine commensurate with its world position.

Government Aid

Close political, military, and economic relationships between Government and Merchant shipping, throughout history, have, to a variable degree, always influenced shipping legislation, which is based on the two objectives of trade and defense.

The Merchant Marine Act, of 1936, prescribed a fleet sufficient to carry all of our water-borne domestic commerce, and a "substantial portion" of our foreign commerce. This Act further required a Merchant Marine "capable of serving as a naval and military auxiliary in time of war or national emergency." Of the two factors necessitating a strong merchant marine—trade and defense—the latter is more crucial, since we are beset by international tensions.

To permit our trade to be transported in foreign bottoms at possible lower cost, as recommended by certain economists, is a fallacious policy, for it would neglect our national security. Additionally, our Merchant Marine gives us a voice in the determination of rates, enables us to maintain continuity and quality of service, and furnishes us a potential weapon if foreign lines should attempt to discriminate against our goods.

These considerations, all international in character, have induced governments to extend various kinds of aid to their national merchant marines, among which the following five are the best known: (1) tariff enactments, (2) contract mail services, (3) construction-differential subsidies, (4) operating-differential subsidies, and (5) tax-exemptions and deferements.

Adopting similar methods, the United States Government has extended its support to our merchant marine. Alert to the realities of the era, through witnessing a rapid succession of wars and other political disturbances during the past two decades, the United States is implementing the Merchant Marine Act of 1936.

Modern, efficient merchant vessels require shipyards in this country for their construction and repair and experienced seamen for their operation. Prevalent labor and material costs, which arise from our high standard of living and wages, result in correspondingly higher domestic production costs. Labor and material costs range from fifty to one hundred percent lower in foreign shipyards. To offset these higher differentials of building and operating ships under the American flag, construction subsidies are regarded as the only feasible solution and are granted under careful restrictions. Contrasting with American manufacturers, who may enjoy tariff protection against commodities produced by cheap labor abroad, American shipowners cannot obtain such relief. American ship operators cannot charge a higher freight rate for transportation than their foreign competitors, whose labor costs are a fraction of his own. To counteract this disadvantage, the government provides—again under limitations—operating subsidies. These subsidies are calculated to equalize the higher American costs with the existent lower costs, if the vessel were operated under a foreign competitor's flag.

Operating subsidies do not guarantee a profit. They are granted only to an operator who agrees to maintain regular cargo or passenger service on trade routes which are declared by the government to be essential to our foreign commerce. A subsidized operator is, also, contractually obligated to replace each of his ships, as soon as it reaches the age limit of twenty years, with a new vessel approved in speed and design by the Department of Defense and the Federal Maritime Board. United States citizens must compose the entire crew of a cargo vessel, and at least 75 percent of the crew of a passenger ship. Furthermore, the American flag operator must agree to share profits with the government on a 50-50 basis. Any excess, over and above a reasonable return on his investment, is "recaptured" until the total subsidy has been paid back. This feature, which renders the subsidy a loan rather than a grant, differs from terms applicable to farm and dairy subsidies. A subsidized line pays a minimum of twenty-five percent of the construction cost in cash, with the balance payable in annual installments, plus interest charges of 3½% on the due amount, within twenty years.

Imposing these conditions on construction and operating subsidies places, in essence, the government in the shipping business, which it neither intends to own or administer. These arrangements, also, seem to cause continuous controversies between the Maritime Administration and shipping industry on one hand, and the Comptroller-General, on the other, who criticizes the "deeds" of the former. This anomalous situation could be prevented if the ships were built for private accounts and purchased at prices equivalent to those prevailing in the world market.

An operating subsidy is granted to only *one* American flag operator on an essential trade route, unless it can be shown that, in order to provide adequate service, subsidizing a competing operator is desirable. In effect, this discourages, and may even prevent, the granting of such subsidy. It also creates a definite obstacle to the development of an adequately strong merchant marine. Another unfortunate result of this restriction is that it places a great number of efficient American ship operators at great disadvantage. Unsubsidized owners declare that they would encounter no financial difficulties, if they were permitted to sail their ships with foreign crews, paid at foreign wage levels. "They contend, since national interest and security dictates the employment of American seamen, it is logical to equalize the wage and salary differential between the foreign level and the American standard through subsidies. Adoption of this policy would also abate the continuous loss of bulk cargo, comprising 63 per cent of our foreign trade to foreign flag vessels, which now haul 52 per cent of our bulk cargo, compared to 37 per cent in 1950."

Additional assistance granted to the American Shipping industry included the mail contract system, which was established under the Merchant Marine Act of 1928, but abandoned in 1936 because of abuses.

Tax exemptions, tax deferments, and taxwise treatment of depreciation have assumed significant status in the subsidy framework.

We reserve exclusively to American ships the right to carry goods in the coastwise and intercoastal services. These services include traffic between any parts of the continential United States, or between the United States mainland and its non-contiguous possessions of Hawaii, Alaska, and Puerto Rico. Known as "cabotage," this policy dates back to the early years of the Republic (1817), and is based on the principle which regards the Merchant Marine as a naval auxiliary and a segment of our national defense force.

Considerable criticism, both at home and abroad, has recently been directed to the American subsidy program, with particular respect to the so-called 50-50 cargo preference legislation. This enactment rules that United States government-financed Foreign Aid cargoes must be shipped half in American flag ships and half in foreign bottoms. Although ostensibly controvertible, the wisdom of this policy is dictated by considerations of self-preservation. Lacking the nucleus of vessels, experienced shipping organizations, construction and repair facilities, and the trained officers, crews, and ship yard-workers, which have been created by the joint efforts of private enterprise and government, the task imposed upon our Merchant Marine in times of emergency would prove insurmountable.

CHAPTER VIII

Liner and Tramp Service

TYPES OF SERVICES

The transition from sail to steam in ship propulsion, accompanied by the change from wood to iron in ship construction, revolutionized water transportation. The size, speed, and reliability of the steamer, coupled with its superior motive power, and the possibility of scheduling cargo shipments transformed ocean commerce and the organization of the shipping industry.

Preceded by the individualistic, adventurous wanderings of transients, or "tramps," the early 19th Century saw the oceans dotted with sailing packets and staunch cargo ships, which marked the beginning of the transatlantic shuttle by "liners." Freight and passenger service, in modern definition, evolved fifty years later, when steamship lines supplanted the former fleets of sailing vessels.

The modern shipping industry may be classified variously according to construction, purpose, structure, services, and motive power: the passenger, cargo, combination, refrigerator, tanker, and ore carrier. Viewed from the relevance to traffic management, it suffices to restrict the discussion to two focal areas: (1) service, that is, the relationship between carrier and owner of the cargo, and (2) operation or the functional setup of the carrier.

Classified on a service basis, three types of ocean carriers may be distinguished: (a) the regular steamship lines, (b) the chartered or "tramp" vessels, and (c) the industrial carriers.

Each of these services has its variations as to use or purposes, each fulfills definite functions, and each is so organized and conducted as to attain the appointed goal. We also may divide the off-shore fleet into dry-cargo and tanker ships.

From the legal point of view, we differentiate between common carriers and private, or contract, carriers. A common carrier is usually defined as, "one who undertakes for hire to carry from place to place the person or the goods of all who apply." One who only occasionally performs carriage service or especially serves one and the same principal is not a common carrier, but is a private carrier. Whether a carrier operates as a private or as a common carrier is determined by the circumstances in each case. This distinction is significant. Common carriage, but not private transportation, is specifically subject to regulation by law. It is based on standard and uniform conditions and equal treatment for all comers, whereas contract carriage is flexible and is characterized by freedom to agree mutually on conditions which will satisfy both transporter and shipper. Hence, unjust discrimination by common carriers, whose legal status and responsibilities are fixed by various statutes dealing with their functions (Interstate Commerce Act 1887, Section 302 and Shipping Act, 1916, Section 1), is prohibited.

LINER SERVICE

Steamship lines generally operate their fleets in common carriage, although exceptions will be found occasionally, when certain economic or service conditions arise. They may operate some vessels in common carriage, simultaneously with others in contract carriage. Conceivably, they can operate a ship under both types of carriage on the same trip, on a regularly scheduled route. This may be accomplished by employing part of the vessel for a number of shippers under published tariffs, freight rates, and contract conditions (Bill of Lading), and placing the remainder of the available space at the disposal of only one shipper under a special contract (charter party) at terms mutually agreed upon by carrier and charterer. Further exception to common carrier operation is when the steamship line may be induced to augment its fleet by reasons of unusual demand on its route for extra shipping space, but which is too temporary in duration to justify the purchase of an additional vessel. Peak movements may be caused by seasonal conditions, such as harvest; unexpected circumstances, such as a sudden increase in duties by foreign countries; or when one of its liners is laid up for repairs, and a substitute vessel is required to maintain the sailing schedule.

However, liner service—comprising passenger, combination, and cargo boats—implies a fleet of ships, which provides regularly scheduled service between named ports on a certain trade route. Further, it implies the obligation to accept as a common carrier cargo from all under uniform conditions. These precepts, and not the size or speed of the ships, nor the number of vessels in the fleet, characterizes liner operation. These precepts, also, distinguish it from the tramp, or general trader, which has no fixed itinerary or schedule. General traders can be hired (chartered), either for a definite period of time (time charter) or a single trip (voyage charter) to carry whatever her charterer demands to or between ports to be determined under the contract.

Liner Organization. The nature of line service requires an extensive, costly organization, with branches at interior points and agencies at all ports of call. Steamship lines are either operated by common management, under ownership, or by agents, who may even manage steamship service companies. They attend to the necessary arrangements in connection with dock facilities, wharves, and warehouses;

STEAMSHIP COMPANY INC.

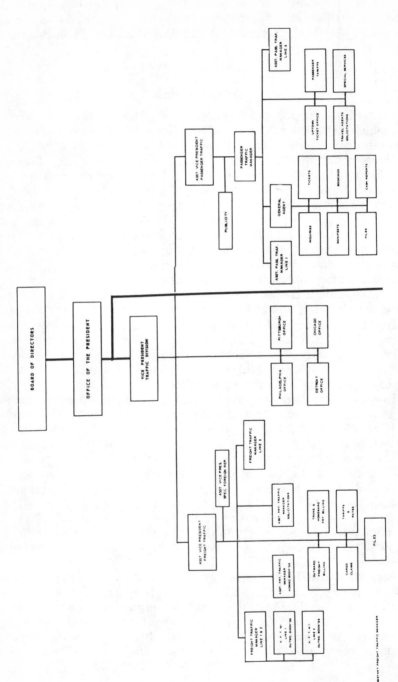

Liner Company Organization Chart

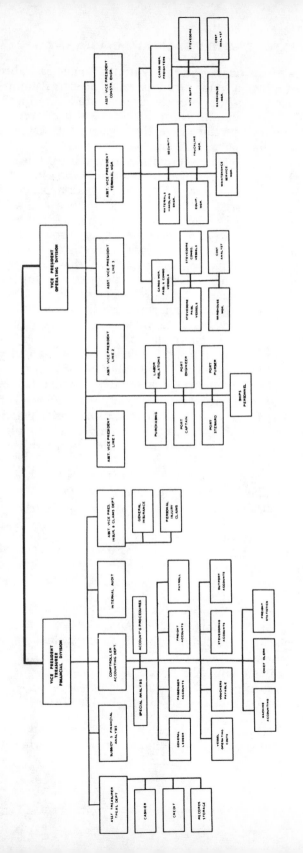

Liner Company Organization Chart (cont'd)

the maintenance of the business organization at home and abroad and the solicitation of traffic, and its advertising needs. Administrative organization varies, depending on the type of trade the line handles, its volume and character, and the types of service offered. Certain organizational standards relating to the departmental structure are found in every ship line's organization.

Among the various departments within a steamship line's business organization, the Freight Traffic Department warrants the most scrupulous attention. The Freight Traffic Department merits this priority because it represents the sales and service end within the organizational structure of the carrier, and because it is almost the sole department with which exporters and foreign freight forwarders transact their affairs. Dealing with these clients is essentially a public relations task. Dependent on the success of these contacts is the line's status within the port community and its earning potential. Platitudinous attributes such as tact, courtesy, precision, skill, cooperation, and the ability to grasp and solve problems, assume new dimensions when they are evaluated as indispensable to the proper conduct of the Freight Traffic Department's affairs.

The Freight Traffic Department is charged with many important functions. The following summary indicates the wide scope of these activities, which range from traffic control to commercial decisions:

1. Establishing of freight rates, either independently, if a nonconference carrier, or in unison with other lines as a member of a steamship conference. This must be accomplished simultaneously with the preparation, issuance, and distribution of freight tariffs and regulations.

2. Solicitation and development of business through advertising media, such as circular letters, sailing cards, trade magazines, personal calls of freight solicitors, and establishing inland branch offices and foreign agencies.

3. Booking of cargoes and issuing freight contracts.

4. Attending to the issuance and respective release of all required carrier documents, such as delivery orders, shipping permits, dock receipts, bills of lading, parcel receipts, freight bills, arrival notices, and other requirements.

5. Exercising strict controls, as to compliance with the regulations imposed by the Export Control Act, 1949, which govern the entry and clearance of vessels, and the discharging, loading, and storing of cargo on piers.

6. Assisting in stowing of cargo.

7. Tracing and expediting of cargo to be shipped.

8. Counseling on matters affecting the general business policy of the carrier and making recommendations thereon.

9. Follow-up the collection of freight charges, and claims as to short-shipments, or non-arrival of cargo at ports of discharge.

10. Cooperating with all other departments for the benefit of the entire enterprise.

Ranking second in importance in the relationship between forwarders and exporters, respectively, and the carrier's organization is the Wharf Department. Actually, it is a sub-division of the Operating Department, and it supervises the manifold functions of physical transactions and maintenance, in contrast to commercial, or traffic operations. The Superintendent of Docks commands a large staff of assistants, whose responsibilities include the following:

1. Supervising the stevedoring organization, which attends to the loading and discharging of vessels.

2. Receiving and storing of goods delivered by truck, or lighter, on dock for outbound dispatch.

3. Checking, weighing, and measuring of cargo, including the rejection of goods unacceptable for shipment.

4. Delivery of inbound cargo to consignees, or their appointed agents.

5. Forwarding of all kinds of documents, or copies thereof, pertaining to wharf operation, to the Freight Traffic or other pertinent department. These include: delivery orders, cargo and tally sheets, stowage plans, cargo capacity sheets, and claim and damage reports.

6. Keeping continually in contact with the Freight Traffic Department of the main office, reporting the progress of loading or discharging vessels and any difficulties or unusual events.

Subordinate to the Manager of Operations, also, is the Chartering Department, which handles the line's ship chartering transactions. These, however, rarely concern forwarders or exporters, but usually affect other vessel owners or operators.

The Cashier's Department is the third department with which exporters, importers, or their respective appointed agents, forwarders and custom brokers have daily relations. The Cashier's Department is a subdivision of the Treasurer's Department. It releases the Bills of Lading, freighted and ready for pick-up, against cash or check payments by occasional shippers or consignees. Bills of Lading are issued against so-called "due bills' which are signed, in lieu of a receipt for documents, by regular clients, who enjoy a limited payment extension for due freight. Upon request, the cashier affixes the various annotations which are required on the Bills of Lading for banking purposes, such as the "On Board" clause. Notations may be required also for presentation to the United States Treasury Department, as "For Internal Revenue" or "For Custom House Purposes Only." Filed with him, also, are the brokerage or commission bills of bona fide foreign freight forwarders. These range from $1\frac{1}{4}\%$ to 5% of the due freight, according to conference regulations or other arrangements with ocean carriers.

Seaboard and District Traffic Offices. Steamship lines maintain home offices. Those lines which maintain cargo services to and from so-called "outports," also have at these points their own branch offices, or employ the organization of a reputable freight agent. This agent performs functions identical to those of the main office. Keen competition has impelled ocean carriers to extent their solicitation activities to the origin of the cargo they wish to acquire. To achieve this, they establish district offices in large industrial centers, which are convenient for manufacturing plants located in the interior. These branches don't require any extensive office staff for the solicitation and booking of cargo. Practiced for decades by foreign freight forwarders, this technique has been successfully adopted by steamship lines. Motivated by a similar—although reverse—objective, ocean carriers maintain also overseas offices in ports of destination or in foreign capital cities. These offices aim to secure the patronage of the consignee, or buyer, who is induced to route the orders he has placed with the American exporter through the soliciting steamship line.

TRAMP SERVICE

"Tramp Shipping" is representative of the multitudinous vessels which are employed world-wide, but not over a fixed trade route, or under a regular scheduled service. These boats are generally made available by their owners to a single shipper for a full load of bulk commodity, such as coal or grain under a specific contract (charter). Complementing the common carrier service provided by steamship lines, as an integral part of a complete seaborne transportation service, the tramp ship offers flexibility, economy, and space supplementation, which regularly scheduled lines cannot furnish.

The tramp shipowner offers a ship operating for a trip from one port to another; it may be coal to Italy, grain to India, or asbestos fibre from South Africa. He may charge a fixed rate to load, deliver, and discharge; or he may render available his fully manned vessel for a specified period, at a fixed charge per month. The contracting party may be another steamship company, which is operating a liner service on a regularly scheduled route, or a governmental agency, such as the Military Sea Transportation Service (M. S. T. S.). This Service was organized by a directive of the Secretary of Defense in 1949. MSTS was designed to control, operate, and administer ocean transportation for personnel, material, mail, and other cargo for all agencies of the Department of Defense, and as authorized, or directed, by other government agencies of the United States. Political and military conditions, past and present, necessitate that governmental agencies, such as the MSTS, continuously require additional shipping space, immediately available. This must exceed the amount that its own fleet or the regularly scheduled liners can provide, or because of the urgency to move cargo for destinations that liner operators cannot meet. The tramp ship is prepared to move whenever called upon to satisfy the varying demands of world trade and shipping, or to implement foreign policy decisions. These latter include relief and rehabilitation needs, and the requirements created by world tension.

Tramp cargo is identified by four characteristics: (1) Low value, which demands cheap transportation; this outweighs the advantage of speed and regularity of sailing. (2) Great bulk or weight, or goods of objectionable character (chemicals), which carriers in the liner trade are neither interested in nor equipped for. (3) Simple handling, which requires no special facilities for loading or discharging. (4) Location in remote ports, consequently, out of the range of scheduled liner service.

These reasons account for most of the world's movements of wheat, grains, coal, ore, sulphur, sugar, and other bulk commodities being carried in full shipload lots by tramp vessels. Prior to World War II, there had been a pronounced trend in ocean transportation away from irregular service toward regular service. Thereafter, the situation changed and a sharp reversal in this trend has ensued. Liner vessels, which before the war carried about two tons of cargo in our foreign trade for each ton carried by tramps, now transport only one ton for almost every two tons conveyed in tramp ships.

Contrasting with the fixed, stable freight rates that are applicable to the liner service, the rates and terms of hire in the tramp charter market are highly flexible. They are sensitive to market conditions, because of low-valued commodities and equally low overhead cost in producing service. On the other hand, liner rates are protected by steamship conference agreements, provided for by the 1916 Shipping Act. This measure, to date, excludes United States tramp shipping, but definitely is worth reconsideration, for the same reasons that apply to the remainder of our merchant marine industry, the American flag liner service.

Charter Parties (Charters)

A "charter party," or "charter," is a maritime contract, which enables the owner of a tramp vessel either directly or through a ship broker or managing ship operator to lease a vessel, or part thereof, to a shipper (charterer), a steamship line, or any vessel-operating enterprise, such as an industrial carrier. As in any lawful contract, whether in the form of a "charter party," or other commercial agreement, two primary factors are required: (1) Mutual consent of the parties to the contract. (2) Consideration; that is payment of a definite sum of money (compensation) by the charterer, either in a lump sum or in a monthly rate based on the tonnage or time element. This compensation is called "hire."

Contrasting with the "charter party," as a maritime contract, in which the underlying shipping document is known also, as "charter" or "charter party," clarification requires that we call an agreement to generally carry goods by water for a consideration a "contract of affreightment"; the compensation we call "freight"; and the legal document involved, "bill of lading."

Conspicuous among the various charters used in ocean shipping, are three classifications: (1) voyage or trip charters, (2) time charters, and (3) bareboat or demise charters. Each of these may contain individual variations.

1. Voyage Charter. Under a voyage charter, the owner (lessor) carries a charterer's complete cargo from one port to another, or delivers a complete ship for the same purpose. The compensation is more or less a tonnage freight rate, based on a ton of 2240 pounds, for the entire transportation service. Regarding loading, unloading, and port charges, voyage charters differ to some extent. The "net form charter party" excludes these services, whereas the "gross form charter" places the entire burden upon the owner.

2. Time Charter. Under a time charter agreement, the charterer (lessee) ought to be fully informed about the vessel and the trade conditions involved, since he has to pay for fuel, pilots, port and consular charges for ship and cargo. Consequently, he should be familiar with the speed, the fuel consumption, the dead weight of the vessel, its cubic capacity, the size of the hatches, and the deck arrangements. The owner pays only for provisions, wages, consular fees incurred in shipping and the discharging of officers and crew, and for the insurance of the vessel and all its stores. Briefly, the owner is committed to man, provision, maintain, and to insure. He must turn over a fully equipped vessel—without fuel—to the charterer, and is compensated for his operation by a monthly hire on a lump sum or tonnage basis.

Voyage and time charters contain a number of important clauses, with the time charter going into greater detail. Both charters indicate the names of the contracting parties; name, size, and position of the vessel; cancelling date; exceptions: act of God; enemies; fire; restraint by princes; etc., general average; brokerage; seaworthiness; rate of freight hire; and method of payment clauses.

Additional clauses are peculiar to each type of charter. Among those applicable only to voyage charters are the so-called "lay-days" and demurrage clauses, which specify the number of days for loading, or unloading, and the number of tons per day to be loaded, or unloaded. Should the charterer cause the delay of the vessel beyond the fixed time limit, he has to pay the owner, in addition to the freight, a penalty called "demurrage." On the other hand, the owner is obligated to pay "dispatch money" to the charterer for each "lay-day" not used.

Whereas voyage charters specify the loading and discharging ports, time charters indicate the ports of delivery and redelivery of the vessel. To insure the vessel's efficient performance, the time charter includes the so-called "breakdown or cesser" clause, which applies in the event of loss of time caused by a deficiency of men or stores, breakdown of machinery, stranding, fire, or damage which prevents the operation of the vessel for more than twenty-four hours. The payment of hire shall then cease until the vessel is again in an efficient state and able to resume its service. This clause is designed to relieve the charterer of paying for the hire during the period when he is denied the vessel's utility. Another important clause in the time charter is the "dry-docking" clause. This stipulates that the vessel be docked and its bottom be cleaned and painted whenever master and charterer think necessary, but at least once in every nine months, and that payment of hire is to be suspended until the ship is in proper shape for service. The obligation to dock the vessel is an absolute one. In case of failure to perform, the charterer may claim among others, damages due to loss of speed of the vessel.

3. **Bareboat or Demise Charter.** Under the *bareboat* or *demise charter*, the owner of the vessel relinquishes the full control and operation of the vessel to the charterer, who is required to maintain, man, provision, fuel, and insure. The owner just leases the bare boat—like a house—to the charterer, who pays to the owner the charter hire agreed upon, either at a monthly or per diem rate based on the type, age, speed, and dead weight of the vessel. The bareboat charter was in general use during both World Wars. The United States Government, through the Shipping Board in World War I, and the Maritime Commission (War Shipping Administration), in World War II, contracted with private shipping firms, as general agents for the operation of vessels. In accord with present government policy and congressional enactments, the bareboat charter is still employed today, with respect to government-built and owned ships.

Today's great variety of *charter parties* has gradually evolved, and they depend upon trade customs and commodity types. Grain, coal, produce, cotton, and other maritime exchanges have attempted to codify the principal conditions pertaining to compensation, risks, obligations, rights, and expenses, and others. Among the well known charters classified by commodity are: coal, grain, wheat, rice, timber, iron ore, stone, cement, bauxite, fertilizer, and innumerable others. They demonstrate the importance of tramp shipping as an integral part of our ocean transportation system and economic life.

Shipbrokers and Steamship Agents

Similar to the foreign freight forwarder, who assists directly in bringing about a transfer of title but does not himself take title to goods, the ship broker acts as functional middleman between owners of vessels and shippers. When representing the owner, who is looking for a charterer, he is called *owner's broker;* and when he is acting on behalf of a shipper, *freight* or *cargo broker.* Obtainment of available vessels is the shipbroker's responsibility. To see that ships are properly maintained, and that their affairs are handled efficiently and diligently while in port, is the steamship agent's responsibility. Though the tasks involved are quite different in nature, their functions overlap in many respects. Due to the close relationship, numerous firms perform both ship brokerage and agency work.

The broker's principal functions include: (1) fixing of charters for cargo liners and tramp vessels, in which case he acts as chartering broker; (2) acting as charterer, or *chartering broker*, for large trading concerns; (3) engaging in the sale and purchase of vessel property; (4) "shopping around" for competitive rates and conditions; and (5) serving his principal as a consultant on prevailing market, or expected transportation conditions.

The following functions apply in varying degree to the management of the steamship agency business: (1) arranging for berthing, and clearance of vessels and goods including customs formalities; and (2) handling of ships while in port (loading, unloading, provisioning, bunkering), delivering and receiving cargo, collection of freight, solicitation of cargo, settling claims, and storing; (3) preparing and issuing documents (Bills of Lading, Manifests etc.) ; (4) attending to repairs; and (5) appointing sub-agents.

To compensate brokers for their services in negotiating and arranging the charter party, it is customary to pay a commission, ranging from $1\frac{1}{4}$ to 5% of the freight amount, payable by the owner of the vessel. An *address commission*, is occasionally granted in charter transactions. This refers to a remuneration paid apart from the regular fee by the owner of vessels, not to the broker, but to the charterer or his designee.

Agency fees may vary according to the size and nature of cargo, the ship's tonnage, and functions performed. They are based, usually, on a fixed scale of charges set up by local agents or their organizations. These scales provide charges for either a certain percentage of the freight or a stated sum per day, or time, or both.

Corresponding to the economic characteristics of a functional middleman, the business organization of the ship broker is relatively small. He is not confronted with the operational burden which is indigenous to carrier's business. In contrast is the steamship agent's situation. Proportionate to the number of ocean carriers he represents, his organization is comparable to that of the average steamship line.

CHAPTER IX

The Conference System

NATURE AND ORGANIZATION

Political, economic, and financial instabilities, with their attendant traffic fluctuations and losses through unrestricted competition, exert a pronounced influence on international liner operation. Contrasting with the chartered or tramp service, liners are exposed and responsive to politico-economic influences in considerably higher degree. Persistent reduction of ocean freight rates among competing ocean carriers on the international shipping routes resulted in a non-compensatory rate level. To surmount this economic obstacle, steamship lines concurred in formulating rules, or agreements, to assure voluntary cooperation for the control of internal and external competition. Thus, those line operators who maintain regular services over the same trade routes are grouped in an unincorporated organization, which is called a "shipping conference."

Inherent in such an institution is the inclusion of elements of both competition and monopoly, with their attendant advantages and drawbacks. Therefore, some form of regulation and supervision is required to limit competitive squanderings and monopolistic practices. Control is exercised internally by self-regulation and externally by government restraint.

Ocean shipping's international character, particularly from the American viewpoint of successful competition and maintenance of parity with low-cost foreign carriers, makes it apparent that self-governing conferences are advantageous to: (1) reduce conflicts of national interests, (2) prevent unrestricted competition, (3) establish workable rates and tariffs, and (4) protect the United States foreign trader and the American Merchant Marine from discriminatory treatment.

Steamship companies emerged towards the end of the nineteenth century. Sir Samuel Cunard, in 1868, organized the North Atlantic Steam Traffic Conference in New York. Conferences, although dominated by a few powerful foreign shipping interests, were well established on American foreign trade routes by the turn of the century. This was an era when our Merchant Marine's position was conspicuously surpassed by those of several countries that, although for smaller in size and wealth, could claim vastly superior maritime strength. American vessels transported only ten per cent of our foreign trade. Steamship lines, which succeeded our former fleet of clippers and sailing packets, operated in the coastwise traffic, composed largely of trade with our neighboring countries like Canada, Mexico and Cuba. We remained content to welcome with acclaim, in New York harbor, the fastest contender of luxurious transatlantic travel and winner of the "Blue Ribbon."

British, Dutch, French, and German interests used the conference vehicle to monopolize steamship business on American and world trade routes. Even before conferences were organized, these foreign lines customarily granted preferential rates to large shippers who were willing to give them all their business. This practice was adopted by the conferences. Increasingly vexatious, in order to make such exclusive agreements "stick," they contrived the so-called "Treue Rabatt" or "Fidelty Rebate." Under this procedure, the exporter would receive a refund—usually ten percent—of the actually paid freight from the carrier, not at once, but only after elapse of a certain period, generally fifteen months. Thus, the conference had its "client" under "control" for at least two years, for it was impossible for the shipper to utilize a non-conference vessel at substantially lower rates, unless he took the risk of breaching his contract covering a period of 12 months and paying an excessive fine. This type of freight discount became known as a "deferred" rebate, and was only one of many abusive, oppressive practices. These grew so extreme that large numbers of American foreign traders were prompted to appeal for Congressional relief, which was granted, in 1916, with the enactment of the Shipping Act.

Today, conferences dominate the berth operations in world trade; the number of "outsiders," or independent carriers, is rather negligible.

Conferences usually operate in only one direction to a specific trading area. Vessels which operate southbound to the West Coast of South America cover the territories and respective ports of Panama, Colombia, Ecuador, Peru, and Chile. The conference operating in this area comprises all the lines which want to be members. Varying conditions and problems which prevail in each directional area have resulted in the organization of individual, independent conferences for the various trade area routes. A carrier maintaining a far-flung service from several coasts, such as Atlantic, Gulf or Pacific, may be a member of several conferences.

In addition to regular members, sometimes a conference may include associate members. This classification includes carriers which, under Federal Maritime Commission regulations, are defined as carriers, and, although they are not regular members, operate a service parallel to that of conference members. Associate members agree to observe conference rules, regulations, rates, and conditions on traffic in the trade area covered by the conference agreement.

United States law decrees that any common carrier, which is engaged in foreign trade by water, and which desires to operate on a trade route, must be admitted to membership if he applies. Despite this, a few shipping companies prefer not to join any conference and thus are not bound to charge uniform conference rates. Non-membership permits them to remain free, not primarily to undercut the conference rate schedules per se, but because they violently disapprove of certain conference tactics and practices, applied to members and shippers alike, which they feel are unjust, discriminatory, and unfair. This competition has brought about bitter controversies before the American authorities and courts in recent years.

Conference activities are extensive, as illustrated by the fact that about 360 common ocean carriers are engaged in the foreign commerce of the United States and that approximately forty of these are American flag operators. More than one hundred conference agreements exist, plus about four hundred supplementary arrangements pertaining to trans-shipment of cargo, joint service, pooling of revenue, and sailing schedules.

Conferences are usually administered by a well-organized staff, headed by a permanent chairman, who serves as executive officer. According to the size of territories and the respective number of steamer services involved, the business organization may be subdivided on a geographical basis, or otherwise.

The general duties and powers of the chairman are: (1) to examine the books, accounts, and correspondence of the lines; (2) to receive from, and communicate to, the members appropriate statistics, manifests, and information; (3) with the concurrence of the lines, to fix, control and supervise rates, regulations, tariffs, agents' commissions, brokerage fees of foreign freight forwarders, and rebates; (4) to enforce contractural obligations of members or shippers, and to collect payment resulting from imposed penalties; (5) to call meetings of the members and keep minutes of such meetings; (6) to act as arbitrator between the members, and (7) to organize special committees to deal with particular situations; for example, to consider rate problems propounded by the shipping public or complaints lodged by industrial or commercial trade bodies.

Headquarters of conferences covering outbound traffic are located in the large shipping centers of New York and San Francisco; most operational centers of conferences administering inbound traffic are situated abroad.

MEMBERS OF CONTROLLING COMPETITION AS TO MEMBERS AND OUTSIDERS

Control of competition is the unequivocal basic purpose of a conference. Methods accomplishing this may include: (1) fixing or regulating rates, (2) apportioning traffic, by allocating the ports of departure and restricting the number of sailings, (3) proportioning the volume of cargo among the members, and (4) combating non-conference lines.

All members are bound to uniform rates, minimum charges, rules and regulations, tariffs, and brokerage fees. Rate-cutting or preferential treatment of shippers or consignees is thus eliminated. However, certain types of cargo may be excluded and remain "open"; that is, the corresponding rates are not fixed, in order to meet instantaneously "outsider" competition.

Definite standards and provisions govern the relationship between carriers and shippers and carriers and consignees, since it has been found that certain members, particularly foreign lines, tend to grant "hidden" preferences to their nationals, such as extension of freight credit on "collect" shipments, and refunds by declassification of goods.

Often, there is an undercurrent of suspicion among the carriers, when another member of the conference exclusively handles the cargo of some powerful exporter or importer, that it may be unlawfully competing against the other members of the conference. To obtain irrefutable evidence of any violation of the conference working agreements are usually impossible, apart from the fact that similar discriminations by other carriers tend to cause those investigations that are acted upon to be conducted indulgently.

All conference agreements, tariffs, rates, fares, arrangements, accommodations, privileges, etc. must be submitted to the Federal Maritime Commission for approval to obtain relief from prosecution under the Sherman Anti-Trust Law, of 1890. Without this approval, such concerted action among competitors would clearly run afoul of that act and also of the Shipping Act of 1916, the latter one having been strengthened in its anti-monopoly tendency through the enactment of Public Law 87-346 (87th Congress, H.R. 6775) of October 3rd, 1961 which brought about the first major overhaul of the 1916 legislation by legalizing the dual rate contract system and requiring the filing of tariffs with the Commission by adding a new Section 14C and amending the old Section 15 in the Shipping Act, 1916.

Intermittently, the Federal Maritime Commission has ordered modifications in individual conference agreements. On the whole, however, there was no objection on the part of the shipping public insofar as measures concerning the control of competition by the industry itself were involved, and although no conference allows any member the right of independent action. A case in question would be an attempt by a shipper to secure a rate reduction through a conference carrier of his liking. This carrier would be in a quandary, were it not for the fact that all conference decisions require either unanimous, or at least two-thirds majority consent to any action. To avoid embarrassment in his relations with such shipper, and to avoid any friction with his colleagues in the conference, it is usually provided that all rate adjustments be exclusively negotiated with the conference chairman.

This orderly pattern of businesslike activities, designed to control competition among conference members, does not apply to non-conference members. Illustrating their respective positions in the foreign trade community, the revealed situation is confused and disappointing. Here, we note the revelation of monopolistic tendencies, and the regrettable indetermination and apprehensiveness of the shipping public, as well as of their trade organizations and press. Shipping interest would be well-served if these groups, instead of merely taking "note" or just "reporting" would also "score" and "attack" malpractices, without fear or hesitation, when necessary.

The conference system, currently again under legal attacks from some vocal "outsiders" and government departments, is not being fortified if reasonable complaints are brushed aside without any valid explanation. For example, about 25 per cent of all conferences refuse to publish or make available tariffs. This peremptory attitude of the conferences is not determined by self-defense against competition from without, because shippers or exporters will support non-conference carriers only if and when forced to do so. This occurs when they lack power to do otherwise, or because they may believe a certain conference requirement to be an unjust and oppressive measure, which may unduly restrict their freedom of action. The first case refers to exporters who, under their FOB or FAS sales contract terms, cannot oppose the routing instructions of foreign buyers. The second instance affects the foreign freight forwarder, who, while holding a conference contract in his own name to secure lower ocean rates for his overseas clientele, on whose behalf he effects shipments, is directed on occasions by his foreign principal to employ the services of a non-conference line for f.o.b. or f.a.s. purchased merchandise. More will be said below about the forwarder-conference relationship when the exclusive patronage, or dual-rate system is discussed. It suffices to say that, from a public relations point of view, some conferences have failed to show the anticipated understanding of the trading public's needs and have betrayed a lack of grasp of the intricate operations in international commerce, as far as buyer-seller relationship is concerned.

To protect themselves against the competition of non-conference carriers, commonly called *outsiders*, conferences have applied since their existence a number of measures. Some of these, because of their discriminatory and abusive character, have been outlawed as being contrary to the public interest, by the promulgation of the 1916 Shipping Act. Congress created an investigating committee, in 1912, which was later known worldwide as the "Alexander Committee," to conduct a thorough inquiry into the formation and practices of conferences, and to report its findings and recommendations back to Congress. Noteworthy is the fact that, prior to then, our law lacked absolutely any provisions for the regulation of ocean carriers, and this situation permitted the development of monopolistic steamship cartels in our offshore foreign traffic. Succeeding an exhaustive study, which took more than two years to complete, this committee reached the conclusion that. (1) Conferences provide a valuable contribution to the promotion of regularity of service, and the stability and uniformity of rates. (2) No effective policing of the industry could be undertaken because of the international character of the business. (3) Conferences should be brought under governmental control because of the inherent evils. (4) Certain monopolistic practices and abuses should be outlawed.

These recommendations led to the creation of the Shipping Act of 1916 and the establishment of the United States Shipping Board, as the regulatory body to deal with water transportation in foreign commerce. The present Federal Maritime Commission is its descendant via the U.S. Federal Maritime Board, which preceded the present body's organization.

Four competitive, illegal practices, directed against non-conference lines, were prohibited under the "Act." First, it was unlawful for any ocean carrier to persuade or influence any insurance company or underwriters not to furnish any competing line operator as favorable an insurance rate on his vessels or cargo as they granted to such carrier or any other person subject to the Act.

Secondly, the "deferred rebate" system was prohibited. This feature was the primary target of Congressional objections. Under this system conferences could coerce shippers into signing contracts to ship only over their member lines and thus prevent their using an independent carrier. This practice also discriminated against tramp ships which ordinarily carried most of American bulk cargo. Tramp ships provided a competition Congress considered desirable, since the tramp, as a private or contract carrier not maintaining a regular service, was exempt from all regulation.

Thirdly, the use of "fighting ships" was declared illegal. This practice had scheduled conference sailings to parallel those of independent carriers to the same port of call and dropped the rates to ruinous levels to drive out the competitors.

Finally, any kind of discrimination was forbidden. This includes making, or threatening reprisals or discrimination in any way,—not only unjust or unreasonable discrimination—against shippers who have patronized any other carrier, including non-conference operators.

However the emergence and strengthening of the Russian and similar state-controlled and independant third-flag carriers had undermined rate structures, reduced cargo inflow and revenues from United States and other conference carriers, and resulted in instability, malpractices and chaos to a number of our trade routes, to the disadvantage of both shippers and carriers. These state-owned fleets, particularly the Soviet-flag fleet, operate largely in cross trades not involving their home country, and have caused a remarkable loss to U.S.-flag and other privately-owned, for-profit operators. To control this rate-cutting by state-controlled merchant fleets, the United States has now responded by enacting Public Law 95-483 (H.R. 9998) October 18, 1978, called the "Ocean Shipping Act of 1978", by amending the 1916 Shipping Act, Sections 2, 3, and 4 accordingly.

Freight Rate Practices

To protect carriers from ruinous competition and to prohibit them from engaging in illegal practices were the primary functions of the previously described regulatory measures. However, these regulations also benefit to a similar extent the shipper, since common carriers by water in foreign trade are prohibited from granting undue preferences or advantages to any person, locality, or description of traffic. They are also prohibited from allowing any shipper to obtain transportation for less than established rates by false billing, false weighing, or other unfair means. Entirely illegal, in fact, is any kind of discrimination between shippers relating to rates, cargo space, or facilities, the loading or landing of freight in proper condition, or in the adjustment and settlement of claims. The underlying principle is that there shall be no favored shippers, whether large or small. Penalties range from $1,000 for each day of violation to $25,000 for each offense. The "Act" applies to American and foreign flag carriers that transact business in this country.

Government control over the rate-making power of conferences and the equitableness of rates is a minor one, due to the international character of the shipping business. However, should the Federal Maritime Commission find a rate to be so unreasonably high or low as to be detrimental to the Commerce of the United States, then the law authorizes the Commission to disapprove such a rate. The pertinent section 18 b 5 of the law is intended as a safety valve but it does not mean that the Commission can decide what is a reasonable rate. If the United States Government were to declare a rate unreasonable, any affected foreign nation at the other end of the transportation line could retaliate unfavorably and, thus, make any workable operation of conferences impossible. However, as mentioned earlier, Public Law 87-346, by amending the Shipping Act of 1916, through adding subsection 18 b to it, required the filing of tariffs with the commission and also duly publishing them.

To strengthen their position in the freight market against "outsiders," and to secure as large a share as possible of any future traffic, conferences have devised the previously mentioned "contract rate" practice. Hereby, the shipper is given the opportunity to obtain a lower than tariff rate by signing a "freighting agreement" or contract, usually running for a period of one year, and agreeing to patronize exclusively the members of the conference group. This prevents him from utilizing non-conference carriers. There is a clause in the contract which, under certain circumstances, permits the signatory to "breach" the agreement. Its effect is practically non-existent because it is based on such unusual, but still burdensome premises. This exclusive patronage system, similar in purpose to the deferred rebate method, differs from the latter only insofar as it provides "immediately" for the application of the lower of the two rates. The fact that the exporter under such a contract is forced to abrogate his freedom of action, which is needed more than ever under today's competitive foreign trade conditions, makes him a quasi-prisoner of the conference system. This situation, regarded by many as a restraint of trade, had brought about a series of complaints, and had led to lawsuits, resulting finally in a 1958 Supreme Court decision wherein the court declared the "Contract Rate System" of the Japan-Atlantic & Gulf Freight conference as illegal. This decision had, of course, cast doubt upon the legality of all dual rate contract systems in effect at that time. So, later in 1958, Congress amended Section 14 of the 1916 Shipping Act to permit the continued use of such contracts by common carrier conferences that had such contracts as of the date of the Supreme Court decision. Meanwhile, investigations into the subject matter were conducted on every level by the Federal Maritime Commission and Congressional Committees for the next three years, culminating in the enactment of Public Law 87-346, effective October 3rd, 1961, authorizing the use of Common Carrier Dual Rate Contracts by adding after Section 14 a, a new Section 14 b and amending Sections 15, 16, 18 and 20 in the Shipping Act, 1916.* It was provided that the legalization of the Contract Rate System was subject to approval by the Federal Maritime Commission and that each contract or freighting agreement should contain the following provisions:

1. Permitting prompt release of the shipper from the contract with respect to any shipment for which the carrier or conference of carriers cannot provide as much space as the shipper shall require on reasonable notice.

2. Providing that no rate may be increased for a period of 90 days after such rate becomes effective.

3. Covering only those goods of the shipper as to the shipment of which he has the legal right at the time of shipment to select the carrier.

4. Not requiring the shipper to divert the shipment from natural routings not served by the carrier or conference where direct carriage is available.

5. Limiting damages recoverable for breach by either party to actual damages determined in accordance with principals of contract law, except that in the case of a breach by the shipper the contract may specify damages in an amount not exceeding the freight charges computed at the contract rate on the particular shipment less the cost of handling.

6. Permitting shippers to terminate at any time upon 90 days notice.

7. Providing for a spread between contract and non-contract rates which the Federal Maritime Commission finds to be reasonable in all the circumstances but in no event be more than 15%.

8. Excluding dry cargo loaded and carried in bulk without mark or count and full shiploads of liquid cargoes except chemicals.

9. Providing such other provisions not inconsistent with the foregoing as the Commission may require.

*See Appendix F.

Conferences applied a sliding scale of rates, depending on the type and quality of service involved, a decade ago. This differentiation, however, has been abandoned. All rates are uniform today, irrespective of frequency of sailings, time in transit, or quality of service performance. Removing any justification for the retention of a sliding rate scale, is the fact that after World War II new, fast ships have been placed into service. Rate uniformity, moreover, was instrumental to their increased stability. Planning export and import transactions over relatively long periods, in turn, is greatly facilitated.

ADVANTAGES OF CONFERENCES

No effective, complete control of freight rates can be exercised because of the international character of trade. However, the existence and operation of steamship conferences do provide benefits, albeit limited, in the way of uniform rates and sailings.

Conferences are conducive to traffic development by maintaining regular sailings, by providing better, safer ships due to stable earnings, and by the elimination of unrestricted, cutthroat competition. All these advantages, however, are merely relative, because it is not the conference system *per se*, but rather its implementation, and the management of the respective conferences which provide effective maritime instruments. This situation implies a dual approach to the problem. Firstly, for our shipping public to have the benefit of tramp and common carrier competitive service, as well as genuine protection from the usual cartel abuses, independent liner service should be protected and encouraged. Secondly, conferences should be compelled to observe the laws and regulations enacted to guard the public interest, and to stimulate the promotion of our foreign commerce. To this end, Public Law 87-346 promulgated some new conference requirements for self-policing and consideration of shipper complaints. First, conference agreements are more closely supervised to the obvious benefit of ocean carriers who faithfully observe their conference tariffs and also to the benefit of the honest and conscientious shipper who does not seek more favorable rates or conditions than are accorded others but who does wish to be assured of the same treatment as his competitor. Second, conferences are to set up proper procedures for hearing and considering shippers' requests and complaints. The consequence will be a greater degree of awareness of both shipper and carrier problems and in the end a closer and more fruitful cooperation between the conference carriers and their supporting merchants.

COMPLAINTS AGAINST CONFERENCES

Foreign traders, non-conference carriers, and government agencies direct trenchant criticism not at the conference system itself, but rather at certain practices which have developed in their operation.

If conferences were operating now as they had been prior to the 1916 Shipping Act, or if they did not provide certain advantages secured by government regulations since 1916, they would not be tolerated in this country. However, it is the degree, or effectiveness, of this control which is in direct relation to the extent of dissatisfaction manifesting itself in foreign trade circles. Enumeration of some of the generally known complaints include the inherent dangers of monopolistic practices; the possibility of excess profits through overly-rigid control of the rate level; careless handling of cargo and claims; improper treatment of shippers; indifference to requests for rate adjustments; inconsistency in the application of rules and regulations; overstepping legal boundaries through usurpation of authoritarian power; and arbitrary changes in conference agreements, such as elimination or reduction of brokerage fees and inadequate notices of rate changes. Appraisal of these factors makes it apparent that there is latitude for voluntary improvement in the restoration of the advantages of the conference system to the trading community.

The Exclusive Patronage Contract. Although no conference will acquiesce in any independent action by its members, there is always the possibility that one of them may resign and then oppose the group. However, with few exceptions, a potential "outsider" cannot gainfully operate over conference trade routes, without somehow being attacked by some conferences. These conferences seek to dominate the shipping lanes through the promotion of the *exclusive patronage contract*. These contracts create the very condition conferences are condemning, namely that of lowering rates. Of course, a distinction must be drawn between steamship lines known as notorious "rate cutters", and those who wish to remain independent.

Attempting self-defense against monopolistic threats, such as the exclusive patronage system, the independent line has no choice except to quote lower-than-conferences rates. In its fight for survival, the independant line indirectly applies the same method by which the conference secures its clientele. To state that the stability of rates is endangered by the existence of independent carriers appears to be an overstatement, in view of the relatively small number of "outsiders."

Therefore, it is suspected that the underlying motive for the insistence on the "exclusive patronage" system by conferences is not one of stabilizing competition through securing equitable and remunerative rates, but of removing competition. The fact that independent carriers and conference lines share in the traffic at stable rates on certain trade routes, without arguments or difficulties, seems to prove this point. Modification of the exclusive contract system, allowing the shipper a greater freedom of action as to the choice of carriers, both within and outside the conference group, would apparently alleviate the entire situation. The disadvantages of the exclusive patronage arrangements to the exporter, namely the elimination of price competition among conference members and the impossibility of patronizing the independent lower rates charging liner operators, have not been eliminated by Public Law 87-346 but even compounded through "built-in" confusions, evidenced by a report of the Federal Maritime Commission issued on March 27th, 1964 on "The Dual Rate Cases." This report combined many dockets involving agreements of carrier conferences for dual rates or two levels of rates providing a spread of not more than 15 per cent, obligating the Merchant, shipper or consignee, to utilize conference carriers exclusively for his shipments in return for a lower rate.

In the introductory statement of this report, it is conclusively shown that not only broad segments of the trading public but also governmental bodies have objected on various grounds to this type of contract, which contains many pitfalls and unreasonable restraints. Even the Federal Maritime Commission, the regulatory agency entrusted with the control of the conference system, is not now more unanimous as to the propriety of the dual system than it was when it was first instituted.

The dual rate system has been under attack since 1948, when a large independent carrier, the Isbrandtsen Company, filed complaint in the Federal Court in New York. Maintaining that dual rates, *per se,* are invalid as a violation of the anti-trust acts, the Court granted an injunction, conditioned on a required investigation by the Federal Maritime Board. The finding of the Board in 1950, approving dual rates, was set aside in the following year by the Federal Court at New York on the ground that the 20 per cent spread between contract and tariff rates was "arbitrary." However, no opinion was expressed as to the validity of the system itself. The Supreme Court affirmed the lower court's decision, in 1952. The Federal Maritime Board, taking cognizance, notified all conferences that they would have to submit such facts and evidence to permit the Board to pass the reasonableness of the rate "differential." Some of the conferences objected to the Board's "authority" to impose such regulations on them, but were rebuffed. In January, 1953, the Board ruled that conferences could establish "dual rates" without a formal hearing whereupon Isbrandtsen Company petitioned the U. S. Court of Appeals for the District of Columbia to stay the Board's order. The court granted an injunction against the Japan-Atlantic and Gulf Freight Conference staying the initiation of the proposed dual system agreement until approved by the Board which in turn, after long deliberations on December 14, 1955, in Docket 730, ruled that the pact was lawful permitting at the same time the aforementioned conference to institute the same with a 9½% spread. The Board pointed out that the system would not result in detriment to the commerce of the United States but would decrease the possibility of rate wars and benefit exporters through more stable rates. The Board, however, did take exception to the contract insofar as it was meant to cover FOB and FAS shipments, declaring that the person named on the bill of lading is the shipper although even here the exporter should be excluded from liability as a party to the conference contract where he only renders assistance at the buyer's request in securing documents needed for exportation.

Again, Isbrandtsen Company went to the Court of Appeals asking for an injuction to stay the institution of the dual rate system until such time as its legality can be finally determined by the courts. In mid January, 1956, the U.S. Government, through the Department of Justice, joined Isbrandtsen Company in requesting the same court to stay an order of the Federal Maritime Board approving the contract/ non-contract rate system. The stay order of the Appeals Court was issued on February 13, 1956, and, on November 9, 1956, the case decided in favor of Isbrandtsen Company, holding that the major features of the dual rate contract system are discriminatory, setting aside the pertinent orders of the Board.* Thereupon, the maritime agency appealed to the Supreme Court for redress.

Finally in 1958 the Supreme Court, in Federal Maritime Board v. Isbrandtsen Co., 356 U.S. 481, set aside the Boards' approval of the contract system on the ground that it was a "resort to other discriminating or unfair methods to stifle outside competition in violation of "section 14 Third Paragraph of the Shipping Act, 1916."

As mentioned previously, this decision of the Supreme Court created a "legal vacuum" with respect to all dual rate systems in effect at that time and necessitated an interim legislation on the part of Congress in the same year to permit continued use of such contracts by the appropriate conferences, through amending Section 14 of the Shipping Act accordingly, with Public Law 87-346 following in 1961.

Having decided to preserve the exclusive patronage system for the use of carrier conferences under certain safeguards for the protection of shipper and consignee and in the best interest of U.S. foreign trade, Congress entrusted the Federal Maritime Commission with the supervision and enforcement of competition restricting agreements among carriers, recognizing that there is some justification in the waterborne foreign commerce for making exceptions to our normal antitrust policies. These safeguards, in accordance with the statutory guidelines set forth in Public Law 87-346, are laid down in the terms of the various dual rate contracts, whereby the agency has sought to resolve different viewpoints by requiring the Merchant's Rate Agreements or contracts to contain specific language as prescribed in Public Law 87-346.

In its report of March 27th, 1964, covering about 60 dockets, the Federal Maritime Commission did emphasize its determination to deal with all the contracts in a single report for several reasons: 1). In accordance with congressional intent dual rate contracts should be standard or uniform. 2). An additional consideration to adjudicate all contracts for a single decision by the Commission was the fact that the contract clauses which should be permitted in each instance

*U. S. Court of Appeals No. 13027, *Isbrandtsen Company, Inc. petitioner V. United States of America and Federal Maritime Board, respondents*, decided November 9, 1956. See Appendix G.

depend generally upon construction of the Statute rather than upon the peculiar facts of a particular trade. 3). In reaching its conclusions, the Commission considered all the pros and cons presented in each of the many dockets under discussion since the enactment of Public Law 87-346 in 1961.

Of the many issues discussed and analyzed in the Dual Rate Report, the following are of greatest importance to the exporter (shipper) and the Foreign Freight Forwarder—to the latter one as advisor and/or agent of shipper respectively consignee,—and will be treated below.

1. *Definition of Contract Shipper.* The desire of conference carriers to bind all affiliates of the signatory Merchant without regard to the Merchant's control over his such affiliates was disapproved by the Commission. Instead it was decided that conferences which wish to bind an affiliate must use a uniform clause which binds only those affiliated companies over which the signatory merchant regularly exercises working control in shipping matters. The further requirement in this clause that all companies over which the merchant exercises this control be listed in the contract, serves two additional purposes: a), it furnishes the conference a complete list of the companies entitled to contract rates, and b), obliges the merchant to warrant that he has the authority to bind the named affiliates to the contract. Further, each contract shall contain a clause which declares it to be a breach if the merchant ships through an affiliated company as an evasion or subterfuge. By another required clause, the conference agrees not to give contract rates to non-signers and the shipper agrees not to obtain contract rates for anyone not entitled to them by shipping cargoes under the terms of the contract for the non-signer. The phrase "regularly exercising working control over an affiliate" is a question of fact in each instance. If a parent company has the authority and actually exercises some caution in shipping matters on behalf of the subsidiary, then there is no doubt that this control is legally and factually applied. The term "affiliate" means ordinarily that this "subsidiary" is either owned or controlled by the parent, the Merchant, by reason of stock ownership or through interlocking officers, directors, or stockholders.

2. *Legal Right to Select Carrier.* This is the most controversial issue of the Statute (Section 14 b (3)). By this provision Congress intended to specify that the dual rate contracts should encompass only those shipments over which the contract shipper has the "legal right to select the carrier" as a condition of the contract of sale, either by implied or expressed terms of the sales agreement.

In the opposite case, the buyer having reserved the legal right to select the carrier as a condition of the contract of sale, the Merchant cannot be required under the seller's dual rate contract to ship by conference carrier. However, if the buyer does not reserve this right, or if he does so but fails to exercise it or otherwise permits the Merchant to select the carrier, the Merchant is bound to ship by conference carrier. The question of whether or not the Merchant had the legal right to select the carrier in instances where the shipment moves by non-conference carrier, requires a specific finding of fact and cannot rest upon conclusive presumptions arising from the appearance of the Merchant's name on the bill of lading or export declaration, or otherwise participating in the arrangement for ocean transportation. The report does not elaborate as to what is meant by participating in the accomplishment of the shipment, but it may reasonably be assumed that if the Merchant books the consignment or otherwise engages in acts which bring about the transportation, he has "arranged" for it. Whether the employment by the Merchant of a foreign freight forwarder by itself can be construed as "participating in the arrangement for ocean transport," remains a question for future determination. In substance, it can be concluded that if the Merchant can legally ship by conference carrier, he must; that if the shipment is made via conference carrier, it is entitled to the contract rate; that the appearance of the Merchant's name on a non-conference bill of lading or other participation in the arrangement for ocean transportation shall give rise to rebuttable but not a conclusive presumption that he had the legal right; but that, in no event, may the Merchant be required by a dual-rate contract to refuse to sell goods on terms which vest the legal right to select the carrier in the buyer or any other person. The use by a conference of the rebuttable presumption clause will place upon the Merchant the obligation to show that he did not have the legal right to select the carrier. While the conference has the burden of proving a violation,—and this procedure follows the general law principle that he who claims a breach must prove the breach—, if the conference presents facts as to the participation of the Merchant in the arrangement for ocean transportation by showing the Merchant as shipper on the bill of lading or export declaration, then the conference has made out a "prima facie" case which the Merchant must refute by other evidence or face the consequences for a breach of contract.

Since neither Public Law 87-346 nor the Commission has ever defined the phrase "legal right," it would appear that the export sales contract of the Merchant would be evidence, but not conclusive proof, as to prove or disprove the Merchant's legal right to select the carrier. As to the definition of "legal right," law courts have previously considered the expression in various contexts and have found that it includes natural rights, that is one of property, one arising as a result of contract, one that is protected against tortious invasion or one created or recognized by law. A fundamental principle of our legal system is "The Law Merchant," or "Lex Mercatoria," which as part of our common law rests not only on the institutions and local customs of any particular country, but consists of certain principles of equity and usages of trade which general convenience and a common sense of justice have established to regulate the dealings of merchants and mariners in all the commercial countries of the civilized world.

It is a known rule and habit of dealing in a particular trade constituting such a custom in relation to contracts in that trade that it forms a part of every agreement in that trade in the absence of an express condition to the contrary. By common consent among merchants and bankers, the Revised American Foreign Trade Definitions—1941, as well as the Incoterms of 1936—determine the appropriate rights and obligations of buyers and sellers in our foreign commerce. These Definitions explicitly provide that—except for F.O.B. DESTINATION, C. & F., C.I.F. and EX DOCK abroad sales—"the obligation to obtain ocean freight space, etc. rests with the buyer." It is, therefore, obvious that under the Law Merchant the seller has "no legal right" to select the carrier or book freight space.

If the latter should be asked by the foreign buyer to book space in the importer's name on a non-conference vessel, the exporter must follow through and does not breach his conference contract; the reason being that the selection of the Ocean carrier under the principle, applicable to the sales contract (unless specific terms stipulate the contrary), rests with the foreign buyer, and the exporter in the U.S. acting as agent of the foreign buyer and thus not being a partner to the conference contract, is removed from the jurisdiction of the CONFERENCE like the buyer himself.

There exists an analogous situation, and no one, so far, has come up with an opinion to the contrary, if and when the foreign buyer appoints a Foreign Freight Forwarder as his agent in this country, instructing him to book space with a non conference line vessel and attend to export clearance procedure of the FOB/FAS purchased goods.

It is, therefore, obvious that conditions in the conference contract vitiating the above outlined principles represent a violation resp., disregard of internationally recognized trade principles and/or definitions all of which are an integral part of established sales terms.

With respect to the issuance, negotiation and presentation of bills of lading respectively the transfer of title, it is generally understood that, under an agreement to sell ascertained goods, title passes at the time when the parties intend it to pass. So, where there is an unconditional contract to sell specific merchandise in a deliverable state, title passes at once, i. e., at the point where the intent of the parties to change title to the property is supposed to take place, and this is the point where cost and risk change from one party to the other. Payment for the goods and/or delivery is, therefore, immaterial to that extent, unless stipulated to the contrary in the sales contract.

Any conclusions to the opposite effect are not only legally untenable but detrimental and damaging to the desired development of our Foreign Commerce.

The converse is true under a C.I.F. sale where the American Exporter pays the ocean freight. This would generally entitle him to book space and select the ocean carrier. However, it is well possible that there are many instances where under a specific condition of the sales contract, the buyer allows the seller to select the carrier. In such cases, there is a moral obligation upon the signatory to use a conference vessel, but this could easily be made a contractual obligation. It is essential that the condition as to the selection of the carrier was arrived at in a "bona fide" manner and was not a device used by the Merchant to abrogate his obligations under the dual rate contract. "Good Faith" requires not that the seller demands control of routing but, rather, that the seller holds the buyer to a consistent pattern of behaviour, namely, either that he leaves to the seller all routing of his goods for a definite period of time, in which case the seller has the legal right to ship such goods in his own name under his dual rate contract, or, conversely, for buyer to retain the prerogative of routing, in which case the seller must deny the buyer the advantages of seller's dual rate contract, and whenever buyer selects a conference vessel, the seller should declare the shipment not covered by his contract. However, should the buyer be a signatory to a dual-rate contract, he should be designated as the "Shipper" on the bill of lading and would be bound hereby.

The relationship between conferences and foreign freight forwarders merits attention in this connection.

During the last two decades, the American foreign freight forwarder has assumed an ever-increasing importance in the world of trade, because of his eminent position as a coordinator of traffic and as an American representative of buyers abroad. It is through this close relationship with his foreign clientele, whose interest he protects in every possible manner, that the forwarder has gained a definite control of routing. For this reason, certain conferences, covering the trade routes from the Atlantic and Gulf coasts to Venezuela, Colombia, and the West Coast of South America, agreed to let forwarders sign conference contracts on behalf of all their foreign clients. In this way, the lower contract rate was applied, regardless of whether or not the individual exporter had executed his own freighting agreement. On the other hand, the forwarder, upon being directed by one of his clients abroad to ship via an independent carrier, could not comply; the conference held that, as a signatory to the contract, he is prevented from such compliance. Although forwarders protested against this ruling, pointing out that their principal, residing abroad, was not under the jurisdiction of the conference, this objection was overruled. This policy created a condition which placed forwarders in an equivocal position concerning their relationship to their principals. Potentially this policy could have caused them great detriment, since it could have led to the loss of clients. Moreover, this intransigent attitude on the part of the conference was apt to disturb the business relations between buyer and seller with resulting losses to both. Instances could be cited where the buyer directed his forwarder to ship simultaneously via conference and non- conference lines. Here, the conference insisted on the application of the higher tariff rate when the goods were handled by the forwarder and routed via its member lines; however, when shipped in the name of the seller himself, the lower contract rate was assessed.

Conference treatment of this type discloses inconsistency, and shortsightness, and limited comprehension of foreign trade needs. Display of this confusion is not a tribute to American business policy, and it may lose the goodwill of our overseas customers. Conferences' functions, it should be remembered, are to serve the advancement, rather than the disruption, of this nation's commerce. Efficacious solution of this disputed problem, which will equitably satisfy all participants of our foreign trade, is increasingly imperative.

3. *Release of Merchant from Contract.* The dual rate law makes it mandatory for the conference that a signatory be promptly released from his contract on any shipment for which the carrier or conference cannot provide as much space as the Merchant requires on reasonable notice. The Commission requires that all contracts, by their terms, fix the time period by which the conference must furnish space. Variations in the time periods are being permitted among the various trades depending upon what appears to be the reasonable commercial needs in the particular trade.

4. *Rate Increases.* Each conference contract must provide that the Merchant must have a minimum of ninety (90) days notice of any rate increase. Should such increase be not acceptable to the Merchant, he may tender notice of termination of the agreement by giving thirty (30) days written notice of such intention to the Conference. However, should the Conference within thirty (30) days subsequent to the expiration of the Merchant's notice notify the Merchant in writing that it elects to continue the dual-rate contract under the existing effective rates, then the agreement shall remain in effect. The Conference shall also offer, under the terms of the contract, to the Merchant a subscription to its tariffs at a reasonable compensatory price. Further, the tariffs shall be open to the Merchant's inspection at the Conference offices as well as the individual carrier's offices during regular business hours. To subscribe to the many tariffs covering the many trade routes over which an exporter may operate, is a very costly expense since the prices of tariffs range from $25.00 to $100.00, but it may be still more economical to buy the tariffs than to parade from one steamship office to another all the time checking tariffs.

5. *Diverting Cargo from National Routing.* Public Law 87-346 stipulates that all contracts include a provision which expressly does not require the contract shipper to divert a shipment from natural routings not served by the conference carrier where direct carriage is available. The F.M.C. has construed the "Natural routing" provision of section 14 b to mean that the Merchant will be free under his contract to use non-conference vessels if in fact the use of conference vessels would require him to divert his cargo to unnatural routes. However, the Merchant will not be permitted to escape his contract obligations, when the non-conference service is no more natural, as it were, than that of the conference. The Commission considers a natural transportation route to be a traffic path reasonably warranted by economic criteria such as costs, time, available facilities, the nature of the shipment and any other economic criteria. A Merchant who intends to ship non-conference on a natural route shall so notify the conference in accordance with the provisions on "Prompt Release," discussed under #3 above, so as to allow the conference to provide the service desired.

6. *Damages for Breach of Contract.* The law limits damages recoverable for breach by a contract shipper to actual damages which means to be an amount not exceeding the freight charges computed at the contract rate on the particular shipment, less the cost of handling, i. e. the cost of loading and unloading. The term "actual damages" would mean to be the dollar loss in the amount of dead freight by a conference carrier. No punitive suspensions or terminations by conferences of merchants' contracts are permitted under the statute as long as the merchant acts promptly in any dispute concerning an alleged breach of contract and, in case an adjudged damage is promptly, i. e. in due time, paid, the contract is never suspended.

7. *Other Contract Provisions.*

a). *Notice of Shipment via Non-Conference Vessel.* Although the statute does not require that a signatory give notice to the conference of the movement of goods via non-conference vessels, the police power given by Public Law 87-346 to the Commission under Section 14b (9) namely, that dual-rate contracts shall contain such other provisions "not inconsistent herewith as the Commission shall require or permit," induced the F.M.C. to allow a clause in all contracts requiring a Merchant who does not have the right to select the carrier to notify the conference within 10 days after a shipment has been made by non-conference vessel, giving the name of his client (or vendor) and all particulars as to type and quantity of the commodity involved. Even if the Commission declares that this provision will help assure the signatory's good faith, although he has not the legal right to select the carrier, it must be said that this clause makes the Merchant implicitly to an "informer" and might place him in an awkward position in relation to his customer, a situation not conducive to the promotion of our foreign trade.

b). A conference may also include a contract clause requiring the Merchant to allow the conference to examine pertinent documents at the signatory's premises, provided that there shall be no disclosure of data or information as to prices and similar details in violation of Section 20 of the Shipping Act, 1916, as amended.

c). Further, all contracts must also specify that a Merchant shall be permitted to transport cargo on his own vessel or on a vessel chartered by the Merchant, provided the term of the charter is at least six months or more. By limiting this requirement to charters for periods of not under six months, the conferences are protected from spot raiding of cargoes and merchants accorded the right to engage in bona fide proprietary carriage under reasonable conditions.

d). Merchants may terminate contracts upon ninety (90) days written notice without penalty.

e). Dual-rate conference contracts must be made available to shippers and consignees on equal terms. While the statute allows dual-rate agreements to a shipper who agrees to "all or any fixed portion" of his patronage to a conference member, the Commission does not construe the quoted language to require that under a dual-rate contract a lower rate has to be offered for a fixed portion of the merchant's cargo. A Merchant who executes such a dual-rate contract must ship all of his goods via conference lines if the contract provision so demands.

Shippers' Credit Agreement. The credit agreement—a new arrangement adopted by steamship conferences, effective September 1st, 1966 —inaugurated new procedures covering the release of freight prepaid bills of lading to shippers and forwarders whereby the shipper or his authorized representative or forwarder may either pay the freight and charges to the ocean carrier when picking up the signed bill of lading, or alternatively execute a special shippers' credit arrangement. The credit agreement involves extension of credit by the conference carriers to shippers for up to 15 days after the date of sailing from the ports of loading.* These credit agreements are issued by the conferences in duplicate like Merchant's Freight Contracts and are to be executed by the dual-rate contract holders if they wish to avail themselves of the credit privileges. Bills of lading calling for freight "prepaid," "to be prepaid," "prepaid at destination," "prepaid at London" or any form other than "collect," shall not be released by the carrier until 1), the freight charges have been received by the carrier or 2), shipper has executed a valid "Credit Agreement."

*See Appendix L.

NORTH ATLANTIC UNITED KINGDOM FREIGHT CONFERENCE
17 Battery Place, New York 10004

MERCHANT'S FREIGHT CONTRACT, Effective: _____

The undersigned Merchant and Carriers, for their common benefit in the stabilization of rates, services and practices and for the development of international maritime commerce in the trade covered by this contract, hereby mutually agree as follows:

1. (a) The Merchant undertakes to ship or cause to be shipped all of his ocean shipments for which both contract and non-contract rates are offered, moving in the trade on vessels of the Carriers, unless otherwise provided in this contract.

(b) The term "Merchant" shall include the party signing this contract and any of his parent, subsidiary or other related companies or entities, who may engage in the shipment of commodities in the trade covered by this contract and over whom he regularly exercises direction and working control (as distinguished from the possession of the power to exercise such direction and control) in relation to shipping matters, whether the shipments are made by or in the name of the "Merchant", any such related company or entity, or an agent or shipping representative acting on their behalf. The names of such related companies and entities, all of whom shall have the unrestricted benefits of this contract and be fully bound thereby, are listed at the end of this contract. The party signing this contract as "Merchant" warrants and represents that the list is true and complete, that he will promptly notify the Carriers in writing of any future changes in the list, and that he has authority to enter into this contract on behalf of the said related companies and entities so listed.

(c) In agreeing to confine the carriage of his shipments to the vessels of the Carriers the Merchant promises and declares that it is his intent to do so without evasion or subterfuge either directly or indirectly by any means, including the use of intermediaries or persons, firms or entities affiliated with or related to the Merchant.

(d) The Carriers agree that they will not provide contract rates to anyone not bound by Merchant's Freight Contract with the Carriers. The Merchant agrees that he will not obtain contract rates for any person not entitled to them, including related companies not bound by this contract, by making shipments under this contract on behalf of any such person.

(e) This contract shall include all cargo, transported by sea from United States North Atlantic ports in the Eastport, Maine/Hampton Roads range, both inclusive, to ports in England, Scotland, Wales, Northern Ireland and Republic of Ireland, except the following:

   (i) Cargoes loaded and carried in bulk without mark or count, except liquid bulk cargoes (other than chemicals and petroleum products) in less than full shipload lots;

   (ii) Any commodity shown in the Conference Tariff for which the rate is open;

   (iii) Any commodity transported in the Merchant's owned vessels or in vessels chartered by the Merchant where the term of the charter is for six months or longer and the chartered vessel is used exclusively for the carriage of the Merchant's commodities.

2. (a) If the Merchant has the legal right at the time of shipment to select a carrier for the shipment of any goods subject to this contract, whether by the expressed or implied terms of an agreement for the purchase, sale or transfer of such goods, shipment for his own account, operation of law, or otherwise, the Merchant shall select one or more of the Carriers.

(b) If Merchant's vendor or vendee has the legal right to select the carrier and fails to exercise that right or otherwise permits Merchant to select the carrier, Merchant shall be deemed to have the legal right to select the carrier.

(c) It shall be deemed a breach of this contract if, before the time of shipment, the Merchant, with the intent of avoiding his obligation hereunder, divests himself, or with the same intent permits himself to be divested, of the legal right to select the carrier and the shipment is carried by a carrier not a party hereto.

(d) For the purposes of this Article, the Merchant shall be deemed prima facie to have the legal right at the time of shipment to select the carrier for any shipment:

   (i) With respect to which the Merchant arranged or participated in the arrangements for ocean shipment, or selected or participated in the selection of the ocean carrier, or

   (ii) With respect to which the Merchant's name appears on the bill of lading or export declaration as shipper or consignee.

(e) Nothing contained in this contract shall require the Merchant to refuse to purchase, sell or transfer any goods on terms which vest the legal right to select the carrier in any other person.

(f) This contract does not require the Merchant to divert shipments of goods from natural transportation routes not served by conference vessels where direct carriage is available; provided, however, that where the Carriers provide service between any two ports within the scope of this contract which constitute a natural transportation route between the origin and destination of such shipment, the Merchant shall be obligated to select the Carriers' service. A natural transportation route is a traffic path reasonably warranted by economic criteria such as costs, time, available facilities, the nature of the shipment and any other economic criteria appropriate in the circumstances. Whenever Merchant intends to assert his rights under this Article, to use a carrier who is not a party hereto, and the port through which Merchant intends to ship or receive his goods is within the scope of this contract, Merchant shall first so notify the Conference in accordance with the provisions of Article 6 hereof.

3. (a) The freight rates to be charged to the Merchant by the Carriers for the transportation of contract commodities shall be fifteen (15%) percent (rounded out to the nearest twenty-five (25¢) cents per Ton Weight or Measurement or five (5¢) cents per freight unit where goods are not freighted on a ton basis, nearest thereto but no more than fifteen (15%) percent below the non-contract rates shown in the Conference Tariff, which would otherwise be applicable to such goods (not including additional handling or accessorial charges). Rates under this contract may be decreased without advance notice. The rates of freight under this contract are subject to increase from time to time and the Carriers, insofar as such increases are under the control of the Carriers, will, except as provided in Article 11 hereof, give notice thereof not less than ninety (90) calendar days in advance of the increases by publishing them ninety (90) days in advance in the North Atlantic United Kingdom Freight Conference Tariff. Should circumstances necessitate increasing the rates by notice as aforesaid and should such increased rates be not acceptable to the Merchant, the Merchant may tender notice of termination of this contract to become effective as of the effective date of the proposed increase by giving written notice of such intention to the Conference within thirty (30) calendar days after the date of notice, as aforesaid, of the proposed increase; further provided, however, that the Carriers may, within thirty (30) calendar days subsequent to the expiration of the aforesaid thirty (30) calendar day period, notify the Merchant in writing that they elect to continue this contract under the existing effective rates and, in the event the Carriers give such notice, this contract shall remain in full force and effect as if the proposed increase had never been made and the Merchant's notice of termination had never been given.

(b) The Conference shall offer to the Merchant a subscription to its tariffs at a reasonably compensatory price; however, the Merchant shall be bound by all notices accomplished as aforesaid without regard to whether it subscribes to the Conference Tariff. Tariffs shall be open to the Merchant's inspection at the Conference offices and at each of the offices of the Carriers during regular business hours.

(c) The rates initially applicable under this contract shall be deemed to have become effective with their original effective date rather than to have become effective with the signing of this contract and notices of proposed rate increases which are outstanding at the time this contract becomes effective shall run from the date of publication in the tariff rather than from the date of this contract.

4. The Merchant and the Carriers recognize that mutual benefits are derived from freedom on the part of the Carriers to open rates, where conditions in the trade require such action, without thereby terminating the dual rate system as applicable to the commodity involved; therefore it is agreed that the Conference, to meet the demands of the Merchants and of the trade, may suspend the application of the contract as to any commodity through the opening of the rate on such commodity (including opening subject to maximum or minimum rates), provided that none of the Carriers during a period of ninety (90) days after the date when the opening of such rate becomes effective shall quote a rate in excess of the Conference contract rate applicable to such commodity on the effective date of the opening of the rate and provided further that the rate shall not thereafter be closed and the commodity returned to the application of the contract system on less than ninety (90) days' notice by the Carriers through the filing of contract/non-contract rates in their tariff.

5. The term "Carriers" as used herein shall include all lines which are members of the North Atlantic United Kingdom Freight Conference on the effective date hereof and any additional lines which may from time to time thereafter become members of said Conference. Any line which, for any reason, shall cease to be a member of said Conference shall simultaneously cease to be a Carrier hereunder and shall not thereafter have the benefits of this contract or be bound thereby. The Merchant shall be promptly notified of the admission, withdrawal or expulsion of any Carrier to or from the Conference, and in case of withdrawal or expulsion the notice shall be at least twenty (20) days before the effective date of the withdrawal or expulsion.

6. All arrangements for the booking and carriage of contract commodities are to be made with individual Carriers selected by the Merchant. It is the spirit of this contract that, so far as reasonably convenient to the Merchant, there shall be equitable division of shipments among the Carriers. The Merchant agrees to make application to one or more of the Carriers for space as early as reasonably practicable before the desired sailing date. If such space is not secured, the Merchant shall then request the aid of the Conference office, at its address as shown from time to time in the Conference Tariff, in obtaining such space. The Merchant shall be free to secure space elsewhere without prejudice to this contract if, within three (3) business days after such request, the Conference office fails to arrange for space in a vessel scheduled to sail within fifteen (15) days of the request or within seven (7) days after the requested future desired sailing date, whichever is later.

(Continued over page)

Merchant's Freight Contract

7. This contract and any shipments made thereunder are subject to sailing schedules and to all terms, provisions, conditions and exceptions of the then current Conference Tariff and of the permits, dock receipts, bills of lading and other shipping documents regularly in use by the individual Carriers and to all laws and regulations of the appropriate authorities. Receipt and carriage of dangerous, hazardous or obnoxious commodities shall be subject to the special facilities and requirements of the individual Carrier.

8. (a) In order that the Conference may investigate the facts as to any shipment of the Merchant that has moved or that the Merchant or the Conference believes has moved, via a non-conference carrier, and upon written request clearly so specifying, the Merchant, at his option, (1) will furnish to the Conference Chairman, Secretary or other duly authorized Conference representative or attorney such information or copies of such documents which relate thereto and are in his possession or reasonably available to him, or (2) allow the foregoing persons to examine such documents on the premises of the Merchant where they are regularly kept. Pricing data and similar information may be deleted from the documents at the option of the Merchant, and there shall be no disclosure of any information in violation of Section 20 of the Shipping Act, 1916, as amended.

(b) Within ten (10) days after the event in any transaction in which the Merchant is a party and the legal right to select the carrier is vested in a person other than the Merchant, and if he has knowledge that the shipment has been made via a non-conference carrier, the Merchant shall notify the Conference in writing of this fact, giving the names of the Merchant and his customer, the commodity involved and the quantity thereof, and the name of the non-conference carrier; provided, however, that where the activities of Merchants are so extensive in area or the nature or volume of his sales makes it impracticable to give notice within ten (10) days, the Merchant shall give notice as promptly as possible after the event.

9. Any controversy or claim arising out of or relating to this contract, or the breach thereof, shall be promptly submitted to arbitration at New York, N. Y., before an arbitration committee consisting of three persons: one to be appointed by the Carriers, one by the Merchant and one by the two so chosen or by the American Arbitration Association in case of disagreement. All of the arbitrators shall be commercial men. Either party may call for such arbitration by mailing to the other a written notice, by registered or certified mail, specifying the name and address of the arbitrator chosen by it and a brief description of the controversy or claim to be arbitrated. If the other party shall not, by a reply mailed within thirty (30) days of the mailing of the first party's notice, appoint its arbitrator, then the first party shall have the right, without further notice, to appoint a second arbitrator, who shall be a disinterested person, with precisely the same force and effect as if such second arbitrator had been appointed by the other party. Each of the parties shall make available to such arbitration committee all information and data requested by it in connection with the subject matter of the controversy or claim. The decision in writing of two or more members of said committee of three, acting jointly throughout the arbitration, shall be binding on the respective parties, and any award shall be paid within thirty (30) days after a copy of the decision has been mailed by the arbitrators to the party held liable, failing which judgment upon the award may be entered in any court having jurisdiction.

10. (a) Damages recoverable by either party for breach of this contract shall be limited to actual damages determined in accordance with principles of contract law, except that, where any shipment is made via an ocean carrier not a party to this contract in violation hereof, liquidated damages shall be paid in lieu of actual damages which would be impracticable to determine. Such liquidated damages shall be the amount which the Merchant would have paid for transportation of such shipment on a vessel of the Carriers in accordance with the effective contract rate less the cost of loading and unloading (stevedoring in and out).

(b) Upon the failure of the Merchant to pay or dispute his liability to pay liquidated damages as herein specified for breach of the contract within thirty (30) days after receipt of notice by registered mail from the Conference that they are due and payable, the Conference shall suspend the Merchant's rights and obligations under the contract until he pays such damages.

(c) If, within thirty (30) days after receipt of such notice, the Merchant notifies the Conference by registered mail that he disputes the claim, the Conference shall within ninety (90) days thereafter proceed in accordance with Article 9, to adjudicate its claims for damages, and if it does not do so, said claim shall be forever barred. If the adjudication is in the Conference's favor and the damages are not paid within thirty (30) days after the adjudication becomes final, the Conference shall suspend the Merchant's rights and obligations under the contract until he pays the damages.

(d) No suspension shall abrogate any cause of action which shall have arisen prior to the suspension.

(e) Payment of damages shall automatically terminate suspension.

(f) The Conference shall notify the Federal Maritime Commission of each suspension and of each termination of suspension within ten (10) days after the event.

11. (a) In the event of war, hostilities, warlike operations, embargoes, blockades, regulations of any governmental authority pertaining thereto, or any other official interferences with commercial intercourse arising from the above conditions, which affect the operations of any of the Carriers in the trade covered by this contract, the Carrier or Carriers may suspend the effectiveness of this contract with respect to the operations affected, and shall notify the Merchant of such suspension. Upon cessation of any cause or causes of suspension set forth in this Article and invoked by any Carrier or Carriers, said Carrier or Carriers shall forthwith reassume its or their rights and obligations hereunder and notify the Merchant on fifteen (15) days' written notice that its suspension is terminated.

(b) In the event of any of the conditions enumerated in Article 11(a), the Carrier or Carriers may increase any rate or rates affected thereby, in order to meet such conditions, in lieu of suspension. Such increase or increases shall be on not less than fifteen (15) days' written notice to the Merchant, who may notify the Carrier or Carriers in writing not less than ten (10) days before increases are to become effective of its intention to suspend this contract insofar as such increase or increases is or are concerned, and in such event the contract shall be suspended as of the effective date of such increase or increases, unless the Carrier or Carriers shall give written notice that such increase or increases have been rescinded and cancelled.

(c) In the event of any extraordinary conditions not enumerated in Article 11(a), which conditions may unduly impede, obstruct or delay the services of the Carrier or Carriers, the Carrier or Carriers may increase any rate or rates affected thereby, in order to meet such conditions; provided, however, that nothing in this Article shall be construed to limit the provisions of Section 18(b) of the Shipping Act, 1916, as amended, in regard to the notice provisions of rate changes. The Merchant may, not less than ten (10) days before increases are to become effective, notify the Carrier or Carriers that this contract shall be suspended insofar as the increases are concerned, as of the effective date of the increases, unless the Carrier or Carriers shall give notice that such increase or increases have been rescinded and cancelled.

12. This contract may be terminated by either party giving the other ninety (90) days' written notice of intention to do so.

13. Any notice provided for herein shall be addressed to the Chairman, North Atlantic United Kingdom Freight Conference, 17 Battery Place, New York, N. Y. 10004, or the Merchant at the address below designated, as the case may be.

14. This contract shall become effective on the date above set forth. If the Merchant was on that date a signatory to a prior dual rate agreement with the Conference lines, this contract shall be deemed to supersede in its entirety any such prior agreement.

CARRIERS

ANCHOR LINE
Anchor Line Limited

BRISTOL CITY LINE
Bristol City Line of Steamships, Ltd.

CUNARD LINE
The Cunard Steam-Ship Company Limited

FURNESS WARREN LINES
Johnston Warren Lines, Ltd.

HEAD LINE AND LORD LINE
Ulster Steamship Co., Ltd.

IRISH SHIPPING LTD.

MANCHESTER LINERS, LTD.

SEA-LAND SERVICE, INC.

UNITED STATES LINES
United States Lines Company

By ....
Chairman, North Atlantic United Kingdom Freight Conference

MERCHANT

* ....
(Merchant's full corporate, company or individual name)

*By ....
(Signature of company official and title)

* ....
(Street address, city, postal zone and state)

* ....

Please fill in required data in space indicated by stars (*)

If related companies or entities are to be included in this contract pursuant to Article 1(b), attach supplementary list hereto, in duplicate.

DIRECTIONS: This agreement is submitted in duplicate. Both copies should be signed in ink by the Merchant and returned to the Conference Office promptly. After accomplishment by the Conference, an executed copy will be returned to the Merchant.

Rev. 1/11/67

Merchant's Freight Contract (cont'd)

CHAPTER X

Ocean Freight Rates and Tariffs·

SIGNIFICANCE OF OCEAN FREIGHT RATES

Ocean freight rates influence foreign trade in may ways. They affect, first, the routing of the cargo; second, the type of ocean service; and third, the selection of the ocean carrier. Although ocean freight rates on most commodities seldom handicap overseas trade, they must nevertheless receive particular attention from the trading public. Rates require scrutiny because of possible savings on freight charges. These savings are measured on the volume of a year's turnover, which involves hundreds of different consignments, rather than on the basis of a single shipment.

The selection of the port of exit, the type of ocean service, and the carrier may be governed also by the time element. Indeed, speed is becoming an increasingly prominent factor in international competition. Transit time influences the extension of foreign credits, the turnover of funds, the carrying of stocks by importer and exporter, warehousing facilities and practices, channels of distribution, the condition of perishable freight, and even production policies. Considerations regarding delivery costs, then, are superseded by those concerning delivery arrangements, frequency of sailings, speed of the vessel, and directness of inland and ocean routes. The shipper may even be willing to pay a substantially higher rate, and may select a line which operates the fastest available passenger vessels. This choice would enable the goods to reach the port of destination in the shortest scheduled time. Conversely, the shipper may be guided exclusively by the cost factor. He may choose a regular freight line operating on a schedule satisfactory to his purposes and from a port nearest to the point of production or origin. The exporter's decision will depend on general custom; on the extent to which the particular trade is competitive; the stability, or lack of stability, of ocean freight rates and marine insurance premiums; the sales contract and export price quotation. Significantly, the exporter will also depend on the advice of the international forwarder whose skill, experience, and familiarity with all these problems will assure him superior forwarding service, and will enhance the good will of his overseas customers. Perpetually prepared to assist the exporter in all problems of export traffic and shipping, the forwarder will enlighten his patron on all questions of ocean freight and with their interpretation and application.

RATE MAKING FACTORS

There are two determining factors in building up the rate structure in ocean transportation: (1) the carrier's cost of producing the service, and (2) the price a shipper is willing and able to pay for the transportation. Both elements represent the minimum and maximum levels respectively. The range between both these levels provides adequate allowance for the effects of other factors which, in varying degree, influence the construction of rates.

Important considerations in determining rates include: (1) competition: (a) market, (b) port; (2) type of service: (a) Regular versus irregular (Conference vs. Tramp or "outsider"), (b) fast or direct versus slow or indirect (express liner vs. cargo steamer); (3) volume of business; (4) possibility of claims for damage and theft; (5) value of the commodity; (6) cost of loading and discharging; (7) stowability of goods; and (8) density of goods.

Analysis of these factors reveals that they will all relate to one or the other basic factor or both. Although additional, similar items can be listed, such as packing, extra-length or heavy-lift cargo, port facilities and port charges, as well as others, the aforementioned conclusion remains valid.

Primarily to obtain a certain degree of rate-stability and uniformity, steamship lines organized themselves in ocean conferences. The lines also hoped to attain other objectives, namely, traffic development, and protection against competition. These conferences determine, or limit, the rates of their members, particularly those applicable to general cargo, as well as the minimum freight charges. Steamship companies levy a minimum freight charge for small shipments; they will not issue an ocean bill of lading for less than a certain payment. The minimum may be the regular freight charge for one or two tons, or from forty to eighty cubic feet, or fraction thereof, but still a multiple of the actual freight otherwise applicable. "Minimum" bills of lading, therefore, mean a disproportionate charge of ocean transportation cost for the exporter. The international forwarder can avoid this situation by combining small shipments from several sources and directed to the same destination. This consolidation may suffice to aggregate a total freight over and above the minimum charge.

OCEAN FREIGHT CLASSIFICATIONS

Contrary to the complexity of railroad rates, which are established through the device of classification or interpretive lists, ocean carriers have not followed the practice of publishing formal classifications. Uniformity is non-existent in making such classifications and in applying them. Rates in one direction may be in one form; in the opposite direction, quite different.

The failure to adopt freight classifications in ocean shipping is due, partially, to the confusing, existent method of quoting ocean freight rates in a multitude of ways.

These methods are frequently beyond the comprehension of the average shipper and require the professionally competent skills of the foreign freight forwarder to elucidate their working and application. Until the enactment of Public Law 87-346 of October 3rd, 1961, amending Section 15, Shipping Act, 1916, carriers claimed that competitive reasons made them forego the publishing of formal classifications. They were apprehensive that they would incur great expenses in attempting to issue continuously supplements when rate changes should become necessary. They also believed that, lacking a list, they were in a better position to avoid arguments with shippers as to the proper application and interpretation. Now, this has thoroughly changed. Not only must all common carriers by water in foreign commerce of the United States file tariffs specifying the freight rates with the Federal Maritime Commission but the law also authorizes the Commission to review, regulate, approve or conditionally disapprove these rates and to enforce their publication and inspection by the shipping public. Exporters and importers require instantaneous rate information to calculate their sales - or purchasing costs to make advance quotations of delivered prices with some degree of assurance. To obtain this information either by calling in person at the steamship lines' office, or over the telephone, is vexatious. Telephone communication, particularly, may yield misinterpretations. Moreover, shippers and consignees should be placed in the position to describe accurately their merchandise for proper rating on the bill of lading. The foreign freight forwarder, solely, renders effective assistance on rates and other vital matters to the overwhelming majority of foreign traders, particularly to those in the interior.

Today, prices, as well as production conditions, are based on long-range marketing considerations, which make allowance for fluctuations of the rate level. It is for this reason that the Shipping Act, 1916, requires that increases in freight rates may be accomplished only upon 30 days' advance notice unless the Commission finds that good cause exists for making increases on shorter notice. So that carriers and traders alike will at all times be in a competitive position, reductions may be effected simultaneously with filing.

OCEAN FREIGHT TARIFFS

Whereas the device of freight classification, or grouping of commodities, and its application in the freight tariff is generally known in railroad traffic, it is only slightly applied in ocean transportation. Usually, the classification is combined with, or incorporated in, the freight tariff. This process not only catalogues the various commodities into certain groups, but also compiles the rates applicable to these groups. In addition, the tariff contains other charges and rules which govern a particular traffic.

Rigid standards don't exist in the composition of an ocean freight tariff, but certain provisions are found practically in every tariff. These provisions are:

1. Rates are subject to change without notice.

2. Commodity rates (covering specific goods) take precedence over class rates (covering a great number of various goods).

3. Mixed goods contained in the same shipping package take the highest rate for any comodity included.

4. Freight must be prepaid, with exceptions provided for.

5. Rates do not include marine insurance.

6. Goods exceeding a specified length or weight are subject to additional fixed charges.

7. *On deck* cargo is accepted at owner's risk.

8. Application of *Minimum Freight,* below which transportation will not be offered.

9. Cargo measurement rules.

10. Ports of call.

11. List of participating carriers.

12. Consular requirements.

13. Packing and marking regulations.

14. Acceptability of *To Order* bills of lading.

15. Rules pertaining to the aceptance and carriage of dangerous cargo.

16. Export Control regulations.

How to Read a Freight Tariff. To prescribe a simple formula to be used in reading and interpreting all types of freight tariffs naming various classes of rates, special and terminal charges, and rules and regulations, which govern all sorts of services because of radical differences in material and make-up, is impossible. To suggest definite steps in the use of tariffs that are valuable to the student of traffic management, who is able to exercise care in reading tariffs and patience in their use, is practicable.

The most valuable parts of tariff regulations to those who are unfamiliar with them, are the title page and the tables of contents. These two parts of the tariff schedule are the bases of operation from which to proceed from the known to the unknown.

The following steps should be regarded as general guides to be applied in meeting the varying requirements of different types of tariffs:

1. The table of contents should be consulted, so that the pages and sections of the tariff devoted to the material content of the tariff, i.e., rules and regulations governing the tariff, notes, reference marks or symbols, rate bases, rate tables, and other information can be readily located.

2. The table of contents should be examined carefully to determine the date of issue, the effective date of the tariff, and if it is issued to become effective in whole, or in part, on less than the statutory period of notice.

3. If the tariff has been supplemented, the supplements must be checked to determine the number of each supplement, and the numbers of effective supplements that contain the effective changes in the original tariff.

4. The items in the effective supplements should be checked, to be sure that they take precedence over the corresponding items in earlier supplements or in the original tariff.

5. The next step is to look for the geographical list of ports of destination, to spot the location and group, if any, of the port of destination.

6. Reference marks or symbols and notes pertaining to the destination ports should also be checked, because these minute items have a disconcerting way of transforming the ordinary application of rates to particular points.

7. If no complications have been interposed, the problem has now been reduced to checking a rate from or to a certain rate base, or group, to which reference has been made in the geographical lists of points of destination. The rate base should next be checked in order to find the rate reference or rate scale number applicable to the port or group of ports of destination.

8. The rate scales may then be consulted to find the class or commodity rate desired.

9. If commodity rates or exceptions to the classification are required, reference should first be made to the alphabetically arranged list of commodities. The items referred to in this list should then be checked until the rate sought is found, or careful search indicates that no commodity rates, or exceptions to the classification, are to be found in the tariff.

10. The rules governing the tariff should next be examined, with special attention to rules regulating the substitution, or alternation of class, exceptions to classification, and commodity rates.

11. The minimum freight, as the minimum amount below which no cargo will be carried, must be checked in the tariff.

12. If the tariff provides special and terminal rules, regulations, charges, or allowances, these provisions must be checked to see if the services required in connection with the movement of traffic in any way influence the basic rates.

13. Attention should be paid to tariffs cancelled wholly, or in part, by the tariff used in seeking the rate desired, in order to guard against the use of inapplicable rates.

14. The table of contents must be checked, as a final precaution, to examine any explanatory statements, reference marks, notes, or

other special factors, which may increase or decrease the total charges, or affect the application of the rates in any manner.

OCEAN FREIGHT RATE QUOTATIONS

Ocean freights are payable in various ways in the different world trades. Many rates on general cargo are quoted at a fixed rate per ton, weight or measurement, ship's option. This means that the rate named will be applied either per ton of 2,240 pounds (long ton or gross ton) in some trades; 2,000 pounds (short or net ton) ; or per 40 cubic feet (measurement ton). The choice is dictated by whichever application will yield the highest revenue to the carrier. Computations are based on the principle that a weight ton is the equivalent of 40 cubic feet.

The following example will clarify how the application of rates quoted on this basis, works out in practice.

Assume the general cargo rate to be $20 per ton, weight or measurement, ship's option. Goods that weigh exactly 56 lbs. (50 lbs.) per cubic foot will stow at 40 cubic feet to the ton of 2,240 lbs. (2,000 lbs). On such goods, the question of whether the freight is to be applied on a weight or measurement basis does not arise, since the rate is the same whichever way it is applied.

Now let us assume a shipment of goods that weighs 50 pounds per cubic foot, but is applicable to a long ton of 2,240 pounds. This is *measurement* cargo. Such goods will occupy 44.8 cubic feet per ton (2,240 divided by 50, the weight of 1 cubic foot). Therefore, one long ton of such cargo occupies more than a measurement ton of space (40 cubic feet). The steamship company, quoting on the basis of $20 per 40 cubic feet, will charge $22.40 for 44.8 cubic feet. If they accept the goods on a weight basis, they would receive only $20 for the same amount of goods, namely, one long ton.

Another way of quoting is to name two rates, like 45/80, which means that the specified cargo will pay 45 cents per cubic foot, or 80 cents per 100 pounds, whichever basis provides the greater revenue. This type of quotation is designed to provide an equal, or approximately equal, revenue from goods which stow at 40 cubic feet per ton, which is the dividing line between weight and measurement cargo. This, in the present instance, 40 cubic feet of cargo (a measurement ton) would pay 40 x 45¢, or $18.00. On a weight basis, such cargo would pay 22.4 x 80¢, or $17.92.

The units on which rates are based are not the same in all trades. More commonly they are quoted per hundred pounds or cubic foot, or per 2,240 pounds or 40 cubic feet. In some instances, however, there are special bases. For example, lumber per thousand feet board measure or thousand superficial feet; poles and piling, per linear foot; kerosene, per case of two five-gallon cans; and lubricating oil, per barrel.

The assessment of rates per case, barrel, bale, bag, or other similar unit is possible in some trades, because standard containers have been adopted by the shippers. Rates for animals are quoted per head.

Still another basis of rates is percent of the value, with articles of exceptionally high value frequently being charged ad valorem rates. The carrier usually reserves the option of charging on either the weight or measurement basis, and in the case of valuables, the additional option of charging on the ad valorem basis. In many cases, however the basis is specifically provided.

It seems appropriate to enumerate certain descriptive designations appearing most frequently in the ocean rate terminology. Among these are the following:

1. *Class rates* are those which apply to the groups or classes into which the various articles of commerce are divided. Due to the relatively small number of ports of shipment and destination covered by a given service, a classification may be used which refers to the rate book or rate section which lists the applicable rate, and thus gives rise to class rates.

2. A *commodity rate* is a special rate on specific articles, usually removing the application of the class basis. In contrast to the railway service, water rates are predominantly quoted on a commodity rather than class basis.

3. An *arbitrary rate* is a stipulated amount over a rate between two points, and is used to make a through rate. It is *sometimes* called a *differential*, though strictly speaking a differential may be made by either adding or subtracting from a basic rate. The arbitrary rate is usually applied by adding a fixed amount covering transference and carriage to an inland point, or a nearby port, to the base port-to-port charge.

4. *Minimum rates* are rates below which by law or agreement the rates of a carrier may not fall. Conference rates are often of this type. However, many rates on desirable berth cargo are excepted, or put at such a low minimum that they afford little protection to fellow conference members.

5. *Heavy-lift* and *extra-* or *long-length rates* are those which, because the cargo weight or length exceeds the specified maximum, are added to the basic rate or quoted separately. These are sometimes referred to as penalty charges.

6. *General cargo rates* are those which are applicable in the absence of specific commodity rates or class rates.

7. *Charter rates* are those paid under the contract of charter for the use of an entire vessel.

8. *Optional cargo rates* are those assessed in return for the privilege of declaring an option as to the port of call at which the cargo shall be discharged.

9. *Ad valorem rates* are charged in cases where the value of the shipment is declared to be in excess of the bill of lading limits of liability. They may be assessed on value alone or in addition to the regular charges assigned.

10. *Refrigerated cargo rates* are those assessed in addition to the usual charges for similar items, because of the services involved in transporting the cargo under refrigeration.

11. *Deck cargo rates* are those which are charged for the carriage of goods on the deck of the ship rather than in the holds. Such charges are usually somewhat under the level of the under-the-deck stowage rates.

12. *Dangerous cargo rates* are the rates which are assessed by special arrangements with the transporting company upon hazardous or dangerous cargo. Movements of this sort are usually under Board the transportation of small parcels not forwarded upon a bill of lading.

13. Parcel rates are those which are assessed by some carriers for the transportation of small parcels not forwarded upon a bill of lading. Some lines may issue instead a bill of lading for small parcel shipments, collecting as their recompense the minimum charges made for the service of issuing a bill of lading.

14. *Open rates* are rates upon which the carriers in a conference cannot agree; so each carrier is allowed to charge what it pleases or can get. If no conference agreements in any trade are in force, all rates are open rates.

The diversity of ocean rates necessitates the forwarder's being familiar with tariff classification and rates, and obliges him to pay strict attention to the correct declaration of the goods entrusted to him. Exact declaration of the freight is imperative because; (1) the freight charges of the ocean carrier are based on the declaration; (2) the declaration determines the treatment of the cargo in, or on, the vessel; and (3) the declaration is a decisive factor in the clearance of goods through customs in foreign ports.

The dispatch of dangerous cargo, or other material labeled for cautious handling, is subject to certain security regulations. The declaration of the goods notifies the carrier to recognize the dangerous character of the freight and to act accordingly. Reference should be made as to whether the goods in question are deck cargo, highly inflammable, corrosive, or explosive. Severe penalties are provided by United States statutes for failure to declare inflammable, explosive, or other dangerous goods when delivering them to steamship lines for export. Passenger vessels are forbidden to carry hazardous cargo, and many cargo liners do not have facilities for handling, or do not wish to handle certain types of freight. Port regulations hold steamship lines strictly accountable for loading and discharging in certain areas, and underwriters of marine insurance have rules regarding the parts of the ship where acids, gases, and highly inflammable products can be stowed.

Liability to carrier and vessel causes the forwarder great risks in shipping dangerous cargo. This also applies to fines, which are assessed by foreign customs authorities for misdeclarations in ocean documents. Every forwarder, therefore, should wisely insist on the proper and exact declaration of goods received from exporters, who are obliged to furnish a true description of the cargo to be shipped.

OCEAN FREIGHT RATE ADJUSTMENT PROCEDURES

Whereas the preceding sections of this chapter concerned themselves with the significance of ocean freight rates, rate making factors, ocean freight classifications, tariffs and modes of quotations, the following section concerns itself with the ways and means of seeking ocean freight rate adjustments and of conference practices for handling such requests.

Individual exporters, their appointed agents such as the foreign freight forwarder, or trade associations may enter into negotiations with conferences or independent carriers to secure rate modifications. The generally accepted practice is to conduct negotiations with the secretary of the conference at their headquarters which is usually situated at the major ports. Although conferences do not have uniform requirements regarding applications by exporters for rate adjustments, they insist that the requests are submitted to the conference office rather than to a member line. Even after a request for a rate modification or for the setup of a new rate has been received, it is common practice in most conferences not to reveal the applicant's identity in order to prevent a conference member from seeking to ingratiate itself with the petitioner by unconditionally supporting the applicant's request without regard to its merit.

In order to properly evaluate the application and pass intelligently upon the information submitted by the exporter, conferences need specific data which may be classified into four general groupings: 1). Transportation characteristics of the commodity; 2). Rate information concerning the current delivered cost of the article; 3). Estimated volume of movement at the rate requested; 4). A statement of reasons why the suggested rate is necessary.

To this end, conferences make available to the applicant a one-sheet or two-page form, called, by different conferences, Rate Adjustment Application, Traffic Analysis Form, Application for Modification In Ocean Freight Rates, etc.* While these forms vary from Conference to Conference, they call for specific information on the following subjects:

1). Name of commodity, its trade name, if any, and complete description of the article;

2). Nature of commodity with respect to being liquid or solid, hazardous or inflammable or perishable;

---

*See two sample forms in Appendix L/A.

3). Particulars concerning the shipping package including material from which made, and its shape, such as case, carton, barrel, drum, crate, etc.;

4). Gross weight of package, its three dimensions in feet and inches, and cubic content;

5). Cubic-feet required per short and long ton, using gross weight and measurement or shipping package;

6). Can the cargo be pre-palletized?

7). F.A.S. value of commodity at port of exit per pound, per ton (long and short), and per package;

8). Use of the article;

9). Name of competitive of substitute article;

10). Point of origin;

11). Cost of making shipside delivery, i. e. inland freight and port transfer charges;

12). Schedule B Commodity No. (U.S. Dept. of Commerce Statistical Classification of Commodities Number);

13). Sources of foreign competition involved, including difference in production costs and duty imposed also competitive price of article at foreign market place;

14). Ocean freight rates quoted from foreign ports of the countries of production to port of entry of competitive market place;

15). Present and proposed ocean freight rate;

16). Volume in which commodity ordinarily moves, i e. continuous, seasonal or sporadic;

17). Reason for the requested change in rate (just to make a higher profit is not a valid one).

The foregoing listed characteristics to be furnished by the shipper will suffice as a proper basis for an evaluation by the conference of the pertinent cost and demand factors for each rate decision. The transportation peculiarities influence the carrier's handling the goods such as loading, unloading and stowing; data on the volume of movement will provide some clues for an estimate of the revenue potential at the suggested rate; the conference's curiosity relating to foreign competition will allow a proper evaluation of the true competitive situation of the export product and the need for a rate reduction.

Most conferences have established standard procedures for handling rate adjustment requests. Once received, they are usually referred to the conference chairman and conference staff. The application is then docketed and presented to the member lines at a conference meeting. In some conferences, it is submitted to Standing Rate Committee made up for the purpose by the conference chairman; after reviewing the rate request, the committee prepares a recommendation on the proposal and submits the recommendation for decision to the representatives of all the Conference members at a rate making meeting called in by the conference secretary or chairman. In some conferences a unanimous vote by the members is required; in others, it is only two-thirds or three-fourths of the members, and again some require only a simple majority. As a rule, the all-member conference meetings are held on a regular basis, but there are instances where on urgent requests by exporters in special cases a telephone poll is undertaken by the conference chairman or secretary replacing the usually regular scheduled conference rate-making meeting; however, in such a case, a unanimous approval is required, otherwise the decision is deferred and the subject matter transferred to the next official plenary session of the conference members. It is also common practice that all votes taken are kept secret. One conference has adopted a rule that "no member shall advise how he or any other member voted"; another one adopted a guideline whereby the "conference secretary will take a secret ballot and shall announce the result of the motion as to whether it has carried or not, but make no record of the votes cast pro or contra." Under these circumstances it is difficult to determine the range of influences affecting rate decisions and, therefore, well possible that a justified rate modification may be denied by a conference. In such a case, the exporter may wish to seek remedy by requesting the Maritime Commission to investigate the negative rate decision of the conference, and can avail himself of two methods to secure the assistance of the Commission: (1) He may file an informal complaint in writing; or (2) file a formal complaint with the Commission in accordance with Section 22 of the Shipping Act, 1916. In the first case, the Commission tries to secure an adjustment with the conference and at the same time will determine whether any violation of the Shipping Act has incurred and what corrective measures should be taken. In the second case, which involves a formal complaint and judicial procedures, the employment of a competent attorney for counsel is highly recommended.

CHAPTER XI

Terminal And Port Charges

Services provided at ports are divided into terminal and port charges, according to the facilities offered to either cargo or ship. Charges are levied for these services by the Federal Government, state government, municipalities, and commercial enterprises.

The Federal authorities impose fees, or taxes, for quarantine, including disinfection and fumigation, customs clearance and entry of vessels, immigration of passengers, tonnage dues and light-house fees. State governments may assess toll taxes and further pilotage fees and, if dock or piers are state-owned, dockage charges. Municipalities and private enterprises may collect charges pertaining to any of the following services rendered in connection with the use of port facilities by vessel and cargo: towage, dockage, handling of cargo, lighterage, bunkering, elevating, watchmen, electric current, water, ballasting, dunnage, stevedoring, storing, switching, cartage, drayage, demurrage, weighing, and the miscellaneous fees of forwarders, ship brokers, surveyors, interpreters, etc. Uniformity generally prevails among the charges assessed by the Federal Government at the various ports; all other charges differ considerably as to application and use.

TERMINAL CHARGES

Terminal charges, as a rule, apply to cargo; port, or harbor charges are levied against the vessel. Among the terminal charges which, sometimes, are termed wharfage charges, the following items are included:

Direct Transfer: (1) Between open cars and vessel: *Direct transfer* means the handling, loading, or unloading of freight directly between open cars and vessel by ship's gear or by mechanical equipment. (2) Box cars alongside vessel: Unless otherwise specified, freight handled (loaded or unloaded) directly between a vessel and box cars spotted alongside, or freight trucked through a transit shed directly between a box car and shipside without being deposited on wharf, will not be considered as direct transfer freight. This freight will be assessed the same charges to which freight would be subject if unloaded from cars to place of rest on wharf, and handled from said place of rest to shipside, and vice versa.

Handling. A charge assessed for the service of handling freight, *viz.*, the service of moving or conveying freight between the ship's gear and the place of rest on wharf. Ordinary sorting, piling, tiering, breaking out, elevating, and trucking are included in this service. This charge is paid by the ocean carrier.

Heavy Lift. Articles of heavy lift, or extra length, are subject to man-hour rates, plus equipment and materials, levied against the cargo.

Lighterage. The cost for conveying the goods by lighters or barges between ship and shore and vice versa, including the loading into, and discharging out of, lighters.

Loading and Unloading. Charges assessed for service of loading freight on, or into railroad cars, and unloading freight from railroad cars. These services include ordinary sorting, breaking down from piles, and piling.

Service Charge. A charge assessed on the basis of cargo tons handled, and levied against vessels—or their owners, agents, or operators—which load or discharge cargo at the terminals; for use of terminal facilities; for berthage while loading or discharging cargo; for administrative expense in serving the carrier, and for performing other varied services.

Wharfage. Usually defined as a charge assessed on all cargo passing or conveyed over, on, through or under a pier, wharf, dock, or quay, or a charge made for receiving export cargo from truck, conveying to dock loading platform, and delivering to ship's tackle. Occasionally called "Port or State Toll."

Switching. The movement of railroad cars by the Belt Railroad from one location on the Belt to another location also on the Belt.

Car Float Delivery Charge. This charge is levied if a lesser number than six railroad cars, or less than six times the minimum carload weight, is moved on a scow or barge, fitted with railroad tracks, from ship to shore or vice versa.

Demurrage. A penalty for failure to unload carloads, which is assessed by railroads after the allowed free period for cars has elapsed. This period is usually seven days, excluding Saturdays, Sundays, and holidays.

Storage. A charge for goods held in railroad, or other warehouses, under fixed agreement for periods of time, and which is not included in other service arrangements.

Drayage or Trucking: A charge for delivery of goods or pick-up of goods from docks or other port terminals.

Port or Dockage Charges

Among the port or dockage charges we find:

Pilotage. A charge assessed according to the draft, tonnage, and type of vessel in line with established rate scales or tariffs.

Tonnage Tax. A Federal tax collected from all commercial vessels for the privilege of entering, leaving, or lying in a United States port and doing business within United States territory.

Towage. A charge payable by the vessel employing tugs to assist in bringing the ship into and out of a port, or in docking, undocking, and shifting from one pier to another within the harbor area.

Dockage. A charge collected from a vessel for the utilization of the dock accommodation, for the purpose of loading and unloading cargo. Dockage rates are charged on an hourly basis, or if the vessel's owner or operator holds a preferential assignment to a wharf area, on a monthly basis. This charge is assessed in some ports on the gross tonnage; in others, on the net tonnage and, although rarely, on the over-all length in feet of the vessel.

Stevedoring. A charge, generally so much per ton, agreed upon between the ocean carrier and a stevedoring, or terminal, operator covering the allocation of men (longshoremen), gear, and all other equipment for working the cargo in or out of the vessel, under the supervision and control of the ship's master.

Dunnage Charges. They represent the cost of acquiring and installing dunnage material in the hold and decks of a vessel for loading operations.

Port or Harbor Dues. Local charges levied against the vessel in connection with the maintenance and administration of harbor facilities, such as channels, anchorage grounds, buoys, lights, harbormaster fees.

Port charges are usually published in tariff form, filed with regulatory agencies and are subject to change.

Bunker Surcharge. In times of drastic increases in the price of bunker fuel, a surcharge, assessed on a percentage basis, will be applied to all freight rates and charges governed with deliveries to carrier's vessel alongside or on the dock.

Port Congestion Surcharge. Due to congested pier conditions, lack of adequate discharging facilities and deficiency of the available labor force, resulting in an alarming increase in the overall costs of operation, a congestion surcharge, assessed on a percentage basis, is being applied to all freight rates.

CHAPTER XII

Cargo Handling

Low cost and rapid handling constitute the bulwark of the efficient operation of world seaborne trade and its continuous expansion. Strengthening this framework is the satisfactory layout and operation of port facilities.

Contrasting with the swift development of bigger, faster merchant vessels and the improvement of air, rail, and motor transportation, the progress in terminal operations has greatly lagged. Practically, this has nullified the advances in other phases of ship operation. Cognizance was granted only a few years ago to the fact that bottlenecks in the free flow of goods, in terms of exorbitant cargo-handling costs, threatened the ability of our exporters to compete successfully for business abroad.

Ships earn only when in action. When at standstill in port, they lose money. Each day an average cargo vessel lies in port costs from two to five thousand dollars, an amount which equals the vessel movement costs for five to six thousand miles.

Consequently, the time spent by a ship in port for the turn-around should be definitely reduced to permit increased earning power by scheduling more voyages per year. This can, and will be accomplished, if the cargo transference problems (the handling of cargo on the dock, and the handling of the freight into, and in, the ship's hold) are boldly attacked. To implement this solution, a scientific approach is requisite to critically consider all factors relevant to ship operation and cargo handling. Notable advances have been made during the last few years to attain this goal.

Particular recognition must be given to the work done by one of the most effective organizations in the field of international commerce, The International Cargo Handling Coordination Association. Dedicated to the continuous investigation of ways and means of expediting all phases of moving oceanborne cargo throughout the world, this group was established in London on December 1, 1951. The unit acts as a clearing house for over five hundred members in fifty leading seafaring nations. Stevedores, packers, shippers, shipowners, shipbuilders, equipment manufacturers, insurance companies and port authorities exchange ideas concerning methods of increasing the efficiency of the packaging, transporting, handling, and stowing of oceanborne cargo.

Problems typical of those which this professional body explores and attempts to solve through special studies include: (a) layout of port facilities in relation to docking and cargo handling; (b) design of ships in connection with loading, discharging; and stowing; (c) loading and unloading of vessels lying offshore; (d) railroads and their relationship to cargo handling; (e) bulk cargo handling; (f) standardization of packing methods and materials; (g) waterfront labor force (education or other means of overcoming resistance to mechanization); and (h) administrative matters concerning customs and port authorities.

TERMINAL OPERATIONS

Efficient cargo handling operations require modern marine terminals and service which provide the following facilities:

1. A wide pier, or quay, with transit shed of enough capacity to allow the berth to be used for laying out cargo and for the intensive utilization of motorized equipment such as trucks, trailers and tractors.

2. A wide apron fitted with at least one railroad track.

3. If the transit shed has more than one deck, the upper decks should be equipped with adequate loading platforms.

4. Sufficient land and water area around the pier to avoid congestion of the approach area.

5. Up-to-date mechanical equipment for use by the terminal operator, or stevedore, as we usually call him.

6. Enlightened management, first class supervisory personnel, and trained labor.

Cargo transference from ship to dock, or vice versa, either via side-port over a gang plank by hand or motorized truck, or via hatch by means of the ship's tackle, double boom, or cargo mast is broken down in four component parts.

A. When discharging cargo:

1. Operations in the hold, or between decks breaking out the freight, making up the sling or pallet loads, and moving the cargo from the stowage location to the square of the hatch or side-port.

2. Movement between hold and apron by the ship's gear.

3. Movement between apron and storage place in the transit shed by the terminal's vehicles.

4. Sorting, piling and tiering of cargo in the transit shed.

B. When loading:

1. Receiving and laying out truck or rail cargo opposite the hatch.

2. Movement between storage pile and apron by the transit shed vehicles.

3. Movement between apron and hold or between decks by ship's gear.

4. Stowing in the ship's hold and decks.

This cycle clearly demonstrates that the efficiency of the stevedore in handling a given type of cargo, in loading and discharging a given type of ship, depends to a large extent upon the type of transit shed, pier deck, and equipment available at the terminal. Further key factors in smooth functioning are the efficiency of the rail and motor transportation which backs up the terminal, and the accessible transportation methods to the floor of the transit shed and the apron of the dock.

Specialized cargo handling techniques have recently been developed and successfully applied in limited degree. However, a solution of the thorny problem of reducing cargo-handling cost through greater dispatch of the loading and discharging cycle, will be achieved only upon the fulfillment of all the previously indicated requirements. Efficient, economic service demands continuous research, coupled with long range planning to overcome any possible lethargy, from whatever direction it may originate.

Among the various contributions towards the solution of improving cargo handling methods is the "Ship and Shore Loading System." This technique is designed to carry unit loads of various types, such as super-pallets, medium or large containers, right from the pier into the ship. The basic unit of the system is a low-slung, wheeled carriage, which moves along rails on the decks within the vessel and on the pier floor via large side-ports. The vertical movement within the ship is performed by elevators.

Another system, termed "The Farrell Coordinated Rolling Wing Decks," has been successfully installed and utilized.

Modernized materials-handling equipment, such as cranes, forklifts, pallets, conveyors, truck-loaders, car-unloaders, tractor-trailer combinations, and other time-and-work-saving devices are now used extensively in the transit shed, as well as on the vessel.

In contrast hereto, the ship's gear has scarcely changed in many years, except for some slight refinements. One new idea was to dispense with the old-fashioned, complicated, and slow method of moving cargo to and from the ship's hold by winches, masts, spars, and booms. By applying side-door loading, most cargo would not have to be lifted, but could roll directly from pier to hold by means of an overhead monorail. This monorail can be shifted without ado inside the vessel, thus placing the cargo exactly where needed. Bowdoor loaded ships—the "roll-on, roll-off vessels" that carry truck-trailers and railroad freight cars—are envisaged as the ships of the future. Utilization of this radical advance in ship construction will decisively shorten turn-around time for vessels and transit time for cargo.

The Container Problem: The use of shipping containers to expedite cargo-handling and to protect goods from pilferage and breakage in transit, as far as ocean transportation is concerned, was given great impetus by conditions during World War II. Shortly thereafter, the development of the standardized container became a reality. It was the result of the experience gained in connection with effective coordination of transportation and interchangeability of equipment. The solution to effective coordination of transportation was the standardization of the container dimensions. The National Defense Transportation Association recommendations for basic dimensional standards for containers was one of the considerations that led to the enactment of Public Law 87-271 of September 21st, 1961, amending Section 607 (b) of the Merchant Marine Act, 1936, providing important tax advantages to subsidized ocean carriers by allowing them to utilize their reserve funds in the purchase and construction of standard-size containers.

Originally, the first post-war containers' dimensions were dictated by the limitations imposed by the linear measurements of holds, hatches and 'tween decks of vessels, and the design best fitted to the needs, had a bale capacity of about 280 cubic feet, a structural strength to carry up to six tons of cargo, and measured approximately 7' 9" in length, 6' 5" in width, and 6' 10" in height. The qualifications for a modern and practical shipping container were that it be durable, portable, lightweight, weathertight, adaptable and theftproof. These physical and functional characteristics were successfully developed after many tests.

Evaluated from the steamship operator's viewpoint, the cargo container has evidenced a great reduction in theft and damage in the carriage of small, highly pilferable commodities such as watches, cutlery, costume jewelry, clocks, and liquor, to enumerate but a few. Cargo claims for theft and damage have been reduced to a minimum. Goods shipped in containers are protected during all stages of the voyage, from the arrival at the pier until the discharge at destination. Simultaneously, the container serves as an advertising medium, which displays the steamship line's name. Stenciled on the sides, the name can attract the eye, and possible business, of a potential shipper. Containers have proved particularly useful to those ocean carriers whose vessels have to load and discharge their cargo at open roadsteads where, due to lack of proper pier facilities, cargo handling has to rely on the use of lighters or barges.

In the early 1950's, foreign traders realized how great an impact containerization could have on their over-all transportation costs.

Ten years later, this idea had progressed to a point where the dawn of a container era could be reported. Containers of every type and size were built and leased by firms specializing in the supply of containers. A demand by exporters for containers and the resulting competitive situation had stimulated international ocean carriers and their conferences into expanding container services from the various U.S. ports, especially to Europe. The Intermodal Van Container transport had arrived and with it, the modern container ship concept which is by now firmly established in United States foreign trade. Arrangements on international level developed patterns of standardization on containers* which found approval in Europe so that the

* Through the I.S.O. (International Standard Organization).

smaller European units are joined by a full set of larger American containers for worldwide use. At the same time, through-transportation arrangements by Railroads and Motor Carriers for export shipments, to satisfy the needs toward intermodal coordinated transport accelerated the construction of a container fleet by the leading ocean carriers and the creation of special port facilities needed for unhampered container ship operation in Europe as well as in the United States such as the Stapleton, Staten Island, New York and the Elizabeth-Port Newark complex in the Port of New York area.

We distinguish three different types of containerships, some of which have roll-on/roll-off capacity and can be converted to pallet ships:

a). The All-Containership. All cargo spaces are fitted with vertical cells for container or trailer stowage. Additional vans are carried on deck. Each vessel according to size carries between 226 and 1300 containers.

b). The Semi-Containership. It is a conventional general cargo carrier with one or two holds fitted with vertical cells. The construction of the vessel provides the conversion of additional holds to cell stowage if container traffic requires.

c). The Combination Containership. In addition to the cellular van-container fitting, the vessel's design and structure allows Roll-on/Roll-off Trailer and Container Service through ramps to docksides, and stern-and-side-port openings, as well as palletized cargo handling in addition to the loading of bulk cargo into the lower holds.

d). The LASH System (Lighter-Aboard-Ship) provides steel barges, each measuring about 30 feet by 60 feet, being hoisted by the ship's crane onto the vessel. This type of vessel carries containerized, unitized, bulk, liquid and almost any type of break-bulk general cargo.

These vessels, some of them moving at a speed of 40 knots, will complete an Atlantic round trip from base port to base port in just about one week's time. The containership deserves full credit for advancing the acceptance of containerization in general. How fast containerization will further grow and progress depends on many factors among them the attitude of, and measures taken by the various regulatory agencies, on the degree of support and coordination these agencies and ocean carriers can mutually develop, the cooperation of international agencies on state and private level, the availability of standardized equipment, and last but not least on continuous care and maintenance of all facilities involved.*

STOWAGE

The placing of cargo into a vessel is called *stowage*. Good stowing is an art. Stowing demands experience, skill, knowledge, imagination, and endurance. Loading or stowing of miscellaneous cargo does not follow a fixed pattern. This is applicable, particularly, when goods are received in advance of the vessel's arrival, sometimes several days prior to the drawing up of cargo sheets and storage plans. Proper stowage of cargo is of paramount importance to the shipper. It aims to protect merchandise against damage during the ocean voyage

---

*See Appendix R for a list of container terms and definitions.

and assures prompt discharge at port of destination. It also avoids over-carriage of cargo to other ports and the disappointment of short-shipment at port of unloading. To assure this goal, cargo for the first port of call is loaded last, and vice versa.

Responsibility for planning and supervising this demanding operation is delegated to the *stevedore*. His job requires agility, foresight, and patience. Incessantly confronted by challenging situations, he is accountable for the proper layout of cargo on the dock. He must be certain that packages are in good condition and note exceptions if they exist. He must supervise the measuring and weighing and pass judgment on the adequacy of containers. Significantly, to retain their good will, he must satisfy shippers, forwarders and consignees. He must be an effective coordinator; for although he should arrange and advance course of action whenever possible, he must be flexible, in order to change his plans on a moment's notice. He must confer with, and receive approval of, the ship's master or his representative. He must know and adhere to the rules of the United States Coast Guard, with special reference to the acceptance and loading of dangerous cargo. He is generally responsible to the ship owner for proper stowage, and thereby, indirectly, for the safety of ship, cargo, and crew. This principle was reaffirmed in a 5-to-4 decision of the Supreme Court on January 9, 1956. This decision ruled that liability of the stevedore exists where the contractor, "without entering into an express agreement of indemnity, contracts to perform a shipowner's stevedoring operations. The contractor has no logical ground for relief from the full consequences of its independent contractual obligation, to load the cargo properly." The stevedore asserted that the shipowner was obligated to supervise the stowage, but since he failed to do so, he, the owner, should be prevented from recovering damage costs. This contention was dismissed by the court on the grounds that the owner's neglect does not excuse the stevedore from his own failure to discover his breach of contract.

The power of a vessel to right itself from a sideward rolling position is called *stability*. Improper loading or distribution of cargo in a ship's hold greatly influences stability. Moderate changes in stability can cause a vessel to ride or roll badly and create the possibilities that its cargo may shift, that it may lose some of its propulsive power and speed, or that, in the extreme case, it may capsize. When bow and stern have the same draft, a ship is said to be *in trim*. Most ships perform best when they have a slight *drag;* that is, when the ship draws more water aft than forward. The *stability* and *trim* must be given advance consideration, and must continuously be watched. Heavy cargo loads placed at both ends of the vessel will cause the ship to pitch, and may permanently damage its structure. Concentration of more weight on one side than on the other reduces her speed, makes her unstable, and puts her in danger of listing. An aggressive and conscientious stevedore must be cognizant of ship design and must be familiar with the characteristics of each vessel he is to load. If the ship is narrow and deep, heavier weights of cargo should be placed low in the holds; if she is wide and shallow, the heavy pieces should be put into the 'tween decks. The stevedore must see that cargo is stowed in a manner which will not crush or damage other packages. He must consider the possible leakage of liquid freight; damage from "sweat," or condensation of moisture; damage arising from climatic conditions during the voyage; and be aware of dangers resulting from odors.

Dunnage is one of the stevedore's chief aids in handling the wide variety of cargo, packaged in different styles. Dunnage is but one of the many types of equipment at his disposal. Consisting mainly of rough pine boards, *dunnage* is used as flooring for the hold before loading is begun. Also, it is placed against the sides, to separate the cargo from the "skin" of the vessel, and from the bulkheads, which separate the holds from each other. Prior to stowing a succeeding tier of cargo, a platform of dunnage is placed on the previous tier. It is also employed to protect the cargo from the moisture and sweat which often collect on the steel bottom, sides, and bulkheads in a ship, and from water leaking from bilges and tanks. In addition, dunnage serves as a cargo binder, which prevents the shifting, loosening, and movement of freight during the trip. It supplies, also, ventilation space for air to circulate in the holds. Unboxed automobiles are loaded chockablock, secured with special lashings, or placed in cradles. Other special dunnage devices are sometimes applied for shoring of decks in the lower holds and to reinforce the vessel's structure when exceptionally heavy and bulky pieces must be carried as "deck" cargo.

All these functions, plus many more, conclusively demonstrate that trained personnel hold the key to cargo-handling costs. This concept, in the stevedoring field, embraces the boss and continues directly down the occupational scale to the longshoreman. Stowage represents a complicated operational process. Skill and planning are required to load a vessel "full and down" to its marks, to obtain maximum revenue.

To accomplish this goal, the stevedore applies certain rules concerning the relationship of cargo weight to cargo measurement. Except for some minor deviations, the generally accepted standard for cargo measurement is 40 cubic feet to the ton of 2000 or 2240 pounds, depending on the various trades. Contrasting with the weight ton, the measurement ton, equalling 40 cubic feet, is also called the *Stow Ton*. Cargo measuring less than 40 cubic feet to the ton, as outlined in Chapter X on ocean freight rates, is rated under the principle known as *weight or measurement, ship's option,* on a weight basis, since the carrier's revenue will be higher. To achieve the most economical combination of weight and measurement cargo in loading a given vessel and to obtain simultaneously the highest possible revenue, the ship operator and the stevedore must know the available space. They must know the cubical carrying capacity of the ship for each actual weight ton of cargo to be loaded. They must also know the weight-carrying capacity, called *cargo deadweight tonnage*. This is the number of tons of 2240 pounds of cargo the vessel can lift after the weight of fuel, stores, water and other necessary items have been deducted from the total deadweight tonnage of the ship. (*Total deadweight* is the number of long tons required to submerge a vessel to her loaded draft and includes besides cargo, fuel, water, stores, and passengers.) The figure which expresses the number of cubic feet taken up by one long ton (2240 lbs.) of a commodity as packed for shipment, with no allowance added for "broken stowage" or waste space, is the stowage factor which is arrived at by dividing 2240 pounds by the weight, in pounds, of a cubic foot of the particular commodity. For example: a wooden box containing cellophane measures 1.9 cubic feet and weighs 65 pounds gross. To ascertain the stowage factor, we first have to find the weight of one cubic foot by dividing 1.9 into 65 pounds, which results in 34.2 pounds. Then we divide 34.2 into 2240 lbs., thus arriving at the number of cubic feet occupied by one long ton, or the stowage factor—in this instance, 65 cubic feet. To facilitate in advance the loading of a vessel, ocean carriers found it expedient to prepare a comprehensive list of commodities indicating their stowage factors. It is impossible to know in advance the various kinds and amounts of cargo to be stowed in a given vessel, or the manner in which the cargo is to be stowed. It is, also, difficult to determine what the broken stowage will be on any given commodity. For these reasons, the aforementioned list includes a certain allowance for broken stowage, ranging from two to forty per cent. This means that if a broken stowage of fifteen per cent is applicable to a certain type of cargo, then fifteen per cent of the hold capacity remains unused, because there is lost space around the units of cargo. Experienced stevedores refer, as an example, to the stowage of newsprint in rolls. They declare its net stowage factor of eighty (that is, 2240 pounds require 80 cubic), as entirely too small. In laying out the vessel, they allow 100 to 110 feet to the ton for broken stowage, according to the size of the rolls.

Allowance for waste space varies, in accordance with the location of the cargo in the ship. More broken stowage will occur in the number one hold and the aftermost hold, since these compartments taper toward bow and stern. This considerable space between the cargo and the "skin" of the ship can not be utilized, but must be filled with dunnage. Other factors which influence the amount to be allowed for broken stowage are the type of cargo (whether subject to damage from leakage, odor, heat or other elements) ; proximity to engine room bulkheads; order of call of various ports; distribution of freight for proper stability; and need for prompt loading or discharge.

A more detailed outline as to the actual procedure of practical stowing as a function of the carrier's traffic department, in cooperation with the dock force based on the booking sheet, cargo capacity sheet and stowage plan, will be found in Chapter XIII, "Documents Required by Ocean Carrier."

TONNAGE TERMINOLOGY OF VESSELS

The preceding discussion concerned itself predominantly with cargo or traffic tonnage, in contrast to vessel tonnage. Tonnage, in such cases, was expressed either in weight (*long tons*), or measurement (*stow tons* of 40 cubic feet). As applied to vessel tonnage, the measurement ton is equivalent to 100 cubic feet of space. We distinguish five kinds of vessel tonnage: gross, net, displacement, deadweight, and cargo dead weight. This latter tonnage is a modification, or adjustment for cargo purposes, of the total dead weight tonnage.

Gross Tonnage. All the enclosed space in the ship, which is measured at 100 cubic feet per ton, resulting in a space ton. Gross tonnage should not be confused with the cargo measurement ton of 40 cubic feet. This tonnage measurement usually refers to the size of the vessel.

Net Tonnage. Gross tonnage, less deductions for crew space, machinery, stores, and provisions. Net tonnage is an indication of the earning capacity of the vessel and is used as a basis for the assessment of tonnage taxes, port dues, canal tolls, and other commercial charges.

Displacement Tonnage. The weight of the volume of water displaced by the vessel. *Light displacement* is equal to the weight of the ship, whereas *loaded displacement* equals the weight of steamer and cargo.

Deadweight Tonnage. Actual weight of fuel, provisions, water, cargo, and passengers that a vessel can carry, when loaded to its marks.

Cargo Deadweight Tonnage. Actual weight of cargo which will submerge the vessel to its marks, less bunker, water, provisions, and so forth.

Freeboard. Height of side of the vessel measured amidships, from the center of the disc to the top of the weather deck.

Loadlines Marks assigned by governmental maritime agencies, above which a steamer must not be submerged. The load line is also known as Plimsoll line, named after Samuel Plimsoll, an Englishman, whose effort resulted in legislation requiring governmental inspection of ships and its approval of loading marks.

CUBAGE

Manufacturers, exporters, and foreign freight forwarders are frequently called upon by steamship lines when booking space, or for "freighting" purposes, in order to figure and post the applicable freight on the ocean bill of lading, to furnish the weight, dimensions, kind, and number of shipping packages. Usually, a packing list is submitted, which serves the desired purpose. Factory measurements, however, are not always correct. Frequently they do not conform to steamship lines' practice with respect to the methods of measuring cargo, with the result that freight charges are miscalculated either by the shipper or carrier.

Computing cubage for ocean freight purposes refers exclusively to the method of measuring cargo in ocean transportation, as expressed in tariffs issued by various liner conferences, or as customarily applied. Computing cubage does not deal with the cubic capacity of a container, since this would indicate only cubic contents or inside capacity; nor is it cubic displacement. To understand the problem involved, we have to consider the shapes of the various shipping packages, whether unboxed, or cases, crates, kegs, barrels or drums. Almost all of them cause waste space or broken stowage. None of this space could be profitably utilized by the carrier, unless it were included in the revenue by charging the total space, which equals the used and the lost, to the shipper of the package. This is accomplished by a measuring method which attempts to obtain the smallest rectangular cubic space to enclose the shipping package. Ocean freight cubage thus is derived by multiplying the three outside dimensions—length, breadth, and depth. When measuring barrels, kegs, casks, and drums, the measurements are taken on the square of the bilge. To elucidate: the diameter is taken at the bilge, then is multiplied by itself, before being multiplied by the height (depth) of the cylindrical container. When irregular packages are measured, the three greatest dimensions should be used to determine the cubic space they will occupy.

Further attention must be given to the treatment of fractions of an inch by ocean carriers. Common practice decrees that all fractions under one-half inch are dropped, whereas a fraction of one-half inch and over in one dimension of a package is to be included as a full inch. Where there are fractions of one-half inch on two dimensions of a package, the one on the smaller dimension is to be included as a full inch, and the other dropped. In the case of fractions of one-half inch on three dimensions, the ones on the largest and smallest dimensions are included as a full inch, and the fraction on the other is dropped. All fractions exceeding one-half inch are to be included as full inches. When computing measurements to ascertain the applicable rate, where weight rate is predicated on measurement per ton, the actual fractions may be used.

To compute the correctly determined dimensions into cubage for freighting purposes, all feet and inches must be reduced to inches. Each of the three "inch" dimensions then should be multiplied together (length times width times depth), and the total inches should be divided by 1,728. To avoid lengthy computations, so-called *standard cubic contents tables* may be obtained at commercial printers and stationary stores. These tables are fixed on a "feet and inch" basis and contain a tabulation of measurements to the nearest inch by length, breadth, and depth. The "figured-out" results are presented in terms of cubic feet and "twelfths" of a cubic foot. For example, if the table indicates that the "cube" of a shipping package is 3/5, it *means* three and 5/12 cubic feet, *not* three and 5/10 cubic feet. When billing freight on the total shipment, ocean carriers, as a rule, do not charge for a fraction of a cubic foot. They ordinarily drop fractions of a cubic foot when it is less than one-half cubic foot, and round up a full cubic foot when the fraction is one-half cubic foot, or more.

Cargo handling, and its ramifications, may seem complicated to a beginner in ocean traffic matters. Patience, practice, and study will, however, help to overcome anticipated difficulties. Thorough knowledge of the "cubage" problem and the accurate measuring of packages in accordance with practices established by ocean carriers will eliminate misunderstandings. Costly errors are apt to disturb the harmonious relations between the diverse elements in shipping operations; so maximum effort should be exerted to reduce computation errors to a minimum.

INTERMODALISM, MINIBRIDGE AND MICROBRIDGE

The growth of containerization has brought about the following new phrases: "INTERMODALISM," "MINIBRIDGE" and "LAND-BRIDGE." Intermodalism is a door-to-door through service of freight in a single unit, under a single bill of lading and under uniform liability & regulations by whatever mode of transportation the shipper selects, be it by sea, land or air. Minibridge traffic differs from pure "Landbridge" service in that the foreign traffic begins or terminates at some U.S. port, as distinguished from foreign-to-foreign freight moving across the U.S. continent. Thus, cargo from the Far East is transferred from ship to train at a West Coast U.S. port for delivery to East Coast, Gulf or Midwest consignees. Conversely, cargoes from Europe destined for West Coast consignees are supposed to tranship at the ports of the other coasts. The export movements travel their destined way along the same logic.

Lately, a new export shipping service that provides door-to-door service for shippers in the United States, midwest and other inland points, was introduced by a San Francisco based ocean carrier. Called "MICROBRIDGE", its rates combine the price of rail and ocean transportation into a single tariff which comes out to a lower rate than the two rates paid separately. In contrast to MINIBRIDGE, which merely transports cargo from port to port, MICROBRIDGE provides carriage from door to door. Its advantage is that it competes successfully with rate-cutting non-conference carriers and facilitates export/import goods price quotations for the seller/buyer of goods.

CHAPTER XIII

Documents Required By Ocean Carriers

Those who conduct business with foreign markets or participate in the cargo carrying trade called ocean transportation are charged with the responsibility of performing efficiently and economically. Incessant increases in both foreign and domestic governmental controls have effected an inundation of documentary requirements to contend with the resultant restrictions and regulations. The international forwarding agent is a specialist whose services are essential for the successful management of the agglomeration of required business papers. These, by reasons of law, either contractual or political, or because of financial security, or for purely functional purposes must be attended to in order to permit the unhampered exchange of international goods.

Documents in the field of international shipping are classified in groups, depending upon their use and intent: (1) Cargo and vessel documents, (2) Documents required by foreign governments, and (3) Documents used in international forwarding.

This chapter will outline the purposes and describe the contents of the essential documents required by ocean carriers.

The Freight Contract. This is a formal agreement between the ocean carrier, or his appointed agent, and the shipper (exporter or forwarder) for booking (engaging) steamer space, committing the vessel operator to reserve the required space for a certain sailing, and authorizing the shipper to deliver accordingly. The contract specifies the commodity, weight, cubic feet, rate, ports of loading and discharge, the means of delivery (truck or rail), name of vessel, delivery date of cargo, and the ship's sailing date. A clause subjecting the booking to all terms and conditions of the vessel's usual bill of lading is also included. The dock receipt, whether issued or not, and the current tariff of the carrier, are all, hereby, a part of this contract. This agreement is subject to the safe arrival of vessel. The carrier exempts strikes, accidents, or other hindrances of any kind that prevent the carrying out of this contract. If, because of conditions either existing or anticipated, such as strikes, lockouts, labor troubles (including those of officers and/or crews of vessels), accident or other hindrances, acts or restraints of governments, princes, rulers and peoples, war, or any circumstances beyond the carrier's control, the carrier or its agents should consider it impossible, unsafe, or (having regard to the ship's despatch and further prosecution of her voyage) inadvisable to proceed to, call at, or remain at port of loading, the carrier shall have the option of postponing or cancelling shipment of all or any part of the cargo covered by this contract, and the vessel shall not be bound to proceed to, call at, or remain at the port of loading. Unless by the owner's option, the vessel is not to be detained at port beyond the scheduled sailing date.

S/S Santa Margarita
Voyage 17 on berth P 58 N.R.

CARGO CAPACITY SHEET
Tons of 2240#

Delivery Dates:
Truck   8/5-12
Lighter 8/7-12
Sailing date 8/13/48

Stowage Factor:
60 cu.ft. per ton, which is derived by dividing the cubic contents of cargo space (478,520 Cu.ft.) by deadweight, less fuel, water, stores, dunnage, mail, and baggage = 7,952 tons.

	Weight Tons	Cubic Meas. Ton
Total Deadweight @ 26' 9" (Draft. S. Line)	9,102	10,022 - Dry bale
Less: Fuel .... 350 Tons		2,341 - Reefer
Water 300		
Stores 150		
Dunnage 200	1,000	
	8,102T	12,363 MT
Less: Mail	100	300
	8,002	12,063
Less: Baggage	50	100
	7,952T	11,963 MT

RECAPITULATION OF CARGO BOOKINGS

	Buenaventura		Guayaquil		Talara		Callao		Chanaral		Valpo		TOTAL
	Wgt.T.	Stow.T.	Wgt.T.	Stow.T.	Wgt.T.	Stow.T.	Wgt.T.	Stow.T.	Wgt.T.	Stow.T.	W.T.	St.	
Cargo under 10T	300	750	100	250	-	-	200	500	-	-	400	1,000	1,000 W.T. / 2,500 S.T.
Cargo over 10T	1,600	1,800	700	1,000	.550	600	460	610	400	300	900	1,600	4,610 W.T. / 5,910 S.T.
Automobiles	140	2,800	160	900	-	-	80	440	-	-	90	380	4,70 W.T. / 4,520 S.T.
Reefer Cargo	-	-	-	-	2#	0/7	180#	18/-	-	-	489#-	20/-	671# / 38/7
TOTALS	2,040	5,350	960	2,150	550	600	740	1,550	400	300	1,390	2,980	6,080 W.T. / 12,930 S.T.

AUTOMOBILES UNBOXED

	Jeeps	Passenger Cars	Trucks	TOTAL
Buenaventura	50	25	15	90
Guayaquil	-	6	-	6
Callao	-	4	1	5
	50	35	16	101

Cargo Capacity Sheet

The contract may stipulate further that, if one copy of the contract is not signed and returned to the agent for the carrier within four days from date shown thereon, the carrier shall have the privilege of cancelling the reservation.

All cargo bookings are entered on the booking sheet immediately upon execution of the contract. The Booking Sheets are maintained by the Traffic Department of the steamship line. From there, the bookings are transferred to the Cargo Capacity Sheet, which is a rough drawing of the ship. The Cargo Capacity Sheet illustrates how and where the booked cargo will be stowed, as well as all pertinent weight and measurement capacities for cargo, provisions, and fuel.

The use of freight contracts is currently limited to bulk cargo. Bookings for general cargo, however, occasionally originate from interior shipping centers, and are made by so-called "engagement notes." The availability of foreign freight forwarding services throughout the country, particularly at all major sea ports, precludes the extensive execution of "freight contracts," plus the fact that exporters, in order to keep a free hand in their dispositions, do not like to be tied down or drawn into possible legal entanglements. In summary, it may be stated that the freight contract is a product of emergency or wartime exigencies, when steamer space is scarce. In normal times, the problem of securing space is practically nonexistent. As shipments arrive they are lined up and delivered to the next due vessel, the exceptions being as previously mentioned, only those unusually bulky and heavy goods which require special stowing and for which the necessary arrangements with the carrier should be made in advance. However, this can be achieved either orally or by a written request, asking for immediate booking and confirmation thereof, without any formal contract between exporter, or forwarder, and carrier.

The Shipping Permit. The Shipping Permit, sometimes called *Delivery Permit,* is a document used chiefly in the Port of New York. It is issued by the Traffic Department of the ocean carrier, after the booking of cargo has been made. It directs the Receiving Clerk of the pier at which the vessel will load, to receive from a named party (exporter or forwarder) to a named port on a specified day, or time, the goods described by number and kind of packages, contents, gross weight, and measurement. This permit must be presented, prior to delivery of cargo, together with the regular Dock Receipt of the carrier, and is issued subject to certain conditions. Among these conditions, the following are important to the shipper:

1. The export declaration number issued by the United States Customs, which indicates approval of the exportation of the shipment, must be shown on the permit and dock receipt.

2. No liability of the carrier for any delay or detention of trucks, lighters, or other craft or from any cause whatever beyond its control.

3. No cargo received, unless properly marked and numbered.

4. Lighterage delivery subject to the lighterage rules of the port.

55 8903 18M 3-55 B.P.

GRACE LINE INC.	SHIPPING PERMIT
3 HANOVER SQUARE NEW YORK 4, N. Y. DIGBY 4.6000	Permit No. 29984

GRACE LINE TERMINAL   New York, _____, 19____

To the Receiving Clerk
PIER 57 NORTH RIVER ☐ } _ _ _ _ _ _ WAtkins 9-8400
PIER 58 NORTH RIVER ☐ }
JAVA ST. PIER, BROOKLYN ☐ _ _ _ _ _ _ EVergreen 3-3600

It is in order to receive from_____

for account of_____

for shipment per S.S. _____scheduled to sail_____
(OR SUBSTITUTE)

the following cargo destined_____to be delivered by

Lighter ☐   A.M. ☐
Truck ☐ on_____P.M. ☐ Delivering Carrier will be

_____Railroad Car Numbers are:_____

SHIPPER'S DESCRIPTION OF GOODS

NO. OF PACKAGES	KIND OF PACKAGES	CONTENTS	WEIGHT

SHIPPER'S EXPORT DECLARATION NUMBER MUST BE SHOWN ON ALL DOCK RECEIPTS AND BILLS OF LADING.

This permit is issued upon and subject to the terms and conditions stated on the reverse side hereof.
GRACE LINE INC.

Export Declaration No._____   Per_____

This permit must be presented to the pier at time of or prior to delivery of cargo together with regular form of Grace Line Dock Receipt.

Shipping or Delivery Permit

It should be mentioned that the permit system, as far as the Port of New York is concerned, applies in varying degree only to carload lots, particularly when delivered by lighters. In other ports, which maintain either a belt line or a similar terminal system, the steamship agents or stevedores order the cars alongside vessel to the wharf, in accordance with the requirements of the stowage operation.

The Dock Receipt. Delivery of goods accepted at the pier for dispatch on a specific vessel or for *hold on dock* storage, is acknowledged with a dock receipt. After being obtained by the shipper from the respective steamship line, the shipper prepares this receipt in quadruplicate and makes certain that it is signed by the ocean carrier's receiving clerk. It is a document of evidence and sometimes serves as proof of fulfillment of a sales contract or for payment purposes. The dock receipt enumerates the shipper's and/or forwarder's name, the steamer or the "hold on dock" clause, the destination of the goods, the marks and numbers, the number and kind of shipping packages, the description of the cargo, weights and measurements of the accepted goods, and the ocean carrier's name. The original, non-negotiable copy, is returned to the delivering agent. It indicates the "in and out;" that is, the time of presentation by and return to the deliverer. This notation is made after the check and acceptance of the freight,

This permit is issued upon the following terms and conditions:—

1. Shipment will not be received unless accompanied by Grace Line Inc. form of Dock Receipt properly filled out. Export declaration numbers, must be also noted on dock receipt.

2. Grace Line Inc. shall not be liable for any delay or detention of trucks, lighters or other craft resulting from any cause of whatever nature beyond its control, including without limitation, riots, strikes, lockouts, stoppage of labor and like disturbances, or extraordinary weather conditions; but in any event no liability shall be assumed unless delivery is made, at permit time and manifests filed in the office of the Clerk of the dock, the time of such filing to be deemed the time of arrival. Cargo will be accepted weekdays: Monday to Friday inclusive from 8 A.M. to 4 P.M., except on Holidays or on sailing day for forwarding on vessel scheduled to sail that day, unless otherwise endorsed hereon. No cargo received unless properly marked and numbered. Cargo for different ports to be properly segregated on lighters and trucks.

3. If the existence or the continuance of warlike conditions or hostilities or civil commotion shall impede, obstruct or prevent the performance by the Carrier of any of its obligations by reason of seizure or loss of any of its vessels, or by reason of any governmental requisition, control or use thereof, either in whole or in part; or if conditions shall arise, exist or continue which indicate to the Carrier that there is danger of such or similar interference with its operation, or which might expose the vessel, its crew and/or cargo to any danger whatsoever; or if any other condition or situation whatsoever, whether similar or dissimilar to those hereinabove specified, shall result or threaten in the judgment of the Carrier to result, either directly or indirectly, in the imposition upon the Carrier of any undue financial or other hard ship, burden or interference in the performance of its obligations; then in any such case the Carrier shall have the right, at any time before actual loading of the goods on the vessel, to cancel or once or oftener suspend any of its obligations, whether express or implied, and any cancellation or suspension hereunder shall apply to all such obligations whether the same be contained in this permit, or in tariff, freight engagement, booking note or dock receipt. The Carrier's right of cancellation shall not be prejudiced by any suspension or suspensions. This clause shall not prejudice or modify any cancellation or suspension right of the Carrier in any contract relating to the goods.

4. Lighterage subject to the Lighterage rules of the port.

5. Subject to contingencies beyond our control.

6. This permit may not be assigned.

GRACE LINE INC.

Shipping or Delivery Permit (cont.)

issuing the receipt number, and noting the possible exceptions as to the conditions of the cargo. The duplicate copy is retained by the receiving clerk and is then transmitted to the steamship line's bill of lading department. Here it is filed as a record of the delivery and receipt of goods on the dock. The duplicate also serves as a basis for rating the freight transportation charges on the bill of lading, which is issued in lieu of the dock receipt. The triplicate copy of the dock receipt is kept by the receiving clerk as a dock record, whereas the fourth copy remains with the shipper or forwarder for his file. The control of the cargo by the carrier is evidenced through the dock recepit until the ocean bill of lading is executed, whereupon the ocean bill of lading becomes the document which indicates the control of the goods. Cargo delivered to the pier for *hold on dock* storage only, re-

FLOTA MERCANTE GRANCOLOMBIANA S. A.

Principal Office — **BOGOTA, COLOMBIA, SOUTH AMERICA**

Shipper/Exporter

DOCK RECEIPT

(Issued Subject to the Terms and Conditions Stated Herein)

D/R NO.

	Forwarding Agent — References
	Point and Country of Origin/Place of Receipt
Notify Party	Domestic Routing/Export Instructions
(WITHOUT LIABILITY TO CARRIER. SEE CLAUSE 24 OF STANDARD BILL OF LADING.) Pier	

Vessel	Flag	Port of Loading	Onward Inland Routing/Place of Delivery
Port of Discharge	For Transhipment To		

PARTICULARS FURNISHED BY SHIPPER

MARKS & NUMBERS	NO. OF PKGS.	DESCRIPTION OF PACKAGES AND GOODS	GROSS WEIGHT KILOS POUNDS	MEASUREMENTS CU. FT.
B L NO.		TOTAL		

All obligations herein are subject to being postponed, suspended, or cancelled in whole or in part in so far as they may in the Company's judgment be affected by strikes, labor disturbances, conditions of war or hostilities, or by acts, restrictions or requests of any Governmental authority or war risk insurer covering the vessel. There shall be no responsibility for the goods as Carrier until they are actually loaded. Until such loading the only liability shall be that of an ordinary bailee but subject to the terms, conditions, exceptions and limitations of liability and value contained in the Company's bill of lading in use at the time.

Shipper's marks and numbers and port of destination must be marked on each package in letters not less than 2 inches high. Shipper's weights and descriptions as inserted herein will be relied on in handling the goods, and, if incorrect, the shipper, consignee and owner of the goods shall be responsible for any loss or damage to the Company or others resulting therefrom.

NOTICE: Explosives and inflammable Articles: Attention is called to Sections 4278, 4279, 4288, 4472, 4473, 4475, 4476, 5353, 5354 and 5355 of the Revised Statutes of the United States. Explosives, inflammable, Hazardous, Noxious or Dangerous Articles must be fully described.

FORM TFF ISA-EPCO REV. 6/73

1

ORIGINAL

NOT NEGOTIABLE

RECEIVED THE ABOVE-DESCRIBED MERCHANDISE FOR SHIPMENT AS INDICATED HEREON, SUBJECT TO ALL CONDITIONS OF THE UNDERSIGNED'S USUAL FORM OF BILL OF LADING COPIES OF THE UNDERSIGNED'S USUAL FORM OF BILL OF LADING MAY BE OBTAINED ON APPLICATION TO ANY OFFICE OF FLOTA MERCANTE GRANCOLOMBIANA S. A., OR TO THE MASTER OR AGENT OF THE MASTER AT THE PORT OF SHIPMENT OR PORT OF DISCHARGE.

Flota Mercante Grancolombiana S. A.
(Grancolombiana (New York), Inc.)

By_____

Receiving Clerk

Date _____

PRINTED IN U.S.A.

The Dock Receipt

quires special release in writing. Presentation of a "passed" export declaration is required, also, if and when it should be shipped on a certain vessel. This is extremely important, for export control regulations demand that no goods be delivered to steamer pier, and no cargo may be accepted by carriers, for loading, unless clearance through customs has been obtained.

The *Dock Receipt* is subject to the terms and conditions of the bill of lading subsequently to be issued. In addition, it stipulates that liability for the goods, as a carrier, does not attach until the cargo is loaded. Until such loading, the liability is only that of an ordinary bailee or warehouseman. Further, dock receipts variously specify

LIGHTER   SHIP   DATE

TRUCK   START. TIME   FINISH TIME

CHECKER MUST VERIFY MARKS, NUMBERS, WEIGHTS AND MEASUREMENTS
CHECKER MUST NOTE ALL LABEL AND HAZARDOUS CARGO
CHECKER MUST REQUEST LIGHTER CAPTAIN TO TALLY AGAINST HIM
CHECKER MUST REPORT ALL DAMAGE OR EXCEPTIONS TO RECEIVING CLERK FOR INSTRUCTIONS BEFORE
RECEIVING SHIPMENT

MARKS	No. of Pkge.	MEASUREMENTS										Gross Weight
		Length		Breadth		Depth		Cubic Ft.		Total Measurement		
		Ft.	In.	Ft.	In.	Ft.	In.	Ft.	In.	Ft.	In.	

REMARKS:

The Dock Receipt (cont'd)

that the complete shipping marks and numbers and the weight and description of goods must be reliably indicated. If this information proves incorrect, the shipper, consignee, and owner of the cargo will be held responsible for any loss or damage to the carrier, or others, resulting therefrom. It also refers to the federal statutes concerning explosives and hazardous or inflammable articles.

Resembling the shipping permit, dock receipts are not in general use in all ports of the world. In Europe we have the so-called *mate's receipt*. At some American ports the dock receipt is partially replaced by the railroad's, trucking company's, or shipper's own inland bill of lading or waybill, or special receipt issued by terminal operators. These substitutes are receipted by the carrier or his agent.

Dock Sheets or Returns, and Tally Sheets. Prepared by the wharf department of the carrier, and occasionally called a *Return*, the "dock sheet" records all shipments which have been received either by truck, lighter, or railroad cars for loading. Recorded, also, is information regarding the number and kind of packages, marks and numbers, descriptions, measurement, weight, permit and dock receipt numbers, name of steamer, and port of destination. Constituting a control document for the booking sheet, which the Traffic Department maintains and against which it is checked daily, it serves as a preliminary list in drawing up the stowage plan by the Pier Superintendent. The wharf department secures a complete detailed record of each consignment as received on dock and loaded on board of the vessel. This is obtained by initially transferring the dock sheet's contents to the tally sheet and converting thereon the individual measurements and weights of a shipment into total cubic and/or weight figures. Thereafter, a separate copy of the tally sheet is composed for each individual shipment. Copies of these tally sheets, assembled in book form, are then channeled to the chief officer of the vessel and to the traffic department of the steamship line.

The Stowage Plan. The cargo stowage plan graphically outlines the disposition of the cargo within the holds and on the deck of the ship, as contemplated by the office and dock staffs. It is subject to modification during the loading process. The final stowage plan indicates the exact position of each shipment carried. This plan serves as a guide for discharging cargo at the various ports of call and for preparing the ship's manifest. It also furnishes a breakdown of weight tons per hatch and 'tween decks; the weight of fuel, water, stores, and ballast; the amount of draft before and after the loading of the vessel; the ports of call; the name of the ship, the sailing date, and the voyage number; the hour when loading commenced and was finished; and the pier where the vessel was on berth.

THE OCEAN BILL OF LADING

General aspects. The ocean bill of lading is the principal shipping paper between shipper and ocean carrier, shipper and consignee, and carrier and consignee. Fundamentally important, it is a basic document in foreign commerce. The ocean bills of lading, together with consular invoices, insurance certificates, commercial invoices, and others, constitute the so-called *shipping documents*. The bill of lading serves three distinct purposes:

1. It defines the terms and conditions of the carriage of the goods and establishes evidence of contract between the shipper and the carrier for the conveyance of the goods described, from one port to another, for freight charges as billed.

2. It is the final, signed receipt from the ocean carrier for the goods shipped.

3. It is a certificate of ownership, which covers the goods noted thereon and, if and when made out "to order," endorsed and delivered to another party, passes the title in the goods. The "order" party, or further "endorsee," can demand delivery of the goods at the port of destination. Such bill of lading is, therefore, one of the essential documents for the purpose of negotiation, sale, banking and delivery.

The bill of lading blanks are supplied by the ocean carrier or his agent, but are prepared by the shipper or the foreign freight forwarder. The required number of bills of lading are, generally, as follows:

1. For shipper: original, duplicate, triplicate, sometimes, a quadruplicate; all signed, and a variable number of non-negotiable copies.

BOW

STOWAGE PLAN

DECK/STERN

	1	2	3	Reefer	4	5
	Callao 1 boxed truck-30T, Guayaquil 6 cars-5T	Callao 4 Autos 10T, 1 boxed truck 40T	Valparaiso boxed trucks 30T		Buenaventura 25 unboxed jeeps 30T	Buenaventura 25 unboxed jeeps 30T
	Buenaventura 20T unboxed Autos & Trucks	Guayaquil 100T General Cargo	Buenaventura 400T Asbestos Fiber		Buenaventura 60T boxed Autos, Trucks	Buenaventura 350T General Merchandise
	Valparaiso 70T unboxed trucks, Guayaquil 90T Cement, 10T Medicines	Guayaquil 155T boxed Trucks	Talara 150T General Cargo		Buenaventura 300T Auto Tires, Guayaquil 90T Plateglass	Buenaventura 250T Ord. Glassware
	Callao 60T Mach. Parts, 160T Soda Ash, Talara 120T Steel Pipe, Valparaiso 140T Nail Wire	Callao 360T Steel-Plates, Valparaiso 120T Machry., Chanaral 200T Steel-Billets	Guayaquil 200T Machry., 310T Steel, Valparaiso 440T Steel-Plates	ENGINE & BOILERS	Buenaventura 400T Mach. Parts, Talara 280T Steel, Chanaral 200T News Print, Valparaiso 500T Steel	Callao 80T Steel pipe, Buenaventura 200T Steel Bars, Valparaiso 100T Steel

    2. For steamship company: Three to eight copies, non-negotiable.

    3. For foreign consuls: Two to four copies, non-negotiable.

Only one of the original, signed bills of lading is needed to secure delivery at destination. After delivery is effected, the remaining signed or original bills of lading become void. There are no limitations as to the number of signed or unsigned bills of lading.

A time-consuming and costly practice established long ago by the international trade community concerning the issuance of "full sets" of "original bills of lading" with a minimum of 3 "originals" and the preparation of up to 25 identical duplicates thereof on a single shipment, came to an end on October 1, 1975, when an overwhelming number of United States and foreign ocean carriers, induced by the efforts of the National Committee on International Trade Documentation (NCITD), started to issue only 1 original bill of lading, unless specifically requested otherwise.

Fortunately, many banks had joined this program of documentation simplification by implementing same through the publication of a new code of "Uniform Customs and Practice for Documentary Credits," put in effect by the Paris-based International Chamber of Commerce (ICC), a world business organization, represented by national committees in 50 countries including the United States of America. These revisions, set out in Publication #290 of the U.S. Council of the ICC were prompted by new trends in multinational transport and unitized cargoes, including goods loaded in containers or on pallets, and aim for the acceptance of bills of lading bearing notations such as "shipper's load and count" or "said by shipper to contain," also for easier production and processing of documents in "short form" and the elimination of "stale" documents.

Bills of lading should specify the vessel, the shipper's and consignee's name, the "notify" party, to whom arrival notice is to be sent, port of loading and discharge, destination of goods, exact marks and number of packages, kinds of packages, and description of goods. Forwarders must show, also, their Federal Maritime Board registration number. Particular attention should be accorded to an accurate description of the merchandise. Diligent execution of this detail helps avoid dissension with the carrier about the proper application of ocean freight rates, difficulties with foreign governments as to misclassification, and violations of the United States regulations pertaining to explosives or other dangerous articles; and export control.

United States Lines, Inc.

SHIPPER / EXPORTER	DOCUMENT NO.
	EXPORT REFERENCES
	FORWARDERS REF. NO.
	SHIPPERS REF NO
CONSIGNEE	FORWARDING AGENT — FMC. NO.
	POINT AND COUNTRY OF ORIGIN
NOTIFY PARTY	DOMESTIC ROUTING / EXPORT INSTRUCTIONS

PIER

| EXPORTING CARRIER (Vessel) | PORT OF LOADING | ONWARD INLAND ROUTING |
| PORT OF DISCHARGE | FOR TRANSSHIPMENT TO | |

OUTWARD SHORT FORM BILL OF LADING — PARTICULARS FURNISHED BY SHIPPER — NOT NEGOTIABLE UNLESS CONSIGNED TO ORDER

MARKS AND NUMBERS	NO. OF PKGS.	DESCRIPTION OF PACKAGES AND GOODS	GROSS WEIGHT	MEASUREMENT

FREIGHT AND CHARGES PAYABLE AT

ALL CHARGES EX
TACKLE FOR ACCOUNT OF CARGO

	$
	$
	$
	$
	$
	$
	$
	$
TOTAL $	

RECEIVED the goods or the containers, vans, trailers, palletized units or other packages said to contain goods herein mentioned, in apparent good order and condition, except as otherwise indicated herein, to be transported to the port of discharge named (TERMS OF THIS BILL OF LADING CONTINUED ON REVERSE SIDE HEREOF) IN WITNESS WHEREOF,
THE MASTER OR AGENT OF SAID VESSEL HAS SIGNED 3 BILLS OF LADING, ALL OF THE SAME TENOR AND DATE, ONE OF WHICH BEING ACCOMPLISHED, THE OTHERS TO STAND VOID.

UNITED STATES LINES, INC.

BY

PLEASE REFER TO THIS INVOICE NUMBER WITH ALL REMITTANCES.

B/L No.

FORM #OD-5 REV. 2/73

FOR THE MASTER

MO.   DAY   YEAR

Ocean Bill of Lading

Custom dictates that all freight charges due to ocean carriers be prepaid before the carriers release executed bills of lading. However,

SHORT FORM BILL OF LADING

NOT NEGOTIABLE UNLESS CONSIGNED TO ORDER

(TERMS OF THIS BILL OF LADING CONTINUED FROM OVERPAGE)

herein and/or such other port or place as authorized or permitted hereby, or so near thereunto as the ship can get, lie and leave always in safety and afloat under all conditions of tide, water and weather, and there to be delivered to consignee or on-carrier on payment of all charges due thereon.

1. It is agreed that the receipt, custody, carriage, delivery and transshipping of the goods are subject to the terms appearing on the face and back hereof and also to the terms contained in the carrier's regular long form bill of lading currently used in this service, including any clauses presently being stamped or endorsed thereon which shall be deemed to be incorporated in this bill of lading, which shall govern the relations, whatsoever they may be, between shipper, consignee, carrier and ship in every contingency, whetesoever and whensoever occuring and whether the carrier be acting as such or as bailee, and also, in the event of, or during deviation, or of conversion of the goods. The terms of this bill of lading shall not be deemed waived by the carrier except by written waiver, signed by a duly authorized agent of the carrier. Copies of the carrier's regular long form bill of lading and clauses presently being stamped or endorsed thereon are available from the carrier on request and may be inspected at any of its offices or its agents offices.

2. It is specifically agreed, without any limitation, that all goods, containers, trailers or vans may be transferred, transshipped and carried on several vessels enroute from the port of shipment to the port of destination, and such transfer, transhipment or change in vessel shall not constitute a deviation and such transfers and transhipments on various vessels are contemplated.

3. This bill of lading shall have effect subject to the provisions of the Carriage of Goods by Sea Act of the United States, approved April 16, 1936, or, if this bill of lading is issued in a locality where there is in force a Carriage of Goods by Sea Act or ordinance or statute of a similar nature to the International Convention for the Unification of Certain Rules Relating to Bills of Lading, dated at Brussels, August 1924, it is subject to the provisions of such act, ordinance, or statute and rules thereto annexed. All the provisions of the applicable Act, ordinance or statute and rules thereto annexed are deemed to be incorporated herein (except as otherwise specifically provided for herein) and nothing herein contained is to be deemed a surrender by the carrier of its rights, immunities, exemptions or liabilities or an increase of any of its responsibilities or liabilities thereunder.

4. All agreements or freight engagements for the shipment of the goods are superseded by this bill of lading. If required by the carrier, a signed original bill of lading, duly endorsed, must be surrendered to the carrier on delivery of the goods.

DO NOT USE THIS SPACE FOR DESCRIPTION OF SHIPMENT

RECORD OF DELIVERY OF CARGO

RECEIVED IN GOOD ORDER
FROM UNITED STATES LINES   BY MESSRS._____

THE FOLLOWING GOODS:

DATE	TRUCK OR LIGHTER	NO. OF PACKAGES AND MARK	SIGNATURE

Ocean Bill of Lading (cont'd)

in some trades, shipments are accepted on a freight collect basis. Large shippers or well-known foreign freight forwarders are privileged, as a matter of convenience, to sign "due bills' when picking up ocean bills of lading from the carrier's cashier's office, instead of paying cash or by check. This type of credit extension by steamship lines to their clients should not be regarded as a magnanimous gesture, for it is a well-considered economical business practice. Receipt of only "one" payment for a dozen or more shipments on any one vessel, as perpetually occurs in the case of forwarders, considerably reduces and simplifies bookkeeping and accounting procedures for the carriers.

Issuance of a signed bill of lading does not necessarily imply that the cargo has been loaded on board of the vessel. It serves as proof that the martime engagement has commenced, and that the goods were "received for shipment." This presents a question: "Is there a possible limited redress against the carrier, in case of loss of the goods before loading or the loss of the vessel on which the cargo was to be placed, or the possible controversy between exporter and importer, if the dispatch of the goods is delayed under a C. I. F. sales contract?" To overcome this obvious deficiency inherent in "received for shipment" bills of lading, foreign traders demand "ON BOARD" or "SHIPPED" bills of lading in business transactions where payments on the strength of Letters of Credit are involved. Here, the carrier makes a special notation on the bill of lading, certifying that the goods are actually loaded on the vessel.

An additional feature, the "clean" bill of lading requires further comment. When freight is delivered to the steamer in poor condition, that is, either damaged, broken, inadequately packed, or in repaired, recoopered, or otherwise objectionable condition; or, in the case of containers filled with liquids, leaking, such status is noted on the dock receipt and, subsequently, on the bill of lading. This, then, is called a "foul" bill of lading, or "not clean." This type bill of lading is seldom accepted by banks when financial transactions are involved, and a letter of guarantee is usually furnished, holding the bank free from any claim arising from the bill of lading which indicates such exceptions, or a letter of indemnification to the carrier which, when accepted allows him to omit the notation. To safeguard the interest of their clients, forwarders see to it that only undamaged goods, properly packed, and for which clean bills of lading can be issued, will be delivered to the steamer pier. They also instruct the receiving clerks at the docks of the steamship companies, with whom they maintain regular dealings, not to load any damaged cargo on board of the vessel. The receiving clerks inform the forwarder, who takes appropriate measures to put the goods in proper condition, to assure the issuance of a clean bill of lading. Redounding to his credit, this type of service is frequently performed by foreign freight forwarders. Since much damage occurs en route to port, shippers have no way of knowing about it, prior to the loading of their goods, unless the forwarder informs them thereof. Forwarders merit the recognition of both shipper and carrier for this function, for it reduces to a minimum any conceivable friction in the relationship of seller and buyer, carrier and shipper, or carrier and consignee.

Occasionally, the expression, "stale bill of lading" is used in banking circles. This means that an ocean bill of lading has been presented with undue delay or not promptly after its issuance. Acceptance of this bill of lading, together with the other documents pertinent to certain financial transactions, is refused by the bank. This will always happen when the shipping date on the bill of lading reveals that the vessel will reach the port of destination prior to the bill of lading, which has been tendered to the bank for negotiation and successive forwarding to the port of discharge. The bank's acceptance of the bill of lading, on a date which makes it impossible to have the document at the port of discharge on time, would jeopardize the interests of the consignee, and make the bank liable as a contributor to possible damages. Shipping documents must be available for customs clearance in arrival ports about the same time as the vessel docks, otherwise fines and storage charges will be assessed against the cargo.

Depending on the method of obtaining payment in foreign trade, according to the export sale's terms, bills of lading may be drawn straight or to order.

A straight bill of lading is one which shows the shipment consigned directly to the consignee, and is considered as "not negotiable." In accordance with Section 6, of the United States Bill of Lading Act, 1916 (Pomerene), a straight bill of lading shall have clearly marked upon its face, the clause, "non-negotiable" or "not negotiable." It can not be negotiated free of existing equities, and the endorsement of such a bill of lading does not give the transferee any additional right. Goods, when shipped on a straight bill of lading basis, may be delivered to the consignee without the signed bill of lading being presented to the carrier. Steamship lines sometimes ask for a satisfactory indemnity, instead of the signed bill of lading, if and when circumstances warrant precautionary measures against unauthorized delivery. Conversely, for reasons of financial security, shippers occasionally request their forwarders to issue so-called "release letters." Addressed to consignees, who are functioning as port agents or brokers for importers, they are requested not to release goods after clearance through customs, until advised by the collecting bank that the shippers' drafts have been paid or accepted.

Order bills of lading are of two types: a) those made out "to order" of the foreign consignee, or "to order" of a foreign bank, b) those made out "to order" of shipper, or "to order" of a bank in this country, or another especially designated party. They are negotiable, and should bear the endorsement of the shipper, or order party, and of all transferees. The purpose of a "to order" shipment is to safeguard the shipper's or transferee's interest. Therefore, if the party to whose order the bills of lading are drawn wishes to transfer the title of the goods to another party, all negotiable, original, signed copies—the so called "set" of bills of lading—must be endorsed before possession of the goods can be taken by the receiving party, if such endorsement is stipulated. The endorsement entitles the person presenting the documents to receive the goods at the port of destination, inasmuch as the holder of a bill of lading is deemed to be the true owner of the goods. If there is no endorsement stipulated, any one copy of the original, signed bill of lading (in some countries it must be legalized and/or visaed original), provided that it has been honestly acquired, is sufficient to prove title to the goods.

There is, however, an exception to the rule that possession of the goods can be obtained only by presenting properly drawn and endorsed bills of lading. This eventuates when the party claiming the goods furnishes a bond of sufficient amount to indemnify the delivering steamship agent and foreign customs authority against all possible claims on the part of others.

Order bills of lading require that a "notify party" be shown thereon, to enable the carrier to dispatch a notification of arrival of goods. This party may be the ultimate consignee, his port agent or a designated bank. The person so notified does not thereby obtain control of the goods, since the signed and endorsed original bills of lading must be transmitted to the carrier in order to secure delivery.

In concluding this outline of the bill of lading's general aspects, we must stress that any alteration, addition, or erasure in a bill of lading after its issuance without authority in writing from the carrier, is void, and the document will be enforceable according to its original tenor.

When a straight bill of lading has gone astray, has been destroyed or stolen, the consignee may arrange to obtain delivery of the cargo by satisfactory proof of its ownership, or by posting a bond, or letter of indemnification. In case of loss, destruction or theft of an "order" bill of lading, release of the goods by the "order party" may be secured either by giving the carrier a satisfactory indemnifying bond, or through legal action, after approval of an adequate bond by a court of competent jurisdiction.

Legal Aspects: Contrasting with land carriers, and by custom, water carriers have enjoyed less strict treatment under common and statutory law, with respect to the liabilities in the carriage of goods. In view of the hazards involved on the high seas, the water carriers were granted special exemptions and limitations of their liabilities.

However, modern international commerce expanded about the mid-1800's at a time when the United States had lost its leading position as a shipping nation. European ship owners then started to restrict their liabilities by inserting negligence clauses in the bills of lading. These, in effect, removed any liability for negligence on the part of master, officers, and crew. However, courts in the United States had ruled on several railroad cases of similar nature. Their rulings propounded that clauses of such character were contrary to public policy and, therefore, void. The same clauses were held invalid with regard to ship owners, American and foreign. The resulting conditions, whereby carriers could be sued successfully in United

States courts, but not on the continent, wrought confusion and discord in foreign trade circles. The need for uniformity in the application of admiralty law became imperative. Thus, "Rules" on an international level were agreed upon by the leading maritime nations and incorporated in the bills of lading. These rules were the so-called "York Rules" of about 1878, and were modified in 1890 as "York-Antwerp" Rules. Achieving a measure of international uniformity, they were extended later by the "York-Antwerp" Rules of 1924, and the "Hague" Rules of 1932. These rules have been incorporated, since 1924, in relevant statutes enacted by almost all shipping nations.

The Harter Act, of February 13, 1893, was the first piece of major legislation in the United States, which dealt with the limitation of the ship owners' liability. This act was named after Michael Harter, an exporter and member of the House of Representatives, who had experienced serious difficulties as a shipper, and who felt that ocean carriers were trying to evade their obligations.

The relative provisions of the Harter Act make it unlawful to insert in any bill of lading a clause relieving the owner, manager, or master of the vessel from liability for loss and damage arising from improper loading, stowage, and delivery; further, carriers are prohibited from limiting their obligation to carefully exercise due diligence in equipping, manning, and provisioning their vessels and making them seaworthy. However, carriers are exempt from liability for loss and damage caused by errors and faults in navigation, or management of the vessel, and for other matters not due to negligence. They are also relieved from liability for loss and damage due to: dangers of the sea; acts of God; acts of public enemies; inherent defect, quality or vice of the cargo carried; insufficiency of packing; seizure under legal process; acts of omission on the part of the shipper and owner of merchandise; saving, or attempting to save, life or property at sea. However, in all the aforementioned cases, the carrier would always be liable if he fails to exercise proper skill and diligence in the discharge of his duties. The term "carrier's duties" means the duties of the master, officers, and crew. Therefore, liability for damage to goods during shipment may be imposed, though caused by a peril excepted in the bill of lading.

A troublesome, vague aspect in the rule of law is to be seen in the fact that the carrier may be at fault "in the navigation or in the management of the ship" and yet not be liable. This might lead to a conflict of interests between liability in proper handling or management of the cargo, on one side, as distinguished from the vessel, on the other. It could happen that an entire consignment of cargo may become a total loss through the ship's engineer turning the wrong water valve, yet without liability to the carrier. It is obvious that many similar or related situations might arise which would bring up the question of where the liability rests, or if there is any at all.

The Harter Act provides, in Section 3, that the responsibility of the carrier for goods delivered to him commences at the pier; that is, when the voyage begins, and ends with the delivery of the cargo to the consignee at destination, that is, again at the dock. When enacted in 1893, it applied simultaneously to domestic (coastwise and inter-coastal) and foreign carriage of goods, to goods shipped to and from ports in the United States of America, but not, for instance, to shipments from Canada to Brazil.

The Carriage of Goods by Sea Act, of 1936, was the second major statute, thereon, legislated here. It endeavored to control the limitations of liability which were incorporated in the carrier's bills of lading issued before its enactment; and secured a greater uniformity, created by the promulgation of the "Hague" Rules, and actually included the rules by having the bill of lading specifically refer to them. However, the Act does not replace the Harter Statute or any other law which would be applicable in absence of the 1936 Legislation, insofar as the stipulations of the older laws relate to the duties, responsibilities, and liabilities of the vessel or carrier prior to the time when the cargo is loaded on, or after the time it is discharged from the ship (Section 12).

The Carriage of Goods by Sea Act supersedes, however, the Harter Act in two instances:

a) With respect to on deck, or under deck cargo (carrier's option), if such carrier selects to incorporate a specific proviso to that effect in his bill of lading in domestic commerce, and, what is more important,

b) In connection with cargo carried under deck from tackle to tackle in foreign trade. Here, it is conceivable, that Section 3 of the Harter Act will be enforced as to cargo damaged on the pier, either before loading or after discharge, thus overcoming the restricted liability of the 1936 Act.

With regard to the amount of liability for any loss or damage, there is another significant difference between the two statutes. The 1936 Act places a ceiling of $500.00 per package, or per customary freight unit if cargo is shipped unpacked, which sum cannot be decreased by the carrier. The Harter Act did not provide this limitation. We recognize, therefore, a tendency on the part of Congress to ease the rather strict liabilities imposed upon the carrier by the Harter Act. From a legal point of view, this tendency is confirmed by the fact that the 1936 Act grants the carrier immunity in cases where previously it had been held accountable; the shipowner is permitted to claim the limitations of liability, even if his vessel was not seaworthy at the start of the voyage, provided he can prove that the loss or damage was not in any way caused by such unseaworthiness.

Representing the rights and obligations of the carrier under the maritime contract, the conditions and clauses of the ocean bill of lading are, for various reasons, of primary consequence to the foreign trader. Experience indicates, however, that there is a perplexing lack of knowledge about the import of the shipping business' most extensive document.

It behooves us, therefore, to examine some of the clauses that are of common interest to all exporters.

The clause wherein a carrier receipts for goods as being "in apparent good order and condition," constitutes prima facie evidence that superficially, only insofar as the external appearance of the shipping packages is concerned, the goods were in proper condition and order when delivered into the care and custody of the carrier. Should, however, the cargo itself be damaged on arrival and legal action be taken against the carrier, although the carrier shows that the damage might have occurred prior to shipment, the burden of proof is on the shipper to show that the merchandise was in sound condition at the time of delivery to the steamship company.

The notation on the bill of lading, reading "On Deck at Owner's Risk," does not relieve the carrier of its liability, if loss or damage is the result of neglect in the care of the cargo and is not contributed to by a peril of the sea. However, if the shipper has consented to have the goods stowed on deck, the steamship line is required only to exercise reasonable skill and care, which means his liability is only a limited one; whereas failure on the part of the carrier to secure approval from the shipper to place his cargo on deck, makes the vessel fully liable.

Damage to cargo by sea water, caused by an unavoidable accident, is regarded as a peril of the sea. However, were the water damage due to faulty equipment, such as defective hatches, the carrier would be liable, unless he establishes proof that due diligence has been exercised in making the vessel seaworthy.

Damage to goods by harmful odors or fumes, because of proximity in stowage, may make the carrier liable as he, by experience, should calculate the possible consequences and should stow accordingly.

Bills of lading vary as to the time allowed for the filing of claims and the institution of suits. Therefore, as soon as loss or damage of the shipping package is discovered, goods should be inspected. This should be done immediately after formal notice, with the intent to claim, has been filed with the carrier. Immediate notification gives the steamship line's surveyor an opportunity to be present, if he will attend. This implies that this notice should be given before the cargo is removed from the dock. Underwriters should be notified simultaneously.

The Maritime contract, as evidenced by the bill of lading, usually terminates upon completion of carriage by the: (1) delivery of cargo to the consignee; (2) delivery of cargo to connecting carrier, in apparent like order as received; (3) notice of arrival to the consignee, and expiry of the free time provided for; (4) delivery into the custody of the customs authorities against signed receipt; and (5) seizure of cargo through public authority.

Finally, the so-called "Clause Paramount" refers to the introductory statement in the American Carriage of Goods by Sea Act, effective July 15, 1936, which makes all bills of lading on shipments to or from the United States in foreign commerce subject to its provisions (See Appendix E).

Through Export Bill of Lading. A through export bill of lading combines the features of a domestic and an ocean bill of lading, but includes two distinctly different sets of terms applicable, respectively, to the domestic haul and to the ocean voyage. It is issued only for carload shipments from point of origin in the U. S. A. to the foreign port of discharge, and sometimes even to the ultimate inland destination of the goods. It must itemize the rates and charges pertaining to the inland haul, transit fees, and ocean transport. Therefore, no savings are obtained regarding charges incurred. Information to be indicated on an "Export Bill of Lading" has to cover the combined contents of the inland and ocean bills of lading. Usually, all charges must be prepaid. The through export bill of lading must be signed by the railroad's foreign freight representative. When "on board" Bills of Lading are involved under letters of credit, banks will require an endorsement by the ocean carrier's duly authorized agent, to the effect that the goods are loaded "On Board" of the vessel indicated. Regarding the limited usefulness or the serviceability of the through bill of lading, reference is made to Chapter III (*Railroad Traffic Department*).

Through Ocean Bill of Lading. The through export bill of lading is not to be confused with the Through Ocean Bill of Lading. The latter evidences a maritime contract which involves transportation by means of a two-carrier service over an ocean through route. The contract is based on a through rate, whereby the necessary transhipment arrangements are attended to by the originating carrier, who issues to the shipper the sole bill of lading, and, thus, becomes responsible for proper delivery of the cargo to final port of discharge.

Ship's Manifest: The ship's manifest is a compilation of all the loaded cargo, as specified in the individual bills of lading issued for a particular voyage. The form and contents are currently uniform, with only a few exceptions prevailing because of foreign consular requirements. Manifests are required by law under United States and foreign government regulations. They present a reproduction of the bills of lading, together with freight rates and charges, names of captain, ports of call, and port agents of the line attending to clearance of the vessel, and the ship's registered tonnage and nationality. The ship's manifest is prepared for use by:

1. United States Customs, for clearance of the outgoing vessel and its cargo. The port collector retains a signed copy of the manifest, together with one copy of each export declaration attached thereto, for each shipment listed, for export-control and statistical purposes. With respect to import shipments, it serves as an entry document.

2. Foreign customs authorities, for clearance of the vessel and nationalization of the cargo discharged.

3. The carrier, himself, as a check on cargo loaded, carried and discharged, and on revenue due or earned.

FLOTA MERCANTE GRANCOLOMBIANA S. A.

MANIFEST OF CARGO   AT

ON BOARD THE M/V_____OF_____TONS NET REGISTER.   CAPT

| B/L No. | SHIPPERS | CONSIGNEES | PACKAGES OR LOOSE OBJECTS | | | |
			MARKS	NUMBERS	Q'TY	DESCR.

Ship's Manifest

4. Governmental authorities and men of war, as a means of identification of eventual contraband.

The Delivery Receipt is a document which represents a release, signed by the consignee, for goods received from the carrier upon their discharge from the vessel.

Parcel Receipt: To facilitate the shipment of small export packages, ocean carriers waive the usual minimum ocean freight charge. For this transportation ocean carriers issue "parcel receipts," subject to the terms, conditions, and exceptions contained in the steamer's usual bill of lading, not negotiable or transferable. It must be surrendered on delivery of goods. The carrier's liability for damage, loss or delay is usually restricted to $25.00, which is the approximate maximum value above which the carrier will not accept shipment under parcel receipt. Inasmuch as steamship lines impose limitations upon the weight and dimensions of parcel packages, savings obtained in comparison to shipment by regular parcel post vary. In many instances, foreign freight forwarders offer greater advantages and better facilities through their own arrangements of combining shipments at regular, but considerably cheaper, ocean freight charges.

Regarding pier deliveries of Hazardous Materials the most important document is a properly executed Dock Receipt. The U. S. De-

Page No._____

Sailed_____

Port of Discharge_____

DESCRIPTION	WEIGHT LBS.	MEAS. CU. FT.	RATE	NET FREIGHT	PKG. CHG.			TOTAL PREPAID

Ship's Manifest (cont'd)

partment of Transportation as well as the U.S. Coast Guard warn shippers to prepare carefully the dock receipt in accordance with D.O.T.,C.F.R.—49 (Code of Federal Regulations). The details are stated in parts 172.200 through 172.204, and specifically in parts 100-199. By learning how to use the hazardous materials table and becoming familiar with the previously mentioned parts, the proper preparation of shipping documents for hazardous goods will be greatly facilitated. It is the shipper's responsibility to determine the proper and accurate shipping name and classification.

AMERICAN REPUBLICS LINE
PACIFIC REPUBLICS LINE
MOORE - McCORMACK LINES, Inc.

BRAZIL SERVICE   RIVER PLATE SERVICE

NON-NEGOTIABLE PARCEL RECEIPT
EMBODYING CONTRACT FOR TRANSPORTATION

RECEIVED AT THE PORT OF_____ NEW YORK _____, from

M ____A. B. C.__MOTORS CORPORATION,__REFRIGERATOR DIVISION_____

in apparent good order and condition, weight, contents and value unknown to steamer for shipment on board the

S. S. ___BRAZIL_____Port of Discharge from Ship_RIO DE JANEIRO

PARTICULARS FURNISHED BY SHIPPER OF GOODS

MARKS AND NUMBERS	NO. OF PKGS.	DESCRIPTION OF PACKAGES AND GOODS	GROSS WEIGHT IN KILOS	GROSS WEIGHT POUNDS.
UGO ROSS RIO DE JANEIRO "AMOSTRA DE ENGENHARIA- SEM VALOR" ENGINEERING SAMPLES - NO VALUE #2422 - #2423	ONE-1-CASE	ELECTRIC HOUSEHOLD REFRIGERATOR PARTS	81	178#
	ONE-1-CASE	ELECTRIC HOUSEHOLD REFRIGERATOR PARTS	52	115#

Subject to the terms, and conditions and exceptions contained in the Steamer's usual Bill of Lading in use for

similar shipments except as hereinafter set forth consigned to __UGO ROSS,__AVE.__GRAC ARANHA 22,

_____RIO DE JANEIRO,__BRAZIL_____

    This receipt is not negotiable or transferable but must be surrendered before delivery of the property. Possession of the receipt by any person applying for delivery of the property shall be sufficient evidence that he is entitled to receive it in behalf of the owner, and the steamer shall not be liable for delivering the property to any person presenting this receipt at destination or elsewhere.

    Anything in the bill of lading to the contrary notwithstanding, if the steamer shall become liable for any loss, damage or delay of or to the above described property, such liability shall not exceed $25.00, which sum it is agreed that the value of said property does not exceed said sum.

FREIGHT PAYABLE AT   **NEW YORK**

_____cf. @_____per 40 cf. $_____   VALUE FOR CONSULAR PURPOSES

_____lbs. @_____per 2240 $_____

Consul fee _____ $_____ $__23. 00_____

                     Total $_____   10. 00

                                      Dated at   **NEW YORK**_____

FOR THE MASTER, By MOORE-McCORMACK LINES, INC.,

    By_____   Parcel Receipt No._____

THIS RECEIPT MUST BE SURRENDERED ON DELIVERY OF THE GOODS

11-56 33459A

Parcel Receipt

CHAPTER XIV

Documents Required By Foreign Governments

Shipper's Commercial Invoice: This should represent a complete record of the transaction between exporter and foreign importer as to goods sold. It differs from the "bill" used in domestic commerce in many respects, due to international trade requirements. Mental memo should be retained that the buyer is a person outside the jurisdiction of the United States, and is subject to the rules and regulations of his government. His customs, language, and business habits differ from ours in many ways. In addition, not only the seller and the buyer have an interest in the invoice; third parties who are rightful participants in any transaction between consignor and consignee are also concerned. Included among such third parties are banks, underwriters and customs authorities, etc. These facts demand that utmost care be exercised in the preparation of the commercial invoice, which becomes a legal document, subject to all ramifications in the field of international law.

Minimum requirements for the commercial invoice usually indicate the date; the names and addresses of exporter and importer; the invoice and order (seller and buyer) numbers; description of goods; and, price per unit and total price. This invoice should include; also, the exact sales and payment terms; the carrier; port of shipment; discounts; Import Licenses Numbers; consular declarations, if any; and, importantly, a certified statement as to the correctness of its contents. All data contained in the invoice must conform to the particular entry regulations of the foreign country to which the goods are exported. The fact that the invoice serves as a basis for the determination of foreign duties or taxes makes it imperative that any charges beyond the sales point, such as, insurance premium, freight and handling charges, be added, as far as possible, to arrive at the landed cost the buyer has to pay. On the other hand, all facts and figures appearing in the invoice must conform in every detail with the balance of the documents. Packing specifications, whether in the form of a separate packing list, or as part of a "combination" invoice, deserve special attention as to accuracy and completeness. Included among numerous details to be checked are: weights in pounds and, if necessary, kilos must agree as to their proper conversion; measurements in metric unit should be exact to secure the proper freight amount; marks and numbers must be accurate, avoiding repetition in numbering; description of the containers must conform to the facts. Substituting the exact description of goods by mere catalogue or price list numbers is an existent, thoughtless habit. United States export control regulations require the indication of the exact and pertinent "Schedule B" commodity number. Every exporter should know that a "laissez faire" attitude in this sphere will ultimately cause friction between him and his client.

The Consular Invoice: This is a document which covers all the usual details of the commercial invoice and packing list, prepared in the language of the foreign country for which goods are destined, on special forms obtainable from the Consulate or authorized commercial printers. Four or more copies are usually required. Consular fees, which may be a fixed amount or a percentage charge, are payable to the Consulate certifying and legalizing the documents. The consular invoice must be fully and exactly executed under strict observance of the customs law of that country, and must be presented and sworn to by the shipper or his representative, the foreign freight forwarder, at the corresponding foreign Consulate in the American port of shipment. Exporters in the interior, not having establishments of their own at the seaboard, are therefore dependent on the forwarder to handle this formal procedure for them.* No indefinite or vague statements are permissible, and no corrections are allowed, except by a specially prepared letter of correction, for which an extra fee is assessed by the Consul. The slightest error, if not corrected in due time, will place on the foreign buyer exceedingly heavy fines that are certain to react on the exporter. The goods must be described in strict accordance with the official customs classification and nomenclature of the country of destination. Only skilled, experienced clerks are able to master these intricacies, despite the fact that a few countries permit English, and others, English and Spanish, or English and Portuguese. Many foreign governments offer generous rewards to their customs officers for the detection of mistakes or inaccuracies in consular invoices, with the result that a painstaking search for errors makes it practically impossible to have them passed unnoticed.

In some instances, consular invoices must be supported by commercial invoices or certificates of origin; in others, by bills of lading, or both, requiring one or the other to be visaed, too, when being presented for legalization at Consulates.

Stipulation in the sales contract is recommended, even under F.A.S. or F.O.B. vessel sales terms, that the buyer should bear the cost of consular certification, or fees therewith, in order to exclude any later arguments.

Certificate of Origin: In addition to the consular invoice, many countries require a "Certificate of Origin", which is a document

---

*Legalization of consular invoices pertaining to international air cargo and parcel post will be attended to by Consuls at the point of shipment or nearest location.

certifying that the goods referred to were manufactured in the United States and no other country. Whenever certificates of origin are required, they apply to countries with which the United States maintains special trade agreements, and in which countries United States products are favored by lower than usual tariff rates and duties. Certificates of origin are incorporated in the consular invoice form, in certain cases; they are submitted in place of, or in addition to the consular invoice, in others. Certificates of origin must be certified either by a recognized trade institution, such as a Chamber of Commerce or a Merchant's and Trade Association, which is sometimes authorized to act in lieu of the foreign Consul, or by the Consulate of the country of destination located at the port of exit, or by both.

Health and Purity Certificates: Consular regulations of foreign countries frequently ask for the presentation of official certificates issued by governmental authorities attesting to the absence of disease or pest, or certifying purity, to be visaed by a Consul of the importing country. This practice is in connection with the exportation and importation of live animals, plants, trees, seeds and certain food products, such as, lard, meat, meat products and alcoholic beverages. For example: live animals and meat products must first be inspected by the Bureau of Animal Industries, Department of Agriculture, prior to issuance of a certificate of health which, in turn, requires certification by a foreign Consul, together with the rest of the necessary documents, before exportation can be effected.

The complexity of foreign consular requirements and regulations demand the utmost care on part of the exporter and expert advice from competent traffic specialists, particularly as each case will have to be treated individually. Again, the foreign freight forwarder can be depended on to assist in overcoming these barriers, thus contributing in great measure to the promotion of our foreign commerce.

A compilation of consular and shipping documents required on ocean and air cargo shipments to all countries of the world are included in the appendix.

CHAPTER XV

Documents Used in Foreign Freight Forwarding

Questing patronage as a functional middleman, the foreign freight forwarder can seek shipper's accounts in the great industrial areas of the United States or solicit consignees in the world-wide foreign markets.

The Routing Order. When he secures a foreign account, he will induce the client to sign routing orders, which direct his suppliers in the United States or elsewhere to ship the orders placed with them

Federal Maritime Board Registration No. 717

ROUTING ORDER
ORDEN DE RUTA

To..   Date..
A   (Fecha)

Dear Sirs:
Muy Señores nuestros:
    Until otherwise instructed please ship all goods for our account in care of
    Hasta nuevo aviso rogámosles despachar todas nuestras mercancías al cuidado de

D. C. ANDREWS & CO., Inc.
27 & 29 Water Street, New York 4, N. Y.

with whom we have arranged to handle all our shipments.
a quienes hemos encargado del manejo de todos nuestros embarques.

                               Signed
                               (Firmado)..

                               Address
FORM 218 10M 10-50 C.P.   Dirección)..

through the forwarder's medium; he will also leave with the customer so-called "Routing Stickers," to be pasted on any future orders. The forwarder will then communicate with the American exporter and, under enclosure of the routing order, advise him of the arrangements made with the foreign buyer. This will mean to the importer, having now the forwarder as his United States representative to follow up his orders, that the latter will try to consolidate as many shipments from different suppliers as is practical. These shipments will be forwarded on one set of shipping documents to obtain considerable savings on handling charges, consular fees, ocean freight, and foreign clearance expenses at the port of destination. It will mean compliance with the importer's instructions as to insurance and disposition of clearance and collection papers, thus guaranteeing the prompt receipt of shipping documents promptly and in good order, and thereby eliminating the drawing of drafts through various foreign banks with which the buyer abroad does not deal. Improved, faster service at a lower cost will ensue.

It should be noted that a foreign buyer is entitled to select his forwarder or ocean carrier as soon as title to the goods has passed from the seller under the terms of sale. This legal question poses problems in many cases. Their solution require great skill on the part of the forwarder acting on the behalf of, and for the account of, the importer abroad.

Proper adjudication requires a thorough knowledge of the rights and duties of the buyer and seller in international trade transactions. Extensively existent among exporters is the erroneous opinion that title passes only when payment has been made or received, or the goods taken by the buyer. Unless the sales terms provide to the contrary, title of the property passes at the point where the seller agrees to effect delivery. Usually, it is the place up to which the seller is prepared to pay the freight or cost of transportation, which also serves as the dividing line where the seller's liability terminates and the buyer's risk and responsibility begins. Confirming this fact are the Revised American Foreign Trade Definition of 1941 and their counterpart, the *Incoterms* of 1953. *Incoterms* is a set of standard international trade definitions, which were adopted by the International Chamber of Commerce at its biennial Congress at Vienna in May, 1953. It is, therefore, unfortunate to encounter frequently an unwarranted animosity, or even disregard of buyer's instructions by exporters who, under f. o. b. or f. a. s. sales, refuse to honor their routing orders. They not only antagonize their clients, but also endanger their future business relationship by unwittingly inviting foreign competition. This attitude reveals a regrettable lack on the part of the seller of understanding his position under the law. In a tactful, adroit manner the forwarder will be able to remove obstacles in many instances, thus serving as a true coordinator and arbitrator in foreign trade relations.

The Shipping Instruction Blank. To secure an efficient procedure in handling export shipments, the foreign freight forwarder supplies both his regular and occasional clients with export shipping instruction forms. These should be completed by the shipper and should serve the forwarder as a guide in executing the exporter's shipping instructions.

This shipping instruction blank is a form covering all essential points and factors. It enables the forwarder to proceed, without hindrance or further inquiry, in arranging the prompt movement of goods overseas to final destination. Its proper use should assist the exporter in making his cargo shipshape. By requesting the shipper to furnish him in concentrated form all details of an important business transaction, which involves great distance and high value, the forwarder is, also, cast in the role of an educator.

"Know-how," possessed by forwarders in full measure, perfects the sale of cargo. In case of incomplete or confusing shipping instructions, the forwarder will ask the shipper for clarification. Where consignees have furnished applicable general and standing instructions, these will govern the handling of the consignment. In addition to checking the routing, the insurance coverage, the banking instructions, and other details, it is necessary that the shipper's invoice be verified for proper consular declarations. Requiring verification, also, is the packing list for proper markings and for separate net, legal, and gross weights applicable to commodity items under each separate consular declaration. Customs regulations of the various South American countries necessitate this verification.

Shipments to some Latin American countries require import licenses which serve currency exchange purposes, and must cover either the full c. i. f. dollar value or f. o. b. vessel value of the consignment. Prepared in the forwarder's office before steamer sailing, these licenses must be submitted, together with consular invoices and ocean bills of lading, to the respective foreign consulates for legalization. This is a general prerequisite for acceptance and delivery of merchandise by ocean carriers to overseas destinations. Only upon completion of all these preliminary requirements necessary for additional export documentation is the forwarder able to proceed. He is then permitted to release the freight from the interior, or start preparation for transfer of goods from a port terminal, or from a place within the greater port area, to steamer pier.

In times of emergency it is always advisable to furnish the forwarder with the shipping advice attached to the required export documents, such as commercial invoice, packing list, license for export or import to foreign countries, and banking papers. This should be done before dispatching the goods to the port of exit, as the scarcity of space for commercial cargo necessitates the rationing of available freight space. For this reason, cargo permits must first be obtained for booking and delivery to port.

In normal times, however, shipping instructions and export documents are mailed to the forwarder simultaneously with the inland bill of lading. This indicates that the freight is already on the way to the port of exit.

The Arrival Notice: Notification by the carrier, railroad, carloading company, or over-the-road trucker is called the Arrival Notice. Addressed to the port consignee, it notifies as to the arrival of goods and usually indicates the railroad car number and the shipping marks, package numbers, description of the cargo, gross weight, freight amount prepaid or payable, pickup location, and the allowed free time. The latter varies according to the mode of transportation and weight involved (car or truckload; less-carload or less-truckload). This notification advises the consignee that the goods will be placed in storage at the owner's risk and expense, unless removed by 5:00 p.m. of a specified date. Arrival notices are combined sometimes with freight bills. Motor carriers customarily substitute the arrival notice with a telephonic notification because the allowed free time is only 48 hours. Definite dangers inhere in this method, for the telephoned message may be forgotten, misunderstood, or belatedly recalled. Acquiescence to this condition has no alternative, in view of the short time made available for removal of the goods.

Shipping Permit. The shipping permit instructs the receiving clerk at the pier to accept delivery of specific goods for shipment by a named vessel to a certain port at a given time. This document is issued in triplicate: the original, for the shipper; duplicate, for the booking department of the ocean carrier; and the triplicate, for the dock organization. Further references to the shipping permit may be found in Chapter XIII.

Export Declaration. Export goods have to be cleared through the United States Customs at the port of shipment before steamship companies, air carriers, or the United States Post Office are permitted to issue bills of lading or accept the cargo for loading and shipment. The "shipper's export declaration," prepared in triplicate—in fourfold if shipment subject to export license and/or U.S. Government sponsored —must designate the ship carrying the goods, the flag, the loading pier, the destination, the marks and numbers of the packages, the kind of articles contained, their value, weight, statistical code number, and other data. Then the exporter or forwarder must present the duly executed export declaration to the exporting carrier. Power of attorney to arrange export clearance is given usually to a clerk in the forwarding house. This formal authority is filed in the custom house.

An export declaration is not required for any shipment, other than a shipment made under a validated export, to Country Group T or V if the shipment is valued at $500.00 or less. All exceptions as to the non-requirement of individual export declarations are listed in Subpart D of the Census Bureau Foreign Trade Statistics Regulations.

Lighterage and Truck Delivery Orders. Export freight carried by railroads into a port area may be moved "shipside," either by direct "rail-to-keel" operations or by means of a flexible "water belt line" —the *lighterage system.* The latter method is peculiar to the Port of New York. Here, the railroad's foreign freight department is charged with operating and coordinating the overseas shipments of carload lots. Upon arrival, the carloads are ferried into the waterfront marshalling yards, the so-called lighterage terminals. They are then placed alongside the vessel, either after discharge onto lighters or fully loaded on carfloats.

Immediately upon the export carload's arrival at the railroad terminal in the port district, the marine department is notified by teletype. A copy of the arrival notice is sent from there to the shipper's repre-

---

F.N. ... NO. 922

D. C. ANDREWS & CO., Inc.
One Whitehall Street   New York, N. Y. 10004

WHitehall 4-0780

FOREIGN FREIGHT FORWARDERS—FOREIGN CONTRACTORS—CUSTOM BROKERS—OCEAN FREIGHT BROKERS

DELIVERING CARRIER TO STEAMER | DELIVER TO: | DELIVERY DATE

1. Forwarding Agent—ADDRESS—REFERENCE NOS. | EXPORT DEC. No.

2. Method of Transportation (check one)
☐ VESSEL ☐ AIR ☐ OTHER (SPECIFY)

DELIVERY INSTRUCTIONS

SHIPPER ▶

Ship | Flag | Pier | Port of Loading

Port of Discharge from Ship | For Transshipment To

PARTICULARS FURNISHED BY SHIPPER OF GOODS

MARKS AND NUMBERS	NO. OF PKGS.	DESCRIPTION OF PACKAGES AND GOODS	CUBIC MEAS. OR KILOS	GROSS WEIGHT IN POUNDS
		ONLY CLEAN DOCK RECEIPT ACCEPTED.		

ATTACHED:

☐ D/R

☐ STEAMER PERMIT

☐ ORDER B/L

☐ ARRIVAL NOTICE

SPECIAL NOTICE - IMPORTANT

DELIVERY TO VESSEL INDICATED ABOVE IS ESSENTIAL. IF DELIVERY CANNOT BE ACCOMPLISHED, CALL THE UNDERSIGNED AT WH 4 - 0780.

D. C. ANDREWS & CO., Inc.

DCA 243

By...

Delivery Instructions

---

sentative, usually the foreign freight forwarder, for disposition instructions. Seven days free time, not counting Saturdays, Sundays, and full legal holidays, is permitted for arranging delivery of the goods to steamer. Meanwhile, after booking the cargo for a specific sailing, the forwarder secures a delivery permit from the steamship line, and prepares his multiple lighterage order and dock receipt. Lighterage instructions indicate the railroad car number; the location of the car; the reference number of the railroad; the arrival date of the car, or, in case the car is only expected to arrive, the notation: "due to arrive;" full details as to the kind of material to be delivered by marks, numbers, description, and weight; and steamer name and designated pier. The lighterage order refers also to the shipping permit and attached dock receipt and usually contains a clause requesting the railroad to notify the forwarder in case of damage to the goods or a shortage in delivery.

These documents are sent immediately to the lighterage department of the railroad. This department then will transmit the documents' contents by teletype, and the papers by messenger to the freight agent at the railhead for further action. The lighterage order is usually prepared in a multiple number of copies. One or two copies are for the railroad; one to be attached to papers going to the railroad terminal, another copy is receipted and returned to the forwarder; and the remaining copies are held in the forwarder's shipping file for follow-up purposes.

In ports where delivery of complete export carloads—not consolidated carloads—is effected by a so-called "belt railroad," the delivery order, without a dock receipt, is tendered to the trunk line carrier. He holds the carload in his own yard until ordered to the pier, in accordance with the wishes of the consignee and the stowing requirements of the steamship line. Then the trunk line railroad issues corresponding switching instructions to the belt railroad.

Consolidated export carloads are not accepted for switching in ports where belt railroads function. These carloads are directed to warehouse railroad sidings for discharge. The individual lots are then trucked to designated piers.

The *Truck Delivery Order* is made up similarly to the lighterage order. Then it is forwarded to local or over-the-road truckers, together with the dock receipt and arrival notice. The latter serves as a document of identification.

The Pick-up Order is used when city or suburban export cargo has to be delivered to dock, or for pick-up of goods from storage places. It is addressed and forwarded to the shipper in the greater port area, or to the warehouse or trucking company that delivers, or arranges for delivery of cargo, to steamer pier. Attached thereto is the dock receipt, which has to indicate the shipping permit and export declaration number. The pick-up orders refers to the dock receipt by indicating the steamer name, the pier and the delivery date.

The dock receipt is supplied by ocean carriers on a special form, usually in fourfold, to shippers or forwarders for delivery of cargo to pier. Prepared by them, it represents when signed by the receiving clerk of the steamship line, evidence of receipt of cargo, against which the ocean bill of lading is issued. Further details may be found in Chapter XIII.

Ocean Bill of Lading. The bill of lading is the basic document in connection with the carriage of goods, and serves: (1) as a receipt for the cargo, subject to modification and explanation; (2) as an evidence of contract subject to its terms; and (3) as a document of ownership, taking the place of the goods, themselves, under certain conditions for negotiation, sale, or other purposes. Further data, on this is included in Chapter XIII.

The Forwarder's Receipt and Waybill. United States Maritime Commission General Order 72, Part 244, Section 244.12 of May 18, 1950, reads: "Forwarder's receipts for cargo shall be clearly identified as such and shall not be in form purporting to the ocean carrier's bills of lading."

This rule is the outgrowth of the Port of New York Freight Forwarder Investigation, Docket No. 621, decided November 17, 1949, by the predecessor of the Federal Maritime Board. That body found that among various objections raised against certain practices of foreign freight forwarders, the forwarder's issuance of a receipt for cargo, which purports to be a bill of lading, is an unreasonable practice in violation of Section 17, of the Shipping Act, 1916. The pertinent passage of this statute provides that "every other person subject to this Act shall establish, observe, and enforce just and reasonable regulations and practices relating to or connected with the receiving, handling, storing, or delivering of property. Whenever the board finds that any such regulation or practice is unjust or unreasonable it may determine, prescribe, and order enforced a just and reasonable regulation or practice."

As in many other decisions of regulatory bodies, composed of erudite men who lack practical experience and thereby fail in properly evaluating the gist of the matter, this finding was wholly unsupported by any reasoning. The record discloses that one of the commissioners opposed the majority's decision, pointing out that "There is no indication that that particular complaint and the damage complained of (based on a single case) would have been avoided had the document in question been identified as a cargo receipt rather than a bill of lading. Moreover, due to absence of definitions, indefiniteness in language, and lack of supporting discussion, the finding leaves it open to conjecture whether we condemn, as an unreasonable practice, the issuance of a cargo receipt which purports to be, and actually is, a bill of lading, or only the issuance of a receipt for cargo which purports to be, *but actually is not,* a bill of lading."

To clarify matters, it should be pointed out that the "forwarder's bill of lading," now *Forwarder's Receipt,* was and is used mainly on combination shipments consigned to the forwarder's agent at the

F.M.C. No. 922   **D. C. ANDREWS & CO., Inc.**   WHitehall 4-0780

One Whitehall Street New York, N. Y. 10004

FOREIGN FREIGHT FORWARDERS—FOREIGN CONTRACTORS—CUSTOM BROKERS—OCEAN FREIGHT BROKERS

DELIVERING CARRIER	DELIVERY DATE

1. Forwarding Agent—ADDRESS—REFERENCE NOS.	B/L NO.

2. **Method of Transportation** (check one)

☐ VESSEL   ☐ AIR   ☐ OTHER (Specify)

FORWARDERS RECEIPT

3. Exporter or
SHIPPER ▶

4. Consigned To ▶

5. Ultimate Consignee/Arrival Notice Party *(Give name and address)*	6. Intermediate Consignee *(Give name and address)*

Vessel	Flag	Pier	Port of Loading

Foreign Port of Unloading	For Transshipment To

PARTICULARS FURNISHED BY SHIPPER OF GOODS

MARKS AND NUMBERS	NO. OF PKGS.	DESCRIPTION OF PACKAGES AND GOODS	CUBIC MEAS. OR KILOS	GROSS WEIGHT IN POUNDS

PARTY WHO MAY BE NOTIFIED............................

....

....

FOR DELIVERY APPLY TO............................

....

....

(CONDITIONS CONTINUED FROM REVERSE SIDE HEREOF)

ISSUED AT............................

IN (   ) ONE OF WHICH

BEING ACCOMPLISHED THE OTHERS STAND VOID.

D. C. ANDREWS & CO., Inc.

Per............................

Date............................

Forwarder's Receipt

port of destination for distribution and delivery of goods to ultimate consignees. Intent of the "Forwarder's Receipt" is a) to overcome the effect of the minimum ocean freight charge, and b) to assist the exporter in retaining indirect possession of the merchandise until the importer or buyer has complied with terms of the sales contract. In

CABLE ADDRESS "BOCKAND"

ESTABLISHED 1884

D. C. ANDREWS & CO., Inc.

27 & 29 Water Street
NEW YORK 4, N. Y.

LONDON, ENGLAND
LIVERPOOL, ENGLAND
NOTTINGHAM, ENGLAND
BUENOS AIRES, ARG.
RIO DE JANEIRO, BR.
SAO PAULO, BR.

CHICAGO BOSTON BALTIMORE CLEVELAND NEW ORLEANS

Received on behalf of the shipper and/or owner and/or consignee named here-on (hereinafter referred to as the sender), bill of lading or receipt of Railroad Company, Steamship Company or other carrier and/or other documents, subject to all the contracts, clauses, rules, regulations and conditions (printed, written or stamped) appearing in the tariffs, bills of lading or receipts of the American or Foreign inland and/or ocean carriers; said to control the packages described here-on for the purposes, hereinafter set forth and subject to the terms, provisions and conditions printed, written or stamped on the face and back hereof, said packages being in apparent good order and conditions except as noted, said to contain merchandise, the contents, value, weight, quantity, conditions of contents or the marks on said packages not being known to the person, firm or corporation named in the heading hereof hereinafter designated as the Company, to be forwarded to the port of destination named here-on.

SUBJECT ALWAYS TO THE TERMS, CONDITIONS AND EXCEPTIONS OF THIS CONTRACT AND WHICH ARE HEREBY MUTUALLY AGREED AS FOLLOWS:

1. The company assumes no liability as a carrier, and undertakes only to use reasonable care in the selection of carriers, truckmen, forwarders, lightermen, warehousemen, agents and others to whom it may entrust the goods for transportation, handling and/or delivery and/or storage or otherwise.

2. The Company is authorized to select and engage carriers, truckmen, lightermen, forwarders, agents, warehousemen and others, to transport, store, deal with and deliver the goods, all of whom shall be considered the agents of the Sender, and the goods may be entrusted to such agencies subject to all conditions as to limitation of liability for loss or damage, and to all rules, regulations, requirements and conditions whether printed, written or stamped, appearing in bills of lading, receipts or tariffs issued by such carriers, truckmen, lightermen, forwarders, agents, warehousemen and others.

3. Inasmuch as carriers limit their liability to a nominal sum for loss or damage, unless a freight rate based on valuation is made with said carriers,—the Company must receive at the time when forwarding instructions are given, special written instructions from the Sender to pay such higher freight rate based on valuation; otherwise the valuation placed by the Sender on the goods shall be considered as solely for customs and insurance purposes, and the goods will be delivered to the carriers, subject to all their limitations of liability. Such special written instructions indicating value do not in any manner relate to insurance.

4. The Sender has the option of paying a special compensation to the Company based upon a value in excess of $50.00 per package, in case of any loss or damage from causes which would make the Company liable, but such option can be exercised only by special written agreement made with the Company, prior to shipment, which agreement shall indicate the limit of the Company's liability and the special compensation for the particular risks by it to be assumed, and be attached hereto or endorsed hereon by a duly authorized officer of the Company;—otherwise the Sender agrees that the Company's liability for any loss or damage to the goods for any cause which would make the Company liable, shall not exceed the sum of $50.00 for each package (or the invoice value thereof, if less) and any partial loss or damage for which the Company might be liable, shall be adjusted pro-rata on the basis of the valuation of $50.00 per package, or the invoice value thereof if less.

5. In no event shall the Company be liable for any act, omission or default in connection with the within shipment, unless a written claim therefor shall be presented to it at its office in New York within six (6) months from date of shipment of the goods to the Company, in a statement to which sworn proof of claim shall be attached. No suit to recover for any claim or demand hereunder shall in any event be maintained against the Company unless instituted within three (3) months after presentation of the said claim as above provided. The provisions of any and all Statutes of Limitations are hereby expressly waived.

6. It is agreed that any claim or demand for loss, damage or delay, or any other cause, shall be only against the carriers, truckmen, lightermen, forwarders, agents, warehousemen or others in whose actual custody the goods may be at the time of such loss, damage or delay, and that the Company shall not be liable or responsible for any claim or demand from any cause whatsoever, unless in each case the damages alleged to have been suffered be proven to be caused by the negligence of the Company, its officers or employees, in which event the limitation of liability set forth in paragraph number 4 hereof shall apply.

7. The Company shall not be obliged to incur any expenses or advance any money in connection with the forwarding of the goods, unless the same is previously advanced to the Company by the Sender on demand.

8. The Company shall have a general lien on any property of the Sender in its possession, for all claims for charges and expenses incurred in connection with any shipments of the Sender, and if such claim remains unsatisfied for thirty (30) days after demand for its payment is made, the Company is given the right to sell at public auction or private sale, without notice to the Sender, the goods, or so much thereof as may be necessary to satisfy such lien, and apply the net proceeds, less the expenses of such sale, to the payment of its charges.

9. The seizure of the goods by any Government, or by legal process, shall not affect the liability of the Sender to the Company in respect to the payment of all charges.

10. If the forwarding of the goods from the seaboard is, or in the opinion of the Company is likely to be prevented or delayed beyond the usual time thereof, either directly or indirectly by war, civil commotion, insurrection, blockade or other hostilities, or by strikes, labor disturbances or stoppage of labor of carriers, employees, or others, or by lockout by the carriers or others, the Company may at its discretion but at the risk and expense of the Sender store the goods, and charge all expenses and services incurred thereby to the Sender, and the Company shall be entitled to and have a lien upon the goods for such services and expenses.

11. It is agreed that the shipper of the goods is, and shall remain, primarily responsible to the Company for all charges and expenses incurred by the Company in connection with the forwarding of the goods. In the event the goods are refused at destination or acceptance thereof is delayed or they remain unclaimed at destination or any transhipping point in the course of transit or are returned for any reason or under any circumstances, the said shipper shall nevertheless pay the Company for all charges and expenses in connection therewith, including those incurred in storing or rerouting the goods or in arranging transportation back to the original shipping point, if the Company so undertakes on behalf of the shipper. Nothing herein contained, however, shall obligate the Company to arrange for the return or storage of the goods. Nor shall anything herein contained effect any rights which the Company may also have against the consignee or the owner of the goods.

12. The Company in fixing charges for freight, insurance and other items shall have and is hereby given the right (subject to existing statutes and local law) to charge rates in excess of those charged by any and all carriers, insurers and other agencies, selected to transport and deal with the goods, and the difference between the rates and charges made by such carriers, insurers and agencies and those made by the Company shall be considered as part of the Company's profit or compensation for its services. The Company's compensation shall also, subject above, include all brokerages, commissions, profits and sums, if any, received by the Company from carriers, insurers and others in connection with the shipment. The Company shall have the option, in assessing or fixing charges for freight, insurance and other items in which it may include its profits, of basing such charges on the weights, measurements, values and other information furnished by the Sender.

13. Charges do not include charges in foreign countries for duties, customs or revenue items, service for customs clearance, port or terminal charges, or expenses or cartage to consignee's local address, none of which expenses are required to be advanced by the Company.

14. The Company shall be under no obligation to arrange for any insurance on the packages herein described on behalf of the Sender or holder hereof, and any insurance to be effected by the Company shall be provided by special written agreement; but, insofar as the Company may be responsible to the Shipper, the Company shall be entitled to the benefit of any insurance effected on the goods and to any payments or loans made by the insurer thereon in any manner whatsoever.

15. It is further agreed that, since neither the carriers which will transport and handle this shipment, nor the Company, will have any control over the shipment while in custody of government officials, a full and complete delivery shall be deemed to be made when the goods have been delivered to custom house, government or other authorities as required by the law or customs regulations then and there in force.

16. The Company may cause the goods to be stored at the expense and risk of the Shipper, and/or of the goods, if unusual delay occurs enroute, or delivery is prevented by causes beyond the Company's control, and if acceptance is refused, or the goods unclaimed, at destination, the Company shall not be obligated to arrange for disposition or return of the goods, but the goods shall be at sole risk of Shipper, consignee and/or owner thereof.

17. In the event that this shipment originates at an interior point in the United States or Canada, the Company shall be under no obligation to take any action until a reasonable time after the Company has received a notice from the railroad company, express company or other carrier of the arrival of such shipment at the port of exportation.

18. The Shipper undertakes to mark plainly the contents of all packages containing explosives or other dangerous articles, and assumes all responsibility for failure to do so; also, for not conforming with customs, quarantine or other laws, regulations or requirements, and for undervaluation or misdescription of the goods; and the Shipper agrees to pay and reimburse the Company for all fines and expenses incurred by non-compliance with any of the laws and regulations aforesaid, and to hold the Company harmless therein; and the Company may direct the stoppage, storage, sale, or any other disposition of the goods necessitated by the Shipper's defaults therein.

19. If specifically stated in the place reserved on this contract, the Company will make reasonable effort to select and arrange with forwarders, carriers or other agencies for the reforwarding of the packages hereinafter described; beyond the port of discharge of the steamship transporting the same. In selecting such agencies, carriers, truckmen, lightermen, forwarders, warehousemen and others to reforward, transport, store, deal with or deliver the packages, the Company only undertakes to use reasonable care in their selection, and may entrust to the foregoing agencies or any of them the said packages, subject to all conditions as to limitation of liability for loss or damage, and to all rules, regulations, requirements, whether printed, written or stamped, appearing on bills of lading, receipts, or in tariffs issued by such agencies, carriers, truckmen, lightermen, forwarders, warehousemen and others, and subject likewise to local and general customs affecting the same and to the terms of this agreement.

20. The sender, holder or transferee hereof agrees to accept from the Company, or from carriers, truckmen, lightermen, forwarders, warehousemen and others who may be selected by the Company to transport, store, deal with and deliver the goods at the port of discharge or other places, a bill of lading, delivery order or other document entitling such sender, transferee or holder to receive delivery of the goods from the carrier, truckman, lighterman, forwarder and other agencies to whom the goods may be entrusted, in whose possession the said goods may be at the port of discharge or destination, and the delivery of such bill of lading, delivery order or other document to the sender, transferee or holder hereof, shall be full performance of all the Company's obligations hereunder with respect to the forwarding and reforwarding of said goods.

21. If a carrying vessel, because of blockade, interdict, war, insurrection, internal disturbance, mistake, or for any other similar reason, shall land the goods at any port other than the port of discharge, such landing shall be deemed a full and complete delivery at the said port of discharge and the Company shall in no way be held responsible therefor or be obligated in respect thereof. If the Company shall have previously undertaken to arrange for the reforwarding of the goods to a destination beyond the aforementioned port of discharge, the Company, in such event, upon cancellation or refund of that portion of its charges covering shipment of the goods from the port of discharge to the said destination beyond, shall be deemed to have completed its undertaking and shall in no way be obligated in respect thereof.

22. If the packages herein are consigned to "ORDER," the surrender of this contract duly endorsed shall be required before the delivery of the packages at destination, and if so consigned the Company is hereby authorized by the Sender or holder hereof to effect delivery of said packages to any person presenting this contract so endorsed; and, the effecting of such delivery to any person presenting this contract so endorsed, shall be a full performance of the duty of the Company hereunder. The Company shall not owe any duty to notify the consignee or others of the arrival or disposition of the packages nor be liable for any loss or damage arising from failing so to do. If the packages herein are NOT consigned to "ORDER," then said packages may be delivered without requiring the production or presentation of this contract.

23. All disputes and suits hereunder shall be determined in accordance with the laws of the State of New York.

24. No agent or employee of the Company shall have authority to alter or to waive any of the provisions of this contract.

25. In accepting this contract the Sender and the holder of this contract expressly ratify and agree to be bound by all its stipulations, exceptions and conditions whether written, printed or stamped hereon or affixed hereto, as fully as if they were all signed by such Sender and holder and to expressly waive any right to prior inspection of bill of lading or receipt of any carrier or others to whom the packages are or may be entrusted for transportation, or for any other purpose.

Forwarder's Receipt (cont'd)

short, it serves as a receipt and a quasi-title document to the seller, supporting his claims against the final consignee and forwarder. Showing clearly the forwarder's name, it cannot, under any circumstances, be confused with a steamship bill of lading, although it embodies the usual clauses defining the liability of the ocean carrier, as contained in the regular forms of bills of lading in use by steamship lines. It provides that the forwarder acts only as an agent of the shipper, and is in no way responsible for the carrier's acts or defaults. In case of damage or loss to the goods, the ocean bill of lading issued to the forwarder by the steamship line becomes available for filing claim. Besides a number of non-negotiable copies, the forwarder issues three original negotiable copies. Upon transfer to the shipper, should one of these be accomplished, the others stand void. This clause is indirectly referred to in the forwarder's waybill by the stimpulation therein that goods are to be delivered only when a properly endorsed original copy of the bill of lading is produced.

The *waybill*, like the carrier's manifest, is a summary of cargo shipped under one ocean bill of lading. Containing pertinent instructions, it is sent by the "dispatching" forwarder to his overseas agent, the "receiving" forwarder. The waybill is prepared in triplicate; one copy is retained as a record of the transaction; the other two copies are transmitted to the correspondent abroad. He is requested to acknowledge receipt thereof, to furnish immediate notification of any undelivered consignment and to comply with given instructions as to delivery, billing, and collection of charges.

The Rebilling Invoice. Prepared by the foreign freight forwarder, the Rebilling Invoice is a type of commercial document which has assumed increased importance in contemporary foreign trade. Appraisal of its functional value has enhanced the position of the forwarder as an efficient coordinator in the commercial sphere and as an indispensable link in international transportation.

Two types of transactions require the rebilling services of the forwarder:

1. Purchase by importers, to be delivered and billed to their clients, instead of to them. This is done either to insure the foreign buyer's freedom from local tax or special tariff or as a matter of substantive mandate. The importer will request the forwarder, in whose name the Import License, if any, will be taken out, to bill on his letterhead at given prices which are different from, and usually higher than those quoted by the original supplier.

2. The other mode concerns orders placed by foreign buyers with two or more vendors whose products require assembling, mounting, or consolidating. For instance, an automobile or truck manufacturer delivers the chassis, and a body builder, the equipment, such as, a hearse, ambulance, dump, or crane. The invoices of the different sellers must then be combined into one invoice, indicating the total value involved. Under letter of credit payment terms, the forwarder will be the beneficiary, collect by means of his own invoice and remit to the various suppliers. Of course, the consignment will be made in the forwarder's name as agent of buyer, indicating the correspond-

F.M.C. No. 922

D. C. ANDREWS & CO., Inc.
One Whitehall Street   New York, N. Y. 10004

WHitehall 4-0780

FOREIGN FREIGHT FORWARDERS—FOREIGN CONTRACTORS—CUSTOM BROKERS—OCEAN FREIGHT BROKERS

DELIVERING CARRIER	DELIVERY DATE

1. Forwarding Agent—ADDRESS—REFERENCE NOS.	B/L NO.

2. Method of Transportation (check one)
☐ VESSEL   ☐ AIR   ☐ OTHER (Specify)

WAYBILL

3. Exporter or
SHIPPER ▶

4. Consigned To ▶

5. Ultimate Consignee/Arrival Notice Party (Give name and address)	6. Intermediate Consignee (Give name and address)

Vessel	Flag	Pier	Port of Loading

Foreign Port of Unloading	For Transshipment To

PARTICULARS FURNISHED BY SHIPPER OF GOODS

MARKS AND NUMBERS	NO. OF PKGS.	DESCRIPTION OF PACKAGES AND GOODS	CUBIC MEAS. OR KILOS	GROSS WEIGHT IN POUNDS

PROPORTIONATE OCEAN FREIGHT.............................

PARTY WHO MAY BE NOTIFIED...........................

WAYBILL TO..................................

COLLECT FOR OUR ACCOUNT $........................

WAYBILL INSTRUCTIONS   ....

EXPLANATION OF INSTRUCTIONS
A   Debit us all charges to destination excepting duty.
B   Debit us ocean freight and collect all other expenses from Consignee.
C   Consignee pays all charges.
D   Delivery entirely free and debit us all charges, including duty.
X   Special Instructions
No. 1 Please Note. You are ONLY to deliver these goods against presentation of the original of the enclosed agents copy of our bill of lading properly endorsed.
No. 2 Quickest Route.
No. 3 Cheapest Route.

VALUE OF THIS SHIPMENT $......................................

DCA 125 25M-11-59-PPC.

Forwarder's Waybill

ing manufacturers only as suppliers on the shipping documents.

The Expense Bill. The forwarder's itemized statement of expenses and fees for advances made and services rendered to either shipper or consignee, or both—whoever employs his assistance—is called an *Expense Bill*. This serves as the basis for settling the transaction in question. Prepared in a multiple number of copies, it is distributed to the interested parties, such as, bank, shipper, consignee, and to the forwarder's accounting and solicitation departments.

Banking Collection Letter. In handling the collection for shipper's invoice value, whether on a draft or letter of credit basis, the forwarder is guided primarily by the instructions he receives from the exporter as expressed in the shipping instruction form. However, he also has to consider general standing directions from consignees, which govern the handling of "routed" shipments. Discrepancies which emerge must be settled first to both parties' satisfaction.

When submitting the necessary documents for collection, the forwarder operates under the directive of the so-called *collection letter*. Specifying all the required information to be used by the collecting bank, domestic or foreign, this instruction sheet enumerates the documents attached, the drawer and drawee, the mode of payment or acceptance, where to remit, and other necessary details.

To keep the exporter informed, a copy of the collections letter is sent to him, together with the required balance of the shipping documents.

Insurance Policy and Certificate: Export freight protection is secured primarily by marine insurance which, in itself, is a highly specialized field. Conditions range from the simplest, the general average while waterborne, to that of protection against loss and damage from external causes, including strikes, riots and civil commotions, travel between warehouses, and war. Marine insurance can be negotiated, with policies or certificates issued instantaneously, by the foreign freight forwarder. As an experienced traffic specialist, he is in a position to efficiently accommodate both shipper and consignee.

Headed by a licensed insurance broker, the forwarder's insurance department "writes" cargo insurance policies based on a contract between the underwriter (Insurance Company), or insurer, on the one hand, and the forwarder, shipper, consignee or owner of cargo (assured) on the other hand. Herein the insurance company agrees, in consideration of a specified premium, to idemnify the insured party for any loss and damage that may befall the goods during the specified voyage. Indemnification will be made for causes incident to the maritime venture that arise from the perils of the sea, from fire, or from other causes enumerated in the policy. Indemnification does not exceed the sum insured; consequently, proper valuation is a significant factor.

Two types of policies are currently used: One, a *special risk policy;* the other, *a floating* or *open policy.* If an exporter wishes to insure a single cargo risk, such as, grain, coffee, or cotton, he would take out a special policy. Manufacturers who export a line of products must select an open policy, which covers any type of shipment. Advantages possessed by an open policy, as against the special risk policy, include:

1. The insurance automatically attaches to the goods which become the property of the assured; whereas, under the special policy, it is indispensable to place the insurance with the insurer before the risk attaches.

2. The premium is paid only on the shipments actually made.

3. The assured can issue certificates of insurance.

4. The policy can be written in a manner to cover all kinds of merchandise or commodities.

The *insurance certificate* refers to the marine insurance policy and describes the quantity and nature of the goods shipped, their identifying numbers, their value, an identification of the vessel carrying the shipment, and the terms of insurance provided by the master policy. The facility of issuing certificates enables the forwarder to assemble promptly a complete set of shipping documents, before or upon steamer sailing, for banking purposes or mailing abroad.

CHAPTER XVI

Marine Insurance

Insurance is a device whereby the risks caused by human failures or misfortunes are shared with others. Confronted by risks to his transactions, the businessman attempts to overcome them by buying protection from some of the perils. Upon payment of a relatively small percentage of the policy's coverage to the one who assumes the risk, he receives a guaranty of indemnification against the possible loss. Since in most instances the loss does not materialize, the risk bearer is able to pay the loss if and when it does occur. Conversely, by pooling the risk through the medium of insurance, the burden of any loss is shared by many and does not fall upon any one individual. This fact has accounted for the extraordinary growth of the insurance business in general and of marine insurance in particular. Marine insurance, as applied to international commercial intercourse, has become one of the dominant institutions in our economic life.

HISTORICAL BACKGROUND

The origin of modern marine insurance is said to date back to the 12th century. According to Giovanni Villani, a Florentine historian (A.D. 1275-1348), the Jews devised a system resembling modern insurance for the protection of their evacuated property. Villani states that this occured during their temporary resettlement in the Lombardy, after their expulsion from France in the 12th century. However, long before the Middle Ages, ancient commerce on land and sea applied provisions whereby the trader induced the money-lender to assume the transportation risk through loans, which pledged his vessel or cargo, and were repaid with interest only upon the safe arrival of the goods. Early maritime nations, such as the Phoenicians and Greeks, and later, the Roman Empire, commonly used this method. Money-borrowing, by the vessel owner on security of his ship, was effected by a so-called *bottomry bond;* if the cargo was pledged, a *respondentia contract* had to be executed.

Traceable to the embryonic era of ocean-borne commerce, about 900 B.C., is another insurance-like system. In case of jettison, this system required contributions from all parties in the common interest. Due amounts were determined by assessing the value of the goods thrown overboard, proportionally over the entire value of the ship and cargo, including the property which had to be sacrificed in order to save the vessel. Based on the distribution of loss among the participants of a venture, this practice embodied all the characteristics of the *General Average* principle, as we know it today. This was the original procedure whereby several people shared insurance in different percentages by signing their names individually, with the amount of risk assumed, which led to the modern institution called, Underwriters.

Marine insurance was well-established among the maritime nations of Europe by the middle of the 14th century. World trade leaders were Venice and Genoa, both city-states. Their wares crossed the Alps to the Low and Nordic countries; their ships sailed the known oceans. Controlling commerce on the North and Baltic Seas was their counterpart, the Hanseatic League. Originally composed of individual traders to foreign lands, this protective association later comprised about 70 towns of different political affiliations.· The Hanseatic League promulgated directives which included references to the handling of bottomry bonds in connection with ocean-borne commerce.

Influences exerted by the Lombard cities and the Hanseatic League patterned the development of British trade and marine insurance, and culminated in the establishment of that preeminent institution, Lloyd's of London, in 1696. Lloyd's was founded by merchants, ship owners, and underwriters at the Coffee House of Edward Lloyd. Aiming to promote the patronage of his shop and to stimulate further interest in maritime matters, Lloyd, who was a shrewd, competent businessman, had already started to publish his *Lloyd's News* in 1692. Thirty years later he changed its title to *Lloyd's List;* today it still appears under this name. Correlating with the expansion of British commerce, marine insurance developed rapidly. Multiple risks of foreign trade commercial transactions caused complex difficulties and costs. This situation posed serious financial problems for the various underwriters, each of whom signed the insurance policies as an individual and placed his name opposite the amount of the risk taken. Efforts to surmount these trade impediments led to the chartering of "Assurance Companies." Organizing themselves into a permanent body under the name of Lloyd's in 1769, the group of underwriters who patronized Lloyd's Coffee House secured the control of *Lloyd's List* and established quarters at the Royal Exchange. Ten years later the group adopted a standard form for marine policies which succeeded in winning approval by the British Parliament.

The first stock company to engage in insurance on the American continent was chartered in Charleston, South Carolina, in 1735. The Insurance Company of North America was the first American insurance corporation to receive its formal charter, which was issued by the General Assembly of Pennsylvania on April 14, 1794. However, the company issued its first insurance policy on December 15, 1792, prior to the official date of incorporation. This policy covered the ship *America,* sailing from Philadelphia to Londonderry, to a value of $5333.33 at a premium of $120.00. Newly-established marine insurance companies benefited in fair measure from the growth of the young Republic about the turn of the 19th Century. Sharp declines followed the War of 1812, but the marine insurance industry revived 30 years later, during the era of the clippers. Mutual marine insurance companies were organized by traders, who, in their dual capacity as shipowners and commercial merchants, tried to enhance their profit by adding underwriting to their regular line of business.

With the advent of the "Ironclads" and steamers, the American Merchant Marine commenced to deteriorate, adversely affecting the cargo marine business. This trend came to a halt only after World War I. Fortunately, however, coastwise and Great Lakes trade prospered throughout this period and helped to sustain the underwriters, particularly with respect to hull insurance. Congress in 1919 undertook a comprehensive study of marine insurance, which resulted in beneficial legislation. Contained in the Merchant Marine Act of 1920, Section 29, this legislation effected the formation of three marine insurance syndicates to assist in the reconstruction of the American merchant fleet. Favored by the postwar development of our foreign commerce, the marine insurance business became stabilized. Underwriting companies formed cooperative groups to solve the various problems of the business as they relate to uniform practices and increasing difficulties of overseas trade. The American Institute of Marine Underwriters, The Board of Underwriters of New York, The School of Insurance of the Insurance Society of New York, and others significantly express the continuous, cooperative efforts to keep pace with the perpetual demands of international commerce and to stimulate our dynamic national economy.

DEFINITION OF MARINE INSURANCE

Contained in an Elizabethan statute of 1601 is the following definition of marine insurance: "By means of a policy of insurance it cometh to pass that upon the loss of perishing of any ship there followeth not the undoing of any man but the loss lighteth rather easily upon many than heavily upon too few." Although quaint in language, and relatively restrictive when compared with modern terminology, this definition encompasses the pith of the subject. Current meaning of the term "marine insurance" differs principally in that it now has a considerably broader application. Today, it not only provides for protection of a shipowner against the loss of his vessel or the cargo carried therein, but it also comprises many forms of coverage not precisely within the confines of a maritime venture. Marine cargo insurance may cover losses or damages arising from non-seagoing types of transportation, such as freight moving over land by train, truck, mule, or camelback. Coverage can include the period from the time a shipment leaves its point of origin until it reaches the premises at its final destination. Marine Insurance can be issued to cover extraordinary items, such as bullion, securities and other valuables, or almost any conceivable risk.

However, since our purpose here is to explore problems affecting ocean traffic and its management, we may limit our definition. *Marine insurance*, here, can be defined as a contract between the insurer and the insured, specifically between the insurance company, on the one hand, and the shipper, consignee, or owner of the cargo, on the other hand, whereby the insurance company agrees in consideration of a specified premium to indemnify the insured party for any loss or damage, not exceeding the sum insured, that may happen to the merchandise during the specified voyage, incident to the maritime venture, that arises from the perils of the sea, from fire, or from other causes enumerated in the policy.

The *assured* (insured) is any person who has an insurable interest to such an extent that he will be benefited by the safe arrival of the merchandise or injured by its loss or damage.

The *premium* is the consideration paid to the underwriter which validates the marine insurance contract. The premium is flexible, and is based entirely upon the amount of risk accepted by the underwriter.

With respect to the subject matter of insurance, the contract, or policy, may cover all kinds of lawful goods and merchandise.

Essential factors which must prevail for the existence of a valid insurance contract are, in summary: (1) the signatories must be legally competent; (2) there must be an insurable interest on the part of the assured; (3) there must be a valid consideration; (4) there must be an agreement as to the intention of the parties to the contract; and (5) the contract must have a legal purpose.

Extensive alterations have been wrought on the original concept of marine insurance, with respect to its meaning, extent and application. Factors exerting potent influence on insurance companies' efforts to meet changing needs include: the expanse of international trade with its political, legal and economic ramifications; the mode of transportation; and the technical intricacies in connection with consular regulations.

Various reasons render it imperative for international traders to purchase additional protection. Confronted by uncertain conditions and potential dangers over which they have no control, they nevertheless, wish protection against these perils.

Among these modern hazards are those of a financial nature, like the relative instability of many foreign currencies. Similar in character are the measures taken by certain foreign governments to the effect that insurance must be placed by the buyer in any and all circumstances. Through this endeavor to protect their own insurance industry, United States dollars will not be available for premiums, except on c.i.f. sales contracts. This insurance discrimination, upsetting the established pattern of sales terms, based on definite international trade definitions, requires special precaution on part of the foreign trader who may not be aware of the shortcomings of the buyer's policy. A loss may be incurred because of damage before the title to the goods passes to the importer and before payment under the Letter of Credit is made. In many cases, the buyer's policy provides coverage only after title has been passed, or only from port of exportation instead of from points of origin.

Prudence demands that the exporter exercise scrupulous care to prevent unsuspected monetary losses. Securing proper coverage for himself, to supplement the buyer's coverage, will permit him effective control of any situation, which otherwise might adversely affect his interest. Payment of his premium would be a pittance for this purchase of commercial equanimity.

CHAPTER XVII

The Forwarder as Insurance Broker

Insurance brokerage history, particularly in the United States, has been closely connected with the development of the marine insurance companies and overseas commerce. Increased business volume during the flourishing clipper ship era caused the separation of the originally combined functions of merchant trader and carrier. Emerging then as middleman between underwriter and shipper, the broker, or agent, provided indispensible services as an adviser to the merchant on the purchase of the proper amount of protection with the most advantageous insurance company at favorable rates. Absorbed by foreign trade's complexities relevant to sources of supply, shipping procedure, and the search for new markets, the merchant welcomed the independent broker's assistance in protecting his sales by obtaining proper insurance coverage. Experience during the past century has indicated that there is no adequate substitute for a competent insurance agent as an intermediary between exporter and underwriter. The insurance agent acts on behalf of his principal, the assured, although he receives his compensation from the insurance company with whom he arranges the contract for the account of the party buying property or liability protection.

The professional, licensed insurance broker will arrange that:

1. The policy or contract of indemnity is "made to measure" to fit the particular situation of his client.

2. The rates charged are based upon the client's premium and loss experience.

3. The settlement of claims are taken care of efficiently and quickly, while simultaneously considering possible improvements as to packing and handling.

4. In case of differences of opinion between exporter and underwriter, the interests of the assured are skillfully, properly, and fully protected so that his client will receive complete recovery in accordance with the terms of the policy.

5. The insurance declarations are processed rapidly.

6. The best qualified insurance company is selected, as he is not limited to a single underwriter.

7. His service is always of the highest standard.

Determined by the competitive nature of the insurance business, there exist, with few exceptions, no tariff rates or standard conditions. These circumstances, plus other factors, yield an advantage to the foreign freight forwarder who maintains his own insurance department under a licensed broker as Manager, or who acts in a dual capacity as forwarder and insurance agent. This advantage over any average insurance broker with whom an exporter, particularly a customer of the forwarder, might contract his insurance coverage, is illustrated by the following:

1. In all cases where the insurance is for the account of the consignee, the consignor is relieved of any responsibility because the forwarder takes care of it.

2. Whenever an exporter or a manufacturere employs the services of a forwarder for all of his export trade, the forwarder will perform all the necessary details in connection with insurance. Transferring an essential part of his own obligations to his agent, the exporter may save time, money, and possible expense and trouble, because his experienced forwarder can capably manage his insurance affairs. The forwarder's routine in insurance matters makes him best suited to suggest the correct form of policy or insurance coverage for the needs of his client to obtain favorable rates and to arrange the filing and collecting of future claims.

3. The large volume of insurance business handled by the forwarding agent creates an atmosphere of confidence and fairness between the underwriter and himself and an obliging attitude on the part of the insurance companies he employs. Advantages resulting from this situation place the forwarder in a position superior to that of the average insurance broker and redounds to his customer's benefit. This fact has been demonstrated in cases where the insurance coverage has been delayed or belatedly placed, where placement of unusual risk was involved, and particularly where the settlement of claims has been entailed.

Placing and handling insurance coverage through the forwarding agent proceeds as follows:

Acting either through his broker, who usually has a desk in the forwarder's office or dealing directly as independent broker and forwarding agent, the forwarder has negotiated in advance for one or more insurance contracts which will protect and apply to all shipments entrusted to and insured by him, made within a specified time and over certain described commercial routes. These contracts are known as *open policies*. Under such policies, the forwarding agent, as the assured, enjoys the privilege of issuing, on specially prepared forms, certificates of insurance that incorporate the important conditions and terms of the insurance policy. Under these arrangements, the forwarding agent makes out one set, original and duplicates, to go with the shipping documents. He sends one copy to the insurance company, one to the shipper, and retains one for his files. The certificate states that there has been insured, with the insurance company in question, in the name of the assured forwarding agent, a specific number of packages covering a specified freight, marked and numbered as indicated, for a certain amount of money, by named or described means of transportation, from the point of shipment (interior or port of exit, as the case may be) to the point of destination, against the perils enumerated therein or in the original open policy to which reference is made. An important point is that the certificate is made to the order of the assured, the forwarder. Thus, like the bill of lading, this certificate becomes a negotiable instrument, which through endorsement is made available to the holder thereof, to whom it has been transferred in good faith.

Declaring cargo value for marine insurance purposes necessitates that forwarding agents consider, in addition to the invoice value of the goods, all incurred shipping expenses, such as packing, inland freight, storage fees, transfer charges, ocean freight, handling fees, consular fees, and insurance premium. Customarily, also, it includes a reasonable amount (usually about ten per cent) to cover the anticipated profit or against possible losses which might result from the non-arrival of the goods. This additional amount serves as a protective element for profit in favor of shipper or consignee, as the case may be. Some foreign traders, however, advise the forwarder to increase the usual amount of 10 per cent to 15, 20, or 25 per cent, when justified by special circumstances.

Although insurance is frequently referred to as a "passive" service on the part of the forwarder, it entails a considerable portion of his time and attention and routinely merits adequate renumeration. However, upon arranging claim settlements, he will charge, in addition to direct expenses, a service fee ranging from one-quarter per cent to one per cent, according to the value involved, or a flat service fee.

The insurance rates the forwarder charges to his clients are his out-of-pocket costs plus a small mark-up both of which he must show on his invoice as per Federal Maritime Commission regulation.

Coverage furnished by the forwarder's open policy is vitally important for all interested parties, inasmuch as the shipper or consignee desires to obtain the best possible protection. Customers sometimes propound indefensible complaints when they compare the forwarder's rates with those of his competitors who quote lower rates. Further analysis will disclose that the lower rates do not cover the risks to the same extent. Relative completeness of the coverage in marine insurance, as in other areas, will affect the level of the insurance rate. Application of utmost skill and foresight in the placement of proper and complete insurance for goods entrusted to him for shipment is requisite to the forwarder's prestige. The client should be cautious not to compare incomparables; and by regarding these aspects, in the long-run his financial status will not be desiccated.

CHAPTER XVIII

Types of Marine Insurance Policies and Certificates

Various types and forms of insurance policies are in use today. Trade, custom, and the kind of goods involved are the determining factors for classification of present-day policies. Commonly rooted in the marine policy, which has been written for centuries, they nonetheless vary considerably in phraseology. No standard form of policy is legally required in the United States.

Modern policies provide comprehensive coverage from house to house by all means of transportation and include protection while the goods are in transit. When the term, "transit," means, "in course of being conveyed" from place to place, it is phrased, "in due transit." This phrase applies, also, when the goods may be temporarily delayed through unforseen events, such as, congestion in the port of discharge, or through intended interruption when placed in a bonded warehouse or free zone, awaiting either more favorable market conditions, or for other reasons. This type of additional coverage can be obtained by writing corresponding policies. Although insurance companies' policies are all essentially similar in meaning, they differ in their verbal construction. Utmost caution is indispensable when the assured or broker examines the policy as to its propriety and individual application.

THE OPEN OR FLOATING POLICY

Modern cargo insurance is written, almost exclusively, under what is known as open or *floating policies*, which are insurance contracts that remain in force until cancelled. They cover all shipments of the exporter afloat or in transit within the indicated geographical trade areas, as described in the policy. Controlled by the limit of their liability and valuation clause, individual shipments and values are reported successively, and premiums paid "as they go." They are called "open" because the amounts to be applied to the contract are declared only when the goods are shipped, and "floating" because the name of the vessel, or other details as to packing, marks, and contents of a particular consignment are furnished only at the time of actual dispatch.

Manifold advantages characterize the open policy.

1. The assured has automatic protection up to the maximum limits, as stipulated in the contract, from the time goods leave the

warehouse, or even thirty days prior to actual commencement of transit, until they reach final destination.

2. Goods are held insured even if the policyholder unintentionally, due to business pressure, fails to report that the goods already have been forwarded from the place of shipment. This, in effect, represents protection against errors and omissions.

Atlantic Mutual Insurance Company

ATLANTIC BUILDING, 49 WALL STREET, NEW YORK 5, N. Y.

$..

No. CP ....

New York,...

By this special policy of insurance

do make insurance and cause to be insured lost or not lost, for account of

at and from

to

in the sum of

on

Marks and Numbers

Dollars

Valued at sum insured. Shipped per

Loss, if any, payable to   or order,
upon the surrender of this policy at the office of this Company in New York City, or at the office of its nearest settling agent, as per back hereof, computed at the current rate of exchange on the day of payment, and, on the payment being made, liability under this insurance shall be thereby discharged.

Attention of the holder of this document is directed particularly to the SPECIAL NOTICE clause, as per back hereof, outlining the proper procedure in the event of the goods hereby insured arriving in a damaged condition.

The Revenue Laws of Great Britain require that this policy be stamped within ten days after receipt in the United Kingdom, otherwise loss cannot be collected there. Such stamps to be at the expense of the assured.

This Special Policy is subject to the following terms and conditions and also those printed on the reverse side hereof.

This insurance attaches from the time the goods leave the Warehouse and/or Store at the place named in the policy for the commencement of the transit and continues during the ordinary course of transit, including customary transhipment if any, until the goods are discharged overside from the overseas vessel at the final port. Thereafter the insurance continues whilst the goods are in transit and/or awaiting transit until delivered to final warehouse at the destination named in the policy or until the expiry of 15 days (or 30 days if the destination to which the goods are insured is outside the limits of the port) whichever shall first occur. The time limits referred to above to be reckoned from midnight of the day on which the discharge overside of the goods hereby insured from the overseas vessel is completed. Held covered at a premium to be arranged in the event of transhipment, if any, other than as above and/or in the event of delay in excess of the above time limits arising from circumstances beyond the control of the Assured.

NOTE:—It is necessary for the Assured to give prompt notice to this Company when they become aware of an event for which they are "held covered" under this policy and the right to such cover is dependent on compliance with this obligation.

Where this insurance by its terms covers while on docks, wharves or elsewhere on shore, and/or during land transportation, it shall include the risks of collision, derailment, overturning or other accident to the conveyance, fire, lightning, sprinkler leakage, cyclones, hurricanes, earthquakes, floods (meaning the rising of navigable waters), and/or collapse or subsidence of docks or wharves, even though the insurance be otherwise F. P. A.

The following Warranties shall be paramount and shall not be modified or superseded by any other provision included herein or stamped or endorsed hereon unless such other provision refers especially to the risks excluded by these Warranties and expressly assumes the said risks:—

(A) F. C. & S. Notwithstanding anything herein contained to the contrary, this insurance is warranted free from capture, seizure, arrest, restraint, detainment, confiscation, preemption, requisition or nationalization, and the consequences thereof or any attempt thereat, whether in time of peace or war and whether lawful or otherwise; also warranted free, whether in time of peace or war, from all loss or damage caused by any weapon of war employing atomic fission or radioactive force; also warranted free from all consequences of hostilities or warlike operations (whether there be a declaration of war or not) but this warranty shall not exclude collision, explosion of contact with any fixed or floating object (other than a mine or torpedo), stranding, heavy weather or fire unless caused directly (and independently of the nature of the voyage or service which the vessel concerned or, in the case of a collision, any other vessel involved therein, is performing) by a hostile act by or against a belligerent power; and for the purpose of this warranty "power" includes any authority maintaining naval, military or air forces in association with a power.

Further warranted free from the consequences of civil war, revolution, rebellion, insurrection, or civil strife arising therefrom, or piracy.

(B) S. R. & C. C. Warranted free of loss or damage caused by or resulting from strikes, lockouts, labor disturbances, riots, civil commotions or the acts of any person or persons taking part in any such occurrence or disorder.

The following clauses shall have precedence of all others if in conflict therewith.

Where goods are shipped under a Bill of Lading containing the so-called "Both to Blame Collision" Clause, this Company agrees as to all losses covered by this insurance, to indemnify the Assured for this policy's proportion of any amount (not exceeding the amount insured) which the Assured may be legally bound to pay to the shipowners under such clause. In the event that such liability is asserted the Assured agrees to notify this Company who shall have the right at its own cost and expense to defend the Assured against such claim.

Warranted free from Particular Average unless the vessel or craft be stranded, sunk, or burnt, but notwithstanding this warranty this Company is to pay any loss or damage to the interest insured which may reasonably be attributed to fire, collision or contact of the vessel and/or craft and/or conveyance with any external substance (ice included) other than water, or to discharge of cargo at port of distress. The foregoing warranty, however, shall not apply under broader terms of Average are provided for herein or endorsed hereon.

American Institute Clauses: This insurance, in addition to the foregoing, is also subject to the following American Institute Cargo Clauses (1949):

1. Craft, etc.	5. Bill of Lading, etc.
2. Deviation	6. Inchmaree
3. General Average	7. Warehousing & Forwarding Charges
4. Explosion	8. Constructive Total Loss

Warranted free of claim for loss of market or for loss, damage or deterioration arising from delay, whether caused by a peril insured against or otherwise, unless expressly assumed in writing herein.

This policy is not transferable unless countersigned by a duly authorized representative of the Company.

Countersigned

....

Underwriter

O-2099

In Witness Whereof, the President of the said Atlantic Mutual Insurance Company hath hereunto subscribed his name, and caused the same to be attested by its Secretary, and this policy is made and accepted upon the above express conditions, the day and date first above written.

J. Harold ....

Secretary

President

Special Policy of Insurance or Insurance Certificate

ADDITIONAL TERMS AND CONDITIONS

Losses arising from breakage or leakage are excluded from this insurance unless caused by stranding or collision with another vessel, except when included in the average terms of this policy.

In case of damage affecting labels, capsules, or wrappers, this Company, if liable therefor under the terms of this policy, shall not be liable for more than an amount sufficient to pay the cost of new labels, capsules or wrappers, and the cost of conditioning the goods, but in no event shall this Company be liable for more than the insured value of the damaged merchandise.

When the property insured under this policy includes a machine consisting when complete for sale or use of several parts, then in case of loss or damage covered by this insurance to any part of such machine, this Company shall be liable only for the proportion of the insured value of the part lost or damaged, or at the Assured's option, for the cost and expense, including labor and forwarding charges, of replacing or repairing the lost or damaged part; but in no event shall this Company be liable for more than the insured value of the complete machine.

(A) Except as otherwise provided in (B) and (C) below, it is agreed that in the event the interest insured is covered by other insurance the loss shall be recoverable under the several policies in the order of the date of their attachment except that insurance attaching on the same date shall be deemed simultaneous and shall contribute pro rata.

(B) Warranted that any fire insurance granted herein shall be null and void to the extent of any fire insurance which the Assured or any carrier or other bailee has, at the time of the fire, and which would attach if this policy had not been issued.

(C) Warranted by the Assured free from liability for loss of or damage to goods in the possession of any carrier or other bailee who may be liable therefor. However, this Company agrees to pay to the Assured the difference between the amount which would be a claim under this policy if it did not contain this warranty and the amount recoverable by the Assured from such carrier or bailee, plus the costs and expenses of prosecuting the claim against such carrier or bailee. Pending collection from such carrier or bailee this Company agrees to advance as a loan such amount which would be a claim under this policy if it did not contain this warranty, repayable only to the extent of any net recovery from such carrier or bailee.

TOUCHING the adventures and perils which the said ATLANTIC MUTUAL INSURANCE COMPANY is contented to bear, and takes upon itself in this voyage, they are of the seas, men-of-war, fires, enemies, pirates, rovers, assailing thieves, jettisons, letters of mart and countermart, reprisals, takings at sea, arrests, restraints, and detainments of all kings, princes or people, of what nation, condition or quality soever, barratry of the master and mariners, and all other perils, losses and misfortunes that have or shall come to the hurt, detriment or damage of the said goods and merchandises or any part thereof. AND in case of any loss or misfortune, it shall be lawful and necessary to and for the assured, their factors, servants and assigns, to sue, labor, and travel for, in and about the defense, safeguard and recovery of the said goods and merchandises, or any part thereof, without prejudice to this insurance; nor shall the acts of the insured or insurers, in recovering, saving and preserving the property insured, in case of disaster, be considered a waiver or an acceptance of an abandonment, to the charges whereof, the said Insurance Company will contribute according to the rate and quantity of the sum herein insured.

MEMORANDUM. It is also agreed, that bar, bundle, rod, hoop and sheet iron, wire of all kinds, tin plates, steel, madder, sumac, wickerware and willow (manufactured or otherwise), salt, grain of all kinds, tobacco, Indian meal, fruits (whether preserved or otherwise), cheese, dry fish, hay, vegetables and roots, rags, hempen yarn, bags, cotton bagging, and other articles used for bags or bagging, pleasure carriages, household furniture, skins and hides musical instruments, looking-glasses, and all other articles that are perishable in their own nature, are warranted by the assured free from average, unless general; hemp, tobacco stems, matting and cassia, except in boxes, free from average under twenty per cent, unless general; and sugar, flax, flax-seed and bread, are warranted by the assured free from average under seven per cent, unless general; and coffee in bags or bulk, pepper in bags or bulk, and rice, free from average under ten per cent, unless general.

Warranted by the Insured free from damage or injury from dampness, change of flavor or being spoiled, discolored, musty or mouldy, except caused by actual contact of sea water with the articles damaged, occasioned by sea perils. In case of partial loss by sea damage to dry goods, or other hardware, the loss shall be ascertained by a separation and sale of the portion only of the contents of the package so damaged, and not otherwise; and the same practice shall obtain as far as practicable. Not liable for leakage on molasses or other liquids unless occasioned by stranding or collision with another vessel.

If the voyage aforesaid shall have been begun and shall have terminated before the date of this policy, then there shall be no return of premium on account of such termination of the voyage.

THIS SPACE IS RESERVED FOR ENDORSEMENTS IN TRANSFER OF THIS DOCUMENT

SPECIAL NOTICE—IN CASE OF LOSS OR DAMAGE to the goods hereby insured, immediate application for survey, appraisal and authentication of proofs of loss should be made to the settling agent of the Company or to its correspondent, as the case may be, at the port of destination if there be one at such port, otherwise to the correspondent of The Board of Underwriters of New York, or, if there be none, to Lloyd's agent.

Any apparent loss or damage or irregularity in this shipment SHOULD BE NOTED ON RECEIPT given to the carriers and preliminary CLAIM should be FILED with them IN WRITING IMMEDIATELY. When survey is held to ascertain loss or damage the carrier should be given an opportunity of being represented and claim for actual loss MUST BE FILED AGAINST THE CARRIER IN WRITING.

Copies of notation on receipts and correspondence in connection with claim against carrier must form part of proof of loss under the Insurance Policy.

A full list of settling agents and correspondents of this Company appear below.

After a proper adjustment settlement of the loss may be made at the office of the nearest settling agent in the manner herein indicated.

This Company hereby agrees to a British Domicile for the purpose of any legal proceedings and will accept service of process in London at the office of Morgan, Grenfell & Co.

SETTLING AGENTS

ACCRA (West Africa)..........The United Africa Company Limited
ADELAIDE (So. Australia)..................The Union Marine and General Insurance Co., Ltd.
ALEXANDRIA (Egypt)..........Manley & Co.—Successors Givam, Besly & Co.
AMSTERDAM (Netherlands)..........................De Vos & Zoon
ANTWERP (Belgium).....................................P. Varles
BARCELONA (Spain).....................Macandrews & Co., Ltd.
BOMBAY (India)............................Andrew Yule & Co., Ltd.
BREMEN (Germany)...............................P. Reck & Co.
BRISBANE (Australia).............Thomas Brown & Sons, Ltd.
BUENOS AIRES (Argentina)....F. B. O'Grady & Co., Soc. Resp. Ltd.
CALCUTTA (India)..............Gillanders, Arbuthnot & Co., Ltd.
CAPE TOWN (So. Africa)...........Thomson, Watson & Co.
CARACAS (Venezuela)...........................Imataca S.A.
CHITTAGONG (Pakistan) ....James Finlay & Company, Ltd.
COLOMBO (Ceylon)..........................Henderson & Co.
COPENHAGEN (Denmark)..........................Jansen & Co.
DAR-es-SALAAM (East Africa)........Smith Mackenzie & Co., Ltd.
DJAKARTA (Batavia) (Indonesia)....O. W. J. Schlencker N. V.
DURBAN (So. Africa)..................John T. Rennie & Sons
EAST LONDON (So. Africa)..............Dyer & Dyer, (Pty.) Ltd.
GENOA (Italy)...........................Thomas L. Carr & Son
GLASGOW (Scotland)....................The Union Marine and General Insurance Co., Ltd.
GUATEMALA CITY (Guatemala).........Agencias Unidas, (S. A.)
HAMBURG (Germany).....................H. J. Burmester & Co.
HAVRE (France).......................................Paul Giblain
HONG KONG (China)...........................Gilman & Co., Ltd.
HONOLULU (Hawaii)......................American Factors, Ltd.
JOHANNESBURG (So. Africa)..............John T. Rennie & Sons
KARACHI (Pakistan) ....James Finlay & Company, Ltd.
LAGOS (West Africa).............The United Africa Company Limited
LISBON (Portugal).............................James Rawes & Co.
LIVERPOOL (England)....................The Union Marine and General Insurance Co., Ltd.
LONDON (England)..................Joseph Hadley (Insurance) Ltd.
For change, alteration or extension of this special policy required in Great Britain or European Countries apply to Joseph Hadley (Insurance) Ltd., King William Street House, Arthur Street, London, E.C. 4.

LOURENCO MARQUES (Delagoa Bay) (East Africa)..John T. Rennie & Sons
...........................Parry, Leon & Hayhoe, Ltd.
MADRAS (British India)..........T. A. Taylor & Co. (Madras) Ltd.
MANCHESTER (England)..........The Union Marine and General Insurance Co., Ltd., at Liverpool
MANILA (Philippine Islands)......................E. E. Elser, Inc.
MEDAN (Indonesia)..................Harrisons & Crosfield, Ltd.
MELBOURNE (Australia)..................The Union Marine and General Insurance Co., Ltd.
MOMBASA (East Africa)..............Smith, Mackenzie & Co., Ltd.
MONTEVIDEO (Uruguay)...........................A. O. Crocker
PERTH (Australia)....................Keith Barker, Pty Ltd.
PORT ELIZABETH (So. Africa)..........Mackie Dunn & Company
PORT LOUIS (Mauritius).............................Scott & Co.
PORT-OF-SPAIN (Trinidad)..............Greil & Company, Limited
RANGOON (Burma)..............Gillanders, Arbuthnot & Co., Ltd.
RIO de JANEIRO (Brazil)......Companhia Immobiliaria Financeira Americana S.A.
ROTTERDAM (Netherlands)..................Wambersie & Zoon's Avaril-Bureau N. V.
SAN FRANCISCO (California)....Atlantic Mutual Insurance Company
SANTOS (Brazil)..............Companhia Immobiliaria Financeira Americana S.A.
SAO PAULO (Brazil)..........Companhia Immobiliaria Financeira Americana S.A.
SINGAPORE (Straits Settlements)..........Boustead & Co., Ltd.
SOURABAYA (Indonesia)..............O. W. J. Schlencker N. V.
SYDNEY (Australia) ....The Union Marine and General Insurance Co., Ltd.
TIENTSIN (China)......................William Forbes & Co., Ltd.
TOKYO (Japan)......................AFIA France Corporation
TRIESTE (Italy)..............Edgar H. Greenham & Company
VALPARAISO (Chile)..................Hanna & Company, Ltd.
ZANZIBAR (East Africa)..........Smith, Mackenzie & Co., Ltd.

CORRESPONDENT

NEUCHATEL (Switzerland)..........................Dr. Carl Ott

Special Policy of Insurance or Insurance Certificate (cont'd)

3. The exporter is relieved of the irksome necessity of arranging individual coverage for each shipment.

4. The open policy has an attached rate schedule, which provides the assured, in advance, with the rate or premium to be charged for various commodities and merchandise to different places in the world. This enables him to calculate the exact insurance amount and facilitates the quotation of the landed sales price. If a certain commodity is not listed, insurance is attached thereto nevertheless, but the rate will have to be negotiated with the insurer.

5. Under an open policy the premium is paid only on the actual shipment made. It will be in no way higher, and may be even lower, than when placing special risks on each shipment. Benefiting both parties to the contract, i.e., the open policy, the underwriter is in a position to acquaint himself over a long period of time with the special requirements of the assured.

6. The assured has the privilege of issuing certificates of insurance or "special marine policies," as they are called now, which are payable to holder or order, making them negotiable instruments.

7. Under the open policy, increased value and/or profit coverage can be arranged to provide automatically for any increase in value during the time the goods are in transit. This procedure is applied on import shipments when full information as to the value is not available at the time the "provisional" report or declaration is sent to the underwriter. The "provisional" report is terminated when the final value is known.

8. The open policy is individually adapted to fit the needs of the assured.

Reports, declarations and special marine policies are compiled in book form by the insurer and placed at the disposal of the assured for completion and return whenever shipments are made.

The open or floating policy has proved its extraordinary value to underwriter, brokers, and their clients. Additionally, by saving time and expense for all concerned, it has directly influenced the general growth of commerce.

The Blanket Policy

The blanket policy, in contrast to the open or floating policy, is a closed contract by which the assured pays a lump-sum premium, fixed in advance. The premium based on the estimated total amount for which insurance protection has been asked during the contract term, subject to mutual adjustment of premium payments, depending whether or not, at the end of the term, the coverage exceeded the originally insured amount or fell below it. Similar to the open policy, the blanket policy describes the kind of goods to be covered, trade areas, and time limits under the contract. However, it limits liability on any one vessel or in any one location at one time. In case of payment of a loss, the proportional annual premium for the amount of the loss must be paid up in order to reinstate the policy to its full insurable amount. This provision could render the blanket policy very costly if serious losses should incur. Elimination of the chore of filing detailed reports upon each shipment constitutes the blanket policy's sole major advantage. However, if insurance rates should rise during the period of the contract's term, some savings might be effected with respect to the lump-sum payment of the premium. Although used extensively in Europe, the blanket policy is selected in lesser degree in the United States export trade.

THE SPECIAL RISK POLICY

Covering a single cargo risk, such as, grain, cotton, or refrigerated products, this policy requires that the insurance be placed before the risk attaches. No privilege of issuing insurance certificates attaches thereto. Rates must be negotiated every time a shipment is made. Available coverage is applicable equally to the open or special risk policy.

CHAPTER XIX

Basic Fundamentals of Coverage

The fundamental purpose of marine insurance is to secure indemnity as protection against loss or damage to property while enroute from point of origin to final destination, subject to the restriction that it cannot and will not guarantee the replacement of the property, itself, or its continuity. The assured is promised protection for the interest in the goods, or the value of same; therefore, protection covers only the market or appraised value. Protection, also, adheres only if the loss or damage is a casual one, or beyond the control of the assured, and not caused by the inherent nature of the goods, the condition of the shipping container, or the nature of the voyage. Consequently, irrespective of emanation, neglect or carelessness will not be condoned; any loss or damage resultant therefrom will render the party who fails to perform imposed duties, liable and subject to redress.

Insurable interest usually is claimed either by those who will gain through the safe arrival of the cargo or will be injured by its damage, loss, or detention. These parties may be regrouped into two classes, namely, into holders of owner's interest and nonowner's interest. Determining the ownership situation are the sales terms agreed upon between seller and buyer, usually based on the *Revised American Foreign Trade Definitions*, 1941, or *Incoterms*, 1953. The exporter who wishes insurance coverage must either have a provable interest in the goods or act on behalf of the buyer. For example, on f.o.b. sales, under which the title passes to the importer at some inland point of shipment, the seller still has a financial interest in the goods until payment has been received. This interest can be fully protected, even where certain countries require their nationals to control the marine insurance, regardless of credit terms, by taking out contingent interest insurance. Then, should the foreign insurance fall short in a given situation, the exporter is nonetheless protected by the supplementary coverage in the American insurance market.

In applying for insurance, it is most important to disclose all pertinent facts, such as the kind and quantity of goods, amount to be covered, means of transportation, and origin and destination of cargo. Detailed disclosures enable the underwriter to issue a legally valid policy or contract, and thereby exclude later misunderstandings as to liability. This principle of fair play applies equally to the need for a valid consideration and purpose. Bargaining, with respect to an agreed premium in case of loss or safe arrival, and gambling are taboo.

VALUATION CLAUSES

Insurance, in general, may be divided into as many different classes as there are kinds of risks. Depending on the contract, an allocation of a fixed sum for the insured property in the event of a loss may have been stipulated; in this case, the policy is called a valued one.

If there is no agreement as to the specific value of the property because the payable amount is awaiting determination by appraisal, proof, or mutual understanding when loss has occurred, the insurance contract or policy is a *non-valued* or *open* one.

Cargo insurance, in contrast to fire insurance, is "valued." In case of total loss, the agreed amount is paid; in the event of a partial loss, a corresponding percentage will be payable.

Proper valuation of goods for insurance in foreign commerce equals the total amount of the landed cost of the merchandise at the port of discharge or, sometimes, at an interior point. "Whole" value includes all the costs, expenses, and other factors, for which the exporter wishes indemnification in case of loss, partial, or total. Valuation includes the invoice value, charges for export packing, trucking cost, consular and other fees, ocean freight, eventual inland freight, insurance premium, and anticipated profit. The latter is ordinarily computed by a percentage increase; in the case of a general average, this anticipated profit may be applied for the assessment of the necessary contribution. Determination of value in advance prevents disputes and secures fair relations between the parties to the insurance contract. A valuation clause in a common cargo policy will read, "The said goods and merchandise hereby insured, are valued (premium included) at ...." This "premium included" method normally is applied in cargo insurance when rates are low. However, it is not employed during emergencies, when rates, particularly those connected with war risk, mount considerably and reach or exceed ten per cent.

PERILS INSURED AGAINST

Marine cargo insurance does not cover every loss which occurs in shipment; *coverage is limited to those losses caused by perils named in the contract.* Cargo policies usually cover loss or damage caused by fire, stranding, collision and/or sinking of the vessel, and sea water entering the vessel during severe storms. All other risks, such as ordinary sea water damage, fresh water damage, theft and pilferage, leakage and breakage are not covered unless added by endorsement.

Indicating its century-old origin, the modern marine insurance policy has retained many quaint terms and words, with respect to the perils insured against. Thus, it may read:

"Touching the adventures and perils which the said . . . . . . Insurance Company is contented to bear, and takes upon itself in this voyage, they are of the seas, men-of-war, fires, enemies, pirates, rovers, thieves, jettisons, letters of mart and countermart, reprisals, takings at sea, arrests, restraints and detainments of all kinds, princes, or people, of what nation, condition or quality soever, barratry of the master and mariners, and all other perils, losses and misfortunes that have or shall come to the hurt, detriment or damage of the said goods and merchandise, or any part thereof."

Ostensibly, this enumeration of perils is all-inclusive. Actually, court interpretations has set a reasonable limit to their proper application, and has evolved the doctrine of "proximate cause." This doctrine bases liability on the direct, immediate cause; it excludes the indirect, remote, and secondary cause. To exemplify: if two perils were operative at the time of a misfortune, it must be determined which of the two was the decisive, primary one that caused the loss or damage. Concretely: if a vessel has been torpedoed but, still afloat, is trying to make for port, and later runs aground through the loss of the rudder, the predominant cause is the act of war.

Explanation of the numerous hazards contained in the policy must emphasize that the policy covers only those which are the direct consequence of actual perils *of* the sea, and not *on* the sea.

"Perils of the sea" include heavy weather, stranding, collision, lightning, and sea water damage when caused by insured perils.

"Fire" includes direct damage, and losses resulting from fire, or from attempts to extinguish a fire.

"Assailing thieves" refers to an act of forcible taking, rather than to clandestine theft, or theft by crew or passengers.

"Jettison" is the throwing overboard of part of the cargo to lighten the ship in time of peril.

"Barratry" is a willful, fraudulent, and illegal act on the part of the master or crew, and would involve any wrongdoing, or injury to ship or cargo.

"All other perils, losses and misfortunes" means hazards like "perils of the sea," but does not imply "all risks" as understood today.

Conditioned by the needs of modern seaborne commerce, other perils are or may be, included as extension of basic coverage. The *Inchmaree Clause* (named after the Inchmaree case, concerning a vessel of that name) provides for the extension of protection against loss resulting from either a latent defect of the vessel's hull or machinery, not discoverable by due diligence, or from errors of navigation or management of the vessel. A further protection in the policy refers to the hazards to which goods may be exposed while in due transit. The "shore clause" includes risks of collision, derailment, overturn, sprinkler leakage, windstorm, earthquake, flood, and collapse of docks and wharves.

Additional premium payment can secure specific coverage for a third group of hazards. To this category belong theft, pilferage, non-delivery, fresh water damage, sweat and oil damage, breakage, leakage, steam-of-hold, and hookhole damage.

Exporters have recently insisted on inclusion of the "all risk" clause in the policy.

This clause affords one of the broadest, obtainable protections; however, it excludes war risks, strikes, and 1iots, unless covered by special endorsement and premium.

Contrasting with the aforementioned special risks, the "warehouse to warehouse" clause is one of the basic coverages found in every cargo insurance policy. It attaches from the time the goods leave the initial point of shipment, and continues during the ordinary course of of transit, including customary transhipment, if any, until the goods are delivered to the final warehouse at the destination named in the policy, or until the expiry of 15 days (or 30 days, if the destination is an interior point) whichever shall first occur.

AVERAGE TERMS

While the *Flying Enterprise*, an Isbrandtsen steamer, was battling the raging seas of the Atlantic in 1952, newspaper reports of this dramatic effort to stay afloat, referred repeatedly to the term, *General Average*. Foreign traders are cognizant of this expression, since their cargo insurance policies contain the clause: "General Average and Salvage charges payable according to United States laws and usage ...., if in accordance with the Contract of Affreightment."

While the hazards mentioned specifically in the policy determine the nature of the losses recoverable under the insurance contract, the "average terms" define the extent of coverage. According to the Supreme Court of the United States, the "General Average" is "a contribution by all the parties in a sea adventure to make good a loss sustained by one of the number on account of sacrifices voluntarily made of part of the ship or cargo to save the residue and lives of those on board from an impending peril, or for extraordinary expenses necessarily incurred by one or more of the parties for the general benefit of all the interests embarked in the enterprise."

Coincident with this definition is Rule A of the York-Antwerp Rules, 1950, which states: "There is a general average act when, and only when an extraordinary sacrifice or expenditure is intentionally and reasonably made or incurred for the common safety for the purpose of preserving from peril the property involved in a common maritime adventure." Four factors are required to constitute a general average act: (1) an imminent peril common to ship and cargo; (2) a voluntary sacrifice or extraordinary expenditure to avert such peril from the common interest; (3) a successful result; and (4) an absence of fault on the part of those claiming contribution.

The word "average" derives from the French word, *avarie*, which means "damage to ship and cargo;" however, it actually originated from the Arabic *awarijah*, standing for "merchandise damaged by sea water." Testifying to the past domination of seaborne commerce in the eastern Mediterranean by the Moslems, numerous maritime expressions are traceable to the Arabic idiom, including the word, "Admiral."

Although the principles of General Average are recognized by all martime nations, there is no uniformity in their application. The closest approach to uniformity of customs and practices is found in the previously cited *York-Antwerp Rules of 1950*. Examples of General Average acts are: jettison; water, steam, or chemical damage to cargo while extinguishing fire aboard the vessel; damage to a ship's engines, winches, and gear, incurred while attempting to refloat a stranded vessel; all other salvage expenses so incurred, such as, warehouse cost.

A *Particular Average* (P. A.) is a partial loss which solely affects "particular" interests. It may be a partial loss of goods or a partial damage concerning a particular interest, both of which were accidental in nature and resulted from the perils of the sea. These damages or partial losses are not contributed for by other interests, but are borne exclusively by the parties who have suffered the damage and are excepted in the ocean carrier's bill of lading. Therefore, except if negligence is involved, claims under particular average cannot be directed against the steamship line.

The phrase, *Free of Particular Average* (F. P. A.) means that the underwriter will cover, in addition to total losses, partial losses resulting from perils of the sea, but only when caused by stranding, sinking, burning, or collision. American and English Underwriters employ diverse clauses. American insurance companies, under their clause, agree to pay particular average damage if caused by stranding, sinking, burning, or collision of the vessel. The English clause reads "unless the vessel or craft be stranded, sunk, burnt or in collision." Here, the underwriters do not require that the damage be caused by the named accidents, but merely that such accidents must occur before their liability accrues. For cargo loaded under deck, it is established practice to use a modification of the English version of the clause (*F. P, A.—E. C.*), which reads, "Free of particular average or unless the vessel or craft be stranded, etc." The American conditions form of the F. P. A. clause (*F. P. A.—A. C.*) is usually applied when cargo is stowed on deck. However, under both F. P. A. clauses, General Average and salvage charges are recoverable.

With Average (W. A.) coverage is broader than *F. P. A.*, and represents one of the most inclusive protections for partial damage caused by the perils of the sea. To obtain payment from the underwriter, the damage must be at least three per cent of the value of the whole shipment or of a shipping package. In case of stranding, sinking, burning or collision, the three per cent franchise is waived and losses from the perils of the sea are fully recoverable. Additional named perils, such as, theft, pilferage, non delivery, and fresh water damage can be added to the W. A. Clause, which became the "forerunner" of the now widely demanded "all risk" clause.

Types of Losses Excluded

The *All Risk* (A. R.) clause may read: "To cover against all risks of physical loss or damage from any external cause irrespective of percentage, but excluding nevertheless, the risks of war, strikes, riots, seizure, detention, and other risks excluded by the F. C. & S. (*Free of Capture and Seizure*) Warranty and the S. R. & C. C. (*Strikes, Riots and Civil Commotion*) Warranty in this policy, excepting to the extent that such risks are specifically covered by endorsement." Protection is not as complete as the name would indicate, however, because: 1) numerous risks, including the marring, scratching of unboxed automobiles, are still excluded, and 2) only physical loss and damage from external causes is covered. The excluded risks can be provided for by special endorsement and additional premium.

Another common exclusion from the cargo insurance policy is the "Delay Clause," which precludes claims for loss of market and for damage or deterioration caused by delay. Occasionally, the latter ones are included, by special endorsement, if and when the assured proves the necessity of inclusion in a particular trade. Then the delay must result from accidental perils.

All cargo insurance policies imply two noteworthy warranties, namely, that of the legality of the undertaking, and that of seaworthiness. Seaworthiness is admitted to exist by inserting a corresponding waiver in the policies. However, the underwriter cannot waive the implied warranty of legality, inasmuch as this would amount to a violation of established public policy and, therefore be unlawful. Consequently, certain basic conditions must be regarded as implied requirements, even if not written into the policy. Among these are that : (1) when applying for coverage, the assured will furnish without hesitancy all facts essential to the risks; (2) the assured will comply with the generally valid trade customs and practices pertaining to the covered subject matter; and (3) the assured will abstain from everything that could contribute to loss or damage by omission or commission. In addition, the exclusion of losses or damages caused by inherent vice or internal cause is automatically implied. However, as previously stated, some exclusions can be modified or eliminated by endorsements as a result of mutual negotiation between underwriter and assured, upon payment of an adequate premium increase.

The fact that the ocean carrier is liable for damage or loss resulting from neglect or carelessness in loading, stowing, handling, or discharging cargo under the provisions of the various "Carriage of Goods by Sea" acts does not warrant any relaxation on the part of the exporter in exercising due care in all his undertakings.

EXTENSIONS OF COVERAGE

Many years ago, the ordinary cargo insurance policy limited its coverage from the time the goods were actually loaded on board of the vessel until they were discharged and landed at the port of destination. Proving insufficient for modern needs, this protection has been extended to include warehouse to warehouse coverage.

Conditions engendered by World War II, particularly the scarcity of available steamer space, effected shipment delays in ports of exit. Increased demand to cover interruption or suspension of transit led to the adoption of the Marine Extension Clauses in 1942. However, this broadened coverage is contingent on the fact that the interruption of due transit is beyond the control of the assured. In case of an intended suspension of transit, the underwriter must be notified and additional protection obtained.

American Institute   87 B 28
(February 1949)

Endorsement to be attached to and made part of Policy No. .... of

S. R. & C. C. ENDORSEMENT (Form No. 6)

This insurance also covers damage, theft, pilferage, breakage or destruction of the property insured directly caused by strikers, locked-out workmen, or persons taking part in labor disturbances or riots or civil commotions and destruction of or damage to the property directly caused by persons acting maliciously; but the foregoing shall not be construed to include or cover any loss, damage or expense caused by or resulting from (a) delay, deterioration or loss of market, or (b) hostilities, warlike operations, civil war, revolution, rebellion or insurrection or civil strife arising therefrom; or (c) any weapon of war employing atomic fission or radioactive force.

While the property insured is at risk under the terms and conditions of this insurance within the United States, its incorporated territories and its possessions in the Western Hemisphere, Canada and Newfoundland, this insurance is extended to cover damage, theft, pilferage, breakage or destruction of the property insured directly caused by "Vandalism," "Sabotage" and "Malicious Mischief," and as so extended shall include such losses directly caused by acts committed by an agent of any government, party or faction engaged in war, hostilities or other warlike operations, provided such agent is acting secretly and not in connection with any operation of military or naval armed forces in the country where the described property is situated. Nothing in the foregoing shall be construed to include or cover any loss, damage or expense caused by or resulting from (a) delay, deterioration or loss of market; or (b) hostilities, warlike operations, civil war, revolution, rebellion or insurrection, or civil strife arising therefrom, excepting only the acts of certain agents expressly covered above; or (c) any weapon of war employing atomic fission or radioactive force.

The Assured agrees to report all shipments attaching under this cover and to pay premiums therefor at the rates established by the Company from time to time.

This endorsement may be cancelled by either party upon forty-eight hours written or telegraphic notice to the other party, but such cancellation shall not affect any risks which have already attached hereunder.

All other terms and conditions remaining unchanged.

Dated ...., 19..........

For Sale by Joseph Lazard, 496 Broome Street, New York 13, N. Y.   PRINTED IN U. S. A.

S. R. & C. C. Endorsement

STRIKES AND WAR RISKS

As a logical consequence of warehouse to warehouse coverage, this protection might be impeded by unlawful acts, such as strikes, riots, and civil commotation (S. R. & C. C.). However, underwriters cannot be expected to assume additional liability for losses or damages without being duly compensated by corresponding endorsement.

A similar view-point is applicable to war risk. Distinction must be drawn between the war acts of a belligerent government and warlike acts, like capture or seizure, committed by authorities whose status as a recognized power is legally doubtful, or whose acts contradict international law. Examples of such warlike acts are the shelling of an Isbrandtsen vessel by the Chinese Nationalists, and the removal of cargo destined for Israel from an Isbrandtsen vessel, by Egypt, during the passage of the Suez Canal.

Cargo policies today invariably include an F. C. and S. Clause (*free of capture and seizure.*) Separate policies are issued solely for war risk coverage. Considering the possibility of the sudden eruption of full-scale warfare, as potentially foreshadowed by the current, tense, international political situation, any exporter who failed to arrange appropriate coverage would be remiss in judgment and caution.

CHAPTER XX

Analysis of the Insurance Policy

Analysis of the function of insurance, namely the redistribution of loss to share risk, discloses that this process, as formalized in the insurance contract, is based on certain legal prerequisites. Law obligates the parties involved in the venture to perform definite duties but provides them with proper legal protection. Each interested party has a special, different interest at stake; and the conditions, terms, and clauses of the insurance policy signify their individual rights, obligations, and compensation. Contrasting with other types of insurance coverage, this diversity of interests accounts for the fact that the rates applicable to marine cargo insurance are not standardized. These rates are generally determined by the experience of the risk contained and the judgment thereof by the insurance company.

Evaluation of risk involves the underwriter's consideration of these three basic elements: (1) the cost of loss incurred by major disasters in specific voyage categories; (2) particular average experience based on commodity types; and (3) particular average, classified as to shippers.

Insurance risks will vary as these factors change, and the rates for coverage will follow correspondingly. This observation will be substantiated by study of all phases connected with the production, handling, and movement of goods from the factory to their final destination abroad. Packing, routing, choice of inland carriers, port facilities, types of ships and ocean carriers, climatic conditions, customs handling at port of destination, and the commodity itself, require protracted attention on the part of the insurer, for they decisively influence the make-up of the insurance rate.

To assure a logical, equitable distribution of risk, each party under the insurance contract has certain rights and responsibilities which will affect even third parties insofar as recovery facilities are concerned. A basic concept of insurance law is that the insurer, upon settlement of loss or damage, is entitled to secure and pursue any rights the assured may exercise against a third party. Therefore, the cargo insurance policy indirectly represents a tri-partite agreement between underwriter, merchant, and transporter or carrier. Thus, an exporter who experiences a loss or damage caused by a peril of the sea will collect from the insurer, but he will discover that he must also give assistance to the insurer. Low-cost insurance could not be sustained without the aid of this reciprocal technique.

OBLIGATIONS AND RIGHTS OF THE OCEAN CARRIER

Derived from the right of subrogation, the rights of recovery are available to the underwriter to secure indemnification for payment of losses or damages to the assured. The extent to which an ocean carrier can be held liable for damage incurred to goods in custody depends on three factors: (1) the provisions of the bill of lading; (2) common law modifications applicable to admiralty matters; and (3) statutory legislation, such as,

a) The Harter Act, of 1893, which determines the liability of the carrier for goods received prior to loading and after discharge from vessel before delivery, and

b) The Carriage of Goods by Sea Act, of 1936, (COGSA) which, generally speaking, applies from "tackle to tackle," for goods shipped in foreign trade.

As a rule, the carrier is responsible for the proper loading, handling, stowing, carriage, custody, care and discharge of cargo entrusted to him. However, he is not ordinarily liable for damage arising from errors of navigation and management; from unseaworthiness of the vessel, unless caused by neglect or lack of due diligence; from insufficiency of packing, marking, or description of cargo; or from the perils of the sea, fire, and several other stated reasons, whereby the burden of proof in fixing liability rests in some cases with the shipper and in others with the carrier. Expert knowledge is required when filing suit or claims because of the complexity and intricacies inherent in matters affecting admirality law.

OBLIGATIONS AND RIGHTS OF THE ASSURED (MERCHANT)

The exporter or assured is obliged to pack and mark the shipping packages properly; to furnish the insurer accurate and specific information regarding shipments made or to be made; to notify the underwriter immediately as to damages or losses occured; to cooperate to the fullest extent, that is, to sue and labor with the insurance company to minimize the damage or loss incurred; to transfer or waive his rights and claims to the insurer (subrogation clause) for the purpose of recovering any indemnification made to the assured; to pay promptly bills rendered by the underwriter or broker for due premiums. In return, the exporter is entitled to the protection and compensation by the insurer as laid down in the policy. Special care should be taken to avoid under-insurance or double-insurance. The law provides that where the assured is insured for an amount less than the insurable value or, in the case of a valued policy, for an amount less than the policy valuation, he is deemed to be his own insurer in respect to the uninsured balance. In the case of double insurance, which occasionally happens, due to a misunderstanding between the exporter and his client abroad, American theory customarily holds that the prior insurance is valid and bears the whole risk, thereupon voiding the subsequent coverage.

OBLIGATIONS AND RIGHTS OF THE UNDERWRITER

One of the most important clauses in the ocean cargo policy is represented in the phrase, *Lost or Not Lost*. Inclusion of this phrase signifies that the holder of an open policy is fully protected if damage or loss had occurred before he learned about it and, thereby, was unable to notify the underwriter in time. However, any concealment of this knowledge would amount to a breach of good faith, which automatically would void the contract.

Similarly, the underwriter can expect the assured to advise him immediately if the goods are not loaded under deck, inasmuch as coverage of on deck cargo is attached only if special notice is given to the insurer, and the additional risk is accepted by him.

Limits of coverage as to the time and place insurance attaches and terminates is defined in the policy by the words "at and from," which follow the "lost or not lost" clause.

Required in the policy, also, are the name and type of the vessel on which the goods are *laden or to be laden on board*. Fitness of the ship determines the risk the insurance company is prepared to assume. Therefore, even if the name of the ship should change, the vessel itself may not be changed without invalidating the insurance contract, unless the underwriter has given his consent.

This principle also applies in case of *deviation*, that is, a change of voyage by the vessel, or departure from the usual, intended route, except when necessary for compelling reasons. Immediately upon notification of the deviation, the assured must notify the insurer and, if warranted, agree to a higher premium for added coverage. Because the exporter receives additional protection for this possible rate increase, it is fair.

In conclusion, written or stamped words, phrases, or clauses are often found inserted in the ocean cargo policy.

Presumed to have been the subject of mutual agreement between insurer and assured, they supersede the printed text of the policy. Consequently, clarity in policy-writing is indispensable to express the actual intention of the parties and minimize potential disputes which might emerge from apparent ambiguities or inconsistencies in the contractual phraseology.

CHAPTER XXI

Adjustments of Claims—Requirements and Procedure

Claim adjustment primarily requires that the assured, exporter or consignee, as the case may be, must act with speed and care to keep his loss or damage at a minimum.

Prudent exporters advise their clients abroad on what steps they must take to comply with this standard, since effectiveness is essential. Reasonable expenses or charges incurred to prevent additional damage are recoverable under the policy. For example, when a consignment of paints arrives with some leaking cans in each of several wooden boxes, these damaged cans must be removed immediately to avoid further harm. Timely, accurate presentation of intent to claim, or claim, being paramount for the recovery of any loss or damage, the exporter and his foreign customer are impelled to attend to numerous details either directly or through port, foreign claims, and/or settling agents.

Special attention must be given to the fact that clauses contained in the ocean bills of lading prescribe the time within which claim must be filed and suit instituted against the carrier. Whatever the clauses referring thereto stipulate, they must give a reasonable period to be valid and enforceable. Under the United States *Carriage of Goods by Sea Act,* of 1936, notification of loss or damage must be submitted to the carrier at the port of discharge before or at the time of removal of the goods into the custody of the party entitled to receive them. Prompt notice concerning damage or loss, whether concealed or not, also must be given to the claims agent of the underwriter, as listed on the insurance certificate or policy, with the request for an immediate survey in presence of the carrier for the purpose of issuance of a survey report. In case of concealed damage, or in the event the carrier will deliver only against clean receipt, the consignee or his agent should file with the carrier an intent to claim, describing the condition of the cargo as received, and reserving the right to institute claim for any loss or damage that a later survey may disclose. Damaged cargo and containers must be held aside until the survey has been completed, unless additional damage would hereby result. The surveyor's fees and expenses, payable by the consignee, are recoverable as part of the claim under the insurance contract. In filing a preliminary claim, or letter of intent to claim, with the ocean carrier, it is not necessary that details as to quantity, prices, or value be submitted. Adequate for this purpose is a brief statement as to the loss or damage sustained. To be included herein are the marks and numbers of the shipping packages, the description of the goods, the bill of lading number, the name of the vessel, and the phrase that "claim is hereby filed and carrier held responsible."

Copies of all correspondence directed to the carrier and, if available, the original reply received from him or his agent should be filed with the underwriter's representative abroad, together with the following documents for adjustment and payment of the claim:

1. Original or copy of ocean bill of lading.

2. Original and copies of insurance certificate or special cargo policy.

3. Original commercial invoice, or certified copy thereof.

4. Packing list, and any other statement evidencing the condition of the cargo at the time of shipment, such as, signed dock receipt.

5. Survey or inspection reports, concerning proof of loss or damage.

6. The claimant's detailed statement of the loss or damage.

Under no circumstances should the filing of the claim with the insurance company be delayed because the carrier's acknowledgement of claim is still lacking. A claim may be changed or amplified at any time after filing, but prior to settlement. Resubmission with undiminished qualification is permitted in case of rejection, as long as the previously mentioned time limitations have not elapsed. Should the bill of lading require that suit be commenced within one year after the delivery of cargo by the ocean carrier, the claimant must strictly adhere to this provision; otherwise, he will lose all rights of recovery from the steamship line.

Adjustment of an *actual total loss* presents no difficulty. Total loss is construed when the cargo is either completely destroyed, or to such an extent that it ceases to be the matter for which insurance was obtained, or when the assured is definitely and irrevocably divested of the goods.

In case of a *constructive total loss*, that is, one in which the property insured is damaged so extensively that the cost of its repair would exceed its salvaged value, insurance companies usually pay full insured value, with the understanding that the assured agrees to abandon the cargo, as well as to relinquish any recoverable salvage value to the underwriter.

With respect to the adjustment of *particular average claims*, we have to distinguish between two different types of *particular average losses*: namely, (1) the total loss of a portion of cargo, and (2) the arrival of the cargo in a damaged condition. In the first case, pertinent to general export cargo, an apportionment of the total insurance amount for which claim is being filed, will have to be contrived. For instance:

Total invoice..$1,500
Insured Amount...$1,650
Insurance Ratio.. 110%
Invoice value of lost items..............................$ 100
Insured in proportion 110%...............................$ 110

With reference to goods arriving in damaged condition, the *percentage of depreciation* method is applied, if the assured and the surveyor achieve a mutual agreement. When their viewpoints are disparate, the damaged goods' value is determined after their sale, after calculating the difference between their *sound and damaged values*.

When a *General Average* is declared by a vessel owner, or operator on behalf of its owner, an intentional sacrifice of ship or cargo has been made, or an extraordinary expenditure has been incurred for the common good in time of danger. The vessel owner then has a lien on the cargo and has the right to retain it in his possession until the shippers (1) contribute their estimated proportional share of security; (2) furnish the required information as to the landed value of their respective consignments; and (3) agree to pay the general average contribution when the assessement eventually is collected.

The apportionment of loss and expenditure over the parties interested in the maritime venture includes the vessel owner, for the value of his ship and the freight, both of which usually represent the largest amount involved. For this reason, if the shipowner appoints the Average adjuster, it is incumbent for him: (1) to determine the names of the cargo owners, and the landed costs of their goods; (2) to draw up an Average Bond for signature by the individual shipper, concerning the contribution he is to make after final assessment; (3) to prepare the Average Statement, indicating detailed information as to the contribution of each party in proportion to the value of their interest in the goods involved; and (4) to distribute the completed statement among the participants in the General Average.

In the contingency that an insured cargo owner wants his merchandise released by the steamship line before the final assessement is known, he will have to furnish security for the payment of his proportional share in the General Averge. This collateral may be in the form of a *cash deposit* or a bond, and a guarantee is issued by the underwriter. The cash deposit receipt, being negotiable, may be endorsed by the assured and turned over to the insurance company, which will then reimburse the cargo owner and issue their own guarantee to the vessel owner. The eventual payment of the insured exporter to the General Average contribution will be effected by his underwriter.

A shipper who was not insured but whose goods were saved also has to produce either a cash deposit or a corresponding security; otherwise, the delivery of his cargo is withheld. His contribution will be offset by his deposit, and the balance will be refunded to him. In order to provide a margin of safety, the adjuster usually calculates the cash deposit or guarantee on a higher percentage basis, with respect to the anticipated contribution. A shipper who wholly fails to insure and loses his cargo through a General Average act is regarded as a self-insurer. He is obliged to absorb his loss, but he will receive a refund of a certain percentage, based on the General Average settlement.

Perusal of this chapter's contents reveals that the complexities of General Average are manifold and baffling. Concomitant features entail serious financial obligations for which the exporter is held responsible, and for which he must obtain protection by contracting for adequate insurance coverage.

CHAPTER XXII

Credit and Payment Terms

Attracting increased attention recently, the subject of export credit and financing facilities has come to the fore primarily because the buyer's choice of his supplier is influenced increasingly by the terms of payment offered. American business policy has been criticized, and many of our overseas friends have declared that we are insufficiently realistic to compete successfully with other nations, such as, Germany, Japan, Belgium, and France, whose export credit policy ostensibly is adapted more favorably to the market conditions and requirements of the foreign buyer. Witness of the substantial increase in the volume of United States' exports during the last decade testifies to the vital importance of credit policy and payment terms with respect to the future success of our export efforts.

Admittedly, many firms inadequately equipped for conducting export business entered the field in recent years. Having failed to respond to their customers' reasonable credit needs, many withdrew from the export market. Fear of hazards involved, or lack of interest, due to the rising boom in the domestic market, accounted for this group's retreat. These so-called "fair-weather exporters," are definitely in a minority. Difficulties encountered by thousands of American exporters are caused by circumstances which bear no relationship to the usual commercial credit risk, but belong in the category of the so-called "political risks," which have become prevalent. Indispensable for proper appraisal of both risks is a thorough understanding of all the documents affecting the formulation of a sound credit policy. Additionally, continuous reexamination of our attitude and practices is requisite to our continued pursuit of our export market's expansion. Export credit policies are fundamentally similar to those we apply in our domestic market. Supplementary factors, however, impart a distinct flavor to export financing. Currency, legal system, distance, language, and custom of doing business, exemplify those factors which influence the sense of financial security. In the final analysis, this assurance is the decisive consideration in the granting of export credit.

The foreign buyer's choice in selecting his sources of supply is influenced, more than formerly, by the proffered credit and payment terms. Additional factors influencing an importer's decision as to where and from whom to purchase include: transit time for his purchases; the necessity to pay duties and taxes immediately upon landing of goods; the high cost of borrowing funds; and the turnover rate of goods after their receipt. Conversely, the exporter must visualize these elements to understand the problems which confront his prospective customer or client. In examining his own position, the exporter must weigh those cogent considerations against the credit practices in his line, here and abroad; the buyer's credit standing; the supply situation of his goods; his own financial strength; the availability of dollar exchange; the imposition of exchange controls; and, as previously mentioned, the prevailing economic and political conditions in the importer's native land. This analysis is basic to his comprehension of the reasons why, when other things are fairly equal, the buyer abroad could conceivably prefer to transact business with his competitor.

To guide and protect him in his sales efforts, the exporter can avail himself of a number of tools. When effectively employed, they can facilitate the development and maintenance of safe, sound, and profitable business relations in overseas markets.

With the exception of the United States, every major industrial nation provides protection to its exporters against both credit and political hazards. This protection is achieved by the payment of a small premium, ranging from one-half per cent to one per cent of the export sales value, to an export credit institution. These programs are run by governmental agencies or private insurance companies with governmental support. Attempts are in process to arrange similar protection for United States exporters. Until this project materializes, the American export trade must rely on existing facilities which, to date, have been adequate to the situation.

Credit information pertaining to the customer and trading area can be obtained from many sources and should include data on the: (1) integrity and efficiency of the buyer; (2) financial standing; (3) payment experience; (4) payment terms allowed; (5) size of territory covered; (6) number of salesmen employed; (7) all lines handled, previously and currently; (8) banking and commercial references; and (9) financial and earning statements.

To evaluate political and economic conditions in the foreign country, the following sources should be consulted: (1) the United States Bureau of Foreign Commerce; (2) commercial banks active in foreign trade; (3) the Federal Reserve Banks; (4) the export trade press; (5) private credit agencies, such as, the Foreign Credit Interchange Bureau, New York; the American Foreign Underwriters Corporation, New York; Dun & Bradstreet, New York; and (6) Foreign Freight Forwarders who engage extensively in business in the contemplated trading area.

The contractual sales terms should designate the methods of payment. Banking has developed, through years of experience, patterns of handling collections for almost any method the exporter may formulate. These may range from cash, sight draft payment against documents, to time drafts, delivery of documents on acceptance, open account, or letter of credit. Discussed herewith are the usual and principal methods.

CASH IN ADVANCE WITH ORDER AT TIME OF SHIPMENT

Terms of *cash in advance* are most desirable from the seller's standpoint, for risks are eliminated. Although high in safety, this method is not conducive to a maximum of sales. Any buyer will oppose these terms, which tie up his working capital, in view of the long period elapsing between the placement of the order and the shipment of goods. However, these terms are justified and accepted in many cases where goods, expressly manufactured to order, or substantial values are involved. In the latter instance, a down payment of approximately 20 per cent by the buyer is not unusual, with the balance to be settled through a series of installment notes, running up to the date of shipment or delivery in the foreign port. Governmental restrictions in some countries, where dollar exchange is in short supply, or economic or political conditions are unstable, usually prevent importers from making cash or advance payments. Generally speaking, the volume of business transacted on this basis is negligible.

OPEN ACCOUNT: INHERENT RISKS AND DANGERS

Representing the opposite extreme from the cash or advance payment pattern, the *Open Account* is employed either when the shipper has received direct payment, has available funds, or has sufficient confidence in the customer to ship the merchandise, sending his client the documents free of any restrictions for later payment. This payment method provides no documentary basis of obligation or of ownership. Since the buyer can assume possession of the goods on arrival without any hindrance, this method is used only with clients whose long-standing relationship with their suppliers warrant this practice. Nonetheless, the exporter must exercise constant vigilance, because of existent risks and dangers, due to the absence of any material or documentary obligation. Conceivably, also, these risks might increase, due to circumstances beyond the control of the importer, such as, the deterioration of the financial position of the buyer's country.

Transactions under open account terms provide payment as agreed or specified. Alternatives include: *R/M:* return mail; *E.O.M.:* end of the month; *30 days:* 30 days from date of invoice; *2/10/60:* 2% discount for payment in 10 days, net if paid 60 days from date of invoice. If no terms are specified, *O/A* (open account) generally implies payment by return mail.

DRAFTS

Promptly convertible to bank financing, due to their negotiability, *bills of exchange,* more commonly called *drafts,* constitute the most prevalent method of extending credit and securing payment in international trade. Moreover, drafts have two favorable attributes for use in international commerce: (1) documentary evidence of a contractual and transferable obligation. (2) a determinable maturity of the credit or payment instrument. Contractual provisions of the sales contract, as well as correlation with an established, properly-defined terms pattern operative in the respective trading area, will determine prior agreement between the buyer and seller as to the type of draft— *sight* or *time*—to be drawn. Following a summary of the legal aspects concerning their status as negotiable instruments, the concomitant features of different drafts will be examined.

Modern business uses negotiable instruments, such as checks, promissory notes, and drafts as the most common credit device. Constituting a special class of contracts or written obligations, they possess conspicuous, distinctive advantages for commercial use. Otherwise unavailable in combination, these features are salability and negotiability.

An instrument to be negotiable must meet the following test: (1) it must be in writing and not oral; (2) it must be signed by the maker or drawer; (3) it must be payable to order or to bearer; (4) it must be payable in money only; (5) it must be payable in a sum which is specific in amount; (6) it must be payable unconditionally; (7) it must be payable at a fixed or determinable future time; and (8) where the instrument is addressed to a drawee, he must be named or otherwise indicated therein with reasonable certainty.

Three Parties Involved. A negotiable draft or *bill of exchange* may be defined as an unconditional written order, in which the person drawing the draft (drawer) instructs another person (drawee) to pay a certain sum of money on a definite date, on demand or at a fixed future time, to a third person (payee), or to his order, or to bearer. Three parties are concerned in transactions involving a draft or bill of exchange, namely: (1) *The drawer:* executes the draft or orders the payment; (2) *the payee:* to whom the negotiable instrument is made payable; (3) *the drawee:* to whom the draft is addressed and who is ordered to pay the instrument.

The payee usually is a bank with whom the drawer maintains his account. In some instances, the payee and drawer are the same person.

Foreign drafts are usually issued in duplicate as a means of protection. The *First of Exchange* is usually attached to the original shipping documents, if and when they control title to the goods; the *Second of Exchange* is sent under separate cover with the duplicate documents. The second set becomes void upon arrival of the first, or vice versa. Original ocean bills of lading, made out to order, may under appropriate sales contract terms reserve or control title to the property, notwithstanding the delivery of the goods to the buyer or to the carrier for the purpose of delivery to the buyer. Disposition of each case depends on the intentions of the seller as expressed in the terms of the sales agreement.

TYPES OF DRAFTS

We distinguish two different categories of drafts: one, concerning the delivery, conditional or unconditional, of the merchandise; the other, affecting the time element, or the maturity of the respective payment or acceptance.

Clean and Documentary Drafts. A draft to which there are no, or only non-negotiable, documents attached, is known as *clean draft.* The documents, if any, are sent directly either to the customs broker designated by the importer, the buyer, or the collecting domestic or foreign bank. When the exporter has confidence that the buyer will honor the draft, he utilizes the clean-draft procedure. This permits the buyer to obtain possession of the goods before payment or acceptance of the draft. In some trading areas, particularly Latin America, forwarders, provide for the execution of so-called *release letters.* Directed to foreign port agents handing the import clearance, this letter requests them not to release the merchandise to the buyer upon it nationalization, until advised by the collecting bank that the shipper's draft has either been paid or accepted. This measure facilitates the clearance of goods through customs and avoids fines for the late presentation of documents to the customs authorities, and possible storage expenses thereby incurred. While contributing to the retention of good will between buyer and seller, this procedure also protects the exporter's financial interests.

If the seller wishes to subject the delivery of the merchandise to the acceptance or payment of a draft, he may then utilize the *documentary draft.* This instrument is formed by attaching to the draft a complete set of original documents, prepared in a manner so as to control the possession of the shipment. A complete set of shipping documents generally consists of: the commercial invoice, consular invoice and certificate of origin, if any; full set of bills of lading, signed, claused "On Board," legalized if necessary; and insurance policy, or advice, if covered under buyer's policy, accompanied further by all instructions necessary to direct the collecting bank how to proceed. To avoid delayed clearance of goods, this procedure should be applied only when the prompt arrival of shipping documents at the port of discharge is assured.

Sight—Time—Date—Arrival Drafts. As previously noted, a negotiable instrument must be made payable at a "time certain" to arrive, which means it must be payable in all events. Therefore, drafts may be issued payable: (1) At sight, presentation on demand; (2) At X days or months sight; (3) At X days or months date; (4) At a fixed date; or (5) At arrival.

Drafts *at sight* must be paid on presentation or demand; those at a *fixed date* on the indicated day. If the date of payment is not shown, the draft is considered at sight.

For *drafts at X days,* or *X months at sight,* the computing of the maturity date is done by counting from the day immediately following that of acceptance, or of the protest, in case the draft is dishonored by non-acceptance. An *acceptance* is the assent of the drawee to make payment at the stipulated time by either endorsing the draft, or indicating thereon in any manner his intent to accept the draft subject to stipulated future payment. Months are counted for their actual number of days in the case of drafts at X days sight or date.

For *drafts at X months sight or date,* the maturity falls in the corresponding month, the same day as that of acceptance. A draft at X months date which has been issued—or a draft at X months sight which has been accepted—on the last day of any month, comes to maturity the last day of the month of maturity. For example, a draft issued the 30th of November at three months date, falls due the 28th of February. If the maturity date is a holiday, the draft is considered due the following working day. Should there be a difference between the sum indicated in figures and that given in writing, the latter is always considered valid.

The aforementioned drafts, if payable at a given number of days after date of the instrument, are called *date drafts;* if payable at a given number of days after initial presentation to the drawee, such as 30 days after sight, they are known as *sight drafts.* These drafts respectively are abbreviated 30 d/d and 30 d/s. When an exporter sells, for example, on a 120 days date draft, the draft matures 120 days from its date, regardless of the time of acceptance, and exclusive of days of grace legally permitted by the country of payment. Both types of drafts are also called *time drafts.*

A modified sight draft which does not require payment upon presentation or upon demand, but only when the goods covered by the draft have arrived, is known as *arrival draft.* The term, "arrival," definitely refers to the shipment; the word, "sight," in *sight draft,* refers to the bill of exchange as a credit instrument. Various factors affected the creation of this type of sight draft. Firstly, since the inauguration of airmail services, many importers had to effect payment prior to the arrival of the merchandise. This situation was regarded as unfair, inasmuch as prior to the use of airmail services, the shipping and collection of documents, received by steamer, were presented for taking up the draft shortly after the goods had arrived. Moreover, some countries completely prohibit the granting of exchange until goods have been nationalized, and permit only a provisional deposit in local currency. In these cases, the importer is usually responsible for any exchange differential. Nowadays, even in markets where neither dollar shortage nor any other import restriction exists, almost all importers pay the sight draft upon the goods safe arrival.

Finally, the so-called *interest bearing draft* requires the drawee to pay interest at the current rate from the date of the draft to the approximate date that remittance is received by the drawer. Other things being equal, the exporter can sell this draft for the face amount, without deductions.

Financial Symbols. The various methods of collection under demand or time drafts on one hand, and the different requirements as to the transfer or employment of shipping documents in connection with the payment or acceptance of drafts, on the other, have led to the usage of certain standard designations or symbols. Illustrative of these symbols are:

A/S = After sight;

D/A = Document against acceptance;

D/D = Demand Draft;

D/P = Documents against payment;

S/D B/L = Sight draft, bill of lading attached;

30 days S/D-D/A = Draft payable 30 days after presentation and acceptance, documents delivered against acceptance;

60 days D/D-D/A = Draft payable 60 days after date, documents against acceptance.

DRAFT COLLECTION PROCEDURE

All documents required for banking transaction must be in perfect order. If any real or fancied error or discrepancy between evidences of shipments and details of the buyer's order has crept into this set of documents, the consignee will complain promptly to the shipper and, consequently, to the "guilty" forwarder or the banks involved. He might even refuse to accept the documents for banking collection, so the need for accuracy can not be over-emphasized.

Points which must be considered in the instructions to the bank are essentially:

1. Description of the draft and documents attached: (a) number of drafts, (b) date, (c) amount, (d) usance, that is, the number of days after sight, or sight when draft matures, (e) name of the drawer, (f) name and address of the drawee, (g) number of copies of the draft, (h) number of copies of bill of lading, (i) insurance certificates, (j) commercial invoices, (k) consular invoices, or certificates of origin, if required, (l) any special certificates or documents necessary for the particular shipment, (m) the name of the vessel by which the documents should be forwarded, and its sailing date.

2. Whether or not the documents conveying title to the goods are to be surrendered against acceptance of the draft, or only against

payment; in the case of sight drafts, the acceptance instructions are unnecessary.

3. Whether acceptance or payment may or may not be deferred until the arrival of the goods, even in the event that the documents reach the collecting bank at destination and are presented to the drawee.

4. Whether the drawee may or may not inspect the goods before acceptance of the draft.

5. Whether or not the bank at the foreign destination shall file protest for nonacceptance or for nonpayment of the draft upon presentation.

6. Whether or not the drawer shall be notified by cable of nonacceptance or nonpayment.

7. Whether or not the drawer shall be notified by cable when the draft is paid.

8. Whether or not the drawee is to be allowed an interest rebate if he pays the draft before maturity; if such allowance is to be made, at what rate per annum.

9. Whether or not interest and collection charges are to be borne by the drawer or by the drawee; and whether or not such charges (if for the account of the drawee) are to be waived if payment is refused.

10. Whether remittance of the proceeds of the draft is to be made by mail or by cable.

11. Full instructions as to the disposition of goods in the event that the draft is dishonored.

12. Whether or not in case of difficulties arising in connection with the collection of the draft, the foreign bank is to communicate with some local representative of the drawer. "In case of need refer to: (name and address)": a. whose instructions with respect to this draft and documents (if any) you are authorized to follow; b. who will assist in having the drawee honor the draft as drawn, and c. who is empowered to grant delays or extensions not exceeding____days or reductions not exceeding____per cent of the value of the merchandise.

In handling the collection for shipper's invoice value, the forwarder is guided mainly by the instructions he receives from the exporter, as laid down in the shipping instruction form. He also has to consider general standing instructions from consignees, which govern the handling of their shipments with regard to the collecting bank in the country of destination. In cases where shippers collect on open account or clean draft basis, the forwarder is relieved of any attendance with regard to the collection of merchandise value. He will have to collect only his own expenses, either by drawing on sight, documents attached, or, if the consignee is a reliable account of the forwarder, simply by sending his bill of charges.

Whenever shippers wish to collect their invoice value on sight draft or time draft basis, and desire to exercise control over their goods until the draft has been paid or accepted, the covering shipping documents must be attached for protection purposes. This procedure may cause certain difficulties if shippers should decline to advance or prepay incurring expenses on ocean freight, insurance, and other charges, on the ground that the goods were sold on f.o.b. factory or on f.a.s. port of exit terms; nonetheless, they want the controlling documents for attachment to their draft. On the other hand, the forwarder is entitled by custom either to ask for prepayment of his outlays on freight, insurance, and other charges, or to retain the controlling documents to protect his draft drawn against the consignee and covering the amount of his bill of charges. Under the former circumstances, the forwarder will suggest that the shipper forward his draft in blank to him, to be completed by the forwarder for shipper's invoice amount and his charges. The charges are billed to the shipper, who will be remitted the total collection amount, as the draft is drawn in his name.

After receiving the collection documents either from the forwarder or the exporter, the American bank completely records and mails them to its own, or designated foreign correspondent, with the attendant instructions, simultaneously furnishing the deliverer (forwarder or exporter) an acknowledgment. Later, an advice regarding acceptance and payment of draft is sent. Collection charges are usually for the account of the drawee. These fees run unreasonably high in some countries, particularly in Latin America. This fact induces many importers to refuse their payment, and exporters consequently must absorb them. As no uniform practice exists with respect to those incidental charges such as collection, stamp, and remittance taxes, exporters benefit by completing advance arrangements with their clients. Operating on this policy will avoid both delays in remittance and deductions from their principal amounts.

REJECTED DOCUMENTS—PROTESTING DRAFTS— MORAL SUASION—ARBITRATION

Rejection of acceptance or payment of drafts seldom occurs, as ordinarily foreign importers invariably honor their obligations.

Rejection might be caused by a sudden deterioration of the market situation caused by financial or political upheavals. Conceivably, this circumstance might make an extension of presentment or payment of the draft desirable. Refusal to accept or pay sometimes is based on the fact that the goods do not conform to the specifications contained in the order. In all cases, great skill and sound judgment is needed in the adjustment of delinquent or disputed export accounts. Overdue bills, for which draft payment has been refused, may be protested, particularly when the buyer's good faith or financial position is in question. Due deliberation should precede this drastic step, for to recover the debt, subsequent legal action must be sustained.

Modern business thinking, however, prefers non-legal methods, believing them usually to be more effective and practical in the collection of export receivables. Moral suasion and arbitration, as a means of solving serious trade disputes without losing the client's good will, are forward-looking measures.

The Inter-American Commercial Arbitration Commission, with headquarters in New York, and allied branches abroad, is the United States organization which was established for the purpose of advancing both the knowledge and use of voluntary arbitration. Serving as an intermediary between seller and buyer, this group's decisions are recognized here and in many countries overseas. Consequently, the sales contracts of most exporters provide that any disagreements be submitted for arbitration to this commission. This group serves a genuine need, since the average foreign trader lacks the facilities and experts required to protect him against the adverse occurrences which cause disputes. Additionally, he cannot afford costly foreign litigation, which could wipe out his anticipated profits and threaten his future business.

CHAPTER XXIII

Commercial Letters of Credit

Stimulated by the widespread imposition of import and export controls, an emergent trend has been the acceleration of requests for foreign buyers to establish commercial letters of credit, as the preferred form of export financing. Resulting from disadvantageous trade balances with the United States, these trade restrictions are operative in many countries.

Defined as an undertaking by a bank on behalf of the foreign buyer, an *export letter of credit* assures payment up to a certain sum of money to the beneficiary, on compliance with stipulated requirements, evidencing the shipment of the described goods on or before a fixed expiration date. The beneficiary of these transactions ordinarily is the seller. Requirements for commercial letters of credit usually imply the presentation of specified and qualified documents.

PARTIES INVOLVED

Procedurally, the transaction ensues thus: the importer abroad (the opener) purchases a letter of credit from his bank (*the issuing bank*), on strength of which there is established in some American bank (*the notifying bank*) a fund to the credit of the buyer, against which he may authorize the exporter (*seller or beneficiary*) to draw drafts for goods ordered by the buyer and shipped by the seller. When the beneficiary receives the credit advice directly from the foreign bank, without the intermediary of an American banking institution, the *notifying bank* and *issuing bank* are the same. Rarely occurring, except when the issuing bank instructs a branch in this country to notify, accept, and pay the exporter's draft, this situation effectuates the American subsidiary acting as a notifying and negotiating agent. Further distinction must be delineated between a *negotiating, notifying* and *paying bank,* on the one hand, and a *confirming bank,* on the other. In the first instance, the American bank serves only as an advising medium of the foreign principal; in the latter case, the issuing bank has arranged with the notifying and paying American bank to add its own confirmation to the letter of credit.

When requesting his bank to establish a letter of credit in favor of his American supplier, the foreign buyer will base his application on the nature of the transaction, as agreed upon in the sales contract.

Accompanying his request will be details regarding the goods to be shipped, the amount to be paid, the documents required, and the validity or expiry date to be set. With this information at its disposal, the issuing bank will draw up the letter of credit, including the pertinent terms and conditions, and forward it to its correspondent in the United States. Not having any direct contact with the foreign buyer, or any knowledge of the transaction involved, the American bank cannot waive or modify the terms or conditions stipulated in the credit, unless authorized by its principal abroad. Occasionally, if the letter of credit were to conflict with certain stipulations of the sales contract, the exporter would be placed in an equivocal situation, which would, nevertheless, cause consternation.

Appraised objectively, the institution of the letter of credit attains emphatic significance. Affording a dual protection, not available alternatively in export financing transactions, it assures payment to the beneficiary if he complies with the terms and assures the importer that the shipper will not receive payment until he submits valid documents evidencing shipment, as required. Notably, a letter of credit is not a merchandise guarantee, as it is an undertaking relating solely to documents; nor does it pretend to protect either buyer or seller against frauds, with respect to documentation or merchandise.

TYPES OF EXPORT LETTERS OF CREDIT

Letters of Credit are usually divided into four categories:

1. *An irrevocable letter of credit issued by a foreign bank.* Under this type of credit, the foreign issuer has an arrangment with the U. S. bank, which advises the details to the beneficiary and adds its own confirmation or liability. Included in the letter of credit, this confirmation is formulated thus: "We confirm the credit and undertake that all drafts drawn and presented in accordance with its terms will be duly honored." Constituting an irrevocable undertaking by the American bank, this statement thereby increases the exporter's protection.

2. *An irrevocable letter of credit issued by a United States bank.* This instrument differs from the type just discussed, only insofar as it carries the obligation of one bank, the American bank. By issuing its own irrevocable letter of credit, the U. S. bank can eleminate its own confirmation. Demonstrating the contrast, the opening statement of the letter of credit issued by a foreign bank reads: "We are instructed by X = bank to inform you that *they have established their* irrevocable letter of credit No. . . . ." Conversely, a letter of credit established by the American bank commences: "In accordance with instructions received from the X = bank, *we have established our* irrevocable letter of credit No. . . . ."

3. *An irrevocable letter of credit issued by a foreign bank, but unconfirmed by the American bank.* Here, the latter acts merely as a

IRVING TRUST COMPANY

ONE WALL STREET
NEW YORK 15, N. Y.

Confirmed Irrevocable
Credit No. 0014/268

Dated July 15, 1956

General Export Corporation
65 Main Street
New York 11, New York

Gentlemen:

We are informed by Banco Comercial de Bogóta, Bogota, Colombia

that they have issued their Irrevocable Credit No.   268   in your favor, to the extent of -
$10,000.00 (Ten Thousand Dollars)- -

for account of Importadores Fernandez Cia., Bogota, Colombia
available by your drafts on us at   sight   accompanied by the following documents (complete sets unless otherwise stated) evidencing shipment(s) of:
Complete portable chlorinators for aqueducts, FOB Vessel New York, from New York to
Barranquilla.

Copy of invoice.

Copy of Consular Invoice including Certificate of Origin and mentioning Import Permit
Number 90143.

Copy of your airmail letter to Seguros Int_____ ___ ____ __ S.A., Bogota, stating the details
of shipment necessary for insurance purposes.

Non-negotiable copy of onboard ocean bill of lading issued to order of Embarcadores
Nacional S.A., Barranquilla, Colombia.

Copy of your airmail letter to Embarcadores Nacional S.A., Barranquilla, Colombia, enclosing the originals of the invoice, consular invoice, including certificate of origin, and
onboard ocean bills of lading.

I

Drafts must clearly specify the number of this credit, and be presented at this Company not later
than   September 15, 1956.
Except so far as otherwise expressly stated, this credit is subject to the Uniform Customs and Practice
for Commercial Documentary Credits fixed by the Thirteenth Congress of the International Chamber
of Commerce. For the definitions of certain export quotations reference is made to the general descriptions of those terms included in the "Revised American Foreign Trade Definitions, 1941." Any amendment of the terms of this credit must be in writing over an authorized signature of this Company.
The above mentioned correspondent engages with you that all drafts drawn in conformity with the conditions
of this credit will be duly honored. At the request of our correspondent we confirm their credit and also engage
with you that drafts drawn in conformity with the conditions of this credit will be duly honored by us.

Note
*Documents must conform strictly with the terms of
this Credit. If you are unable to comply with its terms,
please communicate with us and/or your customer
promptly with a view to having the conditions changed.*
*I-1129 (5-56)

Yours very truly,

Authorized Signature

Confirmed Irrevocable Letter of Credit Issued by a Foreign Bank

notifier and payor on behalf of the foreign bank, without assuming
any obligation of its own. This form of credit does not afford genuine
protection to the beneficiary. To evidence non-confirmation, it is
customary for the American bank to indicate in such a letter of credit
a clause, which may read similarly to: "This letter is solely an advice
and conveys no engagement on our part." Reformulated, this state-

The Chase Manhattan Bank

New   York

INTERNATIONAL DEPARTMENT
18 PINE STREET
NEW YORK 15, N. Y.

CORRESPONDENT'S IRREVOCABLE STRAIGHT CREDIT ·   April 20, 19**

┌   ┐
    American Cotton Export Co.   ADVICE NO. E-89052
    4900 Broadway
    New York, N. Y.   SPECIMEN
└   ┘

GENTLEMEN:
  WE ARE INSTRUCTED BY The Imperial Bank of Bombay, Bombay, India.......

TO ADVISE YOU THAT THEY HAVE OPENED THEIR IRREVOCABLE CREDIT IN YOUR FAVOR FOR ACCOUNT OF
  Mohamed & Co., Ltd., Bombay, India ....
UNDER THEIR CREDIT NUMBER 45676   FOR A SUM OR SUMS NOT EXCEEDING A TOTAL OF
  US$20,000.00 (TWENTY THOUSAND U.S. DOLLARS)......................

AVAILABLE BY YOUR DRAFTS ON US AT sight D/P without recourse to you in duplicate

TO BE ACCOMPANIED BY

  Commercial invoice in triplicate - signed, describing the merchandise
  as shown below,

  Negotiable marine insurance policy and/or underwriter's certificate,
  including war risks, endorsed in blank, showing steamer named in bill
  of lading and/or other steamer or steamers,

  Full set of on board ocean steamer bills of lading to order of shipper,
  blank endorsed, marked "FREIGHT PREPAID",

  evidencing shipment of 55,000 (fifty five thousand) yards of cotton
  textiles C.I.F. Bombay from any U.S.A. port.

ALL DRAFTS SO DRAWN MUST BE MARKED "DRAWN UNDER CHASE MANHATTAN BANK ADVICE NO. E -89052 "

  THE ABOVE MENTIONED CORRESPONDENT ENGAGES WITH YOU THAT ALL DRAFTS DRAWN UNDER AND
IN COMPLIANCE WITH THE TERMS OF THIS ADVICE WILL BE DULY HONORED ON DELIVERY OF DOCUMENTS
AS SPECIFIED IF PRESENTED AT THIS OFFICE ON OR BEFORE June 30, 19**
  EXCEPT SO FAR AS OTHERWISE EXPRESSLY STATED, THIS ADVICE IS SUBJECT TO THE UNIFORM
CUSTOMS AND PRACTICE FOR COMMERCIAL DOCUMENTARY CREDITS FIXED BY THE THIRTEENTH CONGRESS
OF THE INTERNATIONAL CHAMBER OF COMMERCE.
  *THIS LETTER IS SOLELY AN ADVICE OF CREDIT OPENED BY THE ABOVE MENTIONED CORRESPONDENT AND
CONVEYS NO ENGAGEMENT BY US.*

YOURS VERY TRULY,

ASSISTANT TREASURER
ASSISTANT VICE PRESIDENT
PER PROCURATION

Unconfirmed Irrevocable Letter of Credit Issued by a Foreign Bank

ment explicitly implies that, if upon presentation of proper documents
the American bank refuses to make payment, the beneficiary would
have no recourse therefrom, and would have to apply to the foreign
bank for satisfaction.

4. *A revocable letter of credit, also unconfirmed by the American
bank.* Lacking any assurance of payment, because it can be modified

MORGAN GUARANTY TRUST COMPANY
OF NEW YORK
INTERNATIONAL BANKING DIVISION
23 WALL STREET, NEW YORK 8, N. Y.   April 2, 19*

Raw Cotton Export Co.
Houston
Texas

> EXPORT CREDIT No. R-532744

Dear Sirs:

In accordance with instructions received from

Commercial Bank of London, Ltd., London, England (their No. 79328) . . . .

we have established a REVOCABLE credit in your favor for account of Green & Buckley Textile Co.,Ltd.,
London, England

for U.S.$65,000.00 (SIXTY FIVE THOUSAND U.S.DOLLARS) . . . .

available by your drafts at sight on us, accompanied by documents consisting of:

Commercial Invoice in triplicate, describing the merchandise as indicated below

Full set of on board ocean steamer Bills of Lading to order of shipper, blank endorsed,
marked "Freight Prepaid",

evidencing shipment of 500 (five hundred) bales of COTTON, middling 7/8 inch, from U.S.
to C and F United Kingdom.

Except as otherwise expressly stated herein, this credit is subject to the Uniform Customs and Practice
for Documentary Credits (1962 Revision), International Chamber of Commerce, Brochure No. 222.

THIS CREDIT IS SUBJECT TO REVOCATION OR MODIFICATION AT ANY TIME, EITHER BEFORE OR AFTER
PRESENTMENT OF DOCUMENTS, AND WITHOUT NOTICE TO YOU.
Drafts and documents must be presented to our Commercial Credits Department, 55 Exchange Place,
New York 8, N. Y., on or before July 15,19*   on which date this credit expires UNLESS SOONER
REVOKED.

SPECIMEN   **SPECIMEN**

Yours very truly,

Authorized Signature   Authorized Signature

Immediately upon receipt please examine this credit, and if its terms are not clear to
you or if you need any assistance in respect to your availment of it, we would welcome your
communicating with us. Documents should be presented promptly and not later than 3 P.M.

Unconfirmed Revocable Letter of Credit

at any time, or even cancelled without notice, this instrument is employed less frequently. The corresponding notation in such a letter of
credit may read: "This credit is subject to revocation or modification
at any time either before or after presentation of documents, and
without notice."

When an American bank issues its own letter of credit, instead of
adding its confirmation to the opening bank's irrevocable instrument,

it may contain the following: "We hereby engage with the drawers, endorsers and bona fide holders of drafts drawn under and in compliance with the terms of this credit that the same shall be duly honored on due presentation and delivery of documents as specified if negotiated, etc." Known as negotiation, this procedure permits the presentation of drafts through other channels. For example: instead of the beneficiary collecting directly, he may receive the proceeds through his own bankers with whom he usually deals. The alternate form of confirmation, requiring presentation for payment at the advising bank only, is customarily referred to as a *straight letter of credit*.

Virtually all letters of credit issued or advised by American banks refer to: (1) The Uniform Customs and Practice for Documentary Credits (1962 Revision); the International Chamber of Commerce Brochure No. 222, adopted by the United States banks which have subscribed to these regulations, as of July 1st, 1963, and (2) Revised American Foreign Trade Definitions—1941.

Virtually an integral part of every letter of credit, both regulations contain interpretations and clarifications of all pertinent banking and shipping terms and conditions. They constitute a standard for the foreign trader, and proper application of their provisions can help avert numerous documentary exceptions and consequent irritation to beneficiaries of letters of credit.

Letters of credit represent the most intricate form of payment. Perception reveals why bankers achieve the anomalous repute of being technical when they refuse to effect payment under letters of credit against presentation of documents deemed incompatible with the stipulated requirements! Nevertheless, the confirming bank is fully responsible to its principal, the opening bank; and no technical, or other, deviations from the provisions of the letter of credit would incur which, in the final analysis, could jeopardize the rights and position of the importer abroad. Minor exceptions will not pose consequential problems if responsible traders are involved in the transaction. Sanctioned by experience, confirming banks can have confidence in their good judgment that their action, making payments, will be approved by the opening bank and its client. When doubt exists, the confirming bank should secure permission from its principal to pay the document as presented.

To obtain payment, the various stipulations in the letter of credit relevant to the preparation of ocean bills of lading, consular documents, merchandise, prices, invoicing and other details must be effected in strict accordance with the stated conditions. When a consignment is handled under the terms of letters of credit, exporters rely extensively on the skill and experience of their shipping agents. The forwarder, therefore, first will check whether the amount indicated therein is sufficient to cover the shipper's invoice value and all shipping expenses. He must verify, also, whether he can comply with the stipulated conditions before arranging for exportation. Any deficiency which hinders full compliance with the terms must be reported promptly to the shipper for transmittal to the bank concerned, in order to amend the credit instrument accordingly.

Documents usually required on letter of credit shipments must be tendered to the bank either by the forwarding house, if it acts as the shipper's agent, or by the exporter himself. These documents are:

1. Three original bills of lading, endorsed by the forwarder, if the shipment was made in his name; and, further indorsed by him, in the shipper's name, if he submits the documents directly.

2. Several memoranda of copies of bills of lading (need not be endorsed).

3. Two original marine (and war) risk insurance certificates, endorsed by him and for account of the seller; or, if insurance is covered by the buyer, a corresponding advice to his underwriter.

4. Three copies (original and two copies) of the commercial invoice.

5. Consular invoices (original and, sometimes, one additional copy) and certificates of origin, when required.

6. Drafts, in duplicate, payable to the order of the seller.

The forwarder will have to verify that the ocean bills of lading are clean, bearing no notations qualifying their apparent good order and condition, and that they are not stale because of lapse of time. Most credits require in some manner that shipments be forwarded prepaid to overseas destination. Therefore, the payment of incurring charges, such as ocean freight and insurance, will have to be proved. Proof is established by presenting to the bank ocean bills of lading, carrying the prepaid stamp, unless ocean freight must be on a collect basis under regulations of the destination country, and the forwarder's bill of charges covering all transportation and insurance expenses, which will be added, sometimes, to the shipper's invoice.

Banking the necessary documents through the forwarding house engenders this collection procedure:

1. Six copies of the bill of charges are prepared in accordance with the top sheet of the shipping file. In case of prepayment of charges, one original and three copies go to the shipper or the bank; the fourth and fifth copies, to the consignee for customs clearance purposes; the sixth, to the accounting department. In case of charges *collect*, one original and four copies go to the consignee; the fifth copy to the shipper; the sixth, to the accounting department.

2. The shipper's draft, when in blank, is completed. If the forwarder is requested to collect for the shipper's account, he prepares the draft in the shipper's name, in accordance with instructions.

3. The instruction sheet to the bank is prepared. It enumerates the enclosed documents and the details regarding protest, collection

IRVING TRUST COMPANY
NEW YORK, N. Y.

DATE __JULY 15, 1956__

GENTLEMEN:

WE ENCLOSE [X] FOR COLLECTION / [ ] FOR NEGOTIATION   THE DRAFT(S) DESCRIBED BELOW:

				DOCUMENTS ATTACHED				
NUMBER	DRAWN ON	TENOR	AMOUNT	B/L	INV.	INS.	CONS.	MISC.
268	IMPORTADORES FERNANDEZ CIA., BOGOTA, COLOMBIA	SIGHT	$10,000.00	3	3	2	1	3P/L

SPECIMEN

PLEASE FOLLOW INSTRUCTIONS INDICATED BELOW:

[X] FORWARD DOCUMENTS VIA AIRMAIL. POSTAGE FOR [X] A/C DRAWEE / [ ] A/C DRAWER

[X] PRESENT ON ARRIVAL OF VESSEL CARRYING GOODS.

[ ] DELIVER DOCUMENTS TO DRAWEE ON ACCEPTANCE.

[X] DELIVER DOCUMENTS TO DRAWEE ON PAYMENT.

[ ] PROTEST FOR NONACCEPTANCE.

[ ] PROTEST FOR NONPAYMENT.

[X] DO NOT PROTEST.

[ ] NONACCEPTANCE TO BE ADVISED BY [ ] AIRMAIL / [ ] CABLE

[X] NONPAYMENT TO BE ADVISED BY [X] AIRMAIL / [ ] CABLE

[X] INCUR NO CABLE EXPENSES.

[ ] WAIVE CHARGES IF REFUSED.

[X] DO NOT WAIVE CHARGES IF REFUSED BY DRAWEE.

[ ] PAYMENT TO BE ADVISED BY CABLE.

[X] HAVE PROCEEDS REMITTED BY [X] AIRMAIL / [ ] CABLE : CHARGES FOR [ ] OURSELVES / [X] DRAWEES

[X] IN THE EVENT U. S. DOLLAR EXCHANGE IS NOT IMMEDIATELY OBTAINABLE A PROVISIONAL DEPOSIT IN LOCAL CURRENCY MAY BE ACCEPTED WITH DRAWEES WRITTEN UNDERTAKING TO ASSUME FULL RESPONSIBILITY FOR ALL EXCHANGE RISK AND TO TAKE SUCH STEPS WITH THEIR EXCHANGE CONTROL AUTHORITIES AS MAY BE NECESSARY TO BRING ABOUT FINAL SETTLEMENT IN U. S. DOLLARS AT THE EARLIEST POSSIBLE DATE.

REBATE AT THE RATE OF_____% P. A. MAY BE ALLOWED FOR ANTICIPATION.

COLLECT INTEREST AT THE RATE OF__5__% P. A. FROM DATE OF DRAFT (JULY 15, 1956) TO ARRIVAL OF FUNDS IN NEW YORK

[ ] WE WILL / [X] DRAWEES PAY COLLECTION CHARGES.

TRANSMIT DRAFT AND DOCUMENTS TO [ ] YOUR CORRESPONDENT [X] BANCO COMERCIAL DE BOGOTA, BOGOTA-COLOMBIA FOR COLLECTION.

IN CASE OF NEED REFER TO__JUAN DIXON, APARTADO 2312, BOGOTA__

[X] WHOSE AUTHORITY IS LIMITED TO SECURING HONOR OF DRAFT AS SHOWN.

[ ] WHOSE INSTRUCTIONS YOUR CORRESPONDENTS ARE AUTHORIZED TO FOLLOW WITHOUT RESERVE.

SPECIAL INSTRUCTIONS__KINDLY INSTRUCT COLLECTING BANK TO ADVISE YOU BY AIRMAIL IMMEDIATELY AFTER DRAWEE PAYS IN LOCAL CURRENCY, DATE REGISTERED WITH F.X. CONTROL AUTHORITIES.__

IN CASE OF NEGOTIATION, YOU MAY REQUEST ADVICE OF DISHONOR BY CABLE AT OUR EXPENSE ON ITEMS OVER $1,000 OR EQUIVALENT.

IN RECEIVING ANY ITEM HEREIN MENTIONED AND FORWARDING IT FOR COLLECTION TO THE BANK OR OTHER PARTY DESIGNATED ABOVE, OR TO ANY CORRESPONDENT SELECTED BY YOU WITH REASONABLE CARE, YOU SHALL NOT BE RESPONSIBLE FOR ANY ACT, OMISSION, DEFAULT, SUSPENSION, INSOLVENCY OR BANKRUPTCY OF ANY SUCH COLLECTING AGENT, OR SUB-AGENT THEREOF, OR FOR ANY DELAY IN REMITTANCE, LOSS IN EXCHANGE, OR LOSS OF ITEM OR ITS PROCEEDS DURING TRANSMISSION OR IN THE COURSE OF COLLECTION, BUT YOUR RESPONSIBILITY SHALL BE ONLY FOR YOUR OWN RISK.

THIS COPY TO BE SENT TO **IRVING TRUST COMPANY**	VERY TRULY YOURS GENERAL EXPORT CORPORATION BY _____ (AUTHORIZED SIGNATURE)

D 582/00 (1-56)

Customers Letter of Instruction for Foreign Collections

AIR MAIL   CRQ   IRVING TRUST COMPANY   EJG

STANDING INSTRUCTIONS
(unless otherwise noted on face hereof)

1. If necessary, please guarantee delivery of documents listed on the face hereof.

2. Advise fate promptly by AIR MAIL giving reasons for any delay in acceptance or payment.

3. In the event of dishonor of items over $1,000 or equivalent, cable us stating reasons.

4. Present on receipt.

INSTRUCTIONS REGARDING PROVISIONAL DEPOSITS

If so indicated on the face hereof, a provisional deposit in local currency may be accepted with drawees *written undertaking* to assume full responsibility for all exchange risk and to take such steps with your Exchange Control Authorities as may be necessary to bring about final settlement in U. S. Dollars at the earliest possible date, in the event U. S. Dollar exchange is not immediately obtainable.

PLEASE COLLECT YOUR CHARGES INCLUDING COST OF YOUR AIRMAIL REMITTANCE FROM DRAWEE PLUS OUR COMMISSION.‖₁₀‰AND $0.50 POSTAGE FOR US.

Instructions to Collecting Bank

charges, discounts and allowances, delivery of documents, and the action to be taken if the draft is not accepted or paid.

4. A shipping notice is sent to either the buyer or the seller, advising him as to the steamer on which the goods cleared. This advice also includes any further data or documents, such as, canceled import license, or originals or copies of bills of lading.

At this point, the shipping file is *split-up*. The documents are distributed and mailed in accordance with given instructions, to the parties involved—such as the bank, the buyer, or the seller—whereupon the file is transmitted to the accounting department to organize the financial records. Succeeding this phase, the shipping file is closed and put in its proper place. However, the forwarding agent is not yet discharged from his responsibility. Perhaps many months have passed, his bills have been paid and shipments have arrived at their destinations; however, it may now occur that delayed claims are arising within the due course of the statute of limitations and necessitate reopening the file. To reconstruct the record readily and accurately for any transaction to which the forwarder has been a party, the record must be available.

In addition to the four basic forms of commercial letter of credit as already discussed, there are a number of adaptations which merit brief attention.

A so-called *Red Clause Credit* is a confirmed irrevocable credit which is arranged and applied for when a particularly large order is being executed in stages. Progress payments, corresponding to the respective stages, are made against certification by the beneficiary that the required portion has been completed. Upon shipment of the balance of the order, the beneficiary presents his draft, with the stipulated documents, for collection of the final amount.

A *Revolving Credit* may assume different forms. However the basic concept is that the amount originally drawn by the beneficiary will recur in availability within the time limits and credit terms. To exemplify: Several years ago, a hospital in Colombia, South America, was to be established over a period of 18 months. Available funds were insufficient to cover the total project; they were based on a continuous inflow through collections and contributions. To obviate the establishment of innumerable separate credits, the hospital foundation requested the various American suppliers to submit their invoices for payment to a reputable foreign freight forwarding house, in whose name a revolving credit had been opened. Whenever a shipment was made, the forwarder drew against the credit and effected payment to the supplier.

An *Assignable letter of credit* is usually irrevocable and confirmed. Providing as beneficiary a definite named party, plus an assignee, it reads, for instance: "John Doe and Company or Assignees." Under this type of credit, the named beneficiary is in a position to assign his interest to another party, or arrange for the establishment of a secondary *Back to Back* credit. Requiring identical documentary terms and conditions as stipulated in the basic credit, except for an earlier expiry date, the Back to Back credit is drawn for a lesser amount, and in favor of a third party.

Letters of credit opened for an *about* or *approximate* amount, or quantity, indicate that the exporter is entitled to draw, or ship, up to 10% in excess of the stipulated figures.

With respect to partial shipments, banks are permitted to pay, accept, and negotiate for same, unless expressly prohibited under the terms of the credit.

AUTHORITY TO PURCHASE. AUTHORITY TO PAY

Although in some respects similar to a letter of credit the *Authority to Purchase* differs from the letter of credit in that it authorizes the

FORM A

FIRST NATIONAL CITY BANK

CABLE ADDRESS "CITIBANK"

399 PARK AVENUE, NEW YORK, N.Y. 10022

ADVICE OF AUTHORITY TO PAY

NEW YORK   May 1,1963

An American Corporation
100 Main Street
Dallas, Texas

> ALL DRAFTS DRAWN MUST BE MARKED:
> DRAWN AS PER ADVICE   CCF 10500

DEAR SIRS:

WE ADVISE YOU THAT   A Milan Bank, Milan, Italy

HAVE AUTHORIZED US TO HONOR YOUR DRAFTS UNDER THEIR CREDIT NO   2114

FOR ACCOUNT OF   A Milan Company, Milan, Italy

FOR A SUM OR SUMS NOT EXCEEDING A TOTAL OF $18,000.00 (Eighteen thousand dollars)

TO BE DRAWN AT   sight   ON US TO BE ACCOMPANIED BY

1. Full set on board ocean bills of lading issued to order blank endorsed evidencing shipment from U.S.A. port to Genoa dated latest June 30,1963. Partial shipments not permitted.

2. Marine and war risk insurance certificate in full set.

3. Certificate of origin.

4. Commercial invoice in triplicate stating it covers 50,000 lbs U.S.A. raw cotton, U.S. strict middling 1-1/32" Texas growth cif Genoa.

DRAFTS SO DRAWN, WITH DOCUMENTS AS SPECIFIED, MUST BE PRESENTED AT THIS OFFICE
NOT LATER THAN July 9,1963 unless sooner revoked.

THIS ADVICE IS SUBJECT TO THE UNIFORM CUSTOMS AND PRACTICE FOR DOCUMENTARY CREDITS (1962 REVISION), INTERNATIONAL CHAMBER OF COMMERCE BROCHURE NO. 222.

THIS ADVICE, WHICH IS SUBJECT TO REVOCATION OR MODIFICATION AT ANY TIME WITHOUT NOTICE TO YOU, CONVEYS NO ENGAGEMENT ON OUR PART OR ON THE PART OF THE ABOVE MENTIONED CORRESPONDENT AND IS SIMPLY FOR YOUR GUIDANCE IN PREPARING AND PRESENTING DRAFTS AND DOCUMENTS.

YOURS VERY TRULY,

COM 512 (L) REV. 3-68

AUTHORIZED SIGNATURE

Advice of Authority to Pay

American bank to purchase for the account of the foreign bank the documentary drafts of the beneficiary, drawn *With Recourse*. This means that the seller (drawer) remains liable until his draft has been paid by the buyer (drawee).

Occasionally *Authority to Pay* is used in connection with export shipments. It incurs no obligation to either the foreign or American bank. This credit instrument merely advises the shipper, or beneficiary of a revocable and unconfirmed arrangement between buyer and foreign bank to pay or accept drafts which, upon payment by the advising bank, releases the drawer from liability.

TRUST RECEIPT

A *trust receipt* is a document signed by a buyer, on the strength of which a bank releases merchandise to him for the purpose of manufacture or sale, but retains title of the goods. The buyer obligates himself to maintain the identity of the goods—or the proceeds thereof —distinct from the rest of his assets, and to hold them subject to repossession by the bank.

Trust receipts are used extensively under letters of credit, so that the buyer may obtain possession of the goods before he has completed his credit contract with the issuing bank. They are also used extensively in the Far East, where it is customary to sell documents against payment on terms of 60 or 90 days. Under a trust receipt contract, the collecting bank permits buyers of good standing to clear the goods before the maturity date of the draft.

COMMON DISCREPANCIES IN CREDIT DOCUMENTS

Discrepancies in documents to be presented under letter of credit transactions are still a major factor in the rejection of shipping papers. These errors lead to interminable difficulties and delayed payment of drafts for all parties concerned.

These mistakes refer to invoices, bills of lading, consular documents, insurance certificates or declarations, packing lists, and so forth. Below, the most frequent irregularities are listed:

As to invoices:

1. Merchandise description does not agree with that indicated in the letter of credit.
2. Insufficient copies.
3. Excess drawing or excess quantity.
4. Not certified or notarized, as stipulated by the credit.
5. Omission of the price quotation specified in the credit, (F.O.B., F.A.S., or C.I.F.).
6. Shipping marks do not agree with those given in other documents.

As to Bill of Lading:

1. The goods are consigned to order of, instead of to a named consignee.

2. The "To order of Shipper" bill of lading is not endorsed.
3. The "On Board" notation is not signed, nor dated.
4. The bill of lading is "Stale;" this precludes its arrival at the port of discharge, before the steamer carrying the shipment arrives.
5. Notations qualifying the conditions of the goods as not being in good order, which thereby violate the requirement of presenting "Clean bills" of lading.
6. Shipment has been effected from a port, or to a destination, other than that stipulated.

As to Consular Documents:
1. Total kilos differ from those in the packing list.
2. Consignment deviates from that shown on the bill of lading.

As to Insurance:
1. The amount is insufficient.
2. Merchandise is not properly described.
3. The insurance policy is dated later than the date of the bills of lading.
4. The set of insurance papers is not complete; duplicate insurance policy missing.
5. The policy is not countersigned or endorsed.

As to Packing List:
1. Packages listed as cartons are described on the bill of lading as cases.
2. Error of conversion, of pounds into kilos.

Need for accuracy cannot be over-emphasized, although its implications frequently are under-estimated.

CHAPTER XXIV

Financing

Requirements for credit accommodation in commercial exports is more extensive than those in our domestic market. Although these factors vitally influence successful export efforts, they apply to our domestic economy to a limited extent. This topic was introduced in Chapter 22, which deals with the credit and payment terms entered into between exporters and importers, and will herewith be amplified.

Among those factors which mold our export credit and financing policy are: (1) Inadequate supply of banking capital in foreign countries; (2) underdeveloped business activity and organization; (3) distance and time; (4) currency fluctuations; (5) competition; and (6) desire to broaden the distribution of goods for exports.

Current developments in export financing take cognizance of a situation which arose during the early 1950's due to the recovery of Western Europe. Exportations of all the world's manufactured goods in 1955 consisted of almost 46 per cent which had originated in that trading area which only ten years ago was destitute. Plans have been prepared to assist the American exporter in grappling with this challenge.

With respect to long term financing, exporters may avail themselves of the services offered by the Export-Import Bank of Washington (EXIMBANK), established in 1934, an independent United States government agency. The functions of the Bank are limited to financing, guaranteeing, and insuring payment for goods and services of U.S. origin. As of the early 1960's, the Bank has increasingly emphasized its desire to offer medium-term guarantees and insurance for U.S. export sales through commercial banking and private insurance facilities. This was done to match similar services offered by other industrialized countries who had completely recovered from the ills of the postwar period, thus strengthening the potentialities of the American exporter and the U.S. balance of payments, leaving the actual handling of the export transactions in the hands of the commercial banks and the Foreign Credit Insurance Association (FCIA), an unincorporated private company of over 50 underwriters, established in 1962 in New York. Only if exporters are unable to secure assistance from the aforementioned entities, will the Eximbank take under consideration direct applications for the accommodation of comprehensive guarantees of, or participations in, credits.

C. C. HARTZELL, Chairman

EXECUTIVE OFFICE
ONE WHITEHALL STREET
NEW YORK, N. Y. 10004

D. C. ANDREWS & CO., INC.
FMB No. 717 FMC No. 922

New York, N. Y. 10004
One Whitehall Street
Whitehall 4-0780 (Area Code 212)

Charleston 5, South Carolina
24 Vendue Range
723-4582 (Area Code 803)

Detroit 26, Michigan
1348 Book Building
Woodward 1-1733 (Area Code 313)

D. C. ANDREWS & CO. OF ILLINOIS, INC.
FMB No. 1134 FMC No. 666

Chicago 4, Illinois
327 South La Salle Street
Wabash 2-1680 (Area Code 312)
Freight Terminal, 262 E. So. Water St.

Honolulu 7, Hawaii
177 South Queen Street
59960-59969

San Francisco 11, California
244 California Street
Douglas 2-0514 (Area Code 415)

D. C. Andrews & Co., Inc.
REPLY TO OFFICE AT:

SHIPPING DEPT. FILE

Date_____

DCA Ref._____

Buyer Order No._____

Your Order No._____

F. R. HARLOCKER, President

Cable Address: "BOCKAND"

D. C. ANDREWS & CO. OF LOUISIANA, INC.
FMB No. 1135 FMC No. 606

New Orleans 16, Louisiana
323 Chartres Street
Jackson 2-0341 (Area Code 504)

D. C. ANDREWS & CO. OF MARYLAND, INC.
FMB No. 1136 FMC No. 586

Baltimore 2, Maryland
403 Maryland Indemnity Bldg.
Saratoga 7-4550 (Area Code 301)

D. C. ANDREWS & CO. OF MASS.
FMB No. 1137 FMC No. 659

Boston 9, Massachusetts
131 State Street
Hubbard 2-7083 (Area Code 617)

LONDON E. C. 3, ENGLAND
Roman Wall House — Crutched Friars
LIVERPOOL, ENGLAND
48 Castle Street
NOTTINGHAM, ENGLAND
Alfred Street North
GLASGOW, SCOTLAND
136 Buchanan Street
BUENOS AIRES, ARGENTINA
Cerrito 388
RIO DE JANF   ?, BRAZIL
Caixa Postal   ; — ZC-00

Gentlemen:

We are pleased to confirm and will pay for the above order under conditions specified below:

Account of:

Specifications, quantity, quality and price of goods; marks, numbers and other pertinent data must be in accordance with the customers order and any changes must be approved by the customers.

Approximate Total Amount $_____

Immediately that shipment is ready contact our Mr._____for shipping instructions and please forward to his attention packing lists and_____copies of the commercial invoice. invoice prepared on the_____Customs form.

Export license, if required, valid for sufficient time to permit shipment, must accompany your invoice. Import license No._____ must appear on your invoice. Import license, if sent to you, must accompany your invoice. To conform with Import License requirements, merchandise must be described as:

Special Remarks:

Payment Terms:

Confirmation is subject to expiration by limitation on_____at which time material must be at seaboard available for shipment. If delivery cannot be accomplished by this time, notify us immediately and we will request authority to extend.

Anything herein to the contrary notwithstanding, this Company shall not be responsible if by reason of strikes, invasion, insurrection, blockade, interdict, war (whether declared or actual) riot, civil war, internal disturbance, commotion or military or usurped power or by order of any civil authority, or for any other similar reason this Company is rendered unable to complete the performance of any of its undertakings hereunder.

Yours very truly,

D. C. ANDREWS & CO., INC.

Approved_____

Per

Notice of Importers Funds on Hand

In addition to the Eximbank, there are a few other official lending institutions, some U.S. government owned, some internationally sponsored, whose task is to facilitate the promotion of U.S. exports. These agencies are:

1. The Agency for International Development (AID), set up in 1961, succeeding the International Cooperation Administration (ICA), the Development Loan Fund (DLF), the Food-for-Peace Program, and the local currency lending activities of the Eximbank, including the Alliance for Progress assistance.

2. The International Bank for Reconstruction and Development (IBRD), a United Nations Agency, also called World Bank, owned by its member countries (about 100), making loans to governments or individual enterprises in a member country as long as the country's government guarantees the loan.

3. The International Development Association (IDA), domiciled like the other mentioned agencies in Washington, D.C., created in 1960 by the World Bank, to assist in the economic growth of less developed member countries for projects which do not qualify for loans from the World Bank and for which financing on conventional terms is not available. As a prerequisite, the project must make a significant contribution to the economic development of the area in question, such as housing and municipal improvements.

4. The International Finance Corporation (IFC). An affiliate of the World Bank, established in 1956, was designed to invest exclusively and directly in privately owned enterprises, without government guaranty, to stimulate economic growth in its less developed member countries. I.F.C. investments have been made in such industrial enterprises as mining, processing and manufacturing.

5. The Inter-American Development Bank (IDB). This Bank, a hemispheric variation of the World Bank, founded in 1960 by the United States and 19 Latin American countries, assists exclusively the economic growth of its Latin American Members by providing financing and technical assistance for development needs.

6. The Private Export Funding Corporation (PEFCO). It was formed on the initiative of the Bankers Association for Foreign Trade (BAFT) to mobilize additional private capital to assist in financing U.S. exports with commercial banks and EXIMBANK and generally will take medium-term maturities. PEFCO, however, has complete flexibility to accept maturities over any length of an export credit. PEFCO purchases medium and long-term debt obligations of foreign importers of U.S. exports, and finances such purchases through the sale of PEFCO's own securities to private investors in the U.S. and abroad. EXIMBANK fully guarantees all debt obligations purchased by PEFCO.

In the field of intermediate and short-term financing, commercial banks and factors implement the requirements of individual credits on a case-by-case basis. Notably, this significant area, too, provides scope for the foreign freight forwarder to manifest his outstanding

EXECUTIVE OFFICE
ONE WHITEHALL STREET
NEW YORK, N. Y. 10004

D. C. ANDREWS & CO., INC.
FMB No. 717 FMC No. 922

New York, N. Y. 10004
One Whitehall Street
Whitehall 4-0780 (Area Code 212)

Charleston 5, South Carolina
24 Vendue Range
723-4582 (Area Code 803)

Detroit 26, Michigan
1348 Book Building
Woodward 1-1733 (Area Code 313)

D. C. ANDREWS & CO. OF ILLINOIS, INC.
FMB No. 1134 FMC No. 666

Chicago 4, Illinois
327 South La Salle Street
Wabash 2-1680 (Area Code 312)
Freight Terminal, 262 E. So. Water St.

Honolulu 7, Hawaii
177 South Queen Street
59960-59969

San Francisco 11, California
244 California Street
Douglas 2-0514 (Area Code 415)

Cable Address: "BOCKAND"

D. C. ANDREWS & CO. OF LOUISIANA, INC.
FMB No. 1135 FMC No. 606

New Orleans 16, Louisiana
323 Chartres Street
Jackson 2-0341 (Area Code 504)

D. C. ANDREWS & CO. OF MARYLAND, INC.
FMB No. 1136 FMC No. 586

Baltimore 2, Maryland
403 Maryland Indemnity Bldg.
Saratoga 7-4550 (Area Code 301)

D. C. ANDREWS & CO. OF MASS.
FMB No. 1137 FMC No. 659

Boston 9, Massachusetts
131 State Street
Hubbard 2-7083 (Area Code 617)

LONDON E. C. 3, ENGLAND
Roman Wall House — Crutched Friars
LIVERPOOL, ENGLAND
48 Castle Street
NOTTINGHAM, ENGLAND
Alfred Street North
GLASGOW, SCOTLAND
136 Buchanan Street
BUENOS AIRES, ARGENTINA
Cerrito 388
RIO DE JANEIRO, BRAZIL
Caixa Postal 3417 — ZC-00

D. C. Andrews & Co., Inc.
REPLY TO OFFICE AT:

ORIGINAL
LETTER OF CREDIT

Date_____

DCA Ref._____

Buyer Order No._____

Your Order No._____

Letter of Credit No._____

Gentlemen:

We are pleased to refer to the above order for the account of:

Invoice to: Approximate Amount $_____

Please note the following:

Specifications, quantity, quality and price of goods; marks, numbers and other pertinent data must be in accordance with the customers order and any changes must be approved by the customers.

Immediately that shipment is ready contact our Mr._____for shipping instructions and please forward

to his attention packing lists and_____copies of the commercial invoice. invoice prepared on the_____Customs form.

Please do not release the merchandise until you have received definite shipping instructions from us.

Export license, if required, valid for sufficient time to permit shipment, must accompany your invoice. Import license No._____ must appear on your invoice. Import license, if sent to you, must accompany your invoice. To conform with Letter of Credit and/or import license requirements, merchandise must be described as:

Special Remarks:

Payments — Letter of Credit has been established in our favor through_____ providing for payment against the presentation of certain shipping documents. We will arrange for the transportation and when such documents are obtained, present them to the bank for payment, MAKING REMITTANCE TO YOU AFTER SUCH PAYMENT HAS BEEN MADE TO US.

Confirmation is subject to expiration by limitation on_____, at which time material must be at seaboard available for shipment. If delivery cannot be accomplished by this time, notify us immediately and we will request authority to extend.

Anything herein to the contrary notwithstanding, this Company shall not be responsible if by reason of strikes, invasion, insurrection, blockade, interdict, war (whether declared or actual) riot, civil war, internal disturbance, commotion or military or usurped power or by order of any civil authority, or for any other similar reason this Company is rendered unable to complete the performance of any of its undertakings hereunder.

Yours very truly,

D. C. ANDREWS & CO., INC.

Approved

Per

Importers Letter of Credit in Favor of Forwarder

qualities as a coordinator and promoter of the free flow of freight in international commerce. Although definitely not bankers, forwarders assume a quasi-banking position when they assist in general their overseas clients or foreign importers. They deem this transposition to be an integral part of their complete service. Financing orders which are intended to be placed, or which they have placed, with American manufacturers furnishes them an additional opportunity to expedite export trade.

To extend his facilities to the realm of export finance the forwarder can resort to these three courses of action: (1) He may attend to quasi financing by utilizing funds or deposits on hand; (2) he applies letters of credit, established in his favor, drawn up for a particular transac-action; and (3) he may finance orders through his own means, or through factors.

IMPORTER'S FUNDS ON HAND

When the forwarder has an importer's funds available, he requests the seller or shipper to furnish him written evidence regarding the amount and the terms stipulated in the orders. Thereupon, executing the buyer's instructions, he will confirm payment under certain conditions, but usually only upon export clearance, or arrival of goods at seaboard. These terms are established for the buyer's protection, since the forwarder is obliged to secure the possession of the merchandise for the importer's account before payment is made. In exceptional cases, either by the insistence of a seller (but then with the explicit approval of the buyer), or upon the request of the importer abroad (whose terms of purchase provide for the advance payment), the forwarding agent will issue his confirmation of payment. This will provide remittance: upon the certificate of manufacture, or presentation of the commercial invoice; upon receipt of delivery order placing the goods at his disposal; or, upon receipt of a complete set of export shipping papers and goods.

IMPORTER'S LETTER OF CREDIT IN FAVOR OF FORWARDER

A type of payment arrangement that is usually made available to the forwarder by the foreign buyer to cover a particular transaction involving two or more American suppliers is called, an *Importer's Letter of Credit in Favor of Forwarder*. This instrument is utilized, also, when a series of orders is placed with a number of manufacturers whose delivery schedules extend beyond the usual period of regular commercial letters of credit. In the latter instance, a revolving letter of credit will have to be opened to satisfy the variable requirements and complications posed by the business. Proving its flexibility, this type or credit is operated in different ways. Firstly, the amount of the credit, when exhausted, renews itself to the original sum for further drawings. Secondly, as soon as shipments and corresponding drawings are made, which have utilized a certain amount, the sum withdrawn again becomes available, thus reinstating the amount of the credit to the original sum. Thirdly, drawings may be restricted to a fixed sum for each period of time, such as, a month during the life of the credit. If the monthly authorized sum is not wholly used, the balance is made available for further drawings; thereupon, the instrument is called a *cumulative letter of credit.*

Application of the usual type of letter of credit in favor of the forwarder will occur, for instance, on shipments of vehicles where the chassis is delivered by the automotive supplier and the equipment (dump body) from another manufacturer. The forwarder, attends to two separate payments, but independently combines the invoices of the different suppliers. The revolving or cumulative credit is used for large projects, such as, the shipments of a plant (steel mill, auto factory), extending over a period up to a year, and involving a considerable number of suppliers.

Under both types of credit, the forwarder agrees to make payment only when he receives the remittance from the bank, upon presentation of documents. Sound policy does not permit him to effect payment in advance, since this would freeze a large proportion of his own funds, which could exceed his financial capacity intermittently. Concretely illustrated, a railroad, longshoremen's or seamen's strike would catapult him into a situation of having funds advanced concomitant with expiring letters of credit, or at least encountering considerable delay in shipping and collection against the letters of credit.

THE FORWARDER IN THE ROLE OF BANKER
BY HIS OWN MEANS OR THROUGH FACTORS

Few forwarders are in a position to extend the service of being a banker by his own means or through factors. Their number is restricted to certain large, eminent firms, which are fortified by a strong capital position, and maintain an extensive network of branch offices on one or more continents. Export trade expansion, in general, is but one facet of their policy when they assume the role of banker. Correlative with this object is the more tangible factor of broadening the base of their general patronage, and increasing their business volume.

When considering the extension of credit abroad, the forwarder proceeds similarly to any other exporter. His sources of information about the reputation and financial ability of the customer are references obtained through New York banks which have developed extensive credit files; reports from his own branches; and correspondents or agencies, such as Dun and Bradstreet. The reports, among other details, cover the financial and organizational basis of the enterprise; the capitalization; the relative size; the integrity of the actual, or prospective, customer; and, the manner in which he, the buyer, meets his financial obligations. When considering the extension of credit or the financing of the importer's orders, the line of goods involved is an important factor in the forwarder's decision. Articles of high valuation are preferred to those in the lower-price bracket. Regular lines of goods that have general marketability receive priority over those made to special order for the importer in a single country.

It is important for the exporter to know that his risk is at a minimum. If necessary, he can easily check the financial responsibility of the forwarder. The forwarding agent, however, will be positive that the goods he has to pay for actually have been received, and not merely placed at his disposal. Acting as a buying agent for the foreign importer, he has all the rights and obligations thereof, as determined under the law of agency.

The importer who engages the forwarder's service enjoys immense advantages. He is able to obtain merchandise from exporters whose sales terms may be either cash before shipment, or against letter of credit. He may even be able to obtain a cash discount. Further, he need pay the forwarder only when the merchandise is approximately at the destination, or at least on the way and shortly available for resale. Thereby, he saves the extra cost for the opening of letters of credit and their extensions, for commissions and exchange charges, and the interest for borrowed capital.

In addition, the opening of a letter of credit necessitates that a corresponding amount of his credit with his own bank is immobilized for weeks or months; it is not available to him for other productive transactions. Moreover, he must pay the forwarder's collection, in the form of a sight draft, only when it is presented to him. This may occur many weeks or months after placing the order. He may pay in dollars, which he could choose to purchase at the cheapest price in his local currency.

Regarding the amount that the forwarder is willing to advance to finance his customer's orders placed with American manufacturers or exporters, the forwarder, generally, will consider the results of his investigation with respect to his client's standing and the currency situation of the country of destination. The amounts will vary from $100 to $5,000 per account, although amounts up to $500 are the rule. Accounting for this is the fact that the cost of opening letters of credit for orders valuing less than $500 is more or less prohibitive for the buyer, if recurrences are considered; whereas, orders of larger value can absorb the cost.

Invariably, where the forwarder attends to financing, he will submit the required documents to banks for collection, or draw from the deposits when making remittance. This should be effected upon the compliance of the exporter with the respective stipulations in the forwarder's confirmation of payment. Regardless of the financing method he employs, whether from deposits or funds on hand, inclusive of letters of credit in his favor, he must not be remiss on this detail.

Forwarders can assist their foreign clients through their contacts with factors, who are interested in promoting export facilities by extending credit to overseas buyers. A factor may be defined as one who helps to finance the merchandise, in which he is interested, or handles. He extends to the importer the credit which makes the purchase possible. He utilizes the services of the forwarder for handling the shipment, and preparing the documentation, in a manner which will secure payment for him. The forwarder acts as intermediary between buyer and factor, factor and seller, and buyer and seller, without being financially engaged. He functions strictly as a forwarding agent, and as a consultant to the parties involved.

The preeminent position the forwarder occupies within the foreign trading community is indicated also by his close contact with financial circles. The forwarder's ability to arrange financing through factors is another element which deserves the international trading public's attention and appreciation.

CHAPTER XXV

Transportation to Seaboard

ROUTING

Too few exporters realize the magnitude of proper traffic control or maximize their efforts to secure effective traffic management. This deficiency may be attributable to ignorance of the available services or to lack of the foresight to institute intelligent traffic planning on the executive level. Top management in many, if not most companies, doing extensive exporting, accepts transportation charges often amounting to more than 20 per cent of sales, with perplexing indifference. Rife among executives is a lack of awareness of ostensibly elementary facts concerning the movement of materials and products, warehousing, materials handling, packing, and package research.

This situation demands reappraisal of present thinking, and a new concept of traffic management. Since billions of dollars are annually spent on transportation costs, and millions of them are wasted, action is imperative. The importance of the traffic function to over-all company operations, including production and distribution, is indisputable. The concept of the traffic manager as a "Rate Clerk" should be relegated to the past; his function today is that of an executive "in charge of movement."

Routing export cargo from interior points to seaport, and from there to the overseas destination, as a part of traffic control, transcends the phase of transportation as a function of movement. Seen from the standpoint of marketing, it assumes a far greater significance. Decisions by exporters in the inland industrial areas of the United States affect the *service industries,* such as truckmen, motor carriers, railroads, forwarders, ocean carriers, airlines, banks, underwriters, and port administrations of our vast seaboards, and, to an even larger extent, their own sales and distribution facilities.

Consequently, it is appropriate to direct attention to those salient aspects which most concern executive interest in shipping and top management decisions, in relation to the value of consulting the company traffic manager or the foreign freight forwarder.

We distinguish five major factors which influence the routing of shipment: (1) The value, size, and nature of the merchandise in relation to the attendant transportation charges; (2) The terms of sale;

(3) The time element; (4) The general traffic conditions from the point of origin to the final destination; and (5) The transportation costs.

Each of these classifications will now be amplified.

1. The value of the merchandise has a bearing on the cost of freight, whether inland or ocean, since the ability and willingness of the exporter to pay a given rate depends in large degree on the cargo's value. Tariff analysis forms of steamship conferences specifically refer to the value of the article at the port of loading; they inquire, also, as to the value of any competitive article. The same consideration applies to the size and nature of the merchandise. It is important to know whether the goods move in small lots, or in bulk; whether packed; moving in box cars; unpacked, or bulk material shipped in open or flat cars; or a hazardous, dangerous, or oversize product requiring special care in transporting, handling, or stowing.

2. In terms of transportation cost, the "landed" price of the merchandise will be the decisive factor on which to base the ability of the exporter to compete. Equally important, however, is the condition, or price term, under which the buyer or seller has contracted, because the traffic control will vary accordingly. On f.o.b. factory sold cargo, the foreign freight forwarder, as the American representative of the foreign buyer, can instruct the supplier to use the means of transportation prescribed by him. Similarly, under f.a.s. sales contracts, shippers are obliged to accept instructions at point of exportation from the forwarder as the port representative of the overseas importer, as to the selection of the ocean carrier, insurance coverage, inclusion of cargo in a consolidation, disposition of original documents for foreign customs clearance, and other items. In his role as traffic coordinator, the foreign freight forwarder invariably will be guided by the interests of his customer—whether he be buyer or seller—and will try, in the long run, to benefit both.

3. The time element is of paramount importance to both seller and buyer. Considerations relating to the supplier's production schedules, contractual delivery dates, the mode of inland and ocean transportation, selection of carriers and ports, frequency of sailing, and the validity of import licenses and letters of credit will influence the routing of shipments. An analysis of the pertinent factors involved in the problems of *speed* or *time-in-transit*, as well as cost and general traffic conditions, is warranted, and will be discussed later in this chapter.

4. It cannot be over-emphasized that general traffic conditions exert a pervasive influence on the routing of cargo. Here, a study of the port's facilities and the degree of cooperative teamwork by the various agencies and services, to which the exporter looks for assistance,, will reveal whether or not the utilization of the port is desirable. As a further objective to be included in this category, there should be an

investigation as to possible delays, which may be caused by labor disputes, or congestions, due to either a poor layout of dock facilities, or lack of proper cargo-handling equipment. Other appropriate subjects for examination include: whether the inland cariers in question are able to perform a speedy, economical transfer of goods by either truck, lighter, or belt railroad upon arrival, and whether suitable storage, banking, and insurance facilities are available. Another consideration refers to the evaluation of a carrier, as to his record in the careful handling of cargo.

5. As far as the transportation costs are concerned, it is imperative, particularly in these highly competitive times, that scrupulous care be exerted to avoid any unnecessary addition to the final landed-cost. To be considered are: rail routes and rates; and the relative advantages of such competitive means of transportation as, long distance truckers, railroads, consolidated carload services, and barge lines. Eventual port differentials in rates must be checked, especially on export-carload shipments. Meriting study, also, the desirability of employing only one inland carrier for the whole haul, instead of many, for reasons which will be set forth below.

ANALYSIS OF COST AND TIME FACTORS

Purchasing transportation service requires a superior degree of skill and experience, due to its complex pricing structure, which is seldom found in ordinary business transactions. Inefficient buying leads to a waste of thousands of traffic dollars, thereby possibly causing the loss of markets. All phases of production and distribution must be thoroughly examined, starting with plant location and the purchase of material, until the finished product is possessed by the foreign buyer. Top management's study should pay strict attention to every operation which may affect the economy of the enterprise without damaging the quality of its product or its ability to sell competitively. To achieve this goal, the following steps should be taken.

1. Securing car sidings and other carrier agreements, such as, credit arrangements;

2. Planning flawless production and delivery schedules;

3. Procuring complete freight and traffic information on inland, as well as ocean rates;

4. Assisting foreign buyers in transportation problems;

5. Advising sales staff on contracts where terms affect traffic;

6. Improving materials handling and packaging;

7. Auditing freight bills;

8. Filing claims for over-charge, loss, and damage;

9. Preparing rate cases for classification changes;

10. Checking and signing conference contracts and attending meetings before rate or regulatory bodies; and

11. Avoidance of departmental rivalry, particularly between domestic and export sales management.

Importers abroad are fully aware. of the importance of the cost factor. They judge the competitive position of product and exporter and instruct their suppliers, whenever possible, how to forward the ordered goods. In the absence of such directions, the seller is obliged to ship the cargo in the fastest and most economical manner to the port of destination. This maxim applies to the inland exporter, as well as the foreign trader at the seaboard.

New York is the largest port in the United States and channels the greatest number of sailings to any port of the world. However, it is not a corollary that it will be the cheapest or most advantageous one, since savings in transportation costs and transit time are customarily predicated on the point of origin and destination of goods to be shipped. For example: cargo originating in the New England Area can frequently be routed out of Boston at a saving in inland freight, provided there is prompt, fast steamer service to the country or port of destination, and no unusual heavy or bulky cargo requiring special, and unavailable equipment. The port of New Orleans, in many instances, serves as an export gateway for the mid-continent industrial area. Shipments originating at certain points east of the Denver-Fargo Line, bound for Trans-Pacific destinations, are generally cleared from West Coast ports, such as San Francisco.

Manifold criteria determine the port of export to which goods should be routed. Ostensible present savings on time or cost may not be equally applicable in the near future. The complexity and intricacy so characteristic of foreign trade activities is even magnified with respect to the transportation function. To complete successfully and economically a through-routing study, consideration must be given to the following: railroad and motor carrier rates, classifications, and quotations; the possibility of car shortages with a particular carrier; charges for transfer and handling at port of exportation; ocean rates by passenger or express steamers, compared with those of cargo vessels; contract rates available, in comparison with higher tariff rates; conference quotations, compared with those by "outsiders" or non-conference lines, must be considered. Attention must also be focused on the problems of selecting the fastest of several roads to the same port of exit; the frequency of sailings; the transit time of a specific vessel, dictated by the number of ports of call during the voyage; the availability of steamer space; the mode of freight payment, prepaid or collect; lower than usual consular fees, by shipping through a specific steamship line; granting of *hold-on-dock* privileges; additional insurance coverage; loading and unloading facilities in the ports of exportation and discharge; price and sales terms; credit arrangements; interest rates; import restrictions, and other factors indigenous to the situation.

INVESTIGATION OF GENERAL TRAFFIC CONDITIONS

The question of "how" to route an export shipment depends, as noted, on so many factors that no particular tangent can be ascribed to be the determinant. Only perpetual, painstaking endeavors, yielding patience and experience, can create a mind capable of mastering the labyrinth called *traffic control,* of which routing is only a minor segment. Good traffic managers should be rated as "artists," rather than as "clerks;" like magicians, they produce mysterous "wonders" of movement, whether by air, rail, motor, inland water, or ocean. It is not without justification, that the foreign forwarder carries the sobriquet, *jack-of-all-trades.*

ROUTING BY AIR

Routing by air is illustrated by the case of a damaged X-Ray apparatus in a hospital somewhere in South America. The American manufacturer's foreign representative has cabled for the replacement tubes to be rushed within the next twenty-four hours to destination. Contacting the suppliers, pressing for immediate delivery, finding the next direct flight, clearing without delay through the United States Customs and the foreign consulate, bringing the parcel directly to the "ready to go" aircraft, cutting the airway bill, and other details requires the full play of mental and physical faculties.

Another example of air routing is afforded by an inquiry concerning shipping, via the cheapest and fastest route, a consignment of ten head of cattle to a point in Central America. In this instance, the possibilities of moving this type of cargo either by air or by surface carrier must be examined. When shipping by steamer, stalls and feed are needed; a transport supervisor must be hired; the freight charges, assessed per head, calculated and compared with total air freight cost; foreign inland transportation from port of discharge added to ocean haul expenses; different insurance rates investigated; and the transit time scrutinized. This latter factor is particularly consequential in this instance, because it bears on the amount of expenses incurred by the attendant, for whom accommodations must be provided on the steamer carrying the livestock. This measure is not required for a flight taking only about six hours, instead of six days by vessel. Modern aircargo liners, carrying up to fifteen tons of freight at a speed of 300 m.p.h., demonstrate that many suitable commodities benefit by the speed and actual savings of air movement. The trend for utilizing air routing for cargo is being accelerated by the constantly expanding inter-through-route and inter-through-rate network, which virtually links this country with the rest of the world.

ROUTING VIA RAILROAD

Completely different problems arise for exporters who effect shipment from interior location via rail to seaboard. Firstly, when utilizing rail and ocean services, the factor of competition influencing price quotations is considerably stronger. Scope for this competition inheres in the delays, multiple handling, and consequent additional fees and costs, which are entailed because of the "Stop and Go" nature of surface movement. It manifests itself in port, as well as carrier competition. Harbor administrations try to counter it by reducing operating expenses for rail and ocean carriers or by improving port facilities in various ways. As a result, existing handling and transfer charges, such as, heavy lift and lighterage fees, have been eliminated, or additional privileges are made available to export shippers. The plan devoloped by the Port of New York Authority provides an example of this type of money-saving device, which benefits shippers of mixed export carloads. Thereby, steamship companies which operate more than one service to ports all over the world from a single, or adjoining piers, accept a single railroad lighterage delivery, consisting of cargo for several vessels at more than one pier.

Ocean and rail carrier competition was instrumental in the creation of the so-called *Port Differentials*. Their inception reverts to about eighty years ago, when the railroads first permitted lower export rates on goods moving from the Middle West to some United States North Atlantic ports. Because of the lack of adequate port facilities and the longer distance to Europe, these ports were handicapped by higher ocean freight rates than were payable on cargo moving out of New York and Boston. This was the era when oceanborne commerce was transported in sailing ships, and these differentials had amounted to about 60 cents per ton. Although ocean freight rates were equalized for all ports in 1935, because the conditions leading to their establishment had been nullified, some twenty odd years elapsed before they were abolished.

Fundamentally requisite for any export traffic manager, in order to arrive at a proper cost account and pertinent routing, is a comprehensive knowledge of all rail rates and routings, tariffs, and freight classifications. He must keep abreast of Interstate Commerce Commission regulations and any other traffic development. He should be in continuous contact with his foreign freight forwarder, as to port and overseas conditions. On important movements, he must examine alternative routings, which often will result in disparate charges. He must be familiar with the distinction between carload, and less-than carload rates; between domestic and export freight rates; different applications of carload minimum weight as to commodity and port of export; the possible advantages for free lighterage to steamer on less-than carload lots; and the merits of utilizing the services of carloading firms.

Some of the larger foreign freight forwarders maintain branch offices at various industrially important interior points. This enables them to reach their exporting manufacturers more directly and to create and operate a regular, consolidated carload service for export. Securing a saving for the individual shipper, they offer rates based on the difference between carload and less-than carload rail or motor-carrier rates, or on the privileges of mixing freight in carload lots, as authorized in certain railroad tariffs. These forwarders also make use of export tariff schedules issued by the transcontinental railroads, or by themselves with approval of the Interstate Commerce Commission. These schedules quote lower class and commodity rates on many specified articles to Pacific, Gulf, or Atlantic ports, when destined to the Far East, Mexico or South American, or European-African countries. They quote also, so-called *all-commodities rates*, which are applicable to all but certain exempt export articles when routed in straight or mixed carloads, subject to certain minimum carload weight. Savings hereby obtained are three-fold: (1) on the overland haul in the United States; (2) on special Overland Ocean Freight Rates, which are considerably lower than the regular ocean freight rates; and (3) by eliminating cartage, possible *waiting time* charges, and warehousing.

The carloading services are speedier than less-than carload deliveries, and cover a large territory, comprising many industrial production centers.

Those foreign freight forwarders who maintain branch offices in the interior and were engaged in the consolidated carloading business, as well as in their own domain as seaport forwarders, were affected by an act of Congress, May 16, 1942 (part IV of the Interstate Commerce Act), which regulates the practices and rates of domestic freight forwarders. Under the terms of this statute, a separation of export carloading business and foreign freight forwarding became necessary. However, this restrictive legislation did not impair the cooperation between the former partners (main and branch office), nor accomplish any actual change in the effective use of the existing transportation facilities.

To assure proper classification, rating of freight, and delivery of goods, precise instructions as to description of merchandise, routing and destination must be given to the carrier for forwarding shipments by railroad, whether in carload lots—straight or mixed—or otherwise. The inland bill of lading should show the export marks and numbers of the shipping packages and a reference as to *export* delivery by indicating the pier, on which the vessel will load, and the name of the steamer. Carload lots, clearing from New York, should be billed *For Export, Lighterage Free*. The use of *Through Export Bill of Lading* and *Through Rates*, is restricted to export cargo shipped from Pacific coast ports. Based on a combination of inland rail rate, transfer charge—if any—at port of export, and ocean freight rate, without any saving on transportation cost, it lacks appeal to foreign traders.

This attitude is strengthened by its inherent disadvantages as pointed out in Chapter XIII.

ROUTING VIA MOTOR CARRIER

The growth of motor haulage for the movement of export cargo, during the past few decades, emphasizes its importance as a dynamic force in our national economy, as well as with respect to the development of our foreign commerce.

Alert export traffic managers also recognize the advantages of this mode of transportation, such as overnight delivery, lower freight charges, flexibility of service, and direct pier delivery. These advantages appeal to shippers who are located in the neighborhood of a greater port area, and to those whose productive capacity does not warrant shipping in carload quantities. Like railroads, the over-the-road carriers charge full truckload and less than truckload rates, in accordance with published tariffs. In many instances, rates include shipside delivery, but exclude unloading charges, if any; in others, long-distance carriers discharge their goods at local terminals for redelivery by their own truckmen, or have the cargo turned over to a local cartman, who attends to dock delivery. When export shipments are transported by the over-the-road trucks, care must be taken that all necessary documents, such as dock receipt, export declaration, and, if necessary, shipping permit have been properly issued. These documents must be either in the hands of the delivering carrier or lodged on the pier; otherwise the delivery cannot be effected and storage will accrue. The allowed free-time period varies for different motor carrier conferences. On less-than truckload freight, forty-eight hours from the first 7 A.M. after tender is the customary period of grace; on truckload freight, it varies from two and on-half hours to forty-eight hours.

ROUTING VIA BARGE CARRIER

This type of transportation, using canals and inland river waterways, caters to bulk commodities, such as grain products, coal, asphalt, pulpwood, newsprint, pig iron, petroleum products. Barges also provide transportation service to a certain extent, to manufactured iron and steel products, such as automobiles and trucks. Traffic is moved in steel barges, towed by diesel-powered motor vessels. The lines operate as common carriers. They join other carriers, including railroads, for the purpose of issuing joint rates and the establishment of through routes. Without this arrangement, barge lines probably could not exist. To cite an example, an auto manufacturer in Detroit can take advantage of the Mississippi water route if he can ship by railroad to St. Louis and have his goods transferred there to a water carrier for forwarding to New Orleans. However, if railroads would not interchange cargo with waterways, the barge line carrier on the Mississippi would have to depend on traffic originating from the communities on its banks. Barge lines are the cheapest means of transportation, but also the slowest; therefore, they have limited usefulness for the average foreign trader.

Finally, a word of caution applying to exporters irrespective of the means of transportation selected for the movement of goods from the interior to the port of export is in order.

Shipments should be released only when the necessary arrangements at seaboard for immediate reshipment abroad are complete, unless a· modus operandi between shipper and forwarder has been established, which removes all anticipated difficulties. However, if the requirements are fulfilled, speedy dispatch of the goods is imperative, as freight is accepted by steamship lines according to special schedules. As a matter of fact, most vessels call at more than one foreign port on their sailing route. Delivery dates for goods are arranged to concur with the loading schedule of the steamer, according to ports of destination. Freight for the last port of call has to be loaded first; whereas, goods for the first port of destination may sometimes be accepted up to the very day of sailing.

Maximum economic efficiency, to be achieved with a minimum of physical confusion, is the desideratum of effective traffic control.

Enforcement of regulations covering shipment of hazardous materials is to be observed. Three steps must be taken for compliance: (1) correct labeling must be on the package; (2) documents must show the hazardous materials as the first items listed and must note the character of the product (for example, flammable gas, solid or liquid, etc.); and (3) certification that the shipment meets DOT (Department of Transportation) must appear on the documents. The certification must show that the hazardous materials are "properly classified, described, packaged, marked and labeled and are in proper condition for transportation according to the applicable regulations of the Department of Transportation." Rules and regulations prescribed are based on Public Law 93-633, 93rd Congress, called the Transportation Safety Act of 1974 and signed into law on January 3, 1975.

CHAPTER XXVI

Port Activities

The foreign freight forwarder occupies an eminent position in the world of trade as a fiduciary of multiple millions of property values and as a transfer agent between exporters, transport carriers, and importers. This fulfillment of his trust is best judged by the competence with which he performs his functions at the center of his activities, the port of shipment.

Basically, the task which confronts a forwarder is to see that export goods arrive at a port on time and are loaded aboard a vessel or plane without any impediment. This implies that all necessary documentation is in order. However, the decisive consideration concerning his function is not so much *what* but *how* he performs. His diligence, reliability, dispatch, and efficiency constitute the standards for measuring his ability, and evaluating his performance.

Booking Cargo

Booking of cargo involves the reservation of space on a specified vessel or vessels for a scheduled sailing, on behalf of a shipper. Technically, it may be effected in two ways, either: (1) by signing a freight contract (see Chapter XIII), a procedure which nowadays applies only to bulk commodities; raw materials; an extraordinary large movement of special cargo, such as, the transfer of a whole manufacturing plant; or for particular types of goods requiring special stowage, like unboxed cars or trucks; or (2) by informal request (verbal) for general cargo, with the possible issuance of a shipping permit, thereafter employed as a sort of booking confirmation, but only when a scarcity of freight space is imminent. This situation will arise during emergencies (war), when steamship companies have less space available for commercial cargo.

In practice, securing freight space to worldwide destinations presents a situation which, due to many causes, imposes serious responsibilities on the foreign freight forwarder. Time elements, weather conditions, human failure, or breakdown of equipment frequently complicate the task of booking. Certain hazardous cargo, goods affected by heat or cold, or of unusual weight or extra-length, all require special attention to insure acceptance by the ocean carrier. The fact that vessels load from two to ten ports necessitates that the

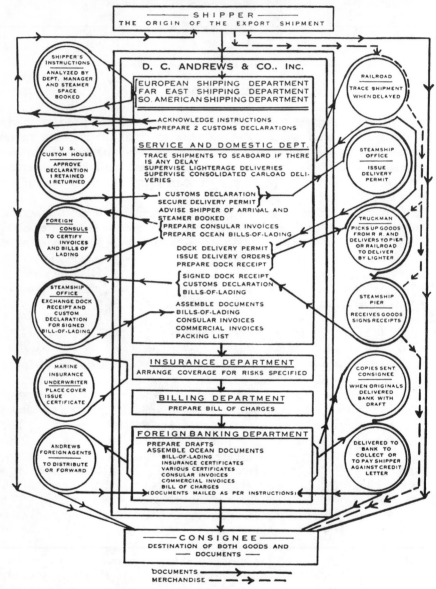

GRAPHIC CHART SHOWING
CO-ORDINATED EXPORT SHIPPING
VIA ATLANTIC OR PACIFIC PORTS

COPYRIGHT APPLIED FOR, MARCH 1938
D. C. ANDREWS & CO., INC.

"A LOT OF SERVICE FOR A SMALL PROFIT"

PREPARED BY
D. C. ANDREWS & CO., Inc.
ESTABLISHED 1884

FOREIGN FREIGHT FORWARDERS - FREIGHT CONTRACTORS - CUSTOMS BROKERS
THE STANDARD OF EXCELLENCE IN SHIPPING FOR OVER SIXTY YEARS
27-29 WATER STREET - - - - NEW YORK CITY

| BOSTON | BALTIMORE | CLEVELAND | CHICAGO |
| 131 STATE ST. | STEWART BLDG. | 1681 COLUMBUS RD. | 327 SO. LA SALLE ST. |

NEW ORLEANS   HONOLULU, HAWAII
238 SO. SARATOGA ST.   800 SOUTH ST.

steamship operator analyze the cargo. Thereupon, he must lay out a corresponding loading program, guided by the capacity of the vessel and the fitness of the offered goods, with respect to their weight, measurement, or type of packing for a particular voyage. Frequently, cargo can only be booked, *subject to room.* This implies that carriers expect certain goods to be delayed in arrival, but, the forwarder will not miss any possible opportunity. Then, there are shippers or consignees who, exercising their right of routing, prescribe the use of a certain line. They are motivated thereto, because of its dependability or reputation; the speed of the vessel; the freight rate quoted; or the number of ports of call on the trade route which, for instance, permits a shipper to consolidate various orders into a mixed carload, destined for those ports served by the ocean carrier. Thus, the forwarder's skill and competence is often accompanied by stress and strain in buying a service, which is intermittently difficult to obtain, namely ocean transportation. His maneuvers may culminate in prompt delivery to the final destination, with satisfaction to the buyer and seller, and as enhancement of the forwarder's repute. Conversely, ineptitude may engender undesirable delays, extra costs, and irritation in the relations between the forwarder and customer. Missing a boat may even involve the rejection of goods by the buyer, in case they had to be available for a seasonal holiday or exhibition. Similar tardiness may cause a considerable financial loss to both the shipper and the importer, should an enterprise, like a factory, be threatened with a shutdown, due to lack of material or essential replacement parts for damaged equipment. Therefore, the interested parties should be kept informed as to the engagement of space and process of shipping at all times.

TRACING

Arrangements for the actual dispatch of goods by ocean steamer are preceded by a series of preparatory steps that are necessary to avoid any delay and extra cost in export clearance.

Shipping instructions and export documents should reach the forwarder before the goods are shipped, or, at least, before they arrive at seaboard, so that they may be checked with regard to their completeness.

After this has been done, and assuming that the goods are either unduly late in arriving, or fail to arrive, at the railroad or truck terminal or pier of the port of exit within the expected time, the forwarder will start immediate tracing activities, in order to assure dispatch in the first available sailing or steamer for which space has been engaged.

Tracing is necessary to locate and effect delivery of delayed shipments and expedite urgently-needed cargo.

The inland carrier will be notified that failure to deliver on time, or delay in arrival, may result in the filing of a claim for non-delivery.

The carriers are required to investigate the movement of the freight while it was in their custody, and to report the record of delivery to the connecting carriers, and to the consignee. The forwarder will also engage the assistance of the steamship line which, in turn, is following up the movement of the over-due cargo with the railroad or motor carrier. Since they are concerned about retaining their proposed revenue, they use their own channels in pursuing the investigation.

The *expediting* of freight shipments, however, must be distinguished from tracing. Freight is *traced* to discover the location of overdue shipments. *Expediting*, on the other hand, consists of hurrying the movement of freight, in order that urgently-needed shipments, which have been booked for a steamer due to load in the very near future, may be delivered on time.

If goods do not arrive in due time, the forwarder will consolidate his tracing or expediting files with the claim files. Then, he will present the claim to the delivering or originating carriers, either for failure of the carrier to transport the freight with reasonable dispatch, or for actual loss.

Arrival Notice

Once the goods have arrived at the port terminals, the railroads, carloading companies, and some of the over-the-road truckers send notices to the consignee, or foreign freight forwarder if consigned to him, who proceeds on one of two courses. He either takes the goods to a storage place, warehouse or dock, in case the shipment for any reason cannot go forward; or he proceeds with the usual formalities and operations required for export clearance.

The arrival notice generally indicates the name and location of the shipper and consignee; the freight-bill number; the route; the date of shipment and arrival; car initials and number; shipping marks; number and kind of packages; description of merchandise; weight; freight rate and amount; the mode of freight payment, that is, prepaid or collect; and the expiration date of the free time period, after which delivery of goods must be taken or storage or demurrage becomes due.

On cargo shipped on a straight *inland bill of lading*, the arrival notice represents the proper identification for the pick-up or disposition of the goods; whereas, in order to take possession of freight consigned *to order*, the bill of lading, properly endorsed, must be delivered to the carrier. Short-haul truckers and other motor carriers do not send arrival notices, but advise consignees over the telephone. This practice is prevalent partially because of the short period of free time allowed and partially for reasons of indolence. In these instances the essential details must be recorded promptly and accurately, in order to avoid undue delays and costly consequences.

Frequently, export shipments arrive and cannot be transferred to shipside because of lack of the required export documents. Hereupon, the forwarder will immediately request the shipper, either by telephone or telegram, to rush the missing shipping papers to him. Exporters, as a rule, are grateful for this type of prompt, though costly notification, because the slightest delay may cause other considerable expenses.

FREE TIME

Free time is a term used in the field of domestic and international transportation by inland, ocean, and air carriers. It denotes the duration of time between the notification made by the carrier to the consignee or shipper as to the availability of goods, or the readiness of vessel or aircraft, and the beginning of storage, demurrage or laydays. Free time stipulates the *no charge* period allowed to consignee or charterer before he has to accept the delivery of cargo, and load or unload the car, truck, vessel or aircraft.

The free time generally granted by railroads on export freight at Atlantic, Gulf, and Pacific ports, is:

Carloads (Boxcars, Gondola & Flat Cars)	3 days, excluding Saturdays, Sundays, and legal Holidays
Less-Carloads	5 days, excluding Sundays and legal Holidays

The same rules apply for consolidated export carloads. Free time starts at 7:00 A.M., the day after arival notice is mailed or delivered. During periods of traffic congestion and car shortages, which unfavorably affect car supply and distribution, the Interstate Commerce Commission may intervene by changing or reducing the free-time period.

For truckborne export freight the free time varies in accordance with regulations issued by the different motor carrier conferences. Truckload freight is allowed only from 2½ up to 48 hours; whereas on less-than-truckload, the usual free time is 48 hours from the first 7:00 A. M. after tender of delivery.

STORAGE AND DEMURRAGE

If export cargo remains at the rail or truck terminal for a period extending beyond the free time limits, storage or demurrage charges will incur. Both are identical in character and purpose. However, some ports, which have direct rail connections to shipside, describe them as *demurrage fees;* others call them *storage charges.* They vary as to port of exportation and, like other port charges, they are contained in published tariffs, which are filed with regulatory bodies, and, are subject to change from time to time. Presently, the demurrage fees in the New York/New Jersey Port District are as follows: $10.00 per day, for the first four days, $20.00 per day, for the fifth and sixth day, $30.00 per day thereafter.

DETENTION OR WAITING TIME

Delays which affect the free flow of traffic adversely influence a port's well-being. Prompt clearance of freight depends on various factors; among them, an unhampered approach to docks, modern pier facilities, and efficient labor. If a port lacks these facilities, it will result in congestion and extra costs, and thus limit its own status as an otherwise desirable port.

New York is an example where certain obstructions retard the smooth movement of goods, particularly with respect to the transference of freight involving the trucking industry. Most difficulties stem from the concentration of business in a relatively small area, like Manhattan, where a considerable part of the shipping business is transacted. In addition, the deplorable conditions of old dilapidated docks and narrow streets leading to and passing along the waterfront work against the motor carrier and its usefulness. Truck detention, or waiting time, is one of the major problems confronting the exporter and foreign freight forwarder. Some piers do not get started until 8:30 A. M. and most of them close for receiving cargo by 4:00 P. M.; with a complete shutdown during the 12:00—1:00 P. M. luncheon recess. Moreover, there are many recorded instances where the irreparability of conditions has led to the formation of long waiting lines of trucks. This situation compels them to cease delivery of goods much earlier that 4:00 P. M., and necessitates that these partly-unloaded vehicles return to their garages with a few pieces for delivery the following day, causing unforeseen additional expenses through no fault of the carrier. This problem has become a cause for concern to the city's government. Aware of the potential threat to the city's economic life, attempts are being made to meet the challenge.

The resourceful competent foreign freight forwarder will counter this problem by arranging with truckmen and steamship lines that the delivery of freight will be coordinated, so that trucks will be available and ready for discharge at the docks in time, and "delay charges" will be eliminated. Here, again, the forwarder renders invaluable service to his clients.

DELIVERY PERMIT

Delivery Permits, also known as shipping permits, have been in limited use since the days of World War II. This has been pointed out in Chapter XII and XV. They are required for certain types and quantities of cargo in the Port of New York only. As a rule, the booking number secured from the steamship line over the telephone, and entered on the dock receipt, lighterage—or truck delivery order, or waybill, will suffice; thereby, the receiving clerk of the vessel at the pier is notified that space has been properly reserved.

PIER DELIVERY BY TRUCK

Pier Delivery by truck may cover shipments arriving in the port area by over-the-road truck, or freight to be picked up within the seaboard area. On out-of town goods, the foreign-freight forwarder will, upon receipt of complete export documents examine them for correctness and then attend to customs clearance. If all essentials are found in order, he will forward to the consignor either the dock receipt, together with the delivery order, or just delivery instructions, whereupon the shipper prepares his own waybill or bill of lading. Herein, the shipper will indicate all pertinent information covering the merchandise, as well as the steamer name, pier location, delivery date, and other details. Then, he instructs his own motor carrier to proceed accordingly. On deliveries made under dock receipt, the forwarder requests his client to have the signed dock receipt returned to him, rather than to the shipper, as soon as delivery has been effected by the trucker. This procedure enables the forwarder to verify proper delivery and secure the bills of lading from the ocean carrier. Moreover, with the signed dock receipt in his possession, the forwarder can expedite the issuance of all export documents, especially in urgent cases such as the imminent expiration of letters of credit.

Similarly, the forwarder proceeds on freight to be picked up within the port area and delivered to shipside, by transmitting to his truckman the delivery order, arrival notice, and dock receipt, if any. Alternatively, he can furnish the necessary delivery papers either to the exporter's drayman or to the motor carrier at whose terminal the goods arrived, always being guided by the instructions received from his customers or by considerations which will serve his clientele most efficiently and economically.

BELT RAILROAD

Contrasting with New York, almost all other major ports in the United States provide direct rail connections on their docks. Among cities thus enabling freight to be delivered alongside ship are Boston, Philadelphia, Baltimore, Newport News, Norfolk, New Orleans, and San Francisco. The procedure for ordering cargo to steamer varies. In some ports, orders for shipside delivery of cargo are placed by ocean carriers with the terminal operator; in others, the shipper or forwarder orders the goods to the belt railroad which, in turn, follows instructions received from the steamship line regarding the placement of the freight alongside vessel. Drayage and lighterage transfer is eliminated.

These so-called *harbor* or *belt railroads* function as switching carriers and terminal operators and do not perform any other service. Their entire trackage is run as a single yard, providing the necessary connections with the trunk line carriers which serve the corresponding port area, and holding loaded and empty cars in their yards until ordered to the piers. This is arranged by a switch list which is prepared by and furnished to the belt railroad by the delivering carrier. The terminal railroad does not issue any bills of lading, nor maintain car seal records. Demurrage incurring on cars moving to the belt railroad is payable to the trunk line carrier that controls the equipment, except demurrage which accrues exclusively within the terminal railroad's domain. Switching charges are billed to the line haul carrier.

RAILROAD LIGHTERAGE

The lighterage system, also called the flexible *water belt line* is, as already pointed out in Chapter XV (Lighterage and Truck Delivery Orders), peculiar to the Port of New York, where at least half of the port's export cargo is moved by lighters. The twelve railroads serving the harbor area have developed and improved this system, with the active and farsighted support of The Port of New York Authority. The system has developed to such an extent that it has become a keystone of the port's success, and one of the major factors contributing to its preeminent position as the nation's chief handler of general export freight.

Marine operations under the lighterage procedure are carried on within specified areas, designated as *free lighterage* limits, which cover almost all waterfront terminals of steamship lines maintaining worldwide services, and are divided into two chief categories: *carfloat* and *lighterage.*

Carfloat operations refer to the transfer by water of fully loaded export freight cars from railroad pier heads to the side of vessels berthed all over the harbor, thus expediting cargo-handling through simultaneous on-and off-shore loading.

Lighterage involves the movement by water of freight which has been unloaded from export carloads at railroad terminals, from rail-pier heads to private or public docks, steamship piers or directly to shipside.

Both these marine operations apply similarly, but in reversed sequence, to import cargo. Waterborne transference of export-import freight has the distinct advantage of facilitating a quicker turnaround for vessels. Hereby, simultaneous inshore and offshore loading and unloading can be effected, while also securing a high flexibility of the cargo-handling process through the shifting of lighters and other floating equipment, wherever and whenever needed.

Marine equipment used by the railroads in both carfloat and lighterage operations generally consist of:

1. *Carfloats,* which are floating steel craft with railroad tracks mounted lengthwise on their decks, having a carrying capacity of some fifteen freight cars.

2. *Scows,* which are flat-decked, open boats, without tracks and hoisting facilities.

3. *Barges,* which can be described as "floating trailers," protect-

ing the cargo against wind and weather. They can carry from 200 to 500 tons.

4. *Lighters,* resembling scows, but equipped with booms and derricks capable of lifting up to fifty tons apiece. Some of the lighters are self-propelled; therefore, they do not require, like the other previously-mentioned craft, the assistance of the "harbor workhorse," the tug.

At the Port of New York, the railroads have at their disposal some twenty-five hundred lighters, scows, carfloats, barges, and tugs in order to accomplish the immense task of moving every conceivable type of freight, be it heavy or light, liquid or bulk, packaged or crated. Refrigeration or heating facilities can be made available, if required.

New York Harbor Lighterage and Terminal Regulations and Tariffs provide free lighterage of export cargo in straight and mixed carloads under certain conditions which are explained in detail later in this chapter.

To increase the efficiency and economy of their rail-to-keel operations, the New York-New Jersey railroads, in conjunction with the Port of New York Authority, constantly try to improve their methods and facilities.

Some of the recently introduced services should attract additional volume to the port's business and gain the good will of the nation's shippers. They are:

1. *Heavy Lift Cargo* is delivered or received on lighters or barges at shipside or alongside the dock of the vessel, free of additional charge, up to twenty-five tons inclusive.

2. *Car floatage delivery* has been liberalized, through a reduction of the minimum requirements, to permit free carfloat movement on minimum quantities of six carloads or more.

3. *Packing-in-transit Privileges,* which affect a wide range of articles, were until recently subject to domestic rail rates during their movement from point of origin to the packing plant, although ultimately destined for export. Savings are obtained through the elimination of the three percent transportation tax on domestic shipments, and, through the usage of lighter containers, or only crating up to the port of export, where heavier overseas repackaging will be performed.

4. *Split Deliveries* are arranged on carload export traffic to various steamship piers. This enables shippers to consolidate into carloads small export consignments, thus avoiding truck transference or additional less-than-carload lighterage charges.

As a rule, railroads provide for one free delivery for mixed or consolidated carloads and for a maximum of four paid lighterage deliveries. The utilization of the multiple services maintained by New York's steamship lines to world-wide ports from single or adjoining piers work as follows:

These companies accept a single railroad lighterage delivery, comprising cargo for more than one vessel, whether loading takes place at one pier or several piers. Should there be more than five consignments in one car, the largest would get one of the free lighterage deliveries; the next three largest would receive the three paid lighterages; and the balance of the car would be delivered to a local railroad pier for truck pick-up, with the second free lighterage applicable. In no case will railroads attend to more than five deliveries under export freight-rate privileges. Therefore, on mixed carload lots requiring more than five lighterage deliveries, the inland-freight rate will be assessed on a domestic—that is, higher—basis.

PREPARATION AND ISSUANCE OF CLEARANCE AND SHIPPING DOCUMENTS

Once the goods are available at the port terminals and are "ready to go," the forwarder proceeds with the usual, but intricate and varied formalities and operations, which signify his reputation as a specialist in export traffic matters.

The shipper's export papers consist of the shipping instruction, (if the consignor has failed to prepare this, it will be made up by the forwarder) ; the commercial invoice; the packing list; and other accessoraial documents, such as, licenses for export or import, and banking papers, such as, drafts or letters of credit. These will be placed together in a file which receives either a top sheet, or is put in a folder carrying both registration numbers for identification purposes and a pro-forma bill for pricing. These files are then forwarded as follows:

1. To the so-called acknowledgment desk, where receipt of the export papers is confirmed to the shipper.

2. To the export declaration department, for preparation of the shipper's export declaration. As export goods are subject to the U.S. Export Control Regulations, this declaration, prepared in triplicate, has to furnish: the name of the ship carrying the goods, and its flag; the loading pier; the foreign port of discharge; the marks and numbers of the packages; the kind of articles contained; their value, weight, statistical code number, and other details. This declaration is then submitted, unauthenticated by the U.S. Customs Service, directly to the exporting carrier who, in turn, will have to file the declaration, before departure of the vessel, with the afore-mentioned governmental authority, since it is the carrier who is responsible for the completeness and accuracy of information on all export declarations concerning the cargo his vessel carries as shown on the ship's manifest. On the other hand, the forwarder, as agent of the exporter and the exporter himself, continue to be fully responsible for all statistical information on the export declaration and for the filing of the declaration with the carrier prior to the departure of the goods, also for indicating the "Destination Control Statement" on the commercial invoices, bills of lading, and in case of

airshipments, on the air waybills. For validated export license shipments, the complete validated license number will continue to be required in the commodity description column of the export declaration. Concerning general license shipments, the proper general license symbol (e.g. G—DEST, GLV, GTE, etc.) must also be shown in the commodity description column.

3. To the bill of lading department for the preparation of: a) Dock receipts, b) Delivery orders, and c) Bills of lading. These documents will now receive our attention.

a). *The dock receipt* (see Chapters XIII and XV), made available by the ocean carrier, must be accurately prepared in quadruplicate. The original, duplicate, and triplicate are rushed to the carrier who is entrusted with the delivery to the steamer dock; whereas the fourth copy is retained in the file.

b) *The delivery order* (see also Chapter XV) is addressed and forwarded, together with the dock receipt, if any, to the transportation company effecting the transfer from the arrival terminal, or pick-up location, to shipside pier.

c) The *ocean bill of lading* requires particular attention, considering the manifold purposes it serves. The greatest care must be taken that the description of the goods is precise, so that the lowest possible, proper, ocean-freight rate will be applied by the steamship line. To do this, the forwarder must possess a comprehensive knowledge of all pertinent ocean freight tariffs and be thoroughly familiar with their interpretation and application. He must examine the exporter's packing specifications accurately, as to weights and measurements, in order to avoid overcharges on the part of the ocean carrier; and, when the occasion arises, he must insist on remeasuring the cargo at the port of destination. Weights given in pounds must be converted into kilos on shipments to Latin American countries. This task requires minute attention, since any error might cause heavy fines and inconveniences to the buyer abroad.

The number of bills of lading generally needed are as follows: (1) For shipper: original, duplicate, and triplicate, all signed, and a variable number of non-negotiable copies; (2) For the ocean carrier: about eight copies, non-negotiable; and (3) For foreign consuls: two to four copies, non-negotiable.

In the preparation of the bill of lading the forwarder must strictly adhere to the consignor's shipping instructions. Thereon, he must reproduce the marks and numbers appearing on the packages; the weight in kilos and pounds; the vessel's name; the port destination; the consignee, or, if to order, the proper "to order" party; the person or firm to be notified upon the arrival of the goods at the port of destination; the consignor or shipper; the required clauses prescribed under United States export regulations; the foreign import license number, if any; and any other requisite data.

The file, then, will be transmitted to the supervisor-in-charge of preparing the documents for examination. If they are found to be in order, they should be passed on to the consular invoice department.

4. The consular invoice department prepares the consular documents (see Chapter XIV). This is one of the most exhausting tasks that confronts the forwarder, since each country has a different procedure as to the forms, number of copies required, weight, values, charges, proof of origin, certification, fees, mode of setup, hours of presentation, and the return of the documents. There is the continuous problem of "beating the deadline;" that is, the consular and shipping documents must be submitted to the consul for legalization within specified hours or days before or after the sailing of a vessel. Additionally, consular requirements, like fashions, habitually change, for they are not designed on a long-run framework.

Some countries require a certificate of origin in addition to or instead of consular invoices (see Chapter XIV). This document must be certified by trade associations; occasionally, they must be visaed also by consulates.

Having all the necessary shipping and consular documents prepared and assembled, the file is turned over for final inspection to the chief clerk or department manager. Hereupon, the *runners* deliver the completed sets of shipping and consular documents to the respective ocean carriers and consulates for legalization and signature and hereby terminate the first phase of documentary functions and procedures affecting approved port clearance.

The second and final part of the documentary process in the forwarder's office begins when the visaed and legalized, signed and claused consular and shipping documents are assembled, upon their return from their various errands. Advanced fees and expenses, then, are recorded on the file for later billing. Thereupon, the *shipping folder* is transmitted to the department manager to conclude the export transaction by indicating thereon: (1) The handling fees to be charged out; (2) the insurable value of the shipment to be covered, either under the exporter's, consignee's or forwarder's open policy, according to the instructions received; and (3) the banking or financing procedure to be followed. It is then transmitted to the forwarder's insurance, billing and collection departments, respectively for corresponding action and completion.

Myriad details perpetually confront, but do not disconcert, that hardy commercial breed, the forwarder of foreign freight.

CHAPTER XXVII

Combination Shipments

ANALYSIS AND APPLICATION OF FOREIGN TRADE DEFINITIONS

The idea of combining or consolidating shipments originating from several suppliers under one bill of lading, destined either for one or a number of consignees abroad, was conceived by the domestic freight forwarder some 100 years ago. Emerging when the railroads took over the freight traffic which had been carried up to then by sailing vessels, canal boats, stage coaches, and horsedrawn wagons, this concept has been skillfully adapted and logically applied by the international forwarder ever since foreign trade began to develop on a large scale. Today the consolidated carloading business, in general, is based on the principle of splitting up the difference between the carload rate and the less-carload rate, on which the shipper and the forwarder participate fairly equally. Hereby, the shipper gains the advantage of moving his freight at lower rates than he would have to pay by using direct railroad service, while the forwarder obtains a profit beyond the regular handling fee.

However, with the expansion of international commerce and the accompanying increase of financial and legal complications, certain aspects relating to price quotations, in terms of place of delivery and ownership, respectively change of title to goods, caused doubts to be raised in the minds of many exporters. These doubts focused on whether or not the foreign freight forwarder, as the appointed agent of the buyer, could lawfully combine their goods with those of other suppliers, and thus ostensibly restrict their otherwise unhampered prerogative in disposing of their shipping documents, which, when negotiable, represent title to the goods.

Unfortunately, there still exists in wide circles of the exporting industry, as already pointed out in Chapter XV (Routing Order), the erroneous idea that title to goods passes only when payment has been made by the foreign buyer and is received by the seller. This is an error in law and in fact, which is caused by ignorance of the state of affairs evoked by the law of sales, as laid down in the Uniform Sales Act and in the Revised American Foreign Trade Definitions, 1941. Usually, these definitions, prescribing certain rights and duties of the exporter and the consignee in foreign trade transactions, are made part of the contract of sale between the seller and the buyer, and then become legally binding upon all parties. The conditions and terms under which an exporter sells his goods are customarily inserted in the price clause in an abreviated form, such as, FOB and FAS, but the import of these terms exceeds price quotations and affect obligations and rights, namely: (1) The point of delivery at which the risk of loss of, or damage to, the cargo passes from the seller to the buyer; (2) The distribution of costs either to be borne by the seller, whether included in the sales prices or not, or by the buyer; (3) The transfer of title to the goods; (4) The documentation incidental to the shipment; and (5) Many other details pertaining to the export sale.

Therefore, it is mandatory for enlightened persons in the sphere of international commerce—and this, of course, includes the foreign freight forwarder—to be thoroughly familiar with foreign trade terms and their definitions (see Appendix). Finally, it may be noted that the retention of title to goods beyond any point stipulated in the usually, quoted price terms must be specifically agreed upon between seller and buyer.

Anent the foreign trade definitions, the other conclusion to be drawn from the preceding brief discussion is that the international forwarder, acting as an agent for the buyer, under f.o.b. and f.a.s. sales, has the right to combine shipments from various suppliers under one ocean bill of lading. This procedure is justifiable since, as a rule, title passes to the buyer at the time the forwarder acts on behalf of the importer abroad.

REDUCTION OF TRANSPORTATION COST

By consolidating various consignments, whether small or large, all destined to one port, the forwarder avoids high ocean-freight, minimum costs, and obtains a considerable saving on the consular fees, and the foreign landing and clearance charges. Significantly, this procedure assists the importer, and—indirectly—the American exporter, in reducing the landed-cost of the goods. The following two examples will demonstrate how this principle works.

Let us assume the forwarder received from five different manufacturers general cargo shipments to the same port of destination. The respective weights involved were: (1) 500 kilos; (2) 600 kilos; (3) 400 kilos; (4) 700 kilos; and (5) 800 kilos.

The ocean freight rate for general cargo is forty dollars per ton of one thousand kilos, but the ocean carrier's minimum bill of lading charge is $40.00. Were each of the five manufacturers to forward his consignmemt by itself, each would have to pay $40.00 minimum freight. By combining all five shipments on one bill of lading, the forwarder has collected a total of three tons or three thousand kilos.

Then, paying $40.00 per ton of 1000 kilos to the carrier, or $120.00 for the combination, he is in a position to charge the manufacturers on a pro rata basis, as follows: (1) $20.00, saving $20.00; (2) $24.00, saving $16.00; (3) $16.00, saving $24.00; (4) $28.00, saving $12.00; (5) $32.00, saving $8.00.

All these savings must be passed on to the respective manufacturers, since the forwarder is not allowed under the law to participate in the savings secured but may charge a special fee for obtaining these profits for the individual shipper. The savings involved range from 20 per cent to 60 per cent for the individual manufacturer.

The second example will illustrate the consolidation of three shipments, each of which is subject to different ocean freight rates, computed on a measurement basis. Assume the following measurements and rates:

    (1) 3 cu. ft., 1 cu. in., @ $1.20 per cu. ft. $3.72
    (2) 4 cu. ft., 6 cu. in., @ $1.35 per cu. ft. $6.08
    (3) 2 cu. ft., 9 cu. in., @ $1.725 per cu. ft. $4.74
                                                                                    $14.54

The minimum ocean freight to the port of destination is $40.00.

The savings obtained by combining the three consignments are as follows; only one minimum freight of $40.00 has to be paid instead of 3 minimum fees, totaling $120.00. Therefore, a saving of $80.00 has been secured.

Indubitably, these illustrations clearly prove that the foreign freight forwarder can offer considerable advantages concerning lesser ocean freight expenses. Without the forwarder's effective service, as far as small consignments are concerned, the free movement, or even the sale of these goods would be handicapped by the high, minimum freight charge, generally required by ocean carriers.

Savings of Consular and Foreign Landing Charges

Besides the savings on ocean freight, other advantages will accrue through the forwarder's combination of shipments on one ocean bill of lading; namely, savings on consular fees and clearance costs at port of destination. For example: On shipments to Colombia, South America, the legalization fee for the ocean bill of lading, and the cost for form blanks as charged by the Colombian Consulate, in New York, amounts to $16.00 per set of documents, including consular invoice blanks. In consolidating several consignments on one set, the consular's fee will be the same, if the ultimate consignee is the same. Assuming that shipments, originating with four different suppliers in the United States, and destined for one consignee or importer in Colombia, is being shipped on a combination bill of lading, and is listed on the same consular invoice, $48.00 will be saved.

With regard to the entrance and clearance fees assessed by customs authorities and brokers at the Colombian port of destination, an even better result will be achieved. Here the fees are not only considerably higher but will be charged only per bill of lading, irrespective of the number of shipments contained therein.

Considering the volume of business transacted between the seller and the buyer during a year's period, the savings obtained through the application of the combination principle may run into thousands of dollars.

TYPES AND PROCEDURES

Manifold operations are applied in consolidating shipments, either from various suppliers to one or several importers, or from one shipper to several consignees in the foreign country. Accounting for thousands of shipments, with hundreds of thousands of packages during a year's time, requires continuous effort and attention, and a prodigious amount of detail and clerical work. All the formalities necessary and applicable to any overseas shipment have to be executed in every detail and exactly reproduced; and in addition to the standard performances of services, special work and services have to be done.

The initiation and accomplishment of a combination shipment which is destined for a foreign buyer requires particular skill and care. Covering a traffic mechanism of its own, it extends far into the diversified field of foreign trade. This type of consolidation originates with the forwarder's overseas client who continuously places orders with a relatively great number of manufacturers in the United States. Upon appointing a forwarding agent, he informs him about those orders by sending him copies of the respective orders, which indicate the routing of the shipments to be made through the forwarder. Otherwise, he can inform the forwarder by regular correspondence and request his agent to follow-up with the suppliers the progress, or status, of the order. The forwarder, as the buyer's representative, will then communicate with the various manufacturers, advises them of: the prospective schedule of sailings; insurance provisions; marks and numbers of cases; and the collection procedure regarding merchandise value and charges. The forwarder will request the suppliers to furnish him with informative data for transmission to his overseas customer so that he can arrange his sales accordingly.

To maintain contact with all the suppliers and the buyer, there will develop an extensive, ceaseless stream of correspondence which requires a comprehensive knowledge of industrial and commercial functions and techniques, and an aptitude for appreciating the diverse modes of thinking and living of foreign customers. The international forwarding agent, acting as a translator of foreign thought through the medium of efficient export traffic management, bears a signal responsibility in creating and nurturing that understanding, which is essential for the satisfactory conduct and expansion of foreign trade.

The technical procedure in handling combination shipments proceeds as follows. Between the departure of two successive steamers scheduled for the same port of call, the forwarder receives a number of routed shipments, which originate from various suppliers, and are destined for his customer. The standing instructions from his client designate the foreign customs broker at the port of entry to whom he must consign the combination shipment. The forwarder draws a bill of lading in his own name, which covers the individual shipments included thereon. He will then advise the foreign broker or correspondent regarding the dispatch of the combination and forward to him the required ocean documents, along with the necessary instructions. He proceeds similarly when he handles free hand shipments, or consignments received from shippers' accounts, and on which he has no specific instruction, except to forward them to the final consignee abroad.

In this connection, reference may also be made to a particular type of small package dispatch service which has been organized and operated by some forwarding companies who maintain branch offices, or have a net of correspondents in the principal foreign markets which yield a high probability of receiving shipments. This parcel service covers precious goods easily endangered by theft, as well as delicate and perishable articles, which require speedy and simple handling. These small packaged goods, such as, samples, flowers, and valuables are usually forwarded on the express, or speedy vessels of steamship lines that accept this type of cargo. When a parcel receipt is issued, it is at rates that are much higher than regular freight rates. Forwarders who specialize in handling this kind of traffic take out a collective bill of lading in their own name, covering all parcels for one port or direction. They have this combination shipment consigned to, and distributed by, their foreign correspondent at the port of destination. In as much as the interested shippers may dispatch their packages like an inland parcel to the forwarder at the port of exit, they save considerable freight expense and are relieved of the time-consuming, laborious effort which is still attached to foreign parcel post shipments. Moreover, all restrictions imposed by the postal authorities with regard to weight and size may be disregarded when using the forwarder's parcel service.

Here, again, is another justification for the forwarder's *raison d'etre* in today's world of international trade.

CHAPTER XXVIII

United States Tariff Policies

TARIFF CONTROL

A tariff is a schedule or table of duties or taxes levied by a government on goods coming into, or going out of, the country. Tariff objectives may be twofold; these factors may exist singly, or in combination. Tariffs may be imposed to provide revenue for the government or to help protect domestic industry from the competition of foreign manufacturers, in an effort to maintain higher living standards for certain segments of the economy. To attain this goal, imports may be excluded entirely, import quotas may be instituted, or bounties may be paid on certain exports. The imposition of duties on the importation of goods, however, is the method to which governments customarily resort.

Since the inception of its national history, the United States has pursued a policy of protecting infant industries. The Revolutionary War had evoked a feeling that the young Republic had been discriminated against. This feeling, plus the cry for protection on the part of the newly-established industries in the Atlantic States, accomplished the first Tariff Act of 1789. Herein, the duties were low and were applicable to only a minor number of imported articles. Succeeding the War of 1812, the situation had changed drastically. The nation had a surfeit of foreign goods; imports had doubled. The Tariff Act of 1816 was this country's response. Evaluated from the viewpoint that the measure represented a product of partisan politics of the worst variety, it was a unique and logical piece of "statesmanship." Nevertheless, it was indicative of the intense battle that was waged for the control of the Federal Government during that period. Strife over the highly protectionist tariff intensified increasingly between the North and South, and between industrialists and farmers. The situation was particularly aggravated when Congress, through the successive tariff acts of 1824 and 1829, twice again raised the duties. The imposts were attacked as a "robbery under government auspices." The 1828 Act, decried as the "Tariff of Abomination," and the resultant revolt in the South impelled President Jackson to request Congress to revise the tariff "downward," and to impose protective duties only on goods required for national defense. The Tariff Act of 1833 provided for a gradual leveling-off period, until the rates had reverted to the 1816 standard. However, the political rivalry between the Whigs (Republicans) and the Democrats continued unabated for the succeeding hundred years; and the peaks and valleys of tariff fluctuations were reflected by the political parties in power.

This cyclical fluctuation, which marked tariff history of the United States, eventually was terminated by the Tariff Act of 1930. The events of 1929, with their worldwide repercussions, rendered the act virtually ineffective. Cash was in short supply, both at home and abroad. Imports had practically ceased, and exports had declined because foreign nations, also, would not buy. The depression had paralyzed foreign trade. High tariff and the governmental debt policies of World War I were contributory factors to the abysmal market collapse. It was not until 1934 that the upward trend commenced. That year, too, witnessed the emergence of a new concept of tariff writing as expressed in the Trade Agreement Act of 1934. Incorporated as Section 350 into the 1930 Tariff Act, it amended that Act by extending the power of tariff-making to the President. Prior to this Act, under Article I, Section 8, of the Constitution, the power to impose tariffs resided exclusively with Congress. With the passage of the Trade Agreement Act of 1934, and its extension of power to the Executive, the President was granted the authority to revise individual tariff rates—up or down—fifty per cent, by concluding reciprocal trade agreements with other countries. This Trade Agreement Act confirmed the so-called "flexible" provisions of the 1930 Tariff, among which were the "peril points" and "escape" clauses. The Tariff Act of 1930, including the 1934 amendment, has been extended several times, for instance, in 1956 by the Customs Simplification Act, but the most recent extension and important legislation was the Trade Expansion Act of 1962 whose purpose was (1) to stimulate the economic growth of the United States and maintain and enlarge foreign markets for the products of United States agriculture, industry, mining and commerce; (2) to strengthen economic relations with foreign countries through development of open and nondiscriminatory trading in the free world; and (3) to prevent Communist economic penetration.

Much of the international trade of the free world is controlled by an organization created in 1947 but still little known compared to similar bodies, outside of the export/import community. Its official designation is "General Agreement on Tariffs and Trade" customarily abbreviated "G.A.T.T.," however, not as its name would indicate, an "agreement," but a permanent organization meeting, as often as conditions warrant, in different countries, but mostly in Geneva where it came into operation in 1948 after having been organized by 23 countries in Torquay, England, the year before. Its aim is to promote the fundamental principle that international trade in a free world should be multilateral with as little discrimination as possible between countries. Under G.A.T.T. procedures, representatives of the member countries assemble to fix tariff rates by multilateral agreements. The first objective successfully achieved was to bring about a scaling down of the high United States tariffs which had been in force since the '20's and '30's. Vice versa, the United States, as the world's greatest exporter, just as anxious as any government to reduce discrimination and thereby enable American goods to reach a maximum of foreign markets, encountered steep tariff-walls, set up to protect the war-torn countries during their years of economic recovery. Since then, G.A.T.T. has developed into a 69-member world body whose rules for the conduct of trade have been accepted by the leading nations. G.A.T.T. itself, which has never been ratified by Congress, expresses the radical alteration of our tariff policy. The power to regulate commerce with foreign nations, although it remains with Congress, is now, for practical reasons, for instance, in order to conclude trade agreements, exercised by the executive branch of the government. This governmental section is now charged with the responsibility of considering questions of injury to the domestic industry and measures for their corresponding relief, in addition to the broad political and economic problems which affect the security and well-being of the entire nation.

The Tariff Act of 1930 provides for a Tariff Commission, which investigates, reports, and recommends rate changes to the President, who, by the power vested in him through the 1934 Trade Agreement Act and Trade Expansion Act of 1962, can overrule the Commission. Commodities are listed in the tariff schedules, with their corresponding rates of duty. All goods imported into the United States are subject to duty, unless specifically exempted. The statutory machinery, under which imports are controlled and duties collected, is known as the Laws of Customs Procedure; thereof the Treasury Department is the supervisory authority.

Customs duties may be assessed in any one of the following three ways: (1) either on weight, measure, or quantity, without regard to value; or (2) on an *ad valorem* basis; or (3) on a compound, or combination method.

As time marches on, it becomes evident, as it is common practice, that changes in guidelines and regulations will be necessary. So, after years of study and negotiations, Congress passed the Customs Procedural Reform and Simplification Act of 1978 Public Law 95-410, signed by President Carter, on October 3, 1978. Many parts of the law, including new judicial review provisions became effective upon signing, others on November 2, 1978, December 2, 1978, January 1, 1979, and April 1, 1979. The changes concern Entry Procedures (Sections 101-103, 207), Record Keeping & Audit (Sections 104-107), Counterfeit Trademark (Section 211), Limitation on Liquidation (Section 209), Penalties (Sections 109, 110, 206, 213), Processing Travelers' (Sections 202, 203, 215 and 216) and other miscellaneous provisions such as Section 113 which requires each person licensed by customs as a customshouse broker to file a report stating whether he is still actively engaged in business as a broker and if so, the name and address under which he is acting as a broker.

The desire of the United States to foster the development of international trade led to the enactment of the "Generalized System of Preferences" (G.S.P.) which was put into effect under the authority of the Trade Act of 1974 as of January 1, 1976 which program allows duty-free treatment on about 2,700 products from 98 developing nations and 39 dependent territories throughout the world and is being administered by the U.S. Customs Service until its scheduled termination in 1985. The idea of G.S.P. had its start in the United Nations Conference on Trade and Development in 1964 with the aim to give "Beneficiary Developing Countries" preferential access to the major trading markets of the world and thus improve their economic growth. The list of the developing countries and territories excludes members of the OPEC (Organization of Petroleum Exporting Countries), most communist countries, the developed countries of Canada, Japan, Australia, New Zealand, South Africa, and most European countries.

ORGANIZATION AND OPERATION OF THE UNITED STATES CUSTOMS SERVICE

The organization and administration of the United States Customs Service is presently based on legislation contained in the Tariff Act of 1930, and the Customs Administrative Act of 1938 (amending the statute of 1930), having been originally established by the Second, Third and Fourth Acts of the First Congress on July 31, 1789. The duties and powers of customs officers include: the general supervision and enforcement of regulations concerning entry; the appraisement and warehousing of imports, including payment of duties, drawbacks, and the compilation of statistics on commerce; and the execution or other provisions, which the Secretary of the Treasury may promulgate under statutory laws, with the Customs Service as the administrative agency-in-charge. Up to 1967, the Documentation of American Vessels was also a function of the U.S. Customs Service but was transferred to the U.S. Coast Guard by Treasury Department Order 67-81, dated January 30, 1967, and the Coast Guard thereafter was transferred from the Treasury Department to the Department of Transportation.

The many changes in tariff legislation, the evolution of new trade patterns, the exorbitant increase and change in international trade and travel since the last comprehensive study of the U.S. Customs organization in 1948, had led to a needed re-examination of all aspects of Customs in 1963, which in turn brought about the recognition for a modernization of the U.S. Customs Service. With this purpose in mind, Reorganization Plan No. 1 was submitted by President Johnson in March, 1965, to Congress which legislative proposal became law effective May 25th, 1965. It authorized the President to place the fast-growing customs service on a career basis, to abolish the offices of collector of customs, surveyor of customs, comptroller of customs and appraiser of merchandise—all of which were Presidential appointed positions—and, at the same time, to simplify the highly complex and technical Customs Service by decentralizing authority and consolidating administrative and supervisory activities into newly created customs regions and customs districts. With Treasury Department Order No. 165-17 of August 10th, 1965, Treasury Decision T.D. 56464, the Secretary of the Treasury confirmed Reorganization Plan No. 1 of 1965, set up 9 Customs regions,* headed by a regional Commissioner, reporting to the U.S. Commissioner of the U.S. Customs Service in Washington. Each of the new regions is subdivided into a number of districts with a District Director of Customs in charge, except Customs Region II of New York City, N.Y., which is divided into three areas: Seaport, J.F. Kennedy Airport, and Newark. Whereas the regional office attends mainly to policy and guidance matters, the district office is responsible for the day-to-day operations involving foreign trade activities, mainly the clearing of import shipments, the enforcement of customs and allied laws, resp. the collection and protection of revenues. The major changes affecting the handling of import shipments have taken place on the district level. Prior to the reorganization, four major steps in the processing of import shipments were performed by separate divisions. They were: (1) entry, or filing of documents; (2) appraisement, or setting the value of a shipment through examination; (3) classification, or setting a duty rate, and (4) liquidation or final determination of duty. Now, these functions have been consolidated, and are the responsibility of a two-or-three-man Import Specialist Team. Each team will handle the entry, appraisement, classification and liquidation on all shipments it processes. On routine importations this system will enable Customs to perform the appraisement aspects and most of the liquidation immediately whereas in the past these last two steps took about 3 months or longer. The advantages to the importer can readily be seen. Another innovation was the introduction of automatic data processing to cope with the rapidly expanding growth of foreign trade and travel.

Each customs region, as well as each of the customs districts within the region has its own headquarters port which is either the seat of the Regional Commissioner of Customs or the official residence of the District Director of Customs respectively Area Director in New York. Each district has, of course, other ports or ports of entry. These terms refer to any place, dry or wet, designated either by the President, the Secretary of the Treasury or by Congress, at which a customs officer is assigned with authority to accept entries of merchandise, to collect duties, and to enforce the various provisions of the customs and navigation laws. The legal procedure prescribed under the law to secure possession of imported goods is known as *entry*. The legal forms to be used are called *entries*.

*See Appendix D/A.

After an entry for other than export òr transportation in bond has been filed with the District Director, the Import Specialist team will designate representative quantities for examination by customs officers, under conditions properly safeguarding the merchandise, in order to determine:

1. The value of the merchandise for customs purposes and their dutiable status.

2. Whether the goods are of a kind which must be marked with the country of their origin or with special markings; and if so, whether they are marked in accordance with applicable regulations.

3. Whether the shipment contains articles which are excluded from entering the country.

4. Whether the goods have been truly and correctly invoiced.

5. Whether an attempt has been made to enter merchandise in excess of the quantities indicated in the invoice, or whether there is a shortage.

Some kinds of goods must be examined, also to ascertain that they meet the legal requirements imposed by the provisions of the Federal Food and Drug Administration and by the Federal Alcohol Administration Act, both of which deny admission of food and beverages unfit for human consumption.

Certain kinds of goods will be weighed, gauged, or measured. If the invoice or entry fails to indicate the weight, quantity, or measure of the goods, the expense of securing such facts may be collected from the consignee or his agent before the merchandise is released from customs custody. In case of neglect to arrange entry for the goods at either the port of lading or at an interior port, within five days after the arrival of the steamer, plane, railroad, truck, or other means of transportation, the District Director of Customs (Area Director at New York) will place them in a general order warehouse at the expense and risk of the owner. If, after the lapse of the allowable storage period, the merchandise is not claimed, it becomes subject to sale at public auction. Perishable goods, goods subject to depreciation, and explosives, which remain unentered, may be sold immediately. Storage charges, expenses of the sale, taxes, duties, and amounts for the satisfaction of liens are deducted from the proceeds, and the available balance, if any, is remitted to the owner of the goods. If the auction sale does not bring enough to pay due taxes, the goods are subject to destruction.

The operations of import activities as they happen to be performed at a Customhouse, like the one in the Port of New York, are best illustrated by a brief summary of the procedure necessary to clear merchandise intended for import through U.S. Customs.

Suppose an importer has requested his appointed customhouse broker to attend to clearance of a due-to-arrive consignment, the broker will present the appropriate documents to the U.S. Customs Service at the Customhouse for an Initial Review, namely: (1) a consumption entry form, (2) a carrier's certificate or proper bill of lading, (3) a valid bond and any other needed document like an invoice, all of which are being examined as to their legal completeness, such as proper signatures, amounts, expiration dates, etc. If found in order, the documents are forwarded to the Import Specialist Team for further review. Here, the documents are checked whether (1) the submitted entry forms have been properly completed, (2) all necessary documents have been filed, (3) the applicable tariff classification and correct value have been chosen. If this review is negative, the entry papers are returned to the customhouse broker for correction, otherwise passed on for numbering, payment of duty, for final examination, and liquidation.

The Customhouse reflects and embodies the lifeblood of a port's international commerce. Like a beehive, it buzzes with activity from morning to night, and is a visible expression of the phenomenal rise of American foreign trade.

CHAPTER XXIX

The Customhouse Broker

DEFINITION AND FUNCTIONS

Coupled with being an extraordinary coordinator with respect to the free flow of export freight, the international forwarder acts also as the intermediary between the foreign seller and the American buyer when the trade relations are reversed. The intricacy of United States import regulations is a permanent source of controversy; and disagreements over the valuation, classification, rate, and amount of duties chargeable, drawback claims, exclusion of goods from entry and delivery, and liquidation of entries are not unusual. These regulations, however, compare no differently in their complexity with those of other countries throughout the world. There are about twenty-two different kinds of customs entries for imported merchandise, each serving a particular purpose. Considering this, it is not surprising that American importers, particularly those in the interior of the country, look for assistance in clearing their shipments from overseas through customs and in having them forwarded to the final destination in bond or otherwise.

Since customs officers are prohibited by law to serve as importers' agents and the average American buyer of foreign goods is not in a position to attend personally to the clearance of his own shipments, the only available, authorized agent, acting as a technical expert for the harassed domestic importer, is the custom house broker. Very often, the foreign freight forwarder is a licensed customs broker. As a customs broker, he is licensed by the United States Treasury Department, and assumes a dual role as both an export and an import specialist.

The nature of the customs brokerage business and the functions of the licensed customs broker are thoroughly defined in a 1944 United States Supreme Court decision (*Union Brokerage Co. vs. Jensen et al.*, 322 U. S. 202).

Justice Frankfurter said:

. . . . We shall outline the nature of this customhouse brokerage business only so far as is relevant to a consideration of our problem.

On goods shipped from Canada into this country the consignee of imported merchandise must "make entry" of them at the office of the Collector of Customs at Noyes either in person or by an authorized agent, and this must be done within forty-eight hours of the report of the vehicle which carried the goods unless the Collector extends the time. To make entry the contents and value of the shipment must be declared and the tariff estimated and the production of a certified invoice and a bill of lading is generally required. Speed in making entry is vital, because goods cannot proceed to their ultimate destination until its completion. Apart from the fact that importers cannot always or even often make entries in person, the procedure makes demands upon skill and experience. The specialist in these services is the customhouse broker. In addition, he advances the duty in order that the goods may be cleared. The competence of the broker also bears on the efficient collection of customs duties in that the likelihood of additional assessment or refund after final determination of the duty is greatly lessened by accuracy in the tentative computation. But since errors and differences of opinion are inevitable, to insure collection of deficiencies the Government requires a bond prior to release.

The business of customhouse brokers, it is apparent, demands a sense of responsibility and skill. To protect importers as well as the Treasury, Congress has authorized the Secretary of the Treasury to prescribe rules and regulations governing the licensing as customhouse brokers of citizens of the United States of good moral character, and of corporations, associations and partnerships, and may require as a condition to the granting of any license, the showing of such facts as he may deem advisable as to the qualifications of the applicant to render valuable service to importers and exporters. Elaborate regulations define the investigation to be made of the character and reputation of the applicant and his experience in customs matters. The applicant is then directed to appear before an examining subcommittee which determines the "applicant's knowledge of customs law and procedure and his fitness to render valuable service to importers and exporters." On approval of a favorable report of the subcommittee by the Committee of Enrollment and Disbarment of the Treasury Department, a license enrollment under the regulations in this part for the transaction within the customs districts in which he is licensed of any business relating specifically to the importation or exportation of merchandise under customs or internal revenue law.

X's license authorizes it to do business in district No. 34. . . The regulations require it to keep records of its financial transactions as customhouse broker and its books and papers must be kept on file available for at least five years. Business relations with those who have been denied a license because of moral turpitude or those whose license has been revoked are prohibited, and the licensee is under a duty not to promote evasion of obligations to the Government. Prompt payment and accounting of funds due to the Government or his client are required of the broker, and responsible and ethical conduct is generally enjoined.

. . . . . The federal regulations are concerned solely with the relations of the customhouse broker to the United States and to the importer and exporter. The limited federal supervision of the financial activities of X is restricted to these federal interests. . . .

. . . . The Tariff Act of 1930 in this case. . . ., confers upon licensees certain privileges, and secures to the Federal Government by means of these licensing provisions a measure of control over those engaged in the customhouse brokerage business.

. . . . The Government exercises that control in the furtherance of a governmental purpose to secure fair and uniform business practices. . .

. . . . What we have said makes it abundantly clear that the business of X is related to the process of foreign commerce. As the trial court found, the customhouse broker in clearing the shipments, "aids in the collection of customs duties and facilitates the free flow of commerce between a foreign country and the United States." The fees exacted by customhouse brokers "are charges for services afforded in the movement of goods beyond the boundaries of the state.

Recently, considerable discussion has been focused about the need for simplification of our customs procedures and tariff laws. Actually, the onus falls not so much upon the American importer, as upon the customs broker, who has to fend through the maze of procedural red tape to assure the smooth, rapid flow of present-day imports. Possessing all the information and intimate knowledge of customhouse practice, he arranges for his client all the detail work in connection with customs procedures, such as preparing the entry blank; filing it, together with other required forms of documents; advising the importer regarding estimated duties; advancing these duties and other incurred costs; making recommendations regarding the advisability of protesting or apealing decisions; and arranging for the delivery of the goods to his client, his truckman, or a carrier for dispatch, to the inland destination.

Customhouse brokers, as pointed out on the above cited decision of the United States Supreme Court, are licensed by the Treasury Department as persons or firms capable of rendering valuable service to the importing public by entering and clearing goods through customs and by performing any other type of customs business. Therefore, the issuance of a license is subject to a rigorous examination by the customs authorities. To check the qualifications of an applicant, he first will be thoroughly interrogated on his knowledge of customs regulations; then in case of successful passing, he must fulfill the requirements of a second test as to character.

Under the regulations governing the licensing of customhouse brokers, it is provided that "no license shall be granted to any corporation, association or partnership unless licenses as customs brokers have been issued to at least two of the officers of such corporation or association, or two of the members of such partnership. In case of a sole proprietorship, only one licensee suffices. However, a person is not required to be licensed if he is transacting business pertaining to his own importations at a customhouse.

Issued licenses may, at any time, for good and sufficient reasons, such as malpractice, be revoked by the Chief Officer of the Customs, in Region II (New York) by the Regional Commissioner; in the other eight Regions by the District Director of Customs, subject to due and prescribed procedure, whereby any final decision rests with the Secretary of the Treasury.

POWERS OF ATTORNEY

Under section 111.3(a) of the Customs Regulations, an importer or exporter transacting Customs business solely in his own account and in no sense on behalf of another is not required to be licensed as a broker, nor are his authorized regular employees or officers who act only for him in the transaction of such business. Furthermore, under section 141.33 of the Customs Regulations, an individual (other than a partnership, association, or corporation) who is not a regular importer may appoint under a power of attorney a relative or friend having knowledge of the facts of the entry in accordance with section 485(f) of the Tariff Act of 1930, as amended, as his unpaid agent to act in his behalf for Customs purposes on a non-commercial shipment. U.S. custom officers and employees are not authorized to act as agents for importers or forwarders of imported merchandise, although they may give all reasonable advice and assistance to inexperienced importers.

Customs Form 5293
TREASURY DEPARTMENT
8.19, C. R.
June 1945

CORPORATION POWER OF ATTORNEY
BUREAU OF CUSTOMS

Know all Men by these Presents, That __Aztec Marine Corporation__
(Name of corporation)

a corporation doing business under the laws of the State of ___Delaware___, and having an office and place of business at __225 19th Street, New York, N. Y.__, hereby constitutes and appoints each of the following persons
__D. C. Andrews & Co., Inc., Licensed Customhouse Brokers who may exercise the powers granted by its employees:-Charles Walter Falkenmayer, Michael Anthony DeLuca and Craig Bradley Huston__

as a true and lawful agent and attorney of the grantor named above for and in the name, place, and stead of said grantor from this date and in this Customs District

No. __10__, and in no other name, to make, endorse, sign, declare, or swear to any entry, withdrawal, declaration, certificate, bill of lading, or other document required by law or regulation in connection with the importation, transportation, or exportation of any merchandise shipped or consigned by or to said grantor; to perform any act or condition which may be required by law or regulations in connection with such merchandise; to receive any merchandise deliverable to said grantor;

To make endorsements on bills of lading conferring authority to make entry and collect drawback, and to make, sign, declare, or swear to any sworn statement, supplemental sworn statement, schedule, supplemental schedule, certificate of delivery, certificate of manufacture, certificate of manufacture and delivery, abstract of manufacturing records, declaration of proprietor on drawback entry, declaration of exporter on drawback entry, or any other affidavit or document which may be required by law or regulation for drawback purposes, regardless of whether such bill of lading, sworn statement, schedule, certificate, abstract, declaration, or other affidavit or document is intended for filing in said district or in any other customs district;

To sign, seal, and deliver for and as the act of said grantor any bond required by law or regulation in connection with the entry or withdrawal of imported merchandise or merchandise exported with or without benefit of drawback, or in connection with the entry, clearance, lading, unlading, navigating, or documentation of any vessel or aircraft owned or operated by said grantor, and any and all bonds which may be voluntarily given and accepted by Customs procedure; to execute, as an agent who has knowledge of the facts, pursuant to the provisions of section 485 (f), Tariff Act of 1930, as amended, consignee's and owner's declarations provided for in sections 485 (a), and 485 (d), Tariff Act of 1930, or affidavit in connection with the entry of merchandise;

To sign and swear to any document and to perform any act that may be necessary or required by law or regulation in connection with the documenting, entering, clearing, lading, unlading, or operation of any vessel or aircraft owned or operated by said grantor;

And generally to transact at the Customhouses in said district any and all customs business, except making, signing, and filing of protests under section 514 of the Tariff Act of 1930, in which said grantor is or may be concerned or interested and which may properly be transacted or performed by an agent and attorney, giving to said agent and attorney full power and authority to do anything whatever requisite and necessary to be done in the premises as fully as said grantor could do if present and acting, hereby ratifying and confirming all that the said agent and attorney shall lawfully do by virtue of these presents; the foregoing power of attorney to remain in full force and effect until __Revoked__ _____ day of _____, 19___, or until notice of revocation in writing is duly given to and received by the Collector of Customs of the district aforesaid.

IN WITNESS WHEREOF, the said corporation has caused these presents to be sealed and signed by its ___President___

City of __New York__, State of __New York__, this __18th__ ~~22~~ day of __April__, 19__56__

                                 Aztec Marine Corporation

[CORPORATE SEAL]   (Signature of President)
[FILE ALPHABETICALLY]   Oath on back of this document must be taken in all cases   [OVER]   16—29495-4

(The following acknowledgment should be taken by the officer who executes the power of attorney)

City __New York__, County __New York__, State __New York__, ss:

On this __18th__ day of __April__, 19__56__, personally appeared before me __Ralph Edwards__ residing at __420 16th St. Greenwich, Conn.__, to me known, who, being by me duly sworn, deposes and says that __he__ is the __President__ of the __Aztec Marine Corporation__, the corporation described in the foregoing instrument; that the seal affixed to said instrument is the corporate seal thereof and was affixed thereto by order of the Board of Directors of said company; that he by like authority subscribed the corporate name to said instrument and signed his own name thereto.

                                   Signature of _____ Notary Public.
(If resolution in any other form is adopted, a certified copy of the resolution must be attached to this power of attorney.
The Collector, when he deems it necessary, should require a certified copy of the articles of incorporation.)

                              - Notary Stamp -
COPY OF RESOLUTION

WHEREAS, it is convenient and often necessary to issue power of attorney for the transaction of the customs business of the company;

NOW, THEREFORE, BE IT RESOLVED that the __President__
of the __Aztec Marine Corporation__
be, and any of them is hereby, authorized severally on behalf of said company to execute such powers of attorney appointing agents and attorneys with such powers as may be necessary and convenient to transact the business of the company with Collectors of Customs, and the company hereby ratifies and confirms whatsoever the said persons, or any of them, may lawfully do by virtue of the authority herein granted to them.

I, __Walter Smith, Secretary__, of the __Aztec Marine Corporation__ do hereby certify that the above and foregoing is a full, true, and correct copy of a resolution passed by the Board of Directors of the said __Corporation__ organized under the laws of the State of __Delaware__, at a regular meeting duly held on the __14th__ day of __January__, 19__46__, a quorum being present, as the same appears on the records of the company, now in my possession and custody as __Secretary__, and I further certify that the above resolution is in accordance with the articles of incorporation and the bylaws of said company.

IN WITNESS WHEREOF, I have hereunto set my hand and affixed the seal of the company, at the City of __New York__ __New York__, this __18th__ day of __April__, 19__56__

                               Aztec Marine Corporation
CORPORATE SEAL   (Signature of Walter Smith)
U. S. GOVERNMENT PRINTING OFFICE   16—29495-3

Corporation Power of Attorney

POWER OF ATTORNEY

The Department of the Treasury
Bureau of Customs
§ 19, 17 2, C.R.; § 19, C.M.

Check appropriate box
☐ Individual
☐ Partnership
☐ Corporation
☐ Sole Proprietorship

KNOW ALL MEN BY THESE PRESENTS, That _____

(Full Name of person, partnership, or corporation, or sole proprietorship (Identify))

a corporation doing business under the laws of the State of _____ or a _____
doing business as _____ residing at _____
having an office and place of business at _____, hereby constitutes and appoints each of the following persons

(Give full name of each agent designated)

IN WITNESS WHEREOF, the said _____

has caused these presents to be sealed and signed (Signature) _____

(Capacity) _____   (Date) _____

WITNESS _____

(Corporate seal)

CUSTOMS FORM 5291 (Jan. 1970)   Certification on reverse must be made in all cases.   (SEE OVER)

Front of Customs Form 5291

INDIVIDUAL OR PARTNERSHIP CERTIFICATION

CITY _____
COUNTY _____ } ss:
STATE _____

On this _____ day of _____ 19 ___, personally appeared before me _____
residing at _____

(Notary Public)

CORPORATE CERTIFICATION

(To be made by an officer other than the one who executes the power of attorney)

IN WITNESS WHEREOF, I have hereunto set my hand and affixed the seal of said corporation, at the City of _____ this ___ day of _____ 19 ___

(Signature) _____   (Date) _____

Back of Customs Form 5291

The only persons who are authorized by the tariff laws of the United States to act as agents for importers in the transaction of their customs business are customhouse brokers who are private individuals and firms licensed by the U.S. Customs Service. In order to prepare and file the necessary customs entries, arrange for the payment of duties found due, take steps to effect the release of the goods from customs custody, or otherwise represent their principals in customs matters, a customs power of attorney must be given by the principal to his customhouse broker showing the broker as consignee, in short this instrument is a formal, written document, which legally appoints the customhouse broker as agent for the principal.

Except in the case where for non-commercial shipments an individual has a relative or friend act in his behalf, the form for the power of attorney is the same for corporations as for associations, partnerships, or individuals. The form used is either Customs Form 5291 (see sample) or a similar statement as explicit in its terms and executed in the same manner as Customs Form 5291. An example of such a statement is found in section 141.32 of the Customs Regulations. The form for the power of attorney to be used when an individual on a non-commercial shipment has a relative or friend act in his behalf, is found in section 141.33 of the Customs Regulations.

If a customs entry is prepared and submitted by a customhouse broker in his own name, he may be relieved, if he so desires, under authority of law, section 485(d), Tariff Act of 1930, as amended, from direct liability for the payment of increased and additional duties found due on the goods, if he (1) files with the District Director of Customs, within 90 days from the date of entry, a declaration of the actual owner of the merchandise, on Customs Form 3347, stating that the contents of the declaration is correct, and (2) submits to the District Director of Customs, also within 90 days from the date of entry, a superseding bond on Customs Form 7601. Neither the owner's declaration nor the superseding bond shall be accepted unless executed by the actual owner or his duly authorized agent, and filed by the nominal consignee.

In case the owner is a foreign principal, the customhouse broker usually insists upon either a guarantee confirming the integrity of the foreign exporter; or upon a power of attorney issued by the foreign shipper, plus a surety bond in the name of the overseas seller, whereby the entry is filed with the customs in the foreign principal's name.

The power of attorney specifies a great number of performances or functions which may, or may not, arise in connection with customs entry or clearance. Those acts that are inapplicable or reserved may be deleted or omitted.

Manifold formalities in relation to the regulations, procedures, appeals, appraisements, and other legal processes have formed a highly technical code of customs, which require a vast knowledge. This situation explains why international freight forwarders, serving foreign trade in general, have added to their organization (although many firms perform customs brokerage services exclusively) an import or customhouse brokerage department. Guided by two or more licensed brokers, these departments specialize in all the routine work associated with the importation and re-exportation of goods from foreign countries.

Import Procedure

Akin to the capacity of the foreign freight forwarder, as such, the customhouse broker acts as the custodian of goods which have been temporarily entrusted to him as the agent of the buyer or seller. He is equipped with the knowledge and has the experience and skill necessary to get a job done efficiently, quickly, and at a minimum of cost to the individual importer or foreign exporter. The import procedure, starting with the preparation of the customs entry, which is based on the foreign shipper's commercial or customs invoice, includes the calculation of the amount of duties in accordance with the schedules and regulations of the Tariff Act; the completion of the entry and the payment of duties due; and continues until the final liquidation by the customs authorities has been accomplished.

Under the laws of the customs procedure prescribing the forms of entry, oaths, bonds, and other papers to be used in carrying out the provisions, rules, and regulations relevant to raising revenue from import, warehousing, or transportation in bond, the customhouse broker is confronted with a maze of red tape which cries for the simplification of regulations. In recognition of this need, the United States Treasury Department eased certain requirements. As of October 1, 1955, exporters to the United States no longer require a certificate of their sales invoice by a United States Consulate on goods shipped into this country. Moreover, certain former requirements on the use of the power of attorney in customs transactions, which in many instances proved impracticable, have been abolished. One of the liberalized rules regarding customhouse brokers permits "any employee duly authorized to act" to enter goods for a corporation. Another rule eliminates the need for the formal power of attorney documentation, in the case of an individual whose importation is non-commercial; here, the formal document is replaced by a simple written statement on the invoice, which confers the power of attorney. Nonetheless, more comprehensive revisions are required to facilitate the complex machinery of import procedures.

ENTRIES

A special permit for immediate delivery of a shipment prior to entry may be issued for perishable goods and other merchandise for which delivery can be permitted with safety to the revenue, when immediate release of such cargo is necessary to avoid unusual loss or inconvenience to the importer or to the carrier bringing the merchandise to the port, or more effectively to utilize Customs manpower or to eliminate or reduce congestion on docks, at airports, or other places. Merchandise intended for either formal or informal entry may be released under a special permit for *Immediate Delivery (I.D.)*. Applications for special permits for immediate delivery shall be made on Customs Form CF-3461 which is the national form replacing Customs Form II-RC-450. Suppliers of Customs Form II-RC-450 have run out and were formerly valid as a regional form only for New York and Newark Seaport Area whereas J. F. Kennedy Airport and the other eight Customs regions did use the national form CF-3461. The afore-mentioned application shall be supported by evidence satisfactory to the district director of Customs of the right of the applicant to make entry of the goods. If the district director approves, a term special permit for immediate delivery may be issued for a class or classes of merchandise particularly described in the application for such permit to be imported during a period not to exceed one year.

If a shipment arrives in the United States, the importer or his autho-rized agent must file at the customhouse an original bill of lading, or a carrier's certificate or, in lieu thereof, any authorized proof of title, the commercial or customs invoice, and the signed entry form. Should the importer wish to pay the duty, in order to have the merchandise re-leased from customs custody forthwith, he uses the *Consumption Entry*. If entry is made without proper evidence of the title to the goods, a bond must be executed, amounting to twice the value of the shipment.

S. STERN CUSTOM BROKERS, INC.
ONE WORLD TRADE CENTER
SUITE 1419
N.Y.C., N.Y. 10048

C. H. BOX 52
CONSUMPTION ENTRY
UNITED STATES CUSTOMS SERVICE

RECORD COPY ☐
CASHIER'S COPY ☐

This Space For Census Use Only				This Space For Customs Use Only		
BLOCK AND FILE NO.	M.O.T.		Form approved. Budget Bureau No. 48-217.6.	ENTRY NO. AND DATE		
	MANIFEST NO.					
FOREIGN PORT OF LADING	U.S. PORT OF UNLADING	Dist. and Port Code 10 01	Port of Entry Name NEW YORK			Term Bond No.
Importer of Record (Name and Address)						
For Account of (Name and Address)						
Importing Vessel (Name) or Carrier	B/L or AWB No.	Port of Lading		I.T. No. and Date		
Country of Exportation	Date of Exportation	Type and Date of Invoice		I.T. From (Port)		
U.S. Port of Unlading NEW YORK	Date of Importation	Location of Goods—G.O. No.		I.T. Carrier (Delivering)		

MARKS & NUMBERS OF PACKAGES COUNTRY OF ORIGIN OF MERCHANDISE (1)	DESCRIPTION OF MERCHANDISE IN TERMS OF T.S.U.S. ANNO., NUMBER AND KIND OF PACKAGES (2)		ENTERED VALUE IN U.S. DOLLARS (3)	T.S.U.S. ANNO. REPORTING NO. (4)	TARIFF OR I.R.C. RATE (5)	DUTY AND I.R. TAX (6)	
	GROSS WEIGHT IN POUNDS (2a)	NET QUANTITY IN T.S. U.S. ANNO. UNITS (2b)				DOLLARS	CENTS

MISSING DOCUMENTS	THIS SPACE FOR CUSTOMS USE ONLY

I declare that I am the ☐ nominal consignee and that the actual owner for customs purposes is as shown above, or ☐ consignee or agent of the consignee I further declare that the merchandise [ ] was or [ ] was not obtained in pur-
name of a purchaser or agreement to purchase. I also include in my declara-tion all the statements in the declaration on the back of this entry.

To avoid double handling, if the importer desires to have his mer-chandise forwarded from the port of original entry to an interior destination for customs clearance, his customhouse broker will ar-range, also, for the transfer of the goods under bond without ap-praisement, by filing an *Immediate Transportation (IT) Entry*.

Should the importer choose to place his merchandise in a bonded warehouse, the customhouse broker will attend to it by having a warehouse entry passed and arrange for the goods to be delivered there through a bonded and licensed truckman, and he will execute a warehouse entry bond. Upon request from his client, he will withdraw the goods, in part or completely, by filing a *Warehouse Withdrawal for Consumption Entry*, with the duty being paid, according to portion, as the goods are withdrawn.

Shipments which are in transit for a foreign country, but which are routed via a United States port do not need to be stored for the short transhipment period in a bonded warehouse. (This type of shipment is illustrated by the routing of asbestos fiber from Durban, South Africa to Buenaventura, Colombia, South America, via New Orleans). In such cases, the steamer pier fulfills the role of a bonded warehouse, and the goods are entered for immediate exportation under an *Immediate Exportation Entry (I. E. Entry)*.

Merchandise arriving in the United States and destined for a foreign country may be transported in bond through United States territory under a *Transportation and Exportation Entry (T. & E. Entry)*. This type of entry applies, generally, to Canadian export shipments handled via United States ports.

Imported material to be used in the manufacture of goods, such articles being exported, with duty being charged upon importation, is entered under a *Consumption Entry with Drawback Privileges*. A certificate of arrival is obtained for drawback purposes.

Merchandise valued at $250 or less may be cleared informally by the use of Custom's Form 5119 A. This is known as *Informal Entry* thus by-passing the normal formal procedures laid down for Consumption and Warehouse Entries.

An *Appraisement Entry* is filed for household goods, new or used, but already owned abroad, and for personal effects not imported in pursuance of a purchase, or an agreement to purchase, and not intended for sale. This entry applies to immigrants' belongings.

A *Baggage Declaration and Entry* is performed when a person arriving in the United States has his baggage cleared through customs, providing the passenger, upon arrival, has declared this merchandise as his own personal effects and his household goods, either accompanying him or to follow.

American goods returned from abroad are cleared under a *Free Entry*, if properly documented.

Of various customs entries which the importer or his broker must attend to regularly, those aforementioned are most prevalent.

Customs import procedure requires, in addition to the making of an entry, the filing of a declaration under oath by the importer, stating:

1. Whether the importation is made on the strength of a purchase of for other reasons;

2. That the prices in the invoice are true or, in case of a gift, etc., are truthfully estimated;

3. That all other statements in the invoice or other documents submitted therewith, including the entry, are true; and

4. That any documents disproving the statements made will be made available to the customs authorities without delay.

It should also be noted that changes in the entry regarding the value or cost of the merchandise, as evidenced by the invoice, may be made at the time the entry is filed.

BONDS

Bonds to be furnished under customs statutes or regulations are divided into three classes: (1) those approved by the Secretary of the Treasury, (2) those approved by the Customs Service, and (3) those approved either by the Regional Commissioner in the Customs Region II, New York or the District Directors of Customs in the other 8 Customs Regions, required by proprietors of manufacturing warehouses, carriers, cartsmen and lightermen, fall into Class I.

Class II pertains to bonds of owners of regular Bonded Warehouses. These have to be submitted for approval to the Customs Service. The same agency must approve also the so-called *General Term Bond* for entry of merchandise. This bond is a surety which covers all the imports of a merchant via all ports of entry in the United States, if so desired, in the amount of $100,000, or more, and is valid for one year. Application should be filed with the Regional Commissioner at the headquarters port most convenient to the importer's main office. The application must name the ports at which goods are intended to be entered, the types of articles, and the total amount of ordinary customs duties which accrued on all merchandise imported during the calendar year preceding the date of application, plus the estimated amount of any other tax or taxes collectible by the Regional Commissioner. To be submitted for approval to the Regional Commissioner are those bonds required by carriers, customs truckmen and lightermen; further, those bonds needed for immediate delivery and consumption entry. The latter can be drawn as a *Term Bond*, with a minimum of $10,000. It is similar to the "General Term Bond," but covers only imports through one port of entry, or as *Single Entry Bond*, applicable to one single entry. Most of the bonds which are required for import procedure must be filed for approval with the Regional Commissioner.

APPRAISEMENT

Under the Tariff Act of 1930, as amended-Section 402a, and the rules and regulations established and promulgated by the Secretary of the Treasury, the Import Specialist Team's task is to secure a just, impartial and uniform examination of imported merchandise and the classification and assessment of duties thereon. To accomplish this, the merchandise must be appraised in the unit of quantity in which it is usually bought and sold; by ascertaining or estimating its value, or the correctness thereof; by properly describing the kind of merchandise to be entered; and by reporting the findings to the Regional Commissioner.

Usually, imported articles have two values: the one which is applicable in the country of origin, where the goods are sold for home consumption; whereas the other is the price at which the goods are offered for sale to all buyers for export to the United States. The appraiser has to apply the higher of these two values.

If the appraising officer finds that there is neither a foreign value nor an export value for the merchandise, he will determine the U.S. value, if any. The U.S. value is the price at which such or similar imported articles are generally on sale in the U.S. at wholesale prices in the open market, *less*: 1) U.S. customs duty; 2) transportation cost, insurance, and other necessary expenses from the place of shipment to the place of delivery; 3) a commission of not more than six per cent, if any has been paid, or profits, not to exceed eight per cent; and 4) a reasonable allowance for general expenses, not to be greater than eight per cent on purchased goods.

If neither foreign home consumption value, export value, nor U.S. value can be determined, the customs value will be based upon the imported merchandise's cost of production. This is the sum of the cost of the materials and of the fabrication, manipulation, or other process used in the manufacture or production of such or similar goods, *plus:* 1) the customary general expenses (not less than ten per cent); 2) profit (at least eight per cent); and 3) the cost of packing.

When the seller places any restrictions, as a condition of the sale, on the use the buyer may make of the goods, such sale does not establish a value under Section 402a. The same principle applies if the seller fixes the prices or terms at which the merchandise may be resold by the buyer.

The cost of labor and material included in the packing of the goods for shipment is a part of the dutiable value.

Ocean freight, port charges, and marine insurance, are described as *non-dutiable charges* and are not a part of the dutiable value. Inland carriage abroad generally is regarded as a *dutiable charge* if it is included in the freely-offered price; but is "non-dutiable" if all buyers are made an allowance therefor when they assume delivery of the goods at the factory.

The date indicating the exportation from the last port of the country of export is the determining valuation date for customs purposes. A correct entry-value is extremely important, because under the law the duties must be assessed on the entered value if it is higher than the final appraised value. However, the importer has the right to apply the protest procedure with the United States Customs Court within a stipulated period.

Now, it may be helpful to examine some practical aspects in relation to the operations of the Import Specialists and of the Appraisers.

When a shipment arrives in a port, customs samplers at the piers, as a rule, examine the goods, particularly that of bulk cargo, such as ore, oil, sugar, and similar commodities. Sometimes they sample its contents for further examination at the customs plant, called *Appraisers Stores*. Package freight, as a rule, is also examined at the wharf except for special needs of the U.S. Customs, in which case usually one out of ten containers, or a sample package, is picked up by one of the licensed truckmen and delivered to the "Store." Here, representative parts, or an entire shipment, of merchandise are processed and examined by a trained army of experts.

Every type of equipment from fork lift trucks or overhead cranes to the finest laboratory microscope is applied for appraisal and assessment of duties, whose levies may range from "nothing," as in the case of an original work of art, to 110 per cent of an article's value. The examination is undertaken by the Import Specialist Team respectively its staff, which, according to the port of entry, may range from as few as three to as many as five hundred employees, and may consist of the chief assistant appraiser and his deputy, assistant appraisers, examiners and their aides, recording clerks, samplers, verifiers, customs guards, and laborers. No article in this world is unknown to these "analysts." The "Store" may even include a "Customs Laboratory," with hundreds of scientific instruments and thousands of chemicals needed for research and the "conviction of violators of the law."

Before the sample or shipment is transferred to the Appraisers Stores, the importer or his broker, prior to or on arrival of the merchandise, has filed the entry together with the attendant documents, at the Customhouse. Hereupon, the invoice is promptly forwarded to the appraisers, so that upon the delivery of the goods at the "Store," the examination can be performed expeditiously. After the merchandise has been appraised, it is moved out as quickly as possible. Only then should the balance of the shipment be disposed of for consumption.

LIQUIDATION

If the importer accepts the findings of the Import Specialist Team or if the dutiable value has been established finally by a decision of the United States Customs Court, the Regional Liquidator liquidates the entry. These custom court decisions are rulings on appeals made by importers to secure the correct classification of specified goods.

Examination of the procedure indicates that the act of liquidation is the Customhouse's final ascertainment of the rate and amount of duty being collected. The notice of liquidation advises the importer of any classification of a rate or amount of duty, either higher or lower, than that under which his goods had been entered, upon payment of the estimated duty. If a protest is duly filed and the Import Specialist Team agrees with the claim, it reliquidates the entry; otherwise, the protest will be sent to the United States Customs Court for its final decision as to the proper classification of the merchandise. Conversely, when a lesser amount of duty is due on the goods than was deposited at the time of their entry, the excess duty originally deposited is refunded without any claim for reimbursement.

DRAWBACK

Goods exported from the United States are often comprised partially of imported, duty-paid, raw materials or components. Typical examples are paints, floor coverings, steel rolls, certain oils, wools and automobiles. Subsequently, the manufacturing exporter sells his products, containing wholly or partly the imported raw material, to foreign buyers.

According to the Tariff Act of 1930, Sections 313 and 557/558, these goods are entitled to a 99 per cent refund, called *Drawback,* and are numbered by the thousand. The procedure in seeking to obtain a drawback starts with submitting an application for authorization of the drawback claim to the United States Treasury Department, which examines its correctness. Upon approval, permission for filing a claim is given. Before the shipment is exported, the Customs Service is to be notified at least one day ahead, and a notice of intent to claim must be forwarded to the Regional Commissioner at the port of exportation, so that the goods in question can be inspected before they are loaded on board a vessel or cross the border.

Manufacturers must maintain accurate records regarding the importation and manufacture of goods, which must be available for inspection by the Treasury Department. The drawback claim must be filed and completed not later than three years from the date of exportation by submitting the necessary certificates, affidavits, and forms required by the customs authorities.

The Customhouse Broker, whose organization is trained and experienced in all matters relating to importation and re-exportation, advises his clients as to the necessary procedures in connection with drawback claims. He relieves his patrons of the intricate detail work, as far as possible, by supplying all the forms, preparing and filing at the Customhouse the preliminary and final entries, and by assembling all the supporting documents. Many forms are applicable to this procedure, among which the most important are: (1) Notice of Intent to Export; (2) Drawback Entry; (3) Drawback Entry and Certificate of Manufacture; (4) Certificate of Manufacture; (5) Certificate of Delivery; (6) Certificate of Importation; (7) Abstract from Manufacturing Record; and (8) *Customhouse Copy* of Bill of Lading.

Prompt settlement of claims depends on the proper, expert use of the applicable forms. The Customhouse Broker spares no effort in attending to the full protection of his clients' interests. For those wishing to engage in the importation of articles assembled abroad from U.S. components, utilizing the provisions of ITEM 807.00 TSUS (Tariff Schedules of the United States) and allowing a reduced duty treatment, a special 807 GUIDE was published in March 1979 by the U.S. Customs Service.

CHAPTER XXXI

The Foreign Trade Zone

HISTORICAL BACKGROUND

The power to tax as a means of providing revenue has transversed historic regimes, and the exercise of this prerogative has resided in the sovereign, be it nobleman, feudal baron, prince, king, emperor, and—later—the state or the government. Merchants opposed taxes a thousand years ago with the same zeal as they do today.

Customs duties, or taxes on imports under tariffs, have occasioned great debates whether levied for the purpose of raising revenue or, as in modern times, aimed at the maintenance of a higher standard of living. As early as A.D. 1189, Frederick I, German emperor of the Holy Roman Empire, granted a charter to the city of Hamburg, releasing that town from the payment of customs duties. Attempts, then, were made to set up trade centers, where no taxes or tariffs were to be imposed, which for these imposts, might threaten ruin to the recently revived maritime commerce, as burdensome tariffs were charged by many petty states. This trend received a further impetus during the thirteenth century. Then political troubles in the Holy Roman Empire and the difficulties of seafaring traders, caused by pirates, oppressive measures against foreign merchants, and excessive taxation on imports led to a protective association of German, Dutch and Belgian cities, the Hanseatic League, which reached its summit in the fourteenth century. This group organized a series of free ports, whose positions were strengthened through the rise of mercantilism, and brought about an extension of this system all over Europe. Among the representative cities, we find the "Freihäfen of Lübeck, Hamburg, and Bremen; the "Ports francs" of Bruges and Antwerp; and the free ports of Stockholm, Amsterdam, London, Leghorn, Venice, Trieste, Genoa, and Marseilles. All goods entering these port cities were duty-free; their citizens received the benefits of tax-free merchandise. If the goods were moved into the adjacent hinterland of which the free port was part, duty had to be paid, but not if they were reshipped to another country. The free trade ports of that era, not to be confused with today's free zones, covered the entire area of a port or port city, including all its citizens.

During the 19th Century, the danger of smuggling, the advent of the Industrial Revolution, and the extension of the laissez-faire policy caused a decline of many free ports. Their importance as transhipping points reached its peak at the beginning of the 20th Century when organized liner service rendered their use as collections and transhipping centers more and more unnecessary. Only a few "true" free ports, more correctly called "free trade ports", such as, Hongkong and Singapore, where goods may be brought in and re-exported without any red tape, customs formality, or payment of duty, are now in existence. The formerly famous free ports of Europe are now nothing more than ordinary free trade zones. Thereon the United States foreign trade zones have been modeled, and adapted in their operation, with the only minor difference being that European zones cover an infinitely larger port area, if not the entire waterfront.

FREE PORTS

The function of a free port (free zone), as we have seen, is to facilitate transhipments, re-exports, and consignment shipments, by exempting goods from customs duties and regulations. Goods on an intransit status, and those destined for stockpiling, manipulation, exhibition, and even manufacturing before importing, will aim at a free course of action in redistributing them over any available market area, in accordance with world trade opportunities. With substantial quantities of the products on hand, free from customs formalities and bonds, and with unlimited time to store, many advantages indubitably are offered, particularly in a country, or in the neighborhood of foreign countries, adhering to a protective tariff system. In this respect the Western Hemisphere affords excellent opportunities for the development of re-export and trans-shipment trade. Efficiency and growth of free ports (free zones) are of course conditioned by their favorable geographical location and progressive harbor administration, a rich hinterland, excellent transportation and shipping facilities, and an enterprising foreign trade community.

UNITED STATES FOREIGN TRADE ZONES

Foreign Trade Zones in the United States are of recent origin. The first attempt in 1894 to introduce corresponding legislation in the Senate was an unsuccessful one, as were later resolutions and bills; moreover, they were defeated by the isolationist and hostile attitude of Congress. United States trade policy, until the advent of the "New Deal," supported a high tariff system, which reached its culminating point in the *Tariff Act of 1930* (Smooth-Hawley Act). The Reciprocal Trade Agreements Program of 1934 indicated the first change of direction, and was followed in the same year by the *Foreign Trade Zones Act*. Sponsored by Congressman Emanuel F. Celler, of New York, the Foreign Trade Zones Act further liberalized our trading position, by providing for the free importation of foreign goods into a restricted "zone," unhampered by restrictive and onerous customs regulations. Indicating an increased understanding of the dominant position of the United States in world affairs, Congress authorized the President to lower import duties in 1945. Despite this, an amendment to the Celler Act, introduced in 1948, to permit manufacturing and exhibiting in Foreign Trade Zones, was surprisingly defeated by an "anti-foreign" minded majority in Congress. However, another attempt to pass this resubmitted amendment was successful in 1949, and it became Public Law 566, effective in June, 1950.

Foreign Trade Zones represent a mechanical device which conforms to the needs of a flexible tariff policy. Considering that the institution of Foreign Trade Zones concurs with their aim of protecting the country from being glutted with imports, the supporters of protectionism are inconsistent in their abhorence of these zones. Conversely, Foreign-Trade Zones definitely are instrumental in encouraging and facilitating our potentialities for foreign trade, which for political and other reasons should be realized to the fullest extent.

Published by the United States Department of Commerce, "Regulations Governing Foreign Trade Zones," include amendments of the Act, passed in 1945 and 1950. According to this publication, the nature and functions of a Foreign Trade Zone are described, as follows:

A zone is an isolated, enclosed, and policed area, under the supervision of a designated board of federal officials; operated as a public utility by a corporation, in or adjacent to a port of entry, without resident population; furnished with the necessary facilities for loading and unloading, for storing goods, and for re-shipping them by land and water; and area into which goods may be brought, stored, and subjected to certain specified manipulation operations. If reshipped to foreign points, the goods may leave the restricted trade zone without the payment of duties and without the intervention of customs officials, except under certain conditions. Such products cannot leave the trade zone for domestic use or consumption without full compliance with existing customs laws. Goods may be manufactured or exhibited in such an area with the exception, as to the manufacturing privilege, of the following commodities: Playing cards, tobacco products, oleomargarine, adulterated or renovated butter, filled cheese, coconut and other vegetable oils, narcotics, white phosphorous matches, firearms, liquor, sugar, watches and clocks. The area is subject equally with adjacent regions to all the laws relating to public health, vessel inspection, postal service, immigration, and to the supervision of federal agencies having jurisdiction on ports of entry, including customs to a limited extent.

The administration of the Act is under the Foreign Trade Zones Board, which consists of the Secretary of Commerce, as chairman; the Secretaries of the Treasury and War; and an Executive Director of Foreign Trade Zones Operations, as public relations officer and supervisor of administrative details.

The major provisions of the act are:

1. The Foreign Trade Zones Board is authorized to grant charters to qualified corporations, for the purpose of establishing, as well as operating and maintaining, foreign trade zones in the United States.

2. Each port of entry is to be allowed at least one zone, with

careful study to be made to indicate a definite economic need. Preferred grantees are public corporations.

3. Both foreign and domestic products are permitted entry into a foreign trade zone, free from customs restrictions, unless goods are otherwise prohibited by law.

4. It is permissible to perform certain manipulations, such as changing articles into different containers and repacking them; to assemble, distribute, sort, grade, clean, or mix with foreign or domestic merchandise, and then to re-export or import the items imported into customs territory.

5. The zone shall be under the protection of customs officers and guards at all times. The grantee of the zone may, with permission of the Foreign Trade Zones Board, permit other persons or organizations to erect such buildings as may be required to meet their needs.

6. Zones must be operated as a public utility; accordingly all rates must be equitable and subject to approval by the Foreign Trade Zones Board.

7. The cost of maintaining additional customs service required by the zone must be paid by the grantee of the zone.

8. Residence within the zone shall be limited to only federal, state or municipal officers or agents, and then only if it is considered necessary by the board.

The first Foreign Trade Zone in the United States was established in New York in 1937, now located at the Brooklyn Navy Yard, Brooklyn, NY. New Orleans Zone No. 2 followed in 1947 and San Francisco, Zone No. 3, in 1948. Los Angeles became Zone No. 4 in 1949 but did not live up to expectations and closed in 1956. Also in 1949, Seattle, WA opened as Zone No. 5. In 1950, San Antonio, TX (Municipal Airport) became Zone No. 6, closing in 1953. In 1961 Zone No. 7 opened in Mayaguez, PR and Zone No. 8 in Toledo, OH. Zone No. 9 opened in Honolulu, HI in 1966 with an additional Zone, 9-A, opening in 1972. Also in 1972 Zone No. 10 opened in Bay County, MI. Bayonne, NJ received its grant to become Zone No. 11 from the Foreign Trade Zone Board, Washington, DC in 1968 but never opened. In 1973 Trade Zone No. 12 opened in McAllen, TX and No. 15, in Kansas City, MO where Zone No. 17 is also located. Foreign Trade Zone No. 14 is located in Little Rock, AR; No. 16 in Sault Ste. Marie, MI; No. 18 in San Jose, CA; No. 19 in Omaha, NE; No. 20 in Portsmouth, VA; No. 21 in Dorchester County, SC; No. 22 in Chicago, IL; No. 23 in Buffalo, NY; No. 24 in Pittston, PA; No. 25 in Port Everglades, FL; No. 26 in Shenandoah, GA; No. 27 in Boston, MA; No. 28 in New Bedford, MA; No. 29 in Louisville, KY; No. 30 in Salt Lake City, UT; No. 31 in Granite-City, IL; No. 32 Miami, FL; No. 33 and Subzone 33-A, Pittsburg, PA; No. 34 Niagara County, NY; No. 35 Philadelphia, PA; No. 36 Galveston, TX; No. 37 Orange County, NY; No. 38 Spartanburg County, SC; No. 39 Fort Worth, TX; No. 40 Cleveland, OH; No. 41 Milwaukee, WI; No. 42 Orlando, FL; No. 43 Battle Creek, MI; No. 44 Morris County, NJ; No. 45 Portland, OR; No. 46 Cincinnati, OH; No. 47 Campbell, KY; No. 48 Tucson, AZ; No. 49, Port Newark, NJ and Elizabeth, NJ.

Applications for the establishment of a foreign trade zone have been filed presently by the following port authorities: Southampton, NY and Portland, OR.

FUNCTIONS AND FACILITIES

Foreign Trade Zones offer certain advantages and services to the import and export trade, as contrasted with those available at custom bonded warehouses. They include:

1. The Zone completely eliminates the expense and delay connected with appraisement, which usually necessitates forwarding one out of ten packages to the Appraiser Stores for examination. Appraise-

ment is required only when goods are ready to be "imported," then it is attended to right in the zone.

2. No expense for bonds or customs inspectors when imports are stored or manipulated, whether dutiable or non-dutiable.

3. Buyers may examine the merchandise and samples thereof may be withdrawn at any time.

4. Imports may remain in storage with no time limit.

5. Substandard foreign products are reconditioned before customs appraisal and liquidation. Goods not meeting the standards of Government inspection agencies may be destroyed or re-exported.

6. Ships, lighters, railroads, motor trucks, or parcel post make direct delivery to or from the zone, insuring efficient and frequent carrier service.

7. Foreign products may be held on consignment for spot delivery without being subject to customs regulations.

8. Domestic products may be assembled, repacked, or combined with foreign products for export. Drawback formalities are unnecessary.

9. Imports arriving improperly marked are re-marked to meet customs requirements, and heavy penalties are thus avoided.

10. Imports under "quota" restrictions may be received in any quantity in excess of the quota and held without customs liquidation while awaiting the next quota period; thereby owners are enabled to obtain loans on warehouse receipts.

11. Alcoholic beverages and other liquids imported in bulk may be bottled, labeled, and packed prior to customs entry, without being subject to state or federal licensing agencies.

12. Inland importers may arrange to examine foreign merchandise here; thus they save costly transportation expense to interior points on defective goods which would be later returned. Examination prior to customs entry precludes the possibility of payment of duties on damaged or unsalable merchandise.

13. Importers may erect their own structures within the zone to perform manipulating operations adapted to their needs.

14. Duty costs can be cut by not paying on "Shrinkage," that is, the part of stored merchandise lost through evaporation or seepage. For example, liquor, tobacco, and nuts lose weight this way.

15. Insurance costs may be reduced, because by storing merchandise in the zone, the actual and not the duty-paid value is applied.

16. On consignment shipments brought into the zone, it is possible to weather unfavorable market conditions by diverting the goods to other markets.

17. If shipments arrive with different commodities in a commingled condition and can not be readily identified, duty is generally assessed on the highest rate applicable to the highest payable commodity. Separation of these commodities at the zone will make it possible to apply the duty separately and hereby reduce the landed duty-paid costs.

18. Warehouse receipts for goods stored may be obtained without

posting bond, as it is required when storing in bonded warehouses; and money may be borrowed against the receipts.

19. Manipulations permitted in the zone make it possible to process goods into a class subject to a lower rate of duty.

20. Traders can withdraw merchandise in partial-amount lots and in any size package.

21. Showrooms can be set up to display merchandise to prospective customers; even international trade fairs can be conducted.

22. Manufacturing is permitted within the zone area, subject to certain exceptions, as previously mentioned.

As with all other zone manipulations, those involving manufacture and display are not subject to restrictions, such as, bonds, taxes, time limits.

The facilities employed in a foreign trade zone are, for all practical purposes, equal to those available in any other part of a well-organized port: namely, docks, piers, transit sheds, quays, warehouses, rail and truck connections, lighterage, modern cargo handling gear, and other trade requisites.

COST AND PROCEDURE

Rates and charges for storing and handling generally are based on the size and weight of goods or packages. Bulk cargo is rated on a tonnage basis, either weight or measurement. Manipulation or special services are charged on the basis of man hour cost; whereas processing space is usually leased on a square-foot rate. All zones in the United States are operated as public utilities; the rates and charges thereof are most reasonable.

To enter the goods in the zone, either the importer or the customhouse broker advises the zone office of an expected consignment, by submitting what is known as Zone Form D, properly executed, to the zone office for concurrence and release. This form is then presented by the broker or importer to the Entry Division of the customhouse where a lot number is assigned to the shipment. Should the goods require transportation through customs territory, a permit is issued for transfer to the zone.

Application for manipulating in the Zone is filed by the importer or his broker and is presented to the Zone Customs officials and the Zone operators for their concurrence. This form is made available and executed in the Zone. Upon its approval, the applicant is permitted to perform the requested manipulations or operations. All manipulations in the Zone are under the supervision of Zone personnel and customs inspectors.

To withdraw goods from the Zone, the importer or his agent requests the issuance of a constructive transfer by the Zone operators. This document, after approval by the Zone management and customs official, certifies that the named goods have been transferred constructively into customs territory. This transfer takes the place of a bill of lading and is presented to the Customhouse by the broker in making his export and import documents. After a permit has been issued at the Customhouse, the shipment may then be claimed for release.

CHAPTER XXXII

Warehousing

Abundant storage facilities are available to the foreign freight forwarder and customhouse broker at the port of export or import. Varying with his requirements, he will utilize privately operated warehouses, railroad warehouses, and municipal warehouses. In case of imports or re-exports, he will select United States bonded warehouses; or, if better suited, place the goods into the Foreign Trade Zone, where—in contrast to the bonded warehouse—"dead" storage is transmitted into a "live" one, due to considerable savings of various kinds. The forwarder seldom acts simultaneously as a warehouseman, for he usually arranges storage as a transportation adjunct. As a warehouseman, his status is that of a bailor in an ordinary mutual benefit agreement.

Any large ocean terminal in the United States takes into consideration the necessity of granting free storage to export shipments at the docks or piers for a few days. Steamship lines which regularly maintain services from certain piers to certain foreign ports permit shippers to store their goods until the next due sailing without collecting a special fee. This advantage is valuable, for if certain sailings are monthly, cargo which has arrived at the seaboard either too early or too late to connect with the originally scheduled vessel, would otherwise be subject to the inland carrier's storage fees, unless removed from the arrival terminal before expiration of the very limited free time. Nevertheless this advantage is noteworthy, because through the skill, diplomacy, and acumen of the foreign freight forwarder, the achievement of this minor privilege was the inception of a comprehensive, intensive campaign to secure a more-or-less general concession from the ocean steamship lines, known as, *Hold on Dock* storage facility. This procedure's extraordinary and far-reaching significance for the export trade will be thoroughly discussed later in this chapter.

Moreover, the foreign freight forwarder is, thus, in a position not only to keep otherwise unavoidable storage charges at a minimum, but also to attend to special activities at the pier or dock such as, weighing, sorting, recoopering, marking and sampling, less expensively than in regular warehouses where he has to pay an extra fee for special handling, in addition to the usual storage charges.

Factors which influence the forwarder's decision in selecting the proper warehouse facilities are the type of goods, the time element, and costs. When transportation is temporarily suspended, the forwarder usually contracts with a warehouse enterprise, to which he entrusts his general cargo. He will enjoy preference fees, which allow earning a small profit for his handling. The warehouseman will perform the usual services for him and will include also certain transportation services; such as receiving the goods from the railroad or truck terminal; checking for loss or damage; weighing; reconditioning; and forwarding to the steamer pier for export. The forwarder will require, also, the performance of financial functions from his warehouseman. In this category belong the issuance of negotiable warehouse receipts, the collection of C. O. D. charges, and the prepayment of transportation charges that may be incurred.

THE TRANSIT SHED

As a "dockside representative" of both the exporter and importer, the foreign freight forwarder must be unsurpassed with respect to the physical movement of goods; and this applies in particular, to all phases concerning the transfer of cargo at shipside, on the dock. The *transit shed* is a covered structure on a pier, quay, wharf or dock, which is erected for the temporary storage of goods in transit between ship and railroad, ship and truck, or ship and warehouse, or vice versa. The transit shed assumes an important position concerning the flow of goods in international commerce. If efficiently managed and well-equipped, the shed will facilitate the turn-around of ships and hereby reduce over-all operating costs. Delay or confusion will lead to excessive charges, with the resultant adverse effect on the port's reputation and activity. This consideration applies particularly to general export cargo which is delivered to the dock from a great number of shippers in many shapes, sizes, and weights; packed in all kinds of containers; transported by various means, such as truck, trailer, railroad, and lighter; and requiring storage on the pier, where it must be checked, measured, weighed, sorted, classified, and assembled for transfer to the ship.

Realizing that both ocean carriers and shippers favor ports which offer the most economical and expeditious loading facilities progressive harbor administrations will be aware of the continuous need for port development and hereby will take into account all the factors which tend to influence port conditions. Among these are: (1) Modernization of existing port terminal facilities, with respect to design and constructions; (2) Extensive use of mechanical equipment; (3) Adequate pier lighting to reduce waterfront crime, pilferage, and theft; (4) Larger transit sheds for larger ships, but with only one floor; (5) Wider aprons; and (6) Sufficient approach area to handle the increasing percentage of cargo moved by over-the-road carriers. This will help to provide adequate space and efficient traffic control, in order to avoid the bottleneck of "waiting lines" of trucks, which come to the pier to pick-up and deliver cargo.

HOLD-ON-DOCK STORAGE

The foreign freight forwarder, exercising his significant role as a coordinator and traffic supervisor in the handling of the immense export and import tonnage which flows through the gateways of international commerce, is keenly aware of the complicated marketing mechanism, with its concomitant traffic fluctuations, posed by the distribution process of transporting commodities from the factories to overseas destinations. He is influenced by the extent to which exporters fulfill their responsibilities in making their goods available for shipment and by the requirements of the importer, for whom he may act as port representative. Almost invariably, there is a time lag between production and consumption which makes storage highly essential. On the one hand, goods must sometimes be stored until consumers are ready to take them; on the other hand, the buyer's needs may require certain performances, with respect to assembling, financing, or purchasing, for which temporary storage becomes indispensable. Between these two poles, and occasioned by the complexity of foreign trade manipulations, there is a wide variety of reasons for storing goods.

Moreover, we must distinguish between the holding of cargo due to incidental causes and the temporary suspension of movement serving certain planned economic, financial, or legal ends.

To the first group belong the following: reconditioning, recoopering, repacking, sampling, marking, discrepancies in shipping papers, and lack of import or export licenses. Should any of these events occur, the forwarder will remove the goods from the carrier's terminal upon their arrival, within the allowed free time, to avoid otherwise accruing storage charges. Thence he delivers the goods to the ocean carrier's dock, to be held there for a limited time, until the following or subsequent sailing, inasmuch as the period of delay can well be anticipated. The holding of the cargo is a casual one.

The other category refers to extraordinary functions which the forwarder performs as a special traffic consultant. These services involve unusual accomplishments—so-called "firsts"—and exemplify the skill and artistry practiced. They represent pioneer work of prime caliber and contribute decisively to the promotion of international commerce.

The following case is illustrative thereof:

About two decades ago, a foreign distributor of a prominent manufacturer inquired of a forwarder whether he could eliminate the storage charges which were constantly accruing on his purchases (consisting of several thousands of tons during a calendar year) between the time of the factory's release of the merchandise and their actual embarkation.

The forwarder, after difficult and lengthy negotiation with a specific ocean carrier, succeeded in obtaining the *no charge, limited time* concession of holding the merchandise on dock. Then, or for competitive reasons, the remaining lines on the particular trade route extended the practice generally, and it has since been extensively accepted as a trade custom.

The total annual saving obtained by the importer on storage fees, plus 40 per cent duty thereof as part of the landed costs, amounted to several thousand dollars.

Similarly, other export cargo originating from various suppliers is now accumulated at steamer docks for purposes of consolidation or combination of special equipment, without paying storage fees. This principle, since then, has become almost universal, affecting most trade routes. This procedure has engendered tremendous advantages, in terms of dollars and cents, to foreign importers and, indirectly, to American exporters in reducing landed-cost of goods shipped.

IN-TRANSIT STORAGE

To promote foreign trade activities, one of the devices widely used by the railroads is the *storage-in transit privilege*. This procedure permits export shippers to stop their goods at a port terminal warehouse, without losing the benefit of export rail rates, in order to be packed, manipulated, or merely stored, until delivered to shipside either by lighter or truck. These terminals offer definite advantages to exporters and importers and are designed to cut the costs of handling and distributing cargo. They are located along the waterfront and have railroad sidings, as well as complete trucking facilities. Lately, export packing for certain commodities is performed extensively at the port of export for several reasons:

1. Inland transportation costs to the seaboard will be reduced, because the manufacturer will not have to pay for the overland movement of the heavy crates or boxes;

2. The need for export-packaging facilities at the plant will be eliminated. Hereby, plant space will be saved and expenses for labor and material will be reduced; and

3. There will be no delay between the completion of manufacture and the shipping from the plant, inasmuch as packing is attended to at the port of export. Resembling the principle of "Storage-in-Transit," the *Packing-in-Transit* or *Stop-over privilege* grants the export shipper the lower export rate.

THE COMMERCIAL WAREHOUSE

Export cargo, as a rule, moves without suspension from the point of origin to the destination. Should interruptions occur, they are usually of a temporary nature, whereby *Hold on Dock* storage suffices. Any suspension in the transportation of goods that is dictated by circumstances which apparently will not permit exportation for a considerable period of time (for instance, the cancellation of an export license, or the bankruptcy of the foreign importer), will force the foreign freight forwarder to place the merchandise in any one of the regular public commercial warehouses available within the port area, with which he has regular contact or special agreements. This is an enterprise which performs all the regular functions mentioned in the introductory remarks of this chapter. It must possess all the prerequisites which similar undertakings offer, such as, protection against fire, deterioration of the goods, theft, and fraud; up-to-date equipment; favorable location; connection with railroad-car supply; a fleet of trucks; low insurance and handling rates; pool car, trans-shipment and distribution services; and reliable management.

THE BONDED WAREHOUSE

Until the enactment of the Foreign Trade Zone legislation in 1934, the American importer or re-exporter, whenever he had no prospect of immediately disposing of his total overseas purchase in the domestic or foreign market, or wished to defer the payment of duty until his sale—effected in the interim—was ready for consummation, had either to place the total shipment in a bonded warehouse or let it go into "general order." If, upon arrival of the goods, he was in a position to sell a portion thereof in the foreign market, he had to file an entry for immediate exportation and order the remainder of the merchandise into a bonded warehouse. However, the petty details and the restrictions imposed by law, requiring burdensome formalities and the filing of bonds, terminated as soon as the importer or re-exporter could avail himself of the advantages offered by the foreign trade zone in allowing him the necessary freedom of action, which the utilization of the bonded warehouse did not.

Bonded warehouses are defined as buildings, or parts of buildings, and other enclosures, so designated by the Secretary of the Treasury, for the purpose of storing imported merchandise entered for warehousing, or taken possession of by the collector of customs, or under seizure, or for the manufacture of merchandise in hand, or for the repacking, sorting, or cleaning of imported merchandise. Like regular warehouses, they are, as a rule, privately-owned and operated, and differ from ordinary warehouses only in that all, or part thereof, is under customs lock and key, in short, under customs supervision. We distinguish eight classes of customs warehouses:

Class 1. Premises owned or leased by the government and used for the storage of goods undergoing examination by the appraiser, under seizure, or pending final release from customs custody. Customs warehouses of this type are also known as *Public Stores*.

Class 2. Importers' private bonded warehouses, used exclusively for the storage of merchandise belonging or consigned to the owner thereof.

Class 3. Public bonded warehouses, used exclusively for the storage of imported merchandise.

Class 4. Bonded yards, or sheds, for the storage of heavy or bulky imported merchandise.

Class 5. Bonded grain elevators.

Class 6. Bonded Manufacturing Warehouses, solely for the exportation of articles made in whole, or in part, of imported materials, or of materials subject to internal revenue tax; and for the manufacturer of cigars, composed entirely of tobacco imported from a single country, for home consumption or exportation.

Class 7. Smelting or refining warehouses, whereof the products are for exportation or domestic consumption.

Class 8. Manipulating warehouses, established for the purpose of cleaning, sorting, repacking, or otherwise changing in condition—but not manufacturing—imported merchandise, under customs supervision and at the expense of the owner.

The transportation to and from warehouses must be made by so-called *bonded carriers*. When employed in the port area, these may be either truckmen or lightermen who are licensed by the Collector of Customs after having executed and filed a bond. Furthermore, they also may be other common carriers, such as railroads, freight forwarders, over-the-road truckers, and inland-water carriers, who, owning or operating a transportation line, may be designated and appointed by the Secretary of the Treasury to perform *in bond carriage*, under fulfillment of the same governmental obligation.

The Collector of Customs assigns to the bonded warehouse a customs warehouse officer, known as *storekeeper*, for continuous duty. Goods may be received, handled, and removed only in his presence and with his permission. His services are compensated by the proprietor of the warehouse.

The owner or lessee of a bonded warehouse has to execute a bond before any goods are accepted for storage, in order to secure the government against any loss or expense arising from the deposit, storage, or manipulation of the merchandise. On all merchandise entered for warehousing, the importer has to file an entry to furnish a bond in the amount of twice the estimated duty. This bond is canceled when the duty is paid. Importers are allowed to store goods in bonded warehouses for the usual period of three years, but can file for an extension of one year.

If the duty has not been paid after that period has elapsed, the government sells the merchandise at public auction. Should the proceeds not cover the amount of the assessed duty, the Collector of Customs looks to the importer and the bond to indemnify the difference. When goods are removed from the warehouse within the due time— for instance, for consumption—a corresponding withdrawal form must be submitted to the customs authorities for approval.

CHAPTER XXXIII

Air Shipping

Air transport, the youngest member in the family of transportation carriers, is rapidly coming of age. It has made such rapid strides and spectacular contributions to the growth of our domestic and foreign markets during the last decade that it not only occupies an important position in the national and international transportation system, but also may be the forerunner of a new marketing revolution measured by its ever-growing vitality and usefulness.

Fostered by forward-looking legislation here and abroad, continuously supported by public demand, and efficiently operated by enterprising management, it has already changed the ways of doing business, particularly in the field of exports, to a degree thought impossible a generation ago.

The basic American law, the *Civil Aeronautics Act of 1938*, the objective of which is to regulate and promote the development of United States domestic and foreign air commerce, created the Civil Aeronautics Board (CAB) as the regulatory body and the Federal Aviation Agency (F.A.A.) as administrative agency in the Department of Commerce. This statute requires that: 1) the airlines serve "the present and future needs of the foreign and domestic commerce of the United States, of the Postal Service, and of the national defense"; and 2) air service meet "the public convenience and necessity, and the public interest."

On the international level, the need for uniformity of law, regulations and equipment finally led to the establishment of the International Civil Aviation Organization (ICAO) in 1947. This agency, affiliated with the United Nations, is dedicated to making civilian air travel and transport safer and easier, by establishing certain standardards and practices through multilateral agreements, and today already comprises sixty-eight nations. Its global headquarters is located in Montreal, Canada.

Noteworthy in this connection is that this United Nations instrumentality indirectly influences the formulation of international air rates and fares, an authority which, under the 1938 Act, was withheld from the Civil Aeronautics Board. The power to establish the above-mentioned rates and fares rests with The International Air Transport Association (IATA), a voluntary organization of international air carriers, which, by means of so-called *Traffic Conferences*, arranges for the necessary rate-making machinery. To be eligible as a member of the IATA, an airline must possess a certificate for a scheduled air service from a member state of ICAO. In this way, each government indirectly controls the eligibility of an airline to membership in IATA.

In spite of the above-mentioned limitation in the United States Civil Aeronautics Act, the Civil Aeronautics Board still has another means of exercising control over whatever arrangements or activities in which a United States air carrier might wish to participate. We shall now see how this control is accomplished. The IATA consists of three traffic conferences: one serves the Western Hemisphere; another is concerned with European, African, and Middle Eastern affairs; and the third group attends to matters involving Asiatic or Australian business. When any of the three conferences has met and acted upon rate or tariff proposals, each airline is required to submit these proposals to its respective government for approval. This means in the case of the United States air carrier that he must secure the consent of the Civil Aeronautics Board, unless he shall expose himself to the risk of violating the strict rules of our anti-trust legislation. A special finding by this Board, approving such contemplated agreements as not being contrary to the public interest, legalizes the participation of the airline. Should the "Board" disapprove all or part of a proposed IATA resolution, the United States carrier is then not only prevented, from being a party to it, but the resolution is virtually void, as the IATA procedure provides for the unanimous acceptance of any proposal by its members. If there is no objection on the part of any one government, the conference airlines may prepare specified tariffs for publication and enforcement.

COST FACTORS

In considering "cost" as part of the landed-value of goods shipped abroad, the firm's export traffic manager or the foreign freight forwarder, a hired traffic manager, will have to evaluate, as indicated earlier (Chapter XXV), all the factors affecting .a particular shipment or type of cargo, in order to select the most favorable method as to the carrier and routing to be used. We know that estimating the cost is more than merely comparing rates, computing them, and choosing the carrier who will transport the freight at the lowest arithmetical figure.

In studying the total freight carriage possibilities from the standpoint of air cargo, three general classes of shipments seem to emerge. One is the rush shipment which must be delivered as quickly as possible, regardless of cost, by any available means. This type of goods probably always will move by air, excepting those whose characteristics, size, and weight prohibit the use of aircraft.

To the second category belong bulk shipments, including oil, ore, and coal, whose low-cost, high-volume relationship are, for all practical purposes, unsuitable for air transportation.

It is the third group, the average cargo, affected neither by "emergency" nor by "mass," which lends itself most appropriately to movement by air and to the development of air transportation.

Despite the fact that air freight is still in its infancy, its capacity limited, and its cost relatively high compared with other transportation media, its outstanding present value consists in its being an important adjunct of surface transportation, which it either complements or replaces under certain circumstances.

Recognizing these limitations, which have developed over the years through practice and experience, the air transportation industry has initiated a comprehensive research program. Geared specifically to the expansion of overseas markets, this program offers American foreign traders advantages which already have shown significant results.

To overcome definite inherent handicaps, an all-out effort is being made to strengthen the air freight potential by : (1) reducing the distribution and financing cost for export shippers; (2) increasing the speed of the aircraft; (3) improving the adaptation of both flight and ground equipment to the needs of the shipping public by utilizing IATA (International Air Transport Association) cartons, igloos or containers, thus securing freight discounts; (4) creating "Interline Through Rates and Routes;" (5) expanding business volume through educational campaigns; and (6) extending the fullest possible assistance to air forwarders.

Foreign traders who intend to utilize air freight services must consider not only the actual transportation cost but also the cost-cutting characteristics peculiar to air shipping as a medium of distribution and financing. These features are simplified packing, which results in lighter weight, requiring lower freight and duties; and lower insurance cost, because of reduced losses. Other cost-saving elements—equally important, although not as obvious—include: lower inventories, quicker turnover of capital and goods, and greatly-reduced warehousing and handling costs.

The greater speed of the aircraft definitely favors a wider market distribution, without necessitating a permanent capital investment for procurement and manufacturing facilities.

The issuance of only one airwaybill from the point of origin to any overseas destination will reduce paper work and its attendant cost.

Each problem must be studied individually as to the appropriate method and procedure, since no single approach applies to the many and diverse situations. Particular conditions will dictate the necessary steps to be taken in order to secure the best result in efficiency and economy.

The creation of lower air-freight rates and special tariffs, which respectively utilize and adapt the principles of surface carriers with reference to the consolidation of goods by air forwarders, will also contribute to cost reduction.

Another feature, borrowed from the field of surface transportation, is the emergence of air charters. Cost-conscious exporters, well-advised by alert air-freight brokers and air forwarders, already are applying this newest type of transport with great success.

Mechanization and modernization of ground-handling equipment, as well as the introduction of new air-cargo liners, capable of being loaded and unloaded rapidly, and assuring more tonnage per day at less cost, is another prerequisite for successful and cost-saving freight operations.

In one respect, the air-transport industry has already gained part of its goal, namely, the creation of Interline Through-Rates and Through-Routes. Modeled after interline passenger freight rates and routes, agreements have been concluded between air forwarders and domestic airlines, as well as carloading companies. These agreements provide for gateway service to shippers in the interior, and hereby facilitate a rapid flow of air cargo to overseas destinations. Simultaneously, this coordination assures a simplification of the heretofore complicated rate structure by enabling the exporter to obtain corresponding through-rates.

Air cargo promotion is another aspect which is receiving greater attention, both by the airlines and by port and city administrations that are vitally interested in the development of air traffic. Recognizing that generalities, such as, "Reducing transportation cost," are inadequate, vigorous efforts are being made to furnish detailed information on all matters pertaining to air freight, as well as cost analyses for particular goods to any exporter. This procedure indubitably will prove beneficial both from the educational angle and from the anticipated increase of cargo volume.

Encouragement by the airlines of international air-freight forwarder's activities, which are regarded as being essential to the further growth of overseas air-cargo business, again confirms the foreign freight forwarder's valuable position as an indispensable link in international commerce. This policy attests also to his recognition as a performer of specialized services which, although outside the scope of the air carriers, are sufficiently substantial to warrant their support.

To arrive at an accurate picture of the over-all cost, every exporter should check and analyze the following factors before deciding upon shipping by air: (1) Cost of documentary preparation by brokers, agents, or carriers; (2) insurance charges; (3) packing costs; (4) local pick-up and delivery charges; (5) inland haul to airport or port gateway; (6) carrier charges from port of exit to port of arrival overseas; (7) surcharges and/or valuation charges; (8) landing and broker's fees at port of arrival abroad; (9) transit charges, including warehousing, from port of debarkation to ultimate consignee's premises, and (10) interest charges on idle working capital.

To reiterate: Any decision in the use of air transport should be made only with a proper awareness of all the circumstances which influence the utilization of this service. Interested parties who are well-informed will comprehend this requirement more readily than will the uninformed. Since it is impossible, because of space limitations here, to detail the rate structure and charges involved in international air transportation, a condensed outline must suffice.

We distinguished two classes of rates, namely, general and specific commodity rates; thereof the latter rates are substantially lower. They are quoted on a per pound basis for airport-to-airport carriage. Rate reductions of 25 per cent commence for shipments exceeding one hundred pounds. The carrier's tariffs provide, also, special advantages for the consolidation of small packages of various shippers into volume shipments, a feature which benefits the individual exporter through the medium of the air forwarder, the consolidator. Minimum charges vary with the destination of the cargo. A valuation charge is collected on shipments of high value; whereon the levy ranges from a minimum of twenty-eight cents per consignment to ten cents per hundred dollars. Rates do not include house-to-house service, but all air carriers transacting international business provide for pick-up and delivery service through local truckmen at published rates. Interairline arrangements between international and domestic carriers furnish the free transfer of cargo at all airports from which the overseas carrier departs. For further information as to tariffs, rates, charges, schedules, and other pertinent data, the foreign trader should consult with carriers, air forwarders, or air freight agents, all of whom are qualified and available to assist him with individual problems.

TYPES OF SERVICE

Fundamentally, all air shipments are handled by the airline—the direct air carrier. However, as in surface transportation, air transport has its "feeder" operators—the indirect carriers—called consolidators, or air forwarders, and the air freight agents, usually a foreign freight forwarder. Air cargo service may be performed in one of four different ways: (1) by the carrier himself; (2) by the consolidator—the indirect carrier; (3) by the air freight agent on behalf of the direct carrier—the airline; and (4) by the air freight agent, through the consolidator. Each method has distinct merits when appropriately applied.

INTERNATIONAL AIR PARCEL POST

International Air Parcel Post service is furnished by the United

States Post Office to a number of foreign nations with which this country has signed reciprocal trade agreements. Air parcels are subject to the same requirements as regular parcel post with respect to weight, size, and documentation. Packages may weight as little as four ounces, or as much as forty-four pounds. They travel "First Class" on scheduled airliners, overcome dockside delays by being cleared through customs at destination post offices, and are not required to pay any "minimum" charge. In addition, in many classifications, the exporter can secure savings up to 50 per cent over the regular International Air Parcel Post Rates by sending shipments of samples, replacement parts, printed matter, commercial papers, and many other small parcels via *AO Mail*, that is, Articles Other Than Letters and Post Cards.

INTERNATIONAL AIR EXPRESS

International Air Express service must be distinguished from international air freight. The latter, a volume movement of goods, is transported by the airlines between airports, with special arrangements as to pick-up and delivery by truckers, forwarders, or consolidators. International Air Express is performed by the Railway Express Agency (REA) as a door-to-door service, via rail and air, at considerably higher rates.

THE AIR FREIGHT FORWARDER

An *Air Freight Forwarder*, according to *Civil Aeronautics Board Economic Regulations* (Section 296.1), is defined as, "any person . . . which in the ordinary and usual course of his undertaking, (a) assembles and consolidates or provides for assembling and consolidating . . . and performs or provides for the performance of break-bulk and distributing operations . . . (b) assumes responsibility for the transportation of such properly . . . and (c) utilizes . . . the services of a direct air carrier. . . ." Originally, the Board regarded the forwarder, in his relation to the direct carrier, as "shipper." In 1949, the Board authorized freight forwarders to engage in overseas air transport, but their status as "indirect carrier" did not change. They were not required to file for a certificate of convenience and necessity; as heretofore, a letter of registration accompanying a tariff indicating the applicable rates and locations served, was sufficient. Subsequently in 1953, occasioned by the imminent expiration of all letters of registration which had been granted in 1948, the Civil Aeronautics Board instituted an investigation to establish a definite future policy with respect to the activities of air forwarders.

In a sweeping ruling, the Board decided in September, 1955, to: (1) renew indefinitely the authority under which air forwarders operate; and (2) sanction, in principle, joint-rate or compensation agreements between direct carriers and air forwarders.

The Board reasoned that the indefinitely-continued operation of the air forwarder was in the best interest of both the shipping public and the airlines, for which the forwarder performs solicitation services. In selling and promoting international air-cargo transportation, the forwarder contributes automatically to the expansion of international commerce. However, the air carrier neither can nor wants to be burdened with all the intricate detail work, which is unavoidable in the consolidation of small-package shipments. As a reward for their efforts in assisting the direct air carrier to secure volume shipments, air forwarders who do not own flying equipment and are not limited to any single airline, receive a lower rate. These forwarders transfer part of this saving to their clients, who, without the services of the consolidator, would have to pay higher individual-package rates or minimum charges. As an indirect carrier, the air freight forwarder issues his own waybill to the shipper; his relationship to the direct air carrier is that of a "shipper," and not that of an "agent." Nevertheless, to his client, he is responsible, as a "carrier," for the complete transportation of the goods from the point of receipt until the point of delivery.

THE AIR FREIGHT AGENT

Air freight agents act strictly as agents for shippers and carriers. Incorrectly, although frequently, they are referred to as "forwarders," with respect to their services in relation to air shipping. They issue the carrier's airwaybill and quote the carrier's original rates. Therefore, liability for carriage rests with the carrier. The majority of air freight agents are foreign freight forwarders who attend to air transportation as only one of their numerous business activities. They will arrange for door-to-door delivery; secure and prepare all necessary export documents; insure, bank, finance; act as customhouse brokers; and attend to other relevant details.

EXPORT DOCUMENTATION

Similar to export cargo dispatched via surface carriers in ocean transportation, all air cargo is subject to similar export documentation. Shipper's export declaration, commercial invoices and packing lists, consular invoices, export licenses and import permits, if required, plus the shipper's instructions letter, are the usual documents to accompany the shipment. The ocean bill of lading is replaced by the airwaybill. The procedure in export clearance approximates that as applied to the surface movement of goods, although there are minor deviations as to the number of certain documents to be submitted to carriers, consulates, and other parties at interest.

CHAPTER XXXIV

Information and Special Services

PROMOTER OF FOREIGN TRADE

One of the erroneous assumptions in the field of foreign trade is that exports do not require trade promotion. When products of an industry have reached a level of surplus production and hereby have achieved a comparative cost advantage, the situation does not imply that these goods will flow automatically to overseas markets without positive efforts on the part of the nation's exporters. To sustain the flow of goods, the ability to produce economically must be complemented by the market demand, which can be stimulated by the development of foreign markets. International competition is conspicuous among the factors which tend to diminish or even eliminate the apparently favorable circumstances created by surplus production and cost advantages. To surmount these varied obstacles and simultaneously stimulate continuous demand for our products, the American exporter must apply all available techniques to promote his product. Post-war history lucidly illustrates this point; for example, the German automobile industry is competing successfully with our manufacturers in foreign markets and is attempting to make inroads in the United States proper.

While it may be reasonable to consider—as many incorrectly do—that the sole function of the foreign freight forwarder is merely to arrange for export shipment, his own concept of his function in international commerce, by logic and necessity, is based on a much broader interpretation. As a connecting link between shipper, carrier and consignee, the forwarding agent finds himself exposed to numerous problems, requirements, and operations which permeate many fields of foreign trade activity. His idea of "Service" is an all-embracing one, which displays the range of his versatility, as well as his mastery of these diverse skills. Guiding shipments from the seller to the buyer —safely, rapidly, and as economically as possible—he handles the intricate paper work and wends his way expertly through all the obstacles imposed by governmental restrictions. To remain competitive and stay abreast of these rapidly changing times, the progressive forwarder must be perpetually alert and an active participant in all facets relevant to world trade. He is neither a "messenger boy" nor a "handyman." His initiative, resourcefulness, and flexibility combine to make him a reliable traffic expert, who streamlines the movement of freight and adapts both shipping and handling methods to benefit all parties concerned. The remarkable rise of United States exports is due, in no small measure, to the endeavors, competence, and accomplishments of the foreign freight forwarding profession. Placing their world-wide services and experience at the disposal of their clientele both at home and abroad, these forwarders are in the vanguard of those forces which are effective in their espousal of international commerce.

CONSULTANT ON EXPORT TRAFFIC

Although large forwarding houses maintain a so-called "Service Department" (the activities of which will be discussed at the end of this chapter), experience qualifies every foreign freight forwarder as an excellent source of reference on foreign trade. For this reason, foreign traders—both novices and veterans—expect to obtain competent advice from him. In many cases, exporters cannot attend to a certain necessary transaction because of local distance, or would not care to, because they are unfamiliar with the export situation. Shipper and consignee, buyer and seller, exporter and importer, the trade's combined functional elements, created an intermediary—the forwarder—in the international exchange of goods. The forwarder, in many cases, is the fount of their fulfillment; to him they not only entrust their merchandise, but upon him they depend, also, for assistance in resolving all problems pertinent to transportation and foreign trade.

The forwarder's service has many aspects. Its range includes providing information regarding: domestic and foreign duties; inland freight by rail or truck; ocean freight rates; domestic or foreign transfer charges at certain ports for trans-shipment purposes; sailing schedules; all types of fees and insurance; and general information about the market situation for a certain commodity in a specified country. In this connection it should be mentioned that the well-known foreign freight forwarding house, similar to a banking house, is solicited frequently to furnish information about clients with whom they maintain regular business relations especially in regard to their financial background and integrity.

Whereas an exporter's inquiries of a general or special character are attended to by various departments handling shipments to certain foreign countries, the forwarder's Service Department is designed to serve the buyer or merchant who is interested either in establishing or extending business relations. This department should contain, also, the forwarder's research facilities, the function of which is to sustain the enterprise's competitive spirit in perpetually operating at top level and to provide scientific training to outservice his competitors. Thus, this department should scrutinize and analyze the foreign customer's problems, whether they concern products, price, transportation, or credit. Diligence thereon constitutes a criterion for evaluating the service rendered. Seeking and expecting guidance in solving his problems, the buyer fully trusts the forwarder's ability to focus all his functions toward extricating his customer from the formidable morass of details in which this fettered individual can only founder. The forwarding house's service department serves, also as the department of advertising and solicitation, and will be discussed further in the section on the business organization of ocean freight forwarding enterprises.

The tendency to increase the scope of usual operations by assuming additional functions is observed currently in international forwarding circles; however, this trend is more apparent on the European continent than in this hemisphere. The consideration that an additional income could be secured without incurring additional costs was the dominant idea which induced leading forwarding houses to add a further field of operation to their present organization. These institutions learned they could thus: (1) favorably influence the total rentability of the enterprise, (2) better utilize the existing business organization, and (3) obtain an increased use of the capital invested. Therefore, we now find the foreign freight forwarder acting not only as an agent or intermediary in moving goods but also as a passenger agent. Earnings therefrom, based on a commission per ticket sold, are relatively high compared with the time-consuming detail work necessary for export or import shipments.

Dovetailing with this activity, the forwarder attends to the clearance and dispatch of the passenger's baggage. Hereby, he assists and advises the traveler on all questions regarding the route and voyage, while he may gain professionally for himself. Having contact with all types of persons, such as, agents, manufacturers, exporters, and importers, he is in a favorable position to extend his business connections, albeit indirectly.

Performing a partially allied-yet distinguishable service is the foreign freight forwarder who acts as ship broker or freight agent for one or more steamship lines, in addition to his regular business. In his capacity as agent for both the shipper and the steamship line, he not only attends to the actual forwarding and handling of export goods, but also undertakes to engage cargo and book space, preferably with the ocean carrier he represents. This additional activity can be performed within the regular scope of duties of his present business organization. As a forwarding agent, as well as a freight agent or a ship broker, he is essentially a middleman, selling a service that is dependent upon his contacts with his or other steamship lines on one hand, and the shippers or customers on the other.

Personalized service, rendered with unceasing loyalty and based on mutual confidence between the shipper and the forwarder, is the ingredient that creates their close relationship—a link which ocean carriers respect. Factually, the large forwarding houses control a tremendous amount of freight; hereby reducing the necessity for the steamship lines to solicit numerous shippers. This fact makes it desirable for the ocean carriers to pay a brokerage fee to foreign freight forwarders for the services which they render in soliciting and booking cargo. This service is of direct value not only to the carrier but also to the exporter, as it covers the important related services of quoting ocean freight rates and of providing all information concerning shipping regulations and practices.

Added to this usual connection between ocean carriers and international forwarding agents, another relationship exists—although rarely—between the forwarder and a railroad. For instance, certain European forwarding houses hold the agencies of various American railroads. These forwarders are in a position to issue so-called "through railroad export bills of lading" from European ports of shipment, indicating and providing transportation to inland stations in the United States of America. However, if compared with shipments handled routinely, business transacted through forwarders on the strength of this type of bill of lading is actually very small.

Diversity characterizes the forwarder's position as middleman and agent for either the seller or the buyer. The manifold manipulations to which the goods might be subjected, according to the instructions of owners, sellers, buyers, or third authorized persons (legal persons), require the forwarder to exert careful attention and great tact. These manipulations include:

1. Treatment of merchandise on the pier or in the warehouse, such as filling up, mixing, sorting, resalting, denaturing, loosening the soil, or picking out.

2. Control of merchandise, such as measuring, weighing, counting, taking value, inspecting, sampling, examining of damages caused by frost, leakage, and shrinkage, or other reasons.

3. Attendance to repacking, such as recoopering, hoopering, and repairing.

Proper execution of all the shipper's wishes and instructions in connection with the treatment and handling of the goods requires a sound and comprehensive knowledge of merchandise, trade, and custom. This knowledge is essential, particularly because the forwarding agent acts as trustee in all these cases; thereby, considering the great value of the goods handled, he is burdened with great responsibilities.

BANKER

The international forwarder also is a banker, although not in the literal or legal sense, when he assumes a quasi-banker's position by: (1) advising his clients on all matters concerning the financing of orders, collection of drafts and letters of credit, and general information about the credit-standing of clients; (2) advancing ocean freight and other charges, including consular fees on behalf of shipper and/or consignee; and (3) by either actually extending credit to the importer, thus financing the foreign buyer's order from his own capital resources or from cash fund deposits or letters of credit established with him or in his name. These services, as described in Chapter 24 (Financing), require considerable skill and experience. Involving a good deal of extra detail work, they greatly facilitate the smooth interchange of goods and are, therefore, of immeasurable value to the trading public. In addition, the official banking community is hereby substantially relieved of many burdens.

Domestic Representative of Buyer

The overwhelming majority of foreign buyers are not represented in the countries where they place their orders. This fact frequently accounts for misunderstandings and errors, as well as disputes and friction concerning the business relationship between exporter and importer. Farsighted forwarders, recognizing the need of assistance, therefore have offered their services and extended their facilities to overseas importers. Motivated by the conviction that their interests were mutual ones, the forwarders invited their overseas friends to consider them not only as their shipping agents but as their American Representatives, by making the forwarder's headquarters their "own" United States office.

For his foreign clientele, the American foreign freight forwarder will perform these services:

1. Instructions received from buyers are recorded and checked against those given by shippers; if contradictory, the forwarder tries to find a solution, satisfactory to both parties.

2. Orders are followed-up with suppliers.

3. Export Licenses are filed on behalf of the importer.

4. Proper ocean freight rates are applied. If the shipper has no conference contract agreement, the forwarder will either see to it that the exporter signs up or he will apply his own freighting contract.

5. Orders are consolidated, if possible, on one ocean bill of lading.

6. Shipments are routed economically from interior points to the most favorable port of exit.

7. Expediting and tracing of shipments.

8. If necessary, coverage of insurance under buyers own floating policy.

9. Payment of suppliers invoices from funds on hand or under letter of credit.

10. Banking and credit information services.

11. Acting as "business directory" for the importer, thus securing sources of supply.

Surely, this summation shows that what the forwarder supplies in full measure through several sources is service—with satisfaction.

CHAPTER XXXV

The Structural And Financial Organization

When referring to the organization of the international forwarding business, we limit our meaning here to the formation or original creation of a specific business enterprise in any one of its several legal forms, and do not include the internal or departmental organization for purposes of operation. Discussion of financial problems in the foreign freight forwarding business signifies the raising, providing, and managing of all the money, funds of any kind, or capital to be used in connection with the enterprise. Consideration of all the financial needs of the business involves an extensive knowledge and mastery of money, credit, securities, financial usages, and management; herewith it comprises a systematic control and regulation of all capital, revenues, and expenses.

Analogous to any type of enterprise, the foreign freight forwarding business, has a general purpose—to assist in supplying human wants—and a specific direct aim—to make a profit for the owner in the accomplishment of which he furnishes a living to the employees. Consequently, the effective performance of the "service" function is dependent upon the intelligent operation of scores of subsidiary functions which, although minor in scope, are indispensable in fulfilling the goal. Among these attendant functions are accounting, advertising, organizing, purchasing, office management, transportation management, personnel management, and many other activities. These diversified functions necessitate that success must depend upon the highest knowledge, ability, and skill of all persons concerned, from the executives and operatives in charge of these and similar departments down to the junior clerk or runner fresh from school.

Selection of a definite form of business organization which is appropriate for the special needs of the international freight forwarding business raises a series of problems that influence any final decision on this subject. The primary criterion in evaluating the form of an organization is whether or not that form is functionally adapted to meet the needs of this particular business. Problems relating to the liability of owner or partner; authority and responsibility of management; stability of organization; taxes and government control; the feasibility of aggregating capital; questions of control and movement; and numerous other details must be resolved.

According to a survey, the facts regarding the international forwarding business indicate that the overwhelming number of foreign freight forwarders in all parts of the world select the corporate organization as their form of business enterprise. This choice is dictated by several reasons. Firstly, there are the corporate form's general and principal advantages, such as (1) the possibility of accumulating large sums of capital, (2) limited liability of stockholders, (3) continuous succession, (4) marketability of ownership, (5) adaptability to efficient organization, and (6) flexibility of expansion and management. These advantages, furthermore, overcome the few apparent disadvantages, such as complicated formation; little influence in the conduct of business on the part of the stockholders; strict government control; and a relatively heavy tax burden.

Nowadays, corporate formation presents few difficulties. Corporation lawyers, experienced in the field, attend to all necessary matters. The stock of the forwarding corporation is, for the most part, privately owned—stockholders, incorporators, and top management being identical. The trend toward government control and supervision, as well as taxation, became so general for business during the last decade, regardless of legal status, that no special hardship can be noted which, practically, would subject corporations to any heavier burden compared with other types of enterprise, particularly in view of its outstanding advantages. The principal advantage, however, in choosing the corporate form lies in the limited liability of the stockholders or owners.

The private nature of the forwarding corporation is of decisive importance, because it is the backbone of any forwarding corporation. When transacting business involving an immense amount of merchandise, the value of which greatly exceeds the invested capital, the corporation obtains the required financial protection against the risk of loss and the security of undisturbed existence. Foreign freight forwarders could not exist successfully had they not protected themselves in this manner. The protection they enjoy under the law is always problematical, inasmuch as, in case of arguments resulting from ostensible negligence, it is always a matter of juridical interpretation whether or not they will be declared liable. Forwarders perform intricate and difficult services; in the execution of these tasks, mistakes are bound to happen, not so much through their own fault, but through ambiguous, incomplete, or inaccurate statements on the part of careless shippers. Damages so occuring may mount into thousands of dollars and be disproportionate to the earnings of the forwarders. An example will illustrate this occurrence:

An exporter shipped machinery equipment, the value of which amounted to $40,000, through his forwarding agent to South America. He had obtained in advance cash payment of 25 per cent, but failed to indicate this in his shipping instructions; these specified only a general reference, without giving any valuation, to insure against the usual risks. The exporter's commercial invoice showed the actual collection value of $30,000. The only true value was contained in the shipper's export declaration, which had been filed at the time of export clearance with the customhouse at the port of exportation and in a letter correspondence attached to the file.

The forwarder's insurance department based the insurable value of the consignment on the shipper's invoice value, thus underinsuring the goods by at least $10,000. The transporting vessel was sunk in a collision when leaving port, and the shipper requested the filing of an insurance claim for the full value of $40,000. The forwarder argued, and in the writer's opinion, correctly, that the shipper omitted to state in proper manner the insurable value. Further this insurable value, according to usage, is gathered from the commercial invoice and/or shipping instructions; therefore, the negligence was that of the shipper.

It is generally recognized that in the world of traffic which daily involves a multitude of details on hundreds of items, principles of liability must be liberally applied. The forwarder cannot be expected to examine his employer's instructions or documents with a microscope or scientific methods, looking for omissions or loopholes. The traffic world is also aware that for the imposition of increased liability in traffic matters, the performance, as such, is not the decisive factor, but only the "financial plus" in connection with the function. It is this purely financial consideration which disposed of the age-old principle of unrestricted liability, and an attentive study of international traffic history confirms this fact. Compared with the value handled by forwarders, their service fees amount to only an insignificant fraction thereof.

The capital investment in foreign freight forwarding enterprises, as a rule, must be regarded as small, for relatively few firms exceed the hundred thousand dollar mark. Contrary to European conditions, financial statements of a forwarding corporation, whose stock is privately-owned, are not published and, therefore, are not assessible for detailed discussion. It is known, however, that the preponderant majority of firms do not exceed a capital investment of $25,000. The popular opinion—that for the establishment and successful operation of the foreign freight forwarding business no large capital funds are needed—may be held correct. This is applicable particularly to the American forwarder, who, contrary to the Continental *Seehafen-spediteur*, owns neither trucks nor warehouses; instead, in both cases, he engages the services of trucking concerns and warehouses by contracting with them on a rental basis. On the other hand, the fact should not be overlooked that some large forwarders who specialize in a certain trade have actually invested considerable sums in real estate, such as, business buildings, warehouses, or storage ground, or in expensive mechanical transference devices, such as, conveyors, hand trucks, tractors, and trailers. However, as noted above, this may be regarded as exceptional.

Interesting to note is the fact that the financial basis of the American forwarder, which has developed in a typically capitalistic and individualistic economic system, is incomparably sounder than that of his European colleague. His disposal of capital is not influenced by any credit manipulations, a practice that is still customary on the Continent and which serves as a competitive weapon. Extensive credits are neither allowed nor taken. Steamship lines, railroads, or motor carriers, all subject to strict government legislation, do not grant any delay in payment of bills due. (Certain steamship conferences extend credit for a short period of 14-30 days under a so-called "Shipper's Credit Agreements"). The same principle applies to duties payable to the Customs. Therefore, the American forwarder who is adequately established has a sufficient amount of working capital and does not need to take up bank credits.

In case of large transactions involving extraordinary amounts of freight, or value, he will insist either on deposits or advance payment to cover incurring expenses. The capital invested, therefore, is mostly liquid capital, represented by assets which, in the ordinary course of business, will be converted into cash. These conditions also contribute to the high degree of confidence with which the American foreign freight forwarder is regarded on the part of his creditors. These conditions have been accomplished by efficient and able management, which is concerned not only with the development of the business, but also with a smooth-functioning, accurate bookkeeping and accounting system that provides orderly control and follow-up. The importance of proper accounting cannot be overemphasized, as it is the indispensable prerequisite of sound business conduct. Perhaps more than in any other profession, the position of the foreign freight forwarder who transacts a million dollar value business for the account of his principals, buyer and seller, is based on trust. His efficiency or ability to provide satisfactory services is appreciated, but his painstaking exactness in financial matters is the final determinant of his reputation, and the measure of the confidence he enjoys.

Therefore, in this type of transportation service where qualiy performance is one of the decisive factors, the small and medium enterprise has vindicated itself successfully and will continue to do so. Personalized service, use of his abilities, comprehensive knowledge in all traffic matters, and efficient advice to his customer, combined, will gain him the confidence of his patronage and will sustain his existence. Compared with the large enterprise, the medium-sized— even more than the small business—enjoys the indisputable advantage of being able to render highly individualized service, and to provide better control and attention to the manifold details. The role of the entrepreneur who actually administers the business is an important factor, because it offers the customer the desired security and satisfaction. In a small firm, the staff is not sufficiently large or efficient to surmount the firm's affairs; nor does the organization carry much weight or influence when dealing with other transportation agencies, such as railroads or steamship lines, because it lacks an impressive business record.

However, the question arises whether "service," alone, fills the need of the day. In the modern economy, the task of the international forwarder extends beyond the function of serving foreign trade as an intermediary in facilitating the movement of goods. Regarded from this viewpoint, the large forwarding enterprise or concern doubtless has advantages. Apart from the financial strength that permits an increase in the volume of business through the financing of export and import, the advantages are found in more effective organization and rationalized management. In addition, it isn't necessary to conclude that, because in a large outfit an account is just one of many, the attention paid to the individual, the regard for the client's instructions, or the respect for operating detail is less than in a medium-sized firm. Good management will provide for efficient service regardless of the size of the enterprise.

Closely connected with the problem regarding the size of the forwarding enterprise, there is the question of the advantages and disadvantages of creating a business concentration by organizing a net of inland and foreign offices. According to the intensity of the existing correlations between forwarding firms, these offices may assume a flexibly loose or rigid form of business cooperation. Herein, the setup can be arranged as follows:

1. The voluntary assignment of shipments among foreign freight forwarders who know each other through hearsay or recommendation —the assignment relation.

2. The selection of a definite forwarding house in a certain place, which agent acts as correspondent and generally has to handle all shipments touching the correspdondent's location. This arrangement is called correspondence relation.

3. The pooling agreement that may provide for the sharing of profit and loss, or even for a capital investment between two or more forwarding concerns.

4. The branch office, or "Filiale." Contrary to European usage, the American forwarder's foreign or inland branch office is easily recognizable; it always bears the name of the parent office and no disguise whatsoever is applied. Firms within the United States that acquire offices from competitors do not continue business under the old firm's name and deceive the clientele about the actual ownership.

The tendency toward expansion in the ocean freight forwarding industry is generally based on three principles: first, to keep shipments from the points of origin to destination in the forwarder's control, regardless of the port via which they have to be routed. Thus, they avoid possible loss either on the way to port or, if routed, via a different port. Foreign importers actually force the international forwarder to open branch offices at various seaports, as they do not wish to employ different forwarding houses at different ports. An example will illustrate this type of operation:

A buyer in Colombia, dealing in paper imports, orders material from mills in Maine, Illinois and Oregon. The cargo originating in Maine will be shipped via New York; the Illinois freight will move via New Orleans; and the consignment emanating from Oregon, via San Francisco. This will intensify business connections with the industrialized interior, especially in the Middle West. This expansion will help establish and develop consolidated carload services from inland points to various ports of exit; thus the forwarders will gain additional revenues by sharing in the resultant economies. The establishment of foreign branch offices in foreign ports will also assure an increase in revenues; hereby additional freight for import to the United States can be solicited and outgoing shipments for various buyers abroad can be combined and consigned to the foreign port branch.

The results of this policy of expansion are manifold. On the positive side, we note an increase in the number of shipments handled; the development of satisfactory relations with the clientele; and the improvement of transportation facilities and information service. On the negative side, we find a tendency toward overorganization, an increased risk of capital losses, and the necessity of large capital investment.

Finally, a few words about the specialization in the foreign freight forwarding profession. This occupation is not comparable to a similar position in commerce or industry, because the ocean freight forwarder represents within the forwarding industry a particular group, characterized by its diversity of functions and tasks. The ocean freight forwarder in his capacity as traffic expert and co-ordinator generally arranges for movement of all kinds of freight in export and import trade at the seaport, irrespective of type, size, and direction. However, the majority of forwarders devote the greater part of their activity to a particular field, whether it be export or import, or a certain traffic relation, such as, South America; or a certain type of transportation, such as goods in bulk; or finally, specialization in handling and shipping certain commodities, such as sugar, canned goods, paper, automobiles, steel, and other products.

These forwarding agents maintain an especially skilled staff that is familiar with the peculiarities of the goods. This, however, does not mean that they do not solocit, accept, and execute any other type of transportation business. The expressions "specialized in" or "specialists in", are frequently used by international forwarding houses for reason of propaganda and solicitation. This need not be a misleading statement to the customer, but should explicitly call his attention to the fact that the forwarder in question, besides his general activity as traffic coördinator, devotes his special interest to a particular field, as stated; it follows that such a forwarder is presumed to possess certain specialized knowledge.

This situation is exemplified by the forwarder who may have a certain traffic relation to a given market. By extensively increasing the volume of his business, he can obtain the most advantageous transportation facilities and charges; thus, he is able to offer more favorable quotations to his patronage than can any of his competitors for the same market. Because of his peculiarly close and intimate relations with his overseas branch office in a given market, he may offer to collect for his client. This being a special service, the merchandise value of all goods shipped during a year's period is collected at a much lower fee than would be available through any banking channel.

We have seen that the foreign freight forwarder applies his various skills to achieve coordination within his structural and financial organization and that by so doing he is enabled to expedite his external relations in serving his clientele.

CHAPTER XXXVI

The Internal Organization

No single form of foreign freight forwarding organization can be regarded as typical. In size, it varies from a one-man outfit with desk space in some other company's office to a large business organization, with hundreds of employees and branches, or affiliated agencies, all over the world. The degree of specialization, the competition, the volume of business transacted, the management's (owners' and executives') views, as well as other factors, determine the set-up of the enterprise.

Custom dictates, however, that the main offices be located at the seaboard. Large freight forwarding concerns maintain branch offices at other ports and at strategically located interior points. This practice facilitates the routing of inland freight through more than one port and enables these firms to share in the freight earnings which result from consolidated export carload services. As in any well-planned organization, the staff is grouped according to functions, the important ones being solicitation, operation, and finance. The first, solicitation, represents the marketing activities of the foreign freight forwarder such as trade promotion and "service" selling. Operation covers all the intricate and detailed clerical work involved in handling the shipments and securing the documents. Under the heading, finance, are found all the activities devoted to bookkeeping, accounting, auditing, and the banking facilities offered to the customer.

EXECUTIVE—OPERATIONS—BANKING—ACCOUNTING— SPECIAL SERVICES

The home office of the foreign freight forwarder is subdivided, as follows: Heading the top level of the organization, we find the executive officers, or owners, whose chief functions are to develop the enterprise, to determine questions of policy, to hold the patronage of the firm, and to exercise control over the personnel. It is upon their ability to offer and produce satisfactory service that the existence and success of the enterprise depends. Customarily, executive officers head respectively functional divisions in the business set-up of the organization. The treasurer will be in charge of finance, the secretary will head the division of operations, and the president will direct solicitation. Each division is divided into departments according to their respective requirements.

The operating department, for instance, is logically subdivided into important sections, such as the traffic division attending to lighterage, trucking, tracing orders, and inland transportation; the import and customs brokerage division; the bill of lading division; the consular invoice division; and the various freight forwarding divisions, which, in turn, are divided on a geographical basis into sections specializing in traffic to Europe, Asia, Africa, and South America. Each section, in charge of a senior clerk and having two to five junior clerks and one to three stenographers, is placed under the supervision of the operating department manager. Each section, continuously handling shipments in the same direction or subjected to the same working procedure develops a high degree of knowledge and technique which benefits customer and forwarder.

As an alternative to this type of operational division, there may be an allocation of clientele among the staff of the freight forwarding department, under which all the shipments of an individual account are handled by the same staff member, regardless of the direction of trade. This system, however, because of apparent disadvantages based on the duplication of work, is usually restricted to the so-called "special accounts."

The accounting department staff attends to the payment and collection of freight and all activities pertaining to bookkeeping, auditing, and financial work. Financing of export orders, brokerage and customer bills, maintenance of the necessary records, and the handling of foreign exchange drafts and letters of credit constitute this department's usual operations.

The service department's functions are to maintain contact with the clientele; seek new patronage through solicitation, advertising, and other means of trade promotion; to assist foreign buyers in obtaining sources of supply; and to exercise a general supervision over the forwarding concern's performance of services and facilities.

STAFF REQUIREMENTS

We have observed repeatedly that the activity of the international forwarding agent is characterized by two fundamentals: expert knowledge of the highest professional nature and ability to cope with extremely diverse situations. Therefore, the work performed by the personnel in ocean forwarding concerns should be evaluated from this point of view. Their activity is not part of a mechanized working procedure, in which the initiative of the individual is lost. There are few other occupations in which the operating detail requires a greater degree of attention, consideration, and accuracy, to avoid an extensive detriment to forwarder and customer and which simultaneously offers the employee ample opportunities to promote the prosperity of the enterprise by displaying the proper versatility and independent decisions.

Certain clerical work, such as, billing, bookeeping, and mailing, is attended to routinely, but the proportion of employees charged with responsible, complex duties, is unusually high, which is attributable to the intricate and diverse nature of the business. To mention only a few, the responsible operating details include: consular invoice work, which requires perfect knowledge of a foreign language, such as Spanish; the preparation of export declarations, which demands an extensive knowledge of goods, in general, for proper classification purposes; the organization of combination shipments for clearance on one consolidated bill of lading, which demands a disposition for prudence in order to properly release and forward goods emanating from various sources of supply.

The continuous pressure of the working procedure, itself, demands great adaptability from each member of the staff, from the "runner" up to the top executive. Particular requirements, as in any other occupation, are placed upon those employees who, as senior clerks, assistant managers, and managers, not only direct the policies and details in their respective fields but also establish or maintain the business relations with their customers. More than in any other country in the world, the position of the forwarder's employee in the United States is enviable; here, unrestrictedly, he can employ his abilities and can assert his independence from narrow-minded business coercion. This attitude undoubtedly is rooted in this nation's political maturity and has contributed much to the growth of American business. This advantage is observed when the forwarder deals with others self-confidently and decisively; foreigners regard this behavior with perplexity and admiration.

A further characteristic of the freight forwarder's staff is its remarkably high level of business knowledge, not only in matters of transportation but in all general matters pertaining to foreign trade. Comprehensive understanding of the intricate export and import procedure enables forwarding personnel to furnish the necessary assistance in assuring an efficient flow of goods. Because the acquired knowledge is valuable for prospective business expansion, it is customary to employ persons who converse and correspond in at least two languages and who have traveled extensively abroad.

Continuous contact with foreign markets and an intimate knowledge of prevailing economic conditions are acquired by experience. The forwarder's solicitor who travels in foreign countries, or the department manager who is in charge of a certain country, or group of countries, is especially well-informed through extensive correspondence and conversation with foreign visitors. He is an invaluable adviser to the clientele seeking his counsel. A few examples will serve as illustrations:

1. Contrary to railroad freight quotations which are based on the hundred weight, ocean freight rates generally are quoted "weight or measurement, ship's option"; thus, they differ from the method of

freight calculation applied in domestic trade. Actually, the ocean freight for many of the regular commercial export shipments, such as textiles and auto parts, is assessed on a measurement basis, which is a multiple of the weight freight rate.

2. In many foreign countries the import duty is assessed on a gross weight basis—for example, textiles in Colombia. Export shippers who use cartons for textiles cause considerable inconvenience, or even losses to the buyer of such merchandise, unless they bale the textiles and protect them by strong—but light—outside wrapping.

3. The proper marking of export shipments is of great importance. Noncompliance with specific instructions will lead to difficulties which may even cause rejection of the cargo by the buyer. Foreign government regulations impose heavy fines in case of deviation.

The constructive aid tendered by the forwarder's personnel in assisting the foreign trader accomplishes both the creation of interpersonal good will and the promotion of international commerce, contemplated from the broader view of global political economy.

DOMESTIC AND FOREIGN SOLICITATION

In the keen competition encountered at home and in foreign markets, the foreign freight forwarder does not hold the favorable position occupied by the American exporter who is aided by the powerful sales-producing force of advertising. Trade-mark, slogan, and trade name, which constantly can confront prospective customers to create attention, develop interest, and inspire action are not available to him. He is not selling a product which, with regard to quality, the prospective buyer can test immediately and easily. He is, instead, selling a function—a service. His means to systematically influence domestic and foreign consumers of forwarding service are purely intellectual.

The desired success, therefore, depends upon the forwarder's relative ability to impress upon the "buyer" the idea that above and beyond the question of price, the quality of service and its excellent performance are the determining factors. This criterion is the sole tool for promotion in this trade, which is composed exclusively of quality of performance and mass turnover. Further, this implies that the promotion must be intensive if and when the existence and expansion of the enterprise is to be secured; and it is the intensity, not the extent to which the promotion is carried, that will prove efficacious.

During the last two decades a decisive change in the solicitation techniques of the American International Forwarding profession has occurred. In addition to demonstrating the forwarders' attainment of maturity, this alteration bespeaks his ever increasing contact with, and influence upon, the domestic industry. In this sphere, he actively aids industry by emancipating it from the isolationistic confines of economic nationalism. Although the forwarder does not attempt to initiate the sale of United States goods for the sale per se, but rather to secure the cargo for handling and transport, he either creates or improves the possibilities for the sale of American goods in foreign markets.

As previously mentioned, large forwarding firms maintain so-called "Service Departments" which follow-up trade opportunities and advise both exporters and importers as to prospective foreign and domestic connections. Hereby—and this should be emphasized—the forwarder is not violating his position as a trustee of the interests of both shipper and consignee, but merely furnishes the names of firms engaging in the production and sale of individual lines. His policy is to give inquirers only such information as could be obtained from business directories, and in no case will he recommend one firm over another. Since many requests of this kind are processed by the forwarder's service department, it is reasonable to assume that this type of trade assistance will bring the forwarder a certain percentage of additional business, if any should develop. Similarly, the international forwarder performs an indispensable service relevant to the promotion of his port. When he goes out to secure patronage among many export shippers, particularly in the hinterland, the forwarder, being well-informed about the advantages of his "home port," will do his utmost to attract business and strengthen the trade position of this gateway; on the other hand, he also must know the opportunities offered by competitive ports. As an expert on traffic control, he will be able to answer all questions concerning inland tariffs, routing, warehousing, transit facilities, frequency of sailings, availability of foreign consulates, and market conditions abroad; moreover, his continuous, close relationship with the various ocean carriers, underwriters, and port and other local, state, and federal agencies will be extremely beneficial to his patrons.

Potent media, useful in the international forwarding business, range from advertising by mail or trade paper to promotion through solicitors. However, specific conditions determine the application of particular methods in accordance with the type and aim of the enterprise. Cursorily, the situation appears as follows:

1. *Oral promotion.* This may be spontaneous recommendation by customers who are satisfied with their forwarder's service, or it may be a contrived recommendation. The latter is influenced by the forwarder through the payment of a commission to export or import agents who, in return, suggest, prescribe, or request their clients to utilize the specified forwarder's services. This method is widely applied, as experience has evidenced that this type of promotion is successful. Moreover, many foreign traders occasionally require the services of an intermediary in foreign ports; consequently, being ignorant of proper assistance, they are responsive to suggestions which recommend engaging a particular forwarding house.

2. *Promotion through solicitors.* This method is probably the most effective, but also the most expensive. Its success depends almost exclusively on the qualifications of the solicitor. Representing his enterprise abroad, he is judged critically by all whom he contacts, and any reflection on him will redound to his employer. To be adequate for his responsible position, a solicitor should possess qualifications that render him an asset when evaluated by his employer and the customer. He should have a pleasant personality and impeccable character. It is desirable that he possess sound, broad social qualities; be free of prejudice; be able to converse in the language of the country to be visited; and have an absolute knowledge about all pertinent transportation and related matters.

Some knowledge of merchandise, where and by whom manufactured, seems serviceable. The foreign freight forwarder's solicitor conducts business with a heterogeneous range of consumers and buyers, particularly abroad. The proprietor of a hardware store, the purchasing director of a department store, the manufacturer of textiles—in their diversity, they present an aspect of unity: candidly each craves to be treated individually.

Essentially, the solicitor should be exhaustively informed on national and international problems which might enter a discussion. Only prolific background, varied experience, continual reading, and a comprehensive knowledge of his field will qualify the solicitor. To reiterate: he does not sell any goods whose qualities or value he can prove, either through the distribution of samples or by comparison with the prices of competitive products. His task is to convince the prospective customer of the efficacy of establishing a mutual business connection, so that his visit, periodically repeated or confirmed through memoranda, will lead to a stable commercial relationship. If he is successful in soliciting the account, he will attempt to induce the client to sign *routing orders* that instruct his suppliers to ship through the forwarding house represented by the solicitor. However, as those routing orders are revocable, they do not guarantee the continuance of the effected business arrangement. Experience shows that some customers, harassed by the excessively frequent appearance of solicitors, seeking other deliverance, resort to expediency and sign these routing orders.

Simultaneously with the soliciting of new accounts, old customers are visited. Special requests and instructions are accepted, complaints or disputes adjusted. Here, the solicitor has an opportunity to learn about the comparable activity of successful competitive firms.

3. *Direct mail advertising, individually written.* This kind of advertising consists either of a letter addressed to a prospective customer, drawing his attention to the advantages offered by the forwarding concern, or of circular letters of similar content. They may differ with respect to the needs of specific foreign countries.

4. *Publication advertising.* Advertising in the mass media news-papers is not common. Important, however, are the export trade papers, journals, and other periodicals, which are read by business men at home and abroad, thus reaching prospective importers and exporters.

5. *The periodical notifications.* These notifications are by regular letters and printed circulars. They contain current trade information, customs and traffic news, sailing schedules, and general freight rates. They enjoy indisputable popularity.

6. *Advertising through gifts.* The usual gifts include calendars, pocketbooks, blotters, pencils, desk covers, and cigarette lighters.

7. *Particular possibilities for trade promotions.* Possibilities exist in advertising at exhibitions, and by seeking contact with foreign buyers or domestic exporters at industrial fairs.

To control the success of his trade promotion is a difficult task for the international forwarding agent, especially in the case of personal solicitation, for the obtainment of an immediate contract with prospective customers is rare. However, many acquaintances can be utilized in diverse manners. Meriting note is the formula that steady, systematic trade promotion by the foreign freight forwarder will prove successful both for the individual enterprise and for the benefit of the entire forwarding business transacted through the respective seaport.

CHAPTER XXXVII

Revenue

COST OF SERVICE AND EXPENSES

The foreign freight forwarding enterprise, being an industry subject to unrestricted competition and trade rivalry, must net the aggregate charges, not only to cover expenses but to earn a reasonable revenue in order to stay in business for an extended period of time. The costs incurred in the operation and maintenance of the enterprise can be divided into two groups: direct or variable expenses, which tend to fluctuate with the volume of traffic; and indirect, fixed or constant, expenses, which, over short periods of time, at least, do not vary and are independent of the volume of business. To the first group belong the expenses which are incurred by advancing duties or freight, insurance premiums or reimbursements, storage or demurrage. The indirect costs consist chiefly of expenditures for salaries, wages, and other operating expenses. Ascertainment of the share of indirect expenses for price or fee calculation purposes is extremely difficult, as the services rendered by the foreign freight forwarder vary considerably. Not only the heterogeneity of services, but also the incalculable element of time needed for the performance of a particular service, influence the forwarder's price calculations and force him to apply average time and cost standards.

Besides the *differential calculation*, which means, "charging more for higher-valued commodities than for mass goods," the foreign freight forwarder usually applies the so-called *addition calculation*. This computation provides, in addition to the particular or out-of-pocket costs of the single shipment, for a proportional increase of the constant expenses, which increase is calculated and based on a uniform percentage and includes, also a certain percentage for profit. To facilitate the calculation of forwarder's fees and to attain conformity among the foreign freight forwarders in a given port area, the professional associations furnish their members *general directives* for calculation purposes. However, due to the prevailing competition and the lack of effective enforcement, these instructions serve only as a theoretical guide; with regard to the observance of the desired price level, they do not have as much practical value as had been expected.

The turnover of the freight forwarding business is usually measured by the receipts for services rendered. The question whether, in times of depression, the enterprise can adapt itself to the changed situation by reducing its operating expenses depends on the financial setup of the individual concern. Where large fixed capital investments are involved, it will be more difficult to overcome unfavorable economic situations. This is not applicable, however, if the invested capital is mainly to cover expenditures for salaries and wages. Considering the distinctiveness of the foreign forwarding business, in which the quality of efficient and diversified service performance is a highly decisive factor, a retrenchment of skilled personnel in times of economic fluctuation is not advisable. Similar to other public utility industries, the foreign freight forwarding business is subject to the *law of decreasing costs;* that is, although an increase in the volume of traffic increases operating expenses slightly, this increase will be more than offset by the net earnings of the enterprise. To utilize this knowledge, every forwarder must exploit potentialities of increasing his patronage through continuous and extensive trade promotion. On the other hand, this condition should not induce the forwarder to accept additional business as a so-called "filler." In short, an increase in the volume of business should never be attempted at the cost of exact calculation.

SERVICE FEES

The revenues of the Foreign Freight Forwarder are of a twofold origin and nature:

1. Compensations incident to the value of service rendered in handling certain shipments, which are usually arranged by mutual agreement between him and his principal, the exporter or foreign importer, as the case may be.

2. Payment of a so-called brokerage fee or commission, ranging from 1¼ per cent up to about 9½ per cent of the ocean freight bill by the carrier. Originally paid as a reward for the "finding of freight" service, this is a custom which dates back to the early beginnings of world trade a few centuries ago. With the development of liner services about the middle of the 19th Century, it was paid as a remuneration for the "securing of cargo" for the ship; since the outbreak of World War II, it has been paid as a commission for "services rendered to the ocean carrier including booking space."

Because of the desirous impact on the forwarder's earnings and the construction of service charges, among a variety of reasons, the subject of *brokerage* became an economic issue of the first magnitude. In addition to affecting the livelihood of the industry itself, it became a political issue. The forwarding profession became embroiled in a congressional investigation relating to alleged abuses in connection with the receipt of brokerage payments, resulting finally in the enactment of the previously mentioned Public Law 87-254 of September 19th, 1961, amending the Shipping Act, 1916, not only licensing the Foreign Freight Forwarders but also regulating the payment of brokerage to them by oceangoing common carriers under Section 44 (e). Consequently a more comprehensive treatment of this topic is definitely warranted and is presented at the end of this chapter.

Included among the various services for which the forwarder will collect corresponding charges are: Arranging Transportation, Preparation and Handling of Bill of Lading as well as Attendance fee, which may be as low as $7.50 or as much as $50.00, and in case of heavy tonnage as much as $1.00 per ton; a charge of about $2.50 to $7.50 for the preparation of either a customs invoice, a consular invoice and/or a certificate of origin, which is largely dependent upon the detail work involved, a fee of $2.50—$5.00 for customs clearance, verification of export license; further, a fee for banking service, concerning either draft attendance or letter of credit collection may range from $3.50 to $10.00. Under the rules of the Federal Maritime Commission pursuant to General Order 4, Amendment #1 through 8, of May 1st, 1963, effective May 1st, 1965, licensed forwarders must itemize or state separately in billing invoices the actual expenditure made on its principal's behalf as well as the fees assessed for the forwarder's own services. As to insurance, the rule is satisfied if the forwarder shows (1) the insured valuation of the shipment, (2) any charge by the licensed forwarder for arranging or placing the insurance, (3) the total charge for insurance, and (4) the net premium cost of the insurance to the forwarder. The forwarder may also lump-sum his own fees for various services into a flat service charge. The practice of foreign freight forwarders in this respect is not uniform since much depends on the customs which prevail in certain trading areas or the special requirements of foreign traders. Sometimes extraordinary service or extra care warrant a "special service fee" as an additional charge.

There is no predetermined scheme of charges to be levied, as the fees depend exclusively on the nature and extent of services that individual circumstances may engender as well as the value of the shipments involved. However, certain standard services are covered by fixed fees, as indicated above, and frequently rate schedules are established on a sliding scale. Other sources of revenue to augment his income are open to the forwarder besides those applicable to cases where extra work in meeting extremely technical requirements demands a special remuneration. This is, for instance, the case when he acts as a quasi-banker in effectuating the payment for goods for account of, or by request of, the foreign buyer, thus indirectly financing the importer's order; or, if the shipper arranges to have the forwarder pay his invoice value, he thus finances the exporter's cargo. These transactions do not constitute a violation of Federal Maritime Rules (General Order 4, Amendment 1, § 510.21 (1) as long as the forwarder can prove that the funds involved are not his own but advanced to him by either a Letter of Credit in the Forwarder's favor or otherwise placed at the forwarder's disposal by his principal to "finance" or pay for the shipment in question. He is then also entitled to a corresponding attendance fee as compensation for "financing" such trade transaction. Further, whenever the forwarder is requested to file a claim with his underwriters (and this happens frequently, because foreign freight forwarders usually act as insurance brokers or agents), a commission is charged for the attendance of the claim. Finally, additional revenues are derived from arranging trucking or warehousing.

Confrontment by war or emergency, when space for commercial cargo is extremely scare, makes the forwarder's obtainment of ocean transportation infinitely more difficult. Solely his personal relations with the ocean carriers and his ability to act as a shrewd, alert buyer of a particularly scarce service will secure for him and his customer this precious desideratum—space. Therefore, it is wholly justifiable that the forwarder, as a reward for all his special efforts to engage steamer space, charges a fee for "booking steamer space." This fee usually amounts to $1.00 a ton, with a minimum charge of $1.00 to $2.00, which varies in accordance with the size of the shipment involved and the effort expended thereon. All other charges billed by the foreign freight forwarder are compensations incident to the value of service rendered in handling certain merchandise, and these are usually established by mutual agreement between him and his principal. Similar tactics apply to the freight rates to be charged in the case of small shipments. These special arrangements are exemplified in the practice pursued by foreign freight forwarders in the consolidation of consignments, which simultaneously obtain considerable savings for the shipper and noteworthy earnings for the forwarder. The forwarder's profit lies in the difference between the ocean carrier's minimum rate per bill of lading and the forwarder's rate, which difference he shows separately as profit on the bill of charges made out to his client.

On the European continent, where a large number of nations maintain an international exchange of goods, the so-called through rate, covering house-door transportation cost, is in general usage. We find this quotation, by which the forwarder assumes not only the effort of calculating the incurring costs but also the selection of the most advantageous route and the coverage of the insurance risk, sporadically applied in this country. This through rate, which is applicable to shipments sufficiently large to be billed on a minimum ocean bill of lading, usually runs higher than the aggregate of freights or costs actually paid to the various transportation enterprises, and thus includes a profit for the forwarder. These through rates are based on tariffs currently in force and which are issued by those transportation companies whose facilities are used. As long as the forwarder itemizes or indicates separately in his invoice the actual expenditure made on his principal's behalf, as well as his profit share, he does not violate any law. The same principle applies to the included insurance rate. The rate is offered to a certain segment of foreign traders, who, either as seller or buyer in foreign countries, will draw two distinct advantages: (1) the rate offers an exact basis for calculating the selling or buying price; and (2) the rate relieves the trader from any transportation risk.

BROKERAGE

As indicated previously, the forwarder—besides his recompense for services rendered to his principal, the shipper or consignee—has an additional, important source of income, the ocean carrier. This feature is common knowledge to those who are familiar with the international shipping business and its customs, which have developed during the past centuries. Lack of realistic economic thinking—even wilful denial of existing circumstances or legalistic meticulous distinctions—do not alter the fact that only the professional forwarders (but never the "dummy" or "quasi," that is, an exporter with an "allied" or "built-in" forwarding department) renders many valuable services to the ocean carrier. Many of these services should be performed by the line operator, but in practice are not accomplished, but which services either create increased revenues or tend to reduce the expenses of the steamship line.

Since the international forwarder of to-day, as the successor and consolidator of functions formerly performed by the freight broker and freight forwarder of some fifty years ago, does provide services benefiting the carrier, a valid consideration exists to support his claim as to the carrier's obligation for the payment of brokerage or compensation. The so-called "historic" concept of the expression *brokerage*, that is, the commission earned by the "professional and experienced intermediary between merchant and shipowner," only confirms the foreign freight forwarder's insistence and the correctness of his contention that he be recompensed for services that are actually performed in the interest of the carrier. This contention unqualifiedly contradicts the definition which the Federal Maritime Board proposed in early 1956 at a hearing before a Congressional Subcommittee in connection with Dockets 765 (1954 Investigation of Foreign Freight Forwarders) and 767 (Pacific Coast European Conference —Brokerage Rules).

Already in 1949, the then United States Martime Commission in Docket 657, a decision which has been sustained by the Federal court, found that:

... The contention that forwarders perform services only for shippers and that there is no consideration for the payment of brokerage by the carriers, is not convincing. The very fact that carriers fear that the removal of the ban against the payment of brokerage will result in all carriers being compelled to pay it because of the competition which will ensue is persuasive of the fact that forwarders do have the power and do direct, in many cases, cargo to the carrier which pays them. Testimony that the volume of cargo movement has increased in spite of no brokerage payments is not conclusive that the payment of brokerage might not have produced a greater volume. The forwarder can, and does at times, increase the movement of cargo when otherwise it might be slack, and the receipt of brokerage is an incentive to create new business as well as to seek to divert cargo from one carrier to another. Furthermore, carriers derive benefits from the activities of forwarders in directing traffic to them even when the carriers maintain their own solicitation tariffs.

Moreover, the Commission declared that:

Forwarding activities have developed American commerce. The maintenance by forwarders of offices in foreign countries has resulted in direct contact between United States shippers and foreign purchasers, thus securing new business and increasing the volume of trade. The studies which many forwarders make of statistical data, trends of trade, market conditions, and the dissemination thereof to foreign purchasers and to United States shippers also tend to develop trade. Consolidation of small shipments, with the saving of overhead costs to shippers, enables them to reach foreign markets which would otherwise be precluded because of high minimum charges by carriers. Consolidation can also save consular fees and improve the exporter's competitive position with foreign exporters to the common market. Moreover, forwarders make a valuable contribution to our foreign trade through their function of relieving the large number of small or occasional exporters from many details and formalities connected with export shipments. Simplification of export trading promotes and develops foreign trade.

The steamship lines, themselves, are divided in their opinion as to the merit, as well as the obligation, of paying brokerage fees. The overwhelming majority of liner conferences acknowledge the fact that forwarders do render numerous functions which redound to the carrier's benefit.

An articulate presentation of forwarder-broker service was tendered by Charles R. Adams, the Chairman of the Transatlantic Associated Freight Conferences, in his testimony before the House Merchant Marine and Fisheries Committee's Special Subcommittee on "Practices of the Forwarding and Brokerage Industry." At this group's hearing in New York, on January 25, 1956, he declared that:

. . . the economic value of brokers does not end with the nomination or designation or securing or collaborating in securing, engaging or booking cargo and the value of their service continues important as a commercial matter.

It is a reasonable observation to make that the existence of a conference in trades is a strong deterrent against unreasonable payment of brokerage by the majority of carriers in the trade," Mr. Andrews said. "However, it does not prevent non-members from attracting cargoes to their vessels by payment of higher rates of brokerage.

Under all the circumstances, our Member Lines consider payment of brokerage reasonably necessary and required to insure the necessary flow of cargoes to their vessels.

Foreign freight forwarders and brokers perform and render many valuable, necessary and essential services from time to time, such as documentation (this involves many technical details and formalities requiring specialized skill and "know-how"; booking of cargo (arranging for space with ocean carrier); marking goods, if necessary; storage of cargo, if necessary; preparation and distribution of documents (bills of lading, dock receipts, export declarations, etc.); supervision of goods at ports of loading and ports of discharge to final destination abroad; and taking care of all other matters incidental to effect export shipment.

There is no uniform practice by the various government agencies on their export shipments. Some governmental agencies (other than United States) in the Transatlantic trades book their cargoes direct with carriers and leave the complete details of handling shipments to freight forwarders. Others turn over cargoes to relief agencies who also leave the complete details of handling to the freight forwarders.

Prior to World War I, when life was simple, the bulk of export trade from the United States was handled from New York with no appreciable services from Pacific Coast to Europe. Service from the Gulf and South Atlantic was restricted largely to Cotton seasons with limited liner service only to main European ports. Business, therefore, originating on West Coast was shipped eastbound all rail, although a larger share moved Southern Pacific to New Orleans than shipped Morgan Line to New York. Mallory Line operated from Galveston and Mobile; Clyde, Merchants & Miners and Savannah Lines, South Atlantic and Old Dominion from Norfolk. Railroads, such as Atlantic Coast and Southern, also owned boat lines extending their services up to Baltimore. Shipping companies had offices at New York and Boston and to some extent Philadelphia and Baltimore. Some Trans-Atlantic Lines maintained Chicago Offices. The business in the interior was largely done through the foreign freight departments of the railroads and generally moved on through bill of lading.

Freight brokerage, as such, was a distinct class of business entirely apart from freight forwarding. The brokers, at that time, generally consisted of one or two partners with limited clerical assistance. The broker actually was the intermediary between the shipper and ocean carrier completing the transaction, and rarely performed any other services. At that time formalities were very limited and when it was necessary for him to prepare a bill of lading the freight broker generally did so without fee.

The United States then was still primarily an agricultural nation and shipments largely were foodstuffs or raw materials and amount of manufactured goods relatively limited. Packing house products were largely booked direct in the West and moved on through bills of lading, and the small general business was mostly handled by manufacturers agents. The firms did the selling, financing and shipping. Such small business not in these categories fell to Express Companies or freight forwarders who then were also relatively limited in number and would take receipt of the goods at some interior point, issue their own bills of lading (now no longer possible) and attend to the forwarding, generally on a lump-sum fee covering all freight charges, etc. At that time and even after World War I, freight brokers and freight forwarders were two distinct trades and while the freight forwarder might act as a freight broker, freight brokers, as a class, would not undertake any freight forwarding, not having the staffs to handle all the details necessary and when business of this kind was forced on them, almost invariably passed it along to some freight forwarder to handle for them.

With the coming of World War I and sudden expansion of shipping, a big change came about particularly as in the expansion of ocean carriers, with limited number of trained people available, many railroads and others came into the trade and introduced new methods of doing business. Manufacturing, of course, increased by leaps and bounds, services were augmented, many new trades opened up and ocean carriers in their expansion established branch offices in the interior to look after their own affairs and hired canvassers. Gradually the activities of the railroads foreign freight departments on behalf of ocean carriers eased and today, execpt in Canada, they no longer do any freight booking. With the extension of shipping, more and more services opened from other ports. We now have ocean carriers operating regularly from all ports to practically anywhere in the world and as result the coastwise trade has ceased to exist and business which formerly moved to New York is now naturally moving on these direct services,

on greatly augmented levels, as well as greatly altered in character. The through
bill of lading is no longer used by the Member Lines. Therefore, thsee changes
necessitated a greatly increased number of freight forwarders, particularly in
view of the great number of further complications with respect to financing,
corresponding, documentation, custom regulations, both export and import.
There are, according to our count, now about 655 freight forwarders in New York
registered with the Federal Maritime Board. The maintaining of a staff to handle
all of these details is very expensive to a merchant, unless his business is of a size
to warrant it. Freight forwarders can do this for merchants much more nominally.
As a result of these conditions the business of freight brokers, who previously were
largely specialists, on handling oil and wax, or fruit, or flour, or cotton, as the
case may be, has also changed. Today except for a few grain broker specialists,
all of them do miscellaneous business falling under the general term of forwarding
and brokerage.

The business of freight forwarders is conducted as a separate and independent
one, distinct from that of ocean carriage. The freight forwarder accepts shipments from the merchant, issues, or causes to be issued, booking notes, arranges
delivery of the goods directly to the Carriers loading berth, or alongside at the
particular port of loading, while the ocean carrier transports the goods overseas
to the port of discharge, where, in some instances, the freight forwarder or his
representative then handles the final destination in Europe.

Our Member Lines consider that the activities of freight forwarders, who
maintain offices, agents and representatives, not only in the United States but
also in Canada, Europe, and throughout the world, having direct contact between
the foreign buyer and the American seller, have developed American foreign
export commerce in our trades and their promotional work and activities tend
to serve, develop, assist, and increase the volume of export goods from the United
States.

The maintenance by merchants of a separate export office and staff at seaboard to handle all the details necessary and required on export shipments would
be expensive, unless the volume and the number of their export shipments are of
size to warrant it. The number of merchants in this class is rather limited. Other
merchants, large and small, also those with the small or the occasional shipment
and not familiar with all the specialized features, documentation, sailings and
services of ocean carriers, their rates, charges, tariff rules and regulations, apparently find it less expensive and more convenient and suitable to turn over their
export shipments to freight forwarders and avail themselves of such services.

There are numerous instances in our Trans-Atlantic trades where freight
forwarders, with their connections in Europe and closeness with the European
purchasers, are vested with the control of the routing of the goods generally
purchased F. O. B. factory, F. O. B. port of loading, or F. S. A. vessel.

Our Member Lines, therefore, consider the foreign freight forwarding
industry an important segment and integral part of export foreign trade *

Adequate evidence substantiates the fact that the basis for payment
of a commission to the commercial forwarder is not, and in the authentic historical import never was, "the securing of cargo for the ship,"
as such, as some captious attorneys content; rather, it is an "over-all
consideration," with respect to "securing business for the carrier."
If it is true that foreign freight forwarders and brokers are a

---

* Charles R. Andrews before the special Sub-Committee of the House Merchant
Marine and Fisheries Committee February 1956, as per reprint in Shipping
Digest, New York, February 6, 1956.

valuable asset, both as trade expediters and trade promoters in the expansion of our foreign commerce—to date, this has not been denied —and if, in pursuance of their essential activities they have received "brokerage," which represents a major portion of their livelihood, it must be irrefutably concluded that the elimination or restriction of brokerage payment to forwarders will be detrimental to our international trade, including our merchant marine; therefore, payment of compensation definitely should not be condemned nor prohibited.

Conversely, unlimited and virtually uncontrolled competition in the forwarding industry—despite warnings from within the industry, as well as from governmental bodies—has not abated. Because patronage has been solicited on the basis of price, instead of service—an unhealthy practice which has led to questionable dealings by a few forwarders—Congress in the autumn of 1955, decided to re-investigate international forwarding with the intent:

1. To determine "if taxpayers' funds are being spent unnecessarily through payment of brokerage to forwarders by subsidized steamship lines";

2. To look into alleged "phony" practices of forwarders, which were cited in a report of the United States General Accounting Office, Washington, D. C.; and

3. To inquire into operations under the Bland Forwarding Act, with respect to the handling of government shipments by forwarders.

This investigation also impelled the Federal Maritime Board, as the regulatory agency concerning forwarders' activities, into the arena. The Board disclosed that it had a revision of General Order 72 under consideration, but that it had to defer its publication until the completion of the Congressional inquiry. The intended amendments to Order 72, as proposed by the Board and announced during the hearing, were justifiably attacked by forwarders and were even criticized by the Congressional Subcommittee as being impracticable, unrealistic, and doctrinaire. These proposals created the impression that the Board's policy lacks the essential experience for comprehension of the problems concerning the conduct of international business.

In the interim, forwarders petitioned Congress for assistance. The outcome was a system of licensing of the forwarding industry by the newly created Federal Maritime Commission, under Public Law 87-254 of September 19th, 1961, Section 44 (a-e) of the 1916 Shipping Act as amended, thereby establishing the means to deal with all legal violations, without imposing undue burdens on a small, but important, segment of our maritime service industry. "Dummy" and "quasi"-forwarders, that is, persons who are engaged in the export sales business either as sellers or agents, and who, incident to such sales, perform forwarding services, were not licensed. Brokerage or compensation was to be paid by a common carrier under the law only to a licensed forwarder who had performed with respect to shipments made on behalf of others the solicitation and securing of the cargo for the ship or booking thereof, and, in addition, at least two of the following services: 1). The coordination of the movement of the cargo to shipside; 2). The preparation and processing of the ocean bill of lading; 3). The preparation and processing of dock receipts or delivery orders; 4). The preparation and processing of consular documents or export declarations; 5). The payment of the ocean freight charges on such shipments.

Regarded from economic viewpoint, income earned by a foreign freight forwarding enterprise may not always reflect the full importance of the services it provides. International exchange of goods, flowing smoothly and transacted efficiently, is essential to secure the degree of general prosperity in which an enduring peace can thrive. To promote and expand that vital international trade, the functions performed by the foreign freight forwarder are incontrovertible, indispensable, and invaluable.

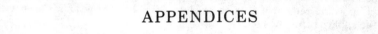

APPENDICES

APPENDIX A

Reprint of

UNIFORM CUSTOMS AND PRACTICE
FOR DOCUMENTARY CREDITS
I.C.C. Publication No. 290
UNITED STATES COUNCIL
OF THE INTERNATIONAL CHAMBER OF COMMERCE

GENERAL PROVISIONS AND DEFINITIONS

a. These provisions and definitions and the following articles apply to all documentary credits and are binding upon all parties thereto unless otherwise expressly agreed.

b. For the purposes of such provisions, definitions and articles the expressions "documentary credit(s)" and "credit(s)" used therein mean any arrangement, however named or described, whereby a bank (the issuing bank), acting at the request and in accordance with the instructions of a customer (the applicant for the credit),

i is to make payment to or to the order of a third party (the beneficiary), or is to pay, accept or negotiate bills of exchange (drafts) drawn by the beneficiary, or

ii authorizes such payments to be made or such drafts to be paid, accepted or negotiated by another bank,

against stipulated documents, provided that the terms and conditions of the credit are complied with.

c. Credits, by their nature, are separate transactions from the sales or other contracts on which they may be based and banks are in no way concerned with or bound by such contracts.

d. Credit instructions and the credits themselves must be complete and precise.

In order to guard against confusion and misunderstanding, issuing banks should discourage any attempt by the applicant for the credit to include excessive detail.

e. The bank first entitled to exercise the option available under Article 32 b. shall be the bank authorized to pay, accept or negotiate under a credit. The decision of such bank shall bind all parties concerned.

A bank is authorized to pay or accept under a credit by being specifically nominated in the credit.

A bank is authorized to negotiate under a credit either

i by being specifically nominated in the credit, or

ii by the credit being freely negotiable by any bank.

f. A beneficiary can in no case avail himself of the contractual relationships existing between banks or between the applicant for the credit and the issuing bank.

A. FORM AND NOTIFICATION OF CREDITS

Article 1

a. Credits may be either
i revocable, or
ii irrevocable.

b. All credits, therefore, should clearly indicate whether they are revocable or irrevocable.

c. In the absence of such indication the credit shall be deemed to be revocable.

Article 2

A revocable credit may be amended or cancelled at any moment without prior notice to the beneficiary. However, the issuing bank is bound to reimburse a branch or other bank to which such a credit has been transmitted and made available for payment, acceptance or negotiation, for any payment, acceptance or negotiation complying with the terms and conditions of the credit and any amendments received up to the time of payment, acceptance or negotiation made by such branch or other bank prior to receipt by it of notice of amendment or of cancellation.

Article 3

a. An irrevocable credit constitutes a definite undertaking of the issuing bank, provided that the terms and conditions of the credit are complied with:

i to pay, or that payment will be made, if the credit provides for payment, whether against a draft or not;

ii to accept drafts if the credit provides for acceptance by the issuing bank or to be responsible for their acceptance and payment at maturity if the credit provides for the acceptance of drafts drawn on the applicant for the credit or any other drawee specified in the credit;

iii to purchase/negotiate, without recourse to drawers and/or bona fide holders, drafts drawn by the beneficiary, at sight or at a tenor, on the applicant for the credit or on any other drawee specified in the credit, or to provide for purchase/negotiation by another bank, if the credit provides for purchase/negotiation.

b. An irrevocable credit may be advised to a beneficiary through another bank (the advising bank) without engagement on the part of that bank, but when an issuing bank authorizes or requests another bank to confirm its irrevocable credit and the latter does so, such confirmation constitutes a definite undertaking of the confirming bank in addition to the undertaking of the issuing bank, provided that the terms and conditions of the credit are complied with:

i to pay, if the credit is payable at its own counters, whether against a draft or not, or that payment will be made if the credit provides for payment elsewhere;

ii to accept drafts if the credit provides for acceptance by the confirming bank, at its own counters, or to be responsible for their acceptance and payment at maturity if the credit provides for the acceptance of drafts drawn on the applicant for the credit or any other drawee specified in the credit;

iii to purchase/negotiate, without recourse to drawers and/or bona fide holders, drafts drawn by the beneficiary, at sight or at a tenor, on the issuing bank, or on the applicant for the credit or on any other drawee specified in the credit, if the credit provides for purchase/negotiation.

c.   Such undertakings can neither be amended nor cancelled without the agreement of all parties thereto. Partial acceptance of amendments is not effective without the agreement of all parties thereto.

Article 4

a.   When an issuing bank instructs a bank by cable, telegram or telex to advise a credit, and intends the mail confirmation to be the operative credit instrument, the cable, telegram or telex must state that the credit will only be effective on receipt of such mail confirmation. In this event, the issuing bank must send the operative credit instrument (mail confirmation) and any subsequent amendments to the credit to the beneficiary through the advising bank.

b.   The issuing bank will be responsible for any consequences arising from its failure to follow the procedure set out in the preceding paragraph.

c.   Unless a cable, telegram or telex states "details to follow" (or words of similar effect), or states that the mail confirmation is to be the operative credit instrument, the cable, telegram or telex will be deemed to be the operative credit instrument and the issuing bank need not send the mail confirmation to the advising bank.

Article 5

When a bank is instructed by cable, telegram or telex to issue, confirm or advise a credit similar in terms to one previously established and which has been the subject of amendments, it shall be understood that the details of the credit being issued, confirmed or advised will be transmitted to the beneficiary excluding the amendments, unless the instructions specify clearly any amendments which are to apply.

Article 6

If incomplete or unclear instructions are received to issue, confirm or advise a credit, the bank requested to act on such instructions may give preliminary notification of the credit to the beneficiary for information only and without responsibility; in this event the credit will be issued, confirmed or advised only when the necessary information has been received.

B. LIABILITIES AND RESPONSIBILITIES

Article 7

Banks must examine all documents with reasonable care to ascertain that they appear on their face to be in accordance with the terms and conditions of the credit. Documents which appear on their face to be inconsistent with one another will be considered as not appearing on their face to be in accordance with the terms and conditions of the credit.

Article 8

a.   In documentary credit operations all parties concerned deal in documents and not in goods.

b.   Payment, acceptance or negotiation against documents which appear on their face to be in accordance with the terms and conditions of a credit by a bank authorized to do so, binds the party giving the authorization to take up the documents and reimburse the bank which has effected the payment, acceptance or negotiation.

c.   If, upon receipt of the documents, the issuing bank considers that they appear on their face not to be in accordance with the terms and conditions of the credit, that bank must determine, on the basis of the documents alone, whether to claim that payment, acceptance or negotiation was not effected in accordance with the terms and conditions of the credit.

d.   The issuing bank shall have a reasonable time to examine the documents and to determine as previously mentioned whether to make such a claim.

e.   If such claim is to be made, notice to that effect, stating the reasons therefore, must, without delay, be given by cable or other expeditious means to the bank from which the documents have been received (the remitting bank) and such notice must state that the documents are being held at the disposal of such bank or are being returned thereto.

f.   If the issuing bank fails to hold the documents at the disposal of the remitting bank, or fails to return the documents to such bank, the issuing bank shall be precluded from claiming that the relative payment, acceptance or negotiation was not effected in accordance with the terms and conditions of the credit.

g.   If the remitting bank draws the attention of the issuing bank to any irregularities in the documents or advises such bank that it has paid, accepted or negotiated under reserve or against a guarantee in respect of such irregularities, the issuing bank shall not thereby be relieved from any of its obligations under this article. Such guarantee or reserve concerns only the relations between the remitting bank and the beneficiary.

Article 9

Banks assume no liability or responsibility for the form, sufficiency, accuracy, genuineness, falsification or legal effect of any documents, or for the general and/or particular conditions stipulated in the documents or superimposed thereon; nor do they assume any liability or responsibility for the description, quantity, weight, quality, condition, packing, delivery, value or existence of the goods represented thereby, or for the good faith or acts and/or omissions, solvency, performance or standing of the consignor, the carriers or the insurers of the goods or any other person whomsoever.

Article 10

Banks assume no liability or responsibility for the consequences arising out of delay and/or loss in transit of any messages, letters or documents, or for delay, mutilation or other errors arising in the transmission of cables, telegrams or telex. Banks assume no liability or responsibility for errors in translation or interpretation of technical terms, and reserve the right to transmit credit terms without translating them.

Article 11

Banks assume no liability or responsibility for consequences arising out of the interruption of their business by Acts of God, riots, civil commotions, insurrections, wars or any other causes beyond their control or by any strikes or lockouts. Unless specifically authorized, banks will not effect payment, acceptance or negotiation after expiration under credits expiring during such interruption of business.

Article 12

a.   Banks utilizing the services of another bank for the purpose of giving effect
       to the instructions of the applicant for the credit do so for the account and
       at the risk of the latter.

b.   Banks assume no liability or responsibility should the instructions they
       transmit not be carried out, even if they have themselves taken the initiative
       in the choice of such other bank.

c.   The applicant for the credit shall be bound by and liable to indemnify the
       banks against all obligations and responsibilities imposed by foreign laws
       and usages.

Article 13

       A paying or negotiating bank which has been authorized to claim reimburse-
       ment from a third bank nominated by the issuing bank and which has
       effected such payment or negotiation shall not be required to confirm to
       the third bank that it has done so in accordance with the terms and condi-
       tions of the credit.

C. DOCUMENTS

Article 14

a.   All instructions to issue, confirm or advise a credit must state precisely the
       documents against which payment, acceptance or negotiation is to be made.

b.   Terms such as "first class," "well known," "qualified" and the like shall not
       be used to describe the issuers of any documents called for under credits
       and if they are incorporated in the credit terms banks will accept documents
       as tendered.

C.1   Documents evidencing shipment or dispatch
                       or taking in charge (shipping documents)

Article 15

       Except as stated in Article 20, the date of the Bill of Lading, or the date of
       any other document evidencing shipment or dispatch or taking in charge, or
       the date indicated in the reception stamp or by notation on any such
       document, will be taken in each case to be the date of shipment or dispatch
       or taking in charge of the goods.

Article 16

a.   If words clearly indicating payment or prepayment of freight, however
       named or described, appear by stamp or otherwise on documents evidencing
       shipment or dispatch or taking in charge they will be accepted as con-
       stituting evidence of payment of freight.

b.   If the words "freight pre-payable" or "freight to be prepaid" or words of
       similar effect appear by stamp or otherwise on such documents they will
       not be accepted as constituting evidence of the payment of freight.

c.   Unless otherwise specified in the credit or inconsistent with any of the
       documents presented under the credit, banks will accept documents stating
       that freight or transportation charges are payable on delivery.

d.   Banks will accept shipping documents bearing reference by stamp or otherwise to costs additional to the freight charges, such as costs of, or disbursements incurred in connection with loading, unloading or similar operations, unless the conditions of the credit specifically prohibit such reference.

Article 17

Shipping documents which bear a clause on the face thereof such as "shipper's load and count" or "said by shipper to contain" or words of similar effect, will be accepted unless otherwise specified in the credit.

Article 18

a.   A clean shipping document is one which bears no superimposed clause or notation which expressly declares a defective condition of the goods and/or the packaging.

b.   Banks will refuse shipping documents bearing such clauses or notations unless the credit expressly states the clauses or notations which may be accepted.

C.1.1   Marine Bills of Lading

Article 19

a.   Unless specifically authorized in the credit, Bills of Lading of the following nature will be rejected:

i Bills of Lading issued by forwarding agents.

ii Bills of Lading which are issued under and are subject to the conditions of a Charter-Party.

iii Bills of Lading covering shipment by sailing vessels.

However, subject to the aforementioned and unless otherwise specified in the credit, Bills of Lading of the following nature will be accepted:

i "Through" Bills of Lading issued by shipping companies or their agents even though they cover several modes of transport.

ii Short Form Bills of Lading (i.e., Bills of Lading issued by shipping companies or their agents which indicate some or all of the conditions of carriage by reference to a source or document other than the Bill of Lading).

iii Bills of Lading issued by shipping companies or their agents covering unitized cargoes, such as those on pallets or in Containers.

Article 20

a.   Unless otherwise specified in the credit, Bills of Lading must show that the goods are loaded on board a named vessel or shipped on a named vessel.

b.   Loading on board a named vessel or shipment on a named vessel may be evidenced either by a Bill of Lading bearing wording indicating loading on board a named vessel or shipment on a named vessel, or by means of a notation to that effect on the Bill of Lading signed or initialled and dated by the carrier or his agent, and the date of this notation shall be regarded as the date of loading on board the named vessel or shipment on the named vessel.

Article 21

a.   Unless transhipment is prohibited by the terms of the credit, Bills of Lading will be accepted which indicate that the goods will be transhipped en route, provided the entire voyage is covered by one and the same Bill of Lading.

b.   Bills of Lading incorporating printed clauses stating that the carriers have the right to tranship will be accepted notwithstanding the fact that the credit prohibits transhipment.

Article 22

a. Banks will refuse a Bill of Lading stating that the goods are loaded on deck, unless specifically authorized in the credit.

b. Banks will not refuse a Bill of Lading which contains a provision that the goods may be carried on deck, provided it does not specifically state that they are loaded on deck.

C.1.2   **Combined transport documents**

Article 23

a. If the credit calls for a combined transport document, i.e., one which provides for a combined transport by at least two different modes of transport, from a place at which the goods are taken in charge to a place designated for delivery, or if the credit provides for a combined transport, but in either case does not specify the form of document required and/or the issuer of such document, banks will accept such documents as tendered.

b. If the combined transport includes transport by sea the document will be accepted although it does not indicate that the goods are on board a named vessel, and although it contains a provision that the goods, if packed in a Container, may be carried on deck, provided it does not specifically state that they are loaded on deck.

C.1.3   **Other shipping documents, etc.**

Article 24

Banks will consider a Railway or Inland Waterway Bill of Lading or Consignment Note, Counterfoil Waybill, Postal Receipt, Certificate of Mailing, Air Mail Receipt, Air Waybill, Air Consignment Note or Air Receipt, Trucking Company Bill of Lading or any other similar document as regular when such document bears the reception stamp of the carrier or his agent, or when it bears a signature purporting to be that of the carrier or his agent.

Article 25

Where a credit calls for an attestation or certification of weight in the case of transport other than by sea, banks will accept a weight stamp or declaration of weight superimposed by the carrier on the shipping document unless the credit calls for a separate or independent certificate of weight.

C.2   **Insurance documents**

Article 26

a. Insurance documents must be as specified in the credit, and must be issued and/or signed by insurance companies or their agents or by underwriters.

b. Cover notes issued by brokers will not be accepted, unless specifically authorized in the credit.

Article 27

Unless otherwise specified in the credit, or unless the insurance documents presented establish that the cover is effective at the latest from the date of shipment or dispatch or, in the case of combined transport, the date of taking the goods in charge, banks will refuse insurance documents presented which bear a date later than the date of shipment or dispatch or, in the case of combined transport, the date of taking the goods in charge, as evidenced by the shipping documents.

Article 28

a.   Unless otherwise specified in the credit, the insurance document must be expressed in the same currency as the credit.

b.   The minimum amount for which insurance must be effected is the CIF value of the goods concerned. However, when the CIF value of the goods cannot be determined from the documents on their face, banks will accept as such minimum amount the amount of the drawing under the credit or the amount of the relative commercial invoice, whichever is the greater.

Article 29

a.   Credits should expressly state the type of insurance required and, if any, the additional risks which are to be covered. Imprecise terms such as "usual risks" or "customary risks" should not be used; however, if such imprecise terms are used, banks will accept insurance documents as tendered.

b.   Failing specific instructions, banks will accept insurance cover as tendered.

Article 30

Where a credit stipulates "insurance against all risks," banks will accept an insurance document which contains any "all risks" notation or clause, and will assume no responsibility if any particular risk is not covered.

Article 31

Banks will accept an insurance document which indicates that the cover is subject to a franchise or an excess (deductible), unless it is specifically stated in the credit that the insurance must be issued irrespective of percentage.

C.3   Commercial invoices

Article 32

a.   Unless otherwise specified in the credit, commercial invoices must be made out in the name of the applicant for the credit.

b.   Unless otherwise specified in the credit, banks may refuse commercial invoices issued for amounts in excess of the amount permitted by the credit.

c.   The description of the goods in the commercial invoice must correspond with the description in the credit. In all other documents the goods may be described in general terms not inconsistent with the description of the goods in the credit.

C.4   Other documents

Article 33

When other documents are required, such as Warehouse Receipts, Delivery Orders, Consular Invoices, Certificates of Origin, of Weight, of Quality or of Analysis, etc., and when no further definition is given, banks will accept such documents as tendered.

D. MISCELLANEOUS PROVISIONS

Quantity and amount

Article 34

a. The words "about," "circa" or similar expressions used in connection with the amount of the credit or the quantity or the unit price of the goods are to be construed as allowing a difference not to exceed 10% more or 10% less.

b. Unless a credit stipulates that the quantity of the goods specified must not be exceeded or reduced a tolerance of 3% more or 3% less will be permissible, always provided that the total amount of the drawings does not exceed the amount of the credit. This tolerance does not apply when the credit specifies quantity in terms of a stated number of packing units or individual items.

Partial shipments

Article 35

a. Partial shipments are allowed, unless the credit specifically states otherwise.

b. Shipments made on the same ship and for the same voyage, even if the Bills of Lading evidencing shipment "on board" bear different dates and/or indicate different ports of shipment, will not be regarded as partial shipments.

Article 36

If shipment by instalments within given periods is stipulated and any instalment is not shipped within the period allowed for that instalment, the credit ceases to be available for that or any subsequent instalments, unless otherwise specified in the credit.

Expiry date

Article 37

All credits, whether revocable or irrevocable, must stipulate an expiry date for presentation of documents for payment, acceptance or negotiation, notwithstanding the stipulation of a latest date for shipment.

Article 38

The words "to," "until," "till" and words of similar import applying to the stipulated expiry date for presentation of documents for payment, acceptance or negotiation, or to the stipulated latest date for shipment, will be understood to include the date mentioned.

Article 39

a. When the stipulated expiry date falls on a day on which banks are closed for reasons other than those mentioned in Article 11, the expiry date will be extended until the first following business day.

b. The latest date for shipment shall not be extended by reason of the extension of the expiry date in accordance with this Article. Where the credit stipulates a latest date for shipment, shipping documents dated later than such stipulated date will not be accepted. If no latest date for shipment is stipulated in the credit, shipping documents dated later than the expiry date stipulated in the credit or amendments thereto will not be accepted. Documents other than the shipping documents may, however, be dated up to and including the extended expiry date.

c. Banks paying, accepting or negotiating on such extended expiry date must add to the documents their certification as follows: "Presented for payment (or acceptance or negotiation as the case may be) within the expiry date extended in accordance with Article 39 of the Uniform Customs."

Shipment, loading or dispatch

Article 40

a. Unless the terms of the credit indicate otherwise, the words "departure," "dispatch," "loading" or "sailing" used in stipulating the latest date for shipment of the goods will be understood to be synonymous with "shipment."

b. Expressions such as "prompt," "immediately," "as soon as possible" and the like should not be used. If they are used, banks will interpret them as a request for shipment within thirty days from the date on the advice of the credit to the beneficiary by the issuing bank or by an advising bank, as the case may be.

c. The expression "on or about" and similar expressions will be interpreted as a request for shipment during the period from five days before to five days after the specified date, both end days included.

Presentation

Article 41

Notwithstanding the requirement of Article 37 that every credit must stipulate an expiry date for presentation of documents, credits must also stipulate a specified period of time after the date of issuance of the Bills of Lading or other shipping documents during which presentation of documents for payment, acceptance or negotiation must be made. If no such period of time is stipulated in the credit, banks will refuse documents presented to them later than 21 days after the date of issuance of the Bills of Lading or other shipping documents.

Article 42

Banks are under no obligation to accept presentation of documents outside their banking hours.

Date terms

Article 43

The terms "first half," "second half" of a month shall be construed respectively as from the 1st to the 15th, and the 16th to the last day of each month, inclusive.

Article 44

The terms "beginning," "middle," or "end" of a month shall be construed respectively as from the 1st to the 10th, the 11th to the 20th, and the 21st to the last day of each month, inclusive.

Article 45

When a bank issuing a credit instructs that the credit be confirmed or advised as available "for one month," "for six months" or the like, but does not specify the date from which the time is to run, the confirming or advising bank will confirm or advise the credit as expiring at the end of such indicated period from the date of its confirmation or advice.

E. TRANSFER

Article 46

a.   A transferable credit is a credit under which the beneficiary has the right to give instructions to the bank called upon to effect payment or acceptance or to any bank entitled to effect negotiation to make the credit available in whole or in part to one or more third parties (second beneficiaries).

b.   The bank requested to effect the transfer, whether it has confirmed the credit or not, shall be under no obligation to effect such transfer except to the extent and in the manner expressly consented to by such bank, and until such bank's charges in respect of transfer are paid.

c.   Bank charges in respect of transfers are payable by the first beneficiary unless otherwise specified.

d.   A credit can be transferred only if it is expressly designated as "transferable" by the issuing bank. Terms such as "divisible," "Fractionable," "assignable" and "transmissible" add nothing to the meaning of the term "transferable" and shall not be used.

e.   A transferable credit can be transferred once only. Fractions of a transferable credit (not exceeding in the aggregate the amount of the credit) can be transferred separately, provided partial shipments are not prohibited, and the aggregate of such transfers will be considered as constituting only one transfer of the credit. The credit can be transferred only on the terms and conditions specified in the original credit, with the exception of the amount of the credit, of any unit prices stated therein, and of the period of validity or period for shipment, any or all of which may be reduced or curtailed.

Additionaly, the name of the first beneficiary can be substituted for that of the applicant for the credit, but if the name of the applicant for the credit is specifically required by the original credit to appear in any document other than the invoice, such requirement must be fulfilled.

f.   The first beneficiary has the right to substitute his own invoices for those of the second beneficiary, for amounts not in excess of the original amount stipulated in the credit and for the original unit prices if stipulated in the credit, and upon such substitution of invoices the first beneficiary can draw under the credit for the difference, if any, between his invoices and the second beneficiary's invoices. When a credit has been transferred and the first beneficiary is to supply his own invoices in exchange for the second beneficiary's invoices but fails to do so on first demand, the paying, accepting or negotiating bank has the right to deliver to the issuing bank the documents received under the credit, including the second beneficiary's invoices, without further responsibility to the first beneficiary.

g.   The first beneficiary of a transferable credit can transfer the credit to a second beneficiary in the same country or in another country unless the credit specifically states otherwise. The first beneficiary shall have the right to request that payment or negotiation be effected to the second beneficiary at the place to which the credit has been transferred, up to and including the expiry date of the original credit, and without prejudice to the first beneficiary's right subsequently to substitute his own invoices for those of the second beneficiary and to claim any difference due to him.

Article 47

The fact that a credit is not stated to be transferable shall not affect the beneficiary's rights to assign the proceeds of such credit in accordance with the provisions of the applicable law.

APPENDIX B

Revised American Foreign Trade Definitions— 1941

Adopted July 30, 1941, by a Joint Committee representing the Chamber of Commerce of the United States of America, the National Council of American Importers, Inc., and the National Foreign Trade Council, Inc.

FOREWORD

Since the issuance of *American Foreign Trade Definitions* in 1919, many changes in practice have occurred. The 1919 Definitions did much to clarify and simplify foreign trade practice, and received wide recognition and use by buyers and sellers throughout the world. At the Twenty-Seventh National Foreign Trade Convention, 1940, further revision and clarification of these Definitions was urged as necessary to assist the foreign trader in the handling of his transactions.

The following *Revised American Foreign Trade Definitions - 1941* are recommended for general use by both exporters and importers. These revised definitions have no status at law unless there is specific legislation providing for them, or unless they are confirmed by court decisions. Hence, it is suggested that sellers and buyers agree to their acceptance as part of the contract of sale. These revised definitions will then become legally binding upon all parties.

In view of changes in practice and procedure since 1919, certain new responsibilities for sellers and buyers are included in these revised definitions. Also, in many instances, the old responsibilities are more clearly defined than in the 1919 Definitions, and the changes should be beneficial both to sellers and buyers. Widespread acceptance will lead to a greater standardization of foreign trade procedure, and to the avoidance of much misunderstanding.

Adoption by exporters and importers of these revised terms will impress on all parties concerned their respective responsibilities and rights.

General Notes of Caution

1. As foreign trade definitions have been issued by organizations in various parts of the world, and as the courts of countries have interpreted these definitions in different ways, it is important that sellers and buyers agree that their contracts are subject to the *Revised American Foreign Trade Definitions - 1941* and that the various points listed are accepted by both parties.

2. In addition to the foreign trade terms listed herein, there are terms that are at times used, such as Free Harbor, C.I.F. & C. (Cost, Insurance, Freight, and Commission), C.I.F.C. & I. (Cost, Insurance, Freight, Commission, and Interest), C.I.F. Landed (Cost, Insurance, Freight, Landed), and others. None of these should be used unless there has first been a definite understanding as to the exact meaning thereof. It is unwise to attempt to interpret other terms in the light of the terms given herein. Hence, whenever possible, one of the terms defined herein should be used.

3. It is unwise to use abbreviations in quotations or in contracts which might be subject to misunderstanding.

4. When making quotations, the familiar terms "hundredweight" or "ton" should be avoided. A hundredweight can be 100 pounds of the short ton, or 112 pounds of the long ton. A ton can be a short ton of 2,000 pounds, or a metric ton of 2,204.6 pounds, or a long ton of 2,240 pounds. Hence, the type of hundredweight or ton should be clearly stated in quotations and in sales confirmations. Also, all terms referring to quantity, weight, volume, length, or surface should be clearly defined and agreed upon.

5. If inspection, or certificate of inspection, is required, it should be agreed, in advance, whether the cost thereof is for account of seller or buyer.

6. Unless otherwise agreed upon, all expenses are for the account of seller up to the point at which the buyer must handle the subsequent movement of goods.

7. There are a number of elements in a contract that do not fall within the scope of these foreign trade definitions. Hence, no mention of these is made herein. Seller and buyer should agree to these separately when negotiating contracts. This particularly applies to so-called "customary" practices.

DEFINITIONS OF QUOTATIONS

(I) EX (Point of Origin)

"EX FACTORY", "EX MILL", "EX MINE", "EX PLANTATION", "EX WAREHOUSE", etc. (named point of origin)

Under this term, the price quoted applies only at the point of origin, and the seller agrees to place the goods at the disposal of the buyer at the agreed place on the date or within the period fixed.

Under this quotation:

Seller must

(1) bear all costs and risks of the goods until such time as the buyer is obliged to take delivery thereof;

(2) render the buyer, at the buyer's request and expense, assistance in obtaining the documents issued in the country of origin, or of shipment, or of both, which the buyer may require either for purposes of exportation, or of importation at destination.

Buyer must

(1) take delivery of the goods as soon as they have been placed at his disposal at the agreed place on the date or within the period fixed;

(2) pay export taxes, or other fees or charges, if any, levied because of exportation;

(3) bear all costs and risks of the goods from the time when he is obligated to take delivery thereof;

(4) pay all costs and charges incurred in obtaining the documents issued in the country of origin, or of shipment, or of both, which may be required either for purposes of exportation, or of importation at destination.

(II) F.O.B. (Free on Board)

NOTE: *Seller and buyer should consider not only the definitions but also the "Comments on All F.O.B. Terms" given at end of this section (page 9), in order to understand fully their respective responsibilities and rights under the several classes of "F.O.B." terms.*

(II-A) "F.O.B. (named inland carrier at named inland point of departure)

Under this term, the price quoted applies only at inland shipping point, and the seller arranges for loading of the goods on, or in, railway cars, trucks, lighters, barges, aircraft, or other conveyance furnished for transportation.

Under this quotation:

Seller must

(1) place goods on, or in, conveyance, or deliver to inland carrier for loading;

(2) provide clean bill of lading or other transportation receipt, freight collect;

(3) be responsible for any loss or damage, or both, until goods have been placed in, or on, conveyance at loading point, and clean bill of lading or other transportation receipt has been furnished by the carrier;

(4) render the buyer, at the buyer's request and expense, assistance in obtaining the documents issued in the country of origin, or of shipment, or of both, which the buyer may require either for purposes of exportation, or of importation at destination.

Buyer must

(1) be responsible for all movement of the goods from inland point of loading, and pay all transportation costs;

(2) pay export taxes, or other fees or charges, if any, levied because of exportation;

(3) be responsible for any loss or damage, or both, incurred after loading at named inland point of departure;

(4) pay all costs and charges incurred in obtaining the documents issued in the country of origin, or of shipment, or of both, which may be required either for purposes of exportation, or of importation at destination.

(II-B) "F.O.B. (named inland carrier at named inland point of departure) FREIGHT PREPAID TO (named point of exportation)"

Under this term, the seller quotes a price including transportation charges to the named point of exportation and prepays freight to named point of exportation, without asuming responsibility for the goods after obtaining a clean bill of lading or other transportation receipt at named inland point of departure.

Under this quotation:

Seller must

(1) assume the seller's obligations as under II-A (page 5), except that under (2) he

must provide clean bill of lading or other transportation receipt, freight prepaid to named point of exportation.

Buyer must

(1) assume the same buyer's obligations as under II-A (page 5), except that he does not pay freight from loading point to named point of exportation.

(II-C) "F.O.B. (named inland carrier at named inland point of departure) FREIGHT ALLOWED TO (named point)

Under this term, the seller quotes a price including the transportation charges to the named point, shipping freight collect and deducting the cost of transportation, without assuming responsibility for the goods after obtaining a clean bill of lading or other transportation receipt at named inland point of departure.

Under this quotation:

Seller must

(1) assume the same seller's obligations as under II-A (page 5), but deducts from his invoice the transportation cost to named point.

Buyer must

(1) assume the same buyer's obligations as under II-A (page 5), including payment of freight from inland loading point to named point, for which seller has made deduction.

(II-D "F.O.B. (named inland carrier at named point of exportation)

Under this term, the seller quotes a price including the costs of transportation of the goods to named point of exportation, bearing any loss or damage, or both, incurred up to that point.

Under this quotation:

Seller must

(1) place goods on, or in, conveyance, or deliver to inland carrier for loading;

(2) provide clean bill of lading or other transportation receipt, paying all transportation costs from loading point to named point of exportation;

(3) be responsible for any loss or damage, or both, until goods have arrived in, or on, inland conveyance at the named point of exportation;

(4) render the buyer, at the buyer's request and expense, assistance in obtaining the documents issued in the country of origin, or of shipment, or of both, which the buyer may require either for purposes of exportation, or of importation at destination.

Buyer must

(1) be responsible for all movement of the goods from inland conveyance at named point of exportation;

(2) pay export taxes, or other fees or charges, if any, levied because of exportation;

(3) be responsible for any loss or damage, or both, incurred after goods have arrived in, or on, inland conveyance at the named point of exportation;

(4) pay all costs and charges incurred in obtaining the documents issued in the country of origin, or of shipment, or of both, which may be required either for purposes of exportation, or of importation at destination.

(II-E) "F.O.B. VESSEL (named port of shipment)"

Under this term, the seller quotes a price covering all expenses up to, and including, delivery of the goods upon the overseas vessel provided by, or for, the buyer at the named port of shipment.

Under this quotation:

Seller must

(1) pay all charges incurred in placing goods actually on board the vessel designated and provided by, or for, the buyer on the date or within the period fixed;

(2) provide clean ship's receipt or on-board bill of lading;

(3) be responsible for any loss or damage, or both, until goods have been placed on board the vessel on the date or within the period fixed;

(4) render the buyer, at the buyer's request and expense, assistance in obtaining the documents issued in the country of origin, or of shipment, or of both, which the buyer may require either for purposes of exportation, or of importation at destination.

Buyer must

(1) give seller adequate notice of name, sailing date, loading berth of, and delivery time to, the vessel;

(2) bear the additional costs incurred and all risks of the goods from the time when the seller has placed them at his disposal if the vessel named by him fails to arrive or to load within the designated time;

(3) handle all subsequent movement of the goods to destination:
  (a) provide and pay for insurance;
  (b) provide and pay for ocean and other transportation;

(4) pay export taxes, or other fees or charges, if any, levied because of exportation;

(5) be responsible for any loss or damage, or both, after goods have been loaded on board the vessel:

(6) pay all costs and charges incurred in obtaining the documents, other than clean ship's receipt or bill or lading, issued in the country of origin, or of shipment, or of both, which may be required either for purposes of exportation, or of importation at destination.

(II-F) "F.O.B. (named inland point in country of importation)"

Under this term, the seller quotes a price including the cost of the merchandise and all costs of transportation to the named inland point in the country of importation.

Under this quotation:

Seller must

(1) provide and pay for all transportation to the named inland point in the country of importation;

(2) pay export taxes, or other fees or charges, if any, levied because of exportation;

(3) provide and pay for marine insurance;

(4) provide and pay for war risk insurance, unless otherwise agreed upon between the seller and buyer;

(5) be responsible for any loss or damage, or both, until arrival of goods on conveyance at the named inland point in the country of importation;

(6) pay the costs of certificates of origin, consular invoices, or any other documents issued in the country of origin, or of shipment, or of both, which the buyer may require for the importation of goods into the country of destination and, where necessary, for their passage in transit through another country;

(7) pay all costs of landing, including wharfage, landing charges, and taxes, if any;

(8) pay all costs of customs entry in the country of importation;

(9) pay customs duties and all taxes applicable to imports, if any, in the country of importation.

NOTE: *The seller under this quotation must realize that he is accepting important responsibilities, costs, and risks, and should therefore be certain to obtain adequate insurance. On the other hand, the importer or buyer may desire such quotations to relieve him of the risks of the voyage and to assure him of his landed costs at inland point in country of importation. When competition is keen, or the buyer is accustomed to such quotations from other sellers, seller may quote such terms, being careful to protect himself in an appropriate manner.*

Buyer must

(1) take prompt delivery of goods from conveyance upon arrival at destination;

(2) bear any costs and be responsible for all loss or damage, or both, after arrival at destination.

Comments On All F.O.B. Terms

In connection with F.O.B. terms, the following points of caution are recommended:

1. The method of inland transportation, such as trucks, railroad cars, lighters, barges, or aircraft should be specified.

2. If any switching charges are involved during the inland transportation, it should be agreed, in advance, whether these charges are for account of the seller or the buyer.

3. The term "F.O.B. (named port)", without designating the exact point at which the liability of the seller terminates and the liability of the buyer begins, should be avoided. The use of this term gives rise to disputes as to the liability of the seller or the buyer in the event of loss or damage arising while the goods are in port, and before delivery to or on board the ocean carrier. Misunderstandings may be avoided by naming the specific point of delivery.

4. If lighterage or trucking is required in the transfer of goods from the inland conveyance to ship's side, and there is a cost therefor, it should be understood, in advance, whether this cost is for ac-

count of the seller or the buyer.

5. The seller should be certain to notify the buyer of the minimum quantity required to obtain a carload, a truckload, or a barge-load freight rate.

6. Under F.O.B. terms, excepting "F.O.B. (named inland point in country of importation)", the obligation to obtain ocean freight space, and marine and war risk insurance, rests with the buyer. Despite this obligation on the part of the buyer, in many trades the seller obtains the ocean freight space, and marine and war risk insurance, and provides for shipment on behalf of the buyer. Hence, seller and buyer must have an understanding as to whether the buyer will obtain the ocean freight space, and marine and war risk insurance, as is his obligation, or whether the seller agrees to do this for the buyer.·

7. For the seller's protection, he should provide in his contract of sale that marine insurance obtained by the buyer include standard warehouse to warehouse coverage.

(III) F.A.S. (Free Along Side)

NOTE: *Seller and buyer should consider not only the definitions but also the "Comments" given at the end of this section (page 11), in order to understand fully their respective responsibilities and rights under "F.A.S." terms.*

"F.A.S. VESSEL (named port of shipment)"

Under this term, the seller quotes a price including delivery of the goods along side overseas vessel and within reach of its loading tackle.

Under this quotation:

Seller must

(1) place goods along side vessel or on dock designated and provided by, or for, buyer on the date or within the period fixed; pay any heavy lift charges, where necessary, up to this point;

(2) provide clean dock or ship's receipt;

(3) be responsible for any loss or damage, or both, until goods have been delivered along side the vessel or on the dock;

(4) render the buyer, at the buyer's request and expense, assistance in obtaining the documents issued in the country of origin, or of shipment, or of both, which the buyer may require either for purposes of exportation, or of importation at destination.

Buyer must

(1) give seller adequate notice of name, sailing date, loading berth of, and delivery time to, the vessel;

(2) handle all subsequent movement of the goods from along side the vessel:

   (a) arrange and pay for demurrage or storage charges, or both, in warehouse or on wharf, where necessary;

   (b) provide and pay for insurance;

   (c) provide and pay for ocean and other tranportation;

(3) pay export taxes, or other fees or charges, if any, levied because of exportation;

(4) be responsible for any loss or damage, or both, while the goods are on a lighter or other conveyance along side vessel within reach of its loading tackle, or on the dock awaiting loading, or until actually loaded on board the vessel, and subsequent thereto;

(5) pay all costs and charges incurred in obtaining the documents, other than clean dock or ship's receipt, issued in the country of origin, or of shipment, or of both, which may be required either for purposes of exportation, or of importation at destination.

F.A.S. Comments

1. Under F.A.S. terms, the obligation to obtain ocean freight space, and marine and war risk insurance, rests with the buyer. Despite this obligation on the part of the buyer, in many trades the seller obtains ocean freight space, and marine and war risk insurance, and provides for shipment on behalf of the buyer. In others, the buyer notifies the seller to make delivery along side a vessel designated by the buyer and the buyer provides his own marine and war risk insurance. Hence, seller and buyer must have an understanding as to whether the buyer will obtain the ocean freight space, and marine and war risk insurance, as is his obligation, or whether the seller agrees to do this for the buyer.

2. For the seller's protection, he should provide in his contract of sale that marine insurance obtained by the buyer include standard warehouse to warehouse coverage.

(IV) C. & F. (Cost and Freight)

NOTE: *Seller and buyer should consider not only the definitions but also the "C. & F. Comments" (page 12) and the "C. & F. and C.I.F. Comments" (pages 14-15), in order to understand fully their respective responsibilities and rights under "C. & F." terms.*

"C. & F. (named point of destination)"

Under this term, the seller quotes a price including the cost of transportation to the named point of destination.

Under this quotation:

Seller must

(1) provide and pay for transportation to named point of destination;

(2) pay export taxes, or other fees or charges, if any, levied because of exportation;

(3) obtain and dispatch promptly to buyer, or his agent, clean bill of lading to named point of destination;

(4) where received-for-shipment ocean bill of lading may be tendered, be responsible for any loss or damage, or both, until the goods have been delivered into the custody of the ocean carrier;

(5) where on-board ocean bill of lading is required, be responsible for any loss or damage, or both, until the goods have been delivered on board the vessel;

(6) provide, at the buyer's request and expense, certificates of origin, consular invoices, or any other documents issued in the country of origin, or of shipment, or of both, which the buyer may require for importation of goods into country of destination and, where necessary, for their passage in transit through another country.

Buyer must

(1) accept the documents when presented;

(2) receive goods upon arrival, handle and pay for all subsequent movement of the goods, including taking delivery from vessel in accordance with bill of lading clauses and terms; pay all costs of landing, including any duties, taxes, and other expenses at named point of destination;

(3) provide and pay for insurance;

(4) be responsible for loss of or damage to goods, or both, from time and place at which seller's obligations under (4) or (5) above have ceased;

(5) pay the costs of certificates of origin, consular invoices, or any other documents issued in the country of origin, or of shipment, or of both, which may be required for the importation of goods into the country of destination and, where necessary, for their passage in transit through another country.

C. & F. Comments

1. For the seller's protection, he should provide in his contract of sale that marine insurance obtained by the buyer include standard warehouse to warehouse coverage.

2. The comments listed under the following C.I.F. terms in many cases apply to C. & F. terms as well, and should be read and understood by the C. & F. seller and buyer.

(V) C.I.F. (Cost, Insurance, Freight)

NOTE: *Seller and buyer should consider not only the definitions but also the "Comments" (pages 14-15), at the end of this section, in order to understand fully their respective responsibilities and rights under "C.I.F." terms.*

"C.I.F. (named point of destination)"

Under this term, the seller quotes a price including the cost of the goods, the marine insurance, and all transportation charges to the named point of destination.

Under this quotation:

Seller must

(1) provide and pay for transportation to named point of destination;

(2) pay export taxes, or other fees or charges, if any, levied because of exportation;

(3) provide and pay for marine insurance;

(4) provide war risk insurance as obtainable in seller's market at time of shipment at buyer's expense, unless seller has agreed that buyer provide for war risk coverage (See Comment 10 (c)

(5) obtain and dispatch promptly to buyer, or his agent, clean bill of lading to named point of destination, and also insurance policy or negotiable insurance certificate;

(6) where received-for-shipment ocean bill of lading may be tendered, be responsible for any loss or damage, or both, until the goods have been delivered into the custody of the ocean carrier;

(7) where on-board ocean bill of lading is re-

quired, be responsible for any loss or damage, or both, until the goods have been delivered on board the vessel;

(8) provide, at the buyer's request and expense, certificates of origin, consular invoices, or any other documents issued in the country of origin, or of shipment, or both, which the buyer may require for importation of goods into country of destination and, where necessary, for their passage in transit through another country.

Buyer must

(1) accept the documents when presented;

(2) receive the goods upon arrival, handle and pay for all subsequent movement of the goods, including taking delivery from vessel in accordance with bill of lading clauses and terms; pay all costs of landing, including any duties, taxes, and other expenses at named point of destination;

(3) pay for war risk insurance provided by seller;

(4) be responsible for loss of or damage to goods, or both, from time and place at which seller's obligations under (6) or (7) above have ceased;

(5) pay the cost of certificates of origin, consular invoices, or any other documents issued in the country of origin, or of shipment, or both, which may be required for importation of the goods into the country of destination and, where necessary, for their passage in transit through another country.

C. & F. and C.I.F. Comments

Under C. & F. and C.I.F. contracts there are the following points on which the seller and the buyer should be in complete agreement at the time that the contract is concluded:

1. It should be agreed upon, in advance, who is to pay for miscellaneous expenses, such as weighing or inspection charges.

2. The quantity to be shipped on any one vessel should be agreed upon, in advance, with a view to the buyer's capacity to take delivery upon arrival and discharge of the vessel, within the free time allowed at the port of importation.

3. Although the terms C. & F. and C.I.F. are generally interpreted to provide that charges for consular invoices and certificates of origin are for the account of the buyer, and are charged separately, in many trades these charges are included by the seller in his price. Hence, seller and buyer should agree, in advance, whether these charges are part of the selling price, or will be invoiced separately.

4. The point of final destination should be definitely known in the event the vessel discharges at a port other than the actual destination of the goods.

5. When ocean freight space is difficult to obtain, or forward freight contracts cannot be made at firm rates, it is advisable that sales contracts, as an exception to regular C. & F. or C.I.F. terms, should provide that shipment within the contract period be subject to ocean freight space being available to the

seller, and should also provide that changes in the cost of ocean transportation between the time of sale and the time of shipment be for account of the buyer.

6. Normally, the seller is obligated to prepay the ocean freight. In some instances, shipments are made freight collect and the amount of the freight is deducted from the invoice rendered by the seller. It is necessary to be in agreement on this, in advance, in order to avoid misunderstanding which arises from foreign exchange fluctuations which might affect the actual cost of transportation, and from interest charges which might accrue under letter of credit financing. Hence, the seller should always prepay the ocean freight unless he has a specific agreement with the buyer, in advance, that goods can be shipped freight collect.

7. The buyer should recognize that he does not have the right to insist on inspection of goods prior to accepting the documents. The buyer should not refuse to take delivery of goods on account of delay in the receipt of documents, provided the seller has used due diligence in their dispatch through the regular channels.

8. Sellers and buyers are advised against including in a C.I.F. contract any indefinite clause at variance with the obligations of a C.I.F. contract as specified in these Definitions. There have been numerous court decisions in the United States and other countries invalidating C.I.F. contracts because of the inclusion of indefinite clauses.

9. Interest charges should be included in cost computations and should not be charged as a separate item in C.I.F. contracts, unless otherwise agreed upon, in advance, between the seller and buyer; in which case, however, the term C.I.F. and I. (Cost, Insurance, Freight, and Interest) should be used.

10. In connection with insurance under C.I.F. sales, it is necessary that seller and buyer be definitely in accord upon the following points:

(a) The character of the marine insurance should be agreed upon in so far as being W.A. (With Average) or F.P.A. (Free of Particular Average), as well as any other special risks that are covered in specific trades, or against which the buyer may wish individual protection. Among the special risks that should be considered and agreed upon between seller and buyer are theft, pilferage, leakage, breakage, sweat, contact with other cargoes, and others peculiar to any particular trade. It is important that contingent or collect freight and customs duty should be insured to cover Particular Average losses, as well as total loss after arrival and entry but before delivery.

(b) The seller is obligated to exercise ordinary care and diligence in selecting an underwriter that is in good financial standing. However, the risk of obtaining settlement of insurance claims rests with the buyer.

(c) War risk insurance under this term is to be obtained by the seller at the expense and risk of the buyer. It is important that the seller be in definite accord with the buyer on this point, particularly as to the cost. It is desirable that the goods be insured against both marine and war risk with the same underwriter, so that there can be no difficulty arising

from the determination of the cause of the loss.

(d) Seller should make certain that in his marine or war risk insurance, there be included the standard protection against strikes, riots and civil commotions.

(e) Seller and buyer should be in accord as to the insured valuation, bearing in mind that merchandise contributes in General Average on certain bases of valuation which differ in various trades. It is desirable that a competent insurance broker be consulted, in order that full value be covered and trouble avoided.

(VI) Ex Dock

(VI) "EX DOCK (named port of importation)"

NOTE: *Seller and buyer should consider not only the definitions but also the "Ex Dock Comments" at the end of this section   in order to understand fully their respective responsibilities and rights under "Ex Dock" terms.*

Under this term, seller quotes a price including the cost of the goods and all additional costs necessary to place the goods on the dock at the named port of importation, duty paid, if any.

Under this quotation:

Seller must

(1) provide and pay for transportation to named port of importation;

(2) pay export taxes, or other fees or charges, if any, levied because of exportation;

(3) provide and pay for marine insurance;

(4) provide and pay for war risk insurance, unless otherwise agreed upon between the buyer and seller;

(5) be responsible for any loss or damage, or both, until the expiration of the free time allowed on the dock at the named port of importation;

(6) pay the costs of certificates of origin, consular invoices, legalization of bill of lading, or any other documents issued in the country of origin, or of shipment, or of both, which the buyer may require for the importation of goods into the country of destination and, where necessary, for their passage in transit through another country;

(7) pay all costs of landing, including wharfage, landing charges, and taxes, if any;

(8) pay all costs of customs entry in the country of importation;

(9) pay customs duties and all taxes applicable to imports, if any, in the country of importation, unless otherwise agreed upon.

Buyer must

(1) take delivery of the goods on the dock at the named port of importation within the free time allowed;

(2) bear the cost and risk of the goods if delivery is not taken within the free time allowed.

Ex Dock Comments

This term is used principally in United States import trade. It has various modifications, such as "Ex Quay", "Ex Pier", etc., but it is seldom, if ever, used in American export practice. Its use in quotations for export is not recommended.

APPENDIX C

FOREIGN CONSULAR REGULATIONS

AFGHANISTAN

SUMMARY OF SHIPPING DOCUMENTS REQUIRED
No Consular Documents Required
1. **Shipping Documents Required**
   (A) **Commercial Invoice**—1—must show FOB and CIF values. All charges must be listed. Must be certified by the New York Chamber of Commerce and Industry. The Chamber requires one additional notarized copy for its files.
2. **Consular Holidays**
   All holidays generally observed in New York City. July 17 - Republic Day.
See Form 10-010.

ALBANIA

SUMMARY OF SHIPPING DOCUMENTS REQUIRED
1. **Shipping Documents Required**
   All Shipments (regardless of value and mode of transportation):
   (A) **Commercial Invoice**—2—no special form—must state full particulars and description of the goods—marks and numbers—number of cases, bales, etc.—net and gross weights—net value of goods—country of origin etc. It is advisable to deduct trade discounts and show on invoices any further discount for cash payment or other consideration.
   (B) **Certificate of Origin**—2—when required—general form—sold by commercial printers—certified by the New York Chamber of Commerce and Industry, which requires one additional notarized copy for its files.
   (C) **Bill of Lading**—no special regulations—must show name of shipper—name and address of consignee—port of destination—description of goods—freight and other charges—the number of bills of lading in the full set—date and signature of the carrier's official acknowledging receipt on board of the goods. The information should correspond with that shown on the invoices and the packages. The air waybill replaces the bill of lading on air cargo shipments.
2. **Import License**
   All imports require licenses.
3. **Holidays**
   All holidays generally observed in New York City.

ALGERIA

SUMMARY OF SHIPPING DOCUMENTS REQUIRED
No Consular Documents Required
1. **Shipping Documents Required**
   (A) **Commercial Invoice**—2—must contain complete information—giving the nature of the goods, any identification marks (including serial numbers), sizes, quantities and prices. Both the factory price and the CIF price should be included. Prices should be shown in dollars as well as Algerian dinars. Invoices must be signed by shipper—country of origin should be shown.
   (B) **Certificate of Origin**—2—when required—on general form—sold by commercial printers—certified by the New York Chamber of Commerce and Industry which requires an additional notarized copy for its files.

341

Form #10-010   Printed and Sold by Unz & Co., Division of Scott Printing Corp., 190 Baldwin
Ave Jersey City, N.J 07306 — N.J. (201) 795-5400 ; N.Y. (212) 344-2270
Toll Free (800) 631-3098

INVOICE AND CERTIFICATE OF VALUE AND ORIGIN FOR IMPORTS INTO AFGHANISTAN

Date of Invoice............... ....

The undersigned (Owner, Agent/ or Company)..declares that the

following goods have been shipped on the S.S. (name of steamer)--on date of................. ....

consigned to (name and address of consignee)...

Customer's Order No..Enclosures..................

Custom Broker....................................... Insurance Company.................................

NUMBER OF CASES	MARKS AND NUMBERS	WEIGHT IN KILOS GROSS	NET	DESCRIPTION

VALUE AND EXPENSES IN U. S. DOLLARS

Selling Price to Purchaser...$
Freight...$
Insurance..$
Buying Commission at..............per cent...$
Other Incidental Charges...$

TOTAL $

I (Name, title,/ Name of firm)...

hereby swear that this invoice is authentic, that it is the only invoice issued for the merchandise described herein, that the prices stated are the exact and current export market prices for the merchandise described. I further swear that origin of these goods is ....

and I accept full responsibility for any inaccuracies or errors in this invoice.

Sworn to before me this........day of..................19....

(Signature of Owner or Agent)

The.., a recognized Chamber of Commerce under the laws of the State of

................................., hereby declares that the prices stated in this invoice are the current export market prices and that the origin of the

goods described herein is the..

Secretary........ ....

CERTIFICATION:

I certify that the invoice has been presented to this Consulate and that the preceding declaration has been signed by the shippers or their duly authorized representative. In witness whereof I sign and affix the seal of this Consulate.

Date of Certification.......................19....
CONSULAR CERTIFICATION NO. ....

CONSUL FOR AFGHANISTAN

Form 10-010. Export Forms, Hazardous Materials Labels, etc. can be purchased from Unz & Co., 190 Baldwin Ave., P.O. Box 308, Jersey City, N.J. 07303.

(C) **Bills of Lading**—should give gross weight (in Kilograms or pounds); measurements (in meters and centimeters preferred, but inches are acceptable); marks of identification; import license number; value of goods; freight; name and address of consignee. Shipping marks and numbers on the bill of lading, containers and commercial invoices should correspond.

2. **Air Cargo Shipments**
Commercial Invoice—2—(See previous listing) must accompany shipment.

3. **Import License**
Required by importer for most goods.

4. **Holidays**
All holidays generally observed in New York City.

ARGENTINA

SUMMARY OF SHIPPING DOCUMENTS REQUIRED
1. **Freight and Air Cargo Shipments regardless of value:**
(A) **Commercial Invoice**—Present 4 copies—in English or Spanish. Consulate retains 2. The original and 1 copy legalized by the Consulate must not be detached. This set must be sent "as is" to Argentina. Must be certified by the New York Chamber of Commerce and Industry prior to presentation to the Consulate. The New York Chamber of Commerce and Industry requires one additional notarized copy for its files. Invoices must contain the following declaration (which may be in English if the invoices are also prepared in English):
> "Declaro bajo juramento que los precios en esta factura comercial son los realmente pagados o a pagarse, y que no existe convenio alguno que permita su alteracion; y que todos los datos referentes a la calidad, cantidad, valor, precios, etc., y descripcion de la mercaderia concuerdan en todas sus partes con lo declarado en la correspondiente Shipper's Export Declaration."

All Commercial invoices must contain the following information: country of origin of merchandise; place, date and full name and address of exporter; place of export of the merchandise; place of entry in Argentina (port or city); unit price of article; and number of packages and their identification marks, together with gross and net weights.

No generic terms are admissible in the commercial invoices—full description of the goods must be shown—for example; medicinal products, spare parts, textiles, etc. are not acceptable, unless followed by an exact and accurate description.

All copies of the commercial invoice must be duly signed in ink by a properly authorized member of the firm, identifying same by typing the full name underneath signature, as well as his position within the firm. Where these commercial invoices are handled or completed in any way by shippers or agents (Freight Forwarders) in the New York area, a responsible representative must sign as well and identify his signature in the same manner, giving the full name and address of his as agents for the exporter or manufacturer. It is suggested that all agents and/or Shippers add their telephone number next to the signature (in pencil).

In this manner, the handler of the documents can be quickly identified and called promptly if necessary, thus avoiding delays in the handling of his documents. The following statement signed in ink must appear on invoices till further notice.
> "Se dejaconstancia que esta compania tiene conocimiento de los terminos de la ley 19.326 con vigencia a partir del 1 de Noviembre de 1971 reconocida con la suspension de las exportaciones al sector oficial de la Republica Argentina asi como sus exceptiones."

Only clear and legible commercial invoice sets will be acceptable. No erasures or alterations in any form are permissible—all originals must be typed out. Copies may be photostats, but all copies must be signed manually in ink (inked-over photocopied signatures are unacceptable).

All values must be clearly stated FOB, C&I, C&F, or CIF, but all invoices must show the FOB value (port of shipment). All charges must be clearly itemized. The consular fee, where it is desired to show it, must appear separately underneath FOB, C&I, C&F, or CIF total. The consular fee must not be included when calculating the legalization fee.

Commercial invoice sets covering live animals, eggs, seeds, birds, queen bees, grains, potatoes, vegetables and certain other foodstuffs cannot be legalized unless the proper sanitary certificate issued by the U.S. Department of Agriculture has already been legalized by the Argentine Consular Office with jurisdiction in the area which issues such certificates. These certificates cannot be countersigned by an equivalent authority in the New York area, neither can they be countersigned by any Agent or Shipper and then processed before a Notary Public and County Clerk. In other words, the signature of the U.S. inspector must be legalized directly by the Argentine Consulate General with jurisdiction in his area.

No Charge Invoices—No charge invoices must show the real value of the merchandise for customs purposes. The consular fees will be based on this amount in the usual manner. If a regular commercial invoice contains no charge items, these items must also show the real value for customs purposes and consular fees must be paid on these items also.

All Commercial invoice sets which consist of more than one sheet must be properly taped through with blue ribbon and fastened by a notarial blank seal in such a way that all pages are well secured to avoid loss or substitution.

*Freight forwarding and/or agents' fees are no longer allowed to be shown on airway bills on freight collect basis.

(B) **Freight—Charges Invoice**—Shippers wishing to have a separate invoice for freight, consular fees, expenses, etc., may have their Freight-Charges invoice legalized by the Consulate following exactly the same procedure as in any other commercial invoice set. If extra copies are requested on a different date than original legalization, shipper must furnish Consulate with the legalization date and number.

(C) **Commercial Invoices not Related to Actual Shipments**—The situation may arise of commercial invoices not pertaining to actual shipments for uses other than clearance of merchandise at Argentine Customs, (for example: pro-forma invoices for presentation in public tenders, banking requirements, credit, etc.). In these cases each commercial invoice must bear the following declaration "Declaro bajo juramento que la presente factura comercial sera utilizada para. . ." ("I swear that the present commercial invoice is to be used for. . .") Legalization fee: $2.00.

(D) **Correction of Legalized Commercial Invoices**—When an error is discovered in a commercial invoice already legalized, shipper must prepare a new set in the usual manner, and present it to the Consulate accompanied by the legalized old set. If the value of the new set is not increased, the consular fee is $5.00. If the new replacement commercial invoice set shows an increase in value, an additional 3% consular fee will apply on the increase. (3% of the difference between the two subtotals shown before the Consular Fee).

(E) **Replacement of Lost Legalized Invoices**—The Consulate will legalize a new set of commercial invoices (original and three copies) provided that a letter is presented explaining the circumstances and stating clearly the date and the numbers under which the originals were processed. Care must be taken that the new set corresponds in every detail to the original, since the Consulate will only issue a new legalization when all details are in accordance with the copies filed in their records. The fee in this case is $5.00.

(F) **Registered Air Mail**—The Argentine Consulate advises shippers that when sending their documents directly to their customers in Argentina they should make sure that the legalized documents are forwarded by Registered Air Mail.

(G) **Extra Copies of Commercial Invoice**—Additional copies of any commercial invoice set, provided they are made up in exactly the same manner as the original, will be legalized at a charge of $2.00 each copy. If extra copies are requested on a different date than original legalization, shipper must furnish Consulate with the legalization date and number.

NOTE—It is therefore specially recommended to all exporters that they keep a careful record of the dates and number under which all their documents are processed in order to facilitate the checking of records.

(H) **Bill of Lading**—Consular legalization not required. "To Order" bills of lading allowed. According to Central Bank Circular No. 256 all bills of lading (or equivalent) must show the freight paid or payable at destination. Must be signed by hand. Facsimile signature will be refused.

(I) **Flag Preference**—According to a decree #5030/69 established by the Argentine Government all imports into Argentina destined for national, provincial and municipal Government entities may be carried on U.S.-flag registry vessels as well as on Argentine-flag vessels. Also all imports which are financed, or guaranteed, by Argentine Government Banks must be carried on Argentine-flag vessels.

2. **Parcel Post Shipments Regardless of Value**

   Commercial Invoice—4—Same as regular shipments, except packages containing noncommercial goods for personal use, valued up to $10.00, which do not require legalization.

3. **Penalties Under New Customs Regulations**

   In connection with the new customs regulations, shippers should take note of the following important points: (a) Shipping documents that are not presented for customs clearance within 15 days after arrival of the ship will be subject to a fine of 2% of the CIF value. (b) Incorrect or false customs declarations regarding quantities or values will be subject to a fine from 2 to 10 times the difference between the false value and the true CIF value. (c) False declarations regarding the quality or characteristics of the merchandise will be subject to a fine of double the actual CIF value (Bases on the correct quality or characteristics). (d) Should there be a false declaration affecting simultaneously both quantity, value, or quality and characteristics, the highest applicable fine will be applied.

4. **Certificate of Origin**

   When merchandise shipped to Argentina originates in any of the other LAFTA countries (Brazil, Chile, Colombia, Ecuador, Mexico, Paraguay, Peru and Uruguay) if required by letters of credit or requested by the importers, shipper must present, in addition to the regular set of invoices in quadruplicate, original and three copies of a Certificate of Origin, certified by a Chamber of Commerce and legalized by the Consulate in the State where the merchandise was manufactured. However, if there is no consulate in the state where the merchandise was manufactured, the certificate of origin must be legalized by a Consulate having jurisdiction over that state.

5. ***Insurance**

   Insurance Decree Law 14135/62 states that for most U.S. imports, insurance must be purchased in Argentina. Exception: AID Shipments, the United Nations, and its Specialized Agencies, including IAEA.

6. ***Import Permits**

All imports now require a statement of necessity import permit issued by the Ministry of Commerce. Approval is being granted only for certain products which are considered necessary for the economy of the country.

7. **Consular Fees**

Paid by cash, certified check or money order made to order for Ministerio de Relaciones Exteriores y Culto de la Republica Argentina. Payment may only be made at Banco de la Nacion 299 Park Avenue, corner of 49th Street from 9 a.m. to 1 p.m. only. The Bank will issue receipts to the shipper which must be attached to documents prior to presentation at Consulate. The Consulate advises that consular fees are based on terms of sale e.g., FOB, C&F or CIF. In the case of CIF, shippers should show FOB value plus insurance plus freight and other charges arriving at a total CIF value. Consular fees are then based on this amount at 3 percent. After determining the amount of consular fees, add that to the CIF value. If discounts are allowed, this amount must be shown after the CIF and consular fee.

Example: (CIF sale, with discount)	Cost:	$500.00
	Insurance:	5.00
	Freight:	50.00
	CIF:	555.00
	Consular Fee:	16.65
		$571.65

Consular fees must be calculated and deposit slips in the exact amount presented. Since errors of a few cents are common, and to avoid rejection of documents, exporters are required to round out the third decimal place, e.g. 3.555 becomes 3.56; 7.589 becomes 7.59; 7.844 becomes 7.84; 7.432 becomes 7.43. Please note when the third decimal place is five or over, the next highest cent is applicable. The minimum fee of $2.00 is applicable to invoices valued up to $66.83.

The Consulate urges exporters to avoid making mistakes when calculating and when depositing consular fees since refunds take a long time (whenever approved). Depending on the circumstances of the mistake, 10 percent of the amount to be refunded or a minimum of $5.00 may be deducted from the refund.

If more than one fee is involved, i.e., regular Consular fee $2.00 and an additional invoice is required for an additional $2.00, then 2 separate bank deposit receipts are required for each amount by the Consulate.

Commercial invoices or

freight-charge invoice (set of 4) .... 3% of total invoice value excluding consular fees (figured to the nearest penny, minimum charge valued up to 66.83: $2.00)

Set of replacement invoices .... $5.00 per set

Set of corrected invoices (if value is unchanged) .... $5.00 per set

Set of corrected invoices (if value is increased) .... $5.00 per set plus 3% of difference between the 2 subtotals shown before consular fees

Additional legalized copies (when requested) ....$2.00 each

Sanitary Certificates, County Clerk's signature authentications,

    and Certificate of Origin $8.00

Pro Forma or temporary importation invoice .... $2.00 each

*Holidays

January 6, Holy Thursday, Good Friday, May 1, May 25, Corpus Christi, June

20, July 9, August 15, August 17, November 1, and December 8. All holidays generally observed in New York.

*Denotes changes since previous notice.

Argentina—Non-essential Imports Suspended: The Argentine Ministry of Economy has suspended for the balance of this year the importation of various merchandise classified as non-essential. Some of the items included are textiles, chemicals, pharmaceuticals, some dairy products, minerals, metals, hand tools and processing equipment. Imports of used merchandise have suspended until December, 1977. Exporters are reminded to check with the importer whether or not your goods are classified in this category.

AUSTRALIA

SUMMARY OF SHIPPING DOCUMENTS REQUIRED
No Consular Documents Required
1. **Shipping Documents Required**
   (A) *****Shipper's Commercial Invoice**—2—must be used for all shipments with a value over Australian $40 and must be signed by shipper. All information such as country of origin, marks, numbers, value, etc. must be shown. Legalization not required. All copies must be sent to consignee. It is important that invoices and bills of lading be mailed in sufficient time to arrive before or at the same time the goods arrive in Australia.
   (B) *****Certificate of Origin**—2—when requested by importer or letter of credit requirement—general form—sold by commercial printers—certified by the New York Chamber of Commerce and Industry, which requires one additional notarized copy for its files.
2. **Import License**
   *Must be obtained by the importer: (1) used, secondhand or disposals machinery equipment of the following class or kind; (a) earthmoving, or excavating vehicles, machinery or equipment (e.g. rock buggies, dumpers, graders, loaders, ditchers, draglines, mechanical shovels, excavators, scrapers, bull-dozers) and parts thereof; (b) tractors, road rollers and parts thereof; (c) materials handling equipment (e.g. cranes, forklift trucks) and parts thereof; (d) other vehicles being used or secondhand four-wheel drive vehicles, excluding public service type passenger vehicles, falling within terms 87.02, 87.03 and 87.04 of the Customs Tariff. License guarantees exchange. Not needed as a shipping document. Merchandise must arrive at port of discharge prior to expiration of license. Tolerances are allowed.
3. *****Consumer Holidays**
   January 29, February 19, April 13 and 16, June 11, October 8, December 24 and 26 and all holidays generally observed in New York City.
   *Denotes changes since preparation notice.

AUSTRIA

SUMMARY OF SHIPPING DOCUMENTS REQUIRED
No Consular Documents Required
1. **Shipping Documents Required for all Commercial Shipments**
   (A) **Commercial Invoice**—2—no legalization by Consulate necessary—must be sent directly to consignee and contain detailed description of merchandise.
   (B) **Certificate of Origin**—3—when required—for certain items on the list of liberalized imports—general form—sold by commercial printers—signed by shipper—certified by the New York Chamber of Commerce and Industry, which

retains 1 notarized copy and returns the remaining 2. Certificate of origin, when required, must be in the possession of the Austrian importer at the time the shipment is cleared through Austrian Customs. Certificates of origin must show marks, numbers, weight and value.

2.   **Air Cargo Shipments**
      Commercial Invoice—2—must accompany shipment.
3.   **Import License**
      Required by importer for few commodities which are still non-liberalized. Import licenses are granted automatically for liberalized items. (Most commodities have now been liberalized).
4.   ***Insurance**—Tax discrimination virtually eliminates or impedes U.S. insurance companies.
      ***Consular Holidays**
      January 6, Easter Monday, May 1, Whitmonday, Corpus Christi, May 8, August 15, October 26, November 1, December 8, and December 26. All holidays generally observed by the Federal Government.
      *Denotes changes since previous notice.

BAHAMAS

SUMMARY OF SHIPPING DOCUMENTS REQUIRED
No Consular Documents Required
1.   **Shipping Documents Required for all Shipments regardless of value:**
 (A) ***Commercial Invoice**—1 original—must contain name of exporter and the name and address of consignee—form of transport—marks, quantities and kinds of packages—gross and net weight of shipment—place of origin and shipment—complete description of goods including proper Bahamian tariff schedule number, if possible and all prices must be shown (including unit price). Declaration of the FAS or FOB value is compulsory and the CIF value optional.
 (B) ***Bills of Lading**—no special form but should contain at least an indication of receipt of the goods for shipment—name of shipper—name and address of consignee, port of discharge—destination—description of merchandise and itemized charges. Order bills of lading are acceptable.
 (C) ***Certificate of Origin**—1—when required—general form—sold by commercial printers—certified by the New York Chamber of Commerce and Industry, which requires one additional copy for its files.
2.   ***Import License**
      Most U.S. goods may be freely imported either under a general or individual import license. Individual licenses are valid for six months from date of issuance to the landing of the goods.
3.   **Holidays**
      All holidays generally observed in New York City.
      *Denotes changes since previous notices.

BAHRAIN

SUMMARY OF SHIPPING DOCUMENTS REQUIRED
1.   **Consular Documents Required**
      All Commercial Shipments regardless of value:
 (A) ***Commercial Invoice**—1—copy—none required for consulate—must be prepared on the letterhead of actual seller, and must give an accurate and specific description of the goods, itemizing all expenses. Invoices must be signed and show the name of the steamer and date of sailing. Prior to presentation to the

Consulate, invoices must be certified as to current export market prices and country of origin by the U.S. Arab Chamber of Commerce, which requires one additional notarized copy containing the following affidavit:

"I, (name, title, name of company) hereby swear that the prices stated in this invoice are the current export market prices and that the origin of the goods described herein is the United States of America, and I assume full responsibility for any inaccuracies or errors therein."

(B) *Certificate of Origin—1 copy—general form, sold by commercial printers, must be certified by the U.S. Arab Chamber of Commerce—each copy must be attached to a commercial invoice. Must show name of vessel. Shippers must show on the certificate of origin the names of the manufacturers of the items being shipped. Shippers must also make a notarized statement certifying that it is true and correct. The U.S. Arab Chamber of Commerce, requires one additional notarized copy for its files.

(C) *Insurance Certificate—A certificate issued by the insurance company stating that the insurance company is not on the boycott list is required to be presented to Consulate for all shipments—none required for Consulate. Returned to shipper. If shipment is insured by the buyer, then the insurance certificate is not required by the Consulate. However, shipper must state on commercial invoice that insurance is covered in Bahrain.

(D) *Steamship Company Certificate—Certificate issued by the steamship company stating that the vessel is not an Israeli vessel nor is it scheduled to call at any Israeli port during her voyage—none required for Consulate. Returned to shipper.

2. **Import License**
   None required.

3. *Special Documents
   (A) **Health Certificate**—A certificate issued by an official department—Food & Drug Administration—is required on all imports of plants and plant materials, such as saplings, seeds, fruits and vegetables proving they are free from pests and other agricultural diseases.

   (B) **Phytosanitary Certificate**—A certificate issued by the Department of Agriculture must accompany shipments of flour, rice, seed wheat, agriculture seeds and plants.

4. *Legalization Fees:
   Payable by check or money order payable to order of Consulate.
   Commercial Invoice .... $4.00 per copy
   Certificate of Origin .... $4.00 per copy
   Steamship Certificate .... $4.00 per copy
   Health Certificate .... $4.00 per copy
   Additional documents (if requested) $4.00 per copy

   Prior to presenting documents to the Consulate, freight forwarders, messenger service firms and shippers are required to figure out the total amount due according to the number of copies at the aforementioned rate, i.e., $4.00 per copy.

5. **Consular Holidays**
   Eid Al-Fitre, Aid Al-Adha, and December 16. All holidays generally observed in New York City.
   *Denotes changes since previous notice.

BANGLADESH

SUMMARY OF SHIPPING DOCUMENTS REQUIRED
No Consular Documents Required
1. **Shipping Documents Required**

(A) **Commercial Invoice**—no special requirements as to form—must contain full particulars as—quantities—weights—value per unit—all necessary charges to establish a CIF value. Invoices must be signed—country of origin shown and statement stating that goods are in accordance with pro-forma invoice. Invoice should be certified by New York Chamber of Commerce and Industry.

(B) **Certificate of Origin**—3—when required—general form—sold by commercial printers—certified by the New York Chamber of Commerce and Industry, which requires one additional notarized copy for its files.

(C) **Bills of Lading**—3—no special requirements—should show gross weight in pounds and dimensions in feet and inches—"To Order" bills of lading acceptable.

2. **Air Cargo and Parcel Post Shipments**

(A) **Commercial Invoice**—see 1(A)—2—must accompany shipment. Additional copies should be sent to consignee.

3. **Import License**

Required by importer for most commodities—validity 1 year.

4. **Special Documents**

(A) **Sanitary Certificate**—required for all plants and plant products (except fruits and vegetables). Leaf tobacco should have an additional certificate attesting that the tobacco is free from "ephestia elutella," or that this pest does not exist in the country of origin.

(B) **Fumigation Certificate**—required for used clothing.

5. **Consular Holidays**

All holidays generally observed in New York City.

BARBADOS

SUMMARY OF SHIPPING DOCUMENTS REQUIRED
No Consular Documents Required
1. **Shipping Documents Required For All Shipments regardless of value:**

(A) **Commercial Invoice**—2—The preferred and recommended form is the "Jamaica Invoice and Declaration of Value" Form C23. (Shippers may print their own, provided they conform exactly to the requirements). Extreme care should be exercised when completing all questions regarding charges and expenses. Shippers should state whether each item is included or excluded in the selling price. The origin section on this invoice should be completed only when shipping goods which are entitled to British preferential duties.

All invoices should contain a careful description of the merchandise and all the necessary detailed charges and expenses to arrive at the CIF value. Although the price column of the invoice is marked CIF, shippers must show both the FAS and CIF value.

In addition to these, 2 regular commercial invoices must be prepared.

(B) **Bill of Lading**—No special requirements.

2. **Import License**

Most commodities may be imported under Open General License. Very few items require an Import License.

3. **Special Documents**

Inspection Certificate—An official inspection certificate is required on all shipments of fresh fruits and vegetables grown in Florida stating that they have been fumigated and are free from Mediterranean fruit fly. State of Florida certificates are acceptable. Fresh fruits and vegetables grown in other States and transiting Florida for export by sea or air must be accompanied by proof of origin.

*Consular Holidays

Good Friday, Easter Monday, May 1, May 19, August 1, November 30, and December 1. All holidays generally observed in New York City.

*Denotes changes since previous notice.
See Form 10-900.

BELGIUM

SUMMARY OF SHIPPING DOCUMENTS REQUIRED
No Consular Documents Required
1. **Shipping Documents Required**
   All Shipments for all commercial shipments regardless of mode of transportation.
   (A) **Commercial Invoice**—1—Must contain full particulars.
   (B) **Certificate of Origin**—1—required only for Port and Madeira wines and seafish for industrial purposes or when stipulated in Letter of Credit or requested by importer—on general form—sold by commercial printers. Certified by the New York Chamber of Commerce and Industry, which requires one additional notarized copy for its files.
2. **Import License**
   Most imports have been liberalized and all that is required is the filing of a Notice of Importation, which is automatically approved. Only a limited number of commodities require an Import License.
3. **Special Documents**
   (A) **Sanitary Certificate**—1—required for shipments of fats; meats (Prepared or preserved), and meat preparations. Must be issued by an officially approved veterinary officer in the country of origin. Consular legalization not required.
   (B) **Inspection Certificate**—1—required for shipment of plants, fresh fruits, hop cuttings and potatoes. Must be issued by official authorities and must state that shipment is free of insects, disease and the San Jose Scale must contain in French the words ("L' envoi est exempt de Pou de San Jose"). In the case of shipments of potatoes the certificate must state in French ("L' envoi est exempt de potato wart [galle hoire] et ring rot"). Certificates covering shipments of hop cuttings must state in French that the merchandise is free from wilt ("L' envoi est exempt de Verticillium alboatrum").
   (C) **Health Certificate**—1—required for shipments of dogs, pets, farm animals, etc. Must be issued by a recognized authority. (For cats and dogs—Form must be obtained from the Consulate General's office.) Consular legalization not required.
4. **Consular Holidays**
   Good Friday (½ day), May 31, August 15, November 15, and December 26. All holidays generally observed in New York City.

BENIN, PEOPLE'S REPUBLIC OF

SUMMARY OF SHIPPING DOCUMENTS REQUIRED
No Consular Documents Required
1. **Shipping Documents Required**
   All Shipments (regardless of value and mode of transportation).
   (A) **Commercial Invoice**—2—no special form—must contain names of exporter consignee—number and types of packages—marks and numbers on packages—net and gross weights—CIF value—terms of sale—accurate, specific and complete description of the merchandise. Must be certified true and signed by the exporter.
   (B) **Certificate of Origin**—2—general form—sold by commercial printers—gener-

ally necessary for all goods originating in foreign countries in order to establish true origin of the goods for customs purposes. Certified by the New York Chamber of Commerce and Industry, which requires an additional notarized copy for its files.

(C) **Bill of Lading**—No special regulations—marks of identification and name and address of the consignee should be clearly indicated. To insure prompt clearance by customs, the shipping marks and numbers on bills of lading, on invoices, and on the goods themselves, should correspond exactly.

(D) **Pro-Forma Invoices**—2—for import license purposes—certified by the New York Chamber of Commerce and Industry, which requires an additional notarized copy for its files.

2. **Import License**

Required for most products; the import license carries the right to foreign exchange. Foreign exchange is controlled. Before making shipment, the exporter should provide a pro-forma invoice and should assure himself that the importer has obtained a proper import license.

Validity of license is usually six months. The goods must be shipped before expiration date of license. Extension of license is possible on proving need. Application for extension should be made before expiration. No tolerance in value is permitted.

3. **Consular Fees**

Payable by check only.

Commercial invoice (when requested) $3.59
Certificate of origin (when requested) $3.59
Nonshipping documents (affidavits, powers of attorney, etc.) $5.74

4. **Holidays**

All holidays generally observed in New York City.

BOLIVIA

SUMMARY OF SHIPPING DOCUMENTS REQUIRED
Consular Documents Required

1. **Special Information**

For ocean freight shipments, all documents must be presented to Consulate within (6) working days after sailing of vessel. For air or parcel post shipments, they must be presented within six (6) working days after date shown on air waybill or parcel post receipt. Any documents presented later than the sixth day will be marked by the Consulate—delayed (DEMORADO). Consequent fines will be charged at the Customs House in Bolivia, at the shipper's cost. (Art. 56 Ley Organica de Aduanas). The Consulate will not charge any fines for any reason.

Registered Air Mail: Exporters that send their documents directly to their customers in Bolivia should make sure that the legalized documents are forwarded by Registered Mail.

Duplicates of Shipping Documents: If the shipping documents are lost on their way to the destination point, the Consulate will not legalize duplicates unless valid proof is presented. Documents mailed to Consulate for legalization, must be accompanied by a self addressed stamped envelope, bearing sufficient postage to return them via Certified Mail. (Call Consulate for charges)

Insurance to be covered in Bolivia:—A new insurance law permits only Bolivian domestic insurance firms or foreign insurance firms authorized to operate in Bolivia to write insurance for: a) the Bolivian exporter shipping CIF from Bolivia and; b) the Bolivian importer buying FOB exports to Bolivia.

CERTIFICATE OF ORIGIN

The undersigned...
(Owner or Agent, or &c)

for...declares
(Name and Address of Shipper)

that the following mentioned goods shipped on S/S...
(Name of Ship)

on the date of ....consigned to. ....

....are the product of the United States of America.

MARKS AND NUMBERS	NO. OF PKGS., BOXES OR CASES	WEIGHT IN KILOS		DESCRIPTION
		GROSS	NET	

Sworn to before me

Dated at.............................on the........day of.....................19....

this............day of.............................19....

....
(Signature of Owner or Agent)

The.., a recognized Chamber of Commerce under the laws of the State of

...., has examined the manufacturer's invoice or shipper's affidavit concerning the origin of the merchandise and, according to the best of its knowledge and belief, finds that the products named originated in the United States of North America.

Secretary...

Form 10-900   Printed and Sold by Unz & Co., Division of Scott Printing Corp., 190 Baldwin Ave., Jersey City, N.J. 07306 — N.J. (201) 795-5400 / N.Y. (212) 344-2270
Toll Free (800) 631-3098

Form 10-900. Export Forms, Hazardous Materials Labels, etc. can be purchased from Unz & Co., 190 Baldwin Ave., P.O. Box 308, Jersey City, N.J. 07303.

2.   *All Shipments valued $100.—F.O.B. up to $2.000.—regardless of mode of transportation:

(A) **Factura Comercial Official (Consular Invoice)**—1—original and 5 copies in Spanish—must show FOB value and all itemized charges to CIF value, (ocean freight, insurance, and any other charges). Sets may not be separated (i.e., all six copies must have the same set number). Unless the number on all six invoices is the same, documents will be rejected. If a shipper requests any additional copies, a photostat of the original must be made. In no case is the shipper to break up a sequence of numbers. The Consulate does not accept documents with erasures, obliterations, amendments, insertions, etc. The Consular invoice should have the date of the day being presented to the Consulate and no other. The Consulate will not accept Consular Invoices with stale dates or no date.

3.   *All Shipments valued $2.000.—F.O.B. and over regardless of mode of transportation:

(A) **Factura Comercial Official (Consular Invoice)**—Same as 2.A

(B) Shippers attention is called to the proper preparation of the Factura Comercial (Official) as per sample attached Form-1. Invoices should be certified by the New York Chamber of Commerce or any other Chamber of Commerce and Industry well reputed in the United States.

Remark: The Consulate General of Bolivia reserves the right to request proof of prices, price lists of manufacturers, or any other proof or samples.

Shippers may prepare one Bill of Lading for various vehicles, e.g. passenger automobiles, trucks, etc. Serial and motor number of each vehicle should be shown in all documents. However, a separate consular invoice, with attached commercial invoice is required for each vehicle showing the respective bill of lading. Please note, that each vehicle has to pay all Consular Fees that applies. If one Bill of Lading covers more than two vehicles the following notation must be written in the Factura Comercial (Official):

"CONOCIMIENTO DE EMBARQUE No. xx CUBRE XX VEHICULOS"

A Due Bill (original) must be attached to the first set.

4.   **Commercial Invoice (Supplier's Invoice)**—1 original and 5 copies in Spanish on shipper's letterhead—4 copies retained by Consulate, must show the FOB value and all itemized charges to CIF. If ocean freight and insurance is not pre-paid, shipper must state that it is paid in Bolivia.

The following information must also be shown on Commercial Invoices: a.—Name of Shipper, b.—consignee, c.—Bolivian Customs port of entry, d.—Port of unloading, e.—Date of Invoice, f.—Ultimate destination, g.—The quantity of packages, gross and net weight of merchandise.

Only one consignment to one consignee in each invoice will be permitted. The notation "without mark or number" or similar expression will not be allowed unless merchandise is shipped in bulk or unpacked. One number alone for more than one package is prohibited. Type of package, e.g. case, bag, barrel, etc., must be shown. The contents of each package must be declared specifically. Must also show unit prices and quantities.

When declaring raw materials or natural products, the specific component of the material must be stated. General descriptions such as "iron, foodstuffs, metal, cereals" or other such phrases will not be allowed. General descriptions of manufactured goods such as hardware, accessories, textiles, etc., will not be allowed.

A more detailed description must be given, e.g. printed cotton piece goods, nylon lace, nylon stockings, steel bars, canned tomatoes, etc. Country of origin, price of each item per unit and total amount must be shown.

Invoices must be signed and contain a statement that the information is true and correct. "To order or Order of Shipper" invoices will not be accepted.

Non manufacturing exporters also must submit to the Chambers of Commerce and Industry the invoice or price list of the manufacturer or supplier from whom the merchandise was purchased. This invoice or price list will be returned. When in doubt, the Consulate reserves the right to request proof of prices. Two copies returned to shipper.

5. **Bill of Lading**—2 originals and 4 non-negotiables copies must be presented to the Consulate together with shipping documents, after being signed by steamship company. "To Order or Order of Shipper" bills of lading will not be accepted. Bolivia must be shown as Country of destination. Due Bill original issued by steamship company must be attached to the first original Bill of Lading in the first set.

NOTE: In the case of air or parcel post shipments, substitute 2 original and 4 copies of the air waybill or parcel post receipt for the bill of lading.

Marks and Numbers: The notation—"without mark or number"—or similar expression will not be allowed. One number alone for more than one package is prohibited. Type of packages, e.g. case, bag, barrel, etc., must be shown. The contents of each package also must be declared on the Commercial Invoices, together with unit prices and quantities.

6. **All shipments valued less than $100.—F.O.B. regardless of mode of transportation, no consular documents required.**

Books—Educational, Scientific, Technical, Catalogs, Manuals, does not require Consular documents, however, 6 copies of seller's invoice must be presented to Consulate to be stamped.

7. **Special Documents**

(A) **Sanitary Certificate**—1 original and 5 copies, issued by U.S. Department of Agriculture (shippers may make photostats of document to complete the set of 6) necessary for shipments of food (lard, canned food, seeds, grains, flour, etc.). Also acceptable notarized certificates "apt for human consumption" issued by the manufacturer. This certificate must be attached in each set along with the other documents—in Spanish.

(B) **Certificate of Analysis**—1 original and 5 copies—in Spanish necessary for all shipments of pharmaceuticals, may be issued by manufacturer, if reliable. Certificate must show expiration dates, when such dates are shown on the medicament containers, (as in penicillin, etc.) and must be notarized. This certificate must be attached in each set along with the other documents.

8. **Arrangement of Documents**

Must be arranged in 6 separate sets, each set to be stapled, and the 6 sets clipped together. The following order must be followed for each set:

1. Factura Comercial (Official Consular Invoice)
2. Commercial Invoice (supplier's invoice)
3. Additional documents, if any (health certificate, sanitary certificate, certificate of analysis)
4. Certificate of Origin (when required)
5. Bill of Lading (the 2 originals attached to the first 2 sets)
6. Due Bill must be attached (stapled) to the bill of lading.

NOTE: Unless documents are arranged exactly as described above, Consulate will reject them.

9. ***Consular Fees**

Consular fees are payable by certified check, money order, or cash, made out to the Consulate General of Bolivia. Checks drawn on banks other than banks in the United States are not acceptable. Each set of documents must be covered by its own check for its respective Consular fees. Unless each set is covered by an individual check, the documents will be rejected.

Any payment for any type of service, legalization of documents, extra copies, or special documents (except consular blanks fees) must have the equivalent amount in Consular stamps affixed on the legalized documents.

10.   ***Legalization Fees of Shipping Documents**

All Shipments valued $100.—F.O.B. up to $2.000.—

a. Legalization $20.00

b. Legalization of bill of lading or air waybill, and
postal receipt 5.00

c. 2% of shipping charges, rounded up
to the nearest 50 cents .... minimum   2.00

d. Legalization of extra copies
(Commercial, and Consular) .... 2.00 each

e. Legalization of extra copies of Bill of Lading, Air waybill, or
parcel post receipt .... 1.00 each

f. Legalization of mineral sales .... 50.00 each

g. To legalize trade marks, patents of invention, names, labels,
tags, sketch, and other commercial signs for each case (Must be
notarized, signed by County Clerk or Secretary of State prior
to presentation to Consulate) .... 30.00 each

h. To legalize transfer of trade marks, labels, and names of
Bolivian manufacturers in foreign countries, for each case (Must
be notarized, signed by County Clerk or Secretary of State prior to presentation to Consulate) .... 30.00 each

i. To legalize power of attorney to obtain registration and renewal of
trade marks and commercial signs and its modifications, for each case
(Must be notarized, signed by County Clerk or Secretary
of State prior to presentation to Consulate) .... 20.00 each

Immediate Service

Immediate document service is available by paying a special fee of 25% which is determined by adding the following:

Legalization, plus bill of lading or airwaybill or parcel post receipt, plus the 2% of shipping charge (see Form 1) & (Form 1A). Documents will then be returned immediately. Special fees must have a separate check, money order or cash.

11.   ***All Shipments valued $2.000.—F.O.B. and over**

a. Legalization .... 1% of F.O.B.

                               (Factory) value rounded up to the next 50 cents

b. Legalization of bill of lading $5.00

c. 2% of shipping charges, rounded up to the
nearest 50 cents .... minimum   2.00

d. Legalization of extra copies (Commercial and Consular) .... 2.00 each

e. Legalization of extra copies of Bill of Lading, Air waybill, or
parcel post receipt .... 1.00 each

12.   ***Letters of Correction**

Letters of correction must be prepared on shipper's letterhead according to the following form:

(A) Shipments valued $100.—F.O.B. up to $2.000.—

1. Up to 10 days from date of original legalization $30.00

2. From 10 up to 30 days from date of original
legalization .... minimum   30.00

PLUS: 1½% over the F.O.B. (Factory) value of the merchandise
rounded up to the nearest 50 cents 1½%

(B) Shipments valued $2.000.—F.O.B. and over

1. Up to 10 days from date of original legalization $40.00
2. From 10 days up to 30 days from date of original
   legalization .... minimum 40.00
   PLUS: 1½% over the F.O.B. (Factory) value of the
   merchandise rounded up to the nearest 50 cents 1½%
(C) Rectifying the value over $2.000.—F.O.B. 1% over the net difference
of the original and new value 1%
   One original and 5 copies in Spanish, legalized by Consulate which retains 2
copies. Notarization or certification not required. Letters of correction or rectification must be presented as follows:

Letters of Correction Form

Factura Consular legalizada con el N° de Orden _____
de fecha _____ correspondiente al vapor _____
de la Compania _____ que salio del puerto de _____
el dia _____ con destino al puerto de _____
consignada a _____
y embarcada por _____
                                    Nueva York, _____
Senor Consul General de Bolivia:
   En la factura Consular del rubro hemos cometido el siguiente error debido a
(explicar causa del error)
DONDE DICE: _____

DEBE DECIR: _____

   Rogamos al Sr. Consul General se sirva disponer la legalizacion de la presente Carta de Correccion.
   De Ud. muy atentamente,

13. **Consular Holidays**
   Good Friday, August 6 (Independence Day); and all holidays generally ob-
served in New York City.
   *Denotes changes since previous notice.
See Form 1 and 1A.

BRAZIL

SUMMARY OF SHIPPING DOCUMENTS REQUIRED
Special Information
All insurance must be covered in Brazil, with the exception of AID Shipments.
No Consular Documents Required
Shipping Documents Required
1. **For all Shipments by Steamer, Air Cargo or Parcel Post regardless of value:**
   (A) **Commercial Invoice**—5—on special form sold by commercial printers or shipper's own invoice form—in Portuguese or English. Certified by Commerce and
   Industry Association. One additional notarized copy is required by the Association for its files.
      The invoice should include the following information: name and nationality
   of vessel, name of steamship company, date of departure, port of shipment,
   port of entry in Brazil, marks and numbers (numbering is not required when
   the same goods are shipped in lots of 50 or more identical cases, each having the
   same weight and dimensions) quantity and type of packages, complete description merchandise in Portuguese as per import license, gross and net weight,

FACTURA COMERCIAL

Numero de Orden Leave blank

Número de Aduana Leave blank

FOR ALL SHIPMENTS VALUED $100.- F.O.B. UP TO $2.000.-

Destinado a la Aduana de Custom House Port
(destined to)

S A M P L E

Por las mercaderías que se expresan, embarcadas por ABC Manufacturing Co Inc.

de NUeva York el 19 de Diciembre de 1974 en s. s. "SANTA CLARA"

a la consignación de Grace & Co del puerto de Matarani, Peru

de orden, por cuenta y riesgo de J. Garcia & Cia. de LA PAZ, BOLIVIA

BULTOS				CLASIFICACION DE LA MERCADERIA SEGUN SUS COMPONENTES Y NOMBRE COMERCIAL	PESO BRUTO KILOS	CANTIDAD LEGAL (Docenas, metros, et.)	VALOR DE LA MERCADERIA	
Marcas	Numeros	Cant.	Clase					
JG&Cia	1	1	Cajon	MEDIAS DE ALGODON PARA SENORAS	132	100 Doc	450.	00
L A							(FOB Factory)	
PAZ				GASTOS DE EMBARQUE				
BOLIVIA				Acarreo	45.50			
MATA-				Flete maritimo	98.25			
RANI				Seguro	4.30			
PERU				Documentacion	53.25			
				Otros Gastos	15.00			
				Total gastos	216.30		216.	30
				DERECHOS CONSULARES				
				Legalizacion	20.00			
				Conocimiento maritimo (aereo, recibo postal)	5.00			
				2% sobre gastos de embarque	4.50			
IMMEDIATE SERVICE: 25% of this ──▶ Total					29.50		29.	50
TOTALES	1			TOTAL CIF	132		695.	80

Protestamos que los pormenores de cantidad, pesos, calidades, valores y fechas de las mercaderias detalladas en esta Factura Comercial, son verdaderos y correctos.

El Cónsul (General) de la República de Bolivia en NUEVA YORK, EE.UU. Certifica: la conformidad de la presente Factura Comercial, que representa un valor de Seicientos noventa y cinco con 80/100

SELLO DEL CONSULADO

Nueva York 19 de Diciembre de 1974
(Lugar y fecha)

Nueva York 19 de Diciembre de 1974

MUST BE SIGNED BY SHIPPER AND
STAMPED BY CHAMBER OF COMMERCE ON THE
(Firma de los embarcadores) REVERSE SIDE OF THIS FORM

CONSUL

THIS SPACE MUST BE CLEAR

Form 1. (Front)

FORM 1A

FACTURA COMERCIAL

Número de Orden Leave Blank

Número de Aduana Leave Blank

Destinado a la Aduana de Custom House Port
FOR ALL SHIPMENTS VALUED $2.000.- F.O.B. AND OVER (destined to)

S A M P L E

Por las mercaderías que se expresan, embarcadas por ABC Manufacturing Co Inc.
de Nueva York el 19 de Diciembre de 1974 en S. S. "SANTA CLARA"
a la consignación de Grace & Co del puerto de Matarani, Peru
de orden, por cuenta y riesgo de J. Garcia & Cia de LA PAZ BOLIVIA

BULTOS				CLASIFICACION DE LA MERCADERIA SEGUN SUS COMPONENTES Y NOMBRE COMERCIAL	PESO BRUTO KILOS	CANTIDAD LEGAL (Docenas, metros, etc.)	VALOR DE LA MERCADERIA	
Marcas	Números	Cant.	Clase					
G&Cia	2	1	Carton	MAQUINA COSEDORA DE SACOS	1200	1 Unid.	3.950.	00
LA				METALEROS			(FOB Factory)	
PAZ				GASTOS DE EMBARQUE				
OLIVIA				Acarreo 195.50				
MATA-				Flete maritimo 2.325.25				
RANI				Seguro 75.00				
PERU				Documentacion 68.50				
				Otros Gastos 15.00				
				2.679.25			2.679.	25
				DERECHOS CONSULARES				
				Legalizacion (1%FOB) 39.50				
				Conocimeinto maritimo				
				(aereo, recibo postal) 5.00				
				2% sobre gastos de				
				embarque (2.679.25) 54.00				
IMMEDIATE SERVICE: 25% of this ——▶ Total 98.50							98.	50
TOTALES	1			TOTAL CIF	1200		6.727.	75

Protestamos que los pormenores de cantidad, pesos, calidades, valores y fechas de las mercaderías detalladas en esta Factura Comercial, son verdaderos y correctas.

El Cónsul (General) de la República de Bolivia en
NUEVA YORK, EE.UU. Certifica: la conformidad de la presente Factura Comercial, que representa un valor de Seis mil setecientos veinti-

SELLO DEL
CONSULADO

siete con 75/100

Nueva York 19 de Diciembre de 1974
(Lugar y fecha)

19 de Diciembre de 1974

MUST BE SIGNED BY SHIPPER AND STAMPED BY
CHAMBER OF COMMERCE ON THE REVERSE SIDE OF
THIS FORM
(Firma de los embarcadores)

CONSUL

THIS SPACE MUST BE CLEAR

Form 1A. (Back)

359

country of origin, country from which sent, unit and total price, freight and all other expenses to CIF value. Name of consignee must agree with import license. "To Order of Shipper" not allowed to be shown on invoices. The reverse side of the commercial invoices must show the following information: import license number (or certificate of exchange), date of issuance, expiration date. Shipper must note whether shipment is first, second, third, etc., and the value being used. (We understand that customs authorities have levied fines for lack of information particularly the date of departure of vessel. We, therefore, strongly urge that the following be shown on the invoice. "(Data da Saida do Navio Date of Departure)." We also understand that the authorities have levied fines on erasures, crossouts and for lack of information.

Shipments of books, maps, newspapers, magazines are exempt of the requirement of an Import License. Shippers should insert the following clause in the commercial invoice: "No Import License required in accordance with Paragraph 6 of Article 54, Decree No. 42820 of December 16, 1957."

(B) **Bill of Lading—Air Waybill**—5—non-negotiable copies signed by carrier. "To Order" bills of lading allowed, but "notify party" must be in agreement with license. Must show import license numbers and expiration dates. Where no import license is required, that fact must be so stated.

When shipments originate abroad and are cleared through New York in transit to Brazil shipper must present either: (a) copy of the through bill of lading issued by the foreign carrier for the voyage or (b) copy of the bill of lading issued by the foreign carrier for the voyage, from port of origin abroad to New York, must be attached to invoices.

Bills of lading or air waybills covering shipments to Brazil must show the amount of the freight charges in figures and in words; e.g. $445.00 (four hundred forty-five dollars). Non-compliance with this regulation will prevent the importer from closing or liquidating foreign exchange contracts.

2. **Import License or Exchange Certificate**—Required for most commercial shipments, including samples. Merchandise must be on board carrier prior to expiration date of license and bills of lading or air waybills dated prior to that date. Steamer may sail after expiration date, provided that goods were on board within the validity of the license.

A tolerance of 10% over or under the FOB value at the port of shipment, and 5% on net weight shown on import license is allowed whether merchandise is sold on weight or unit basis.

Shippers are not required to present import licenses with amendments changing the port of destination. Brazilian importers should apply directly to the office or agency holding the original customs permit which, in turn, will transmit the permit or its particulars to its office at the new port of destination.

New Import Procedures—The Bank of Brazil issued on May 5, 1971 a new circular #343 changing certain provisions regulating imports into Brazil. These are some of the provisions: (1) The value limit per shipment of spare parts and accessories for repair of machinery, aircraft, apparatus, instruments, vessels and other equipment when imported directly by the end user for which an import permit is not required, has been raised to $3,000 FOB. (2) Machinery, engines, or equipment imported into Brazil for repairs or testing purposes and re-exported, no longer require an import/export permit. Parts and accessories imported for the repair of such items are also exempted from the import permit requirement. (3) If a Brazilian representative, agent or distributor of a foreign manufacturer and/or exporter has on file with CACEX a statement of his commission, he no longer needs to submit to CACEX a letter of commitment relative to each import.

Free Zone of Manaus—Shipments to the Free Zone of Manaus do not require import licenses. However, 4 commercial invoices and 4 bills of lading are required. The commercial invoices certified by Commerce and Industry Association which required 1 additional notarized copy. The bills of lading must show under marks "Free Zone of Manaus." The commercial invoice must be manually signed by shipper and his name typed under his signature. Both the commercial invoice and the bills of lading must have one of the following two statements typed in the body of the documents, "Zona Franca de Manaus para Consumo," or "Zona Franca de Manaus para Consumo reexportacao." The following items are prohibited: Ammunition and guns, perfume, tobacco, alcoholic beverages, and passenger cars.

3. **Special Documents**

    All documents requiring notarization (such as power of attorney, affidavits, etc.) must be authenticated by the county clerk before they are presented to the Consulate. This requirement will be waived if the Notary has his signature registered at the Consulate. (Regular commercial invoices covering commercial shipments are not affected.)

    (A) **Sanitary & Purity Certificate**—1—required for various products, including animals, seeds, plants, fresh fruits, potatoes, raw cotton, cotton strips and combing, etc.

    (B) **Inspection Certificate**—2—required for used industrial machinery and equipment. Consular legalization fee: $6.00. If shipper requires extra copies, Consulate will legalize them assessing $6.00 consular fee for each copy. Inspection certificates must be issued by any of the following inspecting and testing firms:

    Superintendence Company, Inc.—New York City
    American Appraisal Company, Inc.—New York City
    Bureau Veritas—New York City
    California Testing Laboratories, Inc.—Los Angeles, California
    El Paso Testing Laboratories—El Paso, Texas
    Electrical Testing Laboratories, Inc.—New York, New York
    George A. Hale, Inc.—St. Louis, Missouri
    Robert W. Hunt & Company—New York City
    Loftus Engineering Corporation—Pittsburgh, Pennsylvania
    Pittsburgh Testing Laboratory—New York City
    (also Nationwide Service)
    United States Testing Co. Laboratories—New York City

    In addition to the above names, Consulate may accept other inspecting firms; reports, if references furnished to Consulate prove satisfactory.

    (C) **Pro-Forma Invoices**—(1) The original copy of the pro-forma invoice must be notarized: (2) Exporters must indicate whether or not freight, insurance and general charges are included in the FOB value; (3) It must contain a signed statement by the exporter or manufacturer accepting full responsibility that the prices stated in the pro-forma invoice are the current export market prices for the merchandise described.

    (D) **Samples and Displays**—All documents required as for commercial shipments must state on documents: "Samples—Not for sale—No Commercial Value." Import License required.

    (E) **Aid Shipments**—All shipments made under AID Loan Agreements must be covered by the following AID documents: 3 copies of Suppliers Certificate (AID form 282); 3 copies of Certificate of Carrier (covering cost of ocean or air freight); 3 copies of Certificate of Supplier of Marine Insurance (covering cost of marine insurance if over $50); and, 2 copies of Commodity Approval Application AID form 11 countersigned by AID). This is in addition to commercial invoices, bills of lading, certificates of origin (if required) and any other documents which are called for by the importer and/or terms of credit. Don't forget

FATURA COMERCIAL
(Commercial Invoice)

No. . . . .

Nome da Firma Vendedora . . . .
(Name of Seller)

Nome Embarcação/Aeronave . . . .   Nome da Companhia da Embarcação/Aeronave . . . .   Nacionalidade. . . . .
(Name of Vessel Aeroplane)   (Name of Company (owner) of Vessel/Aeroplane)   (Nationality)

MARCAS DOS VOLUMES (Marks)   Porto de Embarque . . . .   Porto de Destino . . . .
                              (Port of Embarkation)   (Port of Destination)

                              Saída da Embarcação/Aeronave. . . . .   País de Origem. . . . .   País de Procedência. . . . .
                              (Departure date of Vessel/Aeroplane)   (Country of Origin)   (Country from which sent)

                              Vendida a. . . . .
                              (Sold to)

Numeração dos Volumes (Numbers on the packages)	Quantidade (Quantity)	Espécie (Kind)	Item da Tarifa (Tariff Number)	ESPECIFICAÇÃO DAS MERCADORIAS (Description of goods)	QUANTIDADE (Quantity)	PESO BRUTO EM KGS. (Gross weight kgs.)	PESO LÍQUIDO EM KGS. (Net weight kgs.)	PREÇO EM MOEDA ESTRANGEIRA (Price in foreign currency)	
								UNITÁRIO (Unit price)	TOTAL (Total)

Total . . . .
(Total value of merchandise)

Despesas diversas especificadas . . . . . .
(Inland expenses itemised)

Valor total FOB . . . .
(Total FOB value)

Valor frete. . . . .
(Value of freight)

Valor seguro. . . . .
(Value of Insurance)

Valor total. . . . .
(Total value)

Date. . . . .

Signature. . . . .

Condições: FOB ou C & F . . . .
(Terms)

Revised July 1971 Form 10-070—(Bond) 10-471—(Onionskin) 10-472—(Onionskin Carbonized)
Printed and Sold by Uni & Co., An Affiliate of Scott Ptg. Corp. 190 Baldwin Ave., J. C., N. J. 07306

Form 10-070 (front).

Guia de Importação Número da Licença de Importação e/ou Certificado (Number of Import License and/or Certificate)	Data da expedição (Date of issue)	Data da expiração (Date of expiration)	Guia de Importação Utilização da licença/certificado (Utilization of license/certificate. Number of partial shipment. Value F.O.B. being used. Statement that it is first partial or complete shipment or last shipment of license.)

Form 10-070 (back).

Export Forms, Hazardous Materials Labels, etc. can be purchased from Unz & Co., 190 Baldwin Ave., P.O. Box 308, Jersey City, N.J. 07303.

363

one also requires a Vessel Approval Certificate from Washington, according to GECAM Communique No. 8, Paragraph 10 (c).

4. **Origin of Third Country Merchandise**
   (A) For manufactured goods, the country of origin is that in which the raw material has been processed, treated or worked, i.e. where through such processing its inherent nature is altered.
   (B) Raw materials of origin other than U.S., repacked, cleaned, or bottled in this country, are considered third country merchandise so that the origin, as such, remains unchanged and must be so declared on consular papers.

5. **Arrangement of Documents**
   Commercial Invoice, followed by bill of lading, stapled together. Four other sets arranged in the same manner. Signed and notarized copy of commercial invoices retained by this Association on top (separately).

6. **Consular Fees**
   Power of attorney, statements and
   certificate of analysis, etc. .... $6.00 each
   Invoices for "Banking purposes"
   (services, Commissions, etc.) .... $3.00 each
   See Form 10-070 (front and back).

BULGARIA

SUMMARY OF SHIPPING DOCUMENTS REQUIRED
Special Information
All insurance as well as re-insurance must be handled in Bulgaria.
No Consular Documents Required
1. **Shipping Documents Required**
   (A) **Commercial Invoice**—2—no special form—should show complete description of goods and the usual information.
   (B) **Certificate of Origin**—2—when required—general form—sold by commercial printers—certified by the New York Chamber of Commerce and Industry which requires an additional notarized copy for its files.
   (C) **Bills of Lading**—no special regulations—the usual information should be shown.
2. **Import License**
   Required by importer for all imports.

BURMA

SUMMARY OF SHIPPING DOCUMENTS REQUIRED
No Consular Documents Required
1. **Shipping Documents Required for all surface shipments:**
   (A) *Commercial Invoice**—3—must be signed and certified true and correct. Must show FOB value and all itemized expenses to CIF. If an FOB invoice is desired, then a separate invoice showing all charges must be prepared (which also must be signed and certified true and correct.) Invoice must describe merchandise in detail and show unit prices. Import license number and all discounts and their nature must also be shown. Country of origin must be shown.
   (B) **Bill of Lading**—"To Order" bills of lading allowed, but consignee must be shown as the "notifying party." When shipping documents are sent to a Bank in Burma the name of the Bank must also appear on the bill of lading as a "notify party."
   (C) **Certificate of Origin**—2—when required—general form—sold by commercial

printers—certified by the New York Chamber of Commerce and Industry, which requires one additional notarized copy for its files.

2. **Air Cargo Shipments**
   Commercial Invoice—3—as above, must accompany shipment.
3. **Import License**
   All imports require prior authorization. Foreign trade is nationalized and most importing is done by Government agencies. Foreign exchange automatically available for all authorized imports.
4. ***Consular Holidays**
   January 4, February 20, March 2-24-27, April 14-17, July 19.
   *Denotes changes since previous notice.

BURUNDI

SUMMARY OF SHIPPING DOCUMENTS REQUIRED
No Consular Documents Required
1. **Shipping Documents Required**
   (A) ***Commercial Invoice**—2—no special requirements—should contain the usual information and an accurate description of the goods, country of origin, name of importer, etc.
   (B) **Certificate of Origin**—2—when required—general form—sold by commercial printers—certified by the New York Chamber of Commerce and Industry, which requires an additional notarized copy for its files.
   (C) **Bills of Lading**—no special regulations—should show the usual information, marks, numbers.
2. **Import License**
   All imports with few exception require import licenses—validity 12 months—may be extended. No tolerances are allowed. All goods imported into Burundi must be insured with Government insurer, (SOCABU) and, premiums paid for in Burundi currency & shipments valued over 500,000 Burundi francs must be inspected for quality, quantity & price comparison by Superintendence Co.
3. **Holidays**
   All holidays generally observed in New York City.
   *Denotes changes since previous notice.

CAMEROON

SUMMARY OF SHIPPING DOCUMENTS REQUIRED
No Consular Documents Required
1. **Shipping Documents Required**
   (A) ***Commercial Invoice**—3—must contain names and addresses of shipper and consignee—place and date of shipment—number and types of containers—marks and numbers—contents and weight—a careful description of the goods with the value of each item. The ocean freight and incidental expenses should be added to arrive at the C&F or CIF value. The FOB value (in U.S. dollars) and the CIF values must be listed separately. Must show country of origin.
   (B) **Certificate of Origin**—3—when required—on general form—sold by commercial printers—certified by the New York Chamber of Commerce and Industry, which requires one additional notarized copy for its files.
   (C) **Bills of Lading**—must contain gross weight in pounds—volume measurement in feet and inches—marks of identification and name and address of consignee. Shipping marks and numbers should correspond with those on the commercial invoice and containers.

2. **Import License**
    Required by importer—for all shipments on the free list valued over 500,000 CFA francs. Usually valid for 4 months. In some cases 6 months. Extensions can be granted. A tolerance of 2% of the value is allowed. However, it can not exceed $40.
3. **Special Documents**
    Sanitary Certificate—required for the importation of plants and plant products (e.g., banana plants, cacao plants, coffee plants, sugar cane, raw cotton, cotton seeds and cotton plants) and all containers containing earth and/or compost. Issued by the U.S. Department of Agriculture and other U.S. Government entities.
4. **Mission Holidays**
    All holidays generally observed in New York City.
See Form 10-820.
*Denotes changes since previous notice.

CANADA

SUMMARY OF SHIPPING DOCUMENTS REQUIRED
No Consular Documents Required
1. **Shipping Documents Required**
    ***All commercial shipments valued at $200 FOB Canadian Currency and over (regardless of mode of transportation).**
    (A) **Canadian Customs Invoice**—forms sold by commercial printers—three copies required by Canadian importer, for clearance purposes with extra copy for his record. There are two forms for goods of United States origin—Form M-A for goods sold prior to shipment, and—Form N-A for goods shipped without prior sales (i.e., on consignment). Customs Collectors have been instructed to strictly enforce the provisions regarding cash discounts on imported goods. United States exporters may grant Canadian customers the discount for cash ordinarily allowed in U.S., if payment is made in accordance with the terms, i.e., 2/10, net 30; but it is not permissible to deduct a cash discount from either the selling price or the fair market value.
    (B) ***For shipments valued at less than $200 FOB Canadian Currency**
    The sender's regular commercial invoice is usually sufficient. However, many Canadian Importers require the Customs Invoices, although the shipment is valued under $200. Shippers, therefore, should comply with such requests. In the case of non-commercial shipments of a casual nature, the sender need not furnish invoices, as the Canadian Customs Authorities will make delivery on the basis of forms completed by addressee.
    (C) **Special Exporters' Declaration**—Form B-31—required for all shipments valued at $10,000 or more—forms may be obtained from the Customs Division at the Consulate General of Canada or from commercial printers.
2. **Import License**
    Required for only a few items.
3. **Clearance of Merchandise**
    Goods must be cleared within 72 hours of arrival or charges may be imposed. Merchandise may be stored in a bonded warehouse for a period of 2 years.
    Textiles, Buttons, Footwear—Shipments of these products will not be released from customs unless the importer in Canada has in his possession Customs invoices containing the information outlined in Memorandum D46-7, D46-8, D46-9, respectively.

INVOICE AND DECLARATION OF VALUE REQUIRED FOR SHIPMENTS TO West Africa

COMPRISED OF THE FOLLOWING COUNTRIES:

CAMEROON   GAMBIA   SIERRA LEONE

(Place and Date)................................19......

Invoice of (General Nature or)..consigned
            (class of merchandise)

by...of................................

to...of................................

to be shipped per S. S...

Customer's Order No.   Our Order No.   Terms:

Country of Origin	Number of Packages	Marks and Numbers on Packages	Quantity and Description of Goods	Selling Price in Currency of Exporting Country At	Amount

Enumerate the following charges, and state whether each amount has been included in or excluded from the above selling prices:—	Amount in Currency of Exporting Country	State whether included or excluded
(1) Value of outside packages		
(2) Labour in packing the goods into outside packages		
(3) Cartage to rail and/or to docks		
(4) Inland freight and other charges		
(5) Ocean freight		
(6) Marine insurance		
(7) Commissions and other charges of a like nature		
(8) Other costs, dues, charges and expenses incidental to delivery of the articles at port of destination		
(9) If the goods are subject to any charge by way of royalties		
State full particulars of royalties below:—		

(1) Insert Manager, or Chief Clerk (as the case may be).

(2) Name of firm or Company.

(3) Name of city or country.

(4) Words bracketed should be omitted where the Manufacturer or Supplier himself signs the Certificate.

(5) Insert particulars of any special arrangement.

†Cross out paragraph that does not apply.

I, (1)..of (2)..
                                                    Manufacturer
of (3)..Supplier of the goods enumerated in this Invoice amounting to....................
....hereby declare (4) (that I have the authority to make and sign this Certificate on behalf of the aforesaid
Manufacturer and) that I have the means of knowing and do certify as follows:—
Supplier
            1. That this Invoice is in all respects correct and contains a true and full statement of the price actually paid or to be paid for the said goods, and the
actual quantity thereof.
            2. That no arrangements or understanding affecting the purchase price of the said goods has been or will be made or entered into between the said exporter
and purchaser, or by anyone on behalf of either of them either by way of discount, rebate, compensation or in any manner whatever other than as fully shown in this
Invoice, or as follows (5)..
....
            3† (a) That the country of origin of all the goods mentioned in this Invoice is.. or
            † (b) That the countries of origin of the goods mentioned in this Invoice are as declared in the appropriate column of the Invoice.

Dated at........................this..............day of........................, 19

Witness:..Signature..

Form 10-820. Export Forms, Hazardous Materials Labels, etc. can be purchased from
Unz & Co., 190 Baldwin Ave., P.O. Box 308, Jersey City, N.J. 07303.

367

*Holidays
Good Friday, July 1, October 14, and December 26. All holidays generally observed in New York City.
*Denotes changes since previous notice.
See Forms 10-200, 10-282 (front and back) and 10-090.

CENTRAL AFRICAN REPUBLIC

SUMMARY OF SHIPPING DOCUMENTS REQUIRED
No Consular Documents Required
1.   **Shipping Documents Required**
  (A) *Commercial Invoice**—3—must contain names and addresses of shipper and consignee—place and date of shipment—number and types of containers—marks and numbers—contents and weight—a careful description of the goods with the value of each item. The ocean freight and incidental expenses should be added to arrive at the C&F or CIF value. The FOB value (in U.S. dollars) and the CIF values must be listed separately. Must show country of origin.
  (B) **Certificate of Origin**—3—when required—on general form—sold by commercial printers—certified by the New York Chamber of Commerce and Industry, which requires one additional notarized copy for its files.
  (C) **Bills of Lading**—must contain gross weight in pounds—volume measurement in feet and inches—marks of identification and name and address of consignee. Shipping marks and numbers should correspond with those on the commercial invoice and containers.
2.   **Import License**
  Required by importer—tolerance 10% of the value—valid for six months and may be extended. License entitles importer to purchase necessary foreign exchange.
3.   **Special Documents**
  Sanitary Certificate—required for the importation of plants and plant products (e.g., banana plants, cacao plants, coffee plants, sugar cane, raw cotton, cotton seeds and cotton plants) and all containers containing earth and/or compost. Issued by the U.S. Department of Agriculture and other U.S. Government entities.
4.   **Mission Holidays**
  All holidays generally observed in New York City.
  *Denotes changes since previous notice.

CHAD, REPUBLIC OF

SUMMARY OF SHIPPING DOCUMENTS REQUIRED
No Consular Documents Required
1.   **Shipping Documents Required**
  (A) **Commercial Invoice**—3—must contain names and address of shipper and consignee—place and date of shipment—number and types of containers—marks and numbers—contents and weight—a careful description of the goods with the value of each item. The ocean freight and incidental expenses should be added to arrive at the C&F and CIF value. The FOB value (in U.S. dollars) and the CIF values must be listed separately.
  (B) **Certificate of Origin**—3—when required—on general form—sold by commercial printers—certified by the New York Chamber of Commerce and Industry, which requires one additional notarized copy for its files.
  (C) **Bills of Lading**—must contain gross weight in pounds—volume measurement in feet and inches—marks of identification and name and address of consignee.

Form No. 10-200 Bond Paper—No 10-250 Onionskin—1959   Printed in U S A and Sold by Unz & Co., An Affiliate of Scott Ptg. Corp 190 Baldwin Ave., J. C. N J 07306

1959 N-A Invoice approved by Canadian Customs (1959) for goods shipped on consignment without sale by exporter prior to importation, for entry at most Favoured Nation Tariff Rates.

Place and Date..19...

Invoice of...consigned

by...of..

to...of..

to be shipped from..per..

Country of Origin	Marks and Numbers on Packages	QUANTITIES AND DESCRIPTION OF GOODS	Fair Market Value at Time and Place of Shipment in Currency of Country of Export (See Clauses 8 to 9 of Certificate of Value hereon)	
			@	Amount

To be made in British countries before a Collector of Customs, Justice of the Peace, Notary Public or any official authorised to administer oaths; and in other countries before a British or other Consul, Notary Public or other official authorised to administer oaths.

(N) I, ... of ....
do solemnly and truthfully declare as follows:—   (name of party subscribing to this declaration)   (city or town and country)

1. That I am ....
   (a member of the firm of [giving the name of the firm when the shipment is made by a firm], or an officer, director or manager of [giving the name of the corporation when the shipment is made by a corporation])

the owner of the goods shipped on consignment to .... at ....
                                              (name of consignee)
in Canada and described on the annexed invoice;
   2   That the said invoice is a complete and true invoice of all the goods included in this shipment;
   3. That the said goods are properly described in the said invoice;
   4. That there is included in the said invoice the true value of all cartons, cases, crates, boxes and coverings of any kind and all charges and expenses incident to placing the said goods in condition packed ready for shipment to Canada;
   5   That none of the said goods have been sold by or on behalf of the owner to any person, firm or corporation in Canada;
   6   That the said invoice also exhibits the fair market value, at the time when and place from which the goods were shipped directly to Canada, of like goods when sold in the same or substantially the same quantities for home consumption in the ordinary course of trade under competitive conditions to purchasers located at that place with whom the vendor deals at arm's length and who are at the same or substantially the same trade level as the importer;
   7   That where like goods are not sold for home consumption in the circumstances described in the preceding section but where the goods shown on this invoice are similar to those sold for home consumption, the fair market value exhibited thereon is not less than the aggregate of
     a the cost of production of the goods exported; and
     b an amount that is the same percentage of the cost of production of the goods exported as the gross profit on the similar goods is of the cost of production of the similar goods;
   8. That the said fair market value is without
     a any discount or deduction not shown, allowed and deducted on invoices covering sales for home consumption in the country of export in the ordinary course of trade;
     b any deduction on account of any subsidy or drawback of Customs duty that has been allowed by the Government of any other country, or on account of any so-called royalty, rent or charge for use of any machine or goods of any description, that the seller or proprietor does or would usually charge thereon when the same are sold or leased or rented for use in the country of export; or
     c any discount or deduction on account of the amount of consideration or money value of any special arrangement between the exporter and the importer, or between any persons interested therein, because of the exportation or intended exportation of such goods, or the right to territorial limits for the sale or use thereof;
   9. That if the fair market value of the said goods described in this invoice is other than the value thereof as above specified, such fair market value has, to the best of my knowledge and belief, been fixed and determined under the authority of the Customs Act at the value exhibited in this invoice;

   (A)   That each article on this invoice is bona fide the produce or manufacture of the country specified on the invoice as its Country of Origin.
          That each manufactured article on the invoice in its present form ready for export to Canada has been finished in such specified country of origin, and not less than one-half the cost of production of

each such article has been produced through the industry of* .... entitled to the benefits of treaty or convention rates or the British Preferential Tariff.   (*Insert here name of country or countries)

Declared at ....

this .... day of ...., 19....   } (Signature)...
                                                              (Original copy must be signed in ink
before me ....
          (A Commissioner, etc.)

NOTE When invoicing goods which have been finished in a country specified on the invoice as its country of origin from materials originating in a country or countries entitled to the benefits of the Most Favoured Nation Tariff or the British Preferential Tariff, the names of the countries contributing to one-half the cost of production should be shown in the space provided in the certificate.

In the calculation of the cost of production for the purpose of determining the qualification for entry under the Most Favoured Nation Tariff none of the following items are to be included or considered, viz:—
1   Outside packages and expenses of packing thereinto.   4. Customs or excise duty or tax paid or payable on imported materials.
2   Manufacturer's or exporter's profit or the profit or remuneration of any trader, broker, or   5   Carriage, insurance, etc., from place of production or manufacture to port of shipment.
    other person dealing in the article in its finished manufactured condition.   6. Any other charges incurred or to be incurred subsequent to the completion of the manufacture
3. Royalties.   of the goods.

In cases where the vendor does not reside in the country of export or for other reasons the vendor is unable to sign the certificate both as to value and origin, a separate certificate of origin in prescribed form signed by the exporter in the country of export, bearing a full description of the goods and the marks and numbers of the packages, so that it may be identified with the shipment, will be accepted.

Form 10-200. Export Forms, Hazardous Materials Labels, etc. can be purchased from Unz & Co.. 190 Baldwin Ave., P.O. Box 308, Jersey City, N.J. 07303.

SPECIAL EXPORTERS' DECLARATION

B 31
B 72

Name and mailing address of exporter: Name and mailing address of importer:

1. Is your company or any other company entitled to a reduction, deferral or exemption from corporate income taxes in respect of income earned on exports that would be payable if the goods had been sold for home consumption? Yes............No............
(See Note 3 below)

2. If the answer to question 1 is "Yes" please indicate whether this has resulted in changes in the transfer or selling prices of any or all items included in this shipment. (See Note 4 below)

3. If transfer or selling prices have changed, please specify each of the items involved, and by how much. (See Note 4 below)

4. If the answer to question 1 is "Yes", please specify the name and address of the party or parties entitled to the benefit:

5. Specify the name and address of the producer of the goods contained in this shipment:

6. To the best of my knowledge and belief the foregoing is a true statement of the facts.

....
Signature

....
Name   Title   Date

THIS SPACE FOR USE BY THE DEPARTMENT OF NATIONAL REVENUE

Entry No.   Port Date Stamp

Notes to Exporter

1. This declaration is required to be completed in single copy only and signed by a duly authorized official of the exporter for all shipments of goods to Canada where the declared fair market value or the selling price of those goods is $10,000, or more, Canadian funds. (see the currency guide attached to Memorandum D31-1 for determining the equivalent of $10,000, Canadian funds in various currencies)

2. The declaration should be attached to the form of invoice approved by Canadian Customs (original copy) so that it may be presented by the importer at the time of entry.

3. **Notes re Question 1**
   (a) Question 1 refers only to the shipment covered by the Customs Invoice to which the special exporters' declaration relates.
   (b) "Any other company" refers to any other company involved in the production or distribution of the goods contained in the shipment.

4. **Notes re Questions 2 and 3**
   (a) Pricing changes are those that have taken place since July 28, 1972.
   (b) If additional space is required, please attach additional pages.

Form 10-282 (front). Export Forms, Hazardous Materials Labels, etc. can be purchased from Unz & Co., 190 Baldwin Ave., P.O. Box 308, Jersey City, N.J. 07303.

DÉCLARATION SPÉCIALE DES EXPORTATEURS

B-31
8/72

Nom et adresse postale de l'exportateur:

Nom et adresse postale de l'importateur:

1. Votre société ou toute autre société a-t-elle droit à une réduction, au paiement différé ou à une exemption de l'impôt sur le revenu des sociétés qui serait exigible, en ce qui concerne le revenu acquis sur les exportations, si les marchandises avaient été vendues pour la consommation nationale? Oui ....Non ...., (voir note 3 ci-dessous)

2. Si la réponse à la question n° 1 est "Oui", veuillez indiquer s'il en est résulté un changement dans les prix de transfert ou de vente d'un quelconque ou de tous les articles compris dans la présente expédition. (voir note 4 ci-dessous)

3. Si les prix de transfert ou de vente ont subi un changement, veuillez préciser chacun des articles dont il s'agit et la différence de prix dans chaque cas. (voir note 4 ci-dessous)

4. Si la réponse à la question n° 1 est "Oui", veuillez donner le nom et l'adresse de la ou des parties qui en bénéficient:

5. Donnez le nom et l'adresse du producteur des marchandises que contient la présente expédition:

6. Au mieux de mes connaissance et croyance, ce qui précède est un exposé exact des faits.

....
Signature

....
Nom   Titre   Date

RÉSERVÉ À L'USAGE DU MINISTÈRE DU REVENU NATIONAL

N° de déclaration

Timbreur dateur du bureau

Notes pour l'exportateur

1. Cette déclaration doit être remplie en un seul exemplaire et signée par un représentant dûment autorisé de l'exportateur pour toutes les expéditions vers le Canada de marchandises dont la juste valeur marchande déclarée ou le prix de vente est de $10,000 ou plus en devises canadiennes. (voir le guide annexé au Mémorandum D31-1 pour déterminer l'équivalent de 10,000 dollars canadiens en diverses devises étrangères)

2. La déclaration devrait être annexée à une facture dont la forme a été approuvée par les Douanes du Canada (original) de façon à ce qu'elle puisse être présentée à l'importateur au moment de la déclaration.

3. **Note concernant la question n° 1**
   a) La question n° 1 n'a trait qu'à l'expédition visée par la facture douanière à laquelle la déclaration spéciale des exportateurs se rapporte.
   b) "Toute autre société" veut dire toute autre société ayant participé à la production ou la distribution des marchandises que contient l'expédition.

4. **Note concernant les questions n°s 2 et 3**
   a) Les changements aux prix sont ceux intervenus depuis le 28 juillet 1972.
   b) Si vous avez besoin de plus d'espace, veuillez annexer des pages supplémentaires.

Form 10-282 (back). Export Forms, Hazardous Materials Labels, etc. can be purchased from Unz & Co., 190 Baldwin Ave., P.O. Box 308, Jersey City, N.J. 07303.

Form 10-090. Export Forms, Hazardous Materials Labels, etc. can be purchased from
Unz & Co., 190 Baldwin Ave., P.O. Box 308, Jersey City, N.J. 07303.

372

Shipping marks and numbers should correspond with those on the commercial invoice and containers.

2. **Import License**
   Required by importer—tolerance 10% of the value or quantity, valid for six months and may be extended.

3. **Special Documents**
   Sanitary Certificate—required by the importation of plants and plant products (e.g., banana plants, cacao plants, coffee plants, sugar cane, raw cotton, cotton seeds and cotton plants) and all containers containing earth and/or compost. Issued by the U.S. Department of Agriculture and other U.S. Government entities.

4. **Mission Holidays**
   All holidays generally observed in New York City.

CHILE

SUMMARY OF SHIPPING DOCUMENTS REQUIRED
Special Information
Consular fees are payable at point of destination by the importer, therefore, all original documents should be forwarded to importer as soon as possible.
No Consular Documents Required
1. **Shipping Documents Required**
   Freight Shipments regardless of value.
   (A) **Bill of Lading**—Original and 1 copy—must show total weights in kilos and total freight charges. Import license or deposit receipt number must be shown.
   (B) **Commercial Invoice**—4—in Spanish or English—must clearly show FOB or FAS New York value in the extreme right-hand margin of invoice; also CIF value (itemized as to cost, insurance and freight) under and to the left of the FOB or FAS value. Unit prices of each item must be shown. Must contain the following signed declaration in English or Spanish for customs purposes:
   > "Under oath we declare that we are the owners (or shippers) of the above-mentioned merchandise, that the price and other details are exact, that the said merchandise is a product of the soil or industry of (country of origin), and that we accept the legal consequence which might arise through any inexactitude contained in this account."

   For exchange purposes, shippers must include the following declaration: I (We) hereby certify that the "source" of the commodities and the "origin" of the commodities listed on this invoice or invoices herein are shown below. Source _____, Origin of Commodities_____, Signature_____, Date_____, Title_____.
   Authorized Representative
   When bill of lading includes goods covered by more than one commercial invoice, summary invoice should be used containing the preceding oath and identifying each item with reference to the corresponding invoice.
   (C) **AID Supplier's Certificate**—Washington requires AID Supplier's Certificate 282 in quintuplicate signed by the supplier for shipments of U.S.A. origin only when the value exceeds $1,000 and shipments are AID financed. The form must be prepared in its entirety including commission. However, Chile requires either an AID 75 form or their own Supplier's Certificate form for all shipments regardless of value. Form AID 75 will not be required for insurance premiums the cost of which is less than $50. However, the Banco Central de Chile requires the form regardless of the premium amount.
2. **Parcel Post and Air Cargo Shipments regardless of value:**
   Commercial Invoice—4—consular legalization not required—see 1(B).

3. **Import License**

Or Copy of Deposit Receipt from Chilean Bank—Required for all "controlled" shipments—the number must be shown on bill of lading and commercial invoice. Must show FOB value of merchandise at port of shipment. Freight and insurance are only charges that may be added. Other charges—upon proper verification—may be accepted.

A 5% tolerance of the CIF value, not to exceed $1,000, is allowed unless permit states otherwise.

Importers will be fined if shipment is made prior to date of import license. Fines range from 15 to 100% of the value of the shipment.

Non-Commercial Shipments to an individual exclusively for personal use and not for resale do not require import license provided: (1) the CIF value does not exceed $20; (2) the items are not on the Prohibited List; (3) not in commercial quantities. Members are advised to check with Consulate before shipping under this regulation.

4. **Shipment by Chilean Vessels**

When the Import Deposit Receipt is stamped "EMBARQUE LIBRE" shipment may be forwarded on a vessel of any nationality. When stamped "EMBARQUE EN NAVE CHILENA," shipment may be effected on a Chilean Line vessel or a Grace Line vessel, if the shipment originates in a U.S. Atlantic port. When shipments clear from a U.S. Gulf port, routings must be effected on a Chilean Line vessel or the vessels of the Gulf and South America Steamship company.

5. **Origin of Third Country Merchandise**

To be considered of U.S. origin, imported goods must be fully owned and paid for and cleared through U.S. Customs.

6. **Unaccompanied Baggage**

The only document required for shipments of unaccompanied baggage is the bill of lading.

7. *****Holidays**

Good Friday, September 18, and September 19. All holidays generally observed in New York City.

*Denotes changes since previous notice.

CHINA (FORMOSA)

SUMMARY OF SHIPPING DOCUMENTS REQUIRED

Consular Legalization Abolished—Effective immediately, all Consular intervention has been eliminated. In the future the consular invoice is no longer required. The commercial invoice and bill of lading should be forwarded to importer without Consular legalization.

CHINA, REPUBLIC OF (TAIWAN)

SUMMARY OF SHIPPING DOCUMENTS REQUIRED

No Consular Documents Required

1. **Shipping Documents Required**

   (A) *****Commercial Invoice**—1—may show FOB, C&F, or CIF value. Must show import license number.

   (B) **Bill of Lading (Freight Shipments)**—1 copy—all marks and case numbers appearing on the packages must be shown on the bill of lading.

2. **Parcel Post Shipments**

   Commercial Invoice—same as above see 1(A).

3. **Import License**

   Required for all commercial shipments by importer only. Validity—6 months. License carries right to foreign exchange.

4. ***Consular Holidays**
January 1 & 2, February 7 & 8, April 5, June 10, September 28, October 10, October 25, October 31, November 12. All holidays generally observed in New York City.
*Denotes changes since previous notice.

COLOMBIA

SUMMARY OF SHIPPING DOCUMENTS REQUIRED
1. **Special Information**
*Documents must be presented to Consulate by 4 p.m., two working days before sailing of vessel.

Shippers are advised that merchandise valued up to $20 FOB port of shipment may be made without import license or consular invoice, provided articles are not on the Prohibited List at time of shipment, or do not require prior approval by INSTITUTO DE COMERCIO EXTERIOR. Shipments declared at less than $20 will be appraised at customs, and only those appraised at $20 or less will be admitted if they meet above requirements. There is a list of items covered by Decree #1769 which may be imported without an import permit or consular invoices if the factory price does not exceed $100. (List is available by writing to Walter Vasquez and enclosing a stamped self addressed envelope).

Shipments of Foreign Origin Merchandise
Commercial invoices covering foreign origin merchandise shipped from the Port of New York must be certified by a recognized Chamber of Commerce as to the origin of the commodities before presentation to the Consulate in New York with the other consular documents. An additional notarized copy of the invoice will be required for the Chamber's files.

*Sample Shipments
Sample shipments do not require any consular documents. Shippers should show on the commercial invoice "no commercial value—value for custom purposes $_____."

Reasons for Document Rejections:
The Consulate will reject documents for the following reasons: 1) License expired. 2) Failure to present the license to Consulate. 3) Any change made without an INCOMEX-issued amendment attached to the license. 4) Failure to have the original consular invoice signed by shipper or his representative. 5) Failure to have bill of lading and/or waybill signed by carrier. 6) Failure to have signed statement on commercial invoice. 7) Discrepancy in values between license and commercial invoice. 8) Presentation of documents with erasures or crossovers which can cause any doubt at any moment.

2. **Consular Documents Required**
*Freight Shipments valued over $20 FOB steamer or items covered by decree 1769 in which case $100

(A) **Consular Invoice**—4 in Spanish—forms sold by Consulate (1 additional white tissue copy for shipper's files)—3 retained by Consulate—original must be mailed to consignee by shipper after legalization—1 white tissue copy to be retained by shipper for his files. Presentation of this copy will enable Consulate to legalize promptly extra consular invoices at a later date if requested. Must show FOB vessel value—signature of person signing invoice must be registered at Consulate.

If shipments are exempt from consular fees, it must be so stated on the Consular Invoice. A statement that "this shipment is exempt from consular fees in accordance with Decree No. _____ (or Regulation No. _____)" must be placed on the Consular Invoice.

The general description, customs position number, weights, amounts, etc., must be in strict conformity with those appearing on the import license.

On shipments of automobiles, trucks, buses, jeeps, etc., the trademark of the manufacturer, car and engine serial number, must be shown on all documents.

Shipments via Venezuela require 1 additional blue copy—stamped by the Colombian Consulate gratis. After legalization, shipper must present documents to Venezuelan Consulate.

The Colombian Consulate has an immediate service for this type of shipment for which shippers must pay 50% of the regular legalization fees. For example, if shippers use 4 sets of blanks and one bill of lading, the legalization fee will be $25.00. 50% of this fee for immediate service will be $12.50 making a total of $37.50.

The rate of exchange to be used for converting U.S. dollars to pesos on the Consular invoice should be checked by calling the Colombian Consulate.

(B) **Bill of Lading**—Original and 2 non-negotiable copies. Legalized original returned shipper. Two copies retained by Consulate. (1 additional copy showing the FOB) value in dollars and Colombian pesos marked "For Colombian Customs purposes only" must be delivered to the steamship company). It is not necessary for shippers to have the original bill of lading number by the steamship company prior to presentation to the Consulate. Import license numbers must be shown and Bills of lading must show both notify party as well as ultimate consignee.

(C) **Import License**—Required—see 8.

(D) **Commercial Invoice**—3—in Spanish or English—2 copies retained by Consulate. Original returned to shipper. Must show the same value appearing on the consular invoice. It is not necessary to have a separate commercial invoice for each Tariff Declaration (Posicion de Aduana). If several commercial invoices are presented with one consular invoice, a summary commercial invoice showing commercial invoice numbers and values must be attached to the consular invoice. In this case, the summary invoice will be legalized by the Consulate. The following signed clause must be inserted:

"Declaramos bajo juramento que los precios de esta factura son FOB en el puerto de embarque, que son los mismos que cargamos al cliente y que la mercancia a que ella se refiere es originaria de _____ (country of origin). Y en fe de lo expuesto firmamos la presente declaracion en _____ (city, state) el _____ (date) de _____ (month) de _____ (year)."

There is no consular fee for legalizing the commercial invoice. However, and in cases when shippers present a summary invoice (which is also legalized free) Consulate will legalize each invoice covered by the summary, if requested by shipper, at a fee of $.50 each.

(E) *****Certificate of Origin**—As a rule, a certificate of origin is not required. However, if the importer requires this document, it must be presented to the Consulate in an original and two copies all notarized. Certificates of origin must be certified prior to presentation to the Consulate by the New York Chamber of Commerce or Latin American Chamber of Commerce, which requires one additional copy for its files. The Consulate will legalize (gratis) and return the original and will retain the two copies. If additional copies are required, the Consulate will assess a fee of $.50 each.

3.   *****Air Parcel Post & Parcel Post Shipments valued over $20 FOB or items covered by Decree 1769 in which case $100**

(A) **Consular Invoice**—4—in Spanish—Consulate retains 3 (one additional white tissue copy for shipper for his files)—original and white tissue copy will be returned to shipper.

(B) **Import License**—Required—see 8.

(C) **Commercial Invoice**—3—see 2(D). Two copies retained by Consulate. Original returned to shipper.

(D) **Parcel Post or Air Parcel Post Receipt**—1—Returned to shipper. Import license numbers must be shown.

4. **Air Parcel Post & Parcel Post Shipments valued at $20 FOB or less, provided merchandise can be freely imported:**

(A) **Consular Invoice**—Not required.

(B) **Commercial Invoice**—3—See 2(D). Legalization by Consulate not required. Invoices must accompany shipment. Additional copies should be sent to consignee.

(C) **Import License**—Not Required.

5. *Air Cargo Shipments valued over $20 FOB or items covered by Decree 1769 in which case $100.

(A) **Consular Invoice**—4—consular legalization required—see 3(A).

(B) **Commercial Invoice**—3—See 2(D).

(C) **Import License**—Required—See 8.

(D) **Air Waybill**—2—consignee's copy presented to Consulate for legalization. One retained by Consulate. Import license number must be shown.

6. **Air Cargo Shipments valued at $20 FOB or less provided merchandise can be imported freely:**

(A) **Consular Invoice**—Not required.

(B) **Commercial Invoice**—2—see 4(B).

(C) **Import License**—Not required.

(D) **Air Waybill**—1—Consignee's copy. Legalization by Consulate not required.

7. **Insurance**—with the exception of AID shipments, all exports must be insured in Colombia.

8. *Import License

Required For All Shipments Valued over $20 FOB Steamer unless items covered By Decree 1769.

Copy must be presented to Consulate with regular shipping documents. License number must appear on consular invoices, also total or partial quantity being shipped. If partial, amount shipped and balance remaining to be shipped must be specified. License numbers must be shown on Ocean Bills of Lading and Air waybills.

In accordance with resolution #27 of December 19, 1962, all shipments of goods from the U.S., must be covered in addition to the consular invoices and the original bills of lading by the following documents which will be indispensable for obtaining the Foreign Exchange Certificates for the transfer of proceeds from Colombia: (A) Commercial Invoice in triplicate; (B) Two nonnegotiable copies of the Bill of Lading; (C) Certificate of Origin when required on import license.

None of these documents require legalization by Consulate. However, the Certificate Origin must be certified by a recognized Chamber of Commerce.

Tolerance—In no case may the value or the quantity shown on the Import License be exceeded. However, in cases in which the weight is not the unit of sale (as in shipments of automobiles, or air conditioners, etc.) the shipper need not be concerned about differences in weight.

Validity of Import License—Ten months, unless otherwise indicated. Documents must be legalized before the expiration date shown on import license. Merchandise must be delivered and accepted by steamship company prior to expiration date of import license, and documents also legalized by Consulate prior to expiration date of import license. Government will not extend validity once the license has expired.

9.   **Special Documents**
   (A) **Letter of Correction**—4—in Spanish, on Shipper's letterhead—notarization
   not required—legalized by Consulate which retains one copy. Original should
   be sent to consignee—one copy to steamship company—one copy for shipper's
   files. White tissue copy or consular invoice, which was stamped originally by
   Consulate for shipper's files (see 1-A), one commercial invoice and import
   license must be attached to the letter of correction when presented to Consulate. Letter of Correction must state that the merchandise has not yet been
   nationalized as of that date. Fee: $5.00.
   (B) **Certificate of Purity**—2—Required for shipments of alcoholic beverages (must
   indicate alcohol content) and certain other foods (consult Consulate). Certificates issued by manufacturer are acceptable, but must be notarized and countersigned by the county clerk. Consulate retains original and returns legalized
   copy to shipper. Fee: $5.00.
   (C) **Sanitary Certificate**—1—Required for a variety of different commodities (such
   as lard, trees, plants, seeds, cattle, baby chicks, etc.). Issued by Department of
   Agriculture. Legalized and returned to shipper. Fee: $5.00.
10.   **Arrangement of Documents**
   Must be arranged in 3 separate sets, each set stapled separately and then all
   sets clipped together. (For Air Freight and all P.P. shipments prepare 2 sets
   only.)

By Steamer	**By Air**
First Set:	**First Set:**
a) Import License	a) Import License
b) Bill of Lading	b) Air Waybill (one of the 3 first copies)
c) Original Consular Invoice (blue)	c) Original Consular Invoice and a
d) White tissue copy	copy
e) Commercial Invoice	d) Commercial Invoice
f) Certificate of Origin	e) Certificate of Origin
(when requested)	(when requested)
g) Extra copies in original (blue) and	
3 copies (white)—(if requested)	
Second Set:	**Second Set:**
a) Bill of Lading	a) Copy of Air Waybill
b) 2 copies of the Consular Invoice	b) Copy of the Commercial Invoice
(white)	c) Certificate of Origin
c) Copy of the Commercial Invoice	(when requested)
d) Copy of the Certificate of Origin	d) 2 copies of the Consular Invoice
(when requested)	(white)
Third Set:	Note—Documents returned for any
a) Bill of Lading	reason, including error in arrangement
b) Copy of Consular Invoice	of documents, will not be exempt from
c) Commercial Invoice	late presentation fees.
d) Copy of Certificate of Origin	
(when requested)	

11.   **Origin of Third Country Merchandise**
   Goods which have been imported and processed or manufactured in the U.S.
   before being shipped to Colombia must have been transformed as a result of

processing or manufacturing in the U.S. into a product substantially different from the imported material in order to be considered as of U.S. origin. Unless the product shipped to Colombia is different in commercial designation or use from the product imported, it must be declared as of the country in which it actually originated.

12. **Consular Fees**

Original bill of lading, air waybill
   or parcel post receipt $10.00
Additional Copies (when requested) .... 2.00 each
Original (blue) consular invoice 5.00
Each extra original sheet (blue) even though it is a
   continuation of first page 5.00
Each additional copy (when requested) each blue sheet
   (extra copy) 2.00
Letter of Correction 5.00

    Power of Attorney must be prepared in 2 columns, one in English and one in Spanish. It must state the name or names of the companies issuing the power of attorney, the person or persons who will represent the American firm in Colombia, and it must be authenticated by a notary public and the county clerk. The Consulate will legalize the document 5.00

Letter of Correction Form

Nueva York, N.Y.

Honorable Senor
Consul General de Colombia
Nueva York, N.Y.

Senor Consul:
   Nos referimos a la siguiente Factura Consular No.   presentada a
   ese Consulado con fecha   de 196
CASA DESPACHADORA:

VALOR DE LA FACTURA: $
Por vapor: Puerto de Destino:
CONSIGNATARIO:
MARCAS: Peso neto en Kilos:
               Peso bruto en Kilos:
a la cual tenemos necesidad de hacer las siguientes correcciones:
DONDE DICE:

DEBE DECIR:

Las demas partes quedan iguales.

Atentamente rogamos a usted tomar nota de estas diferencias y remitir copia de la presente Carta de Correccion a la Aduana respectiva para los fines consiguientes.

                       Del senor Consul atentamente,

In case of late presentation of documents, shippers must pay 50% of the legalization fees. Example: if shippers use four sets of blanks and one bill of lading, the legalization fee is $25.00; therefore, the additional fee for late presentation would be $12.50 for a total of $37.50. If exporters require immediate service, the charge is also 50% of the consular fees. For example: documents presented late, as stated above, would be $37.50, plus $12.50 for immediate service, or a total of $50.00, or, if documents are presented on time, the consular fees for the four sets mentioned above would be $25.00 plus $12.50 for immediate service, for a total of $37.50. Exporters may purchase pads of 50 sets of the consular invoice for $500.

*Consular Blanks (per set of 4 sheets) $10.00
*Consular Holidays

February 12, February 16, April 15, April 16, May 31, July 4, July 20, August 7, September 6, October 11, October 25, November 11, and November 25. All holidays generally observed in New York City.

*Denotes changes since previous notice

CONGO, PEOPLE'S REPUBLIC OF THE

SUMMARY OF SHIPPING DOCUMENTS REQUIRED
No Consular Documents Required
1.   Shipping Documents
   (A) Commercial Invoice—3—must contain names and addresses of shipper and consignee—place and date of shipment—number and types of containers—marks and numbers—contents and weight—a careful description of the goods with the value of each item. The ocean freight and incidental expenses should be added to arrive at the C&F or CIF value. The FOB value (in U.S. dollars) and the CIF values must be listed separately. Should show country of origin.
   (B) Certificate of Origin—3—when required—on general form—sold by commercial printers—certified by the New York Chamber of Commerce and Industry, which requires one additional notarized copy for its files.
   (C) Bills of Lading—must contain gross weight in pounds—volume measurement in feet and inches—marks of identification and name and address of consignee. Shipping marks and numbers should correspond with those on the commercial invoice and containers.
2.   *Import License
   Required by importer—tolerance 5% of the value, but in no case can it exceed 50,000 CFA francs. Must show weight, quantity, unit price, total price, etc.
3.   Special Documents
   Sanitary Certificate—required for the importation of plants and plant products (e.g., banana plants, cacao plants, coffee plants, sugar cane, raw cotton, cotton seeds and cotton plants) and all containers containing earth and/or compost. Issued by the U.S. Department of Agriculture and other U.S. Government entities.
4.   Mission Holidays
   All holidays generally observed in New York City.

COSTA RICA

SUMMARY OF SHIPPING DOCUMENTS REQUIRED
Special Information
   Customs authorities in Costa Rica are imposing fines on importers for incomplete or improper information on commercial invoices. Some of the reasons for imposing

fines are: an invoice may read "Made in Japan" instead of "pais de origen—Japan," or "Hilo de Coser" instead of "Hilo de Coser de Algodon." Customs will not accept 3 copies or 3 photostated copies; one original must always be presented. Also, they will not accept invoices with erasures, crossouts or corrections. Fines will be considerable for any such discrepancies.

Costa Rican Foreign Exchange Control regulations require that all import documents be submitted in the original by local importers: A number of U.S. exporters reportedly prepare their invoices to the FOB point, leaving shipping agents to complete invoices to the CIF destination. Frequently, completion of the invoices is done in handwriting or on typewriters with type differing from that on the original documents. Such documents, when presented to the Central Bank of Costa Rica, are rejected on the grounds that additional expenses may have been added arbitrarily by local importers, with ensuing delays in payment of drafts.

No Consular Documents Required

1. **Shipping Documents Required for all shipments valued over $25:**
   (A) **Commercial Invoice**—3—in Spanish—shippers must complete invoices up to CIF destination, and must prepare them in accordance with the Costa Rican Commercial law, which requires that the following information be shown: Name and address of shipper, Place and date of shipment, Name and address of consignee, Port of shipment, Port of destination, Vessel and sailing date, Marks and numbers, Weights and measurements in units of the metric system. Quantity and type of package, Itemized contents of each package, Net weight of each article, Gross weight of each package, Value of each article, and Total expenses to port of destination.

   Must contain an affidavit signed by shipper or authorized representative to the effect that the values, weights and quantities shown are true and correct. Affidavit must also show the country of origin in Spanish.

   (B) **Bills of Lading**—"To Order" bills of lading are allowed.

2. **Import License**
   None required, except for pharmaceuticals, foodstuffs, and certain plants.

3. **Special Documents**
   (A) **Certificate of Analysis**—3—required for shipments of flour, lard and seeds must be legalized by Consulate, which returns all copies. May be prepared on shipper's letterhead, but must be signed by chemist who made the analysis or prepared by a laboratory or an inspection company—must be notarized and authenticated by County Clerk.

   (B) **Health Certificate**—3—Required for shipments of all animals. Must include vaccination. May be issued by the Department of Agriculture. Must be legalized by Consulate which returns all copies.

   For dogs, cats or any other domestic animal it is necessary to obtain a previous import permit from the Department of Agriculture in Costa Rica if the animals are going to remain in the country permanently. This does not apply to those going intransit.

4. **Arrangement of Documents**
   Documents should be presented as follows: 1 original and 2 copies of the commercial invoice with 1 original bill of lading if shipment is made by steamer; 1 original and 2 copies of the invoice together with 2 copies of the air waybill if shipment is made by air.

5. ***Consular Fees**

Legalization of Power of Attorney	$20.00 each
Certificate of Analysis	20.00 each
Health Certificate	20.00 each
Legalization of County Clerk's signature	20.00 each

6. *Consular Holidays

Holy Thursday, Good Friday, Easter Monday, September 15, Election Day, December 24, and December 31. All holidays generally observed in New York City.

*Denotes changes since previous notice.

CYPRUS

SUMMARY OF SHIPPING DOCUMENTS REQUIRED

Legalization of Documents

Documents requiring legalization must be mailed to the Consulate accompanied by a stamped self-addressed return envelope and a check—payable to the Consulate for the exact amount of the consular fees. Legalized documents will be returned to shippers the same day they are received. The Consulate does not accept documents for legalization which are presented by hand.

Special Information

The New York Consulate has jurisdiction for Pennsylvania, Connecticut, New Jersey, Georgia, North Carolina, South Carolina, Florida, Alaska and Hawaii. In addition, the Embassy in Washington, D.C. has jurisdiction over Ohio, Maryland, Virginia, West Virginia, Michigan and Washington, D.C. Documents originating in these states should be mailed to the Washington Office.

No Consular Documents Required

1. **Shipping Documents Required**

   For All Commercial Shipments regardless of value and mode of transportation:

   (A) **Commercial Invoice**—2 on shipper's letterhead. Must be signed by shipper and contain all necessary information.

   (B) **Certificate of Origin**—2—on general form—sold by commercial printers. Certified by the New York Chamber of Commerce and Industry, which requires one additional notarized copy for its files. Legalized by Consulate only when requested by importer or requested in letter of credit. Original returned to shipper—copy retained by Consulate. Must show FOB value of merchandise.

Specimen Of Letter Of Correction For Cyprus
On Shipper's Letterhead

New York, N.Y._____

Consulate General of Cyprus
New York, N.Y.

Dear Mr. Consul General:

We refer to: _____

Legalized under number _____dated _____

Shipper: _____

Consignee: _____

Shipped on the steamer: _____

which sailed from New York: _____destined to: _____

Where it says: _____

Should Read: _____

We respectfully request that you note the correction and thank you for your cooperation.

(signature and full name of shipper)

2.   **Letter of Correction**
      Letter of Correction in triplicate on shipper's letterhead, as per sample, certi-
      fied by the New York Chamber of Commerce and Industry prior to presenta-
      tion to Consulate.
3.   ***Consular Fees Based On FOB Price of Merchandise**
      Invoice valued up to $273 .... $ 8.19
      Over $273 up to $1365 .... 19.11
      Over $1365 up to $2730 .... 27.30
      For each additional $2730 or fraction thereof 13.65
      Letter of correction 1.39
      Each additional copy c/o when required only to be
          sealed by Consulate 2.73
      Each additional copy of c/o when required to be signed and sealed by
          Consulate: Up to $273 .... 8.19
                    Over $273 .... 16.38
4.   **Holidays**
      January 6, October 28, October 29, Good Friday, Easter Monday, and De-
      cember 26. All holidays generally observed in New York City.
      *Denotes changes since previous notice.

CZECHOSLOVAKIA

SUMMARY OF SHIPPING DOCUMENTS REQUIRED
No Consular Documents Required
1.   **Shipping Documents Required**
   (A) **Commercial Invoice**—original and 1 copy—ordinary commercial invoice con-
       taining all details
   (B) **Certificate of Origin**—2—required for shipments of wine and wine distillates to
       be cleared according to the most-favored-nation tariff—general form—sold by
       commercial printers—certified by the New York Chamber of Commerce and
       Industry, which requires one additional notarized copy for its files.
   (C) **Bills of Lading**—original required to clear goods in Czechoslovakia—no spe-
       cial regulation—the usual information should be shown.
2.   **Import License**
      Not required
3.   **Special Documents**
      Health Certificates or Phytopathological Certificate—are required for ani-
      mals; meats and meat products; animal raw materials; plants and their parts;
      and fruits.

DENMARK

SUMMARY OF SHIPPING DOCUMENTS REQUIRED
No Consular Documents Required
1.   **Shipping Documents Required**
   (A) ***Commercial Invoice**—2—on seller's letterhead—mailed directly to importer.
       Must show net, gross and tare weights and contain a signed declaration that
       the value stated is full, correct and true. The invoice should be dated and show
       full particulars, such as terms of payment, FOB and CIF values (itemizing all
       expenses), all discounts and their nature, etc. Invoices should show the BTN
       number and commodity description. The invoices should be signed by shipper.

(B) **Certificate of Origin**—2—when required by importer—general form—sold by commercial printers—certified by the New York Chamber of Commerce and Industry, which requires one additional notarized copy for its files.

(C) **Bills of Lading**—2—no special regulations—the usual information should be shown.

2.   **Air Cargo Shipments**
      Commercial Invoice—2—(see above) must accompany shipment.

3.   **Import License**
      The great majority of commodities require no Import license.
      *****Consular Holidays**
      February 12, February 16, April 16, May 31, September 6, October 11, November 2, November 25, December 24, December 25, and December 31. All holidays generally observed in New York City.
      *Denotes changes since previous notices.

DOMINICAN REPUBLIC

SUMMARY OF SHIPPING DOCUMENTS REQUIRED
Special Information
Shippers can present documents for legalization up to 1 p.m., two working days after sailing vessel. Documents presented late will be assessed a fine of $10.00 per set. Documents must be in the hands of the importer prior to the arrival of the vessel in order to avoid fines.

*****Insurance**
Must be covered in the Dominican Republic, except AID shipments.

1.   **Consular Documents Required**
      Freight shipments valued over $100 FOB.

(A) **Consular Invoice**—6—in Spanish—5 forms sold by Consulate and one carbon copy on white paper—5 retained by Consulate—legalized original returned to shipper. Must show FOB and C&F value itemized showing ocean freight and other charges, name and nationality of steamer, and name, of captain. Shipments of used personal effects (clothing, personal toiletries, etc.), books, magazines, newspapers and other publications of any kind do not require a consular invoice. Shipments of personal effects consisting of household furniture, automobiles, home appliances, etc., require a consular invoice.

   Shipper may not consolidate merchandise for several consignees on the same invoice.

   The quantity of merchandise shipped must be indicated in the metric system; i.e., liquids in liters, solids in kilos, etc. Textiles may not be shown by weight only.

(B) **Bill of Lading**—5—four retained by Consulate—original returned to shipper—must be previously numbered by steamship company. May be unsigned—must show complete information (marks, numbers, weights, etc.). Must show freight charges. "To Order" bills of lading are not issued by steamship company.

(C) **Commercial Invoice**—3—in Spanish—2 retained by Consulate. Must show all information, same as consular invoice.

(D) **Additional Documents Required**—all shipments to the Dominican Republic (regardless of mode of transportation) should be covered by an extra set of documents forwarded by the exporter with the remaining documents to facilitate handling of necessary exchange from the Central Bank. The Bank may not grant the exchange without these added documents: (a) 3 non-negotiable bills of lading stamped on board; (b) consular invoice (photostat or plain copy); (c) 3 commercial invoices.

2. **Freight Shipments valued at $100 FOB or less:**
   No Consular documents required.
3. **Parcel Post Shipments valued over $100 FOB:**
   Documents should be presented to the Consulate as soon as possible.
   (A) **Consular Invoice**—6—in Spanish—consular legalization required—see 1(A). Must be accompanied by 3 copies of the commercial invoice in Spanish of which the Consulate retains 2.

   —OR—

   (B) **Commercial Invoice**—6—consular legalization required—must contain same information required on consular invoice.
4. **Parcel Post Shipments valued at $100 FOB or less:**
   No consular documents required.
5. **Air Cargo Shipments valued over $100 FOB:**
   Documents should be presented to Consulate as soon as possible.
   (A) **Consular Invoice**—6—in Spanish—consular legalization required—see 1(A). Must be accompanied by 3 copies of the commercial invoice in Spanish of which the Consulate retains 2.

   —OR—

   (B) **Commercial Invoice**—6—in Spanish—consular legalization required—must contain same information required on consular invoice.
   (C) **Air Waybill**—3 copies.
6. **Air Cargo Shipment valued at $100 FOB or less:**
   Two non-legalized copies of the commercial invoice in Spanish should be presented to the carrier for all shipments.
7. **Import License**
   Required only for a few products. All importations into the Dominican Republic require prior authorization.

   Licenses issued by the Ministry of Agriculture are required for the importation of fruits, plants, flowers and all types of fresh and dried vegetables. A license issued by Secretary of Public Works is required for imports of heavy construction machinery.

   Textile importers must attach samples to their applications.

   Import license need not be presented to Consulate except for wheat, wheat flour and semolina.
8. **Special Documents**
   (A) **Letter of Correction**—Must be prepared in triplicate—in Spanish. The following information must be shown: consular invoice number and date of legalization, name and nationality of steamer, sailing date, name of shipper, name of consignee, port of destination, marks and numbers, contents and total number of packages, gross and net kilos, value and origin of merchandise. Full details of correction must be given, as well as a statement signed by shipper to the effect that all details are true and correct.
   (B) **Sanitary Certificate**—1—required for shipments of fruits, plants, and all types of fresh and dried vegetables. Issued by the Department of Agriculture. Must state that shipment is free from disease and infection.
   (C) **Certificate of Free Sale**—In order to avoid difficulties in clearing goods at Customs in the Dominican Republic, all pharmaceutical and cosmetic products, as well as foodstuffs, being imported must be registered with the government. New York Chamber of Commerce and Industry will prepare a Certificate of Free Sale (for U.S. origin merchandise only) which must be legalized by the Consulate and forwarded to the importer who must then register same with the Secretaria de Estado de Salud Publica y Asistencia Social. This agency will stamp on the consular invoice that the products shown are re-

gistered in accordance with the law. Merchandise will not be cleared unless the consular invoice is stamped by the previously mentioned agency.

9. **Arrangement of Documents**

First and second sets: consular invoice followed by bill of lading and commercial invoice. Third and fourth sets: consular invoice and bill of lading. Fifth set: consular invoice, bill of lading and commercial invoice. The sixth plain copy of the consular invoice should be placed at the end.

10. **Origin of Third Country Merchandise**

There must be a change in form as a result of U.S. processing in order for imported merchandise to be accepted as being of U.S. origin. For example, Spanish olives packed in the United States must be cleared as of Spanish origin.

11. **Shipments to the Dominican Government and other Diplomatic Entities**

Upon written application to the Consul General, shippers may obtain "exonerated" consular invoice blanks at no charge for shipments to the above official entities. These shipments are also exempt of the $5.00 air mailing fee.

12. ***Consular Fees**

3% of the FOB invoice value payable by consignee in the Dominican Republic.

Shippers are subject to the following fees, payable by cash or certified check made out to the Consulate General of the Dominican Republic:

Consular invoice blanks per set (5) .... $ 6.00
Internal Revenue tax stamp for commercial invoices
covering parcel post or air cargo shipments 11.00
Extra copy of consular invoice if attached at the same
time originals are presented 5.00
Extra copy of consular invoice if presented after
legalization 10.00
Extra copy of bill of lading (if requested) 10.00
Registration and air mailing consular documents .... 5.00 (per set)
Letter of correction 20.00
Certificate of origin 20.00
Sanitary certificate 20.00
Certificate of free sale 20.00
Power of attorney, authentication of county clerk's
signature, etc. 20.00
Immediate service 2.00
Late presentation .... 10.00 (per set)

13. **Consular Holidays**

January 21, February 27, Good Friday, May 1, June 13, August 16, and September 24. All holidays generally observed in New York City.

*Denotes changes since previous notice.

ECUADOR

SUMMARY OF SHIPPING DOCUMENTS REQUIRED
Consular Legalization no longer required.

1. (A) **Commercial Invoice**—2—in Spanish—Must contain a statement in Spanish, signed by authorized person, certifying that the value declared is true and correct. Import license number must be shown on all commercial invoices. FOB and all shipping charges such as ocean freight, insurance and other expenses to CIF or C&F.

All commercial invoices must be certified by the New York Chamber of

Commerce and Industry as to Price and Origin. A copy of the invoice containing the following notarized statement—"The prices are the current export market prices for the merchandise described therein and country of origin is...," signed by the actual seller, must be presented to the Chamber for its files.

When preparing Commercial invoices, follow the information shown on import license such as declaration, value, weight, etc.

(B) Bills of lading must show import license numbers and expiration dates. The original bill of lading should be forwarded to importer.

2. **Insurance Regulations**
Insurance for shipments to Ecuador must be covered in Ecuador, except A.I.D. Shipments.

3. **Import License**
Must show on the reverse side the total amount used and the balance left. If total has been used, then it must be stated "Total amount used—no balance." Returned to importer with other documents. Validity—120 days. Once the import permit has expired, it cannot be extended by the Banco Central of Ecuador and must be replaced by a new license. A prior import deposit is required to obtain license. Approved license entitles importer to foreign exchange.

All imports into Ecuador valued over $40.00 FOB must be covered by import license.

Decrees #1315 allows imports of parts for all types of machinery and medicines with a value up to $500 to general importers without an import permit. Shipments of these items made to government entities and their departments may be made without an import license regardless of value.

Note: Shipments of all medical samples must be covered by an Import License. When license is complete, it should be returned to importer.

Tolerance Allowed: FOB and C&F values, quantities, and gross and net weight shown on import licenses may be exceeded by 20%, but such excesses may be subject at destination to fines from 10% to 25% unless importers can satisfy the Import Control Commission as to the factors causing the excesses. If the tolerance exceeds 20%, shippers must request and obtain an amendment from the Banco Central de Ecuador.

4. **Labeling Regulations for Alcoholic Beverages**
Exporters must affix to each bottle a stamped label inscribed: "CONTROLADO POR EL ESTANCO," which they will get from the importer with the import license. It must be noted on the commercial invoice that the regulations have been complied with. When the alcoholic beverages are shipped in containers other than bottles, it will be the responsibility of the importer to see that the labels are affixed when the beverages are bottled. For shipments of whiskey, a declaration must be shown stating that the liquor has been bottled for at least three years.

5. **Shipments to Government Agencies:**
All shipments by steamer to any Ecuadorian Government agency or entity must be made via Grancolombiana (N.Y.) Inc., and air cargo shipments via Ecuatoriana Airlines or Andes Airlines.

6. **Special Documents:**
(A) **Certificate of Purity or Sanitation**—2—required for various products including flour, lard, livestock, edible oils, plants and seeds, canned food and all types of beverages; animal, chemical and vegetable fertilizers. Five copies retained by Consulate; original returned to shipper. Legalization fee—$5.00 each, prepared on Shipper's Letterhead. Certified by the New York Chamber of Commerce and Industry, which requires one additional copy for its files.

(B) **Certificate of Analysis**—6—required for all shipments of pharmaceutical, cosmetic, food and similar products, except tallow (see below). Prepared by the manufacturer, showing the analysis breakdown. A statement to the effect that the product is clean is not acceptable. Must be signed by a responsible officer and notarized. Five copies retained by Consulate—original returned to shipper. Tallow shipments require a U.S.D.A. certificate (original and 5 copies). Five copies retained by consulate—original returned to shipper. Legalization fee—$5.00 each. Must be certified by the New York Chamber of Commerce and Industry, which requires one additional copy for its files, prior to presentation at Consulate.

(C) **Certificate of Inspection**—6—required for shipments of spun rayon textiles or spun rayon and pure rayon mixed textiles—issued by a recognized inspection company, samples must be attached to each copy. Certificate should state that a microscopical examination was made of the fibers in the sample and that the fabric is ____% spun rayon. Five copies retained by Consulate—original returned to shipper. Legalization fee is $5.00.

(D) **Paraffin Wax Certificate**—1—on manufacturer's letterhead—must be signed by an officer and notarized—must contain the following information: "Melting Point ____ AMP ____ FO: oil content (ASTM D721-47) ____%; color, saybolt (ASTM D-156-49) ____: odor ____; taste ____. Guaranteed not to contain synthetic paraffin.

7. **Consular Holidays**
Holy Thursday, Good Friday, May 1, May 24, July 24, August 10, October 9, October 12, and November 3. All holidays generally observed in New York City.
*Denotes changes since previous notice.

EGYPT

SUMMARY OF SHIPPING DOCUMENTS REQUIRED
1. **Consular Documents Required for all commercial shipments:**
   (A) **Commercial Invoice*—3—must be notarized—consular legalization required. Complete particulars must be shown. Certified by the U.S. Arab Chamber of Commerce which retains one copy. One copy required by Consulate and original returned to shipper. The commercial invoice must show country of origin.
   (B) **Certificate of Origin*—3—on general form—sold by commercial printers—must be notarized—certified by the U.S. Arab Chamber of Commerce which retains one copy for its files—one copy retained by Consulate and original returned to shipper—consular legalization required.
2. **Import License**
Required by importer for all commercial shipments.
3. **Special Regulations**
There are special regulations for the importation of fresh and dried fruits, potatoes, preserved green vegetables, plants and seeds. A sanitary certificate is required for shipments of fresh meats stating meat has been free from contagious disease for at least three months before slaughter.
4. ***Insurance**
Nationalization of insurance industry and of importing agencies virtually eliminates freedom of U.S. insurers to compete.
5. **Consular Fees**
The consular fee for legalization of Certificate of Origin, Commercial Invoice, or any other document is .... $25.00 each and for the county clerk's signature or sanitary certificate, etc. is .... $8.50 each.

6. **Holidays**
   All holidays generally observed in New York City.
   *Denotes changes since previous notice.

EL SALVADOR

SUMMARY OF SHIPPING DOCUMENTS REQUIRED
1. **Freight Shipments regardless of value:**
   (A) *Commercial Invoice—3—in Spanish—All copies must contain signed declaration that prices and expenses are true and correct. The original and all copies must be signed in ink. Items exempt from duties must not be included in the same commercial invoice as those paying duties. No legalization required.

   Invoices must show marks, numbers, quantity and type of container of packing. Numbers must be consecutive except on bulk shipments of the same commodity such as iron, lumber, cement, etc. Type of transportation must be shown. Gross, net and legal weights in kilos must also be shown as well as the quantity and measurement per unit and totals.

   For wines and liquors, alcoholic content must be indicated. For lumber, the board feet. Invoices must show customs tariff number and description of merchandise. Must show value per unit and total value of merchandise shipped and be itemized as to CIF value, showing freight charges, insurance premium and other shipping expenses to port of destination.

   Commercial invoices relating to drugs, guns, ammunition, etc., which are considered restricted imports must be legalized at the Consulate General in New York. One original and 7 copies of the invoice in Spanish must be legalized.
   (B) **Bill of Lading**—3—(1 original, 2 non-negotiables)—duly signed by steamship company—Legalization not required. Should be forwarded to importer.
   (C) **Certificate of Origin**—3—Required for all shipments of goods on Preferential List. May be prepared on general form or special Salvadorean form—sold by commercial printers. Certified by the New York Chamber of Commerce and Industry. One additional notarized copy is required for the Chamber's files. Consulate legalization not required.
2. **Parcel Post Shipments regardless of value.**
   (A) **Commercial Invoice**—3—mailed to consignee—consular legalization not required. See 1(A).
   (B) **Certificate of Origin**—See 1(C).
3. **Air Cargo Shipments regardless of value.**
   (A) **Commercial Invoice**—3—prepared as per 1(A)— must accompany shipment. Consular legalization not required.
   (B) **Certificate of Origin**—See 1(C).
4. **Import License**
   Required only in El Salvador by importer for the great majority of commodities. Exception: All shipments consigned to PROVEEDURIA GENERAL DE LA REPUBLICA must be covered by an import license copy of which must be in possession of the Consulate before the documents can be legalized. All documents must bear the import license number, which the shipper must obtain from the importer. Shipper may also receive a copy of the license in which case it must be attached to the documents. Import permit number must be shown, however, even if shipper does not receive a copy.
5. **Special Documents**
   Analysis, Pedigree, Purity & Sanitary Certificates—2 notarized copies—one copy retained by Consulate—required for certain items (see attached list)—

certificate must be that of an inspection company or a laboratory. Pharmaceutical and medicinal preparations also require such certificates in order to obtain registration in El Salvador.

6.   **Consular Holidays**
February 12, Good Friday, May 1, May 31, July 4, August 5, August 6, Labor Day, September 15, Veteran's Day, November 5, Thanksgiving Day, and December 25. All holidays generally observed in New York City.
*Denotes changes since previous notice.

ETHIOPIA

SUMMARY OF SHIPPING DOCUMENTS REQUIRED
No Consular Documents Required
1.   **Shipping Documents Required**
   (A) **Commercial Invoice**—At least 2 copies should be sent to consignee—no special form—should indicate origin of merchandise. Legalization by Consulate not required—certification by the New York Chamber of Commerce and Industry is required. One additional signed and notarized copy is required by the Chamber for its files.
      Invoices must be notarized, countersigned by the county clerk, authenticated by the Secretary of State, that has jurisdiction of the County Clerk's signature, and the Department of State, Office of the Secretary of State in Washington, D.C., before they are presented to the Consulate for legalization. The Consulate requires one additional copy for their files.
   (B) **Bill of Lading**—No special regulations. Must show marks of identification and name and address of consignee clearly.
2.   **Import License**
Not required, but importer must obtain an exchange license from the National Bank before payment can be authorized. Shippers should show license number (including date of issuance) on the commercial invoice. Ethiopian authorities may refuse to make dollar exchange available on imported merchandise not covered by an exchange license.
3.   **Consular Fees**
Original commercial invoice (when requested by shipper) $5.85
Extra copies (when requested by shipper) $2.00
Consular Holidays
All holidays generally observed in New York City.
*Denotes changes since previous notice.

FINLAND

SUMMARY OF SHIPPING DOCUMENTS REQUIRED
No Consular Documents Required
1.   **Shipping Documents Required**
   (A) **Commercial Invoice**—2—Required for clearance through customs—on shipper's letterhead. All invoices must indicate: The date and mode of shipment, trade description (codes consisting of combinations of letters or numbers are not acceptable), prices of goods to be given per unit and total, kind of packaging used, number of packages and marks and numbers on packages, total gross and net weights, if the packages belonging to the same shipment are of different size and the weights and contents of the packages are not specified in the invoice, the seller has to supply a packing list giving these details and referring to the invoice concerned.

Invoices must also contain the following: (a) terms of delivery (C.I.F., etc.) and time of payment; (b) the amount of discount on gross price if any, and (c) country of purchase and origin.

(B) **Certificate of Origin**—Required on U.S. products subject to preferential duty— general form acceptable—certified by the New York Chamber of Commerce and Industry, which requires one additional notarized copy for its files, or visaed by Finnish Consulate. Certificate of origin requirement waived when both goods and packing indicate country of origin, with trademarks, etc.

(C) **Bills of Lading**—2—no special requirements—generally shipments may be made freight collect. "To Order" Bills of Lading are allowed, but must be endorsed in blank or to a specified person.

2.   **Import License**
     Required only for a few commodities by importer—valid for six months—may be extended upon request if application is made before expiration date. Foreign exchange to pay for imports is readily granted.

3.   ***Consular Fee**
     Certificate of origin (when requested) .... $3.40 each
     (Must be notarized and authenticated by county clerk prior to presentation to the Consulate.)

4.   ***Holidays**
     Good Friday, Easter Monday, June 21, December 6, December 24, and December 26. All holidays generally observed in New York City.
     *Denotes changes since previous notice.

FRANCE
(Also applies to all shipments to the French Overseas Community)

SUMMARY OF SHIPPING DOCUMENTS REQUIRED
No Consular Documents Required
1.   **Shipping Documents Required**
     For All Shipments regardless of value or mode of transportation.
     (A) **Commercial Invoice**—1—on shipper's letterhead—must contain shipping terms, full particulars and itemized expenses. Legalization not required.
                                    —OR—
     (B) **Combined Consular Invoice and Certificate of Origin**—1—on French form— sold by commercial printers. Legalization not required. Must contain complete information as stated.
          There may be cases in which shippers will require to have their invoices legalized. In such instance, invoices must be certified by the New York Chamber of Commerce and Industry, which requires one additional notarized copy for its files.
     (C) **Certificate of Origin**—1—general form—sold by commercial printers— necessary for goods originating in Hong Kong, and for goods which have been processed or transformed in countries other than country of origin. Also required for shipments of mineral waters, certain wines, and certain carpets, rugs and coffee. Certified by the New York Chamber of Commerce and Industry which requires one additional notarized copy for its files.

2.   **Import License**
     Most imports into France have been liberalized and may be imported without a license. There are only a few items requiring import permits (such as agricultural commodities, a few industrial products and a limited number of state-traded items, such as energy sources, etc.).
     A tolerance of F500 maximum is permitted in the value of imported merchan-

dise. In case of non-liberalized goods, the tolerance can be higher whenever the Customs consent to clear the merchandise and banks are authorized to effect payment automatically.

3. **Special Documents**
    (A) *****Sanitary Certificate**—Issued by competent authority—required for shipments of food of animal origin and for certain fish products. Also required for shipments of fresh fruit, specifically stating that such fruit is free from the San Jose scale. Must show name of consignee.
    (B) *****Phytopathological Certificate**—1—issued by competent authorities—required for shipments of plants and shrubs. Must show name of consignee.
4. *****Consular Fees**
    Legalization of any document .... $2.89 each
    Certification of true copies .... $3.08 each page
5. *****Holidays**
    Good Friday, July 14, and August 15. All holidays generally observed in New York City.
    *Denotes changes since previous notice.

GABON

SUMMARY OF SHIPPING DOCUMENTS REQUIRED

1. **No Consular Documents Required**
    (A) **Commercial Invoice**1—3—On shipper's letterhead—4—for air cargo. Must contain all information necessary for the application of the customs duty and for compilation of commercial statistics, including a detailed description of goods; name and address of shipper; place and date of origin of shipment; name and address of consignee; number and types of containers; numbers, contents, weight, FOB value in U.S. dollars; CIF costs listed separately.
    (B) **Bill of Lading**—No prescribed form, but must contain gross weight in pounds, volume measurement in feet and inches; marks of identification; name and address of consignee. Marks and numbers should correspond with those on the containers and commercial invoices.
    (C) **Pro-forma Invoices**—2 copies—required for import license purposes—must be certified as to country of origin by the New York Chamber of Commerce and Industry which requires one additional notarized copy for its files.
    (D) **Certificate of Origin**—3—when required—on general form—sold by commercial printers—certified by the New York Chamber of Commerce and Industry, which requires one additional notarized copy for its files.
2. **Import License**
    Required by importer—valid for six months. Tolerance not to exceed 5%.
3. **Special Documents**
    Sanitary Certificate—Required from the U.S. Department of Agriculture and other U.S. government agencies are mandatory under UDE quarantine regulations for import of various plants and plant products, including banana plants, cacao plants, coffee plants, sugar cane, raw cotton, cotton seeds and cotton plants, and all containers containing earth, or compost. Information on sanitary certificate requirements and plant quarantine import restrictions is available from the Bureau of Entomology and Plant Quarantine, U.S. Department of Agriculture.
    *Denotes changes since previous notice.

GERMANY (EAST)

SUMMARY OF SHIPPING DOCUMENTS REQUIRED

Special Information

All foreign trade operations in Germany are a state monopoly and handled through their various Foreign Trade Corporations.

No Consular Documents Required

1. **Shipping Documents Required**
   (A) **Commercial Invoice**—2—(unless otherwise specified by the Foreign Trade Corporation)—no special form—should show complete description of goods and the usual information, plus details requested by the Foreign Trade Corporation.
   (B) **Certificate of Origin**—2—(unless otherwise specified by the Foreign Trade Corporation)—when required—general form—sold by commercial printers—certified by the New York Chamber of Commerce and Industry, which requires an additional notarized copy for its files.
   (C) **Bills of Lading**—no special regulations—the usual information should be shown.

2. **Import License**
   Required by the Foreign Trade Corporation for all imports.

3. **Special Documents**
   (A) **Health Certificate**—required for shipments of live animals, animal products, pork and sausage products.
   (B) **Sanitary Certificate**—required for shipments of flowers, live (growing) plants, shrubs, etc., and parts thereof. Issued by the U.S. Department of Agriculture.

4. **Mission Holidays**
   Good Friday, Easter Monday, May 1, June 3, October 7, and December 26.

GERMANY (WEST)

SUMMARY OF SHIPPING DOCUMENTS REQUIRED

No Consular Documents Required

1. **Shipping Documents Required**
   (A) **Commercial Invoice**—1—signed—on exporter's letterhead—must contain complete information and full details.
   (B) **Certificate of Origin**—2—required in cases of special tariff treatment, non-liberalized goods, and when required by importer or Letter of Credit. On general form—sold by commercial printers—certified by the New York Chamber of Commerce and Industry, which requires one additional notarized copy for its files.
   (C) **Bills of Lading**—May be made direct or "To Order." Shipments may also be made freight collect.

2. **Import License**
   Importer requires individual license for a few items only. Most commodities may be imported under General License for which only an import declaration need be filed. Bona fide trade samples may be imported without an import license.

3. **Special Documents**
   A special inspection certificate issued by the Meat Inspection Services, United States Department of Agriculture is required for shipments of lard. Shipments

of plants, parts of plants, plant products and certain animals require a sanitary certificate.

4. *Holidays
    Good Friday, Easter Monday, May 1, May 4, June 17, July 4, Labor Day, Columbus Day, Veteran's Day, Thanksgiving Day, and December 26.
    *Denotes changes since previous notice.

GHANA

SUMMARY OF SHIPPING DOCUMENTS REQUIRED
No Consular Documents Required
1. Shipping Documents Required
    For All Commercial Shipments regardless of value:
    (A) Ghana Special Customs Invoice Form—2—sold by commercial printers—must be signed in ink by manufacturer or exporter, and must contain the following information: amount and rate of freight; measurements and weights of each package. If goods are not insured by shipper, a statement to this effect must be shown. If the ocean freight and other charges are to be paid in Ghana by the importer, then there is no need for the exporter to show this information on the invoice. All discounts and their nature must be shown as well. Regulations require that the invoice must be that of the producer or supplier. In cases where the exporter is not the actual manufacturer, the following clause, signed by a notary or a banker, should be inserted:
    "I certify that the suppliers' and/or manufacturers' invoices have produced and compared with this invoice, which truly represents all particulars of the goods, their selling price and other charges."
    (B) Commercial Invoice—2—must contain full particulars, as specified previously (including FOB and C&F values, plus all itemized expenses). Generally speaking, this invoice should be the manufacturer's, but in cases where this is impracticable, the name of the "stockist" must appear at the top of the invoice. (We understand that this practice is successfully followed by European shippers.)
    (C) Bill of Lading—"To Order" bills of lading are permitted.
    (D) *Clean Report of Findings—Issued by Superintendence Company, Inc., 17 Battery Place, New York 10004, will be required at no expense to the shipper for all imports with a few minor exceptions.
2. Air Cargo Shipments regardless of value:
    Same requirements as stated except that documents must accompany shipment.
3. Import License
    Required by importer for most commodities. A very short list of items may be imported under "Open General License." We have been informed that all 1975 import licenses have expired as of December 31, 1974 and that they will not be extended into 1975. However, in exceptional cases new licenses will be issued for the same merchandise covered by 1974 licenses.
4. Insurance
    Must be covered in Ghana, except AID shipments.
5. *Consular Holidays
    March 6, Holy Thursday, Good Friday, Easter Monday, August 6, and December 26. All holidays generally observed in New York City.
    *Denotes changes since previous notice.
See Form 10-350.

COMBINED CERTIFICATE OF VALUE AND INVOICE OF GOODS FOR IMPORTATION INTO GHANA

(Place and Date)..19.... Invoice No..........

Invoice of...
(State here general nature or class of goods)

consigned by...of..................................

to...of..................................

to be shipped per..

CUSTOMER'S ORDER NO.   OUR ORDER NO.   TERMS:

Country of Origin	Marks and Numbers of Packages	Quantity and Description of Goods	Selling Price to Purchaser	
			●	Amount

Enumerate the following charges if they are NOT shown in the invoice:

	Amount in Currency of exporting country	State if included in selling price to purchaser
(1.) Value of packages and packing, inland freight and all charges connected with transport to place of shipment (only required for ex works or f.o.r. invoices)...........		
(2.) Royalties on the goods...........		
(3.) Ocean freight...........		
(4.) Ocean and War Risks Insurance...........		
(5.) Buying commission of .... per cent...........		
(6.) All other commissions and costs not elsewhere included...........		

State full particulars of royalties below:

1) Here insert Manager, Chief Clerk, or as the case may be. The person making the declaration should be a principal, chief clerk, secretary or responsible employee.

2) Here insert the name of the firm or company.

3) Here insert the name of city or country.

4) These words should be omitted when the manufacturer or supplier himself signs the certificate.

5) Here insert particulars of any special arrangement.

I, (1)............................, of (2)........
of (3)..., manufacturer/supplier of goods specified in this invoice, amounting to
...................................hereby declare that I (4) (have authority to make and sign this certificate
on behalf of the said manufacturer/supplier, and that I) have the means of knowing and do hereby certify as follows:—
1. That this invoice is in all respects correct and contains a true and full statement of the price actually paid or to be paid for the said goods, and the actual quantity thereof.
2. That no different invoice of the goods mentioned in the said invoice has been or will be furnished to any one; and that no arrangement or understanding affecting the purchase price of the said goods has been or will be made or entered into between exporter and purchaser, or by any one on behalf of either of them either by way of discount, rebate, compensation, or in any manner whatsoever other than as fully shown in this invoice, or as follows:
(5)..

Dated at ....this...........day of.....................19....

Signature of Witness .... Signature...................................

Form 10-350. Export Forms, Hazardous Materials Labels, etc. can be purchased from Unz & Co., 190 Baldwin Ave., P.O. Box 308, Jersey City, N.J. 07303.

GREAT BRITAIN

SUMMARY OF SHIPPING DOCUMENTS REQUIRED
No Consular Documents Required
1.   **Shipping Documents Required**
  (A) **Commercial Invoice**—2—On shipper's letterhead. Invoices no longer have to be signed by the exporter; but must contain all necessary information. It is just possible that some importers may prefer invoices to be signed, but unsigned invoices are perfectly valid in that country. Neither certification by the New York Chamber of Commerce and Industry nor legalization by Consulate required.
  (B) **Certificate of Origin**—The United Kingdom is normally concerned only with certificate of origin for Commonwealth Preference purposes which would not, of course, apply to goods manufactured in the United States. However, if requested by consignee or letter of credit this certificate should be prepared on general form, sold by commercial printers. Two copies will suffice. Certified by the New York Chamber of Commerce and Industry, which requires one additional notarized copy for its files.
2.   **Import License**
Very few items required an Import license. Goods subject to license should arrive before expiration date of import license.
3.   **Exchange Permit**
Permission to make payments must be obtained from an authorized bank who will advise on the necessary procedure.
4.   **Samples**
Samples of negligible value may be imported free of duty.
5.   ***Consular Holidays**
February 12, Good Friday (½ day), October 14, October 28, December 24 (½ day), and December 31 (½ day). All holidays generally observed in New York City.
*Denotes changes since previous notice.

GREECE

SUMMARY OF SHIPPING DOCUMENTS REQUIRED
*Document Presentation
Shippers are requested to take the following steps: (1) Make a note on your letterhead showing shipper's name and indicating how many sets (each set should be in duplicate) of Certificates of Origin and Commercial Invoices are to be legalized; and, (2) Present one check for the legalization fee for each set of documents submitted; that is, one check to cover the C/O's and Commercial Invoice set for each shipment. A separate check to cover Affidavits, Sanitary Certificates, and so forth. Also show check number and amount on the described note.
1.   ***Consular Documents Required**
  For All Commercial Shipments valued over $200.00:
  (A) **Commercial Invoice**—2—one will be legalized and returned to shipper—one retained by Consulate—prepared on shipper's letterhead. Must contain full details (including FOB value and itemized expenses), and the following signed affidavit:
      "I, (name, title, name of company), hereby swear that the prices stated in this

invoice are the current export market prices for the merchandise described, and I accept full responsibility for any inaccuracies or errors therein."

They must be certified by the New York Chamber of Commerce and Industry prior to presentation to Consulate. One additional notarized copy will be required by the Chamber for its files.

(B) **Certificate of Origin**—2—one will be legalized and returned to shipper—one retained by Consulate—general form—sold by commercial printers. Necessary to obtain minimum rates of duty. Certified by the New York Chamber of Commerce and Industry which requires one additional notarized copy for its files.

2. **Air Cargo Shipments**
   Commercial Invoice—2—certified by the New York Chamber of Commerce and Industry—legalization required. One additional copy if required by the Chamber and one copy is retained by the Consulate. (See 1-A).

3. **Origin of Third Country Merchandise**
   Goods imported into the United States and increased in value by 25% or more by the addition of U.S. labor or materials are considered as of U.S. origin provided such processing in U.S. results in a change in form or commercial designation (not necessarily change in use).

4. **Import License**
   Required only for some specified items. Importers must register their foreign exchange applications with the Authorities. If shipments are financed by AID importer must obtain prior approval from the Bank of Greece.

5. **Special Documents**
   *Sanitary Certificate—Required for poultry, plants and seeds, issued by the proper authority. It must be dated within twenty days of the date of shipment. Legalized and returned to shipper.

6. **Consular Fees**
   Legalization of certificate of origin .... $3.68 each
   Extra copies (on request of shipper) .... $2.44 each
   Sanitary certificate $2.52
   Legalization of commercial invoice .... $2.48 each
   Extra copies (on request of shipper) .... $1.24 each
   Legalization of a set consisting of 1 certificate of origin
   and 1 commercial invoice .... $4.92 each

   *Consular Holidays**
   February 25, March 25, Good Friday, Easter Monday, June 3, August 15, October 14, November 29, December 24, December 26, and December 31. All holidays generally observed in New York City.
   *Denotes changes since previous notice.

GUATEMALA

SUMMARY OF SHIPPING DOCUMENTS REQUIRED
Special Information
Legalization Deadline—Documents covering shipments to Guatemala must be legalized within 20 working days from the date shown on the bill of lading. In accordance with articles 148 and 149 of the present Customs Law importers will be fined 3% of the custom duties for each document (bill of lading and commercial invoice) which does not comply with this regulation. No erasures or corrections are permitted.

Legalization of Documents—Documents covering commercial shipments from ports having a Guatemalan Consulate must be legalized at that port or, if no Consulate is located there, by the Consulate having jurisdiction. The New York Consulate cannot legalize documents covering shipments via other ports at which there is a Consulate, or via ports which fall under the jurisdiction of a different Consulate.

****Legalization Exceptions**—Freight and Parcel Post Shipments valued under $200 and all non-commercial shipments do not require Consular legalization.

1.   **Consular Documents Required**
      Freight Shipments—Valued at $200 and over:
   (A) **Commercial Invoice**—5—in Spanish—4 retained by Consulate—must show country of origin—must show FOB steamer value and be itemized as to ocean freight, insurance, packing and other expenses. Final total must be preceded by the words "Total CIF." If there is no insurance state: "No hay seguro." If paid in Guatemala, state: "Se desconoce el valor del seguro por haber sido contratado en el pais de destino." If there is no charge for packing, the statement "EMPAQUE GRATIS" must be shown. If packing charges are included in the value state: "GASTOS DE EMPAQUE INCLUIDOS EN EL VALOR DE LA MERCADERIA" and show the amount. If merchandise is unpacked, state: "NO HAY EMPAQUE." The commercial invoice must contain all the following information:
      (a) Name and address of the shipper or exporter.
      (b) Place and date (—name of month in letters) where document was issued.
      (c) Name and address of consignee.
      (d) Marks, numbers, type and quantity of the packages.
      (e) Detailed content of each package.
      (f) Gross, legal and net weights in kilos. If different items are packed in one container, the net and legal weights for each item must be shown.
      (g) Country of origin.
   In addition, invoices must be signed and contain—when applicable—the merchandise code, the model number, series, or reference number. If such information does not apply, the following statement must be placed on the invoice: "Esta mercaderia no tiene codificacion."
   Note: Shipments covering merchandise with different marks must have a separate invoice for each mark and a summary invoice must be prepared.
   (B) **Bill of Lading**—1 original and 4 copies—must show weight in kilos or measurement that applies to each item and total weight and freight charges—Consulate retains the 4 copies. Original must be signed by the steamship line. "To Order" bills of lading allowed. All endorsements on bills of lading must have the name of the company and that of the signer stamped, typewritten, or printed.
   Note: All ocean shipments to Guatemalan Government departments must be made on steamers of the "Flomerca Line" or "Guatemala Line." Air cargo shipments through "Aviateca Guatemalan International Airlines."
   In addition, and according to Decree Law No. 1675, all concerns entitled to duty exemption privileges must import their cargoes by State carriers through the ports of Champerico or Santo Tomas de Castilla (unless Customs issues a special permit to unload at a different port). Firms or persons having their own vehicles may use them for their imports in lieu of State carriers.
2.   ****Parcel Post Shipments (surface and air) valued at $200 and over:**
      Commercial Invoice—5—Consular legalization required—see 1(A).
3.   **Air Cargo Shipments regardless of value:**
      Commercial Invoice—5—in Spanish—must contain all same information as

required in 1(A) and indicate the origin of merchandise. Must accompany shipment. Consular legalization not required, with exception of arms and ammunition (over 4mm).

4. ***Import License**—Import Licenses not required for most goods. The following items do require an import license: arms and ammunition, explosives, certain poultry, wheat flour, seeds, cigarette paper, tallow and used trucks and trailers.

5. **Unaccompanied Baggage**—The bill of lading (or air waybill) is the only document required for clearance through customs. It is not necessary to have it legalized by the Consulate.

6. **Arrangement of Documents**—Documents must be arranged in the following manner: Originals of commercial invoice and bill of lading stapled together (no pins or clips); duplicates; triplicates; etc., in the same manner. The five sets may be clipped together.

7. **Special Documents**

   (A) **Letter of Correction**—(Specimen supplied by Consulate)—6—in Spanish—on Shipper's letterhead—4—retained by Consulate—certified by the New York Chamber of Commerce and Industry which requires 1 notarized copy—must be presented to Consulate before shipment arrives in Guatemala.

   (B) ***Sanitary Certificate**—5—consular legalization required and must be presented to Consulate with regular shipping documents. Required for livestock, meat products, meat, birds and poultry, bees, plants and seeds—issued by the Bureau of Animal Industry, Department of Agriculture, 26 Federal Plaza, New York City.

   (C) **Purity and Free Sale Certificate**—5—Consular legalization required. Must be presented to Consulate with regular shipping documents—required for foodstuffs and related products for human consumption—issued by Health Department. Also required for alcoholic beverages, soft drinks and soda water.

   (D) **Certificate of Analysis**—5—Consular legalization required. Must be presented to Consulate with regular shipping documents—required on shipments of fertilizers, flour and insecticides—issued by the manufacturer, signed by a chemist and notarized. If not produced, the analysis will be made in Guatemala at the importer's expense.

8. **Origin of Third Country Merchandise**
   Goods manufactured in the U.S., or bearing the trademark of a U.S. manufacturer are accepted as originating in the U.S. Goods which are merely cleaned or repacked in the U.S. retain their original country of origin. It is understood that under this ruling Spanish olives which are cleaned and repacked in the U.S. must still be declared as of Spanish origin, but those imported nuts which are shelled or roasted in the U.S. may be declared as of U.S. origin, provided they bear the trademark of a U.S. manufacturer.

9. **Registration of Manufacturers and Exporters**
   Shippers to Guatemala must register with Consulate. The necessary cards will be furnished by the Consulate.

10. ***Consular Fees**
    Must be paid by check or money order.
    Commercial Invoice $15.00
    Letter of Correction 5.00
    Extra copy of the Commercial Invoice, Bill of Lading,
        Freight Bill, Certificate of Origin .... 2.00 each
    Duplicate set of Commercial Invoices and Bills of Lading .... 5.00 each
    Free Sale Certificate 10.00

Purity Certificate 10.00
Sanitary Certificate 10.00
Certificate of Analysis
    (if presented with other documents) .... Gratis
Certificate of Analysis
    (if presented separately) 5.00
Authentication of county clerk's signature 5.00

11.   **Holidays**
    February 12, Holy Thursday, Good Friday, May 1, October 14, October 28, November 1, December 24 (½ day), and December 31 (½ day). All holidays generally observed in New York City.
    *Denotes changes since previous notice.

See Form 10-370.

GUINEA, REPUBLIC OF

SUMMARY OF SHIPPING DOCUMENTS REQUIRED
No Consular Documents Required

1.   **Shipping Documents Required**
  (A) **Commercial Invoice**—2—no special form—a complete description of the goods showing all costs to CIF value.
  (B) **Certificate of Origin**—2—when required—on general form—sold by commercial printers—certified by the New York Chamber of Commerce and Industry, which requires one additional notarized copy for its files.
  (C) **Bills of Lading**—2—prepared in accordance with commercial practices in the country of exportation.

2.   **Import License**
    Required by the specialist import organizations in Guinea—validity 6 months.

3.   **Special Documents**
    Sanitary Certificate—required for live animals, skins and some other products.

4.   **Mission Holidays**
    All holidays generally observed in New York.

GUYANA

SUMMARY OF SHIPPING DOCUMENTS REQUIRED
No Consular Documents Required

1.   **Shipping Documents Required**
  (A) **Commercial Invoice**—2—no special form, except for goods enjoying preferential treatment (British) Jamaican Invoice Form C-23 is acceptable. Must contain all charges including freight and insurance and show CIF value: Goods must be described according to Guyana's Trade Classification List and Customs Tariff. The name and address of the buyer and seller must be shown, as well as the country of origin, and signed by the exporter and witnessed.
  (B) **Certificate of Origin**—2—when required—general form—sold by commercial printers—certified by the New York Chamber of Commerce and Industry, which requires one additional notarized copy for its files.
  (C) **Bills of Lading**—no special requirements—"To Order" bills of lading are permitted, and are protected against receipt of goods without honoring the drafts.

2.   ***Import License**
    Required by importer for all goods—usually valid for the balance of the calen-

Form No. 10-370   Printed and Sold by Unz & Co., Division of Scott Printing Corp., 190 Baldwin
Ave., Jersey City, N.J. 07306—N.J. (201) 795-5400 / N.Y. (212) 344-2270
Toll Free (800) 631-3098

FACTURA COMERCIAL PARA EMBARQUES DESTINADOS A LA REPUBLICA DE GUATEMALA
COMMERCIAL INVOICE FOR SHIPMENTS TO THE REPUBLIC OF GUATEMALA

FECHA (Date) _____ LUGAR DE VENTA (Place of Sale) _____

EMBARCADOR (Shipper) _____

DIRECCION (Address) _____

Vendido a _____ de _____
Sold to   of

Consignado a _____ de _____
Consigned to   of

Embarcado en _____ con destino al puerto de _____
Shipped from   to the port of

Por _____ fecha de salida _____
By   Date of sailing—shipped

Marca _____ FOB ó FAS _____ Su pedido No. _____
(Mark)   or   Your No.

Condiciones de venta: _____ Nuestra Orden No. _____
Terms of sale   Our Order No.

_____ Pais de Origen de la Mercaderia _____
Country of Origin of Merchandise

NUMEROS (Numbers)	BULTOS (Packages)		PESO EN KILOS (Weight in kilos)			CONTENIDO (Contents)	VALOR (Value)
	CANTIDAD (Quantity)	CLASE (Type)	BRUTO (Gross)	LEGAL (Legal)	NETO (Net)	DESCRIPCION Y PRECIO (Description & Price)	

El infrascrito _____ declara y jura ser _____ de la casa de comercio
The undersigned (insert name of signer)   declares and swears that he is (insert title)   of the business house

_____ de esta ciudad, calle _____ No. _____ que son ciertos los
(name of seller)   of this city,   (name of the street and house number)

precios y demas datos consignados en la presente factura, haciendose solidariamente responsable con la casa destina-
that the prices and other data shown in the present invoice are true and exact, and that he holds himself

taria por cualquier ilegalidad o inexactitud que por ulteriores investigaciones pudiera constatarse en los datos
jointly responsible with the consignee for whatever wrong or illegal statements which through subsequent investigations might be found in the data

anotados.
herein given.

Fecha _____ Firma _____
(Date)   (Signature)

ORIGINAL

Form 10-370. Export Forms, Hazardous Materials Labels, etc. can be purchased from
Unz & Co., 190 Baldwin Ave., P.O. Box 308, Jersey City, N.J. 07303.

dar year in which issued. Goods must arrive at destination within the validity period of the license.

3. *Holidays
    February 23, March 8, Good Friday, Easter Monday, October 24, and December 26. All holidays generally observed in New York City.
    *Denotes changes since previous notice.

HAITI

SUMMARY OF SHIPPING DOCUMENTS REQUIRED
1. **Special Information**
    Documents should be presented before sailing of vessel or as soon thereafter as possible.
    The Consulate General of Haiti in New York is authorized to sign consular documents for all shipments leaving from the United States ports where the Government of Haiti does not maintain a representative.
    Consular Documents Required
2. **Freight Shipments regardless of value:**
    (A) **Consular Invoice**—6—in English or French—forms sold by Consulate—three retained by Consulate—country of origin must be indicated directly under the marks. Must contain all necessary information including the nationality of the vessel, accurate description of merchandise, quantity and unit price, and gross and net weights of each different commodity.
    When the description of the merchandise in a shipment is very lengthy, shippers may summarize it in the consular invoice, adding the note: "As per attached commercial invoice." In these cases, the Consulate will charge an additional fee of $3.20 for the legalization of the commercial invoice.
    (B) **Bill of Lading**—3—originals and 3 non-negotiables—3 non-negotiables retained by Consulate. To order B/L's are permitted but notified party must be shown.
3. **Parcel Post Shipments regardless of value:**
    No Consular documents required.
4. **Air Cargo Shipments valued at $100 FOB or more:**
    Consular Invoice—Special Air Cargo Form sold by Consulate—6—see 1(A). When shipment originates at a point where there is no Haitian Consul, six notarized commercial invoices are acceptable in lieu of the consular invoices, in which case the Consular fee will be paid by consignee.
5. **Air Cargo Shipments valued under $100 FOB;**
    No Consular documents required.
6. **Import License**
    None required.
7. **Special Documents**
    (A) **Sanitary Certificate**—Required for fresh fruit, plants, lard, lard substitutes and fresh vegetables—issued by the U.S. Department of Agriculture.
    (B) **Fumigation Certificate**—Required for shipments of used cotton bags and used clothing.
    (C) **Letter of Correction**—In order to correct errors on original consular invoice, a letter on the company's letterhead, in six copies, must be submitted with the original legalized consular invoice, showing the original consular invoice number, date of legalization, and giving full details about the error. If an error is made, a new consular invoice will have to be prepared and original consular fees will again be assessed.

(D) **Lost Documents**—To replace original invoices that have been lost, a new set must be prepared, containing the following signed declaration:
"This is a duplicate of the Consular Invoice No. _____."

8. **Arrangement of Documents**

The three consular invoices and three original bills of lading returned by the Consulate must be clipped or stapled together. To each of the three consular invoices retained by Consulate, a copy of the bill of lading must be stapled and the whole set clipped or stapled together.

9. **Consular Fees**

Payable by check or cash—checks exceeding $100 must be certified.

Consular Invoice on shipments up to $199.99 FOB .... $ 3.00
plus $1.20 tax stamp
Consular Invoice on shipments $200 FOB and over .... 2% of FOB value
plus $1.20 tax stamp
Bills of Lading 2.00
plus $1.20 tax stamp
Certificate of Origin 3.20
Consular Invoice blanks, per set (6) payable by cash only 2.50
Sanitary, Fumigation or Free Sale Certificates 10.20
County Clerk's Signature 7.20

To legalize a replacement set of documents, the fee will be the same as originally paid.

*Consular Holidays

January 2, Good Friday, May 18, September 22, October 17, and November 18. All holidays generally observed in New York City.

*Denotes change since previous notice.

HONDURAS

SUMMARY OF SHIPPING DOCUMENTS REQUIRED

1. **Deadline**

Documents must be presented to Consulate for legalization within 3 working days after sailing of vessel.

2. ***Outport Shipments**

In addition to legalizing documents from the Port of New York, the New York Consulate is authorized to legalize documents covering shipments from ports in the states of Connecticut, Delaware, Indiana, Maine, Maryland, Massachusetts, New Hampshire, New Jersey, New York, North Carolina, Ohio, Pennsylvania, Rhode Island, South Carolina, Vermont, Virginia, West Virginia and Washington, D.C. However, consular blanks must be purchased at the New York Consulate, and checks must be drawn to the Consulate of Honduras.

3. **Freight Shipments valued over $25.00 FOB (50 lempiras):**

(A) **Consular Invoice**—5—in Spanish, on forms sold by Consulate—4 retained by Consulate. The number of the bill of lading and the number of the commercial invoice must be shown in the description column of the invoice. A separate consular invoice must be prepared for each different mark, even if the consignee is the same. If the consular invoice has more than one page, all pages must be numbered and the following statement must be inserted on the last page: "ESTA FACTURA CONSULAR CONSTA DE ... HOJAS." Sailing date shown on B/L must also be shown on consular invoice.

On shipments of textiles and clothing, the kinds of fibers must be specified on the consular invoice, as well as the percentage by weight of each class of fiber.

(B) **Bill of Lading**—1—signed original and 3 non-negotiable copies—in Spanish; if it is in English, there must be a Spanish translation—non-negotiable copies retained by Consulate. Must show the Vessel's sailing date. "To Order of Shipper" bill of lading allowed. Copy by steamship company's freight bill must be attached to original bill of lading or show freight figures on bill of lading.

(C) **Commercial Invoice**—1—Original and 3 copies in Spanish or English—3 copies retained by Consulate (6 extra non-legalized copies must be sent to consignee for statistical purpose only). Unless one original commercial invoice is presented with the documents, they will be rejected. Photostat copies are not acceptable. In addition, the invoice must be manually signed in ink. If there is not sufficient space on the front of the invoice a second sheet must be used.

Total amount of invoice must be brought forward on second page. Consulate will refuse to sign the invoice with only a statement. Information on the reverse side of the invoice will not be accepted. Must show FOB (port of shipment) and CIF values—must contain statement signed by shipper in Spanish or English that information is true and correct and he assumes all responsibilities for any misdeclarations or inaccuracies therein.

All commercial invoices must contain origin of merchandise, terms of payment, quantity, sale price, terms of delivery, and a full description of the merchandise followed by the Customs declaration number if possible, as furnished by the importer in Honduras. Invoices not having this additional information will be rejected by the Consulate.

Ocean freight, marine insurance charges and any additional charges must be shown on commercial invoices. Sailing date of steamer must also be shown.

When shipments are made on a letter of credit basis, a copy of the credit must be attached to Consular documents, and the commercial invoices must be certified as to origin by our Chamber which requires one additional notarized copy for its files. When merchandise originates in other than U.S., even though it is not covered by a letter of credit, the invoices must also be certified as to origin by our Chamber prior to presentation at Consulate.

The Consulate advises that documents will be rejected if there are any crossouts, or alterations on any of the documents; e.g., if a bill of lading is changed by the S.S. Company (weights are altered or short-shipment on the number of packages, etc.) a new bill of lading must be obtained.

Exporters are urged to abide by these regulations to avoid rejection and delays in the legalization of documents.

4.   **Freight Shipments valued at less than $25.00 FOB (50 lempiras)**
No consular Invoice is required. At least 7 non-legalized commercial invoices should be sent to consignee, together with the bills of lading.

5.   **Parcel Post Shipments regardless of value**
Commercial Invoice—3—in Spanish—consular legalization not required—2 copies to consignee; original enclosed in package. Must contain statement signed by shipper, "certified correct" (or similar phraseology) in Spanish or English.

6.   **Air Cargo Shipments regardless of value**
Commercial Invoice—3—consular legalization not required—must accompany shipment. Must contain statement signed by shipper, "certified correct" (or similar phraseology) in Spanish or English. Additional copies may be airmailed to consignee.

7. **Import License**

Not required. For shipments of seeds, a license issued by the Honduran Ministry of Natural Resources is required. Must be presented to Consulate.

8. **Special Documents**

(A) **Letter of Correction**—It is no longer necessary for the exporter to prepare letters of correction for errors on the consular invoices pertaining to weights, values, etc. According to Custom House Legislation, the importer must present to the Custom House an original copy of official sealed paper plus copies on plain paper requesting the necessary modification.

(B) *Certificate of Health Leather Shipments**—A certificate issued by the Health Department with the following statement: "I hereby certify that the leathers covered by said invoice have originated, tanned, manufactured and processed in the U.S.A., that they are free of virus of foot and mouth disease, rinderpest, pleuropneumonia and African swine fever, and that after the treatment they have not been in contact with products of materials contaminated by said diseases," must accompany the other documents presented to the Consulate for legalization covering shipments of leather. Legalization fee is $20.00.

9. **Arrangement of Documents**

Consular documents must be arranged in the following manner, prior to presentation to Consulate, to avoid rejection and delays in legalization of documents.

First set—Original commercial invoice, original bill of lading and original consular invoice—stapled together.
2nd, 3rd, and 4th sets—Commercial invoice, non-negotiable bill of lading and consular invoice. Each set stapled together.
Last copy of the consular invoice—separate
All 5 sets then clipped together.

10. **Consular Fees**—Checks made out to Consulate of Honduras

*Consular stamps are no longer required to be placed on the Consular invoice and neither are stamps required for Bill of Lading or Commercial invoices. The fee for these consular stamps will be collected by customs, at point of entry in Honduras, from the importer based on 8% of the FOB or FAS value. However, documents must still be prepared and presented to consulate as per instructions in this summary. The Consulate will assess a consular fee of $15.00 for each set of documents to be legalized.

Consular Invoice blanks purchased only at consulate by cash or check (per set of 5)	$ 5.00
Sanitary, Health, Purity, Agricultural Certificates and Certificate of Free Sale	20.00
Immediate Service	20.00
Special Power of Attorney	20.00
General Power of Attorney	100.00
Registering marks or brands	20.00
Legalization steamships manifests	100.00
Letters of Correction	20.00

Consular Fee Exemption—Merchandise shipped to entities which may be exempt from the 8% consular fee (such as the American Embassy) must pay the regular legalization fees for the commercial invoice and bill of lading in Honduras. This however, does not apply to shipments to the Government of Honduras and its branches, which are also exempt from these additional fees.

All documents covering shipments made to firms which are exempt of the 8% consular fee must show the "Official Resolution Number" sending a copy to the Consulate exempting such firms of this consular fee.

Due to the application of the new Central American Common Market Customs Tariff and to the application of certain rights and privileges granted by the Law of Industrial Development, some industries in Honduras are exempt from the payment of consular fees. If the shipper requires a legalized consular invoice to comply with the requirements of a letter of credit, the Consulate will legalize this consular invoice without the payment of consular fees, under the following conditions: (1) the consignee must fall under the rights and privileges of the Laws of Industrial Development, and (2) the shipper must insert on the body of the consular invoice the following statement, "DECLARAMOS QUE HEMOS SOLICITADO LA LEGALIZACION DE ESTA FACTURA CONSULAR PARA CUMPLIR CON LOS REQUISITOS DE LA CARTA DE CREDITO QUE AMPARA ESTE EMBARQUE, ACEPTANDO TODA LA RESPONSABILIDAD DE ESTA LEGALIZACION Y EXIMIENDO AL CONSUL GENERAL DE HONDURAS DE TODA RESPONSABILIDAD" (Name of exporter and signature)

Consular Holidays

January 1, February 16, April 14, April 15, April 16, May 1, May 31, September 6, September 15, October 3, October 11, October 25, November 2, November 25, November 26, and December 25. All holidays generally observed in New York City.

If holiday falls on Saturday, the Consulate will be closed on Friday preceding the holiday, if it falls on Sunday Consulate will close the following Monday.

*Denotes changes since previous notice.

HUNGARY

SUMMARY OF SHIPPING DOCUMENTS REQUIRED
*Special Information**
The New York Consulate has jurisdiction for Connecticut, Delaware, Illinois, Iowa, Indiana, Maine, Massachusetts, Michigan, Minnesota, Missouri, New Hampshire, New Jersey, New York, Rhode Island, Vermont and Wisconsin.
No Consular Documents Required
1. **Shipping Documents Required**
   (A) **Commercial Invoice**—2—must contain—names and addresses of shipper and consignee—country of origin and of purchases of the merchandise—number of packages—a description of the outer packing—quantity and value of the merchandise (in U.S. currency)—its precise commercial designation, corresponding as closely as possible to the classification of the customs tariff of Hungary. It is advisable to state the value both in figures and in letters. Commercial invoice must be signed by the shipper.
   (B) **Certificate of Origin**—2—when required—on general form—sold by commercial printers—certified by the New York Chamber of Commerce and Industry, which requires an additional notarized copy for its files.
   (C) **Bills of Lading**—no special regulations—usual information should be shown.

2. **Import License**
   Required by importer for all imports.
3. **Holidays**
   Easter Monday, April 4, May 1, August 20, November 7, and December 26. All holidays generally observed in New York City.
   *Denotes changes since previous notice.

ICELAND

SUMMARY OF SHIPPING DOCUMENTS REQUIRED
No Consular Documents Required
1. **Shipping Documents Required for all commercial shipments**
   (A) **Commercial Invoice**—2 copies necessary for Customs Clearance—additional copies should be sent to consignee. Consular legalization not required. All invoices must be signed and must show gross and net weights (if different types of merchandise are packed together, the net weight of each commodity must be furnished); marks (both outer and inner container—if any); numbers; terms of payment, and all discounts and deductions and their nature. Invoices must also show all itemized expenses up to CIF value.
   (B) **Certificate of Origin**—2—when required—general form—sold by commercial printers—certified by the New York Chamber of Commerce and Industry, which requires one additional notarized copy for its files.
   (C) **Bill of Lading**—"To Order" bills of lading are allowed only if name and address of the notifying party is shown.
2. **Import License**
   Most commodities have now been liberalized. Import license required by importers for a short list of goods. No tolerance permitted in value shown on license. Exporter should be assured importer has license where required.
3. **Special Documents**
   Must be obtained before shipment.
   A Special License as well as a Sanitary Certificate issud by the appropriate official agency is necessary for all shipments of fresh vegetables.
   A disinfection Certificate is necessary for shipments of used clothing, feathers, human and animal hair (and their related products), and straw and articles made thereof.
   A Special License as well as a Sanitary Certificate issued by an official veterinarian is necessary for shipments of live animals and birds. Special license necessary for import of cats. Import of dogs prohibited.
4. ***Consular Holidays**
   January 1, February 16, Holy Thursday April 15, Good Friday April 16, Easter Monday April 19, May 31, June 7, June 17, July 4, August 2, September 6, November 25, December 24 noon, December 25, December 26, and December 31 noon. All holidays generally observed in New York City.
   *Denotes changes since previous notice.

INDIA

SUMMARY OF SHIPPING DOCUMENTS REQUIRED
No Consular Documents Required
1. **Shipping Documents Required**
   (A) **Commercial Invoice**—Original and 3 copies sent to consignee. Invoice must be

signed and contain complete detailed description of merchandise, quantities, weights, origin, etc., and all itemized expenses to CIF value.

(B) **Certificate of Origin**—3—when required—on general form—sold by commercial printers—certified by the New York Chamber of Commerce and Industry, which requires additional notarized copy for its files.

(C) **Bills of Lading**—2—weights and other measurements should be in metric units —the usual particulars should be shown—"To Order" bills of lading allowed— should show the name and address of the notified party at destination. The negotiable bill of lading, the draft on the importer, and all other relevant documents pertaining to the shipment should be forwarded to the banks through which payment is to be made.

2. **Air Cargo Shipments**
    Commercial Invoice—3—signed by shipper—see 1-A. Must accompany shipment.

3. **Import License**—Required by importer for all imports (except Government imports). No tolerances are allowed. Goods sent to India must be shipped from United States ports before expiration of the import license. Shipment made after expiration of an import license are treated as unauthorized, and are subject to heavy fines or confiscation. Expiration dates on letter of credit generally coincide with expiration of import license. Licenses are usually valid for 1 year and are rarely extended.
    Exchange Regulations—All foreign exchange transactions are restricted and exchange must be purchased through the Exchange Control Department of the Reserve Bank of India. Import license, if granted, automatically provides for foreign exchange.

4. **Consular Fees**
    County Clerk's signature authentication .... $3.25 each

5. ***Consular Holidays**
    February 17, March 27, March 28, August 15, October 2, October 7, October 13, November 3, and November 18. All holidays generally observed in New York City.
    *Denotes changes since previous notice.

INDONESIA

SUMMARY OF SHIPPING DOCUMENTS REQUIRED

1. **No Consular Documents Required**
    (A) ***Commercial Invoice**—3—Must contain name and address of shipper, place and date of shipment, name and address of consignee, number and kind of packages, contents and weight of each package, marks, numbers and date of the Indonesian Letter of Credit.
    Prices, quantities and qualities on the invoice must coincide exactly with the information shown on the Indonesian Letter of Credit.
    (B) **Manufacturer's Certificate**—Necessary for the shipment of medicine and medical material.
    (C) **Bills of Lading**—no special requirements—freight charges must be stated separately.

2. ***Import License**—In general no import licenses are required for import transactions but importers must have a valid registration number (TAPPI) from the Department of Trade. Except for imports specifically authorized by the Minister of Trade sight letters of credit are required.

3.   **Special Documents**
     Sanitary Certificate—required for plants and seedlings and other agricultural products, live animals.
4.   **Insurance**
     Insurance does not have to be covered in Indonesia. Therefore, shippers to Indonesia may insure their goods with American insurance companies.
5.   ***Special Requirements**
     The importing of cloves, fertilizers, sugar, rice, wheat, wheatflour, medicine/ medicaments and milk powder for babies (baby food), narcotics and patent medicines containing narcotics, is restricted to specified approved importers or government agencies. Heavy equipment (earth-moving and road building equipment, etc.), motorized vehicles can only be imported by the national sole agents/franchise holders.
6.   **Consular Fees**
     Commercial Invoice (when requested) .... $5.00 each
     Authentication of county clerk signature .... $5.00 each
7.   **Consular Holidays**
     All holidays generally observed in New York City, and main Indonesian holidays.
     *Denotes changes since previous notice.

IRAN

SUMMARY OF SHIPPING DOCUMENTS REQUIRED
1.   **Special Information**
     Insurance must be covered in Iran, except AID Shipments.
     Documents Required
2.   **Ocean and Air Freight Shipments valued at $5 or more:**
   (A) **Commercial Invoice**—2—should show all charges to CIF. Certified as to current export market prices by the New York Chamber of Commerce and Industry, which requires one additional notarized copy for its files. Invoices must bear the following affidavit:
       "We hereby certify that the prices stated in this invoice are the current export market prices for the merchandise described therein and we accept full responsibility for any inaccuracies or errors therein."
       The interpretation of this statement is that the prices shown on the commercial invoices are the actual prices quoted and charged for the goods to the Iranian importers. Consulate will legalize the original invoice and retain a copy for its files. Shipments should be addressed using the term "Persian Gulf." Three commercial invoices must accompany air cargo shipment.
   (B) ***Certificate of Origin**—2—on general form—sold by commercial printers. Certified by the New York Chamber of Commerce and Industry, which requires one additional notarized copy for its files. Legalization by Consulate required only if specified by letter of Credit. Original legalized copy will then be returned by Consulate. Duplicate copy will be retained by Consulate for its files.
   (C) ***Shipments Covered by Five or More Commercial Invoices**—A summary covering all commercial invoices must be prepared, which will be certified by the New York Chamber of Commerce and Industry. Consulate will then legalize the summary invoice only ($10), and will charge $5 for each invoice detailed in the summary.

Shipments covered by four commercial invoices or less may not be covered by a summary invoice. In these cases each invoice must be certified by the New York Chamber of Commerce & Industry and legalized by the Consulate at a cost of $5.00 each.

3. **Parcel Post Shipments regardless of value:**
   No consular documents required. However, if legalized certificates of origin or commercial invoices are requested, see 1(A), and 1(B). Country of origin must be shown on the invoice.

4. **Import License**
   Not required, but many commodities require prior Government authorization. In addition, all imports are subject to prior deposits. When the Iranian importer furnishes the U.S. exporter with an official import authorization number, such number must be shown on all invoices.

5. **Letter of Correction**
   A letter of correction is not allowed. A new set of documents must be prepared.

6. ***Consular Fees**

Certificate of Origin or Commercial Invoice	$ 5.00 each
Additional copies	5.00 each
Certificate of unsold imported merchandise	5.00 each
Statement of Account	5.00 each
General power of attorney, designation agent in Iran	10.00 each
Proforma Invoice and Sale Certificate	10.00 each
Health Certificate	10.00 each

   NOTE: Power of Attorney, sale certificate, assignments, and documents of non-commercial nature require the Seal of the Secretary of State of the State in which it originates.

7. **Consular Holidays**
   All holidays generally observed in New York City.
   *Denotes changes since previous notice.

IRAQ

SUMMARY OF SHIPPING DOCUMENTS REQUIRED

1. **Special Information**
   The terms Persian Gulf should not be used on shipping documents or correspondence. Shippers should use the term Arabian Gulf.

2. **Consular Documents Required for all commercial shipments valued over $27 FOB:**
   (A) **Commercial Invoice with Origin Certification**—1 certified as to current export market prices and country of origin by U.S. Arab Chamber of Commerce. The original should be mailed for legalization. Please enclose a self-addressed envelope. Legalized original and five additional non-legalized copies must be sent to the consignee or bank. The invoice must show the freight charges separately from the value of the merchandise.
   (B) **Bill of Lading**—3 copies—must indicate the nationality of the vessel.
   (C) **Certificate of Origin**—1—when requested by importer. Certified by U.S. Arab Chamber of Commerce. Legalized by Consulate and returned to shipper.

3. **Air Cargo Shipments**
   Commercial Invoice—3—must accompany shipment—see Shipper's Commercial Invoice with Origin Certification above. Additional copies should be sent to consignee.

4. **Import License**
   Required by importer for all commercial shipments. Validity periods vary from 6 to 12 months. Issuance of license authorizes importer to purchase exchange at official rate. Commodities arriving in Iraq before license is issued are subject to confiscation.

5. **Special Documents**
   Black List Certificate—1—necessary for all ocean freight shipments. Issued by the Embassy upon presentation of a non-negotiable copy of the Bill of Lading. Such certificate must state that the steamer on which the merchandise was shipped is not on the Iraq Government black list.
   *Analysis Certificate**—1—required for all antibiotic products, compounds and preparations. Should be issued by a recognized and specialized laboratory. Should be notarized, then signed by the County Clerk and certified by the New York Secretary of State and authenticated by the U.S. Department of State, and then sent to the Embassy. Fee: Department of State in Albany $5.00— Department of State in Washington $2.50.
   *Agency Agreements**—Must be notarized, signed by County Clerk, Certified by New York Secretary of State in Albany and authenticated by the U.S. Department of State in Washington, and then sent to the Embassy. Certification fee charge by the Department of State in Albany is $5.00—Department of State in Washington $2.50.
   *Power of Attorney**—Same procedure as above.

6. **Samples**
   Samples with no commercial value may be imported free of duty.

7. *Consular Fees**—Checks should be payable to Iraqi Interest Section, Embassy of India.

Original Shipper's Commercial Invoice with Origin
    Certification .... $ .90
Original Certificate of Origin .... .90
Additional copies of Invoice or Certificate
    of Origin .... .35 each
Black List Certificate .... .35 each

8. **Insurance**
   Insurance must be covered in Iraq except AID shipments.
   *Denotes changes since previous notice.

IRELAND

SUMMARY OF SHIPPING DOCUMENTS REQUIRED
No Consular Documents Required

1. **Shipping Documents Required for ocean freight and air freight shipments**
   (A) **Commercial Invoice**—2—No special form required—currency of payment should be shown. All necessary charges to establish the CIF value of the goods should be given. Invoice should state whether charges such as packing, insurance, and inland freight, etc., are included or excluded. Where the invoice does

not specify the separate contents of packages the production of a packing slip or slips is also required. Country of origin should be stated. For textile shipments, percentage of composition by weight must be shown as well as weight per square yard and method of manufacture.

(B) **Certificate of Origin**—A Certificate of Origin is required

(1) In those cases where:

(a) Preferential rates of customs duties apply; i.e., to goods of United Kingdom, Canadian, or Commonwealth preference area origin, and to certain goods produced or manufactured in specified developing countries.

(b) Anti-Dumping duties apply; only to a limited range of goods (e.g. certain pencils and fertilizers).

(c) Import restrictions by country of origin apply; only to certain fertilizers, textiles (yarns, piece goods and made-up articles), tires and tubes for bicycles and tricycles (mechanically propelled or otherwise).

(2) For wool.

(3) For Port and Madeira wine.

*(4) EEC Documents

A status document under, the EEC Transit System is required if the preferential rate of duty applicable to other member states of the EEC is to be obtained.

Under EEC Agreements preferential rates of duty apply to specified goods originating in certain countries, e.g. EFTA Countries. Claims for these rates must be supported by a movement certificate in the prescribed form.

2.   ***Parcel Post Shipments**

Customs declaration showing the full commercial description of the goods and a Certificate of Origin if required. If preference as at A1 (a) above is claimed the Customs Declaration Form should be endorsed "Preference claimed—.....rate (specifying the appropriate preferential rate)." Goods eligible for preference under EEC Agreements should be supported by the appropriate postal form and the number of the form must be entered on the Customs Declaration. Goods from another member state of the EEC will qualify for the appropriate preferential rate unless a prescribed yellow label is affixed to the postal package and accompanying documents. Clearance will normally be facilitated if the Commercial invoice is enclosed also.

3.   ***Origin of Third-Country Merchandise**

Country of origin—The conditions to be fulfilled before goods may be regarded as the manufacture of a particular country for preference purposes are contained in Notices No. 1029, 1219, 1222 and 1223 (available from the Revenue Commissioners, Dublin Castle, Dublin 2).

4.   **Special Requirements**

Shipments of plants, vegetables, cut flowers, etc., require a certificate from the United States Department of Agriculture.

5.   **Consular Holidays**

March 17, Good Friday, Easter Monday,, and December 26. All holidays generally observed in New York City.

*Denotes changes since previous notice.

ISRAEL

SUMMARY OF SHIPPING DOCUMENTS REQUIRED
No Consular Documents Required
1. **Shipping Documents Required**
    For All Commercial Shipments one of the following is required.

—EITHER—

(A) **Israel Customs Invoice**—3—forms sold by commercial printers. All questions must be answered and all charges must be itemized to FAS steamer. Ocean freight charges, insurance premiums, and any other expenses up to CIF port of unloading must be shown.

—OR—

(B) **Shipper's Commercial Invoice**—3—must contain all the information required in official customs invoice described above.
(C) **Bills of Lading**—2—the usual particulars should be shown—"To Order" bills of lading allowed—freight collect shipments are permissible if stipulated in the import license.
(D) **Certificate of Origin**—2—when required—on general form—sold by commercial printers—certified by N.Y. Chamber of Commerce and Industry which requires additional notarized copy for its files.
2. **Import License**
    A large number of imports do not require a license. Imports still subject to prior permits are covered by licenses with a validity of 9 to 12 months. Issuance of an import license guarantees importer the right to obtain the necessary foreign exchange.
3. *__Consular Holidays__
    April 8, April 15, April 25, May 27, May 28, June 6, September 27, October 11, October 14, October 18, and October 28. All holidays generally observed in New York City.
    *Denotes changes since previous notice.
See Form 10-380.

ITALY

SUMMARY OF SHIPPING DOCUMENTS REQUIRED
No Consular Documents Required
1. **Shipping Documents Required For All Commercial Shipments**
    (A) **Commercial Invoice**—3—on shipper's letterhead. Must contain an accurate description of the merchandise and show country of origin. All expenses are to be itemized. Invoices must be signed by hand—in ink—by an authorized employee.
    (B) **Certificate of Origin**—2—on general form—sold by commercial printers. Certified by the New York Chamber of Commerce and Industry, which requires one additional notarized copy for its files.
    (C) **Bill of Lading**—Should contain country of origin. "To Order" bills of lading are allowed.
2. **Consular Fees**
    Invoice—regardless of the amount (when requested) . . . . $8.60 each—Certifi-

cates of Origin (when requested) must show the value of the merchandise:

from $1 to $800	—$ 3.44
from $801 to $3,200	—$ 8.60
over $3,200	—$17.20

*Consular Holidays

Easter Monday, April 25, June 2, August 15, October 14, November 4, and December 26. All holidays generally observed in New York City.

*Denotes changes since previous notice.

IVORY COAST

SUMMARY OF SHIPPING DOCUMENTS REQUIRED

Legalization of Documents

When legalization is requested, for any document, they must be mailed to the Embassy of the Ivory Coast, 2424 Massachusetts Avenue, N.W., Washington, D.C. (Tel: 202-483-2400).

No Consular Documents Required

1. **Shipping Documents Required**

    (A) **Commercial Invoice**—2—no special form—should contain—names of exporter and consignee—number and types of packages—marks and numbers on packages—net and gross weights—CIF value—terms of sale—an accurate specific and complete description of the merchandise.

    (B) **Certificate of Origin**—2—on general form—sold by commercial printers—required by customs to establish the true origin of the goods—certified by the New York Chamber of Commerce and Industry, which requires an additional notarized copy for its files.

    (C) **Bills of Lading**—no special regulations, but marks of identification and names and address of consignee should be clearly indicated. Shipping marks and numbers on bills of lading, on invoices, and on the goods should correspond exactly.

2. **Import License**

    Required by importer for most shipments—validity six months and may be extended for an additional six months. The expiration date is computed from the day of loading.

3. **Legalization Fee**

    Commercial Invoice (when requested) .... $2.00 per sheet
    Certificate of Origin (when requested) .... $2.00 per sheet

4. **Holidays**

    All holidays generally observed in New York City.

JAMAICA

SUMMARY OF SHIPPING DOCUMENTS REQUIRED

No Consular Documents Required

1. **Shipping Documents Required for all commercial shipments**

    (A) **Special Invoice Regulations**—Jamaica Customs authorities insists that shippers use the "Jamaica Invoice and Declaration of Value" Form C23 in duplicate. It is not necessary to complete the origin certification of this form when the merchandise is of U.S. origin. The origin section on this invoice should be

ISRAEL CUSTOMS INVOICE

Name and address of supplier
Country
NVOICE of (state general nature of goods)
Country of origin of the goods
supplied to
er order No.
Name of agent in Israel
Terms (c.i.f., c&f., c&i., f.o.b., allowances etc.)
Rate of exchange, if specific
to be shipped per

Date

Of
Dated
Israel import license No.
From

Shipping marks	Quantity or measure	Full description of goods incl. % of composition if mixed	Tariff heading No.	Gross weight of each package	Net weight of goods in each package (indicate unit)	Total net weight of goods	Price per unit as sold	Amount
		Weight of outer coverings and packing materials						
		TOTAL						

Whenever in addition to the price as specified above any of the following charges are payable by the importer to the supplier or any of their agents or middlemen, those charges are to be specified below in the currency in which they are payable:—

(1) Packing expenses . . . .
(2) Transport expenses in the country of export . . . .
(3) Expenses of shipping or loading . . . .
(4) Dock dues of all kinds . . . .
(5) Agency fees (commission agent's and/or middleman's allowances) . . . .
(6) Freight charges other than those included above . . . .
(7) Insurance charges . . . .
(8) Any other charges incurred in the exportation of the goods to Israel . . . .

TOTAL . . . .

. . . . hereby declare that I have the authority to make and sign this invoice on behalf of the aforesaid supplier and that, to the best of my knowledge and belief, this invoice is in all respects true and correct and contains a full statement of the price of the goods and all charges thereon as per terms indicated.

Stamp . . . .

Signature . . . .

NOTES

Please type or write clearly.

Attention is drawn to the necessity of completing, in full detail, all the columns provided on the form. Failure to do so is liable to cause delay in clearance through Customs.

In the event of more than one package, containing different kinds of goods, being invoiced, the required particulars should be detailed, in respect of each kind, either in the invoice itself or separately.

(d) The metric system being in use in Israel, weights and measures should preferably be in metric units.

(e) All prices are to be indicated in the currency in which goods are sold.

(f) The indication of the relevant heading No. of the Israel Customs Tariff or of the Brussels Tariff Nomenclature, will facilitate clearance.

(g) The "net weight of goods" includes the weight of inner containers in which the goods are usually sold by retail. The weight of outer coverings and packing materials should be added in the columns of net weight.

Form No. 10-380 Printed and Sold by Unz & Co., Division of Scott Printing Corp., 190 Baldwin Ave., Jersey City, N.J. 07306 — N.J. (201) 795-5400 / N.Y. (212) 344-2270
Toll Free (800) 631-3098

Form 10-380. Export Forms, Hazardous Materials Labels, etc. can be purchased from Unz & Co., 190 Baldwin Ave., P.O. Box 308, Jersey City, N.J. 07303.

completed only when shipping goods which are entitled to British Preferential
duties.
  (B) **Bill of Lading**—No special requirements.

2.   *Import License**
      Special licenses are required for all goods imported into Jamaica.
3.   **Consular Fees**

      Any consular legalization (when requested)
        that requires a signature .... $1.65 per signature
      Any consular legalization (when requested)
        that requires an initial .... .55 for three or less
      Authentication of County Clerk's signature .... $1.65 per signature

4.   **Holidays**
      Good Friday, First Monday in August, and Third Monday in October. All
      holidays generally observed in New York City.
      *Denotes changes since previous notice.
See Form 10-400 (front and back).

JAPAN

SUMMARY OF SHIPPING DOCUMENTS REQUIRED
No Consular Documents Required
1.   **Shipping Documents Required**
  (A) **Commercial Invoices**—On shipper's letterhead. Must contain the following
      information: Shipping marks, packages, numbers, gross and net weights, accu-
      rate and full description of the goods, unit value and all itemized expenses. All
      copies must be signed by shipper.
  (B) **Certificate of Origin**—Certificate of origin is essential for importer in order to
      obtain the duty concessions granted by the Japanese Authorities under the
      General Agreement on Tariffs and Trade (GATT). Either the Japanese or
      General Form is acceptable. Must be certified by the New York Chamber of
      Commerce and Industry, which requires one additional notarized copy for its
      files. Legalization by Consulate not required; however, if requested by impor-
      ter or by Letter of Credit, or upon request by shipper, the Consulate will
      legalize certificate, in which case one extra copy must be prepared for their
      files.
2.   **Import Declaration or Approval**
      Simply a declaration of import of an authorized foreign exchange bank in
      Japan is needed for all commercial shipments into Japan, except for a few
      items included in a negative list which require a MITI approval.
3.   **Consular Fees**
      For legalization of Certificate of Origin (when requested) $4.00
4.   *Holidays**
      April 29, November 3, December 29, December 30, and December 31. All holi-
      days generally observed in New York City.
      *Denotes changes since previous notice.

JORDAN

SUMMARY OF SHIPPING DOCUMENTS REQUIRED

*Special Information

Legalization of Documents—all documents that require legalization by the Consulate must be sent by mail with a self-addressed, stamped envelope together with a certified check or money order. However, in emergencies, such as an expiring Letter of Credit, the Consulate will accept documents by messenger if the emergency situation can be established to their satisfaction. Call for appointment.

The importation of chemical coloring materials used in preparation of foods for human consumption (soft drinks, baked goods, etc.) is banned.

1. **Consular Documents Required**

   (A) ***Commercial Invoice**—1—on shipper's letterhead—must contain detailed description of merchandise and itemized expenses. Consular legalization required regardless of value, invoices must be certified by the U.S. Arab Chamber of Commerce (prior to presentation at Consulate) which requires one additional notarized copy for its files. Consulate will return legalized original to shipper. Invoices must contain the following affidavit:

   "I (name, title, name of company), hereby state that the prices stated in this invoice are the current export market prices for the merchandise described above and whose origin is (country of origin); and do accept full responsibility for any inaccuracies or errors therein."

   Commercial invoices must show the freight charges separately from the value of the merchandise. Invoices covering shipments of textiles and woven fabrics must describe the fabrics, the nature of the raw materials used, and the percentage of mixtures of fibers. Shipments will not be cleared if the invoices do not contain the required information, or does not show the name and address of the manufacturer.

   (B) **Certificate of Origin**—2—when required—on general form—sold by commercial printers—certified by the U.S. Arab Chamber of Commerce, which requires one additional notarized copy for its files. Must also show the name and address of the manufacturer.

   (C) **Bills of Lading**—Must indicate the nationality of the carrying vessel.

2. **Air Cargo Shipments**

   Commercial Invoice—prepared as per 1(A)—2 must accompany shipment.

3. **Import License**

   Required by importer. Validity—6 months—no tolerance permitted.

4. ***Insurance**

   Insurance must be covered in Jordan, except AID shipments.

5. ***Consular Fees**

   Consular fees must be paid by certified check or postal money order.

   For legalizing commercial invoices .... $7.00 each
   Certificate of Origin(when requested) .... $1.75 each
   Power of Attorney .... $3.50 each
   Bill of Lading or other documents $1.75

6. **Holidays**

   March 27 and May 25. All holidays generally observed in New York City.
   *Denotes changes since previous notice.

INVOICE

C. 23

(Place and Date) .... 19 ..

INVOICE OF .... consigned by

.... of ....

To .... of .... to be shipped

Per .... Order No. ....

Country from which consigned.

Marks and Numbers on Packages	Number of Packages	Quantity and Description of Goods	Country of Origin	Selling Price to Purchaser CIF.	
				at	Amount

State whether or not the following charges are included in the above selling price to purchasers and if so state each amount in the currency of the exporting country	State if included in above selling price to purchaser	Amount in currency of exporting country
(1) Labour in packing the goods into outside packages		
(2) Value of outside packages		
(3) If the goods are subject to any charge by way of royalties		
(4) Commission; establishment and other charges of a like nature		
(5) Cartage to rail and/or docks		
(6) Inland freight (rail or canal) and other charges to dock area		
(7) Inland Insurance		
(8) Ocean Freight		
(9) Marine Insurance		
(10) Any other costs, dues, charges and expenses incidental to the purchase delivery of the goods in the Island		

State full particulars of Royalties below:—

Form 10-400 (front). Export Forms, Hazardous Materials Labels, etc. can be purchased from Unz & Co., 190 Baldwin Ave., P.O. Box 308, Jersey City, N.J. 07303.

COMBINED CERTIFICATE OF VALUE AND OF ORIGIN OF GOODS

(¹) Here insert Manager, Chief Clerk, or as the case may be.

(ii) Here insert name of firm or company.

(iii) Here insert name of city or country.

(iv) These words should be omitted where the manufacturer supplier, producer or grower himself signs the certificate.

I, (i) **

of (iii)

of (iii)   manufacturer supplier producer grower of the goods specified in this invoice amounting to   hereby declare that I (iv) have the authority to make and sign this certificate on behalf of the said manufacturer supplier producer grower and that I have the means of knowing and do hereby certify as follows —

VALUE

1.   That this invoice is in all respects correct and contains a true and full statement of the price actually paid or to be paid for the said goods, and the actual quantity thereof

(v) Here insert particulars of any special arrangement.

2.   That no arrangement or understanding affecting the purchase price of the said goods has been or will be made or entered into between the exporter and the purchaser, or by anyone on behalf of either of them, either by way of discount, rebate, compensation or in any manner whatever other than as fully shown on this invoice, or as follows v

ORIGIN

(Delete whichever of 3 (a) or 3 (b) is not applicable. If 3 (a) is used, delete 4 and 5. If 3 (b) is used, insert required particulars in 4 and 5).

(vi) Insert "United Kingdom" or name of other part of the British Empire.

3.   (a)   That all the goods mentioned in this invoice have been wholly or partially produced or manufactured in

(vi)

(b)   That all the goods mentioned in this invoice have been either wholly or partially produced or manufactured

(vi)

4.   As regards these goods only partially produced or manufactured in (vi)

(a)   That the final process or processes of manufacture have been performed in that part of the British Empire.

(b)   That the expenditure in material produced and or labour performed in (vi)

calculated subject to qualifications hereunder in the case of all such goods, is not less than (vii)

per cent of the factory or works cost of all such goods in their finished state.

(vii) Here insert the appropriate figure.

†   (See note below).

(c)   That in the calculation of such proportion of material produced and or labour performed in (vi)

none of the following items has been included or considered — "Manufacturers' profit or remuneration of any trader, agent, broker, or other person dealing in the goods in their finished condition, royalties, cost or outside packages or any cost of packing the goods thereinto, any cost of conveying, insuring, or shipping the goods subsequent to their manufacture."

NOTES

* *   The person making the declaration should be a principal or a manager, chief clerk, secretary or responsible employee.

†   In the case of goods which have at some stage entered into the commerce of or undergone a process of manufacture in a foreign country, only that labour and material which is expended on or added to the goods after their return to the British Empire shall be regarded as the produce or manufacture of the British Empire in calculating the proportion of British Empire labour and material in the factory or works cost of the finished article.

Dated at   this   day of   19

Signature

Signature of Witness

Form No. 10-400   Printed and Sold by Unz & Co., Division of Scott Printing Corp., 190 Baldwin Ave., Jersey City, N.J. 07306 — N.J. (201) 795-5400 / N.Y. (212) 344-2270
Toll Free (800) 631-3098

Form 10-400 (back). Export Forms, Hazardous Materials Labels, etc. can be purchased from Unz & Co., 190 Baldwin Ave., P.O. Box 308, Jersey City, N.J. 07303.

KENYA

SUMMARY OF SHIPPING DOCUMENTS REQUIRED
No Consular Documents Required
1.   **Shipping Documents Required**
   (A) **Commercial Invoice**—2—on shippers letterhead—in English—must show quantity of the goods and their true market value in the country of origin—country of origin—unit rate—value of the goods plus costs of packing, insurance and freight up to the port of entry—must show exact nature of any discounts and/or commissions given by the seller to the buyer. Import license number must be obtained from importer and be shown on the invoice.
   (B) **Certificate of Origin**—2—when required—on general form—sold by commercial printers—certified by the New York Chamber of Commerce and Industry, which requires one additional notarized copy for its files.
   (C) **Bills of Lading**—2—no special regulations. Shipping marks and numbers on bills of lading, on the goods, and on the invoices must correspond.
   (D) **Clean Report of Findings Certificate**—required for all imports into Kenya with the exception of special imports by Government Ministries, goods valued under 20,000 Kenya Shillings and a few other items. Issued by Superintendence Co., Inc. in the United States, without cost to the seller.
2.   **Import License**
Required by importer for a short list of goods. Validity six months from date of issuance. Tolerance of approximately 10% to cover slight increases in value is permitted.
3.   **Holidays**
All holidays generally observed in New York City.
See Form 10-310.

KHMER REPUBLIC
(Formerly CAMBODIA)

SUMMARY OF SHIPPING DOCUMENTS REQUIRED
No Consular Documents Required
1.   **Shipping Documents Required**
   (A) **Commercial Invoice**—3—certified as to current export market prices and country of origin by the New York Chamber of Commerce and Industry, which requires one additional notarized copy for its files. Invoice must contain a detailed description of the merchandise, terms, and all other relevant information. Copy retained by the Chamber must bear the following affidavit:
      "I hereby swear that the prices stated in this invoice are the current export market prices for the merchandise described herein and that the origin of these goods is the United States of America, and I accept full responsibility for any inaccuracies or errors therein."
   (B) **Certificate of Origin**—2—when required—general form—sold by commercial printers—certified by the New York Chamber of Commerce and Industry, which requires one additional notarized copy for its files.
   (C) **Bills of Lading**—no special requirements. "To Order" bills are acceptable.
2.   **Import License**
Imports of merchandise into the Khmer Republic are subject to licenses issued by the Direction du Commerce Exterieur which establishes half-yearly schedules for imports. All import transactions must be domiciled with a bank

May 1, 1964

Printed and Sold by Unz & Co., Division of Scott Printing Corp., 190 Baldwin
Form No. 10-310 Ave., Jersey City, N.J. 07306—N.J. (201) 795-5400 / N.Y. (212) 344-2270
Toll Free (800) 631-3098

COMMERCIAL INVOICE FOR EAST AFRICA, KENYA AND UGANDA

(Place and Date)_____19____ Invoice No._____

Sold by_____of_____

to_____of_____

to be shipped per_____

| CUSTOMER'S ORDER NO. | OUR ORDER NO. | TERMS: |

Country of Origin	Marks and Numbers on Packages	QUANTITY AND DESCRIPTION OF GOODS	Selling Price to Purchaser	
			@	Amount

Exact nature and percentage of any discounts and/or commissions given
by the seller to the buyer._____

Enumerate the following charges if they are not shown in the invoice:—

Amount in Currency of Exporting Country.

(1) Value of packages and packing, inland freight and all other charges connected with transport to place of shipment (Only required for ex works or f. o. r. invoices)..

(2) Royalties on the goods..

(3) Ocean Freight..

(4) Ocean and War Risks Insurance..

(5) Buying Commission of..........per cent...

(6) All other Commissions and costs not elsewhere included..............................

Form 10-310. Export Forms, Hazardous Materials Labels, etc. can be purchased from
Unz & Co., 190 Baldwin Ave., P.O. Box 308, Jersey City, N.J. 07303.

approved by the Ministry of Finance upon notice from the Governor of the Banque Nationale du Cambodge. All foreign trade has been liberalized except for: exports of rice and by-products, corn, rubber, and precious and semi-precious stones.

3. **Consular Fees**

   For legalization of commercial invoice (when required) $1.00

KOREA

SUMMARY OF SHIPPING DOCUMENTS REQUIRED

1. **Special Information**

   Documents should be presented to Consulate prior to sailing of the vessel. If it is impossible to show CIF value, the Consulate will accept FOB value only.

   On shipments requiring an Import License, either a copy of the license must be attached to the documents or the import license number shown on the Certificate of Origin. If shipment is covered by a Letter of Credit, a copy of the credit should be attached, and credit number placed on Certificate of Origin. Shipments made under a Letter of Credit must utilize the full amount of the credit, except in cases where the credit allows partial shipments. If there is no Letter of Credit, it must be stated on the Certificate of Origin.

2. **Consular Documents Required for all steamer, air cargo and parcel post shipments valued at $100 or over:**

   (A) *Certificate of Origin—4—special forms supplied gratis by Consulate—all copies must be notarized—certified by the New York Chamber of Commerce and Industry, which requires one additional notarized copy for its files—legalized by Consulate which retains 1 copy—original and 2 copies returned to shipper. Method of payment must be shown on the Certificate of Origin, e.g., Letter of Credit, Sight Draft, etc. If shipment is covered by Letter of Credit, then the number of the credit must be shown. Certificates of Origin are not required in the following cases unless a Letter of Credit specifically requests it: 1. Shipments consigned to government agencies of the Republic of Korea; 2. Shipments consigned to diplomatic members and organizations; 3. Personal effects; 4. Shipments valued at less than U.S. $100.00 in total; 5. Other items considered exempted by the Minister of Foreign Affairs in Korea.

   (B) *Commercial Invoice—2—must be certified as to country of origin by the New York Chamber of Commerce and Industry, which requires one additional notarized copy for its files. One copy retained by Consulate. Shipments consigned to the Government of Korea, personal effects, or shipments to diplomatic organization are exempt from Consular requirements.

3. **All Shipments valued under $100 FOB:**

   No documents required. Commercial Invoice, in duplicate, should be forwarded to consignee. On air shipments, two Commercial Invoices must accompany shipment.

4. **Import License**

   Required by importer for certain commodities.

5. **Special Documents**

   (A) *Pro-Forma Invoice—3—must be notarized—certified by the New York Chamber of Commerce and Industry—legalized by the Consulate—required by the importer prior to opening a Letter of Credit. One copy retained by Consulate—one copy retained by the Chamber.

(B) **Letter of Correction**—When a Letter of Correction is required, shipper must obtain a letter of correction amendment form from the Consulate. The form must be submitted to the Consulate in triplicate. The fee will be $2.50. However, if the legalized documents have already been forwarded to Korea, then the letters of correction will be done gratis and the fees collected in Korea.

(C) **Sanitary Certificate**—Required for shipments of plants and vegetable products. Consular legalization not required.

6. **Consular Fees**

The Korean Consulate General prefers a certified check for payment of consular fees. However, if this creates too great a hardship to the shipper, they will accept cash or a regular business check.

Special Certificate of Origin form .... Gratis
Certificate of Origin $5.00
Duplicate for lost Certificate of Origin 3.00
Additional copies of Certificate of Origin .... 1.00 each
Pro-Forma Invoice 2.50
Letter of Correction (see
    Letters of Correction) 2.50

7. **Holidays**

January 1-3, March 1, July 17, August 15, and October 3. All holidays generally observed in New York City.

*Denotes changes since previous notice.

KUWAIT

SUMMARY OF SHIPPING DOCUMENTS REQUIRED

Special Information—All documents for Kuwait should show the designation Kuwait Arabian Gulf.

1. **Consular Documents Required for all Commercial Shipments regardless of value:**

(A) ***Commercial Invoice**—3—no special form—must contain full packing particulars; show the name of the steamer (if shipment is made by sea), and also show the name of the manufacturer or processor of the goods, when other than shipper. Weight of each type of goods preferably in kilos, should be shown. Consular legalization required, invoices must be presented to the U.S. Arab Chamber of Commerce for certification prior to presentation at Consulate. One notarized copy for the U.S. Arab Chamber's files and one copy retained by the Consulate and the original returned to the shipper. Goods cannot be shipped on blacklisted ships, or on ships calling at any Israeli port. The following statement must be shown on the invoice—"merchandise is not of Israeli origin or contains any Israeli materials."

(B) ***Certificate of Origin**—3—required for all shipments—certified by the U.S. Arab Chamber of Commerce which retains one notarized copy. Legalization necessary, one copy retained by Consulate and the original returned to the shipper. The following statement must be shown on the invoice "merchandise is not of Israeli origin or contains any Israeli materials."

2. **Import License**

No import license is required.

3.   ***Consular Fees**

Commercial Invoices .... $1.50 each
Certificate of Origin .... $1.50 each
Power of Attorney $3.00
Entry Visa $4.00
Transit Visa (For a stay of 48 hours or less) $1.00

4.   **Consular Holidays**

February 25. All holidays generally observed in New York City.
*Denotes changes since previous notice.

LAOS

SUMMARY OF SHIPPING DOCUMENTS REQUIRED
No Consular Documents Required
1.   **Shipping Documents Required**
  (A) **Commercial Invoice**—2—the following information should be shown: Name and address of shipper, place and date of shipment, name and address of consignee, port of shipment, port of destination, vessel and sailing date, marks and numbers, weights and measurements, quantity and type of package, value of merchandise and country of origin. Must contain an affidavit signed by shipper or authorized representative that the information is true and correct. Invoices should be mailed to consignee for customs clearance.
  (B) **Certificate of Origin**—2—when required—on general form—sold by commercial printers—certified by the New York Chamber of Commerce and Industry, which requires an additional notarized copy for its files.
  (C) **Bills of Lading**—2—no special regulations—the usual information should be shown. "To Order" bills are acceptable.
2.   **Import License**
Required by importers only for import under U.S.A. Import Program (A.I.D.).

LEBANON

SUMMARY OF SHIPPING DOCUMENTS REQUIRED
1.   **Special Information**
Documents covering shipments to Lebanon of foreign origin merchandise must be legalized by Consulate in country of origin.
    Shipping documents must be legalized by the Consulate having jurisdiction where the actual shipper is located, regardless of the final port of exit, e.g., if shipper is located in Chicago and the merchandise is shipped from New York, the documents must be legalized in Chicago.
2.   **Consular Documents Required for all commercial shipments regardless of mode of transportation valued at $10.00 FAS or over:**
  (A) **Commercial Invoice**—1—in French or English—must show the FAS value. Must be certified as to current export market prices and country of origin by a recognized Chamber of Commerce, which requires an additional notarized copy for its files, prior to presentation to the Consulate. No copy is required for Consulate. "Summary" invoices covering several commercial invoices are not acceptable. All invoices must show complete description of goods being exported, e.g.: auto parts will not be acceptable. Shippers must show valves,

piston rings, spark plugs, etc. Prices of each must be shown. Marks, numbers, weights, etc. must be shown. The following signed statement must appear on the invoices:

"We hereby certify that this invoice is authentic, the only one issued by us for the goods above mentioned, that the value is true and correct without deduction of any payment in advance and their origin is exclusively U.S.A. and we accept full responsibility for any errors or inaccuracies in this invoice."

(B) **Certificate of Origin**—1—on general form—sold by commercial printers. Must be certified by a recognized Chamber of Commerce prior to presentation to the Consulate. One additional notarized copy is required for the files of the Chamber of Commerce. No copy is required for Consulate.

3. **All Commercial Shipments valued under $10.00 FAS:**
Commercial Invoices and Certificates of origin covering shipments valued at less than $10.00 FAS will be certified by this Chamber when requested. No Consular legalization is necessary.

4. **Whiskey Shipments**
Whiskey shipments must be covered by either a distiller's certificate stating the origin or a separate certificate of origin.

5. **Special Requirements**—There are special requirements pertaining to shipments of medical and pharmaceutical specialties, patent medicines and products of animal origin—for details call the Chamber.
*Health Certificate—required for all food products, frozen foods, live animals, etc., issued by the Department of Agriculture—2 copies required—legalized by the Consulate.
*Free Sale Certificate—signature, notarized and County Clerk's signature required for medicine and pharmaceutical specialties.
All shipments must be covered by legalized documents and if there is no Consulate at port of exit, the New York Consulate will legalize the invoices. Importers without legalized documents, will be assessed double consular fees.

6. **Consular Fees**

Commercial Invoice:
valued less than $2,500	$ 4.50
$2,500 up to $15,000	$ 7.50
$15,000 and over	$11.50

Extra copies of commercial invoice same fee as for originals.
Certificate of Origin	$ 1.50
Fumigation Certificate	$ 2.50
Health Certificate	$ 2.50 each
Free Sale Certificate	$ 3.75
Commercial Invoice covering shipments of personal effects or automobiles	$12.50 per automobile

7. **Holidays**
Good Friday, Easter Monday, Ascension Thursday, and November 22. All holidays generally observed in New York City.
*Denotes changes since previous notice.

LIBERIA

SUMMARY OF SHIPPING DOCUMENTS REQUIRED
No Consular Documents Required
1. **Shipping Documents Required**
    (A) **Commercial Invoice**—2—must show FOB and all charges to C&F or CIF must be signed and notarized. Certified as to price and origin by the New York Chamber of Commerce and Industry (when requested), which retains one additional copy for its files. Invoices should show the following:

FOB value	XXX
Trucking	XX
Preparation of Documents	X
Other charges excluding	
war risk insurance	X
Sub-Total	XXXX
War risk insurance—if any	XX
Total CIF	XXX

    (B) **Bill of Lading**—2—no special requirements—shipping marks and numbers should correspond with those on containers and invoices.
2. **Import License**
    Required by importer for certain commodities only.
3. **Used Clothing**
    Exporters are cautioned that commercial shipments of used clothing are prohibited in Liberia. The only exception is when shipments are consigned to charitable institutions and no commercial transaction is involved.
4. ***Consular Holidays**
    January 7, February 11, March 13, Good Friday, July 26, October 14, October 28, and November 29. All holidays generally observed in New York City.
    *Denotes changes since previous notice.

LIBYAN ARAB REPUBLIC, THE

SUMMARY OF SHIPPING DOCUMENTS REQUIRED
1. **Consular Documents Required for all commercial shipments:**
    (A) ***Certificate of Origin**—2—on general form—sold by commercial printers. The notarized certificate must be certified by the U.S. Arab Chamber of Commerce in New York prior to Consular legalization. The original and the carbon copy (with a self-addressed, stamped envelope and check or money order for $10.50) must be mailed to the Embassy in Washington for legalization. The legalized original will be returned, and the copy will be retained by the Embassy. If goods are not wholly manufactured but only finished in the United States, the "finishing manufacturer" must state that fact on the Certificate, showing the country of origin of the unfinished goods before their arrival in the United States. The name and address of the finished manufacturer must also be stated.

    All documents, other than Certificates of Origin, must bear the authentication of the U.S.A. Department of State when presented to the Embassy for legalization.

    All Certificates of Origin from Texas jurisdiction must be certified by the

American Arab Chamber of Commerce, 500 Jefferson Building, Houston, Texas 77002.

(B) **Commercial Invoice**—1—Consular legalization not required. Certification not necessary. Must be signed by exporter and show full details, itemized expenses and CIF value.

2. *Consular Fee

Check or Money Order made payable to the Embassy of Libya.

Legalization of Certificate of Origin .... $10.50 each

*Denotes changes since previous notice.

MALAGASY REPUBLIC (MADAGASCAR)

SUMMARY OF SHIPPING DOCUMENTS REQUIRED

No Consular Documents Required

1. **Shipping Documents Required regardless of value and mode of shipment:**

   (A) **Commercial Invoice**—6—showing separately all costs and shipping charges. If the invoice is in English, the importer must furnish the customs with a translation in French. Goods must be carefully described with their weights (net and gross) and measurements; must contain the names of the exporter and consignee; give the number and types of packages; marks and numbers on packages; an accurate specific and complete description of merchandise; terms of sale; the unit price and total FOB value; and preferably should add the ocean freight, insurance and incidental expenses. Invoices must be certified true and correct and signed.

   (B) **Packing List**—3—Packing and weighing list—should describe accurately and in detail the contents of each case or container included in the shipment and give the net and gross weights, together with the FOB value of each commodity. Full specifications should always accompany shipments of machinery and appliances.

   (C) **Pro-forma Invoice**—3—required by importer to obtain Import License—must contain FOB, C&F, or CIF unit prices (following the sale contract), approximate date of delivery and terms of payment—signed by exporter.

   (D) **Bill of Lading**—3—originals—1—non-negotiable stamped and dated according to original—should show gross and net weights; volume of measurement; marks and identification; name and address of importer or consignee. Shipping marks and numbers of the bills of lading, containers and commercial invoices should correspond. Must be signed by shipper or his agent. "To order bills of lading are permitted."

   The air waybill replaces the bill of lading on air cargo shipments. Parcel post shipments should be accompanied by a postal receipt.

   (E) **Certificate of Origin**—when required—2 copies—general form—sold by commercial printers—certified by the New York Chamber of Commerce and Industry, which requires an additional notarized copy for its files.

2. **Import License**—Required by importer for all commodities. Licenses are valid for six months. Goods should be shipped within that period. No tolerance in value or weight permitted.

3. **Special Documents**

   Sanitary Certificate—Required for certain imports of live animals or animal carcasses. The importer should be consulted in each case. In addition imports of animals and food grains for animal feed are subject to preliminary authorization. These animals and food grains require a sanitary certificate and a certificate of origin.

4. *Consular Fees: (paid by cash only)
   Commercial Invoice (when required) $2.20
   Certificate of Origin(when required) 2.20
   Pro—Forma Invoice (when required) 2.20
   Other Documents (when required) 2.20

5. *Consular Holidays
   March 29, Easter Monday, May 23, and June 26. All holidays generally observed in New York City.
   *Denotes changes since previous notice.

MALAWI

SUMMARY OF SHIPPING DOCUMENTS REQUIRED
No Consular Documents Required
1. **Shipping Documents Required**
   (A) **Commercial Invoice**—2—must show full selling price to purchaser in Malawi—name and address of the exporter and consignee—date of invoice—date of purchase—number and kind of packages—accurate, specific, and complete description of the goods—net and gross weights—value—if needed an itemized list of expenses—signed by exporter in ink.

   A separate invoice should be made out for merchandise of each country of origin, and a summary invoice prepared, if a shipment is covered by more than one invoice.

   (B) **Certificate of Origin**—2—Malawi Form 18—sold by commercial printers—must be filled out completely, except part B when it does not apply to the exporter—signed in ink by a responsible member of, or person in the employ of the export firm. A separate certificate of origin form is required for goods of each different country of origin.

   (C) **Bills of Lading**—original and 1 non-negotiable—no special requirements—"To Order" bills allowed. Shipping marks and numbers must correspond exactly with those on other shipping documents and on the merchandise.

2. **Import License**
   Required by importer for some items—valid for 6 months from date of issue—favorable consideration given to any reasonable increase in value.

3. **Holidays**
   All holidays generally observed in New York City.
   See Form 18 (front and back).

MALAYSIA
West Malaysia (Malaya) and East Malaysia (Sabah and Sarawak)

SUMMARY OF SHIPPING DOCUMENTS REQUIRED
No Consular Documents Required
Shipping Documents Required
1. **All Commercial Shipments regardless of value:**
   (A) **Commercial Invoice**—3—on shipper's letterhead—must be signed and show

country of origin. Invoices must show quantities, weights, proper description of the merchandise, and all itemized expenses to CIF value. Importer must submit the original copy of the invoice to the customs authorities for clearance purposes.

(B) **Certificate of Origin**—2—on general form—sold by commercial printers— required only when requested by importer, who may need it for banking purposes in cases where dollar exchange is supplied by Malaysian authorities. Must be certified by the New York Chamber of Commerce and Industry, which requires one additional notarized copy for its files.

2. **Import License**
   The vast majority of goods from the dollar area are freely importable under Open General License. Specific import license required by importer for a short list of goods, including arms, ammunition and explosives, live animals, plants and seeds, and a few others.

3. **Special Documents**
   Health Certificate required for live plants, planting materials, live animals and meat carcasses.

4. **Embassy Holidays**
   All holidays generally observed in New York City.
   *Denotes changes since previous notice.

MALI

SUMMARY OF SHIPPING DOCUMENTS REQUIRED
No Consular Documents Required
1. **Shipping Documents Required**
   (A) **Commercial Invoice**—2—must show names of exporter and consignee— number and types of packages—marks and numbers on packages—net and gross weights—CIF value—terms of sale—accurate, specific and complete description of merchandise—signed by shipper.

   Must show declaration of origin on the invoice (preferably in French) should be notarized or certified by the New York Chamber of Commerce and Industry, in which case an additional copy is required for the Chamber's files.

   (B) **Bills of Lading**—no special regulations—marks of identification and names and address of consignee must be clearly indicated. Shipping marks and numbers on bills of lading, on invoices and on the goods must correspond exactly. A packing list is recommended.

2. **Import License**
   Required by importer—valid 6 months—may be extended for 3 months under justifiable circumstances.

3. **Holidays**
   All holidays generally observed in New York City.

MALTA

SUMMARY OF SHIPPING DOCUMENTS REQUIRED
No Consular Documents Required
1. **Shipping Documents Required**
   (A) **Commercial Invoice**—2—must contain all particulars regarding marks and

GOODS EXPORTED TO MALAWI — CERTIFICATE OF ORIGIN

QUANTITY	DESCRIPTION OF GOODS	WEIGHT	INVOICE NUMBER AND DATE	VALUE

I, the undersigned being ....(Status — e.g. Sales Manager, Partner,

Secretary, etc.) of ....

(name of grower ☐, manufacturer ☐, producer ☐, processor ☐, seller ☐, supplier ☐ — place 'X' in appropriate box) of

....

(place and country), being duly authorised and having the means of knowing, do hereby certify that —

PART A
to be completed
in **all cases**

(A)   the goods of the description, quantity, weight and value set out hereon were wholly

grown or produced or were subjected to their last process of manufacture *in ....

....(name of country).

PART B applies only to
manufactures eligible for
preferential duties
(See Note 1)

(B)   ii)   the expenditure in material produced or in labour performed in the said country

was not less than ....% of the actual factory cost
(as defined in Note 2) of the goods in their finished state; **and**

(ii)   for textile fabrics in the piece the following processes were performed in the

said country...

....

Form 18.

430

I further declare that I will furnish to the Customs authorities of Malawi or to their nominee for inspection at any time such accounts and other evidence as may be requested for the purpose of verifying the correctness of this Certificate or of any part of it.

Date..

Signature ....

* See Note 1

For Notes on completing this Form see over

MALAWI CUSTOMS AND EXCISE DEPARTMENT

<u>NOTES</u>

1.   Goods wholly grown or produced or subjected to their last process of manufacture in the countries set out below may be eligible for preferential duties —

(a)   the United Kingdom, the Channel Islands and the Isle of Man;

(b)   the independent countries of the British Commonwealth and any dependent territory, protectorate, or protected state of any independent country of the British Commonwealth;

(c)   any territory administered by the Government of an independent country of the British Commonwealth under the trusteeship system of the United Nations;

(d)   the Republic of Ireland, South West Africa and the Republic of South Africa.

For the purposes of Part A and of this Note the term **Manufacture** is deemed not to include such operations as, inter alia, diluting, packing, bottling, drying, assembling (i.e. the mere putting together of finished parts), sorting, cleaning, mixing or blending which does not result in the formation of different product, heating which does not bring a permanent change, and the mere sub-division of an otherwise finished article.

2.   The actual factory cost means solely the factory cost of such goods in their finished state as represented by expenditure in material produced and/or labour performed and that in the calculation of the percentage the following items have been excluded: Manufacturer's profit, or remuneration of any trader, agent, broker or other person dealing in the goods in their finished condition; royalties, customs or excise duties paid in respect of the goods or materials contained in such goods; cost of outside packages or any cost of packing the goods thereinto, any cost of conveying, shipping or insuring the goods, or other administration selling or distribution expense incurred in connection with the goods subsequent to their manufacture. In the case of goods which have at some state entered into commerce or undergone a process of manufacture in a foreign country, only that material and/or labour which is added to or expended on the goods after their final return to the country shall be regarded as the produce or manufacture of that country in calculating the percentage.

Form 18 (continued). Export Forms, Hazardous Materials Labels, etc. can be purchased from Unz & Co., 190 Baldwin Ave., P.O. Box 308, Jersey City, N.J. 07303.

431

numbers on the packages—description and origin of the goods—unit price of the articles, apart from the total value. The invoice must contain a declaration signed by the manufacturer or supplier, or by a duly authorized person, to the effect that the amount shown on the invoice is correct and contains a true and full statement of the particulars of the goods and of the price inclusive of the cost of transport and insurance actually paid or to be paid for the goods and of the actual quality and that no different invoice of the goods mentioned in the said invoice has been or will be furnished to any one. If the cost of transport and insurance is not paid, or known, by the manufacturer or supplier, a statement to that effect should be added to the declaration. Goods will not be released from Customs if the declaration is not shown on the invoice.

(B) **Certificate of Origin**—2—when required—general form—sold by commercial printers—certified by the New York Chamber of Commerce and Industry, which requires one additional notarized copy for its files.

(C) **Bills of Lading**—must show measurements—gross and net weights—marks of identification—and name and address of consignee. "To Order" bills of lading are acceptable.

2. **Import License**

Several items require licenses to be obtained by importer—validity 8 months— no tolerance permitted on value, weight or quantity.

3. **Special Documents**

(A) **Sanitary Certificate**—required for fresh, chilled or frozen meat and meat products.

(B) **Phytosanitary Certificate**—required for plant and plant products. The requirement is normally waived whenever: (1) the material is deep frozen (in which case a certificate to this effect is required) or (2) the material is no longer in the raw state, i.e., it has been canned, or subjected to industrial processing which would take care of the phytosanitary aspect.

4. **Consular Holidays**

Good Friday, May 1, May 23, June 13, August 15, September 8, and December 26. All holidays generally observed in New York City.

*Denotes changes since previous notice.

MAURITANIA

SUMMARY OF SHIPPING DOCUMENTS REQUIRED
No Consular Documents Required
1. **Shipping Documents Required**

(A) **Commercial Invoice**—2—no special form—must contain names of exporter and consignee—number and types of packages—marks and numbers of packages—net and gross weights—CIF value—terms of sale—accurate, specific and complete description of the merchandise.

(B) **Certificate of Origin**—2—required on general form—sold by commercial printers—certified by the New York Chamber of Commerce and Industry, which requires one additional notarized copy for its files. A combined invoice and certificate of origin may be used in place of the commercial invoice and certificate of origin.

(C) **Bills of Lading**—no special regulations. Marks of identification and name and address of the consignee clearly shown. Marks and numbers on bills of lading, invoices and the goods should correspond exactly. A packing list is recommended.

2.   *Import License
Required by importer for all goods in excess of 4000 Ougiyas—validity 6 months—may be extended in exceptional circumstances for 3 to 6 months. Goods must be shipped before expiration of license. Tolerance of 5000 Ougiyas over and above the value given on the import license.

3.   Consular Holidays
All holidays generally observed in New York City.

MAURITIUS

SUMMARY OF SHIPPING DOCUMENTS REQUIRED
No Consular Documents Required

1.   Shipping Documents Required
(A) Commercial Invoice—2—no special form—must show FOB value—CIF value must be shown in the body of the invoice and then must show the following charges at the foot of the invoice: ocean freight, insurance stating that each has been included in the selling price to the purchaser. Must contain a certificate by the exporter that the particulars are correct and that no other invoice for the goods has been or will be issued. Invoices covering cotton piece goods should show length, width and weight of each piece and the weight per square meter in the metric system. Declaration of all classes of goods containing cotton, wool, artificial silk or fibers must be strictly accurate.

(B) *Combined Certificate of Value and of Origin—2 copies—for U.S. goods in order to benefit from preferential tariff treatment. The information required by the form may be written, typed, or printed directly on the invoice or the form itself may be obtained from the Mauritius Embassy, 2308 Wyoming Avenue, N.W., Washington, D.C. 20008. Must be certified by the New York Chamber of Commerce and Industry, which requires one additional notarized copy for its files.

(C) Bills of Lading—no special regulations.

2.   Import License
Most goods can be freely imported. Some items require a specific license which are freely available—validity usually one year from date of issuance.

3.   Holidays
All holidays generally observed in New York City.
*Denotes changes since previous notice.
See Form 10-505 (front and back).

MEXICO

SUMMARY OF SHIPPING DOCUMENTS REQUIRED
Special Information
The legalization of commercial invoices must be obtained at the Consulate established in the country and place where the seller issued the invoice. If there is no Consulate, then at the nearest Consulate or at the one located in the maritime port of shipment. The Consulate advises that despite the above, documents can be legalized in any Mexican Consulate in the country where the invoice was issued.

Commercial invoices must be legalized before the arrival of the carrier in Mexico (not on the same date but prior to). Heavy fines will be imposed by the authorities on

Port Louis, this _____ *19* _____

INVOICE *of* _____

Consigned by _____

To _____

Shipped by S.S. " _____ "

Indent

Reference No. _____

Country of Origin	Marks and numbers on packages	QUANTITY AND DESCRIPTION OF GOODS	Selling price to purchaser	
				AMOUNT

F.O.B., C.I.F or C.I.F.C.I.

Enumerate the following charges and state whether each amount has been included in or excluded from the above selling price to purchaser:—

(1) Sea Freight _____

(2) Marine Insurance _____

Form No. 10-505 Mauritius   Printed and Sold by Unz & Co., An Affiliate of Scott Ptg Corp., 190 Baldwin Ave., J. C., N. J. 07306

Form 10-505 (front).

434

SCHEDULE II

Combined Certificate of Value and of Origin to be written, typed or printed on Invoice of goods for exportation to the Country

(1) Here insert Manager, Chief Clerk or as the case may be

(2) Here insert name of firm or company.

(3) Here insert name of city or country

(4) These words should be omitted where the manufacturer or supplier himself signs the Certificate

.... (1) ....

of (2) .... of (3) ....

MANUFACTURER SUPPLIER of the goods enumerated in this invoice hereby declare that I (4) have the authority to make and sign this certificate on behalf of the aforesaid MANUFACTURER SUPPLIER and that I have the means of knowing and do hereby certify as follows:—

VALUE

1. That this invoice is in all requests correct and contains a true and full statement of the price actually paid or to be paid for the said goods, and the actual quantity thereof.

2. That no different invoice of the goods mentioned in the said invoice has been or will be furnished to anyone; and that no arrangements or understanding affecting the purchase price of the said goods has been or will be made or entered into between the said exporter and purchaser, or by anyone on behalf of either of them either by way of discount, rebate, compensation, or in any manner whatever other than as fully shown in the Invoice.

(5) Here insert particulars of any special arrangement

or as follows. (5)..

....

3. The F.O.B. value shown includes any purchasing or agent's commission, the cost of packages or packing for export, carriage to the port of shipment, and all otherexpenses, incidental to placing the goods on board ship.

(4a) and (4b) Insert which part of the Empire

ORIGIN

(Delete whichever of 4 (a) or 4 (b) is not applicable. If 4 (a) is used, delete 5 and 6. If 4 (b) is used insert required particulars in 5 and 6.)

4. (a) That every article mentioned in the said Invoice has been *wholly* produced or manufactured in (4) a...................

4. (b) That every article mentioned in the said Invoice has been *wholly* produced or *partially* produced or manufactured in (4) b

(5a) Insert which part of the Empire

(5b) Insert which part of the Empire

5. As regards those articles only partially produced or manufactured in 5 (b)...................

(a) That the final process or processes of manufacture have been performed in that part of

(b) That the expenditure in material produced in 5 (b)................... labour performed in and or 5 (b). subject to qualifications hereunder. in each and every article is not less than 25%, 50% or 75% of the case may be according to the provisions of the Preferential Tariff Regulation, 1958 or works cost of such article in its finished state. (See Note below).

(6) Insert which part of the Empire

6. That in the calculation in such proportion of produce or labour of the (6)................... none of the following items have been included or considered:—

"Manufacturer's profit or remuneration of any trader, agent, broker or other person dealing in "the articles in their finished condition; royalties; cost of outside packages or any cost or "packing the goods thereinto; any cost of conveying, insuring or shipping the goods subsequent "to their manufacture".

NOTE—In the case of goods which have at some stage entered into the commerce or undergone a process of manufacture in a foreign country, only that labour and material which is expended on or added to the goods after their return to the Empire Country shall be regarded as the produce or manufacture of the Empire Country in calculating the proportion of Empire Country labour and material in the factory or works cost of the finished article.

Dated at PORT LOUIS this.....................day of ....19....

Witness............................ *Signature* ....

Form 10-505 (back). Export Forms, Hazardous Materials Labels, etc. can be purchased from Unz & Co., 190 Baldwin Ave., P.O. Box 308, Jersey City, N.J. 07303.

ocean freight shipments, if commercial invoices are not legalized prior to steamer arrival.

*However, if a shipment originates in a third country, is flown to the United States, and trans-shipped from the United States overland or by steamer to Mexico, consular legalization of the invoice must be obtained in the third country. The single exception to the rule concerns shipments to Petroleos Mexicanos. (Consular fees for invoices for Petroleos Mexicanos: Free of Charge).

Consular Documents Required

1. **Ocean Freight & Overland Shipments valued over $80 FOB Carrier:**

    (A) **Commercial Invoice**—5—in Spanish or English. If in English, a Spanish trans-lation of the invoice is required. Consular legalization required. Original and 2 copies returned to shipper. Fourth and fifth copies retained by Consulate. All copies must be signed manually by the actual seller to the effect "that the value and other details in the invoice are true and correct." It is of the utmost importance that legalized invoices are in the possession of the consignee before the arrival of the goods in Mexico, otherwise, heavy fines will be imposed by the Mexican authorities.

    Invoice must show the following information:

    (a) Place and date of issue.

    (b) Name and address of the consignee.

    (c) FOB value and itemized charges to CIF. In the event charges are not avail-able when invoices are prepared, an approximate of charges may be shown.

    (d) Port of entry and name of customs broker at such port.

    (e) Shipper's invoice number and customers order number.

    (f) Total number of packages (indicating whether they are case, cartons, crates, etc.) and total weights in Kilos (gross, legal and net).

    (g) The description of the merchandise must be definite and concise. Use of trademarks, patent names, abbreviations, etc., are not accepted nor recognized.

    (h) Characteristics such as brand name, model and serial number, motor num-ber, manufacturers' trade-marks, etc. (Applicable in shipments of auto-mobiles, machinery, pharmaceuticals, etc.) must be shown on shipments of merchandise having such characteristics. Failure to comply will impose a burden on the customs broker at the Mexican port of entry and will necessi-tate the opening of cases by customs officials.

    When a shipper wishes to furnish his customer with detailed packing information—too lengthy to include in the invoice—a packing list may be attached to the invoice. This packing list needs no consular legalization. Invoice must still have the information requested in (f) above.

    (B) **Missing Invoices**—Quite frequently a set of invoices legalized by the Consulate is subsequently lost or misplaced. Instead of informing the Consulate accord-ingly, the shipper prepares a new set and in the customary manner either mails it or takes it to the Consulate for legalization.

    This has two contrary effects harmful to all concerned: (1) the new legaliza-tion date is later than the arrival of the shipment in Mexico, and a fine is assessed in Mexico against the consignee which creates a problem between him and the U.S. shipper; and, (2) if the missing invoice is located at the Central Customs Bureau in Mexico, an investigation will be made to ascertain whether only one shipment or two shipments of identical merchandise was made to the same consignee by the same U.S. firm.

All of this can be easily avoided if, in each case, the Consulate in New York is notified in writing of the missing legalized invoices at the time he is requested to legalize the new set.

2. **Freight Shipments valued at $80 FOB Carrier or less:**
   Commercial Invoice—3—in English or Spanish—same as in above 1(A)—notarization or consular legalization not required—must be in possession of consignee or agent before arrival of merchandise in order to avoid heavy fines.

3. **Air Cargo & Parcel Post Shipments regardless of value:**
   Commercial Invoice—3—in English or Spanish—see 1(A) signed by shipper—prepared as in Freight Shipments. Consular legalization not required—must accompany shipment. Heavy fines will be imposed for shipments arriving without invoices. If value of merchandise is over $16.00 package must show import license number or bear notation to the effect that no import permit is required.

4. **Import Licenses**
   Agricultural Products
   Importers in Mexico must obtain import licenses in advance for most shipments including plants, plant parts, and plant products, including fresh, frozen, and dried fruits, and vegetable and vegetable oils.

   Applications for licenses should be made to the Jefe, Departamento de Aplicacion Cuarentenaria, Direccion General de Sanidad Vegetal, Secretaria de Agricultura y Ganaderia, Balderas 94, Mexico 1, D.F. Must include the names and addresses of the consignor and consignee, the locality and country of origin, the name and quantity of plants or plant products, the port of entry and the port of embarkation.

   Non Agricultural Products
   Importers in Mexico must obtain licenses for non agricultural products from Secretaria de Industria y Commercio (Ministry of Industry and Commerce) Avenida Cuauhtemoc No. 80, Mexico, D.F.

5. **Special Documents**
   (A) **Sanitary Certificate**—4—in English or Spanish—required on shipment of live-stock and animal products, seeds, plants and plant products—issued by the U.S. Department of Agriculture or other competent state or municipal authorities. Original legalized by Consulate.
   (B) **Letter of Correction**—4—in English or Spanish—1 copy retained by Consulate —must be presented to Consulate before arrival of shipment at the Mexican port of entry.

6. ***Consular Fees**
   The equivalency in United States currency is given at the current/official rate of exchange of $22.727 per one dollar.

***

	Mexican cy.	U.S. cy.
Certificates of analysis	625.00	27.50
Certificates of Masters and Senders	500.00	22.00
Certificates of Constitution of Foreign companies	5,000.00	220.00

	Mexican cy.	U.S. cy.
Correction certificates in manifests	250.00	11.00
Certificates covering imports of firearms, explosives, etc.	1,875.00	82.50
Certificates of Free Sale	625.00	27.50
Immigrants' health certificates	500.00	22.00
Certificates of Origin	500.00	22.00
Certificates petitioned by third party	250.00	11.00
Certificates of residence to foreigners	1,250.00	55.00
Veterinary health certificates	125.00	5.50
Health certificates of animal products	1,250.00	55.00
Health certificates of live vegetable plants	625.00	27.50
Health certificates of vegetable products	1,250.00	55.00
Survival certificates to aliens	500.00	22.00
Certificates to hunters	3,500.00	154.00
Certificates of vaccination	75.00	3.30
Identity & Travel documents	2,500.00	110.00
Duplicates of Cargo Manifests (sea traffic)	750.00	33.00
Commercial invoices, per set	250.00	11.00
Legalization of signatures	250.00	11.00
Passenger lists	1,250.00	55.00
Certification of household effects to aliens	2,500.00	110.00
Crew lists	1,250.00	55.00
Crew lists of yachts and/or similar crafts up to 9 crew members	250.00	11.00
Statements on shortage or surplus of parcels on sea shipments	500.00	22.00
Letters of correction, per set of invoices	250.00	11.00
Cargo Manifests (sea traffic)	2,500.00	110.00
Provisional Bills of (sea) Navigation	2,500.00	110.00
Certification of official transit permits of human remains	500.00	22.00

***

The decree also changes the fees applicable to powers of attorney or other legal documents granted through the Consulates. These fees are not listed here because of the instruments' variety, but are immediately available when arrangement of details is accomplished.

***

	Mexican cy.	U.S. cy.
Visas on aliens' passports when no agreement is existent	500.00	22.00

***

Certain fees for services rendered to Mexican nationals have likewise changed and are posted at the Consulate for their guidance.

***

The fees for Immigration Services remain unchanged as of this date.

***

Should a new official rate of exchange be set in the future, the equivalents given above will vary accordingly as of the setting date.

***

7. **Freight Information Services**—The General Traffic Agency (Secretariat of Communications and Transportation) located at Avenida Insurgentes Sur, No. 377-104 Mexico 11, D.F., invites American shippers and travelers to make free inquiries to that office in connection with Mexican freight rates, ship facilities, rail freight and express rates, passenger fares, etc. Prompt and efficient service will be given to all inquiries.

8. **Mexico Insurance**
All shipments must be insured in domestic insurance markets (except shipments financed by U.S. Agency for International Development or the United Nations and its specialized agencies).

9. **Consular Holidays**
February 5, March 21, Good Friday (½ day), May 1, May 5, September 16, October 12, and November 20. All holidays generally observed in New York City.
*Denotes changes since previous notice.
See Form 10-510.

MOROCCO

SUMMARY OF SHIPPING DOCUMENTS REQUIRED
No Consular Documents Required
1. **Shipping Documents Required**
Commercial Invoice—3—certified as to current export market prices and country of origin by the New York Chamber of Commerce and Industry, which retains one copy. Must contain detailed description of merchandise. Copy retained by Chamber must bear the following notarized affidavit:

"I hereby swear that the prices stated in this invoice are the current market prices for the merchandise described herein and that the origin of these goods is the United States of America, and I accept full responsibility for any inaccuracies or errors therein."

(Signature)

2. **Import License**—Required by importer for most goods. Preference is given to essential commodities. Importer must deposit 25% of the FOB value of the goods when applying for import license, which are usually valid for six months and carry the right to foreign exchange. It is recommended that U.S. shipper ascertain that the necessary license has been issued and is in possession of the importer. There is a list of prohibited imports for which no licenses are issued at this time.

3. **Consular Fees**
Consular legalization for commercial invoice
   (if requested) .... $1.25 each
(Must be notarized and authenticated by County Clerk, prior to presentation to Consulate)

4. ***Consular Holidays**
February 12, Holy Thursday, Good Friday, Easter Monday, May 1, May 23, October 14, October 28, Election Day, November 18, November 29, December 24, and December 31. All holidays generally observed in New York City.
*Denotes changes since previous notice.

NEPAL

SUMMARY OF SHIPPING DOCUMENTS REQUIRED
No Consular Documents Required
1. **Shipping Documents Required**
(A) **Commercial Invoice**—Original and 3 copies sent to consignee—must be signed and contain complete detailed description of the merchandise—quantities— weights—country of origin etc.—must show all itemized expenses to CIF value.
(B) **Certificate of Origin**—3—when required—general form—sold by commercial printers—certified by the New York Chamber of Commerce and Industry, which requires one additional notarized copy for its files.
(C) **Bills of Lading**—2—weights and other measurements should be in metric units —the usual particulars should be shown—"To Order" bills of lading allowed— should show the name and address of the notify party at destination. The negotiable bill of lading, the draft on the importer, and all other relevant documents pertaining to the shipment should be forwarded to the banks through which payment is to be made.

2. **Import License**
Required by importer for all imports.

3. ***Consular Holidays**
February 18, April 13, October 10, December 26, and December 28. All holidays generally observed in New York City.
*Denotes changes since previous notice.

NETHERLANDS, THE

SUMMARY OF SHIPPING DOCUMENTS REQUIRED
No Consular Documents Required

MEXICAN COMMERCIAL INVOICE
Factura Comercial de las Mercancias

(Place and date of sale) (Lugar y fecha de la venta)

Vendor _____ of _____
Vendido por   (Name)   de   (Place and street address) (Lugar y domicilio)

Sold to _____ of _____
Vendido a   (Purchaser)   de   (Place and street address) (Lugar y domicilio)

Consigned to _____ of _____
A la Consignación de   (Mexican Customs Broker if known) de   (Place and street address) (Lugar y domicilio)

Shipped by _____
Despachadas por   (Steamer, Freight, Express, etc.)

via port of _____
(al puerto de)

MARCAS
(Marks)

Invoice Number _____ Customer's Order No. _____
Factura Numero   Pedido del Cliente No.

Vendor's Order No. _____ Terms _____
Envio del Vendedor No.   Terminos

Numbers Números)	Kind of Package (Clase de Bultos)	Weight in Kilos (Peso en Kilos)				DETAILED DESCRIPTION OF MERCHANDISE IN PLAIN COMMERCIAL TERMS (Especificación Comercial de las Mercancias)	Value in U.S.A. Dollars (Valor en Moneda Americana)
		Gross Weight Each Package (Bruto de Cada Bulto)	Net Weight Each Package (Neto de Cada Bulto)	Legal Weight Each Package (Legal de Cada Bulto)			

*I declare under oath that the value and specifications contained in this invoice are true and correct:

Declaro bajo protesta de decir verdad, que el valor y las declaraciones contenidas en esta factura son veridicas y correctas;

....
(Firm or Company Signature) (Firma)

....
(Signature of Individual)

*Must be vissed by consulate if value is over $80. F.O.B.

Form No. 10-510 Printed and Sold by Unz & Co., Division of Scott Printing Corp., 190 Baldwin Ave., Jersey City, N.J. 07306 — N.J. (201) 795-5400 / N.Y. (212) 344-2270

Form 10-510. Export Forms, Hazardous Materials Labels, etc. can be purchased from Unz & Co., 190 Baldwin Ave., P.O. Box 308, Jersey City, N.J. 07303.

441

1. **Shipping Documents Required**
   (A) **Commercial Invoice**—2—signed by shipper and mailed directly to consignee. Must show origin of merchandise, in addition to marks, numbers and type of containers, net gross weights, value, and accurate description of merchandise.
   (B) **Certificate of Origin**—2—when required—general form—sold by commercial printers—certified by the New York Chamber of Commerce and Industry, which requires one additional copy for its files.
   (C) **Bills of Lading**—2—no special requirements—the usual information should be shown. Generally shipments may be made freight collect.

2. **Import License**
   Most items from the United States may be imported freely without an import license. When required, permits are valid during the year of issue and 6 months of the ensuing year.
       Exchange is obtained through authorized banks. No exchange permit is required.

3. **Special Documents**
   (A) **Special documentary requirements**—Shippers should contact the ‚Consulate before attempting to ship any of the following products: butter, margarine, solid milk products, meat and meat products, fresh cherries, certain wines, shrubs, gooseberry shrubs, live plants and part of plants, animals and animal products.
   (B) **Health certificate**—Health certificates signed by the official veterinary surgeon at the place of origin are required for shipments of meat, meat products, animal fats, ground bones, blood meal, and fertilizers made from animal meal and bonemeal.
   (C) *****Type approval certificate**—Required for shipments of portable fire extinguishers, acetylene generators, pressure reducing valves, centrifuges, threshing machinery, lifts, explosive hammers, grinding machines, movable transporters, generators for electrical fencing, steam and vapor generating boilers, neon-transformers, some electricity meters, aerosols, gas apparatus, motorcars and Dutch watersupply equipment.
   (D) **Pre-packed Medicine**—Registration of pre-packed medicine is required.
       *****Consular Holidays**
   Washington's Birthday, Good Friday, Memorial Day, July 4, Labor Day, Columbus Day, Veterans Day, Thanksgiving Day, ˙and Christmas Day. All holidays generally observed in New York City.
   *Denotes changes since previous notice.

NEW ZEALAND

SUMMARY OF SHIPPING DOCUMENTS REQUIRED
No Consular Documents Required

1. **Shipping Documents Required for all commercial shipments.**
   (A) **Special Form Invoice and Certificate of Value and Origin**—3—signed by shipper and witnessed—sent to consignee—forms sold by commercial printers. All questions must be answered.
   (B) **Bills of Lading**—must show name of shipper and name and address of consignee—port of destination—description of goods—freight and other charges—date and signature of the carriers receipt on board of goods for shipment. Information must correspond with that shown on the invoices and on the packages.

2. **Import License**
Still required for certain imports. However, the authorities have progressively undertaken the necessary measures towards the liberalization of imports. At the present time, almost three-fourths of the country's imports require no import license (including most raw materials). Exchange permit is not required. Licenses are usually valid for annual licensing period in which they are issued. Extensions are granted for special reasons only. Carrying vessels must reach New Zealand ports prior to expiration date of import license.
3. **Special Documents**
   (A) **Sanitary Certificate**—issued by U.S. Department of Agriculture required for any plant in a form suitable for feeding to livestock—seeds used for agricultural purposes—cocoanut meal and copra cake—cotton seed meal—linseed, crushed, and linseed meal—soya bean, soya bean meal, soya bean cakes—a number of grains, and in general any grain, processed or unprocessed, in a form suitable for feeding to stock.
   (B) **Plant Health Certificate**—issued by competent authority—required for all fruits—plants and bulbs.
   *Holidays
   February 6, Good Friday, Easter Monday, June 3, and December 26. All Federal holidays observed in New York City.
   *Denotes changes since previous notice.
See Form 10-530.

NICARAGUA

SUMMARY OF SHIPPING DOCUMENTS REQUIRED

Special Information
Consular documents should be presented to Consulate as soon as bill of lading is obtained.

All commercial transactions originating in the New York Metropolitan area or States under the jurisdiction of the New York Consulate which requires legalization of the Commercial invoice, must be legalized at the New York Consulate regardless of port of exit. The jurisdiction of the New York Consulate covers the States of Connecticut, Maine, Maryland, Massachusetts, New Hampshire, New Jersey, New York, Pennsylvania, Rhode Island and Vermont.

No exporter or vendor of firearms and ammunition in the City or State of New York, or anywhere within the jurisdiction of the New York Consulate General may sell such arms or ammunition to Nicaragua without the express authority of the Consulate General. This requirement will be enforced in order to comply with the laws of the Government of Nicaragua and the Government of the United States relating to the sale of such materials.

Consular Documents Required
1. **Freight Shipment valued at $50 FOB or more:**
   (A) **Commercial Invoice**—5—in Spanish—legalized by Consulate—1 retained by Consulate. Must indicate country of origin in Spanish, e.g., "Esta mercaderia es procendente de los Estados Unidos de Norteamerica." Must contain detailed description of merchandise, and itemized signed account of all charges up to CIF.

INVOICE AND COMBINED CERTIFICATE OF VALUE AND ORIGIN FOR EXPORTS TO NEW ZEALAND

NORMAL

Exporter	Status of Seller		Page	Pages
	(delete terms inapplicable)			of
	Manufacturer			
	Grower			
	Producer			
	Supplier			

Sold to	
	Country of Origin

Ship/Airline, etc.	Sea/Airport of loading	
Sea/Airport of discharge	Final destination of goods	

Marks and numbers	Quantity and description of goods (including any discounts)	Current domestic value in currency of exporting country	Selling Price to Purchaser — State currency and whether FOB, CIF, etc.	
			@	Amount

Enumerate the following charge and state if amount has been included in the current domestic value	Amount in currency of exporting country	State if included	I, the undersigned, being the seller of the goods enumerated in this invoice (or manager, chief clerk, or other responsible person in the sole employ of and authorized by the seller to make and sign this certificate) have the means of knowing and hereby certify that this invoice, including continuation sheets if any, is MADE IN ACCORDANCE WITH THE VALUE CLAUSE PRINTED OVERLEAF.
Drawback or remission of duty			

Declaration of Packing Material Used

1. No packing material of any kind is used for the goods on this invoice.
2. I hereby certify that the material(s) used as packing for the goods on this invoice is (are)

3. No hay, straw, chaff, flax rug or rice husks have been used as packing material for the goods on this invoice.
4. I hereby declare that all timber used for the packing of goods listed in this invoice has been inspected and was to the best of my knowledge free of bark and visible signs of insect and fungal attack when goods were shipped to New Zealand.

SIGNED:

Form 10-530. Export Forms, Hazardous Materials Labels, etc. can be purchased from Unz & Co., 190 Baldwin Ave., P.O. Box 308, Jersey City, N.J. 07303.

444

(B) **Bill of Lading**—4—(2 originals and 2 non-negotiable)—legalized by Consulate and returned to shipper, who must send all 4 copies to consignee. Must show freight charges.

2. **Freight Shipments valued under $50 C&F or CIF:**
   No Consular documents required.

3. **Parcel Post Shipments valued at $10 FOB or more:**
   Commercial Invoice—5—in Spanish—legalized by Consulate—1 retained by Consulate—original and 1 copy must be sent to consignee—1 copy must be enclosed in package with a note to that effect on the wrapper. Must indicate FOB and CIF values.

4. **Parcel Post Shipments valued under $10 FOB:**
   No consular documents required. Original and 1 copy of the commercial invoice should be enclosed in package with a note to that effect on the wrapper.

5. **Air Cargo and Air Parcel Post Shipments valued at $100 FOB or more:**
   Commercial Invoice—5 consular legalization required—see (3)

6. **Air Cargo and Air Parcel Post Shipments valued under $100 C&F or CIF:**
   Original and 4 copies of the commercial invoice, signed by shipper, must accompany shipment. Consular legalization not required.

7. **Gifts and Samples**
   No consular fees on shipments of gifts or samples valued under $50 FOB. Documents must specify that this is a gift or sample as the case may be showing the name of the recipient. Legalization not required.

8. **Import License**
   No longer required to be presented to Consulate. Import declarations must be filed for all imports (government institutions and diplomatic legations exempt). Importers are no longer required to effect prior-deposits to obtain import permits whether in the essential or non-essential list.

   Note: We are told that if the merchandise is shipped before the import authorization is given, or if the FOB value of the invoice should exceed the FOB value shown on the import declaration, the importer will be subject to a fine of 25% of the CIF. We, therefore, suggest that shippers ascertain whether the authorization has been granted, and determine the value before shipment is made.

9. **Special Documents**
   (A) **Letter of Correction**—5—in Spanish, addressed to Consulate, explaining error and specifying correction. Commercial invoice number, date, marks, numbers, name of consignee and port of delivery must be shown—1 retained by Consulate.
   (B) **Animal Shipments**—Shippers of live animals or animal products must submit an import permit issued by the Ministerio de Agricultura and Ganaderia together with regular shipping documents to the Consulate for legalization. If the required import permit is not presented, documents will be rejected.
   (C) **Diplomatic Shipments**—For sea, air or mail shipments consigned to the American Embassy in Nicaragua, shippers must submit 4 copies of the commercial invoice and 4 bills of lading (for freight shipments). There are no consular fees.
   (D) **Documents other than shipping documents**—such as powers of attorney, fumigation and other certificates, must be notarized and authenticated by the County Clerk before presentation to Consulate.

10. **Arrangement of Documents before Presentation to Consulate**

For Consulate — 1 Commercial Invoice)

For Shipper — 4 Commercial Invoice)stapled together

2 Original Bills of Lading)

2 Non-Neg copies of Bills of Lading

Both sets must then be clipped together.

11. **Legalization Fees**

All documents must be accompanied by 2 - 15¢ postage stamps to cover mailing charges of documents by Consulate to the proper Government Authorities in Nicaragua.

The following legalization fees are payable by check to the Consulate General of Nicaragua.

Ocean Freight, Air Cargo and Air Parcel Post Shipments CIF value of shipment from:

$50 - $100	$20.00 per set
$501 - $1,000	$25.00 per set
$1,001 — $10,000	$35.00 per set
over $10,000	$50.00 per set

The above charges cover bills of lading and commercial invoices and extra copies, if requested. Documents will be returned immediately.

Regular Parcel Post shipments valued over $10	$10.00
Authentication fee of the signature of the County Clerk on any kind of Documents	25.00
Letter of Correction	15.00
Certificate of Analysis	25.00
Certificate of Origin	25.00
Cargo Manifests	100.00
Additional Cargo Manifests	25.00
Manifests in Ballast	50.00
Passenger Lists	25.00
Crew Lists	25.00
Store List	25.00
Letter of Correction on Manifests	25.00
Certificates covering importation of firearms, explosives, etc.	50.00
Sanitation Certificates	25.00
Legalizing duplicate set of Documents	10.00
Certificates of Free Sale	25.00
Veterinary Health Certificate	25.00
Health Certificates of Animal Products	25.00
Visas for U.S. Citizens (U.S. Citizens require only a tourist card)	Gratis

Holidays

Good Friday, Election Day, and December 31. All holidays generally observed in New York City.

*Denotes changes since previous notice.

NIGER

SUMMARY OF SHIPPING DOCUMENTS REQUIRED

1. **Shipping Documents Required**

(A) **Commercial Invoice**—2—must contain names of exporter and consignee—

number and types of packages—marks and numbers on packages—net and
gross weights—CIF value—terms of sale and an accurate, specific and complete description.

(B) **Certificate of Origin**—2—on general form—sold by commercial printers—
certified by the New York Chamber of Commerce and Industry, which requires
one additional notarized copy for its files.

(C) **Bills of Lading**—marks of identification and name and address of consignee
must be clearly indicated—shipping marks and numbers on bills of lading,
invoices, and the goods themselves should correspond exactly. A packing list is
recommended.

2.   **Import License**
Required by importer for many products—validity 6 months—may be extended for 3 months on reliable proof from the supplier. Goods must be shipped
before the expiration of the license.

3.   **Holidays**
All holidays generally observed in New York City.

NIGERIA

SUMMARY OF SHIPPING DOCUMENTS REQUIRED
No Consular Documents Required
1.   **Shipping Documents Required for all Commercial Shipments regardless of
value:**

(A) **Special Nigerian Form Invoice and Declaration of Value**—2—sold by commercial printers. Certified as to current export market prices and country of origin
by the New York Chamber of Commerce and Industry, which requires one
additional notarized copy for its files bearing the following affidavit signed by
an authorized employee of the company:
"I, (name, title, name of company), hereby swear that the prices stated in this
invoice are the exact and current export market prices for the merchandise
described. I further swear that the origin of these goods is the United States
of America, and I accept full responsibility for any inaccuracies or errors
therein."
Invoices must show FOB and CIF values and all itemized charges. If the shipper is not the actual producer of the goods the manufacturer's or supplier's
invoice must also be submitted to the Chamber for the purpose of checking
prices. This invoice is returned to the shipper.

(B) **Bills of Lading**—a separate set of bills of lading must be prepared for each port
or interior point, that is, bills of lading must not include cargo ultimately destined for more than one Nigerian port or interior point, i.e., cargo destined for
Lagos on one bill of lading, destined for Apapa on another, etc. Description of
cargo must be complete on bills of lading and correct in every detail. Trade
names must be qualified by a brief description of the goods.

2.   **Import License**
Required by importer for a short list of items—valid to the date shown thereon
—goods must be shipped before expiration date—no tolerances allowed.

3.   **Nigerian Government Announces List of Banned and Licensed Goods**
(A) As follow up to Head of States October 1 National Day speech, Permanent
Secretary Minister of Finance Shehu Musa, announced that 9 consumer goods
have been banned from import and 26 other goods require an import license.

Though the measure is effective as of October 1, orders shipped before that date or for which "Irrevocable Letters of Credit" were opened on or before September 21, will be allowed into the country if they arrive in Nigerian territory by October 31 (Air) or December 31 (Ship). The announced purpose of the measure is to reduce revenue fluctuations, conserve foreign exchange and curb the taste for imported goods.

(B) Banned items are as follows: pearls, precious and semi-precious stones, Christmas cards, greeting cards and calendars, almanacs and diaries, toothpicks and packaged or containerized rice of less than 50 kilogrammes.

(C) Goods placed under license are as follows: tomato puree and paste, mattresses, mattress supports, cushions, gramophone records, recorded tapes and toys, salted or dried meat, loudspeakers, amplifiers, microphone, razor blades, soups of all descriptions, spices, cameras, projectors and all cinematographic accessories, musical instruments, socks and stockings, clocks and watches, brandy, gins, wines of all kinds, sunshades, binoculars and sunglasses (other than medical ones).

(D) Other significant measures affecting trade were: that the duty on built-up trucks, lorries, pick-up and delivery vans was reduced from 50 percent to 20 percent; duty on built-up refrigerators was increased from 40 to 50 percent; import shipments valued at more than 100,000 naira (dollars 156.000) will need to receive foreign exchange clearance from Ministry Trade in addition to Central Bank; Letters of Credit will be allocated by sector at beginning of each financial year.

4. **Special Documents**
    Sanitary Certificate—Required from the U.S. Department of Agriculture for certain animals, animal products, plants, seeds and soil.

5. *****Consular Fees**
    Consular Legalization (when requested) .... $3.27 (per signature)
        When a shipper requests consular legalization, shipping documents will generally be returned in the afternoon, if they have been presented early in the day. Otherwise, they will be ready next business day.

6. *****Consular Holidays**
    February 12, February 16, April 16, April 19, May 31, July 4, September 6, October 1, October 11, October 25, November 25, December 25, and December 26. All holidays generally observed in New York City.
    *Denotes changes since previous notice.
See Form 10-620 (front and back).

NORWAY

SUMMARY OF SHIPPING DOCUMENTS REQUIRED
No Consular Documents Required
1. **Shipping Documents Required for all shipments regardless of mode of transportation:**
    (A) **Commercial Invoice**—at least 2 copies—no special requirements as to form, but should show all necessary information to enable customs officials to clear the shipment, including gross and net weights. If shipment is made up of different types of merchandise, packed together, the net weight of each type must be indicated. Should also show the import license number if such license is required.

(B) **Certificate of Origin**—2—when required by consignee—on general form—sold by commercial printers—certified by the New York Chamber of Commerce and Industry, which requires one additional notarized copy for its files.

2. **Import License**

The list of goods subject to import license has been steadily reduced since 1959 for commodities originating in countries of the so called free-list area (which includes the United States). There is a short list of goods requiring import licenses, which may be issued by either the Ministry of Commerce or the Ministry of Agriculture, depending on the type of import. Issuance of license guarantees availability of foreign exchange.

3. **Special Documents**

The following commodities require a prior special permission from the Ministry of Agriculture: Live animals; meat; meat products and guts (fresh or preserved); dairy products; eggs; honey; potatoes; most vegetables; fruits and berries (fresh or preserved); live plants or parts thereof; potato-starch; glucose and foods made of flour; ice cream with fats but not cocoa; starch or malt extract.

4. ***Consular Fees**

For legalization of any document (when requested) .... $2.50 each

5. ***Consular Holidays**

February 16, April 16, April 19, May 1, May 17, May 31, July 4, September 6, October 11, November 2, November 11, November 25, and December 26. All holidays generally observed in New York.

*Denotes changes since previous notice.

OMAN

SUMMARY OF SHIPPING DOCUMENTS REQUIRED

1. **Consular Documents Required for all Commercial Shipments:**

(A) ***Commercial Invoice**—3—must contain an accurate description of goods—weights, quantities and values—and a signed statement that the invoice is true and correct. Must be certified by the U.S. Arab Chamber of Commerce, which retains one copy for its files. Legalized by the Consulate which retains one copy and the original is returned to the shipper.

(B) ***Certificate of Origin**—3—on general form—sold by commercial printers—must contain a statement that the material is of U.S.A. origin—the name of the manufacturer of the material must be shown—certified by the U.S. Arab Chamber of Commerce, which retains one copy for its files. Legalized by the Consulate, which retains one copy and the original is returned to the shipper.

(C) **Bills of Lading**—2—no special requirements—the usual information should be shown. Legalization is not required.

2. **Import License**

Not usually required.

3. ***Legalization Fees**

Commercial invoices, originals .... $7.50 per copy
Commercial invoices, copies .... $3.00 per copy
Certificate of Origin, originals .... $7.50 per copy
Certificate of Origin, copies .... $3.00 per copy
Visas .... $8.50 per copy

INVOICE AND DECLARATION OF VALUE REQUIRED FOR SHIPMENTS TO

NIGERIA

C-16 Amended

(Place and Date) .... 19.......

Invoice of (General Nature or).. consigned
class of merchandise

by .... of ....

to .... of ....

to be shipped per S. S. ....

Customer's Order No.   Our Order No.   Terms:

Country of Origin	Number of Packages	Marks and Numbers on Packages	Quantity and Description of Goods	Selling Price in Currency of Exporting Country	
				At	Amount

Enumerate the following charges, and state whether each amount has been included in or excluded from the above selling prices:	Amount in Currency of Exporting Country	State whether included or excluded
(1) Value of outside packages		
(2) Labour in packing the goods into outside packages		
(3) Cartage to rail and to docks		
(4) Inland freight and other charges		
(5) Ocean freight		
(6) Marine insurance		
(7) Commissions and other charges of a like nature		
(8) Other costs, dues, charges and expenses incidental to delivery of the articles at port of destination		
(9) If the goods are subject to any charge by way of royalties		
State full particulars of royalties below:—		

Form No. 10-620   Printed and Sold by Unz & Co., Division of Scott Printing Corp., 190 Baldwin
Re   Jan 1, 1972   Ave., Jersey City, N.J. 07306; N.J. (201) 795-5400   N.Y. (212) 344-2270
Toll Free (800) 631-3098

Form 10-620 (front).

CERTIFICATE OF VALUE

I ....

of ....

* Manufacturers/Suppliers/Exporters of the goods enumerated in this invoice amounting to

hereby declare that I have the Authority to make and sign this certificate on behalf of the aforesaid * Manufacturers/Suppliers/Exporters and that I have the means of knowing and I do hereby certify as follows:—

(1) That this invoice is in all respects correct and contains a true and full statement of the price actually paid or to be paid for the said goods, and the actual quantity thereof.

(2) That no different invoice of the goods mentioned in the said invoice has been or will be furnished to anyone.

(3) That no arrangement or understanding affecting the purchase price of the said goods has been or will be made or entered into between the said exporter and purchaser or by anyone on behalf of either of them either by way of discount, rebate, compensation or in any manner whatever other than as fully shown on this invoice.

Dated at .... this .... day of .... 19 ....

(Signature) ....

(Signature of Witness) ....

Note: The person making the declaration should be a Principal or a Manager, Chief Clerk, Secretary or responsible employee.
* *Delete the inapplicable.*

CERTIFICATE OF ORIGIN

I ....

of ....

* Manufacturers/Suppliers/Exporters of the goods enumerated in this invoice hereby declare that I have the authority to make and sign this certificate on behalf of the aforesaid *Manufacturers/Suppliers/Exporters and that I have the means of knowing and I do hereby certify as follows:—

(1) That all the goods mentioned in this invoice have been wholly produced or manufactured in ....

(2) That all the goods mentioned in this invoice have been either wholly or partially produced or manufactured in ....

(3) That as regards those goods only partially produced or manufactured,

(a) the final process or processes of manufacture have been performed in ....

(b) the expenditure in material produced and or labour performed in .... calculated subject to qualifications hereunder, in the case of all such goods is not less than 25 per cent of the factory or works costs of all such goods in their finished state. (See note below.)

(4) That in the calculation of such proportion of material produced and/or labour performed none of the following items has been included or considered: Manufacturer's profit, or remuneration of any trader, agent, broker or other person dealing in the goods in their finished condition; royalties; cost of outside packages or any cost of packing the goods thereinto; any cost of conveying, insuring, or shipping the goods subsequent to their manufacture.

Dated at .... this .... day of .... 19 ....

(Signature) ....

(Signature of Witness) ....

Note:

(1) The person making the declaration should be a principal or a manager, chief clerk, secretary, or responsible employee.

(2) The place or country of origin of imports is that in which the goods were produced or manufactured and, in the case of partly manufactured goods the place or country in which any final operation has altered to any appreciable extent the character, composition and value of goods imported into that country.

(3) In the case of goods which have at some stage entered into the commerce of, or undergone a process of manufacture in a foreign country, only that labour and material which are expected on or added to the goods after their return to the exporting territory, shall be regarded as the produce or manufacture of the territory in calculating the proportion of labour and material in the factory or works cost of the finished article.

(4) *Delete the inapplicable.

Form 10-620 (back). Export Forms, Hazardous Materials Labels, etc. can be purchased from Unz & Co., 190 Baldwin Ave., P.O. Box 308, Jersey City, N.J. 07303.

4.   **Holidays**
All holidays generally observed in New York City.
*Documents must be mailed to the Consulate with a self-addressed envelope only.

PAKISTAN

SUMMARY OF SHIPPING DOCUMENTS REQUIRED
No Consular Documents Required
1.   **Shipping Documents Required**
   (A) **Commercial Invoice**—3—no special requirements as to form, but must contain full particulars, such as quantities, weights, value per unit, and all necessary charges to establish a CIF value. Invoices must be signed, and if no separate certificate of origin is required, then the country of origin must be shown.
   (B) **Certificate of Origin**—3—not generally required, but letters of credit or importers may frequently request it. Certified by the New York Chamber of Commerce and Industry, which retains one notarized copy. May be prepared on general form.
2.   **Air Cargo and Parcel Post Shipments**
Commercial Invoice (see above)—2—must accompany shipment. Additional copies should be sent to consignee.
3.   *Import License**—Required by importer for most commodities. Valid usually for six months. Licenses covering capital goods are usually issued for 12 months but importer may obtain extensions of up to 24 months. Most imports must be made on a letter of credit basis. Shipments must be made prior to expiration of import license.
4.   **Special Documents**
Official U.S. Department of Agriculture Certificate—required for all plants and plant products (except fruits and vegetables). Leaf tobacco should have an additional certification attesting that the tobacco is free from "ephestia elutella," or that this pest does not exist in the country of origin.
Sanitary Certificate—required for used clothing. Must be signed by a physician with the letters M.D. following the signature.
5.   **Insurance**
Must be covered in Pakistan, except AID shipments.
6.   *Consular Holidays**
February 16, March 15, March 23, May 31, July 5, August 14, September 6, September 11, September 24, September 27, November 25, December 24, and December 25. All holidays generally observed in New York City.
*Denotes changes since previous notice.

PANAMA

SUMMARY OF SHIPPING DOCUMENTS REQUIRED
1.   **Special Information**
The Consulate is not authorized to legalize documents covering shipments from ports outside of its jurisdiction. Consular invoices for shipments from east coast or gulf ports must be legalized by the corresponding Consulate.
Documents must be presented to the Consulates for legalization within 8

working days after the issuance date of the ocean bill of lading. To avoid fines, the issuance date should be the sailing date of vessel rather than the date the bill is presented to the steamship company. In many cases the difference between the date the bill is presented and sailing date could be 5 or 6 days and therefore documents would be late before they are received from the steamship company. Shippers presenting documents after the deadline will be assessed 1% of the value of the merchandise. It is therefore suggested that the sailing date of vessel be shown on the bills of lading.

Lost Documents—For replacement of Consular Invoices that have been lost, the following declaration must appear on the back of the Consular Invoice in the two places where it reads "OBSERVACIONES DEL VENDEDOR" and "OBSERVACIONES DEL CONSUL": "Esta Factura es un Duplicado, que remplaza la Factura No. _____ legalizado en este Consulado (fecha _____). Shippers are reminded to record the number of the Consular Invoice and legalization date when the original consular documents are returned by the Consulate. If a duplicate set is required at a later date, all the information will be readily available.

2.   **Freight Shipments regardless of value (except to the Free Zone of Colon):**
   (A) **Consular Invoice**—4—in Spanish—forms sold by Consulate—1—retained by Consulate. Must show unit price of item and FOB value port of shipment.

   If other expenses are shown (ocean freight, insurance, etc.) they must be listed separately and not included in the FOB value of the goods.

   The consular invoices must be sent to the following: Original to consignee; Duplicate (Blue Copy) to Customs Office in Panama; Quadruplicate (Pink Copy) to Comptroller Office-Controloria General De La Republica Direccion Consular Commercial, Apartado 5213, Panama, Republica de Panama.
   (B) **Bill of Lading**—Original—signed by steamship company and 3 non-negotiable copies. Legalized original returned to shipper. "To Order" bills of lading are acceptable. Must show freight figures.
   (C) **Commercial Invoice**—5—in Spanish. Must show FOB value. May show itemized expense up to CIF value. 3 retained by Consulate. Must show the following prescribed sworn declaration in Spanish, signed by shipper and dated:

   "Conste bajo gravedad del juramento, con la firma puesta al pie de esta declaracion, que todos y cada uno de los datos expresados en esta factura son exactos y verdaderos, y que la suma total declarada es la misma en que se han vendido las mercaderias"

   It is not permissible to declare a case of hardware as such. Contents must be declared in accordance with the tariff, i.e., hammers, nails, handles, clamps, etc. Gross and net kilos must be given if the items are assessed on weight basis. If not, meter, liters, etc., are required. In addition, the unit value of each item must be shown.

3.   **Freight Shipments to Free Zone of Colon:**
   (A) **Consular Invoice**—not required.
   (B) **Bill of Lading**—original—signed by steamship company—Consulate returns it to shipper.
   (C) **Commercial Invoice**—Original and duplicate—containing sworn declaration shown in 1(C). Must be presented to Consulate, which returns it to shipper—original must be notarized and signed by the County Clerk, unless the notary's signature is registered at the Consulate. Must clearly indicate destination "ZONA LIBRE DE COLON."

4. **Parcel Post Shipments regardless of value:**
Four (4) commercial invoices containing declaration shown in 1(C) should be sent to consignee under separate cover—consular legalization not required. Invoices must be in possession of consignee before the arrival of shipment.

5. **Air Cargo Shipments regardless of value:**
Two (2) copies of the International Cargo Invoice containing the declaration shown in 1(C) must accompany shipment—consular legalization not required. Additional copies may be sent to consignee.

6. **Special Documents**

(A) **Letter of Correction**—5—Legalized original returned to shipper—4 copies retained by Consulate. There is no deadline set for presentation to Consulate. Letter of Correction should be prepared in accordance with the following text:

"Conste por el presente documento que despues de haber verificado los datos expresados en la factura consular numero _____ por mercaderias embaracada en el vapor "_____," a la consignacion de los Senores _____, de _____, por valor de $_____, se ha encontrado un error que consiste en _____ lo que declaro ante Ud., hoy _____ de _____ de 19_____ para los efectos de la rectificacion en los demas enjemplares de la factura consular."

(B) **Import Permit**—Import Permits issued by the Panamanian Department of Animal Health must be presented to Consulate together with other documents on shipments of meats, eggs, milk and milk products and many by-products.

(C) **Phytosanitary Certificate**—Required for all shipments of meat and meat products. Issued by the U.S. Department of Agriculture. Legalized gratis and returned to shipper. Must be presented together with Consular Documents.

7. **Import License**
Not required. Except for narcotics, firearms, ammunition and explosives.

8. **Arrangement of Documents**
The Original Bill Of Lading must be Face Up; all other papers Face Down, arranged in the following order from top to bottom:

(1) Original bill of lading; two commercial invoices (one original and one copy); and original consular invoice, stapled together.

(2) Copy of bill of lading; copy of commercial invoice; and one copy of consular invoice, stapled together.

(3) Copy of bill of lading; copy of commercial invoice; and copy of consular invoice, stapled together.

(4) Copy of bill of lading; copy of commercial invoice; and copy of consular invoice, stapled together.

All 4 sets must then be clipped together.

9. **Consular Fees**
Consular Invoice forms, per set (4) $3.00
Legalization of Commercial Invoice
(for shipments to Free Zone of Colon) 5.00
Letter of Correction 5.00
Legalization of county clerk's signature .... 5.00 (each)
Legalization of Sanitary Certificate .... Gratis
*Legalization of Duplicates of Consular Invoice
(those that have been lost) 5.00

Legalization of documents is $5.00 per set, with immediate return of documents.

10. **Holidays**
January 9, February 12, February 18, Good Friday, May 27, October 11, October 14, October 28, and November 3. All holidays generally observed in New York City.
*Denotes changes since previous notice.

PARAGUAY

SUMMARY OF SHIPPING DOCUMENTS REQUIRED
Special Information

Documents must be presented to Consulate for legalization not more than two working days after sailing of vessel.

For shipments originating in the U.S., Canada or points not having a Consulate, commercial invoices must be certified by a local chamber of commerce and all the other documents listed in this Summary legalized by the Consulate General in New York.

Consular Documents Required

1. **Freight Shipments valued at $100 or more FOB steamer:**
   (A) **Consular Invoice**—4—(certain steamship lines required an additional copy)—in Spanish—forms sold by Consulate—2 retained by Consulate. All shipping expenses, except ocean freight, must be shown on consular invoice as one item under the heading "Gastos de Despacho."
   (B) **Commercial Invoice**—5—in Spanish—certified by the New York Chamber of Commerce and Industry, which retains one notarized copy—2 retained by the Consulate—2 returned to shipper. Shipping expenses ("Gastos de Despacho"), including ocean freight, must be itemized on commercial invoice.
   (C) **Bill of Lading**—3 originals and 1 copy—Consulate retains copy and returns 3 · legalized originals. Unless there is a direct service to the port of Asuncion, bills of lading must be marked either *Buenos Aires* or *Montevideo "en transito para Paraguay."* "To Order" bills of lading allowed but not advisable.

2. **Freight Shipments valued under $100 FOB steamer:**
   No consular documents required.

3. **Parcel Post Shipments valued at $100 or more FOB:**
   (A) **Consular Invoice**—consular legalization required—see 1(A)—4 copies required.
   (B) **Commercial Invoice**—consular legalization required—see 1(B)—5 copies required.
   Parcel Post Shipments valued under $100 FOB:
   No Consular documents required.

4. **Air Cargo Shipments valued at $100 or more FOB:**
   (A) **Consular Invoice**—4—consular legalization required—see 1(A).
   (B) **Commercial Invoice**—5—consular legalization required—see 1(B)—2 unlegalized copies must accompany shipment.
   (C) **Air Waybill**—original and 3 copies—original and 1 copy legalized and returned to shipper.

5. **Special Documents**

(A) **Letter of Correction**—2—in Spanish—1 copy retained by Consulate. No letter of correction is required to make changes when documents are still in Consulate's possession.

(B) **Sanitary Certificate**—1—in Spanish—required for shipments of live animals, seeds, grains—returned to shipper.

(C) **Transfer of Assignment of Trademark**—1—in Spanish—notarized and authenticated by County Clerk or Secretary of State. Legalized by Consulate and returned to shipper.

(D) **Medicinal Certificate**—1—in Spanish, giving ingredients of drugs—notarized and signed by County Clerk or Secretary of State. Legalized by Consulate and returned to shipper.

(E) **Power of Attorney**—in Spanish—notarized and authenticated by County Clerk or Secretary of State. Legalized by Consulate and returned to shipper.

6.   *Import License

Required only for a very few items, Narcotics, Arms and Ammunition require special license from the Ministry of the Interior. Importer must obtain Exchange Permit.

7.   *Consular Fees

All consular fees, except those listed below, are paid in Paraguay by importer.

Additional copies of commercial invoice,
when requested .... $ 2.50 each
Extra copy of Consular invoice at same time set
of 4 is presented .... $ 5.00 each
Extra copy of bill of lading .... $ 2.50 each
Letter of correction $20.00
Extra copy of certificate of origin .... $ 2.50 each
Transfer and assignment of trademark $20.00
Extension and revalidation of trademark $20.00
Medicinal certificate giving ingredients of drugs, etc. $20.00
Sanitary certificate $10.00
Special power of attorney $10.00
General power of attorney $20.00
Consular invoice blanks per set of 4
(sold only at Consulate) .... $ 8.00
Registration Fee $20.00

8.   *Consular Holidays

March 1, Holy Thursday, Good Friday, May 14, May 15, and August 15. All holidays generally observed in New York City.

*Denotes changes since previous notice.

PERU

SUMMARY OF SHIPPING DOCUMENTS REQUIRED

1.   **Insurance**

Must be covered in Peru except AID shipments.

2.   **Freight Shipments regardless of value:**

(A) **No Consular documents required.**

(B) ***Bill of Lading**—Original and 2 copies in Spanish or English—(if in English, the corresponding translation in Spanish must be attached)—showing weight in pounds and kilos or measurements in metric tons—"To order" bills of lading permitted must be forwarded to importer as soon as possible.

(C) *Commercial Invoice—2—In Spanish—must be forwarded to importer as soon as possible. The Spanish translation of every word must be typed underneath each English term in the document. This refers to column headings and all other printed matter on the invoice, in addition to the use of Spanish to describe the particular shipment.

3.   **Parcel Post and Air Cargo Shipments**
Same regulations as above, substitute airway bill and parcel post receipt for bill of lading.

Prohibited Imports—The following items are prohibited entry unless a license is obtained from the Ministry of Agriculture, all types of animals such as horses, dogs, etc. We have been told unofficially that the Peruvian Government has issued a list containing about 4300 items which can be imported. Items not appearing on the list will be prohibited.

4.   **Special Documents**
(A) **Sanitary & Purity Certificates**—required for animals, plants, cuttings and plant parts. One copy issued by manufacturer or competent authority— Certified by New York Chamber of Commerce—forwarded to importer with other documents.

(B) **Phytosanitary Certificate**—required for shipments of seeds and grains. Issued by the U.S. Department of Agriculture. Same procedure as above.

(C) **Purity Certificate**—required for all shipments of flour—Same procedure as above.

(D) **Age Certificate**—required for shipments of whiskey regardless of origin—1 copy issued by distiller—Same procedure as above.

(E) **Sanitary Certificate**—required for shipments of animal products, edible and inedible (such as meats, fats, hides, etc., and all their by-products in all their forms). Must be issued in duplicate by a U.S. Government Agency, certifying as to its wholesome, sound condition, and fitness for human consumption (if applicable).

5.   **Consular Holidays**
All holidays generally observed in New York.
*Denotes changes since previous notice.

PHILIPPINES

SUMMARY OF SHIPPING DOCUMENTS REQUIRED

Note: When documents are presented at the Consulate a pick-up slip will be given to the person who delivers them. After three (3) working days, or sooner, the consular invoice will be returned upon presentation of the pick-up slip. If the papers are sent by mail, a self-addressed stamped envelope should be enclosed. Also, a self-addressed stamped envelope should be provided when purchasing consular blanks.

1.   **Special Information**
Deadline for Presentation of Documents: (1) Ocean Going Vessels—For sailing from the East Coast, the consular invoice together with supporting papers must be submitted to the Consulate for processing within 14 working days after

sailing of vessel and within 10 calendar days for sailing from the West Coast; (2) Air Freight or Air Parcel Post Shipments—consular documents must be submitted within 3 working days after departure of the carrier; (3) Parcel Post Shipments—documents must be submitted within 28 calendar days from the date of postal receipt.

*Place of Certification—Consular invoices may be presented for legalization at Philippine Consulate having jurisdiction over the place: (1) where the merchandise was manufactured; (2) where the merchandise was purchased; or (3) where the merchandise was shipped; except when no. 1 (one) and/or no. 2 (two) are outside the continental U.S.A., in which case the place of exportation determines jurisdiction.

The Territorial jurisdiction of the Philippine Consulates in the United States appears in Annex "A" of this summary.

*Shipments to Government Agencies: (1) All shipments to Philippine Government agencies or government-owned corporations, or companies covered by Presidential Decree No. 894 of February 26, 1976, as well as fifty percent (50%) of the gross tonnage of all shipments to the Philippines consisting of either U.S. surplus goods, AID commodities, or equipment financed under the credit line authorized by the Export/Import Bank, should be loaded on Philippine Flag Vessels, when available; (2) all the foregoing shipments which cannot be loaded on Philippine Flag Vessels, should be accompanied by "Certificate of Non-Availability of Philippine Flag Air Carriers or Shipping Lines" which should be attached to the consular invoices such certificates to be duly signed by the local agent of the Philippine Flag Vessel or the Philippine Air Lines and certified by the Philippine Consulate at the port of shipment; (3) a period of ten days prior to the date of sailing of a Philippine Flag Vessel may be allowed as the period which may be considered in determining whether or not a Philippine Flag Vessel is available at the port of exportation.

2.   **Consular Documents Required**

The following requirements are prescribed as prerequisites for certification of consular invoices and certificates of origin:

A detailed description of the articles in customary term or commercial designation, including the grade or quality, numbers, marks or symbols under which sold by the seller or manufacturer, together with the marks and numbers of packages containing the articles. The destination of the cargo must not be stated only as "The Philippines." It must specify the particular port of entry in the Philippines where the goods will be unloaded.

(A) **Consular Invoice**—a consular invoice is required for every shipment if the export value in the country of exportation is $400 FOB or over. Must show the FOB value separately from the C&F or CIF value of the shipment. (Legalization fee—$30.00).

(B) *Certificate of Origin—(Same form as Consular Invoice, but Consulate only certifies origin). For shipments with export value under $400 FOB. Fee is $5.00.

(C) **Commercial Invoice**—properly accomplished in quintuplicate and duly signed by the seller, manufacturer, exporter or his authorized representative, who must be a responsible official of the exporting company. Must show separately the FOB value from the C&F or CIF value of the shipment. (Take particular note of the information required in the statement under (b) below).

(a) Specimens of signatures of responsible officers (e.g., export manager, sales manager, shipping manager, etc.) authorized to sign for the company should be filed with Consulate indicating his position and signed by the head of the firm.

Revised list must be submitted each time there are changes. The foregoing requirements also applies to freight forwarders and/or brokers handling shipments to the Philippines.

(b) All copies must contain the following statements:

"I hereby certify that all information contained herein is correct; that the value declared is the same value stated in all other declarations made before or filed for official purposes in any agency in or of the exporting country; and that the amount per unit FOB declared is the same value stated in all other documents filed in connection with this exportation for official purposes of the United States."

"I further certify that this invoice is in all respects correct and true and was made at the place from whence the merchandise was exported to the Philippines. The invoice contains a true and full statement of the date when, the place where, the person from whom the same was purchased, and the actual cost thereof. That no discounts, bounties or drawbacks are contained in the invoice except such as have been actually stated thereon."

(D) **Bill of Lading**—3—non-negotiable copies. (3 Air waybills on air shipments), containing freight and other charges, duly signed by the carrier or its agent stamped "For Consular Purposes Only."

(E) **Detailed Packing List**—5—if the detailed information is already included in the Commercial Invoice, no packing list is necessary.

3. **Parcel Post and Air Parcel Post Shipments**

Three copies of the parcel post receipt should be presented to the Consulate with other consular documents for all shipments.

4. **Exemptions from Requirements**

Exempt from the foregoing requirements are Personal and household effects accompanying a passenger as baggage, or arriving with a reasonable time which in no case shall exceed ninety (90) days before or after the owner's return.

5. **Additional Documentary Requirements in Specific Cases**

(a) **Food and Drug Products**—five (5) copies, Form FA No. 53, Declaration of Shipper of Food and Drug Products.

(b) **Insecticides, Paris Greens, Lead Arsenates, or Fungicides**—five (5) copies, Form FA No. 54.

(c) **Meat and Meat Products**—five (5) copies, Form FA No. 55, Certificate of Ante Mortem and Post Mortem Inspection.

(d) **Viruses, Serums, Toxins and Analogous Products intended for treatment of domestic Animals**—permit or veterinary license number (biological products) from the U. S. Department of Agriculture.

(e) **Viruses, Therapeutic Serum, Toxin, Antitoxin or Analogous Products or Arsphenamine or its derivatives (or any other trivalent organic arsenic compound)**—permit or license to manufacture from the Federal Security Agency or its successor.

(f) **Domestic Animals and Livestock**—permit from the Director of Animal Industry of the Philippines, as well as, a health certificate issued shortly before shipment by a veterinary official of the country of origin, duly certified by the nearest Philippine consular official, stating that each of the animals is free from, and has not recently been exposed to any dangerous and/or communicable animal disease a certificate of antirabies shot is required in the case of dogs and cats.

(g) **Fruits, Vegetables, Seed and other plant materials**—Certificate of Disinfection from the Department of Agriculture of the United States or of the corresponding department of any state of the union.

(h) **Firearms and Ammunitions**—permit/license from the Chief of Constabulary, Quezon City, Philippines. Note: Importation to the Philippines.

(i) **U.S. and Canadian Wheat Flour**—information as to the amount of subsidy received by each shipment upon exportation to the Philippines.

(j) **Essences, flavoring extracts and other preparations containing distilled spirits otherwise known as Ethyl Alcohol**—certificate of the manufacturer stating the source and percentage of the alcohol used.

(k) **Resins**—specific nomenclature of the resins.

6. *Letter of Correction**
    After an invoice has been duly legalized any amendment and/or correction to be made thereon must be done on the shipper's/seller's letterhead in quintuplicate, duly notarized, stating the amendment and/or correction, the consular invoice number and date of legalization. Fee is $2.50.

7. **Arrangement of Documents**
    Shippers should present their consular documents as follows: (a) original consular invoice followed by a commercial invoice, and packing list stapled together; b) blue consular invoice followed by a non-negotiable bill of lading, commercial invoice, packing list; (c) pink consular invoice followed by a non-negotiable bill of lading, commercial invoice, packing list; (d) green consular invoice followed by a commercial invoice and packing list; (e) yellow consular invoice followed by a commercial invoice and packing list, stapled together. All sets should then be clipped together in above sequence.

8. *Consular Fees**—all checks should be made payable to the Philippine Consulate General New York.

Consular invoice blanks—FA Form 48/49 per set of five . . . . $ .30
                   —pad of 25 sets 5.00
                   —FA Form 53/54 per set 30
                   —pad of 25 sets 5.00
Certification of consular invoice—FA Form 48/49 . . . . 30.00
Certification of certificate of origin 5.00
Certification of invoice with FA Form No. 53, 54 or 55 . . . .   5.00
Certification of either FA Form 53 or 54 . . . .   5.00
Certification of disinfection of goods 5.00
Certification of invoice of return Philippine goods—
    FA Form No. 52 . . . .   5.00
Certification of amendment and/or correction 2.50
Certification of extra copies 2.50
Quintuplicate copy signed manually 2.50

Free certification on consular invoice of merchandise:

(a) sent to religious or charitable organization as donations for free distribution to the needy.

(b) sent to any foreign diplomatic and/or consular mission in the Philippines provided that the consular invoice is accompanied by a statement or certificate of the foreign diplomatic and/or consular mission concerned showing that the merchandise is for its exclusive use and not for sale, barter or hire.

(c) shipment of goods consigned or addressed to departments, bureaus, offices and other instrumentalities of the Government.

(d) free service does not apply to certification of quintuplicate and extra copies.

9. *__Consular Holidays__

January 1, April 9, Holy Thursday, Good Friday, May 1, June 12, December 25, and December 31. All holidays generally observed in New York City.

*Denotes changes since previous notice.

ANNEX A

Consulate Offices and Jurisdictions

I. Embassy of the Philippines (Consular Section)
1617 Massachusetts Avenue, N.W.
Washington, D.C. 20006
Area Code (202) HObart 2—1400—8

District of Columbia	North Carolina	Virginia
Kentucky	South Carolina	West Virginia
Maryland		

II. Philippine Consulate General
15 East 66th Street
New York, New York 10021
Area Code (212) 879—0800

Connecticut	New Hampshire	Puerto Rico
Delaware	New Jersey	Rhode Island
Maine	New York	Vermont
Massachusetts	Pennsylvania	Virgin Islands

III. Philippine Consulate General
6 North Michigan Avenue—Room 907
Chicago, Illinois 60602
Area Code (312) DE 2—6458

Illinois	Missouri	Kansas
Indiana	Michigan	Nebraska
Iowa	North Dakota	Ohio
Minnesota	South Dakota	Wisconsin

ANNEX A

Consulate Offices and Jurisdictions
(continued)

IV.   Philippine Consulate General
International Trade Mart—Suite 1440-43
2 Canal Street
New Orleans, Louisiana 70130
Area Code (504) 524—2755—56

Alabama	Georgia	Oklahoma
Arkansas	Louisiana	Tennessee
Florida	Mississippi	Texas

V.   Philippine Consulate General
Suite 835—Central Building
810 Third Avenue
Seattle, Washington 98104
Area Code (206) MA 4—7703—4

Alaska	Montana	Washington
Idaho	Oregon	Wyoming

VI.   Philippine Consulate General
170 24th Avenue
San Francisco, California 94121
Area Code (415) 387—3322

California	Nevada
Colorado	Utah

VII.   Philippine Consulate General
2433 Rali Highway
Honolulu, Hawaii 96817
556—3167

Hawaii   Hawaii

VIII.   Philippine Consulate General
Agana, Guam

Guam	Marianas Islands	The Carolines

IX.   Philippine Consulate General
3250 Wilshire Boulevard
Los Angeles, California 90005
413—387—5321

California (Lower Half)	Arizona	New Mexico

POLAND

SUMMARY OF SHIPPING DOCUMENTS REQUIRED
No Consular Documents Required
1. **Shipping Documents Required**
   (A) ***Commercial Invoice**—4—ordinary commercial invoices. If requested by the importer, the commercial invoice should be legalized by the Polish Commercial Counselor's Office, 500 Fifth Avenue, New York, New York 10036, (Telephone: 564-3884). In this case an extra copy is required for the Commercial Counselor's Office. Legalization fee—$7.50.
   Legalization Fees—The Consulate General of Poland advises that there is no fee for legalizing the commercial invoice (when requested). However, there is a fee of $7.50 for legalization of any other documents.
   (B) **Certificate of Origin**—4—when required—on general form—sold by commercial printers—certified by the New York Chamber of Commerce and Industry, which requires an additional notarized copy for its files.
   (C) **Bills of Lading**—no special regulations—the usual information should be shown.
2. **Import License**
   Required by importer for all imports.
3. ***Consular Holidays**
   Easter Monday, May 1, June 18, July 22, November 1, and December 26. All holidays generally observed in New York City.
   *Denotes changes since previous notice.

PORTUGAL

SUMMARY OF SHIPPING DOCUMENTS REQUIRED

Special Information
Country of Origin must be shown on' Air Waybill, otherwise customs duties will be doubled.

1. **Shipping Documents Required**
   All Commercial Shipments regardless of mode of transportation:
   (A) **Commercial Invoice**—2—in Portuguese or English—must give an accurate and specific description of the goods. FOB value must be shown, followed by an itemized description of expenses. Invoices must show country of origin and should be certified true and correct. Certified by the New York Chamber of Commerce and Industry, which requires one additional notarized copy for its files. Consular legalization not required.
   (B) **Certificate of Origin**—2—in Portuguese or English—forms sold by commercial printers. Required only for merchandise originating outside the United States or Europe. Certificate of Origin is required for shipments via a third country, or when requested by consignee. Must have a signed commercial invoice attached covering the material described. For merchandise of European origin the certificate must be legalized by the Portuguese Consulate in Country of origin.
2. **Consular Fees** (paid by cash, except when documents are mailed to the Consulate, in which case fees must be remitted by check or money order).

For Certificates of Origin up to $ 2,250.00 .... $2.93
   From $ 2,250.01 to 4,500.00 .... $1.00 per 1,000 + 30%
   From   4,500.01 to 9,000.00 .... Approx 1.50 per 1,000 + 30%
   From   9,000.01 to 22,500.00 .... Approx 2.00 per 1,000 + 30%
   Above 22,500.00 .... Approx 2.50 per 1,000 + 30%
Immediate return of documents .... Double the consular fee

Consular Holidays

Corpus Christi, Holy Thursday (½ day), Good Friday, June 10, August 15, November 1, Election Day, and December 24. All holidays generally observed in New York City.

*Denotes changes since previous notice.

QATAR

SUMMARY OF SHIPPING DOCUMENTS REQUIRED
1. **Consular Documents Required**
   All Commercial Shipments regardless of value:
   (A) *__Commercial Invoice__—2—must show name of supplier and consignee—quantity—marks and numbers—origin of the goods—an accurate description and value of goods, CIF or otherwise—must be signed by shipper—must contain statement that the "merchandise is not of Israeli origin or contains any Israeli materials." Certified by U.S. Arab Chamber of Commerce. Legalized by the Consulate, which retains one copy.
   (B) *__Certificate of Origin__—2—must contain the name and address of the manufacturer/producer, as well as a statement that the merchandise is not of Israeli origin or contains any Israeli materials. Certified by the U.S. Arab Chamber of Commerce. Legalized by the Consulate which retains one copy.
   (C) *__Insurance Certificate__—2—issued by the insurance company stating that the insurance company is not on the blacklist, must be legalized by the Consulate, which retains one copy. If shipment is insured by the buyer, then the insurance certificate is not required, however, shipper must state on commercial invoice that insurance is covered by the buyer.
   (D) *__Steamship Company Certificate__—2—issued by the steamship company stating that the vessel is not an Israeli vessel nor is it scheduled to call at any Israeli port during her voyage, must be legalized by the Consulate which retains one copy.
2. **Import License**
   None is required.
3. **Special Documents**
   Health Certificate—Shipments of frozen foods must be covered by an inspection certificate issued by health authorities of the country of origin.
4. *__Legalization Fees__
   Payable by Check or money order to the Qatar Consulate.

Commercial Invoice .... $1.25 per page
Certificate of Origin .... 1.25 per page
Insurance Certificate .... 1.25 per page
Steamship Certificate .... 1.25 per page
Additional documents (if requested) .... 1.25 per page

Shipper only pays for the document returned by Consulate.

Prior to presenting documents to the Consulate, freight forwarders, messenger service firms and shippers are required to figure out the total amount due according to the number of pages at the above rate, i.e, $1.25 per page. Consulate copies should be stapled separately and fee mentioned above also applies.

5.   **Mission Holidays**
All holidays generally observed in New York City.
*Denotes changes since previous notice.

ROMANIA

SUMMARY OF SHIPPING DOCUMENTS REQUIRED
No Consular Documents Required
1.   **Shipping Documents Required**
   (A) **Commercial Invoice**—1 original and 4 copies—signed by shipper—should show full description of goods and any other information which the importer requests.
   (B) **Certificate of Origin**—1 original and 4 copies—when required—on general form—sold by commercial printers—certified by the New York Chamber of Commerce and Industry, which requires an additional notarized copy for its files.
   (C) **Bills of Lading**—1 original and 4 copies—no special regulations—the usual particulars should be shown and any other information which the importer requests.
2.   **Import License**
Required by importer for all commodities.

RWANDA

SUMMARY OF SHIPPING DOCUMENTS REQUIRED
No Consular Documents Required
1.   **Shipping Documents Required**
   (A) **Commercial Invoice**—2—no special requirements—should contain the usual information and an accurate description of the goods.
   (B) **Certificate of Origin**—2—when required—general form—sold by commercial printers—certified by the New York Chamber of Commerce and Industry, which requires an additional notarized copy for its files.
   (C) **Bills of Lading**—no special regulations—should show the usual information.
2.   **Import License**
Required for all imports with a few exceptions—validity 7 months.
3.   **Holidays**
All holidays generally observed in New York City.

SAUDI ARABIA

SUMMARY OF SHIPPING DOCUMENTS REQUIRED
Special Information
Shippers are urged to present documents to the Consulate for legalization as soon as

possible, especially in cases where Letters of Credit are involved.

1. **Consular Documents Required**
   All Commercial Shipments regardless of value:
   (A) *Commercial Invoice—3—Consulate retains one copy and returns two to shipper. Invoices must be prepared on the letterhead of actual seller, and must give an accurate and specific description of the goods, itemizing all expenses. All invoices must be signed and show the name of the steamer and date of sailing. Prior to presentation to the Consulate, invoices must be certified as to current export market prices and country of origin by the U.S. Arab Chamber of Commerce which requires one additional notarized copy containing the following affidavit:

   > "I, (name, title, name of company) hereby swear that the prices stated in this invoice are the current export market prices and that the origin of the goods described herein is the United States of America, and I assume full responsibility for any inaccuracies or errors therein. The following statement must be shown on the invoice—merchandise is not of Israeli origin or contains any Israeli materials."

   (B) *Certificate of Origin—3—on general form—sold by commercial printers—must be certified by the U.S. Arab Chamber of Commerce—each copy must be attached to a commercial invoice—one copy retained by Consulate. Must show name of vessel. Shippers must show on the certificate of origin the names of the manufacturers of the items being shipped. Shippers must also make a notarized statement certifying that it is true and correct. Documents covering products from companies and or their subsidiaries which are on the black list will not be legalized. If in doubt check with the Consulate. The U.S. Arab Chamber of Commerce requires one additional notarized copy for its files.

   (C) Insurance Certificate—2 copies of a certificate issued by the insurance company stating that the insurance company is not on the blacklist required to be presented to Consulate for all shipments. Consulate retains copy for its files. One copy returned to shipper. If shipment is insured by the buyer, than the insurance certificate is not required by the Consulate General. However, shipper must state on commercial invoice that insurance is covered in Saudi Arabia.

   (D) Steamship Company Certificate—A certificate in duplicate issued by the steamship company stating that the vessel is not an Israeli vessel nor is it scheduled to call at any Israeli port during her voyage. The original will be returned to shipper.

2. **Import License**
   None required.

3. **Special Documents**
   (A) Health Certificate—A certificate in duplicate issued by an official department is required on all imports of plants and plant materials, such as saplings, seeds, fruits and vegetables proving they are free from pests and other agricultural diseases. The original will be returned to shipper.

   (B) Certificate of Free Sale—The Ministry of Health requires a certificate of free sale to accompany pharmaceutical and medicinal products. Legalized by Consulate only when requested by importer or requested in letter of credit. Original returned to shipper—copy retained by Consulate. The New York Chamber of Commerce and Industry will issue such a certificate in duplicate upon request.

(C) **Phytosanitary Certificate**—A Certificate in duplicate issued by the Department of Agriculture must accompany shipments of flour, rice, seed wheat, agriculture seeds and plants.

4. *****Arrangement of Documents**—Shipping documents must be presented in the following order: 1—Shippers documents must be stapled together and marked "Return to Shipper." 2—Consulate copies must be stapled together and marked "Consulate Copy." 3—All documents not complying with the above will be rejected.

5. **Legalization Fees:**
Payable by check or money order to order of Consulate.

Set of Commercial Invoices (2) and
    Certificates of Origin (2) .... .30 per page
Insurance Certificate .... .30 per page
Steamship Certificate .... .30 per page
Health Certificate .... .30 per page
Additional documents (if requested) .... .30 per page

Prior to presenting documents to the Consulate, freight forwarders, messenger service firms and shippers are required to figure out the total amount due according to the number of pages at the above rate, i.e., 30 cents per page. Consulate copies should be stapled separately and fee mentioned above also applies.

6. *****Consular Holidays**
All holidays generally observed in New York City.
*Denotes changes since previous notice.

SENEGAL

SUMMARY OF SHIPPING DOCUMENTS REQUIRED
No Consular Documents Required
1. **Shipping Documents Required**
    (A) **Commercial Invoice**—2—should contain names of exporter and consignee—numbers and types of packages—marks and numbers on packages—net and gross weights—CIF value, terms of sale—and an accurate, specific and complete description of the merchandise.
    (B) *****Certificate of Origin**—2—on general form, sold by commercial printers—required by customs to establish the true origin of the goods—certified by the New York Chamber of Commerce and Industry, which requires one additional notarized copy for its files.
    (C) **Bills of Lading**—no special regulations, but marks of identification and name and address of the consignee should be clearly indicated. Shipping marks and numbers on bill of lading, on invoices and on the goods should correspond exactly. A packing list is recommended.
2. **Import License**
Required by importer for most shipments—Validity one year—goods must be shipped before the expiration date.

3.   **Mission Holidays**
     All holidays generally observed in New York City.

SIERRA LEONE

SUMMARY OF SHIPPING DOCUMENTS REQUIRED
1.   **Consular Documents Required, regardless of value and mode of transportation:**

   (A) **Customs Invoice and Declaration of Value**—4—(West African Form)—sold by commercial printers—1 copy retained by Consulate—must contain complete information as commercial invoice. Must also be sealed (or stamped) with shipper's name, and signed. Consular legalization required, invoices must be presented to the New York Chamber of Commerce and Industry for certification prior to presentation at Consulate. The Chamber requires one additional notarized copy for its files.
   (B) **Commercial Invoice**—4—on shipper's letterhead—must contain full particulars and itemized expenses. Must be certified true and correct, signed, and show country of origin. Certification by The New York Chamber of Commerce and Industry necessary which requires one additional notarized copy for its files. The certified commercial invoices must be attached to the "Customs Invoice and Declaration of Value"—1 copy retained by Consulate.

2.   **Import License**
     Most goods may be imported freely under open general license. A specific license is required for a short list of items. Validity—usually 12 months. No tolerance is permitted. With the exception of certain items exempted by the Minister of Finance, all imports are now subject to an import license fee of 5% of the CIF value.

3.   *Insurance
     Shipments covered by insurance must be taken out in Sierra Leone.

4.   **Special Documents**
   (A) **Sanitary Certificate**—Shipments of plants, seeds and animal products, must be accompanied by a sanitary certificate, and are subject to government inspection at port of entry.
   (B) **Fumigation Certificate**—is required for cotton waste, used clothing and rags.

5.   **Consular Fees**
     Consular fee must be paid by certified check upon presentation of documents to Consulate.

   Customs Invoice and Declaration of Value
      (with a total FOB value up to $200) $3.00
   Customs Invoice and Declaration of Value
      (with a total FOB value over $200) 1½%
   For legalizing sanitary or fumigation certificates 1.96

6.   *Consular Holidays
     January 1, February 12, February 16, April 16, April 19, May 31, July 4, September 6, October 11, November 25, December 25, and December 26. All holidays generally observed in New York City.
     *Denotes changes since previous notice.

SINGAPORE, REPUBLIC OF

SUMMARY OF SHIPPING DOCUMENTS REQUIRED
No Consular Documents Required
1.   **Shipping Documents Required**

(A) **Commercial Invoices**—3—must show an accurate description of the goods—quantity—weight (to be shown in metric)—unit price—shipping marks—country of origin—name or number of vessel and aircraft—indent/contract note reference—invoice number—value (to be declared as FOB or CIF as the case may be)—commission and discount.

(B) **Certificate of Origin**—2—when required—general form—sold by commercial printers—certified by the New York Chamber of Commerce and Industry, which requires an additional notarized copy for its files.

(C) **Bills of Lading**—should show names of shipper and consignee—name of vessel —marks and numbers and description of goods. In addition to weight in pounds and measurements in cubic feet, the equivalent measurement in cubic meters must be shown.

(D) **Packing Lists**—are required.

2.   **Import License**
Required by importer for some items. Most imports are made under general licenses.

3.   **Mission Holidays**
All holidays generally observed in New York City.

SOMALIA DEMOCRATIC REPUBLIC

SUMMARY OF SHIPPING DOCUMENTS REQUIRED

Special Information—Shipping documents should be forwarded direct to consignee to arrive before the merchandise.
No Consular Documents Required

1.   **Shipping Documents Required**

(A) **Commercial Invoice**—3—must show names of shipper and consignee—gross weight (in kilograms) and measurement (in metric units)—must contain all information necessary to establish the CIF value—signed by shipper. A packing list is recommended.

(B) **Certificate of Origin**—3—when required—on general form—sold by commercial printers—certified by the New York Chamber of Commerce and Industry, which requires an additional notarized copy for its files.

(C) **Bills of Lading**—no special requirements—shipping marks and numbers must correspond with those on the invoices and on the merchandise.

2.   **Import License**
Required by importer for most goods. A tolerance of 10% is allowed on value, weight or quantity.

3.   **Special Documents**
(A) **Sanitary Certificate**—required for plants, seeds, animals and animal products.
(B) **Fumigation Certificate**—required for used clothing.

4.   ***Insurance**

Must be covered in Somali except AID shipments.

5.   **Consular Holidays**
All holidays generally observed in New York City.

SOUTH AFRICA

SUMMARY OF SHIPPING DOCUMENTS REQUIRED
No Consular Documents Required
1.   **Shipping Documents Required for all commercial shipments**

(A) *Commercial Invoice—must show supplier's price to customer and all costs, charges, and commission to arrive at an FOB port of shipment price.

(B) *Declaration of Origin—on special Form DA-59 sold by commercial printers. For shipments that enter the country for goods at a duty rate less than the general rate (i.e.: a M.F.N. or preferential rate).

Note: Customs require that the original Declaration of Origin must be attached to the original Commercial Invoice. Additional copies may be requested by the customer for his files.

(C) **Bills of Lading**—3—can be either "straight" or "to order"—must show all particulars—number and date—port of loading and port of discharge—marks and numbers—number of cases, and a description of the goods.

2.   *For Parcel Post Shipments
It is advisable to enclose a signed copy of the Commercial Invoice and Declaration DA-59 in the package, and to endorse the outside wrapper to that effect.

3.   **Import License**
Required by importer for most commodities. Imports are divided into several categories, according to their essentiality. Capital equipment, raw materials and some consumer goods are granted licenses on the basis of reasonable requirements. Licenses for the imortation of vehicles will be granted on the basis of reasonable requirements. Licenses for the importation of vehicles will be granted to registered importers of such vehicles. Quota goods (essential and non-essential consumer goods and luxury items) may be imported by registered importers on the basis of exchange allocations, which will imply issuance of Import Permit.

4.   **Holidays**
Washington's Birthday, Good Friday, Memorial Day, May 31, July 4, Labor Day, Columbus Day, Thanksgiving Day, Christmas Day, December 26. All holidays generally observed in New York City.
*Denotes changes since previous notice.

5.   **Commerce Departments South African Regulations**
The U.S. Department of Commerces' recent imposition of controls on the export of merchandise and technical data for use by the military and/or police forces of South Africa and Nambia raises questions which exceeds the bounds of South Africa. Controls apply to all goods that might be used by specific institutions in a foreign country regardless of the nature of the goods and their possible uses. Applying not only to direct sales to the enforcement agencies, but also to the items that might be resold by South African importers (or by other foreign vendors outside of South Africa). The stringent controls impose a

total embargo on trade with specific segments of the South African economy, without effecting shipments to other parties in that country. The controls also prohibit exports or re-exports of U.S. goods and technology under General License when the exporter knows, or has reason to know, that they will be delivered to the South African military or police or used in a way that will assist those agencies. General Licenses may, however, still be used for shipment that will not benefit the military or police. The exporter must indicate by a statement on the Bill of Lading and the Commercial Invoice, notifying his customer that use by the military or police is prohibited. The regulations were published in Export Administration Bulletin #15, Feb. 16, 1978. Exporters with questions as to applicability of the controls should contact The Exporters Service Staff, Office of Export Administration, (202) 377-4811.

*Denotes changes since previous notice.

See Form 10-659.

SPAIN & SPANISH TERRITORIES

SUMMARY OF SHIPPING DOCUMENTS REQUIRED

1. **Shipping Documents Required**
   All Commercial Shipments valued at $142.00 FOB or more.

   (A) ***Certificate of Origin**—3—preferably in Spanish—when legalization is requested by consignee or letter of credit, official Spanish forms must be used—sold by the Consulate at 70 cents per set—2 copies retained by Consulate—Original returned to shipper—One copy of the commercial invoice must be presented together with the certificates of origin—retained by Consulate.

   (B) **Commercial Invoice**—2—must show all details and complete description of each class of goods.

2. ***Consular Fees**

Commercial Invoice (when requested)	$ 6.20
Pro-forma Invoice (when requested)	6.20
Certificate of Origin	9.50
Extra copy of certificate of origin (when requested)	9.50
Certificate of Origin blanks (per set)	.70
Bill of Lading (when requested)	12.00
Powers of attorney executed before a Notary Public within 35 miles of New York City	54.00
Powers of attorney executed before a Notary Public outside 35 miles of New York City	12.00
Letters of Certification	6.20
Certificates of Incorporation (merger, amendment, etc.) of corporations to be used in Registro Mercantil de Espana	54.00
Document of agreement, cession, assignment referring to trade marks, etc. notarized and signed by County Clerk	12.00

***Consular Holidays**
Holy Thursday (½ day), Good Friday, July 18, July 25, August 15, October 12, December 24 (½ day), and December 31 (½ day). All holidays generally observed in New York City.

*Denotes changes since previous notice.

DECLARATION OF ORIGIN—
for the export of goods to the
REPUBLIC OF SOUTH AFRICA

Supplier (name, address, country) ....

NOTE TO IMPORTERS

This declaration, properly completed by the supplier, must be furnished in support of the relative bill of entry where goods qualify for and are entered at the rate of duty lower than the general rate

Consignee (name, address, country) ....

Customs date stamp

Particulars of transport ....

1 Item No.	2 Marks and numbers	3 No. and desc. of packages	4 Description of goods	5 Country of origin	6 Gross Mass	7 Invoice No./ Ref.

472

I, (name and capacity) ....

duly authorised by the supplier of the goods enumerated above hereby declare that—

1. the goods enumerated opposite item(s) .... in column 1 above have been wholly produced or manufactured in the country stated in column 5 in respect of such goods from raw materials produced in that country;

2. the goods enumerated opposite item(s) .... in column 1 above have been wholly or partly manufactured from imported materials in the country specified in column 5 in respect of such goods; and

2.1 the final process of manufacture has taken place in the said country;

2.2 the cost to the manufacturer of the materials wholly produced or manufactured in the said country plus the cost of labour directly employed in the manufacture of such goods is not less than .... per cent of the total production cost of such goods;

2.3 in calculating the production cost of such goods only the cost to the manufacturer of all materials plus manufacturing wages and salaries, direct manufacturing expenses, overhead factory expenses, cost of inside containers and other expenses incidental to manufacturing, used or expended in the manufacture of such goods have been included and profits and administrative, distribution and selling overhead expenses have been excluded.

....

Place   **Date**   **Signature of Deponent**

Form No. 10 - 659   Printed and Sold by Unz & Co., Division of Scott Printing Corp., 190 Baldwin Ave., Jersey City, N.J. 07306 — N.J. (201) 795-5400 / N.Y. (212) 344-2270
Toll Free (800) 631-3098

Form 10-659. Export Forms, Hazardous Materials Labels, etc. can be purchased from Unz & Co., 190 Baldwin Ave., P.O. Box 308, Jersey City, N.J. 07303.

473

SRI LANKA, DEMOCRATIC SOCIALIST REPUBLIC OF

SUMMARY OF SHIPPING DOCUMENTS REQUIRED

Special Information—Shipping documents should be forwarded to the consignee under separate cover.

No Consular Documents Required
1.   **Shipping Documents Required**
   (A) **Commercial Invoice**—3—must describe goods in full detail showing prices, discounts, packing—ocean freight and insurance (must be shown separately)—must show gross and net weights and numbers of the articles shipped—origin of the goods must be declared and signed by shipper. On textile shipments the composition of the goods must be stated correctly and in the fullest possible detail.
   (B) **Certificate of Origin**—2—when requested by importer or letter of credit—on general form—sold by commercial printers—certified by the New York Chamber of Commerce and Industry, which requires one additional notarized copy for its files.
   (C) **Bills of Lading**—no special regulations. "To Order" bills of lading acceptable.
2.   **Air Cargo Shipments**
   Commercial Invoice—3—(prepared as above).
3.   *Import License**
   Except for specified items and merchandise subject to controls for security purposes, import licenses are not required.
4.   **Special Documents**
   (A) **Meat Inspection Certificate**—issued by the U.S. Department of Agriculture—required for meat or products, hermetically sealed—cooked, cured, or dried meat—intestines or other meat products in the form of sausage—rendered animal fats—and any other prepared or manufactured meat products.
   (B) **Certificate of Health**—required for livestock—signed by a veterinarian in the country of export.
   (C) **Certificate of Fumigation**—required for used clothing—raw cotton and cotton seed.
5.   **Consular Holidays**
   All holidays generally observed in New York City.

SUDAN

SUMMARY OF SHIPPING DOCUMENTS REQUIRED

Special Information—All Shipments to the Sudan must be covered by insurance companies in Sudan, except AID shipments. All applications for import authorization will be rejected unless insurance has been placed locally.

No Consular Documents Required
1.   **Shipping Documents Required**
   (A) **Commercial Invoice**—2—on sellers letterhead—must show name and address of purchaser; marks and numbers on packages; quantity and gross weight or measurement of packages; nature, quality, and net weight or measure of con-

tents; the cost price to the importer at the place of purchase together with charges incidental to the making of the contract and to the delivery of the goods at the place of import; any discount, allowance, commission, or any similar deduction together with an explanation of its nature. Weights or measurements should wherever possible be in the metric system. A signed statement to the effect that the invoice is in every respect correct and true.

(B) **Certificate of Origin**—2—when required—general form sold by commercial printers—certified by the New York Chamber of Commerce and Industry, which requires one additional notarized copy for its files.

(C) **Bills of Lading**—required for each separate consignment showing name of vessel, port of loading, name and address of consignee and a description of the contents. "To Order" bills of lading permitted.

2. **Air Cargo Shipments**
   Commercial Invoice—2—(see above) must accompany shipment.

3. **Import License**
   Issued for most goods of U.S. origin—required by importer.

4. ***Holidays**
   Good Friday, Easter Monday, and May 25. All holidays generally observed in New York City.
   *Denotes changes since previous notice.

SWEDEN

SUMMARY OF SHIPPING DOCUMENTS REQUIRED
No Consular Documents Required
1. **Shipping Documents Required**
   (A) **Commercial Invoice**—At least 3 copies required for all goods. No prescribed form. According to the Swedish Customs Regulations should show (a) name and address of seller; (b) name and address of purchaser; (c) date of invoice; (d) number of packages, their kind and gross weight and also marks and numbers; (e) description of goods; (f) quantity of goods; (g) price of each kind of products; (h) any discount or allowance, and the nature of same; and (i) delivery and payment terms. Signature of the exporter or his authorized agent not required.

   (B) **Certificate of Origin**—2—when required—general form sold by commercial printers—certified by the New York Chamber of Commerce and Industry, which requires one additional notarized copy for its files.

   (C) **Bills of Lading**—no special regulations. "To Order" bills of lading acceptable.

2. **Air Cargo Shipments**
   Commercial Invoice—3—(see above) must accompany shipment. (Additional copy may be air mailed to consignee.)

3. **Import License**
   Most items from the United States are free from import licenses. There are very few items requiring an import license (which is only granted to importers domiciled in Sweden).

4. **Special Documents**
   Sanitary Certificate—1—Must show country of origin. Required for shipments of specified commodities including the following:

Certain Animal Products,	Oleomargarine
(including meat and meat products)	Potatoes
Foodstuffs	Seeds

Live Animals	Syrup and Molasses
Live Plants	Used Dairy holloware
Margarine, cheese and fatty emulsions	Used sacks

The Sanitary Certificate must be notarized and authenticated by the New York County Clerk. The County Clerk's signature must then be legalized by the Swedish Consulate. No copy is required for the Consulate.

5. **Consular Fees**

Legalization of County Clerk's Signature $6.30

6. **Holidays**

Good Friday, June 22, December 24, and December 26. All holidays generally observed in New York City.

*Denotes changes since previous notice.

SWITZERLAND

SUMMARY OF SHIPPING DOCUMENTS REQUIRED

No Consular Documents Required

1. **Shipping Documents Required**

   (A) *Commercial Invoice—2—must show description of goods—gross and net weight—quantity in pieces or liters or other metric unit—description of packing—marks—numbers—number of packages—country of origin—market value of merchandise prevailing in the place of shipment, as well as all additional cost of transportation to the Swiss frontier.

   (B) *Certificate of Origin—2—Required for shipments of certain wines, liqueurs, seed potatoes and several specified fabrics of silk or artifical silk—on general form—sold by commercial printers—certified by the New York Chamber of Commerce and Industry, which requires one additional notarized copy for its files. Documents covering shipments of the fabrics must state the country where fabric was actually woven. If a beverage, certificate must show the exact name of the beverage, brand, marking, etc. and the place of production or manufacture. This information may appear directly below the description of the merchandise.

2. ***Import Control**

   Import licenses are only required for a short list of items, mostly agricultural products. State trading activities are conducted in grains, flour, butter, oil and fats, seed potatoes, and alcohol.

3. **Exchange Restrictions**

   There are no official exchange restrictions affecting imports from the U.S., although there may be certain restraints (depending on circumstances) placed upon capital imports.

4. **Special Documents**

   (A) *Sanitary Certificate—Required for fresh fruits, vegetables, trees and shrubs, seeds.

   (B) **Official Health Certificate**—Required for live animals, meat and meat products, game, eggs for hatching, bees, beeswax, honeycombs, and shellfish and preserved fish. Imports of fresh frozen meat, poultry and fish are regulated by the Federal Veterinary Office.

5. *Consular Holidays
    January 1, April 13, April 16, May 24, June 3, August 1 (½ day), December 24 (½ day), December 25, and December 31 (½ day).
    *Denotes changes since previous notice.

SYRIA

SUMMARY OF SHIPPING DOCUMENTS REQUIRED
Special Information
Insurance must be covered in Syria, except AID shipments.
Consular Documents Required
1. **All Shipments regardless of value:**
    (A) *Commercial Invoice—2—in French or English—One copy retained by Consulate—It is recommended that both FOB and CIF values be shown on invoice. Invoices must be certified as to current export market prices and country of origin by the U.S. Arab Chamber of Commerce, which requires one additional notarized copy for its files. Invoices must show the number and kind of packages, marks and package numbers, gross and net weights, all copies must bear the following affidavit, signed by an officer of the Company:
    "We hereby certify that this invoice is authentic, that it is the only one issued by us for the merchandise described herein, and that the prices stated in it are the exact prices without deductions of any kind. The following signed statement must be shown.
    "We hereby certify that the merchandise is wholly produced in the United States of America and with labor and materials from the aforementioned country. It is not of Israeli origin nor were any Israeli products used in the manufacture, thus we assume full responsibility for any inaccuracies or error therein."
    Syrian legislation requires that agents or representatives be of Syrian nationality and that his commission be registered in Syria. Therefore, all exporters and shippers that do not have an agent in Syria and who sell directly to the importer must include the following signed affidavit:
    "We declare under our own responsibility that we are not represented in Syria and that Syria is not included in the territory of any other agent who would benefit from any commission whatever on our products imported into Syria."
    If the exporter has a branch office or agency in Syria, the name, address and registration number (with the Department of Companies, Ministry of National Economy) of the branch office or agency must appear on the invoice. Exception: When the nature of the exported goods is such that there would not be an agent for them (Army) surpluses, used small hardware articles, etc. Shipments may be made either on freight collect or prepaid basis provided the goods are not sent on ships of unfriendly countries.
    (B) *Certificate of Origin—Not always required as the origin of the goods is already declared on invoice. However, when Consulate legalization is required by letter of credit or importer, 2 copies prepared on general form—in English or French—must be presented to Consulate which will retain one copy. Prior certification by the U.S. Arab Chamber of Commerce is required. One additional notarized copy is also required for its files.

All certificates of origin and commercial invoices must contain the following statement: "We hereby certify that the merchandise is wholly produced in the United States of America and with labor and materials from the aforementioned country. It is not of Israeli origin nor were any Israeli products used in the manufacture, thus we assume full responsibility for any inaccuracies or errors therein."

For manufactured goods the name of the manufacturer or producer must be shown.

2. **Correction of Documents**
    To correct errors a new set of documents must be prepared. Consular fee will be the same as that charged for legalization of original documents.

3. **Import License**
    Required by importer for all commercial shipments valued over $65.00.

4. **Medical Samples**
    According to a Ministry of Health Decree free medical samples may not be imported unless they conform to the following conditions: the medical sample to be imported must be different in form and size from the item prepared to be sold. It must be clearly labeled "Free Medical Sample."

5. **Exemption of Consular Fees**
    The Consulate has received blanket instructions to exempt from consular fees the following shipments: Syrian Arab Airlines, Ford Foundation; goods to be displayed at the Damascus International Fair; Diplomatic and U.N. personnel.

6. *When the Consular legalization is required for contracts, trade marks, price lists, power of attorney, assignments etc. the document must be signed by a Notary Public, countersigned by the County Clerk, signed by Secretary of State having jurisdiction of the County Clerk and by the Secretary of State in Washington, D.C. prior to presentation to the Syrian Embassy.

7. *Consular Fees
    Consular fees must be paid by check or money order made out to the Syrian Arab Republic.

On documents not specifying a value, Invoice, Contract, Certificate of Origin, Trade Mark, Free Sale Price List, and other, fee is $4.60.

If the invoice total exceeds even one cent, as in example, $20,000.01, the fee is $37.20 and not $36.95.

If the total on Invoice is exclusive of Consular Fee, is more than $55,555.55, proceed as follows:

$$\frac{(\text{Invoice Amount} - 493.85 \times 4.05 \times 1.50/1{,}000)}{3.90} + 6.45$$

= the Total Fee (to be rounded to the nearest dollar).
EXAMPLE:

$$\frac{(75{,}000 - 493.85 \times 4.05 \times 1.50/1{,}000)}{3.90} + 6.45 = 122.50$$

= $123.00

The Fee is per copy and not per set; moreover, the fees are on the total value of the total value of the invoice, FOB or CIF.

*Denotes changes since previous notice.

Syrian Consular Legalization Fees On Commercial Papers—August, 1976

FEE	VALUE UP TO:	FEE	VALUE UP TO:
GRATIS	$ 49.40	$ 20.30	$ 9,382.72
$ 3.85	246.91	20.80	9,629.63
4.10	271.60	21.05	9,876.55
4.40	296.30	21.55	10,123.46
4.65	321.00	21.80	10,370.37
4.90	345.70	22.35	10,617.29
5.15	370.40	22.60	10,864.20
5.40	395.05	23.10	11,111.11
5.65	419.75	23.35	11,358.03
5.90	444.45	23.85	11,604.94
6.15	469.15	24.10	11,851.85
6.45	493.85	24.65	12,098.77
6.95	740.75	24.90	12,345.68
7.20	987.65	25.40	12,592.60
7.70	1,234.60	25.65	12,839.51
7.95	1,481.50	26.15	13.086.42
8.50	1,728.40	26.45	13,333.34
8.75	1,975.32	26.95	13,580.25
9.25	2,222.22	27.20	13,827.16
9.50	2,469.14	27.70	14,074.08
10.00	2,716.05	27.95	14,320.99
10.30	2,962.97	28.50	14,567.90
10.80	3,209.88	28.75	14,814.82
11.05	3,456.80	29.25	15,061.73
11.55	3,703.71	29.50	15,308.65
11.80	3,950.62	30.00	15,555.55
12.35	4,197.54	30.30	15,802.50
12.60	4,444.45	30.80	16,049.40
13.10	4,691.36	31.05	16,296.30
13.35	4,938.27	31.55	16,543.25
13.85	5,185.19	31.80	16,790.15
14.10	5,432.10	32.35	17,037.05
14.65	5,679.01	32.60	17,283.95
14.90	5,925.93	33.00	17,530.90
15.40	6,172.84	33.35	17,777.80
15.65	6,419.75	33.85	18,024.70
16.15	6,666.67	34.10	18,271.60
16.45	6,913.58	34.65	18,518.55
16.95	7,160.49	34.90	19,765.45
17.20	7,407.41	35.40	19,012.35
17.70	7,654.32	35.65	19,259.30
17.95	7,901.24	36.15	19,506.20
18.50	8,148.15	36.45	19,753.10
18.75	8,395.06	36.95	20,000.00
19.25	8,861.98	37.20	20,246.95
19.50	8,888.89	37.70	20,493.85
20.00	9,135.80	37.95	20,740.75

FEE	VALUE UP TO:	FEE	VALUE UP TO:
$ 38.50	$ 20,987.65	$ 58.75	$ 34,074.10
38.75	21,234.60	59.25	34,321.00
39.25	21,481.50	59.50	34,567.90
39.50	21,728.40	60.00	34,814.85
40.00	21,975.35	60.30	35,061.75
40.30	22,222.25	60.80	35,308.65
40.80	22,469.15	61.05	35,555.60
41.05	22,716.05	61.55	35,802.50
41.55	22,963.00	61.80	36,049.40
41.80	23,209.90	62.35	36,296.30
42.35	23,456.80	62.60	36,543.25
42.60	23,703.70	63.10	36,790.15
43.10	23,950.65	63.35	37,037.05
43.35	24,197.55	63.85	37,283.95
43.85	24,444.45	64.10	37,530.90
44.10	24,691.40	64.65	37,777.80
44.65	24,938.30	64.90	38,024.70
44.90	25,185.20	65.40	38,271.60
45.40	25,432.10	65.65	38,518.55
45.65	25,679.05	66.15	38,765.45
46.15	25,925.95	66.45	39,012.35
46.45	26,172.85	66.95	39,259.30
46.95	26,225.50	67.20	39,506.20
47.20	26,666.70	67.70	39,753.10
47.70	26,913.60	67.95	40,000.00
47.95	27,160.50	68.50	40,246.95
48.50	27,407.45	68.75	40,493.85
48.75	27,654.35	69.25	40,740.75
49.25	27,901.25	69.50	40,987.65
49.50	28,148.15	70.00	41,234.60
50.00	28,395.10	70.30	41,481.50
50.30	28,642.00	70.80	41,728.40
50.80	28,888.90	71.05	41,975.35
51.05	29,135.80	71.55	42,222.25
51.55	29,382.75	71.80	42,469.15
51.80	29,629.65	72.35	42,716.05
52.35	29,876.55	72.60	42,963.00
52.60	30,123.50	73.10	43,209.90
53.10	30,370.40	73.35	43,456.80
53.35	30,617.30	73.85	43,703.70
53.85	30,864.20	74.10	43,950.65
54.10	31,111.15	74.65	44,197.55
54.65	31,358.05	74.90	44,444.45
54.90	31,604.95	75.40	44,691.40
55.40	31,851.85	75.65	44,938.30
55.65	32,098.80	76.15	45,185.20
56.15	32,345.70	76.45	45,432.10
56.45	32,592.60	76.95	45,679.05
56.95	32,839.55	77.20	45,592.95

FEE	VALUE UP TO:	FEE	VALUE UP TO:
$ 57.20	$ 33,086.45	$ 77.70	$ 46,172.85
57.70	33,333.35	77.95	46,419.75
57.95	33,580.25	78.50	46,666.70
58.50	33,827.20	78.75	46,913.60
79.25	47,160.50	86.15	51,604.95
79.50	47,407.45	86.45	51,851.85
80.00	47,654.35	86.95	52,098.80
80.30	47,901.25	87.20	52,345.70
80.80	48,148.15	87.70	52,592.60
81.05	48,395.10	87.95	52,839.55
81.55	48,642.00	88.50	53,086.45
81.80	48,888.90	88.75	53,333.35
82.35	49,135.80	89.25	53,580.25
82.60	49,382.75	89.50	53,827.20
83.10	49,629.65	90.00	54,074.10
83.35	49,876.55	90.30	54,321.00
83.85	50,123.50	90.80	54,567.90
84.10	50,370.40	91.05	54,814.85
84.65	50,617.30	91.55	55,061.75
84.90	50,864.20	91.80	55,308.65
85.40	51,111.15	92.35	55,555.55
85.65	51,358.05		

TANZANIA

SUMMARY OF SHIPPING DOCUMENTS REQUIRED
No Consular Documents Required
1.   **Shipping Documents Required**
  (A) **Commercial Invoice**—2—on shipper's letterhead—should show full descrip-
      tion of goods—net and gross weights—marks and numbers—country of origin
      —true market value of goods in the country of origin—unit rate and value of the
      goods plus packing costs, insurance and freight up to the port of entry—must
      also show any discounts and/or commissions.
  (B) **Certificate of Origin**—2—when required—on general form—sold by commer-
      cial printers—certified by New York Chamber of Commerce and Industry
      which requires an additional notarized copy for its files.
  (C) **Bills of Lading**—2—no special regulations—the usual particulars should be
      shown—shipping marks and numbers on the bills of lading, on the goods and
      on the commercial invoices should correspond exactly.
  (D) **Clean Report of Finding (Certificate)**—all shipments to Tanzania require ad-
      vance inspection prior to exportation. The Superintendence Company, Inc. in
      the United States will perform this service and issue the Clean Report of
      Findings at no expense to the shipper.
2.   **Import License**
      Required by importer for most commodities—validity six months. Tolerances
      usually 5% of the value stated on license.
3.   **Holidays**
      April 26 and December 9. All holidays generally observed in New York City.

THAILAND

SUMMARY OF SHIPPING DOCUMENTS REQUIRED
No Consular Documents Required
1.   **Shipping Documents Required for all commercial shipments:**
   (A) **Commercial Invoice**—3—Must show FOB value and all itemized expenses up to
      CIF value. In addition the following charges must be shown: Packing charge (if
      any); Commission (if any); and others. Must show selling price or value of goods
      per unit expressed in the type of currency under transaction. Must show all
      discounts and their nature in addition tin—2—when required—general form—
      sold nature as encouragement to export such goods (if any). Complete descrip-
      tion of the merchandise must be given, including percentages when com-
      modities contain mixtures (such as textiles, metal alloys, etc.). Must also show
      details of merchandise i.e., names, kinds, qualities. Net weights and quantity of
      each package as well as those of all items must be declared. Marks, numbers,
      amounts and description of packages (whether they are crates, drums, bun-
      dles, etc.) as well as gross weights in kilos of all packages must be shown. Must
      also show country of origin as well as country from which goods were pur-
      chased and consigning country. Date of purchase and date of sale in addition to
      a statement showing whether the goods are: (a) sold or contracted to be sold or
      (b) sent on consignment or (c) supplied to branch firm; etc. Exporters must
      certify that all given information is true and correct and sign such declaration.
   (B) **Certificate of Origin**—2—when required—general form—sold by commercial
      printers—certified by the New York Chamber of Commerce and Industry,
      which requires one additional notarized copy for its files.
   (C) **Bill of Lading**—No special requirements. May be made out "to order" provided
      that importer's name is shown as the notifying party. One copy is required by
      the Customs Authorities for clearance.
2.   **Import License**
      Required for a few commodities only, including firearms, explosives, narcot-
      ics, etc. Licenses are valid for six months. For the majority of goods, all that is
      required is that importer presents a simple "entry declaration" to the Customs
      Authorities.
      A 5% tolerance in value is usually allowed. Letters of credit over 9 months
      require prior approval from the Bank of Thailand.
      Holidays
      April 6, April 13, May 9, October 23, and December 5. All holidays generally
      observed in New York City.
      *Denotes changes since previous notice.

TOGO, REPUBLIC OF

SUMMARY OF SHIPPING DOCUMENTS REQUIRED
No Consular Documents Required
1.   **Shipping Documents Required**
   (A) **Commercial Invoice**—2—no special form—should contain names of exporter
      and consignee—number and types of packages—marks and numbers on pack-
      ages—net and gross weight—CIF value—terms of sale—an accurate, specific
      and complete description of merchandise—must also show ex factory price
      and cost of shipping and insurance.

(B) **Certificate of Origin**—2—on general form—sold by commercial printers—certified by the New York Chamber of Commerce and Industry, which requires one additional notarized copy for its files.

(C) **Bills of Lading**—2—no special regulation. Shipping marks and numbers on bills of lading, on the goods, and on the invoices must correspond. A packing list is recommended.

2. **Import License**

Required by importer for all imports. Validity 180 days from date of issuance. Merchandise must be shipped prior to expiration date. License may be extended with proper cause.

3. **Mission Holidays**

All holidays generally observed in New York City.

TRINIDAD AND TOBAGO

SUMMARY OF SHIPPING DOCUMENTS REQUIRED

No Consular Documents Required

1. **Shipping Documents Required**

All Shipments (regardless of value and mode of transportation):

(A) *Commercial Invoice—No special form—3 copies required—2 for customs purposes and 1 for import licensing. Must contain a careful and detailed description of the goods and all details necessary to arrive at the CIF value. All discounts listed must be explained. In the case of imports under general license, a signed declaration of origin must be included as follows: "We hereby declare that the within goods were manufactured (or produced or grown) in (name of country)." The invoice must be signed by the declarer and one witness. Facsimile signatures are not accepted.

(B) **Bill of Lading**—No special form required. "To order" bills are permitted. Goods are obtainable by the consignee without presentation of the bill if a bond is deposited.

2. *Import License

Required for all items; should be obtained prior to the arrival of the goods. Most licenses are valid for 6 months. The validity period is stated on each license. Goods should arrive before expiration of the license. The Consulate General of Trinidad and Tobago informs us that Open General Licenses are still in effect in that country, however, Import Licenses are required for all goods mentioned on the Negative List.

3. *Special Documents

Sanitary Certificate—Shipments of dried beans, peas, lentils, and other pulses, and of shelled and unshelled peanuts must be accompanied by certificates, in duplicate signed by a State or Federal authority, stating that the products are of a type, quality, grade or standard that could be legally sold for human food under federal law in the country of origin and that the products are substantially free from mold, insect damage, or live insects. Meat and meat products should be accompanied by a health certificate issued by the appropriate authority.

4. *Consular Holidays

Good Friday, Easter Monday, August 6, and August 31. All holidays generally observed in New York City.

*Denotes changes since previous notice.

TUNISIA

SUMMARY OF SHIPPING DOCUMENTS REQUIRED
1.   **Documents Required for all shipments, regardless of value.**
   (A) *Commercial Invoice—3 copies—must give full details and be signed by shipper—certified by our Chamber, which retains one notarized copy—must be legalized by the Embassy, which retains one copy.
   (B) *Certificate of Origin—3 copies—must be certified by our Chamber, which retains one notarized copy—must be legalized by the Embassy, which retains one copy.
   (C) **Bills of Lading**—No special regulations. Goods may be consigned either direct or to order.
2.   **Import License**
   Required by the importer for most shipments. Possession of this license entitles the importer to the release of the necessary foreign exchange.
3.   *Consular Fees
   Commercial Invoice .... $4.15 per copy
   Certificate of Origin .... $3.30 per copy
   Legalization of Signatures, Power of Attorney, etc. .... $2.75 each
   *Denotes changes since previous notice.

TURKEY

SUMMARY OF SHIPPING DOCUMENTS REQUIRED
No Consular Documents Required
1.   **Shipping Documents Required for all commercial shipments regardless of mode of transportation:**
   (A) **Combined Certificate of Origin and Consular Invoice**—2—official Turkish form—sold by commercial printers. Both copies must be notarized. Erasures or corrections are not permitted. The value shown on the commercial invoice must also appear on the combined certificate. Official Turkish forms must be certified as to price and origin by The New York Chamber of Commerce and Industry. One copy must contain the following affidavit and will be retained by the Chamber:

   "I, (name, title, name of country), hereby swear that the prices stated in this invoice are the current export market prices for the merchandise described and origin of these goods is (country of origin). I accept full responsibility for any inaccuracies or errors therein."

                                                            (Signature)

   Shippers must show the following declaration on the certificate:
      "'This certificate of origin is covered by import license (or letter of credit) Number _____ issued on (date of issuance) by _____.'"
   (B) **Commercial Invoice**—1—must show all information and complete description of goods.
2.   **AID Shipments**
   Only the commercial invoice is required—consular legalization is not required. When requested, invoices will be certified as to price and origin by this Chamber which retains one notarized copy containing the affidavit shown under 1(A).

3. **Special Documents**

(A) *__Letters of Correction__
Prepared in duplicate—Must be addressed to consignee in Turkey. Must be notarized, certified by County Clerk or by this Chamber, which requires one additional notarized copy for its files, and legalized by Consulate. Fee $3.30.

(B) **Phytosanitary Certificate**—All imports of plants including fresh fruits and vegetables must be accompanied by Federal phytosanitary export certificates. Plants must be substantially free from plant pests and diseases and must have been grown in an area substantially free from prohibited plant pests and diseases. The wrappings and packing must also be free from prohibited plant pests and diseases.

4. **Import License**
Required by importer for all imports. Validity—6 months. Goods must be cleared through customs before expiration.

5. *__Consular Fees__
Letter of correction; county clerk's signature authentication $3.30

6. *__Holidays__
April 23, August 30, and October 29. All holidays generally observed in New York City.
*Denotes changes since previous notice.
See Form 10-790.

UGANDA

SUMMARY OF SHIPPING DOCUMENTS REQUIRED
No Consular Documents Required
1. **Shipping Documents Required**

(A) **Commercial Invoice**—2—must contain the quantity of the goods and their true market value in the country of origin—origin of the goods—unit rate and value of the goods plus packing cost, insurance and freight up to the port of entry—exact nature of discounts and commissions to the buyer. Import License numbers must be shown on invoice.

(B) **Certificate of Origin**—2—when required—general form—sold by commercial printers—certified by the New York Chamber of Commerce and Industry, which requires one additional notarized copy for its files.

(C) **Bills of Lading**—no special requirements—the usual information should be shown. A packing list is recommended.

2. **Import License**
Required by importer—validity usually 6 months—no tolerance on the value is permitted. Exporters should obtain the license number in order to show it on the commercial invoices.

3. **Special Documents**

(A) **Sanitary Certificate**—required for plants and parts of plants and fresh fruits—issued by U.S. Department of Agriculture.

(B) **Health Certificate**—required for animals—issued by a qualified veterinary surgeon.

(C) **Disinfection Certificate**—required for used clothing.

4. **Holidays**
All holidays generally observed in New York City.

CERTIFICATE OF ORIGIN AND CONSULAR INVOICE for
TURKEY

The undersigned . . . . .   *declares that the following*
(Owner, Agent or Company)

goods shipped on the S. S.   *on the date of*
(Name of Steamer)

consigned to . . . . .
(Name and Address of Consignee)

are the product of   *and the point stated a numers*
(Country of Manufacture)

Number of Packages Boxes or Cases in Words	MARKS AND NUMBERS	WEIGHT IN KILOS GROSS	NET	DESCRIPTION	VALUE IN DOLLARS

Dated at _____ : _____ *on the* _____ *day of* _____ *19*

_____
(Signature of Owner, Agent or Company)

Sworn to before me this _____ *day of* _____ *19* . . .

Form 10-790 Printed and Sold by Unz & Co., Division of Scott Printing Corp., 190 Baldwin Ave., Jersey City, N.J. 07306—N.J. (201) 795-5400 / N.Y. (212) 344-2270 Toll Free (800) 631-3098

Form 10-790. Export Forms, Hazardous Materials Labels, etc. can be purchased from Unz & Co., 190 Baldwin Ave., P.O. Box 308, Jersey City, N.J. 07303.

UNITED ARAB EMIRATES

SUMMARY OF SHIPPING DOCUMENTS REQUIRED
1. **Special Information**
    The term Persian Gulf should not be used on shipping documents or correspondence. Shippers should use the term Arabian Gulf.
2. **Consular Documents Required for all commercial shipments:**
    (A) *Commercial Invoice**—1—must contain an accurate description of the goods with their weight, quantities, and values—must contain a manufacturer's or producers certificate stating that the goods are not of Israeli origin or contain any Israeli materials. Must be certified by the U.S. Arab Chamber of Commerce, which requires one additional copy for its files. Legalized by the Embassy. No copies are required for Embassy's files.
    (B) *Certificate of Origin**—1—on general form—sold by commercial printers—certified by U.S. Arab Chamber of Commerce, which requires one additional copy for its files. Legalized by the Embassy. No copies are required for Embassy's files.
    (C) **Bills of Lading**—no special requirements. The information should correspond with that shown on the invoices and packages.
    (D) *Insurance Certificate (Letter)**—1—issued by the insurance company that insures the shipment—must state that the company is not included on the so-called "blacklist"—certified by the U.S. Arab Chamber of Commerce, which requires one additional copy for its files—legalized by the Embassy. No copies required for Embassy's files.
    (E) *Steamship Certificate**—1—issued by the steamship company stating that the ship is not an Israeli vessel, nor is it scheduled to call at any Israeli port—certified by the U.S. Arab Chamber of Commerce, which requires one additional copy for its files—legalized by the Embassy. No copies required for Embassy's files.
2. **Import License**
    Not generally required.
3. *Legalization Fees**
    Consular fees must be paid by certified check, money order, or cash. Checks and money orders should be made payable to the Embassy of the United Arab Emirates.

Commercial Invoice .... $1.25 per document
Certificate of Origin .... $1.25 per document
Insurance Certificate .... $1.25 per document
Steamship Certificate .... $1.25 per document
Discharge Certificate .... $1.25 per document
*Denotes changes since previous notice.

UPPER VOLTA

SUMMARY OF SHIPPING DOCUMENTS REQUIRED
No Consular Documents Required
1. **Shipping Documents Required**
    (A) **Commercial Invoice**—2—no special form—should contain names of exporter and consignee—number and types of packages—marks and numbers on packages: net and

gross weight—CIF value—terms of sale—an accurate and complete description of the merchandise.

(B) **Certificate of Origin**—2—copies—on general form—sold by commercial printers—certified by the New York Chamber of Commerce and Industry, which requires an additional notarized copy for its files.

(C) **Bills of Lading**—2—no special regulations—marks of identification and name and address of the consignee should be clearly indicated—shipping marks and numbers on the bills of lading, commercial invoices and the goods themselves should correspond exactly. A packing list is recommended.

2.   **Import License**

Required by importer for many commodities—validity six months—goods must be shipped before expiration of license. Tolerance of 5% in value or quantity is permitted.

3.   **Consular Holidays**

All holidays generally observed in New York City.

URUGUAY

SUMMARY OF SHIPPING DOCUMENTS REQUIRED

Special Information—Except for air shipments, all documents are presented to Consulate by the steamship company, not by the shipper.

Transit Shipments—Goods sent to Uruguay in transit to another country, or destined to a free port, cannot be shipped on a "To Order" bill of lading. Consignee must be a commercial firm, freight forwarder, shipping agent, etc., who will be responsible for any irregularities resulting from transhipping.

Documents Required

1.   **Ocean Freight Shipments regardless of value**

(A) *Commercial Invoice*—4—in Spanish—must show country of origin and FOB value (port of shipment), as well as all expenses to CIF value—submitted by steamship company to Consulate—legalized by Consulate.

(B) **Bill of Lading**—5—Three originals, two non-negotiable copies in Spanish retained by Consulate. "To Order" bill of lading allowed. May show more than one mark, but only one consignee.

2.   *Parcel Post Shipments regardless of value*

Same as Freight Shipments (see (1) above).

3.   *Air Cargo Shipments regardless of value*

Legalization of Air Shipments—Documents covering air cargo shipments must be presented to the Consulate at least 3 working days prior to the departure of the airplane. Shippers are advised that the Consulate enforces this regulation to the letter.

(A) *Commercial Invoice*—4—in Spanish—3 retained by Consulate

(B) **Air Waybills**—3—in Spanish or English—2 retained by Consulate

4.   **Import License**—Required by the importer for all shipments, but need not be presented to the Consulate except for shipments of the following items when consigned to individual persons (except those having diplomatic immunity): Automobiles, refrigerators, radios, and all domestic electrical appliances.

5.   **Special Documents**

Sanitary Certificate—2—presented to Consulate along with regular documents—legalized and one copy returned to the shipper. Issued by the Department of Agriculture; certifying that the products are fit for human consumption—required for shipments of fresh fruits, plants, seeds, potatoes, parts of plants and all live animals; also for beef, prepared meats, milk and milk products, fish, shellfish, mollusks, poultry and all products of similar nature; and tobacco leaf.

6. *Consular Fees
    Paid by the importer except for the following:
    Extra copy of commercial invoice when requested if over $90.90 .... $10.50
    Extra copy of commercial invoice when requested if under $90.90 .... 21.00
    Bill of Lading not exceeding 15 lines (per set) 6.30
    For each additional 15 lines or fraction 5.25
    Extra copy of bill of lading 5.25
    Airway Bill (per set) 6.30
    Extra copy 5.25
    Letter of Correction (must be presented within 96 hours after
        the legalization of documents) 21.00
    Sanitary Certificate 10.50
    Power of Attorney (Notarized and County Clerk Certification) 21.00
    Pro Forma Invoice (Notarized and County Clerk Certification 21.00
    Immediate return of Documents 16.80

7. *Consular Holidays
    Washington's Birthday, Memorial Day, Independence Day, Labor Day, Columbus Day, Election Day, Veterans Day, Thanksgiving Day and August 25. All holidays generally observed in New York City.
    *Denotes changes since previous notice.

U.S.S.R.

SUMMARY OF SHIPPING DOCUMENTS REQUIRED
Special Information
All foreign trade operations in the U.S.S.R. are a state monopoly and handled through their various Foreign Trade Corporations.
No Consular Documents Required
1. Shipping Documents Required
    (A) **Commercial Invoice**—2—(unless otherwise specified by the Foreign Trade Corporation)—no special form—should show complete description of goods and the usual information, plus details requested by the Foreign Trade Corporation.
    (B) **Certificate of Origin**—2—(unless otherwise specified by the Foreign Trade Corporation)—when required—general form—sold by commercial printers—certified by the New York Chamber of Commerce and Industry, which requires an additional notarized copy for its files.
    (C) **Bills of Lading**—no special regulations—the usual information should be shown.
2. **Import License**
    Required by the Foreign Trade Corporation for all imports.
3. **Consular Holidays**
    March 8, May 1, May 2, May 9, November 8, and December 5.

VENEZUELA

SUMMARY OF SHIPPING DOCUMENTS REQUIRED
1.   *For All Commercial Shipments
  (A) **Bill of Lading**—All "To Order" bills of lading, e.g., shipper, bank or agent, are prohibited. Shipments must be made on a direct consignment basis—must be presented to Consulate to be stamped—returned to shipper. Only one consignee per bill of lading permitted. Due bill must be stapled to the original B/L.

      We understand that difficulties will arise at Customs unless all documents are in order as to proper spelling, address, etc.

      Bills of lading must include the following: date, captain's name, shipper's name, consignee's name (in Venezuela), port of loading, port of destination, number of packages, type, contents, marks, numbers and weight in kilograms.

      The type of package must be shown to agree with the specific type of package, or container involved, such as "case," "carton," "barrel," "bundle," "keg," "drums," "cylinders," "piece," "crate," "demijon," or "in bulk." The generic name "package" by itself is not permitted.

      Packages must be shown on the bill of lading under different numbers, except in the case of packages containing exactly the same type of merchandise. Merchandise may be described on the bill of lading by its generic name, such as "drugs," "perfumes," "dry goods," "hardware," etc. The use of expressions such as "no marks" (N/M) or "no numbers" (N/N) are not allowed, except for bulk shipments.

  (B) **Palletized Shipments**—It has been reported that the custom authorities in Venezuela are imposing fines on palletized shipments when the shipping documents fail to show the break down of the number of pieces and type of packages in the pallet. It is important, therefore, that shippers prepare documents showing the breakdown to avoid possible fines.

  (C) **Commercial Invoice**—Must contain the following information: 1) Name and address of seller; 2) Name and address of buyer; 3) Quantity of merchandise in commercial units; 4) Total description of the merchandise according to commercial denomination; 5) Detailed unit price; 6) Total price; 7) Conditions and terms of payment; 8) terms of sale (FOB, CIF, C&F, etc.); 9) Invoices must be in Spanish. (We also suggest that tariff number and description be shown). If consular legalization is requested the invoice must first be certified by the New York Chamber of Commerce and Industry, which requires an additional notarized copy for its files. The Consulate will stamp the original without charge.

2.   *Special Requirements
  (A) **Import License**—Required by importer for arms and ammunition, live animals and airplanes, for which the Venezuelan Consulate will require the original license before legalizing invoices. Also the following explosive materials require an import license: (1) oxyginated salts of chlorine, (2) oxyginated salts of nitrate, (a) Chlorate, (b) perchlorates, (c) nitrates.

      Import license must be obtained by importers for a variety of commodities. The exporter should be certain that importer has obtained the license before shipment is made.

  (B) **Shipments of Meat**—All meat products require a prior license from the Ministry of Agriculture in addition to a permit from the Ministry of Development. A certificate of Purity is required from country of origin for all meats, except those in sealed containers, which have been subject to a 56 degree centigrade temperature for at least 30 consecutive minutes.

(C) **Frozen and Cold Storage Food Shipments**—Shipments of frozen and cold storage foods must have an identification number which must be obtained from Venezuelan Customs by the importer and forwarded to his shipper in the United States at the time he places his order. This identification number must be shown on the commercial invoice and bill of lading, and must be printed or stenciled with indelible ink, in 4 inch letters or larger, on each carton or case, in addition to usual shipping marks.

(D) **Certificate of Purity**—1—for shipments of food products including meats and fish. Certificate must be obtained from U.S. Department of Agriculture.

(E) **Phytosanitary Certificate**—For shipments of plants, seeds and vegetable products.

(F) **Shipments of Drugs**—Packages and containers of medicinal and pharmaceutical products arriving in Venezuela must be sealed by a strip of paper or plastic in such a way as to prevent their being opened without breaking the seals.

(G) **Certificate of Origin for alcoholic beverage shipments**—on general form—certified by the New York Chamber of Commerce and Industry, which requires one additional notarized copy—stamped by Consulate Gratis. It is to be executed by the adequate authorities of the country in which the beverage is produced, stating that the product was made in accordance with the country's laws and regulations. Liquor shipments not made directly from the producing country must be accompanied by the aforementioned Certificate, and an official certification of the exporting country or of the Customs authorities at place of export, identifying the country of origin of the shipment.

(H) **Certificate of Origin for any other commodity**—(when required) will be stamped gratis by the Consulate if it has been previously certified by the New York Chamber of Commerce and Industry, which requires an additional notarized copy for its files.

3.   ***Origin of Third Country Merchandise**
Goods which have been imported and processed or manufactured, in the United States before shipped to Venezuela, must have been transformed as the result of such processing and manufacturing in the United States, into a product substantially different from the imported material, regardless of the increase in value resulting from the addition of U.S. labor or materials in order to be considered as of U.S. origin.

4.   ***Consular Fees**
(Payable by check made out to the Consulate General of Venezuela.)

Original commercial invoice or certificate of origin,
    if requested .... Gratis
Additional copies of the commercial invoice,
    certificate of origin, or bill of lading .... $1.25 each
Sanitary certificates, etc. 4.50
Special documents, (affidavits, authentication of
    county clerk's signature, etc.) 4.50

5.   ***Consular Holidays**
Holy Thursday, Good Friday, April 19, May 1, June 24, July 5, July 24, October 14, and December 17. All holidays generally observed in New York City.
*Denotes changes since previous notice.
Special Notice to Shippers and Forwarding Agents:
All shipments free or partially free of duty must be insured by insurance

companies authorized to do business in Venezuela. All other shipments must be insured by the exporter.

VIETNAM

SUMMARY OF SHIPPING DOCUMENTS REQUIRED
No Consular Documents Required
1.   **Shipping Documents Required for all shipments**
   (A) **Commercial Invoice**—2—certified as to current export market prices and country of origin by the New York Chamber of Commerce and Industry, which requires one additional notarized copy. Invoice must contain detailed description of merchandise and show all expenses. Copy retained by the Chamber must contain the following affidavit:

> "I hereby swear that the prices stated in this invoice are the current export market prices for the merchandise described herein and that the origin of these goods is the United States of America, and I accept full responsibility for any inaccuracies or errors therein."
>
> (Signature and Title)

   (B) **Pro-forma Invoice**—2—(same as above) required by importer to obtain import license.
2.   **Import License**
   Required by importer for most commodities.
       Most imports into Vietnam from the United States are financed by the Agency for International Development under Letters of Credit issued by Commercial Banks. Shipments not covered by the AID program must have been authorized and approved, prior to shipment, by the Vietnamese National Exchange Office.
3.   **Consular Fees**

   Commercial Invoice (when requested) $5.00
   Any other Documents (when requested) 5.00

4.   **Consular Holidays**
   Lunar New Year (2 days) and November 1. All holidays generally observed in New York City.

YEMEN

SUMMARY OF SHIPPING DOCUMENTS REQUIRED
1.   **Consular Documents Required for all commercial shipments.**
   (A) **Commercial Invoice**—2—should clearly specify, in addition to the usual details (quantity, product, value, etc.) the Country of Origin and show the Import License Number. Invoices must contain the following affidavit.

> "We hereby certify that this invoice is true and correct in all particulars. We further certify that the invoiced goods are not of Israeli origin nor do they

contain any Israeli raw materials, that these goods will not be transported by any carrier stated on the Black list of the Arab League Boycott Committee and that the carrier will not call at any Israeli Port/Air Port."

(B) *Certificate of Origin—4—general form—sold by commercial printers—all copies must be notarized—certified by the U.S. Arab Chamber of Commerce, which retains 1 copy—legalized by Mission, which retains 1 copy. Import license number must be shown. Merchandise manufacturer's name must be shown.

2.   **Import License**
Required by importer for all commercial shipments—validity period 6 or 12 months.

3.   **Special Documents**
Certificate of Free Sale—required for all imports of pharmaceuticals. The New York Chamber of Commerce and Industry will prepare such certificates on its letterhead upon request. These certificates need be presented only once with respect to each item.

4.   ***Insurance Regulations**
All imports must be insured in the Democratic Republic of Yemen (Aden), except AID shipments.

5.   ***Legalization Fees**

Certificate of Origin .... $10.00 per set
Legalization of any other Document .... 5.00 each

6.   **Holidays**
All holidays generally observed in New York City.
*Denotes changes since previous notice.

YEMEN—PEOPLES DEMOCRATIC REPUBLIC OF

1.   ***Consular Documents Required For All Commercial Shipments**
(A) **Commercial Invoice**—2—should clearly specify, in addition to the usual details (quantity, product, value, etc.) the Country Of Origin and show the Import License Number. Invoices must contain the following affidavit:

"We hereby certify that this invoice is true and correct in all particulars. We further certify that the invoiced goods are of (show country of origin)."

(B) **Certificate of Origin**—4—general form—sold by commercial printers—all copies must be notarized—certified by the U.S. Arab Chamber of Commerce, which retains 1 copy—legalized by Mission, which retains 1 copy. Import license number must be shown. Merchandise manufacturer's name must be shown.

2.   **Import License**
Required by importer for all commercial shipments—validity period 6 or 12 months.

3.   ***Special Documents**
Certificate of Free Sale—required for all imports of pharmaceuticals.

4. **Insurance Regulations**

All imports must be insured in the Democratic Republic of Yemen (Aden), except AID shipments.

5. **Legalization Fees**

The legalization fee for a Certificate of Origin is $25 if the value is under $10,000. Over $10,000, the charge is $25 plus 1½% of the invoice amount. The Certificate of Origin must show country of origin (U.S.A., etc.) No Israel clause is required.

Legalization of any other document .... $ 5.00 each

6. **Holidays**

All holidays generally observed in New York City.

YUGOSLAVIA

SUMMARY OF SHIPPING DOCUMENTS REQUIRED

No Consular Documents Required

The Consulate of Yugoslavia in New York does not legalize any documents in connection with shipments to that country, as such legalization is not required by the Yugoslavian authorities.

1. **Shipping Documents Required**
   (A) **Commercial Invoice**—2—on shipper's letterhead—must contain full particulars.
   (B) **Certificate of Origin**—2—not generally required, except when requested by importer—on general form—sold by commercial printers. Must be certified by the New York Chamber of Commerce and Industry, which requires one additional notarized copy for its files.
   (C) **Bill of Lading**—No special regulations. Ladings may be made either on a direct consignment or to order.

2. **Import License**

   Not required for the majority of commodities. However, importing is restricted to licensed firms. Foreign exchange controlled by Government.

   Consular Holidays

   May 1 and November 29. All holidays generally observed in New York City.

   *Denotes changes since previous notice.

ZAIRE

SUMMARY OF SHIPPING DOCUMENTS REQUIRED

No Consular Documents Required

1. **Shipping Documents Required for all shipments regardless of mode of transportation:**

   (A) **Commercial Invoice**—2—On shipper's letterhead—in French, or both in French and English. If in English only, a French translation is required. Should include all necessary information and itemized expenses. Country of origin must be shown.

(B) **Certificate of Origin**—3—when required—general form—sold by commercial printers—certified by the New York Chamber of Commerce and Industry, which requires one additional notarized copy for its files.

(C) **Attestation of Verification**—Required for all imported goods financed by the Zaire International Funding Systems. This Attestation may be issued by a correspondent of "Societe Generale de Surveillance," who will perform the service and issue the Attestation of Verification at no expense to the shipper. Superintendence Co., are the correspondents of the "Societe" in the United States.

Aid financed commodities and PL480 commodities are not affected.

(D) *Import License

Required by importer for some commercial shipments. Usually valid for six months, with extension permitted. Issuance of Import License guarantees foreign exchange. Zaire firms may pay for goods with their own foreign exchange, provided goods are not for resale. It is important that goods be cleared through Customs before expiration of import license.

The Chamber has a list of items which can be imported subject to an import license issued by the Bank of Zaire. These products in the past could be imported by applying only for an import declaration. The list is available by calling the Export Division. In addition, all imports with the exception of a list of foods, raw materials, pharmaceuticals and semi-finished products will now be subject to either minimum payment terms of 180 days with no interest payment allowed, or a price rebate of 6% on the permissible price for the import. The second list of imports which covers foods, raw materials, pharmaceuticals and semi-finished products are subject to minimum payment terms of 90 days with no interest allowed or a price rebate of 3% on the permissible price for the import. With the exception of the second list, import Letters of Credit are limited to 10% of the total value of credits established in 1974.

*Denotes changes since previous notice.

ZAMBIA

SUMMARY OF SHIPPING DOCUMENTS REQUIRED
No Consular Documents Required
1.   **Shipping Documents Required**

(A) **Commercial Invoice**—Commercial Invoice—special form (invoice and certificate value for exports to Zambia)—sold by commercial printers—the form must be completed in every detail and signed. A separate invoice is required for goods for each country of origin. A final summary invoice, (in addition to individual invoices) must be prepared by the seller: (1) if more than one commercial invoice covers a single shipment; (2) if any charges related to the goods are omitted up to and including their lading on board the exporting carrier; or (3) if a person other than the Zambian importer is invoiced for the goods. The summary invoice must show all packages in the shipment, detail all invoices, and itemize all charges up to and including the final cost of the shipment to the

REPUBLIC OF ZAMBIA

INVOICE AND CERTIFICATE OF VALUE FOR EXPORTS TO ZAMBIA

Insert	Exporter	Status of Exporter (*delete terms inapplicable*). Manufacturer Grower Producer Supplier	Date
Full			Reference number
Names			Page of pages
and		For Official Use Only	
Addresses	Consignee		NOTE: If this is an open market sale in terms of clause 5 overleaf this column need not be completed.
	Purchaser (if not Consignee)		Open Market Value in currency of exporting country at factory/ warehouse/port of shipment* subject to cash discount already *deducted/not deducted.
Country	Place and Country from which consigned	Please state whether this is an open market sale (*see* clause 5 overleaf).	
of	Ship/Aircraft, etc.	Port of Loading	Conditions of sale (e.g. f.o.b., c.i.f., consignment, etc. and details of discount and any other special arrangement).
Origin	Port of Discharge	Final Destination of Goods	RATE OF CASH DISCOUNT .... %
	Marks and numbers; number and kind of packages; description of goods:	Quantity (state units)	Selling Price to Purchaser (State Currency)	* *Delete as necessary*.

		Selling Price to Purchaser		Selling Price to Purchaser (State Currency)			
		Amount (state currency)	State if included	@	Amount	@	Amount

| Enumerate the following charges and state if each amount has been included in the total selling price to purchaser | | | | TOTAL | | TOTAL | |

I, the undersigned, being duly authorised in that behalf by the above exporter and having made the necessary enquiries, HEREBY CERTIFY THAT THIS INVOICE, including continuation sheets, if any, IS MADE IN ACCORDANCE WITH THE VALUE

Form 10-840.

CLAUSES PRINTED OVERLEAF, and hereby declare that I will furnish to the Customs authorities of the importing country or their nominee, for inspection at any time, such accounts and other evidence as may be requested for the purpose of verifying this certificate.

1. Value of outside packages/containers ... ... :
2. Labour in packing goods into outside packages/containers ... ... :
3. Inland transport and insurance charges to dock/airport area ... ... :
4. Dock and Port charges ... ... :
5. Overseas freight ... ... :
6. Overseas insurance ... ... :
7. Details of any other charges relating to delivery of goods ... ... :
8. Duty or taxes remitted on selling price ... :
9. Royalties (state full particulars) ... ... :
10. Commission and similar charges (state full particulars)

Place and date

Full name and business designation of signatory

Signature of authorised signatory

Size 297mm × 253mm

1—P960 2-67 S & T

Printed and Sold by Unz & Co., An Affiliate of Scott Ptg. Corr., 190 Baldwin Ave., J. C., N. J. 07306

(*Reverse*)

VALUE AND ORIGIN CLAUSES

1. This invoice is correct in all respects, and contains a true and full statement of the quantity and description of the goods, and of the price actually paid or to be paid for them, and of the country of origin.

2. No different invoice of those goods has been or will be furnished to anyone.

3. Unless otherwise declared overleaf, such or similar goods to those described in this invoice are sold for consumption in the country of exportation.

4. No arrangement or understanding affecting the purchase price of these goods, by way of discount, rebate, compensation, or of any other nature whatsoever which is not fully shown in this invoice, has been or will be made or entered into by the said exporter and the purchaser, or by anyone on behalf of either of them.

5. An open market sale is a sale in which price is the sole consideration and where there is no common business interest, or commercial, financial or other relationship between the buyer and the seller, whether by contract or otherwise (other than the relationship created by the sale).

6. The open market values shown in the column headed " Open Market Value in currency of exporting country " are those at which the said exporter would be prepared to supply identically similar goods in the country of exportation at the time of exportation, on a free sale in the open market to all independent purchasers trading at the same level of trade as that of the importer in Zambia and include any duty or taxes leviable in respect of the goods before they are delivered for home consumption. Any remission or drawback of duty or taxes which have been or will be allowed on exportation by the revenue authorities in the country of exportation are as shown in the table overleaf.

7. " Exporting country " means the country where the goods are physically held prior to export to Zambia, but does not include any country through which such goods may pass in transit to Zambia.

Form 10-840 (continued). Export Forms, Hazardous Materials Labels, etc. can be purchased from Unz & Co., 190 Baldwin Ave., P.O. Box 308, Jersey City, N.J. 07303.

Zambian importer free on board the exporting carrier. The reverse side of the form contains specific wording regarding discounts, rebates, royalties, etc., and any clause not applying, must be deleted and initialed by the person completing the form. There is a special Invoice Continuation Sheet to be used (if needed) with the invoice.

(B) **Certificate of Origin**—2 when required—on general form—sold by commercial printers—certified by the New York Chamber of Commerce and Industry, which requires one additional notarized copy for its files.

(C) **Bills of Lading**—no special requirements—1—original required for customs clearance. However, when goods are cleared at Beira or Lourenco, the original and one non-negotiable copy are necessary. "To Order" bills are allowed.

(D) ***Insurance**—All imports must be insured in Zambia.

2.   ***Import License**—Required by importer for most items. (Issued on a quota basis)

3.   **Mission Holidays**
All holidays generally observed in New York City.
See Form 10-840.

Appendix D
Customs Simplification Act

CUSTOMS SIMPLIFICATION ACT
OF 1956 (HR 6040) AS
PASSED BY CONGRESS
(OFFICIAL TEXT)

AN ACT

To amend certain administrative provisions of the Tariff Act of 1930 and to repeal obsolete provisions of the customs laws.

Be it enacted by the Senate and House of Representatives of the United States of America in Congress assembled. That this Act may be cited as the "Customs Simplification Act of 1956".

Sec. 2. (a) Section 402 of the Tariff Act of 1930, as amended (U. S. C., 1952 edition, title 19, sec. 1402), is redesignated "SEC. 402a. VALUE (ALTERNATIVE)." and such Tariff Act of 1930 is amended by inserting therein immediately before the redesignated section 402a a new section 402 to read as follows:

"SEC. 402. VALUE.

"(a) Basis. - Except as otherwise specifically provided for in this Act, the value of imported merchandise for the purposes of this Act shall be--

"(1) the export value, or

"(2) if the export value cannot be determined satisfactorily, then the United States value, or

"(3) if neither the export value nor the United States value can be determined satisfactorily, then the constructed value:

except that, in the case of an imported article subject to a rate of duty based on the American selling price of a domestic article, such value shall be--

"(4) the American selling price of such domestic article.

"(b) Export Value.– For the purposes of this section, the export value of imported merchandise shall be the price, at the time of exportation to the United States of the merchandise undergoing appraisement, at which such or similar merchandise is freely sold or, in the absence of sales, offered for sale in the principal markets of the country of exportation, in the usual wholesale quantities and in the ordinary course of trade, for exportation to the United States, plus, when not included in such price, the cost of all containers and coverings of whatever nature and all other expenses incidental to placing the merchandise in condition, packed ready for shipment to the United States.

"(c) United States Value. — For the purposes of this section, the United States value of imported merchandise shall be the price, at the time of exportation to the United States of the merchandise undergoing appraisement, at which such or similar merchandise is freely sold or, in the absence of sales, offered for sale in the principal market of the United States for domestic consumption, packed ready for delivery, in the usual wholesale quantities and in the ordinary course of trade, with allowances made for —

"(1) any commission usually paid or agreed to be paid, or the addition for profit and general expenses usually made, in connection with sales in such market of imported merchandise of the same class or kind as the merchandise undergoing appraisement;

"(2) the usual costs of transportation and insurance and other usual expenses incurred with respect to such or similar merchandise from the place of shipment to the place of delivery, not including any expense provided for in subdivision (1); and

"(3) the ordinary customs duties and other Federal taxes currently payable on such or similar merchandise by reason of its importation, and any Federal excise taxes on, or measured by the value of, such or similar merchandise, for which vendors at wholesale in the United States are ordinarily liable.

"If such or similar merchandise was not so sold or offered at the time of exportation of the merchandise undergoing appraisement, the United States value shall be determined, subject to the foregoing specifications of this subsection, from the price at which such or similar merchandise is so sold or offered at the earliest date after such time of exportation but before the expiration of ninety days after the importation of the merchandise undergoing appraisement.

"(d) Constructed Value. — For the purposes of this section, the constructed value of imported merchandise shall be the sum of —

"(1) the cost of materials (exclusive of any internal tax applicable in the country of exportation directly to such materials or their disposition, but remitted or refunded upon the exportation of the article in the production of which such materials are used) and of fabrication or other processing of any kind employed in producing such or similar merchandise, at a time preceding the date of exportation of the merchandise undergoing appraisement which would ordinarily permit the production of that particular merchandise in the ordinary course of business;

"(2) an amount for general expenses and profit equal to that usually reflected in sales of merchandise of the same general class or kind as the merchandise undergoing appraisement which are made by producers in the country of exportation, in the usual wholesale quantities and in the ordinary course of trade, for shipment to the United States: and

"(3) the cost of all containers and coverings of whatever nature, and all other expenses incidental to placing the merchandise undergoing appraisement in condition, packed ready for shipment to the United States.

"(e) American Selling Price. — For the purposes of this section, the American selling price of any article produced in the United States shall be the price, including the cost of all containers and coverings of whatever nature and all other expenses incidental to placing the article in condition packed ready for delivery, at which such article is freely sold or, in the absence of sales, offered for sale for domestic consumption in the principal market of the United States, in the ordinary course of trade and in the usual wholesale quantities, or the price that the manufacturer, producer, or owner would have received or was willing to receive for such article when sold for domestic consumption in the ordinary course of trade and in the usual wholesale quantities, at the time of exportation of the imported article.

"(f) Definitions. — For the purposes of this section—

"(1) The term 'freely sold or, in the absence of sales, offered for sale' means sold or, in the absence of sales, offered—

"(A) to all purchasers at wholesale, or

"(B) in the ordinary course of trade to one or more selected purchasers at wholesale at a price which fairly reflects the market value of the merchandise,

without restrictions as to the disposition or use of the merchandise by the purchaser, except restrictions as to such disposition or use which (i) are imposed or required by law, (ii) limit the price at which or the territory in which the merchandise may be resold, or (iii) do not substantially affect the value of the merchandise to usual purchasers at wholesale.

"(2) The term 'ordinary course of trade' means the conditions and practices which, for a reasonable time prior to the exportation of the merchandise undergoing appraisement, have been normal in the trade under consideration with respect to merchandise of the same class or kind as the merchandise undergoing appraisement.

"(3) The term 'purchasers at wholesale' means purchasers who buy in the usual wholesale quantities for industrial use or for resale otherwise than at retail; or; if there are no such purchasers, then all other purchasers in either of the foregoing categories, then all other purchasers who buy in the usual wholesale quantities.

"(4) The term 'such or similar merchandise' means merchandise in the first of the following categories in respect of which export value, United States value, or constructed value, as the case may be, can be satisfactorily determined:

"(A) The merchandise undergoing appraisement and other merchandise which is identical in physical characteristics with, and was produced in the same country by the same person as, the merchandise undergoing appraisement.

"(B) Merchandise which is identical in physical characteristics with, and was produced by another person in the same country as, the merchandise undergoing appraisement.

"(C) Merchandise (i) produced in the same country and by the same person as the merchandise undergoing appraisement, (ii) like the merchandise undergoing appraisement in component material or materials and in the purposes for which used, and (iii) approximately equal in commercial value to the merchandise undergoing appraisement.

"(D) Merchandise which satisfies all the requirements of subdivision (C) except that it was produced by another person.

"(5) The term 'usual wholesale quantities', in any case in which the merchandise in respect of which value is being determined is sold in the market under consideration at different prices for different quantities, means the quantities in which such merchandise is there sold at the price or prices for one quantity in an aggregate volume which is greater than the aggregate volume sold at the price or prices for any other quantity.

"(g) Transactions Between Related Persons. —

"(1) For the purposes of subsection (c) (1) of (d), as the case may be, a transaction directly or indirectly between persons specified in any one of the subdivisions in paragraph (2) of this subsection may be disregarded if, in the case of any element of value required to be considered, the amount representing that element does not fairly reflect the amount usually reflected in sales in the market under consideration of merchandise of the same general class or kind as the merchandise undergoing appraisement. If a transaction is disregarded under the preceding sentence and there are no other transactions available for consideration, then, for the purposes of subsection (d), the determination of the amount required to be considered shall be based on the best evidence available as to what the amount would have been if the transaction had occurred between persons not specified in any one of the subdivisions in paragraph (2).

"(2) The persons referred to in paragraph (1) are:

"(A) Members of a family, including brothers and sisters (whether by the whole or half blood), spouse, ancestors, and lineal descendants;

"(B) Any officer or director of an organization and such organization;

"(C) Partners;

"(D) Employer and employee;

"(E) Any person directly or indirectly owning, controlling, or holding with power to vote, 5 per centum or more of the outstanding voting stock or shares of any organization and such organization; and

"(F) Two or more persons directly or indirectly controlling, controlled by, or under common control with, any person."

(b) Paragraph 27 (c) of the Tariff Act of 1930 (U. S. C. 1952 edition, title 19, sec. 1001, par. 27 (c), is amended by striking out "(as defined in subdivision (g) of section 402, title IV)," and, "as defined in subdivision (e) of section 402, title IV".

(c) Paragraph 28 (c) of the Tariff Act of 1930 (U. S. C. 1952 edition, title 19, sec. 1001, par. 28 (c), is amended by striking out "(as defined in subdivision (g) of section 402, title IV)," and ", as defined in subdivision (e) of section 402, title IV".

(d) Section 336 (b) of the Tariff Act of 1930 (U. S. C., 1952 edition, title 19, sec. 1336 (b), is amended by striking out "(as defined in section 402 (g)".

(e) In any action relating to tariff adjustments by executive action, including action taken pursuant to section 350 of the Tariff Act of 1930, as amended, the United States Tariff Commission and each officer of the executive branch of the Government concerned shall give full consideration to any reduction in the level of tariff protection which has resulted or is likely to result from the amendment of section 402 of the Tariff Act of 1930 made by this Act.

(f) Redisignated section 402a of the Tariff act of 1930 is amended by deleting the word "merchandise" in the introductory matter of subsection (a) and substituting therefor "articles designated by the Secretary of the Treasury as provided for in section 6 (a) of the Customs Simplification Act of 1956".

Sec. 3. Section 522 (c) of the Tariff Act of 1930 (U. S. C. 1952 edition, title 31, sec. 372 is amended to read as follows:

"(c) Market Rate When No Proclamation. —

"(1) If no value has been proclaimed under subsection (a) for the quarter in which the merchandise was exported, or if the value so proclaimed varies by 5 per centum or more from a value measured by the buying rate at noon on the day of exportation, then conversion of the foreign currency involved shall be made—

"(A) at a value measured by such buying rate, or

"(B) if the Secretary of the Treasury shall be regulation so prescribe with respect to the particular foreign currency, at a value measured by the buying rate first certified under this subsection for a day in the quarter in which the day of exportation falls (but only if the buying rate at noon on the day of exportation does not vary by 5 per centum or more from such first certified buying rate).

"(2) For the purposes of this subsection the term 'buying rate' means the buying rate in the New York market for cable transfers payable in the foreign currency so to be converted. Such rate shall be determined by the Federal Reserve Bank of New York and certified to the Secretary of the Treasury, who shall make it public at such times and to such extent as he deems necessary. In ascertaining such buying rate, the Federal Reserve Bank of New York may, in its discretion—

"(A) take into consideration the last ascertainable transactions, all quotations, whether direct or through exchange of other currencies, and

"(B) if ther is no market buying rate for such cable transfers, calculate such rate (i) from actual transactions and quotations in demand or time bills of exhange, or (ii) from the last ascertainable transactions and quotations outside the United States in or for exchange payable in United States currency or other currency.

"(3) For the purposes of this subsection, if the day of exportation is one on which banks are generally closed in New York City, then the buying rate at noon on the last preceding business day shall be considered the buying rate at noon on the day of exportation."

Sec. 4. (a) The following provisions of law are hereby repealed:

(1) Section 2649, Revised Statutes (U. S. C., 1952 edition, title 19, sec. 12).

(2) The provisions of law now codified in section 13 of title 19 of the United States Code (U. S. C., 1952 edition, title 19, sec. 13).

(3) Section 2651, Revised Statutes (U. S. C., 1952 edition, title 19, sec. 15).

(4) Section 2999, Revised Statutes (U S. C., 1952 edition, title 19, sec. 14).

(5) Section 2940, Revised Statutes (U. S. C., 1952 edition, title 19, sec. 16).

(6) Section 2941, Revised Statutes (U. S. C., 1952 edition, title 19, sec. 17).

(7) Section 2942, Revised Statutes (U. S. C., 1952 edition, title 19, sec. 18).

(8) Section 2616, Revised Statutes (U. S. C., 1952 edition, title, 19, sec. 21).

(9) Section 2614, Revised Statutes (U. S. C., 1952 edition, title 19, sec. 22).

(10) Section 2615, Revised Statutes (U. S. C., 1952 edition, title 19, secs. 23 and 376).

(11) Section 2617, Revised Statutes (U. S. C., 1952 edition, title 19, sec. 24).

(12) Section 2611, Revised Statutes (U. S. C., 1952 edition, title 19, sec. 26).

(13) Section 11 of the Act of February 8, 1875 (U. S. C., 1952 edition, title 19, secs. 24 and 27).

(14) Act of September 24, 1914 (U. S. C., 1952 edition, title 19, sec. 28).

(15) Section 2627, Revised Statutes (U. S. C., 1952 edition, title 19, sec. 40).

(16) Section 2687, Revised Statutes (U. S. C., 1952 edition, title 19, sec. 53).

(17) Section 2646, Revised Statutes (U. S. C., 1952 edition, title 19, sec. 54).

(18) Section 2647, Revised Statutes (U. S. C., 1952 edition, title 19, sec. 55).

(19) Section 2944, Revised Statutes (U. S. C., 1952 edition, title 19, sec. 56).

(20) Section 2648, Revised Statutes (U. S. C., 1952 edition, title 19, sec. 57).

(21) Section 2635, Revised Statutes (U. S. C., 1952 edition, title 19, sec. 59).

(22) Section 2580, Revised Statutes (U. S. C., 1952 edition, title 19, sec. 61).

(23) Act of December 18, 1890 (U. S. C., 1952 edition, title 19, sec. 62).

(24) Section 258, Revised Statutes (U. S. C., 1952 edition, title 19, sec. 67).

(25) Section 2612, Revised Statutes (U. S. C., 1952 edition, title 19, sec. 379).

(26) Section 2918, Revised Statutes (U. S. C., 1952 edition, title 19, sec. 390).

(27) Section 13 of the Act of June 22, 1874 (U. S. C., 1952 edition, title 19, sec. 494).

(28) Section 3089, Revised Statutes (U. S. C., 1952 edition, title 19, sec. 526).

(29) Section 2763, Revised Statutes (U. S. C., 1952 edition, title 19, sec. 541).

(30) Act of February 10, 1913 (U. S. C., 1952 edition, title 19, sec. 542).

(31) Section 3650, Revised Statutes (U. S. C., 1952 edition, title 31, sec. 549).

(32) Section 960, Revised Statutes (U. S. C., 1952 edition, title 19, sec. 579).

(33) So much of section 3689 of the Revised Statutes (U. S. C., 1952 edition, title 31, sec. 711 (7) as reads: "Repayment of excess of deposits for unascertained duties, (customs): To repay to importers the excess of deposits for unascertained duties, or duties or other moneys paid under protest".

(34) So much of section 1 of the Act of September 30, 1890 (26 Stat. 511), as reads, : "And such clerks and inspectors of customs as the Secretary of the Treasury may designate for the purpose shall be authorized to administer oaths, such as deputy collectors of customs are now authorized to administer, and no compensation shall be paid or charge made therefor".

(b) The second sentence of subsection (f) of section 500 of the Tariff Act of 1930 (U. S. C., 1952 edition, title 19, sec. 1500 (f) is amended by striking out "take the oath," " and by striking out the comma after "duties".

(c) Section 583 of the Tariff Act of 1930 (U. S. C., 1952 edition, title 19, sec. 1583) is amended by striking out "the back of".

Sec. 5. Nothing in this Act shall be considered to repeal, modify, or supersede, directly or indirectly, any provision of the Antidumping Act, 1921, as amended (U. S. C., 1952 edition, title 19, secs. 160-173). The Secretary of the Treasury, after consulting with the United States Tariff Commission, shall review the operation and effectiveness of such Antidumping Act and report thereon to the Congress within six months after the date of enactment of this Act. In that report, the Secretary shall recommend to the Congress any amendment of such Antidumping Act which he considers desirable or necessary to provide for greater certainty, speed, and efficiency in the enforcement of such Antidumping Act.

Sec. 6. (a) The Secretary of the Treasury shall determine and make public a list of the articles which shall be valued in accordance with section 402a, Tariff Act of 1930, as amended by this Act, as follows: As soon as practicable after the enactment of this Act the Secretary shall make public a preliminary list of the imported articles which he shall have determined, after such investigation as he deems necessary, would have been appraised in accordance with section 402 of the Tariff Act of 1930, as amended by this Act, at average values for each article which are 95 (or less) per centum of the average values at which such article was actually appraised during the fiscal year 1954. If within sixty days after the publication of such preliminary list any manufacturer, producer, or wholesaler in the United States presents to the Secretary his reason for belief that any imported articles not specified in such list and like or similar to articles manufactured, produced, or sold at wholesale by him would have been appraised in accordance with such section 402 at average values which are 95 (or less) per centum of the average values at which they were or would have been aprpaised under section 402a, Tariff Act of 1930, as amended by this Act, the Secretary shall cause such investigation of the matter to be made as he deems necessary. If in the opinion of the Secretary the reason for belief is substantinated by the investigation, the articles involved shall be added to the preliminary list and such list, including any additions so made thereto, shall be published as a final list. Every article so specified in the final list which is entered, or withdrawn from warehouse, for consumption on or after the thirtieth day following the date of publication of the final list shall be appraised in accordance with the provisions of Section 402a, Tariff Act of 1930, as amended by this Act.

(b) The final list published in accordance with the provisions of subsection (a), together with explanatory data, shall be transmitted promptly to the chairmen of the Committee on Ways and Means of the House of Representatives and the Committee on Finance of the Senate.

Sec. 7. Notwithstanding the provisions of the last paragraph under the heading "Customs Service", of the Act entitled "An Act making appropriations for sundry civil expenses of the Government for the fiscal year ending June thirtieth, nineteen hundred and fifteen, and for other purposes", approved August 1, 1914 (38 Stat. 623, 19 U. S. C. 2), the State of New Mexico shall hereafter constitute a separate customs collection district with headquarters either in Deming or Columbus, New Mexico, and such additional ports of entry as the Secretary of the Treasury may deem necessary.

Sec. 8. This Act shall be effective on and after the day following the date of its enactment, except that section 2 shall be effective only as to articles entered, or withdrawn from warehouse, for consumption on or after the thirtieth day following the publication of the final list provided for in section 6 (a) of this Act, and section 3 shall be effective as to entries filed on or after the thirtieth day following the date of enactment of this Act.

(End of Official Text)

APPENDIX D/A

CUSTOMS REGIONS, DISTRICTS, AND PORTS OF ENTRY

(Extract from Title 19—Customs Duties; Chapter I—Bureau
of Customs; Part I—Customs Districts, Ports and Stations)

Reorganization Plan No. 1 of 1965 (3 CFR 1965 Supp.) provided for reorganization of the Bureau of Customs. Pursuant to that Plan, Treasury Department Order No. 165–17 of August 10, 1965 (T.D. 56464, 30 F.R. 10913), and the amendments thereto created customs regions, customs districts in said regions, offices of regional commissioners of customs for said regions, and offices of district directors of customs for said districts and abolished then existing customs collection districts on specified dates. The last of these changes was effected June 6, 1966.

In order to reflect the changes thereby made in the customs organizational structure, and for other purposes, Part 1 of these regulations is revised to read as follows:

PART 1—GENERAL PROVISIONS

Sec.
1.1 Authority of Customs officers
1.2 Customs regions, districts and ports
1.3 Customs stations; requirements for transaction of customs business at places other than ports of entry

Sec.
1.4 Customs offices in foreign countries
1.5 Customs Agency Service regions
1.6 Customs laboratories
1.7 Hours of business
1.8 Customs seal

Authority: The provisions of this Part 1 issued under R.S. 161, 251, 77A Stat. 14, sec. 624, 46 Stat. 759, 79 Stat. 1317; 5 U.S.C. 22, 19 U.S.C. 66, 1202 (Gen. Hdnote 11), 1624. Reorganization Plan 1 of 1965; 3 CFR 1965 Supp. Other authorities are cited to text in parentheses.

1.1 Authority of customs officers.—(a) No action taken by any person pursuant to authority delegated to him by the Secretary of the Treasury (whether directly or by subdelegation) shall be invalid by reason of the fact that any statute or regulation, including any provision of this chapter, provides or indicates that such action shall be taken by some other person.

(b) Any action perfomed by a person pursuant to authority delegated to him by the Secretary of the Treasury (whether directly or by subdelegation) shall constitute compliance with any requirement of any statute or regulation which provides or indicates that it shall be the duty of some other person to perform such action.

(c) Any failure to perform any function required by statute or regulation, which failure is attributable to a reorganization of the

Customs Service or the consolidation of the functions of two or more persons in one officer, shall not invalidate any action taken by any customs officer.

1.2 Customs regions, districts and ports.—(a) A customs region is the geographical area under the customs jurisdiction of a regional commissioner of customs. A customs district is the geographical area under the customs jurisdiction of a district director of customs.

(b) The terms "port" and "port of entry," as used in these regulations, refer to any place designated by Executive order of the President,[1] by order of the Secretary of the Treasury,[1] or by act of Congress, at which a customs officer is assigned with authority to accept entries of merchandise, to collect duties, and to enforce the various provisions of the customs and navigation laws.[2]

(c) The following is a list of customs regions and districts, with a list of the ports in each district.[3] The first-named port in each district (in capital letters) is the headquarters port, and the asterisk preceding the name of a port indicates that marine documents may be issued at such port.[4] The ports were created by the President's message of March 3, 1913, concerning a reorganization of the Customs Service pursuant to the Act of August 24, 1912 (37 Stat. 434; 19 U.S.C. 1). That organization has been changed by subsequent orders of the President and the Secretary of the Treasury. Orders affecting existing ports are cited in parentheses following the name of the port affected.

---

[1] "The President is authorized from time to time, as the exigencies of the service may require, to rearrange, by consolidation or otherwise the several customs-collection districts and to discontinue ports of entry by abolishing the same or establishing others in their stead: Provided, That the whole number of customs-collection districts, ports of entry, or either of them, shall at no time be made to exceed those established and authorized as on August 1, 1914, except as the same may thereafter be provided by law. * * *." (19 U.S.C. 2.)

By virtue of the authority vested in him by section 1 of the Act of August 8, 1950 (64 Stat. 419), the President, by Executive Order 10289, dated September 17, 1951 (16 F.R. 9499), delegated to the Secretary of the Treasury the authority theretofore vested in the President by section 1, of the Act of August 1, 1914, as amended (19 U.S.C. 2), (1) to rearrange, by consolidation or otherwise, the several customs-collection districts, (2) to discontinue ports of entry by abolishing the same and establishing others in their stead, and (3) to change from time to time the location of the headquarters in any customs-collection district as the needs of the service may require.

[2] The customs district of the Virgin Islands although under the jurisdiction of the Secretary of the Treasury, has its own customs laws. (See 48 U.S.C. 1406l.) This district, therefore, is outside the customs territory of the United States and the ports thereof are not "ports of entry" within the meaning of these regulations.

[3] The customs region of New York City, New York, and the customs district of New York City, New York, are coextensive.

[4] Marine documents may be issued at Washington, N.C., a customs station in the customs district of Wilmington, N.C.; at Biloxi, Miss., a customs station in the customs district of Mobile, Ala.; and at Houma, La., a customs station in the customs district of New Orleans, La. Marine documents may also be issued at the Commercial Port of Guam, under the supervision of the district director of customs at Honolulu, Hawaii. Although the status of the port of Newark, New Jersey, was changed by T.D. 53786 to provide that it shall be operated as an integral part of the port of New York, New York, in the customs district of New York City, New York, marine documents may continue to be issued at Newark.

No.	Headquarters	Name and headquarters	Area	Ports of entry
I	Boston, Massachusetts.	Portland, Maine___	The States of Maine and New Hampshire except the county of Coos.	*PORTLAND, MAINE (including territory described in E.O. 9297, Feb. 1, 1943; 8 F.R. 1479). *Bangor, Maine (including Brewer, Maine) (E.O. 9297, Feb. 1, 1943; 8 F.R. 1479). *Bar Harbor, Maine (including Mt. Desert Island, the city of Ellsworth, and the townships of Hancock, Sullivan, Sorrento, Gouldsboro, and Winter Harbor) (E.O. 4572, Jan. 27, 1927). *Bath, Maine (including Booth Bay and Wiscasset) (E.O. 4356, Dec. 15, 1925). *Belfast, Maine (including Searsport) (E.O. 6754, June 28, 1934). Bridgewater, Maine (E.O. 8079, Apr. 4, 1939; 4 F.R. 1475). *Calais, Maine (including townships of Calais, Robbinston, and Baring) (E.O. 6284, Sept. 13, 1933). *Eastport, Maine (including Lubec and Cutler) (E.O. 4296, Aug. 26, 1925). Fort Fairfield, Maine. Fort Kent, Maine. Houlton, Maine (E.O. 4156, Feb. 14, 1925).

| | REGIONS | | DISTRICTS | |
No.	Headquarters	Name and headquarters	Area	Ports of entry
I (Con.)				Jackman, Maine (including the townships of Jackman, Sandy Bay, Bald Mountain, Holeb, Attean, Lowelltown, Dennistown, and Moose River) (T.D. 54683).
				*Jonesport, Maine (including the towns (townships) of Beals, Jonesboro, Roque Bluffs, and Machiasport) (E.O. 4296, Aug. 26, 1925; E.O. 8695, Feb. 25, 1941).
				Limestone, Maine.
				Madawaska, Maine.
				*Portsmouth, N.H. (including Kittery, Maine).
				*Rockland, Maine.
				Van Buren, Maine.
				Vanceboro, Maine.
		St. Albans, Vermont.	The State of Vermont and the County of Coos, New Hampshire.	ST. ALBANS, VT. (including townships of St. Albans and Swanton) (E.O. 3925, Nov. 13, 1923) (E.O. 7632, June 15, 1937; 2 F.R. 1042).
				Alburg, Vt.
				Beecher Falls, Vt.
				*Burlington, Vt. (including the town of South Burlington) (T.D. 54677).
				Derby Line, Vt.
				Highgate Springs, Vt. (including township of Highgate) (E.O. 7632, June 15, 1937; 2 F.R. 1042).

224–420—66——3

510

REGIONS | | DISTRICTS | |

No.	Headquarters	Name and headquarters	Area	Ports of entry
I (Con.)		Boston, Massachusetts.	The State of Massachusetts	Island Pond, Vt. Newport, Vt. North Troy, Vt. Richford, Vt. *BOSTON (including territory and waters adjacent thereto described in T.D. 56493). *Fall River (including territory described in T.D. 54476). *Gloucester. Lawrence (E.O. 5444, Sept. 16, 1930); (E.O. 10088, Dec. 3, 1949; 14 F.R. 7287). *New Bedford. *Plymouth. *Salem (including Beverly, Marblehead, Lynn, and Peabody) (E.O. 9207, July 29, 1942). Springfield. Worcester.
		Providence, Rhode Island.	The State of Rhode Island	*PROVIDENCE. *Newport.
		Bridgeport, Connecticut.	The State of Connecticut	*BRIDGEPORT. *Hartford. *New Haven. *New London (including Groton) (E.O. 10238, Apr. 27, 1951; 16 F.R. 3627).

REGIONS

DISTRICTS

No.	Headquarters	Name and headquarters	Area	Ports of entry
I (Con.)		Ogdensburg, New York.	The Counties of Clinton, Essex, Franklin, St. Lawrence, Jefferson, and Lewis in the State of New York.	*OGDENSBURG. Alexandria Bay (including territory described in E.O. 10042, Mar. 10, 1949; 14 F.R. 1155). *Cape Vincent. Champlain. Chateaugay. Clayton. Fort Covington. Massena (T.D. 54834). Mooers Morristown. *Rouses Point. Trout River (T.D. 56074). Waddington.
		Buffalo, New York.	The Counties of Oswego, Oneida, Onondaga, Cayuga, Seneca, Wayne, Broome, Tompkins, Chenango, Madison, Cortland, Hamilton, Schuyler, Chemung, Herkimer, Monroe, Ontario, Livingston, Yates, Steuben, Orleans, Genesee, Wyoming, Allegany, Erie, Niagara, Cattaraugus, Chautauqua, and Tioga in the State of New York.	*BUFFALO-NIAGARA FALLS, NEW YORK (T.D. 56512). *Oswego. *Rochester. Sodus Point. Syracuse. Utica.

512

| REGIONS | | DISTRICTS | | |
No.	Headquarters	Name and headquarters	Area	Ports of entry
II	New York City, New York.	New York City, New York.	The counties of Sussex, Passaic, Hudson, Bergen, Essex, Union, Middlesex, and Monmouth in the State of New Jersey and that part of the State of New York not expressly included in the districts of Buffalo and Ogdensburg.	*NEW YORK, N.Y. (including territory described in E.O. 4205, Apr. 15, 1925). (T.D. 53786.) *Albany, N.Y. *Perth Amboy, N.J.
III	Baltimore, Maryland.	Philadelphia, Pennsylvania.	The State of Pennsylvania except the county of Erie, the State of Delaware, and that part of the State of New Jersey not included in the district of New York City.	*PHILADELPHIA, PA. (including Camden and Gloucester City, N.J., and territory described in E.O. 7840, Mar. 15, 1938; 3 F.R. 687; T.D. 53738 and T.D. 54303). Chester, Pa. (E.O. 7706, Sept. 11, 1937; 2 F.R. 1848). *Pittsburgh, Pa. *Wilmington, Del. (including territory described in T.D. 54202) (E.O. 4496, Aug. 12, 1926).
		Baltimore, Maryland.	The State of Maryland and the District of Columbia.	*BALTIMORE, MD. (including territory described in T.D. 55020). *Annapolis, Md. *Cambridge, Md. (E.O. 3888, Aug. 13, 1923). *Crisfield, Md. *Washington, D.C.

DISTRICTS

REGIONS				Ports of entry
No.	Headquarters	Name and headquarters	Area	
III (Con.)	Norfolk, Virginia		The States of Virginia and West Virginia.	*NORFOLK and *NEWPORT NEWS (including the waters and shores of Hampton Roads). *Alexandria. *Cape Charles City. Petersburg. *Reedville. Richmond.
IV	Miami, Florida	Wilmington, North Carolina.	The State of North Carolina	*WILMINGTON (including townships of Northwest, Wilmington, and Cape Fear) (E.O. 7761, Dec. 3, 1937; 2 F.R. 2679, and territory described in E.O. 10042, Mar. 10, 1949; 14 F.R. 1155). *Beaufort-Morehead City (T.D. 55637). Charlotte (T.D. 56079). Durham (E.O. 4876, May 3, 1928) (including territory described in E.O. 9433, Apr. 6, 1944; 9 F.R. 3761). *Elizabeth City. Elkin (E.O. 10042, Mar. 10, 1949; 14 F.R. 1155). Reidsville (E.O. 5159, July 18, 1929) (including territory described in E.O. 9433, Apr. 6, 1944; 9 F.R. 3761). Winston-Salem (E.O. 2366, Apr. 24, 1916).
		Charleston, South Carolina.	The State of South Carolina	*CHARLESTON (including territory described in T.D. 53994). *Georgetown.

REGIONS		DISTRICTS		
No.	Headquarters	Name and headquarters	Area	Ports of entry
IV (Con.)		Savannah, Georgia.	The State of Georgia, except the north shore of the St. Marys River and the city of St. Marys, Georgia.	*SAVANNAH (including territory described in E.O. 8367, Mar. 5, 1940; 5 F.R. 985). Atlanta (including territory described in T.D. 55548). *Brunswick.
		Tampa, Florida---	The north shore of the St. Marys River and the City of St. Marys, Georgia, and all the State of Florida lying east of the east bank of the Ochlockonee River except the counties of Hendry, Indian River, St. Lucie, Martin, Okeechobee, Palm Beach, Collier, Broward, Monroe, and Dade.	*TAMPA (including Port Tampa and Port Tampa City; T.D. 53514.) Boca Grande. *Fernandina Beach (including St. Marys, Ga.) (T.D. 53033). *Jacksonville (including territory described in T.D. 54476). Port Canaveral, Fla. (including territory described in T.D. 55666). St. Augustine. St. Petersburg (E.O. 7928, July 14, 1938; 3 F.R. 1749; including territory described in T.D. 53994).
		Miami, Florida---	The Counties of Hendry, Indian River, St. Lucie, Martin, Okeechobee, Palm Beach, Collier, Broward, Monroe, and Dade in the State of Florida.	*MIAMI, FLORIDA (including territory described in T.D. 53514). *Key West (including territory described in T.D. 53994). Port Everglades (E.O. 5770, Dec. 31, 1931) (including territory described in T.D. 53514 (Mail: Fort Lauderdale, Fla.). *West Palm Beach (E.O. 4324, Oct. 15, 1925) (including territory described in T.D. 53514).

REGIONS		DISTRICTS		
No.	Headquarters	Name and headquarters	Area	Ports of entry
IV (Con.)		San Juan, Puerto Rico.	The Commonwealth of Puerto Rico.	*SAN JUAN (including territory described in T.D. 54017). Aguadilla. Fajardo. Guanica. Humacao. Jobos (E.O. 9162, May 13, 1942). *Mayaguez (T.D. 22305). *Ponce (including territory described in T.D. 54017).
		Charlotte Amalie, St. Thomas, Virgin Islands.	All of the Virgin Islands of the United States.	*CHARLOTTE AMALIE, ST. THOMAS, V.I. Christiansted, St. Croix. Coral Bay, St. John. Cruz Bay, St. John. Frederiksted, St. Croix.
V	New Orleans, Louisiana.	Mobile, Alabama--	The State of Alabama and that part of the State of Mississippi lying south of 31° north latitude, and that part of the State of Florida lying west of the east bank of the Ochlockonee River.	*MOBILE, ALA. (including territory described in E.O. 10042, Mar. 10, 1949; 14 F.R. 1155). *Apalachicola, Fla. Birmingham, Ala. Carrabelle, Fla. (E.O. 7508, Dec. 11, 1936; 1 F.R. 2149). *Gulfport, Miss. Panama City, Fla. (E.O. 3919, Nov. 1, 1923). *Pascagoula, Miss. (including territory described in T.D. 56333). *Pensacola, Fla. Port St. Joe, Fla. (E.O. 7818, Feb. 17, 1938; 3 F.R. 503).

No.	Headquarters	Name and headquarters	Area	Ports of entry
V (Con.)		New Orleans, Louisiana.	The States of Tennessee, Arkansas, and Louisiana, except the parishes of Cameron and Calcasieu and and that part of the State of Mississippi lying north of 31° north latitude.	*NEW ORLEANS, LA. (including territory described in E.O. 5130, May 29, 1929). *Baton Rouge, La. (E.O. 5993, Jan. 13, 1933) (including territory described in T.D. 53514 and T.D. 54381). *Chattanooga, Tenn. *Greenville, Miss. (T.D. 55697 including the territory described in T.D. 55829). *Memphis, Tenn. *Morgan City, La. (including territory described in T.D. 54682). *Nashville, Tenn.
VI	Houston, Texas---	Port Arthur, Texas.	That part of the State of Texas from Sabine Pass north along state line to north boundary line of Shelby County; west to Neches River; down western shore of said river to north boundary of Jefferson County; westerly along said boundary to east boundary of Liberty County; south to Gulf; also	*PORT ARTHUR, TEX. (including territory described in T.D. 54137). *Beaumont, Tex. (E.O. 4502, Sept. 1, 1926) (including territory described in T.D. 54137). *Lake Charles, La. (E.O. 5475, Nov. 3, 1930) (including territory described in T.D. 54137). Orange, Tex. (E.O. 7495, Nov. 14, 1936; 1 F.R. 1867) (including territory described in T.D. 54137). Sabine, Tex. (including territory described in T.D. 54137).

No.	Headquarters	Name and headquarters	Area	Ports of entry
VI (Con.)			the parishes of Cameron and Calcasieu in the State of Louisiana.	
		Galveston, Texas--	The Counties of Galveston, Matagorda, Chambers, Calhoun, Refugio, Brazoria, San Patricio, Nueces, and Aransas in the State of Texas.	*GALVESTON (including Port Bolivar and Texas City). *Corpus Christi (E.O. 8288, Nov. 22, 1939; 4 F.R. 4691). Freeport (E.O. 7632, June 15, 1937; 2 F.R. 1042). Port Lavaca-Point Comfort, Tex. (T.D. 56115).
		Houston, Texas--	That part of the State of Texas lying east of 97° west longitude, except the territory embraced in the Port Arthur and Galveston districts. Also the counties of Dallas and Tarrant and the State of Oklahoma.	*HOUSTON, TEX. (including territory described in T.D. 54409). Dallas, Tex. Fort Worth, Texas (T.D. 55792). Oklahoma City, Okla. (including territory described in T.D. 66–132).

224-420—66——4

No.	Headquarters	Name and headquarters	Area	Ports of entry
VI (Con.)		Laredo, Texas------	That part of the State of Texas lying west of 97° west longitude and east of the Pecos River except that territory included in the Houston and Galveston districts.	LAREDO. *Brownsville, Texas (including territory described in T.D. 54900). Del Rio. Eagle Pass. Hidalgo (E.O. 3609, Jan. 9, 1922). Rio Grande City. Roma (E.O. 4830, Mar. 14, 1928). San Antonio.
		El Paso, Texas----	That part of the State of Texas lying west of the Pecos River and the States of New Mexico and Colorado.	EL PASO, TEX. (T.D. 54407). Columbus, N. Mexico. Denver, Colorado. Fabens, Tex. (E.O. 4869, May 1, 1928). Presidio, Tex. (E.O. 2702, Sept. 7, 1917).
VII	Los Angeles, California.	Nogales, Arizona--	The State of Arizona-----------	NOGALES (including territory described in E.O. 9382, Sept. 25, 1943; 8 F.R. 13083). Douglas (including territory described in E.O. 9382, Sept. 25, 1943; 8 F.R. 13083). Lukeville (E.O. 10088, Dec. 3, 1949; 14 F.R. 7287). Naco. San Luis (E.O. 5322, Apr. 9, 1930). Sasabe (E.O. 5608, Apr. 22, 1931).

No.	Headquarters	Name and headquarters	Area	Ports of entry
VII (Con.)		San Diego, California.	The Counties of San Diego and Imperial in the State of California.	*SAN DIEGO (T.D. 54741). Andrade (E.O. 4780, Dec. 13, 1927). Calexico. Tecate (E.O. 4780, Dec. 13, 1927). *LOS ANGELES-LONG BEACH (including territory described in T.D. 55341; T.D. 56383). Port San Luis.
		Los Angeles, California.	That part of the State of California lying south of the northern boundaries of the Counties of San Luis Obispo, Kern, and San Bernardino, except the Counties of San Diego and Imperial and that part of the State of Nevada comprising Clark County.	
VIII	San Francisco, California.	San Francisco, California.	That part of the State of California lying north of the northern boundaries of the Counties of San Luis Obispo, Kern, and San Bernardino, and the State of Utah and the State of Nevada, except Clark County.	*SAN FRANCISCO-OAKLAND, CALIF. (including all points on San Francisco Bay, and territory described in E.O. 10042, Mar. 10, 1949; 14 F.R. 1155; and T.D. 53738 and including territory described in T.D. 56020). *Eureka, Calif.

DISTRICTS

REGIONS				
No.	Headquarters	Name and headquarters	Area	Ports of entry
VIII (Con.)		Honolulu, Hawaii	The State of Hawaii _____	*HONOLULU (T.D. 53514). Hilo. Kahului. Nawiliwili-Port Allen (E.O. 4385, Feb. 25, 1926, including the territory described in T.D. 56424).
		Portland, Oregon __	The State of Oregon and that part of the State of Washington which embraces the waters of the Columbia River and the north bank of the said river west of 119° west longitude.	*PORTLAND, OREG. (including territory described in E.O. 3390, Jan. 24, 1921; E.O. 5193, Sept. 14, 1929, and T.D. 53033). *Astoria, Oreg. (E.O. 5193, Sept. 14, 1929). *Coos Bay, Oreg. (E.O. 4094, Oct. 28, 1924; E.O. 5193, Sept. 14, 1929; E.O. 5445, Sept. 16, 1930; E.O. 9533, Mar. 23, 1945; 10 F.R. 3173). Longview, Wash. (E.O. 4956, Aug. 31, 1928) (including territory described in E.O. 5193, Sept. 14, 1929, and T.D. 53514). Newport, Oreg.
		Seattle, Washington.	The State of Washington except that part which embraces the waters of the Columbia River and the north bank of the said river west of 119° west longitude.	*SEATTLE (including territory described in T.D. 53576). *Aberdeen (including territory described in T.D. 56229). Anacortes (including the territory described in T.D. 53861). *Bellingham (including territory described in T.D. 53738).

521

	REGIONS	DISTRICTS		
No.	Headquarters	Name and headquarters	Area	Ports of entry
VIII (Con.)				Blaine (E.O. 5835, Apr. 13, 1932).
				Danville.
				Everett.
				Ferry.
				Friday Harbor (including territory described in E.O. 9433, Apr. 6, 1944; 9 F.R. 3761).
				Laurier.
				Lynden (E.O. 7632, June 15, 1937; 2 F.R. 1042).
				Metaline Falls (E.O. 7632, June 15, 1937; 2 F.R. 1042).
				Neah Bay (E.O. 10088, Dec. 3, 1949; 14 F.R. 7287).
				Nighthawk.
				Northport.
				Olympia (E.O. 4780, Dec. 13, 1927).
				Oroville (E.O. 5206, Oct. 11, 1929).
				*Port Angeles.
				*Port Townsend.
				South Bend-Raymond (T.D. 53576).
				Spokane.
				Sumas.
				*Tacoma.

| REGIONS | | DISTRICTS | | |
No.	Headquarters	Name and headquarters	Area	Ports of entry
VIII (Con.)		Juneau, Alaska.	The State of Alaska.	*JUNEAU. Anchorage, Alaska (T.D. 55295). Fairbanks (E.O. 8064, Mar. 9, 1939; 4 F.R. 1191). *Ketchikan (including territory described in T.D. 53738). Kodiak, Alaska (T.D. 55206). Pelican (E.O. 10238, Apr. 27, 1951; 16 F.R. 3627). Petersburg (E.O. 4132, Jan. 24, 1925). Sand Point (T.D. 53514). *Sitka (including territory described in T.D. 55609). Skagway. *Wrangell (including territory described in T.D. 56420).
		Great Falls, Montana.	The States of Montana, Idaho, and Wyoming.	*GREAT FALLS, MONT. Del Bonita, Mont. (E.O. 7947, Aug. 9, 1938; 3 F.R. 1965). (Mail: Cut Bank, Mont.) Eastport, Idaho. Morgan, Mont. (E.O. 7632, June 15, 1937; 2 F.R. 1042), (Mail: Loring, Mont.) Opheim, Mont. (E.O. 7632, June 15, 1937; 2 F.R. 1042). Piegan, Mont. (E.O. 7632, June 15, 1937; 2 F.R. 1042). (Mail: Babb, Mont.)

REGIONS				DISTRICTS	
No.	Headquarters	Name and headquarters	Area	Ports of entry	

No.	Headquarters	Name and headquarters	Area	Ports of entry
VIII (Con.)				Porthill, Idaho.
				Raymond, Mont. (E.O. 7632, June 15, 1937; 2 F.R. 1042).
				Roosville, Mont. (E.O. 7632, June 15, 1937; 2 F.R. 1042). (Mail: Eureka, Mont.)
				Scobey, Mont. (E.O. 7632, June 15, 1937; 2 F.R. 1042).
				Sweetgrass, Mont.
				Turner, Mont. (E.O. 7632, June 15, 1937; 2 F.R. 1042).
				Whitetail, Mont. (E.O. 7632, June 15, 1937; 2 F.R. 1042).
				Whitlash, Mont. (E.O. 7632, June 15, 1937; 2 F.R. 1042).
IX	Chicago, Illinois----	Pembina, North Dakota.	The States of North and South Dakota and the Counties of Kittson, Roseau, Lake of the Woods, Marshall, Beltrami, Polk, Red Lake, Pennington in the State of Minnesota.	*PEMBINA, N. DAK.
				Ambrose, N. Dak. (E.O. 5835, Apr. i3, 1932).
				Antler, N. Dak.
				Baudette, Minn. (E.O. 4422, Apr. 19, 1926).
				Carbury, N. Dak. (E.O. 5137, June 17, 1929).
				Dunseith, N. Dak. (E.O. 7632, June 15, 1937; 2 F.R. 1042).
				Fortuna, N. Dak. (E.O. 7632, June 15, 1937; 2 F.R. 1042).
				Hannah, N. Dak.
				Hansboro, N. Dak.

No.	Headquarters	Name and headquarters	Area	Ports of entry
IX (Con.)		Minneapolis, Minnesota.	The State of Minnesota except those Counties in the Pembina, North Dakota, and Duluth, Minnesota, districts.	Maida, N. Dak. (E.O. 7632, June 15, 1937; 2 F.R. 1042). Neche, N. Dak. Noonan, N. Dak. (E.O. 7632, June 15, 1937; 2 F.R. 1042). Northgate, N. Dak. Noyes, Minn. (E.O. 5835, Apr. 13, 1932). Pine Creek, Minn. (E.O. 7632, June 15, 1937; 2 F.R. 1042). Portal, N. Dak. Roseau, Minn. (E.O. 7632, June 15, 1937; 2 F.R. 1042). Sarles, N. Dak. Sherwood, N. Dak. St. John, N. Dak. (E.O. 5835, Apr. 13, 1932). Walhalla, N. Dak. Warroad, Minn. Westhope, N. Dak. (E.O. 4236, June 1, 1925). *MINNEAPOLIS (E.O. 4295, Aug. 26, 1925) (including territory described in T.D. 56172). St. Paul (E.O. 4295, Aug. 26, 1925) (including territory described in T.D. 56172).

| REGIONS | | DISTRICTS | | |
No.	Headquarters	Name and headquarters	Area	Ports of entry
IX (Con.)		Duluth, Minnesota.	The Counties of Koochiching, Itaschi, St. Louis, Carlton, Pine, Lake, Cook, Clay, Aitkin, Norman, Wilkin, Ottertail, Becker, Mahnomen, Clearwater, Hubbard, Wadena, Cass, and Crow Wing in the State of Minnesota and the Counties of Douglas, Bayfield, Ashland, and Iron in the State of Wisconsin, and the Island of Isle Royale in the State of Michigan.	*DULUTH, MINN., AND SUPERIOR, WIS. (including the territory described in T.D. 55904). Ashland, Wis. Grand Portage, Minn. (T.D. 56073). International Falls-Ranier, Minn. (T.D. 53738).
		Milwaukee, Wisconsin.	The State of Wisconsin, except the Counties of Douglas, Bayfield, Ashland, and Iron and the County of Menominee in the State of Michigan.	*MILWAUKEE. Green Bay (including the townships of Ashwaubenon, Allouez, Preble, and Howard, and the city of De Pere) (T.D. 54597). Manitowoc. Marinette (including Menominee, Mich.). Racine, (including the city of Kenosha and the townships of Mt. Pleasant and Somers). (T.D. 54884). Sheboygan.

224-420—66——5

REGIONS		DISTRICTS		
No.	Headquarters	Name and headquarters	Area	Ports of entry
IX (Con.)		Chicago, Illinois	The State of Illinois lying north of 39° north latitude; that part of the State of Indiana north of 41° north latitude; and the States of Iowa and Nebraska.	*CHICAGO, ILL. (including territory described in T.D. 54137). *Omaha, Nebr. (including territory described in E.O. 9297, Feb. 1, 1943; 8 F.R. 1479). *Peoria, Ill.
		Cleveland, Ohio	The States of Ohio, Kentucky, that part of the State of Indiana lying south of 41° north latitude and the county of Erie in the State of Pennsylvania.	*CLEVELAND, OHIO (including territory described in T.D. 54734). Akron, Ohio (E.O. 4597, Feb. 25, 1927). Ashtabula, Ohio. *Cincinnati, Ohio. Columbus, Ohio. Conneaut, Ohio. Dayton, Ohio. *Erie, Pennsylvania. *Evansville, Indiana. Indianapolis, Indiana. Lawrenceburg, Indiana (including Greendale) (E.O. 6634, Mar. 7, 1934). *Louisville, Ky. *Sandusky, Ohio. *Toledo, Ohio (including territory described in T.D. 54137).

DISTRICTS

REGIONS		DISTRICTS		
No.	Headquarters	Name and headquarters	Area	Ports of entry
IX (Con.)		St. Louis, Missouri-	The States of Missouri and Kansas, and that part of the State of Illinois lying south of 39° north latitude.	*ST. LOUIS, MO. (including East St. Louis, Ill.). *Kansas City, Mo. (including Kansas City, Kans. and North Kansas City, Mo.) (E.O. 8528, Aug. 27, 1940). St. Joseph, Mo.
		Detroit, Michigan-	The State of Michigan except the Island of Isle Royale and the County of Menominee, Michigan.	*DETROIT (including territory described in E.O. 9073, Feb. 25, 1942; 7 F.R. 1588; and T.D. 53738). *Muskegon (E.O. 8315, Dec. 22, 1939) (including territory described in T.D. 56230). *Port Huron (including territory described in T.D. 53576). Saginaw-Bay City (T.D. 53738). *Sault Ste. Marie. South Haven (E.O. 7632, June 15, 1937; 2 F.R. 1042).

AMERICAN CARRIAGE OF GOODS BY SEA ACT, 1936

EFFECTIVE JULY 15, 1936

Be it enacted by the Senate and House of Representatives of the United States of America in Congress assembled:

That every bill of lading or similar document of title which is evidence of a contract for the carriage of goods by sea to or from ports of the United States in foreign trade, shall have effect subject to the provisions of this act.

TITLE I

Section 1. When used in this Act-

(a) The term "carrier" includes the owner or the charterer who enters into a contract of carriage with a shipper.

(b) The term "contract of carriage" applies only to contracts of carriage covered by a bill of lading or any similar document of title, insofar as such document relates to the carriage of goods by sea, including any bill of lading or any similar document as aforesaid issued under or pursuant to a charter-party from the moment at which such bill of lading or similar document of title regulates the relations between a carrier and a holder of the same.

(c) The term "goods" includes goods, wares, merchandise, and articles of every kind whatsoever, except live animals and cargo which by the contract of carriage is stated as being carried on deck and is so carried.

(d) The term "ship" means any vessel used for the carriage of goods by sea.

(e) The term "carriage of goods" covers the period from the time when the goods are loaded on to the time when they are discharged from the ship.

RISKS

Sec. 2. Subject to the provisions of section 6, under every contract of carriage of goods by sea, the carrier in relation to the loading, handling, stowage, carriage, custody, care, and discharge of such goods, shall be subject to the responsibilities and liabilities and entitled to the rights and immunities hereinafter set forth.

RESPONSIBILITIES AND LIABILITIES

Sec. 3. (1) The carrier shall be bound, before and at the beginning of the voyage, to exercise due diligence to-

(a) Make the ship seaworthy;

(b) Properly man, equip, and supply the ship;

(c) Make the holds, refrigerating and cooling chambers, and all other parts of the ship in which goods are carried, fit and safe for their reception, carriage, and preservation.

(2) The carrier shall properly and carefully load, handle, stow, carry, keep, care for, and discharge the goods carried.

(3) After receiving the goods into his charge the carrier, or the master or agent of the carrier, shall, on demand of the shipper, issue to the shipper a bill of lading showing among other things-

(a) The leading marks necessary for identification of the goods as the same are furnished in writing by the shipper before the loading of such goods starts,

529

provided such marks are stamped or otherwise shown clearly upon the goods if uncovered, or on the cases or coverings in which such goods are contained, in such a manner as should ordinarily remain legible until the end of the voyage.

(b) Either the number of packages or pieces, or the quantity or weight, as the case may be, as furnished in writing by the shipper.

(c) The apparent order and condition of the goods:

Provided, That no carrier, master, or agent of the carrier, shall be bound to state or show in the bill of lading any marks, number, quantity, or weight which he has reasonable ground for suspecting not accurately to represent the goods actually received, or which he has had no reasonable means of checking.

(4) Such a bill of lading shall be prima facie evidence of the receipt by the carrier of the goods as therein described in accordance with paragraph (3) (a), (b), and (c) of this section:

Provided, That nothing in this Act shall be construed as repealing or limiting the application of any part of the Act, as amended, entitled "An Act relating to bills of lading in interstate and foreign commerce," aprpoved August 29, 1916 (U.S.C., title 49, secs. 81-124), commonly known as the "Pomerene Bills of Lading Act.."

(5) The shipper shall be deemed to have guaranteed to the carrier the accuracy at the time of shipment of the marks, number, quantity, and weight, as furnished by him; and the shipper shall indemnify the carrier against all loss, damages, and expenses arising or resulting from inaccuracies in such particulars. The right of the carrier to such indemnity shall in no way limit his responsibility and liability under the contract of carriage to any person other than the shipper.

(6) Unless notice of loss or damage and the general nature of such loss or damage be given in writing to the carrier or his agent at the port of discharge before or at the time of the removal of the goods into the custody of the person entitled to delivery thereof under the contract of carriage, such removal shall be prima facie evidence of the delivery by the carrier of the goods as described in the bill of lading.

If the loss or damage is not apparent, the notice must be given within three days of the delivery.

Said notice of loss or damage may be endorsed upon the receipt for the goods given by the person taking delivery thereof.

The notice in writing need not be given if the state of the goods has at the time of their receipt been the subject of joint survey or inspection.

In any event, the carrier and the ship shall be discharged from all liability in respect of loss or damage unless suit is brought within one year after delivery of the goods or the date when the goods should have been delivered:

Provided, That if a notice of loss or damage, either apparent or concealed, is not given as provided for in this section, that fact shall not affect or prejudice goods or the date when the goods should have been delivered.

In the case of any actual or apprehended loss or damage the carrier and the receiver shall give all reasonable facilities to each other for inspecting and tallying the goods.

(7) After the goods are loaded the bill of lading to be issued by the carrier, master, or agent of the carrier to the shipper shall, if the shipper so demands, be a "shipped" bill of lading:

Provided, That if the shipper shall have previously taken up any document of title to such goods, he shall surrender the same as against the issue of the "shipped" bill of lading, but at the option of the carrier such document of title may be noted at the port of shipment by the carrier, master, or agent with the name or names of the ship or ships upon which the goods have been shipped and the date or dates of shipment, and when so noted the same shall for the purpose of this section be deemed to constitute a "shipped" bill of lading.

(8) Any clause, covenant, or agreement in a contract of carriage relieving the carrier or the ship from liability for loss or damage to or in connection with the goods, arising from negligence, fault, or failure in the duties and obligations provided in this section or lessening such liability otherwise than as provided in this Act. shall be null and void and of no effect.

A benefit of insurance in favor of the carrier, or similar clause, shall be deemed to be a clause relieving the carrier from liability.

RIGHTS AND IMMUNITIES

Sec. 4. (1) Neither the carrier nor the ship shall be liable for loss or damage arising or resulting from unseaworthiness unless caused by want of due diligence on the part of the carrier to make the ship seaworthy, and to secure that the ship is properly manned, equipped, and supplied, and to make the holds, refrigerating and cool chambers, and all other parts of the ship in which goods are carried fit and safe for their reception, carriage, and preservation in accordance with the provisions of paragraph (1) of section 3. Whenever loss or damage has resulted from unseaworthiness, the burden of proving the exercise of due diligence shall be on the carrier or other persons claiming exemption under this section.

(2) Neither the carrier not the ship shall be responsible for loss or damage arising or resulting from-

(a) Act, neglect, or default of the master, mariner, pilot, or the servants of the carrier in the navigation or in the management of the ship;

(b) Fire, unless caused by the actual fault or privity of the carrier;

(c) Perils, dangers, and accidents of the sea or other navigable waters;

(d) Act of God;

(e) Act of war;

(f) Act of public enemies;

(g) Arrest or restraint of princes, rulers, or people, or seizure under legal process;

(h) Quarantine restrictions;

(i) Act of omission of the shipper or owner of the goods, his agent, or representative;

(j) Strikes or lockouts or stoppage or restraint of labor from whatever cause, whether partial or general: Provided, That nothing herein contained shall be construed to relieve a carrier from responsibility for the carrier's own acts;

(k) Riots and civil commotions;

(l) Saving or attempting to save life or property at sea;

(m) Wastage in bulk or weight or any other loss or damage arising from inherent defect, quality, or vice of the goods;

(n) Insufficiency of packing;

(o) Insufficiency or inadequacy of marks;

(p) Latent defects not discoverable by due diligence; and

(q) Any other cause arising without the actual fault and privity of the carrier and without the fault or neglect of the agents or servants of the carrier, but the burden of proof shall be on the person claiming the benefit of this exception to show that neither the actual fault or privity of the carrier nor the fault or neglect of the agents or servants of the carrier contributed to the loss or damage.

(3) The shipper shall not be responsible for loss or damage sustained by the carrier or the ship arising or resulting from any cause without the act, fault, or neglect of the shipper, his agents, or his servants.

(4) Any deviation in saving or attempting to save life or property at sea, or

any reasonable deviation shall not be deemed to be an infringement or breach of this Act or the contract of carriage, and the carrier shall not be liable for any loss or damage resulting therefrom:

Provided, however, That if the deviation is for the purpose of loading or unloading cargo or passengers it shall, prima facie, be regarded as unreasonable.

(5) Neither the carrier nor the ship shall in any event be or become liable for any loss or damage to or in connection with the transportation of goods in an amount exceeding $500 per package lawful money of the United States, or in case of goods not shipped in packages, per customary freight unit, or the equivalent of that sum in other currency, unless the nature and value of such goods have been declared by the shipper before shipment and inserted in the bill of lading.

This declaration, if embodied in the bill of lading, shall be prima facie evidence, but shall not be conclusive on the carrier.

By agreement between the carrier, master, or agent of the carrier and the shipper, another maximum amount than that mentioned in this paragraph may be fixed:

Provided, That such maximum shall not be less than the figure above named. In no event shall the carrier be liable for more than the amount of damage actually sustained.

Neither the carrier nor the ship shall be responsible in any event for loss or damage to or in connection with the transportation of the goods if the nature or value thereof has been knowingly and fraudelently misstated by the shipper in the bill of lading.

(6) Goods of an inflammable, explosive, or dangerous nature to the shipment whereof the carrier, master, or agent of the carrier, has not consented with knowledge of their nature and character, may at any time before discharge be landed at any place or destroyed or rendered innocuous by the carrier without compensation, and the shipper of such goods shall be liable for all damages and expenses directly or indirectly arising out of or resulting from such shipment.

If any such goods shipped with such knowledge and consent shall become a danger to the ship or cargo, they may in like manner by landed at any place, or destroyed or rendered innocuous by the carrier without liability on the part of the carrier except to general average, if any.

SURRENDER OF RIGHTS AND IMMUNITIES AND INCREASE OF RESPONSIBILITIES AND LIABILITIES

Sec. 5. A carrier shall be at liberty to surrender in whole or in part all or any of his rights and immunities or to increase any of his responsibilities and liabilities under this Act, provided such surrender or increase shall be embodied in the bill of lading issued to the shipper.

The provisions of this Act shall not be applicable to charter-parties, but if bills of lading are issued in the case of a ship under a charter-party they shall comply with the terms of this Act.

Nothing in this Act shall be held to prevent the insertion in a bill of lading of any lawful provision regarding general average.

SPECIAL CONDITIONS

Sec. 6. Notwithstanding the provisions of the preceding sections, a carrier, master or agent of the carrier, and a shipper shall, in regard to any particular goods be at liberty to enter into any agreement in any terms as to the responsibility and liability of the carrier for such goods, and as to the rights and immunities of the carrier in respect of such goods, or his obligation as to seaworthiness (so far as the stipulation regarding seaworthiness is not contrary to public policy), or the care or diligence of his servants or agents in regard to the loading, handling, stowage, carriage, custody, care and discharge of the goods carried by sea:

Provided, That in this case no bill of lading has been or shall be issued and that the terms agreed shall be embodied in a receipt which shall be a non-negotiable document and shall be marked as such.

Any agreement so entered into shall have full legal effect:

Provided, That this section shall not apply to ordinary commercial shipments made in the ordinary course of trade but only to other shipments where the character or condition of the property to be carried or the circumstances, terms, and conditions under which the carriage is to be performed are such as reasonably to justify a special agreement.

Se. 7. Nothing contained in this Act shall prevent a carrier or a shipper from entering into any agreement, stipulation, condition, reservation, or exemption as to the responsibility and liability of the carrier or the ship for the loss or damage to or in connection with the custody and care and handling of goods prior to the loading on and subsequent to the discharge from the ship on which the goods are carried by sea....

TITLE II

Sec. 9. Nothing contained in this Act shall be construed as permitting a common carrier by water to discriminate between competing shippers similarly placed in time and circumstances, either (a) with respect to their right to demand and receive bills of lading subject to the provisions of this Act; or (b) when issuing such bills of lading, either in the surrender of any of the carrier's rights and immunities or in the increase of any of the carrier's responsibilities and liabilities pursuant to section 5, title I, of this Act; or (c) in any other way prohibited by the Shipping Act, 1916, as amended....

Sec. 11. Where under the customs of any trade the weight of any bulk cargo inserted in the bill of lading is a weight ascertained or accepted by a third party other than the carrier or the shipper, and the fact that the weight is so ascertained or accepted is stated in the bill of lading, then, notwithstanding anything in this Act, the bill of lading shall not be deemed to be prima facie evidence against the carrier of the receipt of goods of the weight so inserted in the bill of lading, and the accuracy thereof at the time of shipment shall not be deemed to have been guaranteed by the shipper.

Sec. 12. Nothing in this Act shall be construed as superseding any part of the (Harter) Act or of any other law which would be applicable in the absence of this Act, insofar as they relate to the duties, responsibilities, and liabilities of the ship or carrier prior to the time when the goods are loaded on or after the time they are discharged from the ship.

Sec. 13. This Act shall apply to all contracts for carriage of goods by sea to or from ports of the United States in foreign trade.

As used in this Act the term "United States" includes its districts, territories and possessions....

The term "foreign trade" means the transportation of goods between the ports of the United States and ports of foreign countries.

Nothing in this Act shall be held to apply to contracts for carriage of goods by sea between any port of the United States or its possessions, and any other port of the United States or its possessions:

Provided further, That every bill of lading or similar document of title which is evidence of a contract for the carriage of goods by sea from ports of the United States, in foreign trade, shall contain a statement that it shall have effect subject to the provisions of this Act.

Sec. 14.   Upon the certification of the Secretary of Commerce that the foreign commerce of the United States in its competition with that of foreign nations is prejudiced by the provisions, or any of them, of Title I of this Act, or by the laws of any foreign country or countries relating to the carriage of goods by sea, the President of the United States may, from time to time, by proclamation, suspend any or all provisions of Title I of this Act for such periods of time or indefinitely as may be designated in the proclamation.   The Presedent may at any time rescind such suspension of Title I hereof, and any provisions thereof which may have been suspended shall thereby be reinstated and again apply to contracts thereafter made for the carriage of goods by sea.   Any proclamation of suspension or rescission of any such suspension shall take effect on a date named therein, which date shall be not less than ten days from the issue of the proclamation.

Any contract for the carriage of goods by sea, subject to the provisions of this Act, effective during any period when Title I hereof, or any part thereof, is suspended, shall be subject to all provisions of law now or hereafter applicable to that part of Title I which may have thus been suspended....

APPENDIX F

SHIPPING ACT, 1916

[As amended through the 89th Congress, first session]

(39 Stat. 728, chapter 451, approved Sept. 7, 1916)

[NOTE.—See excerpts from the Transportation Act of 1940, as amended, infra.] [1]

AN ACT

To establish a United States Shipping Board for the purpose of encouraging, developing, and creating a naval auxiliary and naval reserve and a merchant marine to meet the requirements of the commerce of the United States with its Territories and possessions and with foreign countries; to regulate carriers by water engaged in the foreign and interstate commerce of the United States, and for other purposes.

Be it enacted by the Senate and House of Representatives of the United States of America in Congress assembled, That when used in this Act:

The term "common carrier by water in foreign commerce" means a common carrier, except ferryboats running on regular routes, engaged in the transportation by water of passengers or property between the United States or any of its Districts, Territories, or possessions and a foreign country, whether in the import or export trade: *Provided,* That a cargo boat commonly called an ocean tramp shall not be deemed such "common carrier by water in foreign commerce." 46 U.S.C. 801. 39 Stat. 728. 40 Stat. 900. 75 Stat. 522.

Definitions: "Common carrier by water in foreign commerce." Ocean tramps excepted.

The term "common carrier by water in interstate commerce" means a common carrier engaged in the transportation by water of passengers or property on the high seas or the Great Lakes on regular routes from port to port between one State, Territory, District, or possession of the United States and any other State, Territory, District, or possession of the United States, or between places in the same Territory, District, or possession. *"Common carrier by water in interstate commerce."*

The term "common carrier by water" means a common carrier by water in foreign commerce or a common carrier by water in interstate commerce on the high seas or the Great Lakes on regular routes from port to port. *"Common carrier by water."*

The term "other person subject to this act" means any person not included in the term "common carrier by water," carrying on the business of forwarding or furnishing wharfage, dock, warehouse, or other terminal facilities in connection with a common carrier by water. *"Other person subject to this act."*

---

[1] See section 27(b) of Public Law 85–508 (72 Stat. 351) and section 18(a) of Public Law 86–3 (73 Stat. 12), regarding continuing jurisdiction of the Federal Maritime Board, now the Federal Maritime Commission, after Alaska and Hawaii statehood.

"Person."

The term "person" includes corporations, partnerships, and associations, existing under or authorized by the laws of the United States, or any State, Territory, District, or possession thereof, or of any foreign country.

"Vessel."
46 U.S.C. 801.
40 Stat. 900.

The term "vessel" includes all water craft and other artificial contrivances of whatever description and at whatever stage of construction, whether on the stocks or launched, which are used or are capable of being or are intended to be used as a means of transportation on water.

Shipping Act,
1916, amend-
ment. Ocean
freight for-
warders.
39 Stat. 728.
Definitions.
P.L. 87–254.
75 Stat. 522.

The term "documented under the laws of the United States," means "registered, enrolled, or licensed under the laws of the United States."

The term "carrying on the business of forwarding" means the dispatching of shipments by any person on behalf of others, by oceangoing common carriers in commerce from the United States, its Territories, or possessions to foreign countries, or between the United States and its Territories or possessions, or between such Territories and possessions, and handling the formalities incident to such shipments.

An "independent ocean freight forwarder" is a person carrying on the business of forwarding for a consideration who is not a shipper or consignee or a seller or purchaser of shipments to foreign countries, nor has any beneficial interest therein, nor directly or indirectly controls or is controlled by such shipper or consignee or by any person having such a beneficial interest.

Citizen of
United States.
46 U.S.C. 802,
803.
39 Stat. 729.
40 Stat. 900.
41 Stat. 1008.
73 Stat. 597.
P.L. 86–327.

SEC. 2. (a) That within the meaning of this Act no corporation, partnership, or association shall be deemed a citizen of the United States unless the controlling interest therein is owned by citizens of the United States, and, in the case of a corporation, unless its president or other chief executive officer and the chairman of its board of directors are citizens of the United States and unless no more of its directors than a minority of the number necessary to constitute a quorum are noncitizens and the corporation itself is organized under the laws of the United States or of a State, Territory, District, or possession thereof, but in the case of a corporation, association, or partnership operating any vessel in the coastwise trade the amount of interest required to be owned by citizens of the United States shall be 75 per centum.

Controlling
interest in
corporation.

(b) The controlling interest in a corporation shall not be deemed to be owned by citizens of the United States (a) if the title to a majority of the stock thereof is not vested in such citizens free from any trust or fiduciary obligation in favor of any person not a citizen of the United States; or (b) if the majority of the voting power in such corporation is not vested in citizens of the United States; or (c) if through any contract or understanding it is so arranged that the majority of the voting power may be exercised, directly or indirectly, in behalf of any person who is not a citizen of the United States; or (d) if by any other means whatsoever control of the corporation is conferred upon or permitted to be exercised by any person who is not a citizen of the United States.

(c) Seventy-five per centum of the interest in a corporation shall not be deemed to be owned by citizens of the United States (a) if the title to 75 per centum of its stock is not vested in such citizens free from any trust or fiduciary obligation in favor of any person not a citizen of the United States; or (b) if 75 per centum of the voting power in such corporation is not vested in citizens of the United States; or (c) if, through any contract or understanding it is so arranged that more than 25 per centum of the voting power in such corporation may be exercised, directly or indirectly, in behalf of any person who is not a citizen of the United States; or (d) if by any other means whatsoever control of any interest in the corporation in excess of 25 per centum is conferred upon or permitted to be exercised by any person who is not a citizen of the United States.

75 per centum of interest in corporation.

(d) The provisions of this Act shall apply to receivers and trustees of all persons to whom the Act applies and to the successors or assignees of such persons.

Receivers, trustees, successors, and assigns.

Sections 3–8, inclusive, were repealed by section 903 (a) of the Merchant Marine Act, 1936, supra.

SEC. 9.[2] That any vessel purchased, chartered, or leased from the board, by persons who are citizens of the United States, may be registered or enrolled and licensed, or both registered and enrolled and licensed, as a vessel of the United States and entitled to the benefits and privileges appertaining thereto: *Provided,* That foreign-built vessels admitted to American registry or enrollment and licensed under this Act, and vessels owned by any corporation in which the United States is a stockholder, and vessels sold, leased, or chartered by the board to any person, a citizen of the United States, as provided in this Act, may engage in the coastwise trade of the United States while owned, leased, or chartered by such a person.

Vessels acquired by or from board may engage in coastwise trade. 46 U.S.C. 808. 39 Stat. 730. 40 Stat. 900. 41 Stat. 994. 52 Stat. 964. Vessels acquired from board may be operated under American documentation only.

Every vessel purchased, chartered, or leased from the board shall, unless otherwise authorized by the board, be operated only under such registry or enrollment and license. Such vessels while employed solely as merchant vessels shall be subject to all laws, regulations, and liabilities governing merchant vessels, whether the United States be interested therein as owner, in whole or in part, or hold any mortgage, lien, or other interest therein.

Subject to all laws and liabilities.

---

[2] See the Act extending the steamboat inspection laws to Shipping Board vessels (41 Stat. 305 ; 46 U.S.C. 363).

See also section 27A of the Merchant Marine Act, 1920, as amended. supra (Public Law 85–902, 72 Stat. 1736) regarding the term "citizen of the United States".

The fourth paragraph of this section was added by Public Law 89–346 (79 Stat. 1305), p. 282 herein. Section 4 of that act contains provisions with respect to transfers to noncitizens prior to such enactment or within one year thereafter.

Except as provided in section 611 of the Merchant Marine Act, 1936, as amended, it shall be unlawful, without the approval of the United States Maritime Commission, to sell, mortgage, lease, charter, deliver, or in any manner transfer, or agree to sell, mortgage, lease, charter, deliver, or in any manner transfer, to any person not a citizen of the United States, or transfer or place under foreign registry or flag, any vessel or any interest therein owned in whole or in part by a citizen of the United States and documented under the laws of the United States, or the last documentation of which was under the laws of the United States.

The issuance, transfer, or assignment of a bond, note, or other evidence of indebtedness which is secured by a mortgage of a vessel to a trustee or by an assignment to a trustee of the owner's right, title, or interest in a vessel under construction, to a person not a citizen of the United States, without the approval of the Secretary of Commerce, is unlawful unless the trustee or a substitute trustee of such mortgage or assignment is approved by the Secretary of Commerce. The Secretary of Commerce shall grant his approval if such trustee or a substitute trustee is a bank or trust company which (1) is organized as a corporation, and is doing business, under the laws of the United States or any State thereof (2) is authorized under such laws to exercise corporate trust powers, (3) is a citizen of the United States, (4) is subject to supervision or examination by Federal or State authority, and (5) has a combined capital and surplus (as set forth in its most recent published report of condition) of at least $3,000,000. If such trustee or a substitute trustee at any time ceases to meet the foregoing qualifications, the Secretary of Commerce shall disapprove such trustee or substitute trustee, and after such disapproval the transfer or assignment of such bond, note, or other evidence of indebtedness to a person not a citizen of the United States, without the approval of the Secretary of Commerce, shall be unlawful. The trustee or substitute trustee approved by the Secretary of Commerce shall not operate the vessel under the mortgage or assignment without the approval of the Secretary of Commerce. If a bond, note, or other evidence of indebtedness which is secured by a mortgage of a vessel to a trustee or by an assignment to a trustee of the owner's right, title, or interest in a vessel under construction, is issued, transferred, or assigned to a person not a citizen of the United States in violation of this section, the issuance, transfer, or assignment shall be void.

Any such vessel, or any interest therein, chartered, sold, transferred, or mortgaged to a person not a citizen of the United States or placed under a foreign registry or flag, or operated, in violation of any provision of this section shall be forfeited to the United States, and who-

ever violates any provision of this section shall be guilty
of a misdemeanor and subject to a fine of not more than
$5,000, or to imprisonment for not more than five years,
or both.

Sections 10 and 11 were repealed by section 903(a)
of the Merchant Marine Act, 1936, supra.

SEC. 12. That the board shall investigate the relative
cost of building merchant vessels in the United States
and in foreign maritime countries, and the relative cost,
advantages, and disadvantages of operating in the foreign trade vessels under United States registry and
under foreign registry. It shall examine the rules under
which vessels are constructed abroad and in the United
States, and the methods of classifying and rating same,
and it shall examine into the subject of marine insurance, the number of companies in the United States, domestic and foreign, engaging in marine insurance, the
extent of the insurance on hulls and cargoes placed or
written in the United States, and the extent of reinsur-
ance of American maritime risks in foreign companies,
and ascertain what steps may be necessary to develop
an ample marine insurance system as an aid in the development of an American merchant marine. It shall examine the navigation laws of the United States and the
rules and regulations thereunder, and make such recommendations to the Congress as it deems proper for the
amendment, improvement, and revision of such laws, and
for the development of the American merchant marine.
It shall investigate the legal status of mortgage loans on
vessel property, with a view to means of improving the
security of such loans and of encouraging investment in
American shipping.

It shall, on or before the first day of December in each
year, make a report to the Congress, which shall include
its recommendations and the results of its investigations,
a summary of its transactions, and a statement of all
expenditures and receipts under this act, and of the operations of any corporation in which the United States
is a stockholder, and the names and compensation of all
persons employed by the board.

SEC. 13. That for the purpose of carrying out the provisions of sections five and eleven no liability shall be
incurred exceeding a total of $50,000,000 and the Secre-
tary of the Treasury, upon the request of the board,
approved by the President, shall from time to time issue
and sell or use any of the bonds of the United States
now available in the Treasury under the acts of August
fifth, nineteen hundred and nine, February fourth, nineteen hundred and ten, and March second, nineteen hundred and eleven, relating to the issue of bonds for the
construction of the Panama Canal, to a total amount
not to exceed $50,000,000: *Provided*, That any bonds
issued and sold or used under the provisions of this sec-

Marginal notes:

Investigations
by board.
46 U.S.C. 811.
39 Stat. 732.
Cost of ship-
building.

Rules of con-
struction and
classification.

Marine
insurance.

Navigation
laws.

Vessel
mortgages.

Annual report
and recommen-
dations to
Congress.

Issuance of
$50,000,000 of
Panama Canal
bonds author-
ized.

36 Stat. L., 117,
193, 1013.

Proviso.

To be payable
within 50
years.

Funds of board
permanently
appropriated.

46 U.S.C. 812.
39 Stat. 733.
72 Stat. 574.
P.L. 85–626.
74 Stat. 253.
P.L. 86–542.
No carrier by
water—

To give de-
ferred rebates.

To use "fight-
ing ship."

To retaliate
against any
shipper.

To discrimi-
nate unjustly
or unfairly.

tion may be made payable at such time within fifty years after issue as the Secretary of the Treasury may fix, instead of fifty years after the date of issue, as prescribed in the act of August fifth, nineteen hundred and nine.

The proceeds of such bonds and the net proceeds of all sales, charters, and leases of vessels and of sales of stock made by the board, and all other moneys received by it from any source, shall be covered into the Treasury to the credit of the board, and are hereby permanently appropriated for the purpose of carrying out the provisions of sections five and eleven.

SEC. 14.[3] That no common carrier by water shall, directly or indirectly, in respect to the transportation by water of passengers or property between a port of a State, Territory, District, or possession of the United States and any other such port or a port of a foreign country—

First. Pay, or allow, or enter into any combination, agreement, or understanding, express or implied, to pay or allow, a deferred rebate to any shipper. The term "deferred rebate" in this Act means a return of any portion of the freight money by a carrier to any shipper as a consideration for the giving of all or any portion of his shipments to the same or any other carrier, or for any other purpose, the payment of which is deferred beyond the completion of the service for which it is paid, and is made only if, during both the period for which computed and the period of deferment, the shipper has complied with the terms of the rebate agreement or arrangement.

Second. Use a fighting ship either separately or in conjunction with any other carrier, through agreement or otherwise. The term "fighting ship" in this Act means a vessel used in a particular trade by a carrier or group of carriers for the purpose of excluding, preventing, or reducing competition by driving another carrier out of said trade.

Third. Retaliate against any shipper by refusing, or threatening to refuse, space accommodations when such are available, or resort to other discriminating or unfair methods, because such shipper has patronized any other carrier or has filed a complaint charging unfair treatment, or for any other reason.

Fourth. Make any unfair or unjustly discriminatory contract with any shipper based on the volume of freight offered, or unfairly treat or unjustly discriminate against any shipper in the matter of (a) cargo space accommodations or other facilities, due regard being had for the proper loading of the vessel and the available tonnage; (b) the loading and landing of freight in proper condition; or (c) the adjustment and settlement of claims.

---

[3] See section 3 of Public Law 87–346 (as amended by Public Law 88–5), set out in footnote 6 to section 15 of this Act.

Any carrier who violates any provision of this section shall be guilty of a misdemeanor punishable by a fine of not more than $25,000 for each offense: *Provided*, That nothing in this section or elsewhere in this Act, shall be construed or applied to forbid or make unlawful any dual rate contract arrangement in use by the members of a conference on May 19, 1958, which conference is organized under an agreement approved under section 15 of this Act by the regulatory body administering this Act, unless and until such regulatory body disapproves, cancels, or modifies such arrangement in accordance with the standards set forth in section 15 of this Act. The term "dual rate contract arrangement" as used herein means a practice whereby a conference establishes tariffs of rates at two levels the lower of which will be charged to merchants who agree to ship their cargoes on vessels of members of the conference only and the higher of which shall be charged to merchants who do not so agree.[4]

Penalty.

Dual rate contract agreements.

46 U.S.C. 814.

SEC. 14a. The board upon its own initiative may, or upon complaint shall, after due notice to all parties in interest and hearing, determine whether any person, not a citizen of the United States and engaged in transportation by water of passengers or property—

46 U.S.C. 813.
39 Stat. 733.
41 Stat. 966.

(1) Has violated any provision of section 14, or

(2) Is a party to any combination, agreement, or understanding, express or implied, that involves in respect to transportation of passengers or property between foreign ports, deferred rebates or any other unfair practice designated in section 14, and that excludes from admission upon equal terms with all other parties thereto, a common carrier by water which is a citizen of the United States and which has applied for such admission.

Rebates, fighting ships, retaliation, unfair contracts.
Rebates or unfair practices between foreign ports.

---

[4] This proviso was added by Public Law 85-626, approved August 12, 1958, which reads as follows:

"*Be it enacted by the Senate and House of Representatives of the United States of America in Congress assembled,* That section 14 of the Shipping Act, 1916, is amended by inserting at the end thereof the following: '*Provided,* That nothing in this section or elsewhere in this Act, shall be construed or applied to forbid or make unlawful any dual rate contract arrangement in use by the members of a conference on May 19, 1958, which conference is organized under an agreement approved under section 15 of this Act by the regulatory body administering this Act, unless and until such regulatory body disapproves, cancels, or modifies such arrangement in accordance with the standards set forth in section 15 of this Act. The term 'dual rate contract arrangement' as used herein means a practice whereby a conference establishes tariffs of rates at two levels the lower of which will be charged to merchants who agree to ship their cargoes on vessels of members of the conference only and the higher of which shall be charged to merchants who do not so agree.'

"SEC. 2. This Act shall be effective immediately upon enactment and shall cease to be effective on and after June 30, 1960."

The expiration date in section 2 of Public Law 85-626 was changed to June 30, 1961, by Public Law 86-542 and to September 15, 1961, by Public Law 87-75. Public Law 87-252 amended section 2 of Public Law 85-626 to read as follows:

"SEC. 2. This Act shall be effective immediately upon enactment and shall cease to be effective on and after October 15, 1961: *Provided, however,* That contracts in effect midnight September 14, 1961, shall remain in effect until midnight October 15, 1961, unless such contracts terminate earlier by their own terms, or are rendered illegal under the terms of the first section of this Act."

Dual rate contract agreements.
72 Stat. 574.
74 Stat. 253.
46 U.S.C. 812 note.

Vessels may be denied entry.

If the board determines that any such person has violated any such provision or is a party to any such combination, agreement, or understanding, the board shall thereupon certify such fact to the Secretary of Commerce. The Secretary shall thereafter refuse such person the right of entry for any ship owned or operated by him or by any carrier directly or indirectly controlled by him, into any port of the United States, or any Territory, District, or possession thereof, until the board certifies that the violation has ceased or such combination, agreement, or understanding has been terminated.

Shipping Act, 1916, amendments.
40 Stat. 903.
46 U.S.C. 813a.
Foreign commerce.
Common carriers, dual rate contracts.
P.L. 87–346.
75 Stat. 762.

SEC. 14b.[5] Notwithstanding any other provisions of this Act, on application the Federal Maritime Commission (hereinafter "Commission"), shall, after notice, and hearing, by order, permit the use by any common carrier or conference of such carriers in foreign commerce of any contract, amendment, or modification thereof, which is available to all shippers and consignees on equal terms and conditions, which provides lower rates to a shipper or consignee who agrees to give all or any fixed portion of his patronage to such carrier or conference of carriers unless the Commission finds that the contract, amendment, or modification thereof will be detrimental to the commerce of the United States or contrary to the public interest, or unjustly discriminatory or unfair as between shippers, exporters, importers, or ports, or between exporters from the United States and their foreign competitors, and provided the contract, amendment, or modification thereof, expressly (1) permits prompt release of the contract shipper from the contract with respect to any shipment or shipments for which the contracting carrier or conference of carriers cannot provide as much space as the contract shipper shall require on reasonable notice; (2) provides that whenever a tariff rate for the carriage of goods under the contract becomes effective, insofar as it is under the control of the carrier or conference of carriers, it shall not be increased before a reasonable period, but in no case less than ninety days; (3) covers only those goods of the contract shipper as to the shipment of which he has the legal right at the time of shipment to select the carrier: *Provided, however,* That it shall be deemed a breach of the contract if, before the time of shipment and with the intent to avoid his obligation under the contract, the contract shipper divests himself, or with the same intent permits himself to be divested, of the legal right to select the carrier and the shipment is carried by a carrier which is not a party to the contract; (4) does not require the contract shipper to divert shipment of goods from natural

---

[5] See section 3 of Public Law 87–346 (as amended by Public Law 88–5), set out in footnote 6 to section 15 of this Act.

routings not served by the carrier or conference of carriers where direct carriage is available; (5) limits damages recoverable for breach by either party to actual damages to be determined after breach in accordance with the principles of contract law: *Provided, however,* That the contract may specify that in the case of a breach by a contract shipper the damages may be an amount not exceeding the freight charges computed at the contract rate on the particular shipment, less the cost of handling; (6) permits the contract shipper to terminate at any time without penalty upon ninety days' notice; (7) provides for a spread between ordinary rates and rates charged contract shippers which the Commission finds to be reasonable in all the circumstances but which spread shall in no event be more than 15 per centum of the ordinary rates; (8) excludes cargo of the contract shippers which is loaded and carried in bulk without mark or count except liquid bulk cargoes, other than chemicals, in less than full shipload lots: *Provided, however,* That upon finding that economic factors so warrant, the Commission may exclude from the contract any commodity subject to the foregoing exception; and (9) contains such other provisions not inconsistent herewith as the Commission shall require or permit. The Commission shall withdraw permission which it has granted under the authority contained in this section for the use of any contract if it finds, after notice and hearing, that the use of such contract is detrimental to the commerce of the United States or contrary to the public interest, or is unjustly discriminatory or unfair as between shippers, exporters, importers, or ports, or between exporters from the United States and their foreign competitors. The carrier or conference of carriers may on ninety days' notice terminate without penalty the contract rate system herein authorized, in whole or with respect to any commodity: *Provided, however,* That after such termination the carrier or conference of carriers may not reinstitute such contract rate system or part thereof so terminated without prior permission by the Commission in accordance with the provisions of this section. Any contract, amendment, or modification of any contract not permitted by the Commission shall be unlawful, and contracts, amendments, and modifications shall be lawful only when and as long as permitted by the Commission; before permission is granted or after permission is withdrawn it shall be unlawful to carry out in whole or in part, directly or indirectly, any such contract, amendment, or modification. As used in this section, the term "contract shipper" means a person other than a carrier or conference of carriers who is a party to a contract the use of which may be permitted under this section.

75 Stat. 763.

Notice and hearing.

39 Stat. 733.
46 U.S.C. 814.
Filing of agreements, etc.

SEC. 15.[6] That every common carrier by water, or other person subject to this Act, shall file immediately with the Commission a true copy, or, if oral, a true and complete memorandum, of every agreement with another such carrier or other person subject to this Act, or modification or cancellation thereof, to which it may be a party or conform in whole or in part, fixing or regulating transportation rates or fares; giving or receiving special rates, accommodations, or other special privileges or advantages; controlling, regulating, preventing, or destroying competition; pooling or apportioning earnings, losses, or traffic; allotting ports or restricting or otherwise regulating the number and character of sailings between ports; limiting or regulating in any way the volume or character of freight or passenger traffic to be carried; or in any manner providing for an exclusive, preferential, or co-operative working arrangement. The term "agreement" in this section includes understandings, conferences, and other arrangements.

P.L. 87–346.

75 Stat. 763.

Discriminatory agreements, disapproval.

The Commission shall by order, after notice and hearing, disapprove, cancel or modify any agreement, or any modification or cancellation thereof, whether or not previously approved by it, that it finds to be unjustly discriminatory or unfair as between carriers, shippers, exporters, importers, or ports, or between exporters from the United States and their foreign competitors, or to operate to the detriment of the commerce of the United States, or to be contrary to the public interest, or to be in violation of this Act, and shall approve all other agreements, modifications, or cancellations. No such agreement shall be approved, nor shall continued approval be permitted for any agreement (1) between carriers not members of the same conference or conferences of carriers serving different trades that would otherwise be naturally competitive, unless in the case of agreements between carriers, each carrier, or in the case of agreements between conferences, each conference, retains the right of independent action, or (2) in respect to any conference agreement, which fails to provide reasonable and equal terms and conditions for admission and re-

75 Stat. 764

---

[6] Section 14b was added to the Act, and section 15 was amended to read as shown in the foregoing text, by sections 1 and 2 of Public Law 87–346 (except for the proviso of section 15 which was added by Public Law 88–275), approved Oct. 3, 1961. Section 3 of Public Law 87–346 (as amended by Public Law 88–5) reads as follows:

"SEC. 3. Notwithstanding the provisions of sections 14, 14b, and 15, Shipping Act, 1916, as amended by this Act, all existing agreements which are lawful under the Shipping Act, 1916, immediately prior to enactment of this Act, shall remain lawful unless disapproved, canceled, or modified by the Commission pursuant to the provisions of the Shipping Act, 1916, as amended by this Act: *Provided, however,* That all such existing agreements which are rendered unlawful by the provisions of such Act as hereby amended must be amended to comply with the provisions of such Act as hereby amended, and if such amendments are filed for approval within six months after the enactment of this Act, such agreements so amended shall be lawful for a further period but not beyond April 3, 1964. Within such period the Commission shall approve, disapprove, cancel or modify all such agreements and amendments in accordance with the provisions of this Act.

77 Stat. 5
P.L. 88–5.

Existing agreements, modifications, etc.

Dual rate contracts, extension.

admission to conference membership of other qualified carriers in the trade, or fails to provide that any member may withdraw from membership upon reasonable notice without penalty for such withdrawal.

The Commission shall disapprove any such agreement, after notice and hearing, on a finding of inadequate policing of the obligations under it, or of failure or refusal to adopt and maintain reasonable procedures for promptly and fairly hearing and considering shippers' requests and complaints.

Any agreement and any modification or cancellation of any agreement not approved, or disapproved, by the Commission shall be unlawful, and agreements, modifications, and cancellations shall be lawful only when and as long as approved by the Commission; before approval or after disapproval it shall be unlawful to carry out in whole or in part, directly or indirectly, any such agreement, modification, or cancellation; except that tariff rates, fares, and charges, and classifications, rules, and regulations explanatory thereof (including changes in special rates and charges covered by section 14b of this Act which do not involve a change in the spread between such rates and charges and the rates and charges applicable to noncontract shippers) agreed upon by approved conferences, and changes and amendments thereto, if otherwise in accordance with law, shall be permitted to take effect without prior approval upon compliance with the publication and filing requirements of section 18(b) hereof and with the provisions of any regulations the Commission may adopt. *75 Stat. 762.* *Infra.*

Every agreement, modification, or cancellation lawful under this section, or permitted under section 14b, shall be excepted from the provisions of the Act approved July 2, 1890, entitled "An Act to protect trade and commerce against unlawful restraints and monopolies," and amendments and Acts supplementary thereto, and the provisions of sections 73 to 77, both inclusive, of the Act approved August 27, 1894, entitled "An Act to reduce taxation, to provide revenue for the Government, and for other purposes," and amendments and Acts supplementary thereto. *26 Stat. 209.* *15 U.S.C. 1–7.* *28 Stat. 570.* *15 U.S.C. 8–11.*

Whoever violates any provision of this section or of section 14b shall be liable to a penalty of not more than $1,000 for each day such violation continues, to be recovered by the United States in a civil action: *Provided, however,* That the penalty provisions of this section shall not apply to leases, licenses, assignments, or other agreements of similar character for the use of terminal property or facilities which were entered into before the date of enactment of this Act, and, if continued in effect beyond said date, submitted to the Federal Maritime Commission for approval prior to or within ninety days after the enactment of this Act, unless such leases, *Shipping Act, amendment. Terminal leases 75 Stat. 763. 78 Stat. 148. P.L. 88–275.*

licenses, assignments, or other agreements for the use of terminal facilities are disapproved, modified, or canceled by the Commission and are continued in operation without regard to the Commission's action thereon. The Commission shall promptly approve, disapprove, cancel, or modify each such agreement in accordance with the provisions of this section.

46 U.S.C. 815.
39 Stat. 734.
False billing.

SEC. 16. That it shall be unlawful for any shipper consignor, consignee, forwarder, broker, or other person, or any officer, agent, or employee thereof, knowingly and wilfully, directly or indirectly, by means of false billing, false classification, false weighing, false report of weight, or by any other unjust or unfair device or means to obtain or attempt to obtain transportation by water for property at less than the rates or charges which would otherwise be applicable.

That it shall be unlawful for any common carrier by water, or other person subject to this Act, either alone or in conjunction with any other person, directly or indirectly:

Undue prefer-
ence or
advantage.

First. To make or give any undue or unreasonable preference or advantage to any particular person, locality, or description of traffic in any respect whatsoever, or to subject any particular person, locality, or description of traffic to any undue or unreasonable prejudice or dis-

Filing
of protests.
49 Stat. 1518.
75 Stat. 766.
P.L. 87–346.

advantage in any respect whatsoever: *Provided*, That within thirty days after enactment of this Act, or within thirty days after the effective date or the filing with the Commission, whichever is later, of any conference freight rate, rule, or regulation in the foreign commerce of the United States, the Governor of any State, Commonwealth, or possession of the United States may file a protest with the Commission upon the ground that the rate, rule, or regulation unjustly discriminates against that State, Commonwealth, or possession of the United States, in which case the Commission shall issue an order to the conference to show cause why the rate, rule, or regulation should not be set aside. Within one hundred and eighty days from the date of the issuance of such order, the Commission shall determine whether or not such rate, rule, or regulation is unjustly discriminatory and issue a final order either dismissing the protest, or setting aside the rate, rule, or regulation.

Unfair means
to obtain lower
rates.

Second. To allow any person to obtain transportation for property at less than the regular rates or charges then established and enforced on the line of such carrier by means of false billing, false classification, false weighing, false report of weight, or by any other unjust or unfair device or means.

To influence
insurance com-
panies to dis-
criminate.

Third. To induce, persuade, or otherwise influence any marine insurance company or underwriter, or agent thereof, not to give a competing carrier by water as favorable a rate of insurance on vessel or cargo, having

due regard to the class of vessel or cargo, as is granted
to such carrier or other person subject to this Act.

Whoever violates any provision of this section shall
be guilty of a misdemeanor punishable by a fine of not
more than $5,000 for each offense.

SEC. 17. That no common carrier by water in foreign
commerce shall demand, charge, or collect any rate, fare,
or charge which is unjustly discriminatory between
shippers or ports, or unjustly prejudicial to exporters
of the United States as compared with their foreign
competitors. Whenever the board finds that any such
rate, fare, or charge is demanded, charged, or collected
it may alter the same to the extent necessary to correct
such unjust discrimination or prejudice and make an
order that the carrier shall discontinue demanding,
charging, or collecting any such unjustly discriminatory
or prejudicial rate, fare, or charge.

Every such carrier and every other person subject to
this act shall establish, observe, and enforce just and
reasonable regulations and practices relating to or connected with the receiving, handling, storing, or delivering
of property. Whenever the board finds that any such
regulation or practice is unjust or unreasonable it may
determine, prescribe, and order enforced a just and reasonable regulation or practice.

SEC. 18(a) That every common carrier by water in
interstate commerce shall establish, observe, and enforce
just and reasonable rates, fares, charges, classifications,
and tariffs, and just and reasonable regulations and practices relating thereto and to the issuance, form, and substance of tickets, receipts, and bills of lading, the manner
and method of presenting, marking, packing, and delivering property for transportation, the carrying of personal, sample, and excess baggage, the facilities for transportation, and all other matters relating to or connected
with the receiving, handling, transporting, storing, or
delivering of property.

Every such carrier shall file with the board and keep
open to public inspection, in the form and manner and
within the time prescribed by the board, the maximum
rates, fares, and charges for or in connection with transportation between points on its own route; and if a
through route has been established, the maximum rates,
fares, and charges for or in connection with transportation between points on its own route and points on the
route of any other carrier by water.

No such carrier shall demand, charge, or collect a
greater compensation for such transportation than the
rates, fares, and charges filed in compliance with this
section, except with the approval of the board and after
ten days' public notice in the form and manner prescribed
by the board, stating the increase proposed to be made;

Penalty.

46 U.S.C. 816.
39 Stat. 734.

Common car-
riers in foreign
commerce.

Not to charge
discriminatory
rates or rates
prejudicial to
American
exporters.

Must observe
reasonable
practices con-
nected with
handling, etc.,
of freight.

46 U.S.C. 817.
39 Stat. 735.

Common car-
riers in inter-
state com-
merce:
Must observe
just and rea-
sonable classifi-
cations, rates,
fares, practices,
etc.

Maximum
rates, fares,
etc., to be filed
with board
and kept open
to public.

Not to charge
higher rates
than those
filed.

but the board for good cause shown may waive such notice.

Whenever the board finds that any rate, fare, charge, classification, tariff, regulation, or practice, demanded, charged, collected, or observed by such carriers is unjust or unreasonable, it may determine, prescribe, and order enforced a just and reasonable maximum rate, fare, or charge, or a just and reasonable classification, tariff, regulation, or practice.

(b)(1) From and after ninety days following enactment hereof every common carrier by water in foreign commerce and every conference of such carriers shall file with the Commission and keep open to public inspection tariffs showing all the rates and charges of such carrier or conference of carriers for transportation to and from United States ports and foreign ports between all points on its own route and on any through route which has been established. Such tariffs shall plainly show the places between which freight will be carried, and shall contain the classification of freight in force, and shall also state separately such terminal or other charge, privilege, or facility under the control of the carrier or conference of carriers which is granted or allowed, and any rules or regulations which in anywise change, affect, or determine any part or the aggregate of such aforesaid rates, or charges, and shall include specimens of any bill of lading, contract of affreightment, or other document evidencing the transportation agreement. Copies of such tariffs shall be made available to any person and a reasonable charge may be made therefor. The requirements of this section shall not be applicable to cargo loaded and carried in bulk without mark or count, or to cargo which is softwood lumber. As used in this paragraph, the term "softwood lumber" means softwood lumber not further manufactured than passing lengthwise through a standard planing machine and crosscut to length, logs, poles, piling, and ties, including such articles preservatively treated, or bored, or framed, but not including plywood or finished articles knocked down or set up.

(2) No change shall be made in rates, charges, classifications, rules or regulations, which results in an increase in cost to the shipper, nor shall any new or initial rate of any common carrier by water in foreign commerce or conference of such carriers be instituted, except by the publication, and filing, as aforesaid, of a new tariff or tariffs which shall become effective not earlier than thirty days after the date of publication and filing thereof with the Commission, and each such tariff or tariffs shall plainly show the changes proposed to be made in the tariff or tariffs then in force and the time when the rates, charges, classifications, rules or regulations as changed are to become effective: *Provided, however,* That the Commission may, in its discretion and for good cause,

allow such changes and such new or initial rates to become effective upon less than the period of thirty days herein specified. Any change in the rates, charges, or classifications, rules or regulations which results in a decreased cost to the shipper may become effective upon the publication and filing with the Commission. The term "tariff" as used in this paragraph shall include any amendment, supplement or reissue.

(3) No common carrier by water in foreign commerce or conference of such carriers shall charge or demand or collect or receive a greater or less or different compensation for the transportation of property or for any service in connection therewith than the rates and charges which are specified in its tariffs on file with the Commission and duly published and in effect at the time; nor shall any such carrier rebate, refund, or remit in any manner or by any device any portion of the rates or charges so specified, nor extend or deny to any person any privilege or facility, except in accordance with such tariffs.

(4) The Commission shall by regulations prescribe the form and manner in which the tariffs required by this section shall be published and filed; and the Commission is authorized to reject any tariff filed with it which is not in conformity with this section and with such regulations. Upon rejection by the Commission, a tariff shall be void and its use unlawful.

(5) The Commission shall disapprove any rate or charge filed by a common carrier by water in the foreign commerce of the United States or conference of carriers which, after hearing, it finds to be so unreasonably high or low as to be detrimental to the commerce of the United States.

(6) Whoever violates any provision of this section shall be liable to a penalty of not more than $1,000 for each day such violation continues, to be recovered by the United States in a civil action.

SEC. 19. That whenever a common carrier by water in interstate commerce reduces its rates on the carriage of any species of freight to or from competitive points below a fair and remunerative basis with the intent of driving out or otherwise injuring a competitive carrier by water, it shall not increase such rates unless after hearing the board finds that such proposed increase rests upon changed conditions other than the elimination of said competition.

SEC. 20. That it shall be unlawful for any common carrier by water or other person subject to this Act, or any officer, receiver, trustee, lessee, agent, or employee of such carrier or person, or for any other person authorized by such carrier or person to receive information knowingly to disclose to or permit to be acquired by any person other than the shipper or consignee, without the consent of such shipper or consignee, any information concerning the nature, kind, quantity, destination, consignee, or routing of any property tendered or delivered to such common carrier or other person subject to this act for transportation in interstate or foreign commerce, which information may be used to the detriment or prejudice of such shipper or consignee, or which may improperly disclose his business transactions to a competitor, or which may be used to the detriment or prejudice of any carrier; and it shall also be unlawful for any person to solicit or knowingly receive any such information which may be so used.

Nothing in this Act shall be construed to prevent the giving of such information in response to any legal process issued under the authority of any court, or to any officer or agent of the Government of the United States, or of any State, Territory, District, or possession thereof, in the exercise of his powers, or to any officer or other duly authorized person seeking such information for the prosecution of persons charged with or suspected of crime, or to another carrier, or its duly authorized agent,

for the purpose of adjusting mutual traffic accounts in the ordinary course of business of such carriers; or to prevent any common carrier by water which is a party to a conference agreement approved pursuant to section 15 of this Act, or any other person subject to this Act, or any receiver, trustee, lessee, agent, or employee of such carrier or person, or any other person authorized by such carrier to receive information, from giving information to the conference or any person, firm, corporation, or agency designated by the conference, or to prevent the conference or its designee from soliciting or receiving information for the purpose of determining whether a shipper or consignee has breached an agreement with the conference or its member lines or of determining whether a member of the conference has breached the conference agreement, or for the purpose of compiling statistics of cargo movement, but the use of such information for any other purpose prohibited by this Act or any other Act shall be unlawful.

SEC. 21. That the board may require any common carrier by water, or other person subject to this Act, or any officer, receiver, trustee, lessee, agent, or employee thereof, to file with it any periodical or special report, or any account, record, rate, or charge, or any memorandum of any facts and transactions appertaining to the business

of such carrier or other person subject to this Act. Such report, account, record, rate, charge, or memorandum shall be under oath whenever the board so requires, and

shall be furnished in the form and within the time prescribed by the board. Whoever fails to file any report, account, record, rate, charge, or memorandum as required by this section shall forfeit to the United States the sum of $100 for each day of such default.

Whoever willfully falsifies, destroys, mutilates, or alters any such report, account, record, rate, charge, or memorandum, or willfully files a false report, account, record, rate, charge, or memorandum shall be guilty of a misdemeanor, and subject upon conviction to a fine of not more than $1,000, or imprisonment for not more than one year, or to both such fine and imprisonment. Penalty for filing false reports, etc.

SEC. 22. That any person may file with the board a sworn complaint setting forth any violation of this Act by a common carrier by water, or other person subject to this Act, and asking reparation for the injury, if any, caused thereby. The board shall furnish a copy of the complaint to such carrier or other person, who shall within a reasonable time specified by the board satisfy the complaint or answer it in writing. If the complaint is not satisfied the board shall, except as otherwise provided in this Act, investigate it in such manner and by such means, and make such order as it deems proper. The board, if the complaint is filed within two years after the cause of action accrued, may direct the payment, on or before a day named, of full reparation to the complainant for the injury caused by such violation. 46 U.S.C. 821.
39 Stat. 736.
Complaint of any violation may be filed by any person.

Remedy for violations.

The board, upon its own motion, may in like manner and, except as to orders for the payment of money, with the same powers, investigate any violation of this Act. Investigations by board on own motion.

SEC. 23. Orders of the board relating to any violation of this Act shall be made only after full hearing, and upon a sworn complaint or in proceedings instituted of its own motion. 46 U.S.C. 822.
39 Stat. 736.

All orders of the United States Maritime Commission, other than for the payment of money, made under this Act, as amended or supplemented, shall continue in force until its further order, or for a specified period of time, as shall be prescribed in the order, unless the same shall be suspended, or modified, or set aside by the Commission, or be suspended or set aside by a court of competent jurisdiction. 53 Stat. 1182.
Orders of Commission.

SEC. 24. That the board shall enter of record a written report of every investigation made under this Act in which a hearing has been held, stating its conclusions, decision, and order, and, if reparation is awarded, the findings of fact on which the award is made, and shall furnish a copy of such report to all parties to the investigation. 46 U.S.C. 823.
39 Stat. 736.
Written reports of hearings to be kept.

The board may publish such reports in the form best adapted for public information and use, and such authorized publications shall, without further proof or authentication, be competent evidence of such reports in all courts of the United States and of the States, Territories, Districts, and possessions thereof. Such reports as evidence.

46 U.S.C. 824.
39 Stat. 736.

Board may reverse, modify, etc., orders and grant rehearings.

SEC. 25. That the board may reverse, suspend, or modify, upon such notice and in such manner as it deems proper, any order made by it. Upon application of any party to a decision or order it may grant a rehearing of the same or any matter determined therein, but no such application for or allowance of a rehearing shall, except by special order of the board, operate as a stay of such order.

46 U.S.C. 825.
39 Stat. 737.

Investigation of discriminations by foreign Governments against American vessels.

SEC. 26. The board shall have power, and it shall be its duty whenever complaint shall be made to it, to investigate the action of any foreign Government with respect to the privileges afforded and burdens imposed upon vessels of the United States engaged in foreign trade, whenever it shall appear that the laws, regulations, or practices of any foreign Government operate in such a manner that vessels of the United States are not accorded equal privileges in foreign trade with vessel of such foreign countries or vessels of other foreign countries, either in trade to or from the ports of such foreign country or in respect of the passage or transportation through such foreign country of passengers or goods intended for shipment or transportation in such vessels of the United States, either to or from ports of such foreign country or to or from ports of other foreign countries. It shall be the duty of the board to report the results of its investigation to the President with its recommendations and the President is hereby authorized and empowered to secure by diplomatic action equal privileges for vessels of the United States engaged in such foreign trade. And if by such diplomatic action the President shall be unable to secure such equal privileges, then the President shall advise Congress as to the facts and his conclusions by a special message, if deemed important in the public interest, in order that proper action may be taken thereon.

Board to report on such to President.

President to secure equal privileges for American vessels.

46 U.S.C. 826.
39 Stat. 737.

Power to subpœna witnesses, etc.

SEC. 27. That for the purpose of investigating alleged violations of this Act, the board may by subpoena compel the attendance of witnesses and the production of books, papers, documents, and other evidence from any place in the United States at any designated place of hearing. Subpoenas may be signed by any commissioner, and oaths or affirmations may be administered, witnesses examined, and evidence received by any commissioner or examiner, or, under the direction of the board, by any person authorized under the laws of the United States or of any State, Territory, District, or possession thereof to administer oaths. Persons so acting under the direction of the board and witnesses shall, unless employees of the board, be entitled to the same fees and mileage as in the courts of the United States. Obedience to any such subpoena shall, on application by the board, be enforced as are orders of the board other than for the payment of money.

Fees of witnesses.

Enforcement of subpœnas.

Sec. 28. That no person shall be excused on the ground that it may tend to incriminate him or subject him to a penalty or forfeiture, from attending and testifying, or producing books, papers, documents, and other evidence, in obedience to the subpœna of the board or of any court in any proceeding based upon or growing out of any alleged violation of this Act; but no natural person shall be prosecuted or subjected to any penalty or forfeiture for or on account of any transaction, matter, or thing as to which, in obedience to a subpœna and under oath, he may so testify or produce evidence, except that no person shall be exempt from prosecution and punishment for perjury committed in so testifying.

46 U.S.C. 827. 39 Stat. 737.

Giving of self-incriminating evidence by witnesses may be enforced.

But no witness to be prosecuted on such evidence.

Sec. 29. That in case of violation of any order of the board, other than an order for the payment of money, the board, or any party injured by such violation, or the Attorney General, may apply to a district court having jurisdiction of the parties; and if, after hearing, the court determines that the order was regularly made and duly issued, it shall enforce obedience thereto by a writ of injunction or other proper process, mandatory or otherwise.

46 U.S.C. 828. 39 Stat. 737. Enforcement of orders.

Where suits to be filed. (a) Other than for payment of money.

Sec. 30. That in case of violation of any order of the board for the payment of money the person to whom such award was made may file in the district court for the district in which such person resides, or in which is located any office of the carrier or other person to whom the order was directed, or in which is located any point of call on a regular route operated by the carrier, or in any court of general jurisdiction of a State, Territory, District, or possession of the United States having jurisdiction of the parties, a petition or suit setting forth briefly the causes for which he claims damages and the order of the board in the premises.

(b) For payment of money.

46 U.S.C. 829. 39 Stat. 737.

In the district court the findings and order of the board shall be prima facie evidence of the facts therein stated, and the petitioner shall not be liable for costs, nor shall he be liable for costs of any subsequent stage of the proceedings unless they accrue upon his appeal. If a petitioner in a district court finally prevails, he shall be allowed a reasonable attorney's fee, to be taxed and collected as part of the costs of the suit.

Findings and order of board as evidence.

Costs and attorney's fees.

All parties in whose favor the Board has made an award of reparation by a single order may be joined as plaintiffs, and all other parties to such order may be joined as defendants, in a single suit in any district in which any one such plaintiff could maintain a suit against any one such defendant. Service of process against any such defendant and not found in that district may be made in any district in which is located any office of, or point of call on a regular route operated by, such defendant. Judgment may be entered in favor

Joinder of parties permitted.

Service of process.

of any plaintiff against the defendant liable to that plaintiff.

No petition or suit for the enforcement of an order for the payment of moneys shall be maintained unless filed within one year from the date of the order.

SEC. 31. That the venue and procedure in the courts of the United States in suits brought to enforce, suspend, or set aside, in whole or in part, any order of the board shall, except as herein otherwise provided, be the same as in similar suits in regard to orders of the Interstate Commerce Commission, but such suits may also be maintained in any district court having jurisdiction of the parties.

SEC. 32. That whoever violates any provision of this Act, except where a different penalty is provided, shall be guilty of a misdemeanor, punishable by fine not to exceed $5,000.

SEC. 33. That this Act shall not be construed to affect the power or jurisdiction of the Interstate Commerce Commission, nor to confer upon the board concurrent power or jurisdiction over any matter within the power or jurisdiction of such commission; nor shall this Act be construed to apply to intrastate commerce.

SEC. 34. That if any provision of this Act, or the application of such provision to certain circumstances, is held unconstitutional, the remainder of the Act, and the application of such provision to circumstances other than those as to which it is held unconstitutional, shall not be affected thereby.

Section 35 was repealed by section 903(a) of the Merchant Marine Act, 1936, supra.

SEC. 36. The Secretary of the Treasury is authorized to refuse a clearance to any vessel or other vehicle laden with merchandise destined for a foreign or domestic port whenever he shall have satisfactory reason to believe that the master, owner, or other officer of such vessel or other vehicle refuses or declines to accept or receive freight or cargo in good condition tendered for such port of destination or for some intermediate port of call, together with the proper freight or transportation charges therefor, by any citizen of the United States, unless the same is fully laden and has no space accommodations for the freight or cargo so tendered, due regard being had for the proper loading of such vessel or vehicle or unless such freight or cargo consists of merchandise for which such vessel or vehicle is not adaptable.

SEC. 37.[7] That when the United States is at war or during any national emergency, the existence of which is declared by proclamation of the President, it shall be unlawful, without first obtaining the approval of the board.

46 U.S.C. 835. 40 Stat. 901.

During war or emergency.

(a) To transfer to or place under any foreign registry or flag any vessel owned in whole or in part by any person a citizen of the United States or by corporation organized under the laws of the United States, or of any State, Territory, District, or possession thereof; or

No vessel to be transferred to foreign registry.

(b) To sell, mortgage, lease, charter deliver, or in any manner transfer, or agree to sell, mortgage, lease, charter, deliver or in any manner transfer to any person not a citizen of the United States, (1) any such vessel or any interest therein, or (2) any vessel documented under the laws of the United States, or any interest therein, or (3) any shipyard dry dock, ship-building, or ship-repairing plant or facilities, or any interest therein; or

No vessel, shipyard, etc., to be sold mortgaged, to foreigner. No contract to construct for foreign account.

(c) To issue, transfer, or assign a bond, note, or other evidence of indebtedness which is secured by a mortgage of a vessel to a trustee or by an assignment to a trustee of the owner's right, title, or interest in a vessel under construction, or by a mortgage to a trustee on a shipyard, drydock, or ship-building or ship-repairing plant or facilities, to a person not a citizen of the United States, unless the trustee or a substitute trustee of such mortgage or assignment is approved by the Secretary of Commerce: *Provided, however*, That the Secretary of Commerce shall grant his approval if such trustee or a substitute trustee is a bank or trust company which (1) is organized as a corporation, and is doing business, under the laws of the United States or any State thereof, (2) is authorized under such laws to exercise corporate trust powers, (3) is a citizen of the United States, (4) is subject to supervision or examination by Federal or State authority, and (5) has a combined capital and surplus (as set forth in its most recent published report of condition) of at least $3,000,000; or for the trustee or substitute trustee approved by the Secretary of Commerce to operate said vessel under the mortgage or assignment: *Provided further*, That if such trustee or a substitute trustee at any time ceases to meet the foregoing qualifications, the Secretary of Commerce shall disapprove such trustee or sub-

P.L. 89-346. 79 Stat. 1305.

---

[7] The proclamation by the President of a national emergency in World War I as provided herein was made Aug. 7, 1918.

The state of war with respect to World War II and the national emergencies proclaimed by the President on Sept. 8, 1939 and May 27, 1941 were terminated July 25, 1947 for the purposes of this section by the Act of July 25, 1947 (Public Law 239, 80th Congress; 61 Stat. 449).

The President on December 16, 1950, issued a proclamation (No. 2914) declaring the existence of a national emergency (15 F.R. 9029).

See also section 27A of the Merchant Marine Act, 1920, as amended, supra (Public Law 85-902, 72 Stat. 1736) regarding the term "citizen of the United States".

Subsection (c) of the first paragraph hereof and the third paragraph hereof were added by Public Law 89-346 (79 Stat. 1305), p. 282 herein. Section 4 of that Act contains provisions with respect to transfers to noncitizens prior to such enactment or within one year thereafter.

stitute trustee, and after such disapproval the transfer or assignment of such bond, note, or other evidence of indebtedness to a person not a citizen of the United States, without the approval of the Secretary of Commerce, shall be unlawful; or

(d) To enter into any contract, agreement, or understanding to construct a vessel within the United States for or to be delivered to any person not a citizen of the United States, without expressly stipulating that such construction shall not begin until after the war or emergency proclaimed by the President has ended; or

(e) To make any agreement or effect any understanding whereby there is vested in or for the benefit of any

person not a citizen of the United States, the controlling interest or a majority of the voting power in a corporation which is organized under the laws of the United States, or of any State, Territory, District, or possession thereof, and which owns any vessel, shipyard, drydock, or ship-building or ship-repairing plant or facilities; or

(f) To cause or procure any vessel constructed in whole or in part within the United States, which has

never cleared for any foreign port, to depart from a port of the United States before it has been documented under the laws of the United States.

Whoever violates, or attempts or conspires to violate, any of the provisions of this section shall be guilty of a misdemeanor, punishable by a fine of not more than $5,000 or by imprisonment for not more than five years, or both.

If a bond, note, or other evidence of indebtedness which is secured by a mortgage of a vessel to a trustee or by an assignment to a trustee of the owner's right, title, or interest in a vessel under construction, or by a mortgage to a trustee on a shipyard, drydock or ship-building or ship-repairing plant or facilities, is issued, transferred, or assigned to a person not a citizen of the United States

in violation of subsection c of this section, the issuance, transfer or assignment shall be void.

Any vessel, shipyard, drydock, ship-building or ship-repairing plant or facilities, or interest therein, sold, mortgaged, leased, chartered, delivered, transferred, or documented, or agreed to be sold, mortgaged, leased, chartered, delivered, transferred, or documented, in violation of any of the provisions of this section, and any stocks, bonds, or other securities sold or transferred, or agreed to be sold or transferred, in violation of any of such provisions, or any vessel departing in violation of the provisions of subdivision (e), shall be forfeited to the United States.

Any such sale, mortgage, lease, charter, delivery, transfer, documentation, or agreement therefor shall be void, whether made within or without the United States, and any consideration paid therefor or deposited in connection therewith shall be recoverable at the suit of the person who has paid or deposited the same, or of his successors or assigns, after the tender of such vessel, shipyard, drydock, ship-building or ship-repairing plant or facilities, or interest therein, or of such stocks, bonds, or other securities, to the person entitled thereto, or after forfeiture thereof to the United States, unless the person to whom the consideration was paid, or in whose interest it was deposited, entered into the transaction in the honest belief that the person who paid or deposited such consideration was a citizen of the United States.

Forfeiture. Contracts and agreements in violation of section void. Consideration may be recovered.

SEC. 38. That all forfeitures incurred under the provisions of this Act may be prosecuted in the same court, and may be disposed of in the same manner, as forfeitures incurred for offenses against the law relating to the collection of duties.

46 U.S.C. 836. 40 Stat. 902.

Prosecutions of forfeitures. 19 U.S.C. 1618.

SEC. 39. That in any action or proceeding under the provisions of this Act to enforce a forfeiture the conviction in a court of criminal jurisdiction of any person for a violation thereof with respect to the subject of the forfeiture shall constitute prima facie evidence of such violation against the person so convicted.

46 U.S.C. 837. 40 Stat. 902.

Prima facie evidence.

SEC. 40. That whenever any bill of sale, mortgage, hypothecation, or conveyance of any vessel, or part thereof, or interest therein, is presented to any collector of the customs to be recorded, the vendee, mortgagee, or transferee shall file therewith a written declaration in such form as the board may by regulation prescribe, setting forth the facts relating to his citizenship, and such other facts as the board requires, showing that the transaction does not involve a violation of any of the provisions of section nine or thirty-seven. Unless the board, before such presentation, has failed to prescribe such form, no such bill of sale, mortgage, hypothecation, or conveyance shall be valid against any person whatsoever until such declaration has been filed. Any declaration filed by or in behalf of a corporation shall be signed by the president, secretary, or treasurer thereof, or any other official thereof duly authorized by such corporation to execute any such declaration.

46 U.S.C. 838. 40 Stat. 902.

Transferee must file declaration as to citizenship, etc., with collector of customs.

Whoever knowingly makes any false statement of a material fact in any such declaration shall be guilty of a misdemeanor and subject to a fine of not more than $5,000, or to imprisonment for not more than five years, or both.

Penalty for false statement.

46 U.S.C. 839.
40 Stat. 902.

Board may approve transactions conditionally.

Penalty for breach of conditions.

Penalty for making false statement of fact to secure board's approval.

46 U.S.C. 840.
40 Stat. 903.

Vessels to be considered documented until registry, enrollment, or license is canceled by board.

Rules and regulations.
P.L. 87–346.
75 Stat. 766.
46 U.S.C. 841a.

46 U.S.C. 841b.

Issuance.

SEC. 41. That whenever by said section nine or thirty-seven the approval of the board is required to render any act or transaction lawful, such approval may be accorded either absolutely or upon such conditions as the board prescribes. Whenever the approval of the board is accorded upon any condition a statement of such condition shall be entered upon its records and incorporated in the same document or paper which notifies the applicant of such approval. A violation of such condition so incorporated shall constitute a misdemeanor and shall be punishable by fine and imprisonment in the same manner, and shall subject the vessel, stocks, bonds, or other subject matter of the application conditionally approved to forfeiture in the same manner, as though the Act conditionally approved had been done without the approval of the board, but the offense shall be deemed to have been committed at the time of the violation of the condition.

Whenever by this Act the approval of the board is required to render any act or transaction lawful, whoever knowingly makes any false statement of a material fact to the board, or to any member thereof, or to any officer, attorney, or agent thereof, for the purpose of securing such approval, shall be guilty of a misdemeanor and subject to a fine of not more than $5,000, or to imprisonment for not more than five years, or both.

SEC. 42. That any vessel registered, enrolled, or licensed under the laws of the United States shall be deemed to continue to be documented under the laws of the United States within the meaning of subdivision (b) of section thirty-seven, until such registry, enrollment, or license is surrendered with the approval of the board, the provisions of any other Act of Congress to the contrary notwithstanding.

SEC. 43. The Commission shall make such rules and regulations as may be necessary to carry out the provisions of this Act.

SEC. 44. (a) No person shall engage in carrying on the business of forwarding as defined in this Act unless such person holds a license issued by the Federal Maritime Commission to engage in such business: *Provided, however*, That a person whose primary business is the sale of merchandise may dispatch shipments of such merchandise without a license.

(b) A forwarder's license shall be issued to any qualified applicant therefor if it is found by the Commission that the applicant is, or will be, an independent ocean freight forwarder as defined in this Act and is fit, willing, and able properly to carry on the business of forwarding and to conform to the provisions of this Act and the requirements, rules, and regulations of the Commission issued thereunder, and that the proposed forwarding business is, or will be, consistent with the national maritime policies declared in the Merchant Marine Act, 1936;

otherwise such application shall be denied. Any independent ocean freight forwarder who, on the effective date of this Act, is carrying on the business of forwarding under a registration number issued by the Commission may continue such business for a period of one hundred and twenty days thereafter without a license, and if application for such license is made within such period, such forwarder may, under such regulations as the Commission shall prescribe, continue such business until otherwise ordered by the Commission.

49 Stat. 1985.
46 U.S.C. 1245.

(c) The Commission shall prescribe reasonable rules and regulations to be observed by independent ocean freight forwarders and no such license shall be issued or remain in force unless such forwarder shall have furnished a bond or other security approved by the Commission in such form and amount as in the opinion of the Commission will insure financial responsibility and the supply of the services in accordance with contracts, agreements, or arrangements therefor.

Conditions.

(d) Licenses shall be effective from the date specified therein, and shall remain in effect until suspended or terminated as herein provided. Any such license may, upon application of the holder thereof, in the discretion of the Commission, be amended or revoked, in whole or in part, or may upon complaint, or on the Commission's own initiative, after notice and hearing, be suspended or revoked for willful failure to comply with any provision of this Act, or with any lawful order, rule, or regulation of the Commission promulgated thereunder.

75 Stat. 523.

(e) A common carrier by water may compensate a person carrying on the business of forwarding to the extent of the value rendered such carrier in connection with any shipment dispatched on behalf of others when, and only when, such person is licensed hereunder and has performed with respect to such shipment the solicitation and securing of the cargo for the ship or the booking of, or otherwise arranging for space for, such cargo, and at least two of the following services:

Compensation
of licensees.

(1) The coordination of the movement of the cargo to shipside;

(2) The preparation and processing of the ocean bill of lading;

(3) The preparation and processing of dock receipts or delivery orders;

P.L. 87–254.

(4) The preparation and processing of consular documents or export declarations;

(5) The payment of the ocean freight charges on such shipments:

Provided, however, That where a common carrier by water has paid, or has incurred an obligation to pay, either to an ocean freight broker or freight forwarder, separate compensation for the solicitation or securing of cargo for the ship or the booking of, or otherwise arrang-

Separate compensation.

ing for space for, such cargo, then such carrier shall not be obligated to pay additional compensation for any other forwarding services rendered on the same cargo. Before any such compensation is paid to or received by any person carrying on the business of forwarding, such person shall, if he is qualified under the provisions of this paragraph to receive such compensation, certify in writing to the common carrier by water by which the shipment was dispatched that he is licensed by the Federal Maritime Commision as an independent ocean freight forwarder and that he performed the above specified services with respect to such shipment. Such carrier shall be entitled to rely on such certification unless it knows that the certification is incorrect.

"Title of Act".
46 U.S.C. 842.

SEC. 45. That this Act may be cited as "Shipping Act, 1916."

AMENDMENT TO THE SHIPPING ACT,
August 29, 1972

[Public Law 92-416, 92nd Congress, H.R. 755]

To amend the Shipping Act, 1916, and the Intercoastal Shipping Act, 1933, to convert criminal penalties to civil penalties in certain instances, and for other purposes.

Be it enacted by the Senate and House of Representatives of the United States of America in Congress assembled. That the Shipping Act, 1916 (46 U.S.C. 801 et seq.), is amended as follows:

Federal Maritime Commission.
Shipping laws, civil penalties.
39 Stat. 728.
75 Stat. 763;
78 Stat. 148.
46 USC 814.
46 USC 813a.
49 Stat. 1518.
46 USC 815.

(a) By deleting that part of the first sentence in the last paragraph of section 15, immediately preceding the proviso, and substituting the following:

"Whoever violates any provision of this section or of section 14b shall be subject to a civil penalty of not more than $1,000 for each day such violation continues."

(b) By deleting the last paragraph of section 16 and substituting the following:

"Whoever violates any provision of this section other than paragraphs First and Third hereof shall be subject to a civil penalty of not more than $5,000 for each such violation.

"Whoever violates paragraphs First and Third hereof shall be guilty of a misdemeanor punishable by a fine of not more than $5,000 for each offense."

46 USC 817.

(c) By deleting section 18(b)(6) and substituting the following:

"(6) Whoever violates any provision of this section shall be subject to a civil penalty of not more than $1,000 for each day such violation continues."

(d) By amending the first paragraph of section 23 to read as follows:

"Orders of the Commission relating to any violation of this Act or to any violation of any rule or regulation issued pursuant to this Act shall be made only after full hearing, and upon a sworn complaint or in proceedings instituted of its own motion."

(e) By deleting section 32 and substituting therefor the following:

"SEC. 32. (a) That whoever violates any provision of sections 14 through 21 and section 44 of this Act, except where a different penalty is provided, shall be subject to a civil penalty not to exceed $5,000 for each such violation.

"(b) Whoever violates any provision of any other section of this Act, except where a different penalty is provided, shall be guilty of a misdemeanor, punishable by a fine not to exceed $5,000.

"(c) Whoever violates any order, rule, or regulation of the Federal Maritime Commission made or issued in the exercise of its powers, duties, or functions, shall be subject to a civil penalty of not more than $1,000 for each day such violation continues."

SEC. 2. The last sentence of section 2 of the Intercoastal Shipping Act, 1933 (46 U.S.C. 844), is amended to read as follows:

"Whoever violates any provision of this section shall be subject to a civil penalty of not more than $1,000 for each day such violation continues."

SEC. 3. Any civil penalty provided herein may be compromised by the Federal Maritime Commission, or may be recovered by the United States in a civil action.

Approved August 29, 1972.

46 USC 822.

46 USC 831.

46 USC 812-820, 841b.

79 Stat. 213.

Civil penalty, compromise or recovery.

LEGISLATIVE HISTORY:

HOUSE REPORT No. 92-478 (Comm. on Merchant Marine and Fisheries).
SENATE REPORT No. 92-1014 (Comm. on Commerce).
CONGRESSIONAL RECORD:
　Vol. 117 (1971): Sept. 20, considered and passed House.
　Vol. 118 (1972): Aug.　8, considered and passed Senate, amended.
　　　　　　　　　　　Aug.　18, House concurred in Senate amendments.

Public Law 95-483
95th Congress

An Act

92 STAT. 1€

To provide for the regulation of rates or charges by certain state-owned carriers in
the foreign commerce of the United States, and for other purposes.

Oct. 18, 1

[H.R. 99'

*Be it enacted by the Senate and House of Representatives of the
United States of America in Congress assembled,* That this Act may be
cited as the "Ocean Shipping Act of 1978".

SEC. 2. The first section of the Shipping Act, 1916, as amended (46
U.S.C. 801), is further amended by inserting the following definition
of the term "controlled carrier" immediately following the definition
of the term "common carrier by water":

"The term 'controlled carrier' means a common carrier by water
operating, offering, or proposing to offer service in the foreign commerce of the United States which carrier is or whose operating assets
are directly or indirectly owned or controlled by the government under
whose registry the vessels of the controlled carrier operate. Ownership
or control by such government shall be deemed to exist if a majority
portion of the interest in the carrier is owned or controlled in any
manner by such government, by any agency of the government, or by
any person, corporation, or entity controlled by such government.
Ownership or control shall also be deemed to exist if the government
has the right to appoint or disapprove the appointment of a majority
of the directors or the chief operating or executive officer of the
carrier".

SEC. 3. Section 18 of the Shipping Act, 1916, as amended (46 U.S.C.
817), is further amended by adding at the end thereof, the following
new subsection:

"(c)(1) No controlled carrier subject to this Act shall maintain
rates or charges in its tariffs filed with the Commission that are below a
level which is just and reasonable, nor shall any such carrier establish
or maintain unjust or unreasonable classifications, rules, or regulations
in such tariffs. An unjust or unreasonable classification, rule, or regulation means one which results or is likely to result in the carriage or handling of cargo at rates or charges which are below a level which is just
and reasonable. The Commission may at any time after notice and
hearing, disapprove any rates, charges, classifications, rules, or regulations which the controlled carrier has failed to demonstrate to be just
and reasonable. In any proceeding under this subsection, the burden
of proof shall be on the controlled carrier to demonstrate that its rates,
charges, classifications, rules, or regulations are just and reasonable.
Rates, charges, classifications, rules, or regulations filed by a controlled
carrier which have been rejected, suspended, or disapproved by the
Commission are void, and their use is unlawful.

"(2) For the purpose of this subsection, in determining whether
rates, charges, classifications, rules, or regulations by a controlled
carrier are just and reasonable, the Commission may take into account
appropriate factors, including, but not limited to, whether: (i) the
rates or charges which have been filed or which would result from the
pertinent classifications, rules, or regulations are below a level which
is fully compensatory to the controlled carrier based upon that carrier's

Ocean Shipp
Act of 1978
46 USC 842

"Controlled
carrier."

Notice and
hearing.

actual costs or upon its constructive costs, which are hereby defined as the costs of another carrier, other than a controlled carrier, operating similar vessels and equipment in the same or a similar trade; (ii) the rates, charges, classifications, rules, or regulations are the same as or similar to those filed or assessed by other carriers in the same trade; (iii) the rates, charges, classifications, rules, or regulations are required to assure movement of particular cargo in the trade; or (iv) the rates, charges, classifications, rules, or regulations are required to maintain acceptable continuity, level, or quality of common carrier service to or from affected ports.

"(3) Notwithstanding the provisions of subsection (b)(2) of this section, rates, charges, classifications, rules, or regulations of controlled carriers shall not, without special permission of the Commission, become effective within less than thirty days following the date of filing with the Commission. Following the effective date of this subsection, each controlled carrier shall, upon the request of the Commission, file within twenty days of request, with respect to its existing or proposed rates, charges, classifications, rules, or regulations a statement of justification which sufficiently details the controlled carrier's need and purpose for such rates, charges, classifications, rules, or regulations, upon which the Commission may reasonably base its determination of the lawfulness thereof.

"(4) Whenever the Commission is of the opinion that the rates, charges, classifications, rules, or regulations filed by a controlled carrier may be unjust and unreasonable, the Commission may issue an order to the controlled carrier to show cause why such rates, charges, classifications, rules, or regulations should not be disapproved. Pending a determination as to their lawfulness in such a proceeding, the Commission may suspend such rates, charges, classifications, rules, or regulations at any time prior to their effective date. In the case of any rates, charges, classifications, rules, or regulations which have already become effective, the Commission may, upon the issuance of an order to show cause, suspend such rates, charges, classifications, rules, or regulations on not less than sixty days notice to the controlled carrier. No period of suspension hereunder may be greater than one hundred and eighty days. Whenever the Commission has suspended any rates, charges, classifications, rules, or regulations under this provision, the affected carrier may file new rates, charges, classifications, rules, or regulations to take effect immediately during the suspension period in lieu of the suspended rates, charges, classifications, rules, or regulations: *Provided, however*, That the Commission may reject such new rates, charges, classifications, rules, or regulations if it is of the opinion that they are unjust and unreasonable.

"(5) Concurrently with the publication thereof, the Commission shall transmit to the President any order of suspension or final order of disapproval of rates, charges, classifications, rules, or regulations of a controlled carrier subject to the provisions of this subsection. Within ten days after the receipt or the effective date of such Commission order, whichever is later, the President may request the Commission in writing to stay the effect of the Commission's order if he finds that such stay is required for reasons of national defense or foreign policy which reasons shall be specified in the report. Notwithstanding any other provision of law, the Commission shall immediately grant such request by the issuance of an order in which the President's request shall be described. During any such stay, the President shall, whenever practicable, attempt to resolve the matter in controversy by negotiation with representatives of the applicable foreign governments.

"(6) The provisions of this subsection shall not apply to: (i) any controlled carrier of a state whose vessels are entitled by a treaty of the United States to receive national or most-favored-nation treatment; (ii) any controlled carrier of a state which, on the effective date of this subsection, has subscribed to the statement of shipping policy contained in note 1 to annex A of the Code of Liberalization of Current Invisible Operations, adopted by the Council of the Organization for Economic Cooperation and Development; (iii) rates, charges, classifications, rules, or regulations of any controlled carrier in any particular trade which are covered by an agreement approved under section 15 of this Act, other than an agreement in which all of the members are controlled carriers not otherwise excluded from the provisions of this subsection; (iv) rates, charges, classifications, rules, or regulations governing the transportation of cargo by a controlled carrier between the country by whose government it is owned or controlled, as defined herein, and the United States, or any of its districts, territories, or possessions; or (v) a trade served exclusively by controlled carriers.".

SEC. 4. The provisions of this Act, including the amendments made by this Act, shall become effective thirty days after its date of enactment.

Effective date.
46 USC 801 no

Approved October 18, 1978.

LEGISLATIVE HISTORY:

HOUSE REPORT No. 95–1381 (Comm. on Merchant Marine and Fisheries).
SENATE REPORT No. 95–1260 (Comm. on Commerce, Science, and Transportation).
CONGRESSIONAL RECORD, Vol. 124 (1978):
    July 31, considered and passed House.
    Oct. 3, considered and passed Senate.

O

APPENDIX G
COURT DECISION IN THE ISBRANDTSEN CASE

UNITED   STATES   COURT   OF   APPEALS   FOR   THE   DISTRICT   OF   COLUMBIA

CIRCUIT

DECISION   OF   November 9, 1956   No. 13027
ISBRANDTSEN   COMPANY,   INC.   Petitioner
V.
UNITED   STATES   OF   AMERICA   AND   FEDERAL   MARITIME   BOARD,   RESPONDENTS
THE   SECRETARY   OF   AGRICULTURE,   INTERVENOR
JAPAN   ATLANTIC   AND   GULF   FREIGHT
CONFERENCE,   et. a.,   INTERVENORS

ON PETITION FOR REVIEW OF ORDERS OF THE
FEDERAL MARITIME BOARD
DECIDED NOVEMBER 9, 1956

FAHY, Circuit Judge: Pursuant to 64 Stat. 1130 (1050), 5 U.S.C.S. 1034 (1952),
Isbrandtsen Company, Inc., petitions as a party aggrieved for review of orders of
the Federal Maritime Board which are described as a Report served December 14,
1955, and orders served December 21, 1955, and January 11, 1956. The respondents are the Board and the United States, the latter being a statutory respond-
ent under section 1034, supra. The United States, however, represented by the
Attorney General, has joined Isbrandtsen in attacking the validity of the orders
under review. The intervenors are the Secretary of Agriculture, supporting
Isbrandtsen, and the Japan-Atlantic and Gulf Freight Conference, defending the
orders of the Board.

The conference is a voluntary association of 17 steamship lines operating between
Japan, Korea, Okinawa, and the Gulf and Atlantic Coasts of North America. Five
of the members are American, eight are Japanese, and four are of other nations.
The primary purpose of the Conference is to establish and maintain agreed rates
among the members. The basic agreement under which the Conference operates
was approved by a predecessor agency of the Federal Maritime Board in 1934 under
section 15 of the Shipping Act of 1916, 39 Stat. 733, as amended, 46 USC. S 814
(1952).

Isbrandtsen is not a member of the Conference, although membership is open to
any common carrier regularly operating or intending to operate regularly in the
trade. Since shortly after World War II Isbrandtsen has been the sole non-Conference line which has maintained a berth service in the Japan-Atlantic trade.
This trade is overtonnaged and consequently the vessels of both Isbrandtsen and
the Conference have had a substantial amount of free and usable space after
completion of loading in Japan. Between 1947 and March 12, 1953, Isbrandtsen
maintained its rates on most commodities an average of 10 percent below the
rates established by Conference members under their agreement. Isbrandtsen's
share of the business during this period was substantial, and its average carryings per sailing were much higher than were the average carryings of the Conference lines. In order to meet this Competition, the Conference members voted
to adopt the exclusive patronage contract non-contract/dual-rate system described
below, but when the Conference was restrained by this court from putting this
system into effect, prior to its approval by the Board of Conference, on March
12, 1953, opened the rates on ten major commodities. This permitted the member

562

lines to set their own rates and to compete effectively with Isbrandtsen.

After March 12, 1953, rates dropped sharply, even to noncompensatory levels
with respect to some commodities.   In May 1953, Isbrandtsen established minimum
rates below which it would not go.   This adversely affected its competitive position,
so that since that date Isbrandtsen has carried little cargo in the trade.

On December 24, 1952, before rates had been opened by the Conference, it had
filed with the Board, pursuant to the latter's General Order 76, a statement
advising the Board of the Conference's intention, to institute in 30 days an exclusive patronage contract/non-contract, dual-rate system in the Japan-Atlantic trade,
hereinafter referred to as the dual-rate system.   Under the proposed system shippers who declined to sign an exclusive patronage contract with the Conference would
be charged rates 9 1/2 percent higher for the same transportation service than the
rates charged shippers who enter into such contracts.   Breach of the exclusive
patronage contracts would be sanctioned by means of a liquidated damage clause
under which a shipper who breaches the contract by shipping with a non-Conference
line, would be obligated to pay to the Conference 50 percent of the contract rate
on the shipment.   The contract would be entered into for an indefinite period,
subject to cancellation by either party on three months notice.

Protests against the proposed dual-rate system were filed by Isbrandtsen and the
Department of Justice, who requested the Board to prohibit the Conference from
implementing the system until after a hearing had been held.   The Board granted
the request for a hearing, but declined to suspend operation of the dual-rate system
stating that the system appeared to be in compliance with the Shipping Act.

On petition for review in this court, we held that section 15 of the Act, note 1,
supra, required the Board to approve the dual-rate system before it could legally
be initiated.

Isbrandtsen Co., v. UNITED STATES, 93, US. App. D. C. 293, 211 F. 2d 51,
cert. denied, 347 US 990.   Consequently we set aside the action of the Board
allowing the system to go into effect without such approval, and enjoined the
Conference from acting under the system until it was approved by the Board.
Thereafter the Board's hearings resulted in its approval of the dual-rate system in
the orders which are now here for review.

If the arrangements in question are such as the statute authorized the carriers to
make or the Board to approve, they are exempt from the inhibitions of the anti-
trust laws under section 15, note 1 supra.   In providing for such exemption, however, the statute also places definite limits.   For example, sections 16 and 17
of the Act provide "it shall be unlawful" for any common carrier by water, alone
or in conjunction with another, to

> "make or give any undue preference or advantage
> to any particular person"

or to

> "demand, charge, or collect any rate, fare, or
> charge which is unjustly discriminatory between shippers***"

The Board strongly urges that the dual-rate system cannot be said to give any
"undue preference or advantage" or to constitute a demand, charge, rate of fare

which is "unjustly" discriminatory.   It says that because of competitive conditions
in the trade, the preference is not "undue" or the discrimination "unjust".   In
explaining these conditions in the trade, the Board points to differences in the
operating costs of carriers of different nationalities, to the need for stability of
rates, and services, to freedom of any steamship company to enter this trade in
contrast to the requirements of the Interstate Commerce Act that there be a finding of public convenience and necessity, to the relationship between costs of operating and the quantity of cargo carried, and to other factors, all of which, in the
view of the Board, are shown by the record and support of the Board's findings
that the inauguration of the dual-rate system is a necessary competitive measure
to offset the harmful effect of non-Conference competition in an overtonnaged trade
subject to the injurious practice of undercutting of Conference rates.

The Board points furthermore to its finding that the dual-rate system will decrease
the possibility of continued rate wars with their disastrous consequences to Amer-
ican-flag lines, consequences repugnant to the purposes of the Act to encourage
the development and creation of a naval auxiliary and reserve, and a merchant
marine able to meet the requirements of the commerce of the United States with
foreign countries.

We might agree with the Board that the objectives it seeks in approving the dual-
rate system are consistent with the objectives of the statute; but these can be
furthered only by means permitted by the statute.   It is here that we find an in-
superable barrier.   It is in Section 14, Third, of the Act, provides that no common
carrier by water shall

> "Retaliate against any shipper by refusing, or
> threatening to refuse, space accomodations when
> such are available, or resort to other discrim-
> inating or unfair methods, because such shipper
> has patronized any other carrier *** or for any
> other reason"

As we have seen, shippers who decline to sign an exclusive patronage contract
with the Conference, would be charged for the same transportation service rates
9 1/2 percent higher than those charged shippers who enter into such contracts,
and breach of contract by one who does sign would entail liquidated damages of
50 percent of the contract rate.   While in terms the 9 1/2 percent higher rate is
for failure to enter into an exclusive patronage contract rather than for actually
shipping via a non-Conference carrier, in reality the higher rate is for the latter,
as are the liquidated damages.   Each of these aspects of the dual-rate system
is hinged to a shipper giving patronage to another carrier.   This is explicit in the
provision for liquidated damages, which is part and parcel of the dual-rate system,
and gives color to the whole; and it is implicit in the difference between the contract rate and the higher non-contract rate.   When the latter is charged a shipper
who has not entered into an exclusive patronage contract the substance of the
matter is that a higher rate is charged because he ships by other than Conference
carriers.   The industry is concerned with the business of shipping, to which the
making of contracts is but an incident.   Both provisions, therefore, come within a
fair meaning of retaliation.   Furthermore, even though the shipper has not patronized another the higher rate constitutes retaliation because it is charged for
failure to contract with the Conference.   Section 14, Third, applies not only to
retaliation for shipping by another carrier, but for "any other reason", which
would include failure to enter into the exclusive contract arrangement.   True it is,
as the Board urges with much persuasion, the dual-rate system may be very

potent in promoting stability and regularity of service, and may be warranted by competitive considerations; but when at the same time the system constitutes retaliation and is also discriminatory it runs into the barrier of section 14, Third, however desirable it otherwise might be.   That provision prohibits not only retaliation by a refusal, or threat of refusal, of available space accommodations, but also by "resort to other discriminating" methods.   In the circumstances stated, the charge of a higher rate for the same service and facilities, or the imposition of the liquidated damages, is prima facie discriminatory. Swayne and Hoyt, Ltd. v. UNITED STATES, 300 US 297, and for the reasons we have cutlined we think that it is also a method of retaliation.   This is the thrust of these provisions under a fair reading of the language adopted by Congress.   And since these provisions are unlawful the system containing them cannot validly be approved by the Board.

We cannot accept the argument that section 14, Third, must be read, in view of the terms of the Act as a whole, to condemm only retaliation which the Board might on a particular record find "unfair" or "unjustly discriminatory", terms used in other parts of section 14 and in sections 15 and 17.   Where the conduct is retaliatory and constitutes discrimination, it is unlawful without more, unless its impact is susubstantial, a subject we need not consider.   Absent retaliation a preference or discriminatory rate is unlawful only if undue, unreasonable, unfair or unjust.   Whether or not these characteristics exist depends upon the facts and circumstances of the case as found by the Board; and the courts will not substitute their judgment in this regard for that of the Board.   Swayne and Hoyt, Ltd. v. United States, supra.   There the court in effect aprproved an order of the Secretary of Commerce, the predecessor of the Board, which had condemmed a higher rate for a shipper who used a carrier other than a member of the Conference.   The court said the differential was prima facie discriminatory since the two rates were charged for identical services and the question whether the discrimination was "undue" or "unreasonable".   The Secretary having concluded that it was, the court considering the case under section 16, would not distrub his conclusion, which was in part based upon his finding that the operation of the contract system in the circumstances "does not differ substantially from that of deferred rebates' outlawed in both foreign and coastwise shipping by S 14 of the Shipping Act ***".   Since the dual-rate system here constitutes retaliation it must be condemmed without regard to the question of its reasonableness, as are deferred rebates.   For while it is not one of the methods specifically condemmed by section 14, as are deferred rebates and fighting ships, nevertheless retaliation is specified in subparagraph Third of section 14, as a method which may not be resorted to when discriminatory.

We are aware that the dual-rate system has not been held by any judicial decision to be invalid under section 14, Third;   that is without regard to the reasonableness or justness of the discrimination inherent in the system.   We have already referred to Swayne and Hoyt Ltd. v. United States, supra, which, though it upheld the Board in condemming the dual-rate system, there involved, did not rest upon section 14, Third.   In Far East Conference v. UNITED STATES, 343 US 570, the court, adhering to principles previously laid down in United States Navigation Co. v. Cunard Steamship Co., 284 US 474, required the District Court to dismiss a suit of the United States which attacked the dual-rate system as violative of the Sherman Act without the particular system having been passed upon initially by the Board.

And in A/S J. Ludwig Mowinckels Rederi v. Isbrandtsen Co. 342 US 950, the court by an equally divided vote affirmed Isbrandtsen v. United States, 96 F. Supp.

883, which had invalidated the dual-rate system there involved, not under section 14, Third, but because the spread between the two rates was found to be arbitrary. From this situation in the courts the Board contends that the dual-rate system has not been considered invalid per-se, otherwise the courts would have disposed of these cases on that ground.   This position is an arguable one; but the fact is that the cases do not decide the point.   And for the reasons which we have indicated we are of the opinion that additional legislation would be needed to permit the system, in the form here approved by the Board, to obtain the approval of the courts.   Congress, after long consideration, lodged very substantial powers in the Board; but we find no language in the statute which, given its fair meaning, permits the Board to grant exemption from the antitrust laws, or to make lawful a discriminatory rate, or the impostion of liquidated damages, for patronzaing a competitor, for refusal to enter into an exclusive patronage contract with Conference members, or for not shipping exclusively in accordance with such a contract.

We have considered the legislative history, particularly pertinent parts of H. R. Doc. No. 805, 63d Cong. 2d Session (1914) known as the Alexander Report. The evils afflicting the industry due to uncontrolled competition on the one hand and unregulated carrier combinations on the other, are, analyzed in this basic study preceding the Act.   Reference is also made to H. R. Regp. No. 659, 64th Cong.·, 1st Sess. (1915); H.R. 14337, 64th Con., 1st Sess. (1915); S. Rep. No. 689, 64th Cong., 1st Sess. (1915).   We have found in this history no indication of an explicit intention by Congress to outlaw the dual-rate system, as is found with respect to deferred rebates and fighting ships.   Furthermore, it is clear from its history, as from the Act itself, that not all discriminatory practices and preferences are unlawful.   On the contrary, the Board is authorized to approve many methods, including the formation of the conferences themselves, which would be unlawful except for the Act and Board action thereunder.   But is signaificant, that when Congress came to the matter of retaliation against a shipper, it did not permit this particular type of conduct to be engaged in or to be approved by the Board if it involved any discriminating method.

Finally, we have considered the Board's position that the enumeration of deferred rebates and fighting ships as practices absolutely prohibited, in contrast with the failure to include in such enumeration the dual-rate system, indicates that the latter was not to be considered illegal per se.   We do not accept this position because to do so would seem to us to give little meaning to the important provision of section 14, Third, that retaliation for any reason is also absolutely prohibited if it constitutes discrimination.   We think it clear not only that the liquidated damage provision is discriminatory, but that a 9 1/2 percent differential for exactly the same service and facilities is of like character.   Further discussion of the matter appears in Judge Washington's concurring opinion "in which as in the present opinion, we all concur"., Walker v. Popenoe, 80 US App. D. C. 129, 131, 149 F 2nd 511, 513, (1945).

> The orders of the Board will be set aside in
> so far as they approve the exclusive patron-
> age contract/non-contract rate system.

Washington, Circuit Judge, concurring: I fully concur in Judge Fahy's opinion. However, certain additional observations may be made, with which both my colleagues agree, and which they have asked me to express on behalf of the court.

The crucial question on this appeal is of course whether Section 14, Third, of the Shipping Act of 1916 proscribes the type of contract here involved.

In the first place, it seems clear that in actual practice the contract system is being used to penalize a shipper because he has patronized another carrier, or at least reserved the right to do so. Is this "retaliation" proscribed by the Act. Certainly there seems no reason to limit "retaliation" to the dictionary definitions of "returning like for like" of "evil for evil", which have been selected by the Board. The very example used by the statute, boycotting for use of another carrier, is not "like for like", nor are the boycotting carrier or group of carriers necessary imbued with ideas of doing evil. But detriment of the independent shippers and the independent carrier plainly results.

Are these contracts, then, the sort of "discriminating or unfair methods" that the statute sought to anticipate? That the contract system comes within the literal meaning of this phrase is clear.

As the Supreme Court observed in Swayne & Hoyt, Ltd. v. UNITED STATES 300 US 297, 303 (1937) a contract system under which different prices are charged for the same transportation of identical cargoes to identical ports under identical circumstances is "prima facie discriminatory". Nevertheless, the Board urges that the literal meaning of the statute should not be followed.

The Board's basic contention is this: Since dual-rate contracts were considered by Congress in its survey of shipping practice, the conspicuous absence of this device from the list of those specifically barred - deferred rebates, fighting ships, and boycotts - demonstrates as implied congressional endorsement of this device. Where the premise sound, the argument would have some merit. But the fact is that the contracts examined by the Alexander Committee in 1913, were materially different from the contracts before us now. The 1913 contracts were bona fide requirements contracts. The sellers (carriers) undertook a firm obligation as to the price. And since the price was fixed for the term of the contract (usually six months) the price figure of the contract represented a hedge on the part of both parties against fluctuations in rates. In the contracts in suit the carriers' commitment as to space is almost illusory, being a commitment to carry "so far as regular services are available". The price aspect of the contract is in terms subject to increases. Thus, the two principal considerations normally given to a buyer (the shipper) under a requirements contract - guarantee of supply and guarantee of no rate increase - are here lacking. In their stead are two essential penal provisions - the higher rate and the liquidated damage clause - both imposed to coerce shippers to refrain from using non-Conference carriers.

These differences are dispositive of the Board's principal argument. Implied congressional approval of a bona fide requirements contract, is no basis for exempting the contracts in this case from the plain meaning of "discriminating or unfair methods". They must therefore be condemmed.

SPECIAL REPORT OF THE HEARINGS ON FOREIGN
FREIGHT FORWARDERS AND BROKERS

Summary of the testimony of witnesses before the Subcommittee.

The first witness to appear was Clarence G. Morse, Chairman of the F.M. B. He summarized the jurisdiction of the F.M.B. over forwarders and noted that as a result of the investigation of the activities of forwarders after four years under G.O. 72, certain questionable practices of forwarders came to the Board's attention and as a result the Board now has under consideration revisions to be made in G.O. 72 designed to further reduce improper practices.   While Mr. Morse felt that as Chairman of the F.M.B. it would not be proper for him to discuss in detail any forwarding practices that might come before the Board for ruling he did, however, say that the most important issue connected with the regulation of forwarders is the matter of brokerage paid by steamship lines to them.

He summarized the various brokerage decisions and noted that the crux of the problem is the question as to when brokerage is earned by a freight forwarder. This question, Mr. Morse stated, "has not been definitively answered." He further noted that the forwarder performs services, which "are said to be performed for the carrier" and that the fundamental question is "whether these residual services performed for the carrier constitute brokerage within the intent and meaning of the Board's decisions".

Mr. Morse then reviewed the Board's activities under the Bland Forwarding Act during the war and thereafter and gave the background surrounding the issuance of G.O. 70, May 26, 1949, requiring the use of forwarders by Government agencies on relief and rehabilitation cargoes. He noted that by amendment in June, 1950 this requirement was relaxed to some extent.   Thereafter, as a result of complaints by the forwarders against the forwarding activities of the Department of Defense, the Undersecretary of Commerce for Transportation took this matter up with that Department, which replied that it would be impracticable and uneconomical to segregate civilian goods from military goods.

Mr. Morse further noted that amendments to G.O. 70 were being considered when the present Subcommittee was established and that the Board has since then decided to defer amending G.O. 70 until the Subcommittee has had an opportunity to complete its inquiry.

As a result of the G.A.O. Report, Mr. Morse noted that the Maritime Administration sent letters to the subsidized operators asking them to comment on the charges in the report with respect to alleged improper payment of brokerage.   The replies received from 16 subsidized operators showed that over $2,000,000 in brokerage was paid by them to forwarders in the United States during 1954, but the subsidized lines generally deny any payment of "unearned" brokerage and stated that had they not paid brokerage their revenues would have suffered.

In closing, Mr. Morse stated that he hoped that congressional action would "clarify the scope of the Maritime Administration's authority and responsibility in the so-called 'promotional' field. " He had no specific recommendations regarding new legislation.

The next witness was Charles E. Eckert, Legislative Attorney, Office of the Comptroller General.   His testimony was in effect a brief summary of the G.A.O. Report issued last March and it was not favorable to the forwarders.   He says that his investigation showed that the government department continued to perform many of the functions which in commercial activities were performed by a forwarder, notwithstanding the employment of a forwarder on a shipment.   Of course, what he failed to point out was that it was unnecessary and uneconomical for the agency to maintain its own forwarding organization when private forwarders were available to do the job efficiently and economically. Mr. Eckert also maintained that brokerage payments tend to increase ocean freight charges which in turn affect the government as a shipper and may act as a deterrent to our foreign trade. Other government witnesses subsequently denied that the payment of brokerage had any effect upon the fixing of ocean freight rates.

The G. A. O. witness also referred to the so-called "questionable brokerage practices" involved in commercial shipments and noted that since brokerage paid by steamship lines increases their costs and may indirectly affect government expenditures under its subsidy program, this phase of the matter may also warrant the attention of the Subcommittee.

Further testimony was given by Stanley Blumenfeld, a G. A. O. investigator, who at a later date was hired by the F. M. B. to conduct an investigation on Docket No. 765 in the New York area.

The next witness was Earl B. Smith, Director of Transportation and Communications in the Office of the Assistant Secretary of Defense for Supply and Logistics. As could be anticipated, his testimony was not favorable to private forwarders. He asserted the position of the Department which had been previously taken, namely, that the complicated supply and logistics program could not because of reasons of military security and efficiency find use for the private forwarder. He stated that there could not be any distinction drawn between military and nonmilitary supplies handled at the ports of embarkation since "supplies in the military supply system are all military items since it is a component part of a military operation."

Mr. Smith reviewed the experience of the Army in using private forwarders during 1948 through 1950 and stated that their services "were of little or no value to the Army." He advised that it was as much trouble to supervise the activities of the forwarder, as it would have been for the Army to perform the services directly. He stated that the Chief of Transportation made a restudy of the Bland Act and has now reached the conclusion that the Army is not required to use private forwarders, except where their use can be justified on the basis of efficiency and economy. Furthermore, the Department of Defense experience has been found to be that the brokerage fee claimed by forwarders was far in excess of the fair and reasonable value of the services rendered.

The next witness was Arthur D. Wildberg, Freight Traffic Officer, Transportation and Public Utility Service, General Services Administration. He stated that the G. S. A. considered the services of private forwarders "necessary and desirable" and that in most instances it has been found more economical and in the best interests of the government for G. S. A. to utilize the services of these private forwarders than to undertake the services itself. He also noted that a spot check of foreign aid shipments through New York during January and February of 1955 showed that the average fee per shipment was approximately $2.73. This bears out the position that this association maintained in its memorandum on the subject to the effect that the brokerage received from most governmental departments was so small that it could not properly be charged that the occasional large brokerage fee received represented excessive compensation to the forwarders. The witness stated that it would be very doubtful if any ocean carrier or conference would agree to a shrinkage of their cargo rates in an amount equivalent to the present 1 1/4% brokerage fee if the G. S. A. should perform its own forwarding services.

The next witness was Martin J. Hudtloff, Director, Transportation and Storage Services Division, U. S. Department of Agriculture. He noted that the forwarders performed the usual and customary services for the Department in connection with the International Cooperation Administration's export programs and that the services of forwarders "are needed" in connection with these programs.

Counsel to the Subcommittee and the chairman questioned this witness as to the statements contained in the G. A. O. Report quoting officials of this particular agency to the effect that the services of forwarders had been "generally unsatisfactory." The witness stated that he did not know who had been quoted to that effect in his Division, that these quotations, if made, did not reflect his views as Chief of that Division and that he was convinced that the forwarders performed a necessary and useful job.

APPENDIX H/A

GENERAL ORDER 4 PLUS AMENDMENTS

TITLE 46—SHIPPING
Chapter IV—Federal Maritime Commission
Subchapter B—Regulations Affecting Maritime Carriers and Related Activities
Reprinted from Federal Register

[General Order 4 (Rev.)]

General Order 4
Issue of September 6, 1968

PART 510—LICENSING OF INDE-PENDENT OCEAN FREIGHT FOR-WARDERS

Because of the number and complexity of published amendments to Part 510 of Chapter IV, Title 46 of the Code of Federal Regulations, the part is republished in its entirety as set forth below. No substantive changes have been made in this republication.

Subpart A — General

Authority: The provisions of this Subpart A issued under secs. 43, 44, Shipping Act, 1916 (78 Stat. 522, 523, and 766); sec. 304, Merchant Marine Act, 1933 (49 Stat. 1987, as amended; 46 U.S.C. 1114).

§ 510.1   Scope.

This subpart sets forth regulations providing for the licensing as independent ocean freight forwarders of persons, including individuals, corporations, partnerships, and associations, desiring to carry on the business of forwarding, the procedure for applying for licenses, the qualifications required of the applicants, and the grounds for revocation or suspension of licenses.

§ 510.2   Definitions.

(a) An "independent ocean freight forwarder" is a person carrying on the business of forwarding for a consideration who is not a shipper or consignee or a seller or purchaser of shipments to foreign countries, nor has any beneficial interest therein, nor directly or indirectly controls or is controlled by such shipper or consignee or by any person having such a beneficial interest.

(b) The term "carrying on the business of forwarding" means the dispatching of shipments by any person on behalf of others, by oceangoing common carriers in commerce from the United States, its Territories, or possessions to foreign countries, or between the United States and its Territories or possessions, or between such Territories and possessions, and handling the formalities incident to such shipments.

(c) The term "freight forwarding service or dispatching of shipments" means a service rendered by an independent ocean freight forwarder on behalf of other persons in the process of dispatching or facilitating an export shipment as authorized by such persons. Such service includes, but is not limited to, the following: Examining instructions and documents received from shippers; ordering cargo to port; preparing or processing export declarations; booking cargo space; preparing or processing delivery orders and dock receipts; preparing instructions to truckmen or lightermen, or arranging for, or the furnishing of trucks and lighters; preparing and processing ocean bills of lading; preparing or processing consular documents and arranging for their certification; arranging for or furnishing warehouse storage when necessary; arranging for insurance when so instructed; clearing shipments in accordance with United

States Government regulations; preparing advice notices of shipments and sending copies thereof to banks, shippers, or consignees as required; sending completed documents to _shippers, banks, or consignees as directed; advancing necessary funds in connection with the foregoing; providing supervision in the coordination of services rendered to shipments from origin to vessel; rendering special services on unusual shipments or when difficulties in transit arise; and giving expert advice to exporters as regards letters of credit, licenses, inspections.

(d) The term "person" includes individuals, corporations, partnerships, associations, and other legal entities existing under or authorized by the laws of the United States, or any State, Territory, District or possession thereof, or the Commonwealth of Puerto Rico, or of any foreign country.

(e) The term "Commission" means the Federal Maritime Commission.

§ 510.3   Licenses, when required.

(a) No person shall engage in carrying on the business of forwarding as defined herein unless such person holds a license issued by the Federal Maritime Commission to engage in such business. A license to carry on the business of forwarding may be granted by the Commission upon application submitted in accordance with the regulations in this part.

(b) In order to comply with section 44(b), of the Shipping Act, 1916, as amended (Public Law 87–254, approved Sept. 19, 1961), a freight forwarder who on September 19, 1961, held a valid certificate of registration, issued pursuant to Part 244 of this title (General Order 72 (15 F.R. 3153)) must have filed an application on Form FMC–18, prescribed herein, on or before midnight January 17, 1962, in order to continue in the business of forwarding pending action of the Commission on such application.

(c) Application for a license as an independent ocean freight forwarder shall be made on Form FMC–18 (Application for a License as an Independent Ocean Freight Forwarder), copies of which may be obtained from the Secretary, Federal Maritime Commission, Washington, D.C. 20573.

§ 510.4   Licenses, when not required.

(a) Any person whose primary business is the sale of merchandise may dispatch such merchandise without a license.

(b) An employee of a licensed independent ocean freight forwarder is not required to be licensed in order to act solely for his employer; but each licensed independent ocean freight forwarder will be held strictly responsible for the acts or omissions of his employees.

§ 510.5   Requirements for licensing.

(a) A forwarder's license shall be issued to any qualified applicant therefore if it is found that the applicant is, or will be, (1) an independent ocean freight forwarder as defined herein, (2) fit, willing, and able properly to carry on the business of forwarding and to conform to the provisions of the Shipping Act, 1916, as amended, and the requirements, rules, and regulations of the Commission issued thereunder, and (3) that the proposed forwarding business is, or will be, consistent with the national maritime policies declared in the Merchant Marine Act, 1936; otherwise such application shall be denied.

(b) A person desiring to engage in carrying on the business of forwarding shall submit to the Secretary, Federal Maritime Commission, Washington, D.C. 20573, an application in triplicate, executed on Form FMC–18, hereby prescribed for this purpose. Such application shall be accompanied by an application fee of $100 by money order, certified or cashier's check, made payable to the Federal Maritime Commission. The application fee shall be returned only when application for return is made within 1 year of denial of the license or 1 year from the date of adoption of the rule, whichever is later, and when on the face of the application the applicant fails to meet the requirements of section 44, Shipping Act, 1916, or the regulations promulgated thereunder. In no event shall the application fee be returned where a field investigation of applicant's qualifications has been conducted, or an application has been denied on the basis of hearing pursuant to § 510.8(a). Applications denied prior to hearing, without prejudice, may be refiled on the basis of changed facts within 1 year of the denial or 1 year from the date of adoption of this rule, whichever is later, without additional fee.

(c) Each applicant for a license and each independent ocean freight forwarder to whom a license has been issued, shall submit to the Commission each change of business address, and any other changes in the facts called for in Form FMC–18, within 30 days after such changes occur, and any other additional information required by the Commission.

(d) The applications received will be assigned application numbers and each applicant will be informed as to the number assigned to his application.

(e) In the case of applicants who may continue in the business of forwarding under section 44(b), Shipping Act, 1916, as amended, each such applicant shall, pending issuance of his license, conduct his ocean freight forwarding operations under the registration number previously assigned him under the provisions of Part 244 of this title (General Order 72) and the application number. After a license number has been assigned, such operations shall be conducted under that number only. Such license number shall be set forth on the licensee's letterhead, invoices and shipping documents.

(f) Prior to the issuance of a license to an independent ocean freight forwarder such forwarder shall file with the Commission, a bond in such form and amount as the Commission by rule may require. The said bond shall be kept in effect as long as the license remains effective.

(g) (1) The purpose of this paragraph is to prescribe a temporary bonding rule and establish the form and amount of a surety bond to be filed with the Federal Maritime Commission by applicants for licenses as independent ocean freight forwarders, who on September 19, 1961, were not operating under a registration number issued by the Commission or who were so operating but failed to file an application for license in the prescribed form on or before January 17, 1962. This requirement is not applicable to other ocean freight forwarders.

(2) A rulemaking proceeding will be instituted at a later date for the promulgation of a bond in such form and amount as the Commission may require for industry-wide applicability. All applicants temporarily licensed upon the basis of the bond prescribed herein will be required to comply with any future bonding regulations adopted by the Commission.

(3) No license shall be issued to a person to whom this paragraph is applicable unless such person has filed with the Commission a surety bond in the amount of $30,000 on Form FMC–59 in the following form:

Federal Maritime Commission

Surety Co. Bond No. _____
FMC License No. _____

Independent Ocean Freight Forwarder's Bond

(Section 44, Shipping Act of 1916)

Know all men by these presents. That we _____, as Principal (hereinafter called Principal), and _____, as Surety (hereinafter called Surety) are held and firmly bound unto the United States of America in the sum of _____ dollars ($ _____) for the payment of which sum well and truly to be made, we bind ourselves, our heirs, executors, administrators, successors and assigns, jointly and severally, firmly by these presents.

Whereas, Principal has applied, or is about to apply, for a license as an independent ocean freight forwarder pursuant to section 44 of the Shipping Act, 1916, and has elected to file this bond with the Federal Maritime Commission;

Now, therefore, the Condition of this obligation is such that if the Principal shall, while this bond is in effect supply the services of an independent ocean freight forwarder in accordance with the contracts, agreements, or arrangements made therefor, then this obligation shall be void, otherwise to remain in full force and effect.

The liability of the Surety shall not be discharged by any payment or succession of payments hereunder, unless and until such payment or payments shall aggregate the penalty of this bond, and in no event shall the Surety's total obligation hereunder exceed said penalty.

This bond shall inure to the benefit of any and all persons for whom the Principal shall have undertaken to act as an independent ocean freight forwarder.

This bond is effective the _____ day of _____ 19___, and shall continue in effect until discharged or terminated as herein provided. The Principal or the Surety may at any time terminate this bond by written notice to the Federal Maritime Commission at its office in Washington, D.C. Such termination shall become effective thirty (30) days after receipt of said notice by the Commission. The Surety shall not be liable for any contracts, agreements, or arrangements made by the Principal after the expiration of said thirty (30) day period but such termination shall not affect the liability of the Principal and Surety for any breach of the Condition hereof occurring prior to the date when said termination becomes effective.

The underwriting Surety will promptly notify the Secretary, Federal Maritime Commission, Washington, D.C. 20573, of any claims against this bond.

Signed and sealed this _____ day of _____, 19___.

(Please type name of signer under each signature.)

_____ [SEAL] _____
(Individual   (Business
  principal)   address)

_____ [SEAL] _____
(Individual   (Business
  principal)   address)

_____ [SEAL] _____
(Individual   (Business
  principal)   address)

_____
(Corporate
  principal)

_____
(Business
  address)

By _____

_____
(Title)

_____
(Corporate
  Surety)

_____
(Business
  address)

By _____ [Affix corporate seal]
(Title)

_____

(h) (1) The purpose of this paragraph is to prescribe a temporary bonding rule applicable only to applicants for licenses as independent ocean freight forwarders not otherwise provided for in paragraph (g) of this section.

(2) The Commission shall notify applicants for license subject to subparagraph (1) of this paragraph of their qualification for the issuance of a license. Within 30 days of such notice the applicant shall file with the Commission a surety bond in the form and amount prescribed in paragraph (g) of this section. The Commission may, upon a showing of good cause, extend the time within which to file said surety bond.

(3) If no bond is filed within the period prescribed in this subpart, the Commission shall issue a notice of intent to deny the application in accordance with § 510.8. If no request for a hearing is filed within the time prescribed therein the Commission shall deny the application.

§ 510.6 Publication of applications.

After application has been filed, the Commission shall cause to be published in the *Federal Register* a notice of the filing of each application, stating the name and address of the applicant and if the applicant is a corporation, association, or partnership, the names of the officers or members thereof. Parts 1 and 2 of the application shall be public information and available for inspection at the office of the Commission in Washington, D.C.

§ 510.7   Investigation of applicants.

All applicants shall be investigated and such investigation shall seek information relevant to the applicant's qualifications for a license, including (a) the correctness of the statements made in the application, (b) the business integrity and financial responsibility of the applicant, (c) the character and experience of the applicant, officers or members of the corporation or partnership as the case may be, and (d) such further evidence of the fitness, willingness, and ability of the applicant properly to carry on the business of forwarding as the Commission may require.

§ 510.8   Issuance or denial of licenses.

(a) After evaluation of the results of the investigation, the Commission will issue a license to an applicant found to be qualified within the provisions of applicable statutes and the requirements, rules, and regulations of the Commission thereunder, otherwise such application shall be denied. Prior to the denial of a license the Commission shall advise the applicant of its intention to do so and state the reasons therefor. If the applicant within 20 days after the receipt of such advice requests a hearing on his application, such hearing shall be granted by the Commission pursuant to its rules of practice and procedure.

(b) The Commission will issue licenses only in the name of the person applying therefor. Where such person is a partnership, association, corporation, or similar legal entity, the license will be issued in the legal name thereof. Licenses will not be issued to partnerships unless all partners execute the application.

(c) Except as provided in subparagraph (1) of this paragraph, only one license shall be issued to any person regardless of the number of names under which such person may be doing business.

(1) Each separately incorporated qualified applicant for an independent ocean freight forwarder license may be granted a separate license even though under common control with other independent ocean freight forwarding corporations, if such applicant submits a separate (i) application form FMC–18, (ii) $100 application fee as required by § 510.5(b), and (iii) surety bond in the form and amount hereafter to be prescribed.

(2) Each independent ocean freight forwarder authorized to carry on the business of forwarding under the Shipping Act, 1916, shall indicate on its letterhead stationery and on billing invoices the name or names of all such related freight forwarders.

(d) Licenses shall not be transferable without the prior approval of the Commission.

§ 510.9   Revocation or suspension of licenses.

A license may be revoked, suspended, or modified after notice and hearing for any of the following reasons:

(a) Violation of any provision of the Shipping Act, 1916, as amended, or of any other statute related to carrying on the business of forwarding.

(b) Failure to respond to any lawful inquiries, or to comply with any lawful rules, regulations, or orders of the Commission.

(c) Making any wilfully false statement to the Commission in connection with an application for a license or its continuance in effect.

(d) Change of circumstances whereby the licensee no longer qualifies as an independent ocean freight forwarder.

(e) Such conduct as the Commission shall find renders the licensee unfit or unable to carry on the business of forwarding.

Provided, however, That no license shall remain in force unless a valid surety bond is maintained on file with the Commission. A license will be automatically suspended or revoked, without hearing or other proceeding, for failure of a licensee to maintain a valid surety bond on file. The Commission, upon receipt of notice of cancellation of any bond, will notify the licensee in writing that his license will automatically be suspended or revoked, effective on the bond cancellation date, unless a new or reinstated bond is submitted to and approved by the Commission prior to such date. *Provided further,* That notice of each suspension or revocation effected pursuant to this section shall be published in the *Federal Register.*

Subpart B—Duties and Obligations

Authority: The provisions of this Subpart B issued under secs. 43, 44, Shipping Act, 1916 (75 Stat. 522, 523, 766); sec. 204, Merchant Marine Act, 1936 (49 Stat. 1987, as amended; 46 U.S.C. 1114).

§ 510.20   Scope.

This subpart pertains to the practices of licensed independent ocean freight forwarders, ocean freight brokers, and oceangoing common carriers pursuant to Public Law 87–254.

§ 510.21   Definitions.

(a) The term "licensee" means any person licensed by the Commission as an independent ocean freight forwarder, or any independent ocean freight forwarder who, on September 19, 1961, was carrying on the business of freight forwarding under a valid registration number issued by the Commission, or its predecessors, who filed an application for such a license (Form FMC–18) on or before January 17, 1962, and whose application has not been denied.

(b) The term "in commerce from the United States" means export commerce from the United States, its Territories, or possessions to foreign countries, or between the United States and its Territories or possessions or between such Territories and possessions.

(c) The term "oceangoing common carrier" as used in the rules in this subpart means a common carrier engaged in transportation by water of property in commerce from the United States, as defined in paragraph (b) of this section.

(d) The term "nonvessel operating common carrier by water" means a person who holds himself out by the establishment and maintenance of tariffs, by advertisement, solicitation, or otherwise, to provide transportation for hire by water in interstate commerce as defined in the Act, and in commerce from the United States as defined in paragraph (b) of this section; assumes responsibility or has liability imposed by law for safe transportation of shipments; and arranges in his own name with underlying water carriers for the performance of such transportation whether or not owning or controlling the means by which such transportation is effected.

(e) The term "principal" means the shipper, consignee, seller, purchaser who employs the services of a licensee.

(f) The term "ocean freight broker" means any person who is engaged by a carrier to sell or offer for sale transportation, and who holds himself out by solicitation or advertisement as one who negotiates between shipper and carrier for the purchase, sale, conditions and terms of transportation.

(g) The term "freight forwarding fee" means payment by a shipper, consignee, seller, purchaser, or any agent thereof, to a licensee for the performance of a freight forwarding service as defined in § 510.2(c).

(h) The term "compensation" means payment by an oceangoing common carrier for the performance of services as specified in § 510.24(e).

(i) The term "brokerage" means payment by a common carrier by water to an ocean freight broker for the performance of functions specified in paragraph (f) of this section.

(j) The term "special contract" means lump sum forwarding charges, monthly retainer fees, or similar financial arrangements that may exist between a principal and a licensee.

(k) The term "Act" means the Shipping Act, 1916 (46 U.S.C. 801 et seq.).

(l) The term "Beneficial interest" for the purpose of these rules includes, but is not limited to, any lien interest in; right to use, enjoy, profit, benefit, or receive any advantage, either proprietary or financial, from; the whole or any part of a shipment or cargo, arising by financing of the shipment or by operation of law or by agreement, express or implied, provided, however, that any obligation arising in favor of a licensee by reason of advances of out-of-pocket expenses incurred in dispatching of shipments shall not be deemed a beneficial interest.

(m) The term "reduced forwarding fees" as used herein means charges to a principal for forwarding services that are below the licensee's usual charges.

§ 510.22   Oceangoing common carriers and persons shipping for own account.

(a) An oceangoing common carrier, or agent thereof meeting the requirements of section 44 and these rules, may be licensed. An oceangoing common carrier may perform freight forwarding services without a license only with respect to cargo carried under its own bill of lading, in which case charges for such forwarding services shall be assessed in accordance with published tariffs on file with the Commission. No licensee can charge or collect compensation in the event that he requests the carrier or its agent to perform any of the forwarding services set forth in § 510.2(c) unless no other licensee is wil-

ling and able to perform such services; or unless the Commission has granted a port-wide exemption from this rule to licensee /agents in the port of loading. Such exemptions may be granted by the Commission upon (1) application of any licensed forwarder/agent serving the port of loading, (2) publication in the *Federal Register* of notice of application and an opportunity for interested parties to comment and request a hearing, and (3) a finding by the Commission that an adequate supply of forwarding services is not being held out by nonagent licensees domiciled at the port of loading. Exemptions shall remain in effect until otherwise ordered by the Commission.

(b) Nothing in the rules in this subpart shall be interpreted to prohibit a person whose primary business is the sale of merchandise from performing freight forwarding services on his own shipments or the shipments of a parent, subsidiary, affiliated, or associated company or on consolidated shipments to the same consignee of merchandise sold to such consignee by a parent, subsidiary, affiliated or associated company of such person: *Provided, however,* That such person may not be paid by the carrier for any service which he performs in connection with any such shipment.

(c) A nonvessel operating common carrier by water or person related thereto, otherwise qualified, may be licensed as an independent ocean freight forwarder to dispatch export shipments moving on other than its through export bill of lading. Such carrier or person related thereto may collect compensation under section 44(e) when, and only when, the following certification is made on the "line copy" of the ocean carrier's bill of lading, in addition to all other certifications required by section 44 of the Shipping Act, 1916, and this part: "The undersigned certifies that neither it, nor any related person, has issued a bill of lading covering ocean transportation or otherwise undertaken common carrier responsibility for the ocean transportation of the shipment covered by this bill of lading." Whenever a person acts in the capacity of a nonvessel operating common carrier by water as to any shipment he shall not be entitled to collect compensation under section 44(e) nor shall a common carrier by water pay such compensation to a nonvessel operating common carrier for such shipment.

§ 510.23 Duties and obligations of licensees.

(a) No licensee shall permit his license or name to be used by any person not employed by him for the performance of any freight forwarding service. No licensee may provide freight forwarding services through an unlicensed branch office or other separate establishment without written approval of the Federal Maritime Commission. Such approval may be granted only when it is found that qualified personnel competent to perform complete ocean freight forwarding services are employed in the branch office or other separate establishment. Applications for approval of branch offices or other separate establishment in existence on the date of adoption of this rule must be submitted within 3 months of such date.

(b) No licensee shall, directly or indirectly, (1) accept employment to perform forwarding services on export shipments as an associate, correspondent, officer, employee, agent, or subagent from any person whose license as an independent ocean freight forwarder shall have been revoked or whose license is under suspension; (2) assist the furtherance of any forwarding business of such person; (3) share forwarding fees or freight compensation with any such person; or (4) permit any such person directly or indirectly to participate, whether through ownership or otherwise, in the control or direction of the freight forwarding business of the licensee.

(c) A licensee who has reason to believe that a principal has not, with respect to a shipment to be handled by such licensee, complied with the law of the United States or any State, commonwealth or territory thereof, or has made any error or misrepresentation in, or omission from, any export declaration, bill of lading, affidavit, or other paper which the principal executes in connection with such shipment, shall advise his principal promptly of the suspected noncompliance, error, misrepresentation or omission, and shall decline to participate in such transaction involving such document until the matter is clarified.

(d) Every licensee shall exercise due diligence to ascertain the correctness of any information which he imparts to a principal with reference to any forwarding transaction; and no licensee shall knowingly impart to a principal or oceangoing common carrier false information relative to any such transaction.

(e) No licensee shall withold information relative to a forwarding transaction from his principal.

(f) Each licensee shall promptly pay over to the oceangoing common carrier or its agent within seven (7) days after the receipt thereof, excluding Saturdays, Sundays, and legal holidays, or within five (5) days after the departure of the vessel from each port of loading, excluding Saturdays, Sundays, and legal holidays, whichever is later, all sums advanced the licensee by its principal for freight and transportation charges, and shall disburse to other person(s) when due all sums advanced by its principal for the payment of any charges, debts or obligations in connection with the forwarding transaction, and shall promptly account to its principal for overpayments, adjustments of charges, reductions in rates, insurance refunds, insurance money paid to the forwarder as the result of claims, proceeds of c.o.d. shipments, drafts, letters of credit, and any other sums due such principal.

(g) No licensee shall endorse or negotiate without the expressed authority of his principal any draft, check, or warrant drawn to the order of such principal.

(h) No licensee shall file or assist in the filing of any claim, affidavit, letter of indemnity, or other paper or document, with respect to a shipment handled, or to be handled, by such licensee, which he has reason to believe is false or fraudulent.

(i) Any receipt issued for cargo by a licensee shall be clearly identified as a "Receipt for Cargo," and shall be in a form readily distinguishable from a bill of lading.

(j) Every licensee shall use invoices or other forms of billing which state separately as to each shipment: (1) The actual amount of ocean freight assessed by the oceangoing common carrier; (2) the actual amount of consular fees paid; (3) the insured value, insurance rate, and premium cost of insurance arranged; (4) the charge for each accessorial service performed in connection with the shipment. All other charges or fees assessed by the licensee for arranging the services enumerated in subparagraphs (1), (2), (3), and (4) of this paragraph shall be itemized. Licensees shall not be required to itemize the components of charges with respect to transactions made pursuant to § 510.25: *Provided, however,* That licensees who offer to the public at large to forward small shipments for uniform charges available to all and duly filed with the Federal Maritime Commission shall not be required to itemize the components of such uniform charges on shipments as to which the charges shall have been stated to the shipper at time of shipment, and accepted by the shipper by payment; but if such licensees procure Marine Insurance to cover such shipments, they must state their total charge for such insurance, in-

clusive of premiums and placing fees, separately from the aforementioned uniform charge: *Provided further,* That a licensee who maintains and adheres to a uniform schedule of fees to be charged for arranging insurance and for performing other accessorial services (stated by dollar amount and/or percentage of markup) need not state separately the components of the charges for such insurance and for such other accessorial services. A licensee who elects to maintain such schedules must make the current schedule and every superseded schedule available upon request. A licensee shall not assess different fees than those specified in the effective schedules. Such schedules shall be filed with the Federal Maritime Commission and posted in a conspicuous place in the forwarder's office, and shall be mailed upon request.

(k) Each licensee shall maintain in an orderly, systematic, and convenient manner, and keep current and correct, all records and books of account in connection with carrying on the business of forwarding. These records must be kept in such manner as to permit authorized Commission personnel to determine readily the licensee's cash position, accounts receivable, and accounts payable. As a minimum requirement, the licensee must maintain the following records for a period of 5 years:

(1) A current running account of overall cash receipts, disbursements, and daily balance. This account may be maintained on check book stubs. The account must be supported by bank deposit slips, paid checks, and a monthly reconciliation of the bank statement.

(2) A separate file for each shipment, to include a copy or notation of each document prepared, processed, or obtained by the licensee with respect to each individual shipment or files which will make readily available such copies or notations with respect to each individual

shipment. Records must be maintained which show the date and amount for payments received and disbursed by the licensee for the performance of services rendered or reimbursement for advance of out-of-pocket expenses.

(l) Each licensee shall make available promptly all records and books of account in connection with carrying on the business of forwarding, for inspection or reproducing or other official use upon the request of any authorized representative of the Commission.

§ 510.24 Compensation and freight forwarder certifications.

(a) No oceangoing common carrier shall pay to a licensee, and no licensee shall charge or receive from any such carrier, either directly or indirectly, any compensation or payment of any kind whatsoever, whether called "brokerage," "commission," "fee," or by any other name, in connection with any cargo or shipment unless the name of the actual shipper is disclosed on the shipper identification line appearing above the cargo description data of the ocean bill of lading, and, if the forwarder's name also appears on said shipper identification line, it appears after the name of the actual shipper.

(b) No licensee shall render, or offer to render, any forwarding service free of charge or at a reduced freight forwarding fee in consideration of the licensee receiving compensation from oceangoing common carriers on the shipment: *Provided, however,* That a licensee may perform freight forwarding services for recognized relief agencies or charitable organizations, designated as such in the tariff of the oceangoing common carrier, free of charge, or at reduced fees.

(c) No licensee shall share, directly or indirectly, any compensation or freight forwarding fee with a shipper, consignee, seller, purchaser, or their agents, affiliates or employees; nor with any person or persons advancing the purchase price of the merchandise or guaranteeing payment therefor; nor with any person or persons having beneficial interest in the shipment.

(d) No oceangoing common carrier shall compensate a licensee when such carrier has reason to believe that receipt of such compensation by the licensee is prohibited by these rules, or by the Act.

(e) Before any compensation is paid by an oceangoing common carrier to a licensee, or before a licensee may accept any such compensation, the licensee shall incorporate the certification set forth below on one copy of the ocean bill of lading, parcel receipt, or forwarder's invoice covering such shipment and endorse the certification. Where certification is made on a copy of a bill of lading such copy shall be referred to as the "Line Copy" and shall be retained in the possession of the carrier. The oceangoing carrier shall be entitled to rely on such certification unless it knows that certification is incorrect. The form of certification follows:

The undersigned hereby certifies that it is operating under license No. _____ issued by the Federal Maritime Commission, and has performed in addition to the solicitation and securing of the cargo for the ship or the booking of, or otherwise arranging for space for such cargo, two or more of the following services: (Check services performed.)
(1) The coordination of the movement of the cargo to shipside;
(2) The preparation and processing of the ocean bill of lading;
(3) The preparation and processing of dock receipts or delivery orders;
(4) The preparation and processing of consular documents or export declarations;
(5) The payment of the ocean freight charges on the cargo.

(f) An oceangoing common carrier may compensate a licensee to the extent of the value rendered such carrier in connection with any shipment forwarded on behalf of others when, and only when, such carrier is in possession of a certification in the form prescribed in paragraph

(e) of this section. Every tariff filed pursuant to section 18(b)(1), Shipping Act, 1916, shall specify the rate or rates of compensation to be paid licensed forwarders certifying in accordance with paragraph (e) of this section and the conditions of payment.

(g) No licensee, and no person, firm or corporation directly or indirectly controlled by a licensee or in whom a licensee has a beneficial interest, nor any person, firm or corporation directly or indirectly controlling or having a beneficial interest in a licensee, shall demand, charge or collect any compensation or brokerage from a common carrier by water unless there shall be first filed with such carrier a certificate in the form prescribed in paragraph (e) of this section and in compliance with section 44(e) of the Shipping Act: *Provided, however,* That the provisions of this paragraph shall not be applicable to brokerage paid on cargoes exempted from the tariff filing requirements of section 18(b)(1) of the Shipping Act, 1916 (46 U.S.C. 817(b)(1)).

(h) Where an oceangoing common carrier has paid, or has incurred an obligation to pay brokerage to an ocean freight broker, or compensation to a licensee, then such carrier shall not pay additional compensation for any other forwarding services rendered on the same cargo.

§ 510.25   Special contracts.

(a) Every licensee shall retain in its files a true copy, or, if oral, a true and complete memorandum of every special arrangement or contract with its principal, or modification or cancellation thereof, to which it may be a party or conform in whole or in part. Authorized Commission personnel and bona fide shippers shall have access to such contracts upon reasonable request.

(b) To the extent that special arrangements or contracts are entered into by a licensee, such licensee shall not deny equal terms to others similarly situated.

§ 510.26   Section 15 agreements.

(a) Copies of written agreements and true and complete memoranda of oral agreements between a licensee and other licensee or common carrier or other person subject to the Act, or modifications or cancellations thereof, which are subject to section 15 of the Act, must be filed with the Commission for approval. Copies of memoranda or agreements, modifications or cancellations thereof submitted for the Commission's approval under section 15 shall clearly show their nature, the parties, ports, and subject matter in detail and shall refer to any previously filed agreements to which they may relate.

(b) All such agreements, or modifications or cancellations thereof, shall not be carried out until approved by the Commission: *Provided, however,* That nonexclusive cooperative working agreements in the form prescribed herein between licensed independent ocean freight forwarder's providing for the completion of documentation and performance of other forwarder services on export shipments on behalf of the parties to the agreements are exempt from the provisions of section 15, of the Shipping Act, 1916, and need neither be filed with the Commission for approval nor reduced to writing.

(1) The typical form of agreement to which the exemption applies is as follows:

Nonexclusive Cooperative Working Agreements

Parties to the agreement are:
(a) A.B.C. Co. (Street address) (City and State) F.M.C. No. _____.

(b) X.Y.Z. Co. (Street address) (City and State) F.M.C. No. _____.

(2) Terms of the agreement are:

1. This is a cooperative working arrangement whereunder either of the parties may complete documentation and perform other freight forwarder functions on export shipments on behalf of the other party. It is not an exclusive agreement and either of the above parties may engage or be engaged by other forwarders under another agreement approved by the Federal Maritime Commission, or exempt from the provisions of section 15 of the Shipping Act, 1916, as amended, by reason of 46 CFR 510.26(b).

2. Forwarding and service fees are (the agreed division of freight forwarder fees, or, schedule of fees, or that fees are subject to negotiation and agreement on each transaction).

3. Ocean freight compensation is (the agreed division of compensation or that compensation is to be divided between the parties as agreed). This division of brokerage will be restricted to those shipments handled on behalf of each other.

4. The terms of the agreement shall continue unless one party shall notify the other of the desire to terminate the agreement.

§ 510.27   Separability.

The provisions of these rules are not interdependent. If. any portion hereof shall be enjoined, set aside, suspended, or held invalid, the validity and enforceability of all other rules shall be unaffected thereby, and shall to the full extent practicable, remain in full force and effect unless and until it is otherwise provided by the Commission or a court of competent jurisdiction.

THOMAS LISI,
Secretary.

[F.R. Doc. 68-10317; Filed Sept. 5, 1968; 8:52 a.m.]

AMENDMENTS

Issue of September 24, 1969

Title 46—Shipping

Chapter IV—Federal Maritime Commission

[General Orders 4, 22; Docket No. 69-41]

SUBCHAPTER A—GENERAL PROVISIONS

PART 503—PUBLIC INFORMATION

SUBCHAPTER B—REGULATIONS AFFECTING MARITIME CARRIERS AND RELATED ACTIVITIES

PART 510—LICENSING OF INDEPENDENT OCEAN FREIGHT FORWARDERS

Fees for Services; License Fee

In the *Federal Register* of August 22, 1969 (34 F.R. 13558), the Commission gave notice that it was considering the revision of certain existing charges to recover the costs of services, as set forth below. An evaluation of estimated direct and indirect costs to the Government, made in accordance with criteria established by the Bureau of the Budget, indicated that an increase in the fee schedule was warranted. The notice stated that, in the absence of comments, the proposed changes would become effective October 1, 1969. No comments have been received.

Therefore, pursuant to section 4 of the Administrative Procedure Act (5 U.S.C. 553) and section 43 of the Shipping Act, 1916 (46 U.S.C. 841(a)), and in accordance with the Act of August 31, 1951 (31 U.S.C. 483 (a)), as implemented by Bureau of the Budget Circular No. A-25, dated September 23, 1959, Parts 503 and 510 of Title 46 CFR are amended as follows:

1. Section 503.43(a) is amended to provide that the rate for copying of records will be 30 cents per page.

2. Section 503.43(b) is amended to provide that the rate for certification and validation with the Federal Maritime Commission seal will be $2.

3. Section 503.43(c)(1) is amended to provide that the rate for records' search by clerical personnel will be $4.50 per person per hour.

4. Section 503.43(c)(3) is revised to read:

(3) No charge for records' search will be imposed for the first one-half hour.

5. In § 510.5(b), in the second sentence, the independent ocean freight forwarder application fee is increased to $125.

Effective date. These amendments shall become effective October 1, 1969.

By the Commission.

[seal]   THOMAS LISI,
Secretary.

[F.R. Doc. 60-11360; Filed, Sept. 23, 1969; 3:46 a.m.]

Issue of October 2, 1969

Title 46—SHIPPING

Chapter IV—Federal Maritime
Commission

[General Orders 4, 22; Docket No. 69-41]

SUBCHAPTER A—GENERAL PROVISIONS

PART 503—PUBLIC INFORMATION

SUBCHAPTER B—REGULATIONS AF-
FECTING MARITIME CARRIERS AND
RELATED ACTIVITIES

PART 510—LICENSING OF INDEPEN-
DENT OCEAN FREIGHT
FORWARDERS

Fees for Services; License Fee;
Correction

By *Federal Register* publication of
September 24, 1969 (34 F.R. 14734), the
Commission increased its fee for application for an independent ocean freight forwarders license to $125 by amending
§ 510.5(b) of Title 46 CFR. The application fee is also referred to in
§ 510.8(c)(1)(ii). This section should also
be and hereby is amended to reflect the
increase in the application fee.

In the same *Federal Register* document
the "General Order" amendment numbers were inadvertently omitted in the
agency identification line. The general
order identification should read "General
Order 4 (Rev.); Amdt. 1 and General
Order 22; Amdt. 2."

By the Commission.

[seal]   THOMAS LISI,
                              Secretary.

[F.R. Doc. 69-11782; Filed, Oct. 1, 1969;
8:50 a.m.]

Issue of August 16, 1972

Title 46—SHIPPING

Chapter IV—Federal Maritime
Commission

SUBCHAPTER B—REGULATIONS AF-
FECTING MARITIME CARRIERS AND
RELATED ACTIVITIES

[Docket No. 72-4; General Order 4 (Rev.),
Amdt. 2]

PART 510—LICENSING OF INDE-
PENDENT OCEAN FREIGHT
FORWARDERS

Subpart A—General

Requirements for Licensing;
Who Must Qualify

Pursuant to the authority of sections
43 and 44 of the Shipping Act, 1916 (46
U.S.C. 841(a), 841(b)); and section 4 of
the Administrative Procedure Act (5
U.S.C. 553), paragraph (a) of § 510.5, 46
CFR, is revised by redesignating existing
paragraph (a) as paragraph (a)(1) and by
adding new subparagraphs (2) through
(5). As revised, paragraph (a) reads as
follows:

§ 510.5   Requirements for licensing.

(a)(1) A forwarder's license shall be issued to any qualified applicant therefor if
it is found that the applicant is, or will be,
(i) an independent ocean freight forwarder as defined herein, (ii) fit, willing,
and able properly to carry on the business
of forwarding and to conform to the provisions of the Shipping Act, 1916, as
amended, and the requirements, rules,
and regulations of the Commission issued
thereunder, and (iii) that the proposed
forwarding business is or will be, consistent with the national maritime policies
declared in the Merchant Marine Act,
1936; otherwise such application shall be
denied.

(2) In determining whether an applicant has the qualifications to be considered fit, willing and able properly to
carry on the business of forwarding and to
conform to the provisions of the Shipping
Act, 1916, and the requirements, rules,
and regulations of the Commission, the
applicant's training and experience will be
considered on the following basis:

(i) In the case of the applicant who
owns a sole proprietorship, the individual
applicant must himself qualify.

(ii) In the case of an applicant which is a partnership, at least one of the active managing partners must qualify.

(iii) In the case of an applicant which is a corporation or association, at least one of the active corporate or association officers must qualify.

(3) Any license issued to an individual owning a sole proprietorship runs to the individual and not to the sole proprietorship itself. If the licensee transfers ownership of the sole proprietorship, or in any manner withdraws from the sole proprietorship, the sole proprietorship may not act as an ocean freight forwarder until the new owner receives a license. This may be accomplished by transfer of an existing license, which requires approval by the Commission pursuant to § 510.8(d), or by applying for a license as a new applicant.

(4) When a partnership or corporation or association applicant has been licensed based upon the qualifications of one or more partners or officers as set forth in subparagraph (2) of this paragraph, and the qualifying person shall at any time thereafter leave such position, then such change shall be reported to the Commission within 30 days as required by paragraph (c) of this section. Within the same 30-day period the licensee shall furnish the Commission with the name and detailed ocean freight forwarder training and experience of the active managing partner(s) or officer(s) who will qualify the licensee; provided that the Commission, upon a showing of good cause, may grant an extension or extensions of time in which to report the name of the qualifying active managing partner(s) or officer(s).

(5) A license which has been granted pursuant to qualifications of individuals as required by this paragraph may be suspended or revoked, after notice and hearing, for failure to comply with the requirements of this paragraph and to conform to the provisions of the Shipping Act, 1916 and the requirements, rules and regulations of the Commission.

* * * *

Effective date. This rule will become effective September 15, 1972.

By the Commission.
[seal]   FRANCIS C. HURNEY,
Secretary.
[F.R. Doc. 72-12965 Filed: 8-15-72; 8:51 a.m.]

Issue of March 5, 1976
Title 46—SHIPPING

Chapter IV—Federal Maritime Commission
SUBCHAPTER B—REGULATIONS AFFECTING MARITIME CARRIERS AND RELATED ACTIVITIES
[General Order 4 (REV.) AMDT.3]
PART 510—LICENSING OF INDEPENDENT OCEAN FREIGHT FORWARDERS

Approval of Reporting Requirement

Pursuant to section 3512 of 44 U.S.C. this Commission has received clearance from the U.S. General Accounting Office of an extension without change of the recordkeeping requirement and application form (FMC Form 18) contained in Part 510—Licensing of Independent Ocean Freight Forwarders (General Order 4 (Rev.)).

Section 10.12. *Notification of General Accounting Office Action,* Title 4 CFR requires that notice of such clearance appear in the agency's regulations and forms. Accordingly, Subpart A and Subpart B of Part 510 of Title 46 CFR are amended by adding the following new sentence to Authority:

The recordkeeping requirement contained herein has been approved by the U.S. General Accounting Office under number B-180233 (RO146).

Notice, public procedure and delayed effective date are not necessary for the promulgation of this amendment because of its nonsubstantive nature. Accordingly, this amendment shall be effective March 5, 1976.

By the Commission February 26, 1976.
FRANCIS C. HURNEY,
Secretary.
[F.R. Doc. 76-6438 Filed: 3—4—76; 8:45 a.m.]

Issue of July 28, 1978
Title 46—SHIPPING

Chapter IV—Federal Maritime Commission
[General Order 4; Docket No. 77-53]
PART 510—LICENSING OF INDEPENDENT OCEAN FREIGHT FORWARDERS

Surety Bond

AGENCY: Federal Maritime Commission.

ACTION: Final rule.

SUMMARY: This rule increases the amount of the surety bond required for Commission licensed independent ocean freight forwarders engaged in the business of forwarding in the United States export trade from $10,000 to $30,000. The rule further provides for return of the application for failure to submit such required bond within a specified period. The rule also deletes certain provisions rendered obsolete or unnecessary by the passage of time. The changes are designed to add a greater degree of protection to the shipping public in the event of a forwarder default.

DATES: To become effective September 1, 1978.

FOR FURTHER INFORMATION CONTACT:

Francis C. Hurney, Secretary, Federal Maritime Commission, Room 11101, 1100 L Street NW., Washington, D.C. 20573, 202-523-5725.

SUPPLEMENTAL INFORMATION: This proceeding was instituted by Notice of Proposed Rulemaking published in the FEDERAL REGISTER on October 21, 1977 (42 FR 56139-56140) to: (1) Amend § 510.5(g)(3) of the Commission's General Order 4 (46 CFR 510.5(g)(3)), by raising the amount of the surety bond required for Commission licensed independent ocean freight forwarders engaged in carrying on the business of forwarding in the export commerce of the United States from $10,000 to

$50,000; (2) provide for the return of an application for a freight forwarders license to the applicant for failure to submit surety bond in the required amount; and (3) make other modifications to § 510.5.

In its notice the commission explained that while the bonding requirement was intended to offer some degree of protection to the shipping public in the event a forwarder should cause financial loss to the shipper, experience has demonstrated that in many instances of forwarder default, the present amount of the bond does not reasonably afford the degree of protection originally intended. In this regard, it was noted that inflationary spiral since 1963, the date of the original $10,000 bond, requires that more financial protection be afforded shipper clients of freight forwarders. This, the Commission pointed out, is demonstrated by the fact that freight rates, the moneys received by forwarders from shippers to be paid to carriers, have doubled and tripled since the original bond was established. The Commission also noted that to obtain such a bond would require the applicant forwarder to demonstrate a substantial degree of financial responsibility and that the surety companies would require a higher degree of financial responsibility from the forwarder.

In addition to increasing the amount of the required surety bond, the Commission also proposed to amend the existing provisions of § 510.5 by: (1) Providing for the return of the application to the applicant for failure to submit required bond; (2) establishing a time period within which existing licensees would be required to file the increased bond; (3) eliminating those provisions pertaining to "grandfather" rights of forwarders and temporary bonding which have been rendered unnecessary by the passage of time; and (4) redesignating certain provisions and making other editorial revisions necessitated by the above changes.

The stated reason for additional amendment (1) above was to terminate the existing procedure of issuing a notice of intent to deny an application and affording the applicant an opportunity for hearing where such applicant has failed to file the required bond. The Commission reasoned that because the filing of a bond by an applicant prior to licensing is mandatory under General Order 4 and section 44 of the Shipping Act, 1916, to require a hearing under circumstances where no bond has been furnished is unnecessary and time consuming.

Comments to the proposed rule were received from 134 parties, 122 forwarders, four forwarder associations, two congressmen, two shippers, one insurance association, one Government agency, one surety company, and one group of ocean freight agents. The Commission's Bureau of Hearing Counsel replied to the comments and answers to Hearing Counsel's replies were also submitted.

All of the comments address the proposal to raise the amount of the bond from $10,000 to $50,000. Most of these oppose the proposed increase in the amount of bond. Those opposed, including Hearing Counsel, agree, however, that some change in the present bonding requirement is necessary and a variety of alternatives is suggested.

Several reasons are advanced by those commentators supporting the proposed increase; the increased bond would better protect the shipping public, help "professionalize" an industry in which, at present, an individual may enter with relatively little capital, reduce malpractices and deter undercapitalized individuals from entering the field.

Those opposing changes in the present bonding requirements take the position that the increase would impose a severe burden on small forwarders; that small forwarders would be forced from the business, leaving the field entirely in the hands of large forwarders. Several of these parties, including an insurance association and the Small Business Administration, submit that forwarders will be unable to: (1) afford the premium on such a bond; and/or (2) establish to the bonding companies that a small forwarder has sufficient financial strength to be eligible to receive a bond of the proposed size. [1] While most of those opposing the Commission proposal believe that the present bond is sufficient, some argue that no bond should be required.

A large number of comments was received favoring some change in the present bond, but

opposing the proposed increase to $50,000. This group, which includes hearing counsel, states that small forwarders will be unable to secure a $50,000 bond due to the size of their forwarding operations and inability to pledge the required collateral, thus driving small forwarders from the trade, leaving ocean freight forwarding entirely in the hands of a limited number of large forwarders.

Many of these parties urge that the size of the bond be based upon the volume of the forwarder's business. Other comments suggest that recently licensed forwarders, or those licensed in the future, should be required to maintain a large bond while forwarders with several years of experience should be permitted to operate under the current bond requirements.

Certain of the commentators in favor of some change recommend that the amount of the bond be raised to $20,000; hearing counsel suggest $25,000. Some suggest that the public would be better served by rigorous Commission enforcement of existing regulations governing the conduct of forwarders in addition to imposing stricter requirements on forwarders seeking a Commission license. Several parties believe that the amount of credit extended by carriers to forwarders should be limited and that the bond requirement be replaced by a yearly license fee.

Hearing counsel suggest the initiation of a further rulemaking proceeding to strengthen the Commission's regulation of the forwarding industry by establishing experience requirements for new forwarders and requiring financial data reporting by existing forwarders in order to identify those with potential problems.

Finally, one commentator suggests that the Commission give consideration to allowing the submission of security other than a bond. In this regard, it is noted that while section 44(c) of the Shipping Act, 1916, provides for a bond, "or other security," § 510.5(g)(3), of Commission General order 4, allows only for the filing of a surety bond.

In this proceeding the Commission must weigh the consequences of the following alternatives. An increase in the amount of the forwarder bond to $50,000 could impose hardship on small forwarders and be detrimental to the interests of the shipping public and possibly

---

[1]This is contravened in an answer submitted by another commentator engaged in the bonding of forwarders which submits that the $50,000 bond would not have an adverse impact on the forwarding company. This commentator claims that $50,000 is not beyond the ability of forwarders, even small forwarders, to secure.

reduce the number of forwarders with a corresponding lessening of competition. Conversely, requiring a $50,000 bond could enhance the level of protection to the shipping public by holding forwarders to a higher degree of financial responsibility.

After carefully considering and evaluating all arguments advanced in support of these conflicting propositions, we have decided to increase the amount of the forwarder bond to $30,000.[2] This not only should act to temper the fears of those who believe the existing $10,000 bond is inadequate to protect the shipping public, but also appears to be within the range which many of those opposing an increase to $50,000 would find reasonable.

No comments were made on the remaining proposed amendments to § 510.5 and subject to one minor change in redesignated paragraph (h)(2), will be adopted as proposed.[3]

Hearing counsel have suggested various changes in the Commission's freight forwarder regulations which are outside the scope of this rulemaking and, accordingly, are not addressed here. However, these comments will be considered for possible inclusion in any future rulemaking.

§ 510.5 [Amended]

Therefore, pursuant to sections 43 and 44 of the Shipping Act, 1916 (46 U.S.C. 841a, 841b); and section 4 of the Administrative Procedure Act (5 U.S.C. 553), § 510.5, Title 46 CFR, is hereby amended as follows:

1. Paragraphs (g)(1) and (g)(2) are deleted.
2. Paragraphs (g)(3) is redesignated paragraph (g)(1) and revised as follows:

* * * *

(g) ***
(1) No license shall be issued to a person to whom this paragraph is applicable unless such person has filed with the Commission a surety bond in the amount of $30,000 on form FMC-59 as set forth below.

---

[2]Commissioner Karl E. Bakke dissents on this point. He does not find the proposed $50,000 figure to be unreasonable and would hold to that amount.

[3]The phrase "for failure to prosecute its application in accordance with this section" has been deleted from final paragraph (h)(2) as unnecessary.

3. New paragraph (g)(2) is added as follows:

* * * *

(g)***
(2) Every licensee shall file with the Commission on or before December 1, 1978, a surety bond in the amount of $30,000 on form FMC-59 as set forth below; otherwise such license issued to the licensee shall be revoked in accordance with § 510.9.

* * * *

4. Paragraph (h)(1) is deleted.
5. Paragraph (h)(2) is redesignated as paragraph (h)(1) and revised as follows:

* * * *

(h)***
(1) The Commission shall notify applicants for license of their qualification for the issuance of a license. Within 30 days of such notice the applicant shall file with the Commission a surety bond in the form and amount prescribed in paragraph (g) of this section. The Commission may, upon a showing of good cause, extend the time within which to file said surety bond.

* * * *

6. Paragraph (h)(3) is redesignated as paragraph (h)(2) and revised as follows:

* * * *

(h)***
(2) If the applicant shall not have submitted the surety bond required under paragraph (g)(1) of this section, within the period specified in paragraph (h)(1), or otherwise authorized, the Commission shall return the application to the applicant.

By order of the Federal Maritime Commission.

FRANCIS C. HURNEY,
Secretary
[F.R. Doc. 78-20867 Filed: 7—27—78; 8:45 a.m.]

Issue of September 12, 1978
TITLE 46—SHIPPING

Chapter IV—Federal Maritime Commission
SUBCHAPTER B—REGULATIONS AFFECTING MARITIME CARRIERS AND RELATED ACTIVITIES
[General Order 4, Amdt. 4]
PART 510—LICENSING OF INDEPENDENT OCEAN FREIGHT FORWARDERS

Approval of Reporting Requirements

AGENCY: Federal Maritime Commission.

ACTION: Final rule.

SUMMARY: Rules providing for the licensing of persons including individuals, corporations, partnerships, and associations as independent ocean freight forwarders are amended to reflect an extension of existing General Accounting Office clearance for the reporting and recordkeeping requirements contained therein. The amendment is necessary to comply with GAO regulations.

EFFECTIVE DATE: September 12, 1978.

FOR FURTHER INFORMATION CONTACT:

Francis C. Hurney, Secretary, Federal Maritime Commission, 1100 L Street NW., Washington, D.C. 20573, 202-523-5725.

SUPPLEMENTARY INFORMATION: 44 U.S.C. 3512 requires the General Accounting Office to review certain collections of information from 10 or more persons undertaken by independent Federal regulatory agencies.

This Commission has received clearance from the U.S. General Accounting Office for the reporting and recordkeeping requirements contained in 46 CFR Part 510 (General Order 4). Title 4 CFR, § 10.12, Notification of General Accounting Office Action, requires that notice of such clearance appear in the agency's regulations.

The clearance information is presently included in General Order 4; however, it must be amended to reflect the more specific wording of GAO's latest clearance approval. Accordingly, the clearance information statements presently appearing as the last sentence of the authority citations in subparts A and B are hereby deleted and replaced within the following statement:

The reporting requirements contained in §§ 510.5(a)(4), 510.5(c), 510.5(f), and 510.26 and the recordkeeping requirements contained in §§ 510.23(k), 510.24(e), and 510.25 of General Order 4 have been approved by the U.S. General Accounting Office under No. B-180233 (R0543).

Effective date: Notice, public procedure, and delayed effective date are not necessary for the promulgation of this amendment because of its nonsubstantive nature. Accordingly, this amendment shall be effective September 12, 1978.

By the Commission, August 30, 1978.

FRANCIS C. HURNEY,
Secretary.

[F.R. Doc. 78-25639 Filed: 9-11-78; 8:45 a.m.]

FEDERAL MARITIME COMMISSION

[CIRCULAR LETTER NO. FF 1-78]

LICENSED INDEPENDENT OCEAN FREIGHT FORWARDERS AND

APPLICANTS FOR LICENSING

INCREASED SURETY BOND REQUIREMENT

The Federal Maritime Commission, by Order effective September 1, 1978, in Docket No. 77-53, has increased from $10,000 to $30,000 the amount of the surety bond required of licensed independent ocean freight forwarders. Other administrative modifications to Rule 510.5(g) & (h) are also set forth in that Order, a copy of which is attached.

It should be noted that all applicants approved for licensing, and filing bonds on or after September 1, 1978, must submit a bond in the increased amount of $30,000.

Existing licensees will be required to file a bond in the increased amount with the Commission by December 1, 1978. Such bond shall bear an effective date no later than December 1, 1978. Failure of a licensee to file an effective $30,000 bond on or before December 1, 1978, will result in the automatic revocation of the license in accordance with Section 510.9 of General Order 4.

Licensees may submit the increased surety bond either by the filing of a new bond on Form FMC 59 or by rider to their existing bond.

If you have any questions with respect to this matter, please contact the Federal Maritime Commission's Office of Freight Forwarders in Washington, D.C. 20573, Telephone: 202-523-5843.

Attachment

Arthur Pankopf
Managing Director

Appendix I
Spanish-English
Vocabulary

ENGLISH-SPANISH VOCABULARY

(A)

a	un, una	attempt	intentar
accommodate	ajustar	auction	subasta
accomplish	llevar a cabo	automotive	automotriz
according	conforme, segun	available	disponible
accuracy	exactitud	average	promedio
accurate	exacto	avoid	evitar
acquaint	informar, enteranse	axle	eje
acquire	adquirir		
actual	real, verdadero	**(B)**	
add	sumar, agregar		
adjust	ajustar	backward	hacia atras
adjustment	ajuste	bag	bolsa
advantage	ventaja	bale	fardo
advantageous	ventajoso	ball	bola
afford	proporcionar, capacitar	ballast	lastre
after	despues de	band	faja
all	todos	bar	barra, varilla
allow	permitir, conceder	bargain	ganga, convenio
almost	casi	bark	corteza
along	a lo largo de	barrier	barrera, obstruccion
also	tambien	basket	cesto, envase
although	aunque	bath	bano
always	siempre	beacon	guia, baliza
among	entre	beam	viga, rayo
amount	cantidad	bearing	cojinete
an	uno, una	become	convertir, transformarse
angle	angulo	begin	empezar
another	otro, otra	behind	detras
anvil	yunque	bell	campana
any	cualquiera	below	abajo
anyone	cualquier persona	belt	correa (de tr.)
appearance	apariencia	bent	curvado, doblado
appliance	utensilio, aplicacion	best	lo mejor
apply	aplicar	better	mejor
apron	delantera	between	entre
arc	arco	beverage	bebida
arc-welding	soldadura al arco	bitter	amargo
arrange	colocar, arreglar	blade	hoja, paleta
arrangement	orden, arreglo	block	bloque
arrow	flecha	blow	soplar, inflar
aside	aparte	blower	soplador
assemble	juntar, armar	body	cuerpo
assembly	conjunto	boiler	caldero
asset	ventaja, posesion	bolster	refuerzo
associated	asociado	bolt	perno, cerrojo
assortment	surtido	book	libro
assure	asegurar	bond	lazo, conexion
atomize	rociar, pulverizar	boom	extension, obstruccion
atomizer	rociador	both	ambos
attach	juntar, anexar	bottle	botella
attachment	union, accesorio	bottling	embotellar
attain	lograr, conseguir	bottom	fondo

bowl	taza	cold	frio
box	caja	collar	anillo, collar
bracket	mensula, sosten	commonly	comunmente
brake	freno	compile	recopilar
brass	laton	completeness	completo
break, -age	romper, rotura	acompounded	compuesto
brewery	cerveceria	compressed	comprimido
brick	ladrillo	comprise	abarcar
bright	lustroso	concerning	concernir
brittle	fragil	confidence	confianza
broken	quebrado	connect	conectar
brown	pardo	constituent	componente
brush	brocha	contain	contener
bubble	burbuja	container	envase
bucket	cubo, exacavadora	content	contenido
	de cucharon	contract	contraer, reducir
buffer	amortiguador	converter	convertidor
build	fabricar	convey	transportar
building	edificio	conveyor	conductor
burn	quimar	cool	fresco, (enfriar)
burner	quemador	cooler	enfriador
bushing	forro de metal	copper	cobre
		cord	cuerda
(C)		cotton	algodon
		counter	contador, contrario
cage	jaula	coupling	enganche, acoplamiento
canvas	lona, forro	cover	cubrir, abarcar
cap	tapa, casquete	coverage	cubierta, abarcamiento
car	vehiculo	crank	eje, manivela
carbide	carburo	crankcase	carter del ciguenal
card	tarjeta	crankshaft	cigueñal
carriage	carretilla, jinete	crawl	arrastrar
carry	transportar	creamery	lecheria
cast	viciar, fundir	crossing	cruce
casting	pieza fundida	crucible	crisol
cathead	proyeccion, serviola	crush	triturar, moler
ceiling	cielo, techo	crusher	triturador
cemented	cementado	cup	taza, cubeta
chain	cadena	cushion	cojin, amortiguador
chamber	camara	customer	cliente
change	cambio	cut	corte, (rebajar)
changer	cambiador	cutter	cortador
channel	cauce, conducto		
charge	cargar, carga	(D)	
check	detener, verificar		
chemical	producto quimico	daily	diario
chief	principal	dairy	lecheria
chilled	enfriado	date	fecha
choice	eleccion, selecto	deal	distribuir, negocio
clay	arcilla	dealer	distribuidor
cleaner	limpiador	deck	cubierta, puente
clearance	espacio libre	deduction	descuento
close	cerrar, estrecho	deep	profundo
coat	capa	degree	grado
code	clave	delay	demora
cohesive	coherente	deliver	entregar

delivery	entrega	equipment	equipo
denote	denotar	erase	borrar
dependable	confiable, seguro	establish	establecer
depth	fondo, espesor	estimate	presupuesto
derail	descarrilar	even	igual (en nivel)
derrick	grua	ever	siempre
design	diseñar, proyectar	every	cada uno, todo
detail	prmenor	example	ejemplo
detect	descubrir	excavate	excavar
detector	indicador	exceed	exceder
develop	desarrollar	exchange	cambiar, canje
development	desarrollo, fomento	exercise	ejercicio
device	plan, aparato	exhaust	escape
devote	dedicar	exhausted	agotado
die (tool)	matriz, herramienta	expect	esperar
dilution	diluicion	expend	gastar
dirty	sucio	expense	gasto, costo
discharge	desempeñar, descargar	expensive	costoso
disclose	descubrir, revelar	explanation	explicacion
displacement	desplazamiento	expose	arriesgar, exponer
display	mostrar	extend	prolongar, estirar
distinguish	diferenciar, distinguir	extent	alcance
distortion	deformacion	extremely	sumamente
door	puerta		
doubt	duda	(F)	
draw	dibujar		
drawing	traccion, dibujo	face	cara, superficie
drill	taladro, barreno	fabric	tejido, manufactura
drive	conducir, (impulso)	fact	hecho
drop	caer, caida	fail	fallar, fracasar
drum	tambor	failure	fracaso
dry	seco	fair	justo, claro (col.)
duty	deber, servicio	fate	destino, suerte
		fall	caer, caida
(E)		fan	abanico, soplador
		far	lejos
		fast	rapido, firme, seguro
each	cada (cada uno)	feature	rasgo, caracteristica
earn	ganar, merecer	feed	alimentar
easy	facil	feeder	alimentador
either	uno u otro	feet	pies
elapse	transcurrir	fender	defensa, guardafango
elsewhere	en otra parte	few	pocos
emphasize	recalcar	feel	sentir, tocar
employ	emplear	figure	figurar, calcular (difra)
enable	habilitar, permitir	file	escofina, archivo
enamel	esmalte	filing	limadura
encase	encajonar, encerrar	fill	llenar. rellenar
encounter	encontrar, chocar	finally	finalmente
end	fin, extremo	find	hallar, descubrir
engagement	compromiso, ajuste	fine	excelente, fino
engine	maquina, aparato	finger	dedo, apendice
enough	bastante	finish	acabar, pulir
enter	entrar	fire	fuego, quemar
entire	todo, entero	first	primero
equipped	aviado (equipar)	fit	ajuste, adaptar

flask	frasco, envase	grinder	moledor, molienda
flat	plano, aplastado	grip	mango, asidero
fleet	linea, flotilla	groove	ranura
float	flotar, flotante	ground	suelo, base
floor	piso, suelo	guard	resguardo, proteccion
flow	fluir, correr, desaguar	guide	guia, guiar
fluidity	fluidez	guilt	culpa
fog	niebla	gun	pistola
folder	circular, plegador		
following	siguiente	**(H)**	
foot	pie		
for	para, por	half	medio, mitad
forced	forzado	hammer	martillo, mazo
foreign	extranjero	hand	mano, manecilla
forged	forjado	hand-book	manual
form	formar, (forma)	handle	mango, manejar
foundry	fundicion	handling	manejo, maniobra
fracture	quebradura	harbor	puerto
frame	armar, (armazon)	hard	duro, dificil
free	libre	hardness	dureza, solidez
freight	carga, flete	harmful	nocivo, perjudicial
from	de, desde	hat	sombrero, cubierta
front	frente, exterior	haul	arrastrar, transportar
full	lleno, completo	hazard	arriesgar, riesgo
fund	fondo, reserva	head	cabeza, tapa
furnace	horno	heading	encabezamiento, titulo
furnish	suministrar, equipar	heart	corazon, centro
furniture	muebles, equipo	heat	calor
furrier	peletero	heater	calentador
furthermore	ademas	heavy	pesado
fuse	fusible, fundir	heel	tacon, talon
		height	altura
(G)		here	aqui
		high	alto
gauge (gage)	calibrador, indicador	hoist	izar, (grua)
gale	viento fuerte	hold	tener, coger
gap	portillo, abertura	hole	orificio, cavidad
garden	jardin	hook	gancho, garfio
garnish	guarnecer, adornar	hope	esperar, esperanza
gasket	empaquetadura	hopper	tolva
gather	recoger, acumular	hose	manguera
gear	engranaje	hot	caliente
get	obtener, adquirir	household	casero
girth	faja, periferia	housing	caja, cubierta
give	dar, conceder	how	como
glade	claro, raso	however	sinembargo, contodo
glass	vidrio		
glide	resbalar, deslizarse	**(I)**	
good-will	buena voluntad		
grade	grado, pendiente	ice	hielo
grain	grano, fibra, veta	idle	desocupado, parado
grapple	agarrar, arpeo	impact	choque, presion
grease	grasa	impair	empeorar, deterioro
great	grande	imply	significar, implicar
grid	reja, hierro	impregnate	impregnar,
grind	moler	improvement	mejora, perfeccion amiento

in	en	leave	dejar, salir
inch	pulgada	leaves	hojas, planchas
incorporate	incorporar, unir	leakage	escape, derrame
increase	aumento, aumentar	length	largo, longitud
indoor	adentro, interior	less	menos, menor
initial	inicial, principio	letter	letra, carta
insert	insertar, anuncio	level	liso, al nivel
inside	adentro	lever	palanca
install	instalar	liability	riesgo, responsabilidad
insure	asegurar	life	vida, duracion
integral	integro, integramente	lifetime	toda la vida
intend	intentar, destinar	lift	elevador, alzador
intensify	intensar, reforzar	light	luz, liviano, leve
interchangeble	intercambiable	like	gustar, igual
introduce	introducir, adoptar	likewise	igualmente
investment	inversion	lime	cal
iron	hierro	line	linea, renglon
item	partida, detalle	lining	forro
itself	el mismo, lo mismo	link	eslabon, gozne
		lip	borde, labio
(J)		little	poco, pequeño
		load	carga, cargar
jack	gato, alzador	lock	cerrar, cerradura
jar	tarro, jarra	log	leño, madera
jaw	telera, quijada	logbook	diario, apunte
jet	surtidor, chorro	long	largo
job	trabajo, tarea	look	mirar, examinar
journal	gorron	loose	suelto, flojo
judgment	juicio, opinion	loss	perdida
		lot	lote, muchos
(K)		low	bajo, modico
		lower	bajar, mas bajo
keep	guardar, mantener		
keeper	guardian, tenedor	**(M)**	
kiln	horno		
know	saber	machined	trabajado a maquina
known	sabido, conocido	made	fabricado, hecho
		main	principal, mayor
(L)		maintain	mantener, afirmar
		maintenance	conservacion
labor	trabajo, mano de obra	make	hacer, manufacturar
lack	faltar, falta	male	macho
ladder	escalera, escala	manifold	multiple
lamp	lampara	many	muchos, muchas
large	grande, largo	market	mercado, plaza
last	durar, ultimo	mate	pareja, emparejar
lasting	durable, permanente	mean	mediano, intermedio
lath	liston, lata	meaning	significado, sentido
launder	lavar	measurement	medida
laundry	lavanderia	meet	encontrar, convenir
lay	poner, colocar	melt	derretir, fundir
layer	capa	member	miembro, parte
layout	plan, disposicion	merge	unir, combinar
lead	dirigir, delantera	merely	solamente
		meter	medidor
leading	primero, sobresaliente	mile	milla

mileage	kilometraje	other	otro
mill	fabrica, molino	our	nuestro, nuestra
mine, mining	mina, minar	out, out of	afuera, fuera de
misuse	maltratar, usar mal	outfit	equipo, enseres
mix	mexclar	outlet	salida, desague
mixture	mezcla	outside	exterior, fuera
mold	molde, moldear	outstanding	sobresaliente, pendiente
monorail	mono-riel	overall	total, de extremo a
month	mes		extremo
more	mas	over	sobre, mas de
most	lo mas, lo mayor	oversize	extragrande, mayor
mount	montar	own	propio, poseer
mounting	monteje, montura	owner	dueño
move	mover, movimiento		
much	mucho	**(P)**	

(N)

		packing	empaquetadura
		padlock	candado, candar
name	nombre	page	pagina
narrow	estrecho, angosto	pail	cubo, balde
near	cerca de, proximo	paint	pintar, pintura
need	necesidad	pan	paila
needle	punto, aguja	panel	tablero
neglect	descuido	parent	padre, principal
negligible	insignificante	pass	pase, pasar
neither	ninguno	passenger	pasajero
never	nunca, jamas	patch	remendar, chafallar
new	nuevo	patented	patentado
next	siguiente, entrante	pattern	patron, molde
nice	fino, delicado	pay	pagar, pago
noise	ruido	per	por
noiseless	sin ruido, silencioso	perform	funcionar
nor	ni	performance	funcionamiento
normalize	normalizar	personnel	ampleados
nose	piton, nariz	pickup	alzar, recoger
note	nota, apuntar	piece	pieza, parte
nozzle	gollete	pig	lingote, molde
number	numero, varios	pilot	guia, modelo mecanico
		pin	pasador, perno
(O)		pint	pinta
		pipe	tubo, caño
obtain	obtener, conseguir	piston	embolo
odorless	sin olor	pit	hoyo, poro
offer	oferta, ofrecer	place	lugar, colocar
often	frecuente, a menudo	plain	llano, sencillo
oil	aceite	plant	planta, fabrica
old	viejo, anticuado	plastic	formativo, plastico
one	uno	plate	chapa, platear
only	solamente	please	agradar, satisfacer
operate	funcionar, manejar	plow	arado
opposite	opuesto	plug	tapon, clavija
option	alternativa	pocket	bolsillo, receptaculo
optional	electivo	point	punta, aguja
orange	naranja	polish	pulir, pulimiento
order	pedido, (ordenar)	poor	pobre, mala calidad
ore	mineral	portable	portatil

portray	representar	rate	tarifa, precio
possess	poseer	rating	clasificacion
poster	cartel, aviso	rather	mas bien, un poco
pound	libra, golpear	reach	alcanzar, alcance
power	fuerza	read	leer
powerful	fuerte, potente	ready	listo, disponible
practice	practica, (practicar)	readily	facilmente
predominance	predominio	rear	atras, detras
prefix	prefijar, prefijo	reason	razon, causa
pressure	presion	reasonable	razonable, modico
prevent	prevenir, impedir	receiver	receptor, depositario
price	precio	reclamation	mejoramiento
print	imprimir, impresion	record	registro, apunte
proceed	proceder	recorded	apuntado, inscrito
producer	productor	recover	recuperar
profit	provecho, utilidad	recovery	recuperacion
profitable	productivo, lucrativo	recur	repetirse
promise	prometer, promesa	reduce	reducir, mermar
promote	promover, organizar	reduction	rebaja
proof	prueba, evidencia	reinforce	reforzar
propel	impeler	refer	referir, aludir
property	propiedad	reference	referencia
prove	probar, demostrar	refractory	refractario
provide	proveer, suministrar	regardless	prescindiendo de
provision	provision, medida	regularity	regularidad
pull	halar, tirar de	regulate	regularizar
pulley	polea	relay	relevador, auxiliar
pulverizer	triturador	reliable	seguro, confiable
pump	bomba	reliability	digno de confianza
purchase	compra, comprar	relief	resaltar
purpose	proposito	remain	quedar, continuar
purposely	a proposito	remove	mudar, suprimir
put	poner, colocar	renew	renovar, suprimir
		repair	reparar, reparacion
(Q)		repeat	repetir, repeticion
		replacement	reemplazo, repuesto
quanitiy	cantidad	require	necesitar
quarry	cantera, pedrera	requirement	requisito
quart	cuarto	research	investigacion
quarter	cuarta parte	resist	resistir
quick	rapido	resistant	resistente
quiet	quieto, silencioso	resource	recurso, medio
		result	resultado, (resultar)
(R)		retain	retener
		return	volver, retornar,
race	curso, ranura, canal		ganancia
rack	cremallera, percha	reveal	revelar, manifestar
radiograph	radiografia	reverse	reverso, contramarcha
radius	radio	rich	rico, fertil
rail	riel	right	propio, verdadero
railroad	ferrocarril	rigid	rigido
rain	lluvia, llover	ring	anillo, argolla
raise	levantar, subida	rivet	remache
ramp	rampa, declive	road	camino, via
range	extension, alinear	rod	varilla, barra
rapidly	rapidamente	roll	rollo, rodar

roller	rodillo
rotary	giratorio, rotativo
rough	aspero, en bruto
round	redondo
row	hilera, fila
rubber	caucho, elastico
rugged	fuerte, resistente
rule	regla
run	manejar, moldear
rupture	rotura
rush	prisa, apurar
rust	moho, herrumbre

(S)

saddle	montura, soporte
safe	seguro
safety	seguridad, proteccion
safely	seguramente
sale	venta, negocio
sell	vender
same	el mismo, igual
sand	arena
sausage	embutido
saving	economia, ahorro
say	decir, dicho
schedule	lista, itinerario
scoop	pala, cuchara, cavador
scour	fregar, limpiar
scrap	deshechos, hierro viejo
screen	tabique, cedazo
screw	tornillo, rosca
screwdriver	atornillador
sea level	nivel de mar
seaport	puerto maritimo
seal	sello, sellar, tapar
seam	costura, juntura
seamless	sin costura
seat	asiento, sitio
secure	seguro, asegurar
see	ver
segment	segmento
service	servicio
serviceable	servible
set, set up	juego, colocar, armar
setting	colocacion, armadura
shaft	eje, pozo, tubo
shape	forma, dar forma
share	participar, porcion
sharp	agudo, cortante
shear	esquilar, cortar
sheave	rueda excentrica, polea
shell	casco, revestimiento
shim	cuña, calza
shield	proteccion, resguardo
shingle	ripia, (cinglar)

ship	barco, despachar
shipment	embarque, despacho
shock	choque, sacudimiento
shoe	zapato, zapata
shop	taller, tienda
shovel	pala
show	mostrar, (exhibicion)
shown	mostrado
shrink	contraerse, mermar
shrinkage	encogimiento, reduccion
shut	cerrar, tapar
shutdown	cierre, cesacion
since	desde, hace
single	uno solo
size	tamaño, medida
skid	varadera, rodillo
skill	habilidad, pericia
skilled	perito
skip	saltar, omitir
slash	cortada, cortar
slight	leve, pequeño
slip	deslizar, soltar
slot	muesca, ranura
slugger	golpeador, lingote
slusher	engrasador, lavador
small	pequeño
smelt	deretido, fundido
smelting	fundicion
smoke	humo
smooth	liso, suave
snag	obstaculo, impedir
soap	jabon
socket	enchufe, encaje
sold	vendido, venta
some	algo, un poco
somewhat	algun tanto, un poco
source	fuente, origen
space	espacio, espacear
spare	repuesto
sparkplug	bujia de encender
specify	especificar
speed	velocidad, acelerar
spindle	torno, eje
split	partir, separar
spool	carrete, canilla
spray	rociar, pulverizar
spread	extender, esparcir
spring	muelle, resorte
sprinkle	rociar, regar
sprinkler	rociador
sprocket	rueda dentada
sprung	combado, torcido
spun	girado, enrollado
spur	uña, diente
square	cuadrado, cuadrar
stabilize	estabilizar

staff	cuerpo (de empleados)	tail	extremo, cola, cabo
stage	etapa, grado	take	tomar, coger, recibir
stain	manchar, ensuciar	tap	sacar, perforar
stainless	inmanchable	tapping	el acto de sacar
standpoint	punto de vista	taxicab	taximetro
start	comenzar, partir	teeth	dientes
steady	firme, constante	tell	decir, expresar
steam	vapor	tensile	tension
steel	acero	term	termino, condiciones
steep	empapar, inclinado	test	ensayo, prueba
stem	vastago, espiga	tester	probador
stick	varilla, barra, pegar	theft	robo, hurto
stiff	tieso, duro	their	suyo, suya
stiffen	endurecer, entiesar	then	entonces, despues
still	todavia, no obstante	these	estos, estas
stoke	atizar (el fuego)	thick	grueso, espeso
stoker	atizador	thickness	espesor, grosor
stone	piedra	thin	delgado, fino
storage	almacenaje	this	esto, esta
straight	derecho, recto	thorough	cabal, completo
straighten	enderezar	thoroughly	completamente
stread	raya, linea	those	esos, aquellos
stream	corriente, flujo	thread	hilo, filete
streamline	de forma continua	throat	cuello, gollete
strength	fuerza	through	continuo, a traves de
stress	tension, esfuerzo	throughout	en todo, por todo
strip	tira, fleje	throw	tirar, lanzar, sacudir
stroke	golpe (de embolo)	thus	asi, de este modo
strong	fuerte	tie	altar, ligar
structure	estructura, construccion	tight	hermetico, apretado
stub	talon, cabo, cola	tilt	inclinado, ladeado
study	estudio	time	tiempo
sturdy	fuerte, firme	tip	punta, extremidad
substantial	importante	tire	llanta, calce
success	exito, buen resultado	toe	punta (de en un
successfully	prosperamente		cambiavias)
suction	succion	together	junto, juntamente
suitable	adecuado, satisfactorio	toggle	palanca, cazonete
supersede	sobreseer, reemplazar	tolerance	tolerancia
supervison	superintendencia	tongue	lengua, espiga
supervise	superintendar	tonnage	tonelaje
supply	surir, proveer	too	tambien, demasiado
supplies	provisiones, suministro	tool	herramienta
support	sostener, sosten	top	cumbre, cabeza, apice
sure	seguro	torch	antorcha
surface	superficia	touch	tocar
surge	agitar, agitacion	tough	duro, resistente
surpass	superar, superior	toward	hacia, para con
swift	veloz	trace	trazar, delinear
swiftness	presteza, velocidad	tracer	trazador
swing	oscilar, balancear	track	via, rieles
switch	cambio, cambiavias	traction	traccion
		trade	comercio
(T)		train	tren, entrenar
		tram	tranvia
tag	rotulo, etiqueta	transom	travesano, division

trap	separador, tubo, sifon	wash	lavar
tray	bandeja, artesa	washer	arandela, lavador
tread	sperficie de rodadura	wastage	desgaste, desperdicio
treble	triple, triplicar	wasteful	antieconomico
trench	zanja, surco	water	agua
trigger	gatillo, calzo	wear	desgaste, desgastar
trip	viaje, soltar	wedge	cuna, calzada
trouble	perturbar, molestia	weekly	semanal
truck	carro, acarrear	weight	peso, carga
true	veridico, genuino	well	bien, satisfactorio
trust	confianza, credito	welder	soldador
tumbler	tambor, rotatorio	welding	soldadura
turn	girar, voltear	wheel	rueda
turning	vuelta, torneando	when	cuando
twice	doble, dos veces	where	donde, adonde, en donde
twin	gemelo, hermano	wherever	dondequiera que
type	tipo, simbolo	whether	si, sea que, ora
		which	el cual, que
(U)		while	mientras, entretanto
		who	quien
under	abajo, debajo	whole	todo, integro
underground	subterraneo	wick	mecha
unequaled	sin igual	wide	ancho, amplio
unit	unidad	widely	extensamente
unlike	distinto, de otro modo	width	anchura
unload	descargar	will	voluntad
unloader	descargador	wipe	limpiar
unstable	inestable	wire	alambre
until	hasta que	wise	prudente
upkeep	manutencion, costo	without	sin
upon	sobre, en, a, al	with	con
upper	alto, superior	withstand	resistir
use	uso, aplicacion	witness	testimonio
useful	util, provechoso	wood	madera
usual-ly	usual, ordinariamente	word	palabra, moticia
utility	servicio, utilidad	work	trabajo, (funcionar)
		working	trabajando, (funcionando)
(V)		workmanship	mano de obra
		worn	gastado
vacuum	vacio	worth	valor, merito
vain	inutil, en vano	woven	tejido
valve	valvula	wrap	envolver, cubrir
van	furgon		
very	muy, mucho, mismo	**(Y)**	
vent	respiradero, salida		
view	vista	yard	yarda
volt	voltio	year	año
volume	volumen	yellow	amarillo
		yet	todavia, sin embargo
(W)		yield	rendir, producir
		yoke	yugo, grapa de sujecion
wafer	sello, sellar		
wall	pared, encierro		
want	necesidad, carecer de		
warrant	garantizar		
warranted	garantizado		

ABBREVIATIONS

According to the United States Department of Commerce, Bureau of Foreign and Domestic Commerce, the following abbreviations are customarily employed in international trading (reported from Bulletin No. 175, issued in 1938).

FREIGHT & INSURANCE

a/c or acct.: Account;
a. a. r.: Against all risks (marine);
A/D: Alternate days;
ad. val.: Ad valorem;
A/V: Ad valorem;
A/R: All risks or against all risks;
a/c: (a cargo): Charged to, or drawn on;
A. O.: Account of;
A. T.: American terms;
B/L: Bill of Lading;
B. O.: Buyer's option;
B. M.: Board measure;
B. E.: Bill of exchange
C. I. F.: Cost, insurance, freight;
C. & F.: Cost and freight;
C. I. F. & C.: Cost, insurance, freight and commission;
C. I. F. & E.: Cost, insurance, freight and exchange;
C. I. F. C. & I.: Cost, insurance, freight, commission and interest;
C. I. FC. I.: Cost, insurance, freight, commission and interest;
C. I. F. I. & E.: Cost, insurance, freight, interest and exchange;
C. T. L.: Constructive total loss;
C/P: Charter party;
c/s: Case(s);
D/W: Dead weight;
D/D: Delivered docks;
D/d: Delivered;
D/O: Delivery order;
D/C: Deviation clause;
D/f: Dead freight;
Ex. Ship: Delivered out of ship;
E. E. U. S.: United States;
Exd.: Examined;
E. & O. E.: Errors and omissions excepted;
Ex.: Out of;
F. O. B.: Free on board;
F. A. S.: Free alongside;
F. a. a.: Free of all average;
F. c. s.: Free of capture and seizure;
F/d: Free docks;

F. g. a.: Free general average;
F. O. C.: Free of charge(s);
f. p. a.: Free of particular average;
F. P. A. A. C.: Free of particular average (American conditions);
Fwd.: Forward;
Frt.: Freight;
Fact.: Bill, invoice;
F. o. d.: Free of damage;
G/A: General average;
Inv.: Invoice;
Ins.: Insurance;
In trans.: In transit;
I. p. a.: Including particular average;
J/A: Joint account;
l. t.: Long ton;
M. I. P.: Marine insurance policy;
Mdse.: Merchandise;
n. o. s.: Not otherwise specified;
N/A: No account;
N/A: Nonacceptance;
N/F: No funds;
n. e. i.: Not elsewhere included;
N/B: (nota bene): Mark well;
O/o: Order of;
O. r. b.: Owner's risk of breakage;
O/R: Owner's risk;
P/a: Particular average;
P. L.: Partial Loss;
pm: Premium;
pd.: Paid;
per ann.: Per annum;
p. a.: Per annum;
R. O. G.: Receipt of goods;
S/D: Sight Draft;
S. D. B. L.: Sight draft, bill of lading attached;
S. O.: Seller's option;
S. P. A.: Subject to particular average;
S. T.: Short ton;
S. tn.: Short ton;
SHPT: Shipment;
T. L. O.: Total loss only;
T. T.: Telegraphic transfer;

T. C.: Telegrams to be repeated;
U/w: Underwriters;
W. A.: With average;
W. B.: Waybill

W/M: Weight or measurement;
W. O. G.: With other goods;
W. P. A.: With particular average;
W/W: Warehouse warrant.

COLLECTION AND PAYMENT

A/C: Account current;
A/D: After date;
A/S: After sight;
A/S: At sight;
A/T: American terms;
A. O.: Account of;
B/P: Bills payable;
B/R: Bills receivable;
B. O.: Buyer's option;
B/E: Bill of exchange;
C. W. O.: Cash with order;
C. B. D.: Cash before delivery;
D/A: Documents after acceptance;
D/a: Days after acceptance;
D/D: Demand draft;
D/d: Days after date;
Dft: Draft;
D/N: Debit note;
D/P: Documents against payment;
D/S: Days (after) sight;
D. A. D.: Documents against discretion
          of collecting bank;
EX. INT.: Not including interest;
F. O. C.: Free of charge;
Inv.: Invoice;

Int.: Interest;
J/A: Joint account;
L/C: Letter of credit;
L/A: Letter of authority;
M. P.: Month after payment;
M. D.: Months after date;
M. S.: Months after sight;
Mdse.: Merchandise;
N/A: No account;
N/A: Nonacceptable;
n/d: Not dated;
N/F: No funds;
O/d: On Demand;
O/o: Order of;
O/a: On account;
P/A: Private account;
p. f.: Pro forma;
pd.: Paid;
per ann.: Per annum;
R/A: Refer to acceptor;
R/D: Refer to drawer;
R. O. G.: Receipt of goods;
R. P.: Return of post;
S/D: Sight draft;
S. D. B. L.: Sight draft, bill of
             lading attached;
SHIPT: Shipment;
S. S.: Steamship;
Stg.: Sterling;
TT: Telegraphic transfer;
W. B.: Waybill;
W/R: Warehouse receipt.

ADDENDA TO ABBREVIATIONS

ABBREVIATIONS USED: ANSI—American Nat'l Standards Institute; APHIS—Animal and Plant Health Inspection Svc; ASTM—American Society for Testing and Materials; BATF—Bur of Alcohol, Tobacco and Firearms; CAB—Civil Aeronautics Bd; CITA—Comm for Implementation of Textile Agreements; CPSC—Consumer Product Safety Comm; DEA—Drug Enforcement Adm; DoT—Dept of Transportation; EC—European Community (Common Market); EPA—Environmental Protection Agency; FAA—Federal Aviation Adm; FCC—Federal Communications Comm; FDA—Food and Drug Adm; FMC—Federal Maritime Comm; FTC—Federal Trade Comm; GATT—Gen'l Agreement on Tariffs and Trade; GSP—Generalized System of Preferences; ICC—Interstate Commerce Comm; ITC—Int'l Trade Comm; NBS—Nat'l Bur of Standards; NDA—New Drug Application; NHTSA—Nat'l Highway Traffic Safety Adm; NIOSH—Nat'l Inst of Occupational Safety and Health; OSHA—Occupational Safety and Health Adm; STR—Ofc of the Spec Rep for Trade Negotiations; TSUS(A)—Tariff Schedules of U.S. (Annotated); USDA —Dept. of Agriculture.

COMMON EXPRESSIONS AND STANDARD TERMS

ACT OF GOD. Operation of an uncontrollable natural force.

AD VALOREM. According to value.

AGAINST. In foreign commerce, used as synonym for "upon".

AIR WAYBILL. Contract of carriage, between shipper and air carrier.

APPARENT GOOD ORDER. - Statement denoting that goods are free from damage and in good condition, as far as their external appearance is concerned.

APPRAISER'S STORES. Government-owned warehouse, where examiners (appraisers) inspect and survey designated goods imported from abroad.

ASSIGNMENT. Legal transfer of title, property, or right.

B. A. I. CERTIFICATE. Certificate issued by the U. S. Bureau of Animal Industry, attesting to a careful veterinary inspection of animals and the absence of communicable disease or exposure thereto.

BALLAST. Heavy material which is placed in the ship's hold for stability.

BARTER. Exchange of goods, without the use of money.

BEAM. The width of the vessel.

BERTH. Ship's place at dock.

BERTH RATES. Rates charges by scheduled liner services.

BILGE. The lowest internal part of the hull, next to the keelson, where the bilge water collects.

BILGE. Belly of a barrel or cask.

BLANK ENDORSEMENT. Writing only one's own name on the back of a document.

BROKER. Middleman between buyer and seller.

BROKERAGE. Fee or commission which is paid to a broker for services performed.

BULK. A mass of a product, unpackaged.

BUNKER. Ship's coal-bin or oil storage place.

CABLE CODE. System of letters, figures or words with arbitrary meaning for shortness or secrecy.

CABOTAGE. Coastwise and intercoastal navigation and trading.

CARGO PLAN. Stowage plan which is prepared by the pier superintendent and carried out by the stevedore.

CASHIER'S CHECK. Check drawn by and on the same bank, signed by its cashier.

CHARTER. Lease of ship by owner, or hire by charterer.

CIRCA. About.

CONFERENCE. Liner organization which fixes rates and sailings, for the purpose of limiting competition between members and of "outsiders".

CONSIGNEE. Receiver of goods.

CONSIGNOR. Shipper of goods.

CONSULTATION. Consular fees.

DELCREDERE. Shifting of risk to someone else, or acceptance by a party other than the original creditor.

DEVISEN (GERMAN). Foreign currencies.

DIVISAS (SPANISH).

DUMPING. Sending goods for sale at low prices abroad, with the intent to maintain home prices and capture foreign markets.

DUNNAGE. Lumber used in stowing cargo.

ENDORSE. Sign one's name on back of document (check, B/L).

EXAQUATUR. Government's authorization of another country's consul.

FACE VALUE. Nominal value on coin, paper currency, or other negotiable instrument; may be lower or higher than the market value.

FILIALE. Branch office (German).

FILS. French for "Sons" at the end of a business firm's name.

FORE AND AFT. At bow and stern, all over ship.

GENERAL ORDER WAREHOUSE. A bonded warehouse to which goods which are not claimed within five days after arrival are sent at the owner's expense.

GODOWN. Far East warehouse.

GRACE, DAYS OF. A certain number of days allowed by law for payment of due bill.

HATCH. The cover of--or opening--in the deck of a vessel, through which cargo is loaded.

INSURANCE RIDER. Additional clause, amending or supplementing the insurance policy.

KNOT. Equivalent to one nautical mile, (6,080 ft.) per hour.

LETTER OF INDEMNITY. Issued by the shipper to the carrier, to secure a clean bill of lading for damaged goods--to protect the carrier and for the purpose of avoiding collection difficulties with bank.

LIST (of ship). Lean over to one side, due to shifting of cargo.

MATE'S RECEIPT. Receipt of cargo by the vessel, signed by the mate (similar to dock receipt).

MEET A DRAFT. To pay or honor a draft falling due.

PLIMSOLL LINE. Statutory load line.

RECOURSE. An obligation, if not net, goes back to the original drawer. "Without Recourse" drawing, relieves the drawer of liability.

SALVAGE. Rescue of goods from loss at sea or by fire; also, goods so saved, or payment made or due for their rescue.

SOCIETE ANONYME. French name for corporation.

SHORT-SHIPPED. Cargo manifested, but not loaded.

TALLY SHEET. List of cargo, incoming and out-going, checked by Tally clerk on dock.

USANCE. Time allowed for payment of foreign drafts.

VALUTA. Designation for foreign means of payment (Devisen, drafts), exclusive coins.

WEIGHT, LEGAL. Net weight of goods, plus inside packing.

APPENDIX L

SHIPPERS' CREDIT AGREEMENT

NORTH ATLANTIC MEDITERRANEAN FREIGHT CONFERENCE

40 RECTOR STREET, NEW YORK, N. Y. 10006

R. H. CABRERA
CHAIRMAN

CABLE
NAMFCON
TELEX
12-8187
TELEPHONE
(212) 766-9660

SHIPPER'S CREDIT AGREEMENT

In consideration of the extension of credit, through the issurance and release of bills of lading indicating that freight is payable on other than a "freight collect" basis, by any member of the North Atlantic Mediterranean Freight Conference at United States North Atlantic ports served by such members to us directly or through duly authorized forwarders, we hereby undertake and agree as follows:

1.   Receipts for all bills of lading so issued shall be signed by us or on our behalf by our Forwarder or Agent.

2.   We will be absolutely and unconditionally responsible to the Carrier for payment of all freight and charges due within fifteen business days (Saturday, Sundays, Holidays excepted) of the sailing of the vessel from the respective port of loading and guarantee that they will be paid within that period, irrespective of whether or not funds for payment have been advanced to the forwarder or otherwise.

3.   Credit privileges will be suspended for any failure to comply with the provisions hereof.

4.   Nothing herein contained shall limit any Conference Carrier's absolute discretion to refuse to extend credit of its right, where credit has been extended, to collect payment of all freight and charges prior to vessel's arrival at port of discharge.

5.   This undertaking shall continue in effect until terminated by written notice from the shipper or the Conference to the other; proveded, however, that termination shall not extinguish any existing liabilities hereunder.

DATED this_____ day of_____,   _____
                                              (Shipper)

                              _____
                                              (Address)

                        By _____
                                       (Signature and Title)

Issued 1/1/75

Form of Receipt for Bills of Lading released
pursuant to Shipper's Credit Undertaking

The undersigned hereby acknowledges receipt from_____Line of the bills of lading described below. Said bills of lading indicate that the freight is payable on other than a "freight collect" basis, and the freight and other charges shown thereon must be paid within fifteen (15) business days (Saturdays, Sundays, Holidays excepted) after the vessel sails from the port at which cargo is loaded in accordance with the credit undertaking executed by the shipper on whose behalf this receipt is signed and the North Atlantic Mediterranean Freight Conference.

Bills of Lading

Vessel	Voyage No.	Bill of Lading No.	Freight and Other Charges

                              _____
                                       (Name of Forwarder)

                        By_____
                                 (Signature, authorized to sign)

FOR AND ON BEHALF OF   _____
                                    (Name of Shipper)

NORTH ATLANTIC MEDITERRANEAN FREIGHT CONFERENCE

40 RECTOR STREET, NEW YORK, N.Y. 10006

R. H. CABRERA
CHAIRMAN

CABLE:
NAMFCON

TELEX:
12-8187

TELEPHONE
(212) 766-9000

February 8, 1977

TO: THE SHIPPING PUBLIC

I M P O R T A N T   N O T I C E

PORT CONGESTION SURCHARGE

ON SHIPMENTS TO

CYPRIAN PORTS

The Member Lines have been greatly concerned at the detention of vessels at Cyprian Ports due to congested conditions resulting in an alarming increase in the cost for discharging cargo in this area.

The extended delays to Member Line vessels has materially interferred with their ability to maintain a dependable sailing schedule to and from other Mediterranean Ports in their itineary resulting in increased cost of operation.

Measures to improve the situation have not as yet alleviated the conditions and being unable to continue absorbing these considerable costs, the Member Lines have found it necessary to impose a Congestion Surcharge of Ten (10%) Percent. This Surcharge will apply on all rates and charges covering shipments to Cyprian Ports effective with delivery of cargo to carrier's vessels, alongside or on the dock, on and after March 4, 1977.

ALEXANDRIA SHIPPING &	HELLENIC LINES, LTD.
NAVIGATION COMPANY	ITALIAN LINE
AMERICAN EXPORT LINES, INC.	NORDANA LINE
ATLANTICA LINE	SEA-LAND SERVICE, INC.
CONCORDIA LINE	TORM LINES
CONSTELLATION LINE	ZIM ISRAEL NAVIGATION CO., LTD.
EGYPTIAN NATIONAL LINE	

NORTH ATLANTIC MEDITERRANEAN FREIGHT CONFERENCE

R. H. Cabrera
CHAIRMAN

FREIGHT RATE ADJUSTMENT FORMS

NORTH ATLANTIC UNITED KINGDOM
FREIGHT CONFERENCE

17 Battery Place
New York, N. Y.   10004
HAnover 5- 7400

APPLICATION FOR RATE MODIFICATION

1. Name of Commodity and trade name, if any

2. Schedule B. No.   Railroad Classification

3. Describe Commodity and its uses

4. State if hazardous or inflammable   Label Required
   If answer is in the affirmative, complete particulars are required concerning chemical characteristics, flashpoint,

   etc.

5. Describe Packing

6. Package Dimensions—Length   Width   Height   Cu.Ft. Pkge.

7. Package Gross Wt.   Cubic Feet per 2240 lbs.

8. F.A.S. value per Pkge.   Per Pound   Per 2240 Lbs.

9. Customs Duty at Destination

10. Point of Origin of Commodity

11. Port of Loading   Port of Discharge

12. Present Rate   Rate Requested

13. Volume of present movement

14. Anticipated Volume if rate modification granted

15. Describe competitive commodity, if any, including price

16. Reason for requested modification (if foreign competition, all known data must be furnished including country or origin, ocean freight rate, laid-down cost, and the steps taken by applicant to reduce other costs to meet competition).

17. Application submitted by

              By   Title

              Address

In order to avoid any delays in the processing of this request, this form should be completed in all respects. In addition it is requested that literature such as catalogs, brochures etc., fully describing the commodity in question be enclosed with this application.

ASSOCIATED LATIN AMERICAN FREIGHT CONFERENCES TRAFFIC
ANALYSIS FORM

1. Name of article and its trade name, if any:

2. Description of article:

3. What it is used for:

4. State if hazardous or inflammable:

5. State what label is required for ocean shipment:

6. State if liquid, paste, flake, powdered, granulated or solid:

7. State how packed (box, barrel, bale, carton, crate, etc.):

8. Package Dimensions: Length   Width   Height   Cu. ft. per package:

9. Package gross weight is   lbs.   Cu. ft. per 2,000 lbs.:

10. From U. S. port of: To foreign port of:

11. Present rate: Rate proposed by applicant:

12. Place where material is made or produced:

13. How article is described for railroad movement:

14. How described in Shipper's Export Declaration:

15. Schedule B Commodity No.:

16. Tonnage of present movement to foreign port named in Item 10:

17. Extra tonnage expected to move at proposed rate:

18. State if movement is continuous, seasonal or sporadic:

19. F.A.S. value per pound:

20. Name of competitive or substitute article:

21. F.A.S. value per pound of competitive article:
    (If this information is not obtainable, but the delivered competitive price is
    the basis of this application, it must be indicated at least approximately)

22. Reason for proposed change:

23. Application submitted by:

                    Per:

Date: Address:

Note.—Applicant to keep one completed copy of this form. The remainder to be mailed to
    A. J. Pasch, Conference Chairman, Room 2100, 11 Broadway, New York 4, N. Y.

APPENDIX M

OCEAN FREIGHT CALCULATION TABLES

Rates Per Ton	Equals Rate per cu. ft.	Equals Rate per 100# Net 2000#	Gross 2240#	Rates Per Ton	Equals Rate per cu. ft.	Equals Rate per 100# Net 2000#	Gross 2240#
.05	.00125	.00250	.00223	18.75	.46875	.93750	.83705
.10	.00250	.00500	.00446	19.00	.47500	.95000	.84821
.15	.00375	.00750	.00669	19.25	.48125	.96250	.85937
.20	.00500	.01000	.00892	19.50	.48750	.97500	.87054
.25	.00625	.01250	.01116	19.75	.49375	.98750	.88170
.30	.00750	.01500	.01339	20.00	.50000	1.00000	.89286
.35	.00875	.01750	.01562	20.25	.50625	1.01250	.90402
.40	.01000	.02000	.01785	20.50	.51250	1.02500	.91518
.45	.01125	.02250	.02008	20.75	.51875	1.03750	.92634
.50	.01250	.02500	.02232	21.00	.52500	1.05000	.93750
.55	.01375	.02750	.02455	21.25	.53125	1.06250	.94866
.60	.01500	.03000	.02678	21.50	.53750	1.07500	.95982
.65	.01625	.03250	.02901	21.75	.54375	1.08750	.97098
.70	.01750	.03500	.03124	22.00	.55000	1.10000	.98214
.75	.01875	.03750	.03348	22.25	.55625	1.11250	.99330
.80	.02000	.04000	.03571	22.50	.56250	1.13750	1.00446
.85	.02125	.04250	.03794	22.75	.56875	1.13750	1.01562
.90	.02250	.04500	.04017	23.00	.57500	1.15000	1.02678
.95	.02375	.04750	.04241	23.25	.58125	1.16250	1.03795
1.00	.02500	.05000	.04464	23.50	.58750	1.17500	1.04911
2.00	.05000	.10000	.08928	23.75	.59375	1.18750	1.06027
3.00	.07500	.15000	.13392	24.00	.60000	1.20000	1.07143
4.00	.10000	.20000	.17857	24.25	.60625	1.21250	1.08259
5.00	.12500	.25000	.22321	24.50	.61250	1.22500	1.09375
10.00	.25000	.50000	.44643	24.75	.61875	1.23750	1.10491
10.25	.25625	.51250	.45759	25.00	.62500	1.25000	1.11607
10.50	.26250	.52500	.46875	25.25	.63125	1.26250	1.12723
10.75	.26875	.53750	.47991	25.50	.63750	1.27500	1.13839
11.00	.27500	.55000	.49107	25.75	.64375	1.28750	1.14955
11.25	.28125	.56250	.50223	26.00	.65000	1.30000	1.16071
11.50	.28750	.57500	.51339	26.25	.65625	1.31250	1.17187
11.75	.29375	.58750	.52455	26.50	.66250	1.32500	1.18303
12.00	.30000	.60000	.53571	26.75	.66875	1.33750	1.19420
12.25	.30625	.61250	.54687	27.00	.67500	1.35000	1.20536
12.50	.31250	.62500	.55804	27.25	.68125	1.36250	1.21652
12.75	.31875	.63750	.56920	27.50	.68750	1.37500	1.22768
13.00	.32500	.65000	.58036	27.75	.69375	1.38750	1.23884
13.25	.33125	.66250	.59152	28.00	.70000	1.40000	1.25000
13.50	.33750	.67500	.60268	28.25	.70625	1.41250	1.26116
13.75	.34375	.68750	.61384	28.50	.71250	1.42500	1.27232
14.00	.35000	.70000	.62500	28.75	.71875	1.43750	1.28348
14.25	.35625	.71250	.63616	29.00	.72500	1.45000	1.29464
14.50	.36250	.72500	.64732	29.25	.73125	1.46250	1.30580
14.75	.36875	.73750	.65848	29.50	.73750	1.47500	1.31696
15.00	.37500	.75000	.66964	29.75	.74375	1.48750	1.32812
15.25	.38125	.76250	.68080	30.00	.75000	1.50000	1.33928
15.50	.38750	.77500	.69196	30.25	.75625	1.51250	1.35045
15.75	.39375	.78750	.70312	30.50	.76250	1.52500	1.36161
16.00	.40000	.80000	.71429	30.75	.76875	1.53750	1.37277
16.25	.40625	.81250	.72545	31.00	.77500	1.55000	1.38393
16.50	.41250	.82500	.73661	31.25	.78125	1.56250	1.39509
16.75	.41875	.83750	.74777	31.50	.78750	1.57500	1.40625
17.00	.42500	.85000	.75893	31.75	.79375	1.58750	1.41741
17.25	.43125	.86250	.77009	32.00	.80000	1.60000	1.42857
17.50	.43750	.87500	.78125	32.25	.80625	1.61250	1.43973
17.75	.44375	.88750	.79241	32.50	.81250	1.62500	1.45089
18.00	.45000	.90000	.80357	32.75	.81875	1.63750	1.46205
18.25	.45625	.91250	.81473	33.00	.82500	1.65000	1.47321
18.50	.46250	.92500	.82589	33.25	.83125	1.66250	1.48437

Rates Per Ton	Equals Rate per cu. ft.	Equals Rate per 100# Net 2000#	Gross 2240#	Rates Per Ton	Equals Rate per cu. ft.	Equals Rate per 100# Net 2000#	Gross 2240#
33.50	.83750	1.67500	1.49553	49.00	1.22500	2.45000	2.18750
33.75	.84375	1.68750	1.50670	49.25	1.23125	2.46250	2.19866
34.00	.85000	1.70000	1.51786	49.50	1.23750	2.47500	2.20982
34.25	.85625	1.71250	1.52902	49.75	1.24375	2.48750	2.20298
34.50	.86250	1.72500	1.54018	50.00	1.25000	2.50000	2.23214
34.75	.86875	1.73750	1.55134	50.25	1.25625	2.51250	2.24330
35.00	.87500	1.75000	1.56250	50.50	1.26250	2.52500	2.25446
35.25	.88125	1.76250	1.57366	50.75	1.26875	2.53750	2.26562
35.50	.88750	1.77500	1.58482	51.00	1.27500	2.55000	2.27678
35.75	.89375	1.78750	1.59598	51.25	1.28125	2.56250	2.28794
36.00	.90000	1.80000	1.60714	51.50	1.28750	2.57500	2.29910
36.25	.90625	1.81250	1.61830	51.75	1.29375	2.58750	2.31027
36.50	.91250	1.82500	1.62946	52.00	1.30000	2.60000	2.32143
36.75	.91875	1.83750	1.64062	52.25	1.30625	2.61250	2.33259
37.00	.92500	1.85000	1.65178	52.50	1.31250	2.62500	2.34375
37.25	.93125	1.86250	1.66294	52.75	1.31875	2.63750	2.35491
37.50	.93750	1.87500	1.67411	53.00	1.32500	2.65000	2.36607
37.75	.94375	1.88750	1.68527	53.25	1.33125	2.66250	2.37723
38.00	.95000	1.90000	1.69643	53.50	1.33750	2.67500	2.38839
38.25	.95625	1.91250	1.70759	53.75	1.34375	2.68750	2.39955
38.50	.96250	1.92500	1.71875	54.00	1.35000	2.70000	2.41071
38.75	.96875	1.93750	1.72991	54.25	1.35625	2.71250	2.42187
39.00	.97500	1.95000	1.74107	54.50	1.36250	2.72500	2.43303
39.25	.98125	1.96250	1.75223	54.75	1.36875	2.73750	2.44419
39.50	.98750	1.97500	1.76339	55.00	1.37500	2.75000	2.45535
39.75	.99375	1.98750	1.77455	55.25	1.38125	2.76250	2.46652
40.00	1.00000	2.00000	1.78571	55.50	1.38750	2.77500	2.47768
40.25	1.00625	2.01250	1.79687	55.75	1.39375	2.78750	2.48884
40.50	1.01250	2.02500	1.80803	56.00	1.40000	2.80000	2.50000
40.75	1.01875	2.03750	1.81919	56.25	1.40625	2.81250	2.51116
41.00	1.02500	2.05000	1.83036	56.50	1.41250	2.82500	2.52232
41.25	1.03125	2.06250	1.84152	56.75	1.41875	2.83750	2.53348
41.50	1.03750	2.07500	1.85268	57.00	1.42500	2.85000	2.54464
41.75	1.04375	2.08750	1.86384	57.25	1.43125	2.86250	2.55580
42.00	1.05000	2.10000	1.87500	57.50	1.43750	2.87500	2.56696
42.25	1.05625	2.11250	1.88616	57.75	1.44375	2.88750	2.57812
42.50	1.06250	2.12500	1.89732	58.00	1.45000	2.90000	2.58928
42.75	1.06875	2.13750	1.90848	58.25	1.45625	2.91250	2.60044
43.00	1.07500	2.15000	1.91964	58.50	1.46250	2.92500	2.61160
43.25	1.08125	2.16250	1.93080	58.75	1.46875	2.93750	2.62277
43.50	1.08750	2.17500	1.94196	59.00	1.47500	2.95000	2.63393
43.75	1.09375	2.18750	1.95312	59.25	1.48125	2.96250	2.64509
44.00	1.10000	2.22000	1.96428	59.50	1.48750	2.97500	2.65625
44.25	1.10625	2.21250	1.97544	59.75	1.49375	2.98750	2.66741
44.50	1.11250	2.22500	1.98661	60.00	1.50000	3.00000	2.67851
44.75	1.11875	2.23750	1.99777	60.25	1.50625	3.01250	2.68973
45.00	1.12500	2.25000	2.00893	60.50	1.51250	3.02500	2.70089
45.25	1.13125	2.26250	2.02009	60.75	1.51875	3.03750	2.71205
45.50	1.13750	2.27500	2.03125	61.00	1.52500	3.05000	2.72321
45.75	1.14375	2.28750	2.04241	61.25	1.53125	3.06250	2.73437
46.00	1.15000	2.30000	2.05357	61.50	1.53750	3.07500	2.74553
46.25	1.15625	2.31250	2.06473	61.75	1.54375	3.08750	2.75669
46.50	1.16250	2.32500	2.07589	62.00	1.55000	3.10000	2.76785
46.75	1.16875	2.33750	2.08705	62.25	1.55625	3.11250	2.77901
47.00	1.17500	2.35000	2.09821	62.50	1.56250	3.12500	2.79018
47.25	1.18125	2.36250	2.10937	62.75	1.56875	3.13750	2.80134
47.50	1.18750	2.37500	2.12053	63.00	1.57500	3.15000	2.81250
47.75	1.19375	2.38750	2.13169	63.25	1.58125	3.16250	2.82366
48.00	1.20000	2.40000	2.14285	63.50	1.58750	3.17500	2.83482
48.25	1.20625	2.41250	2.15402	63.75	1.59375	3.18750	2.84598
48.50	1.21250	2.42500	2.16518	64.00	1.60000	3.20000	2.85714
48.75	1.21875	2.43750	2.17634	64.25	1.60625	3.21250	2.86830

Rates Per Ton	Equals Rate per cu. ft.	Equals Rate per 100# Net 2000#	Gross 2240#	Rates Per Ton	Equals Rate per cu. ft.	Equals Rate per 100# Net 2000#	Gross 2240#
64.50	1.61250	3.22500	2.87946	80.00	2.00000	4.00000	3.57142
64.75	1.61875	3.23750	2.89062	80.25	2.06250	4.01250	3.58259
65.00	1.62500	3.25000	2.90178	80.50	2.01250	4.02500	3.59375
65.25	1.63125	3.26250	2.91294	80.75	2.01875	4.03750	3.60491
65.50	1.63750	3.27500	2.92410	81.00	2.02500	4.05000	3.61607
65.75	1.64375	3.28750	2.93526	81.25	2.03125	4.06250	3.62723
66.00	1.65000	3.30000	2.94643	81.50	2.03750	4.97500	3.63839
66.25	1.65625	3.31250	2.95759	81.75	2.04375	4.08750	3.64955
66.50	1.66250	3.32500	2.96875	82.00	2.05000	4.10000	3.66071
66.75	1.66875	3.33750	2.97991	82.25	2.05625	4.11250	3.67187
67.00	1.67500	3.35000	2.99107	82.50	2.06250	4.12500	3.68303
67.25	1.68125	3.00223	3.00223	82.75	2.06875	4.13750	3.69419
67.50	1.68750	3.37500	3.01339	83.00	2.07500	4.15000	3.70535
67.75	1.69375	3.38750	3.02455	83.25	2.08125	4.16250	3.71651
68.00	1.70000	3.40000	3.03571	83.50	2.08750	4.17500	3.72767
68.25	1.70625	3.41250	3.04687	83.75	2.09375	4.18750	3.73884
68.50	1.71250	3.42500	3.05803	84.00	2.10000	4.20000	3.75000
68.75	1.71875	3.43750	3.06919	84.25	2.10625	4.21250	3.76116
69.00	1.72500	3.45000	3.08035	84.50	2.11250	4.22500	3.77232
69.25	1.73125	3.46250	3.09151	84.75	2.11875	4.23750	3.78348
69.50	1.73750	3.47500	3.10268	85.00	2.12500	4.25000	3.79464
69.75	1.74375	3.48750	3.11384	85.25	2.13125	4.26250	3.80580
70.00	1.75000	3.50000	3.12500	85.50	2.13750	4.27500	3.81696
70.25	1.75625	3.51250	3.13616	85.75	2.14375	4.28750	3.82812
70.50	1.76250	3.52500	3.14732	86.00	2.15000	4.30000	3.83928
70.75	1.76875	3.53750	3.15848	86.25	2.15625	4.31250	3.85044
71.00	1.77500	3.55000	3.16964	86.50	2.16250	4.32500	3.86160
71.25	1.78125	3.56250	3.18080	86.75	2.16875	4.33750	3.87276
71.50	1.78750	3.57500	3.19196	87.00	2.17500	4.35000	3.88392
71.75	1.79375	3.58750	3.20312	87.25	2.18125	4.36250	3.89508
72.00	1.80000	3.60000	3.21428	87.50	2.18750	4.37500	3.90625
72.25	1.80625	3.61250	3.22544	87.75	2.19375	4.38750	3.91741
72.50	1.81250	3.62500	3.23660	88.00	2.20000	4.40000	3.92857
72.75	1.81875	3.63750	3.24776	88.25	2.20625	4.41250	3.93973
73.00	1.82500	3.65000	3.25892	88.50	2.21250	4.42500	3.95089
73.25	1.83125	3.66250	3.27009	88.75	2.21875	4.43750	3.96205
73.50	1.83750	3.67500	3.28125	89.00	2.22500	4.45000	3.97321
73.75	1.84375	3.68750	3.29241	89.25	2.23125	4.46250	3.98437
74.00	1.85000	3.70000	3.30357	89.50	2.23750	4.47500	3.99553
74.25	1.85625	3.71250	3.31473	89.75	2.24375	4.48750	4.00670
74.50	1.86250	3.72500	3.32589	90.00	2.25000	4.50000	4.01785
74.75	1.86875	3.73750	3.33705	90.25	2.25625	4.51250	4.02901
75.00	1.87500	3.75000	3.34821	90.50	2.26250	4.52500	4.04017
75.25	1.88125	3.76250	3.35937	90.75	2.26875	4.53750	4.05133
75.50	1.88750	3.77500	3.37053	91.00	2.27500	4.55000	4.06250
75.75	1.89375	3.78750	3.38169	91.25	2.28125	4.56250	4.07366
76.00	1.90000	3.80000	3.39285	91.50	2.28750	4.57500	4.08482
76.25	1.90625	3.81250	3.40401	91.75	2.29375	4.58750	4.09598
76.50	1.91250	3.82500	3.41517	92.00	2.30000	4.60000	4.10714
76.75	1.91875	3.83750	3.42634	92.25	2.30625	4.61250	4.11830
77.00	1.92500	3.85000	3.43750	92.50	2.31250	4.62500	4.12946
77.25	1.93125	3.86250	3.44866	92.75	2.31875	4.63750	4.14062
77.50	1.93750	3.87500	3.45982	93.00	2.32500	4.65000	4.15178
77.75	1.94375	3.88750	3.47098	93.25	2.33125	4.66250	4.16294
78.00	1.95000	3.90000	3.48214	93.50	2.33750	4.67500	4.17410
78.25	1.95625	3.91250	3.49330	93.75	2.34375	4.68750	4.18526
78.50	1.96250	3.92500	3.50446	94.00	2.35000	4.70000	4.19642
78.75	1.96875	3.93750	3.51562	94.25	2.35625	4.71250	4.20759
79.00	1.97500	3.95000	3.52678	94.50	2.36250	4.72500	4.21874
79.25	1.98125	3.96250	3.53794	94.75	2.36875	4.73750	4.22991
79.50	1.98750	3.97500	3.54910	95.00	2.37500	4.75000	4.24107
79.75	1.99375	3.98750	3.56026	95.25	2.38125	4.76250	4.25223

Rates Per Ton	Equals Rate per cu. ft.	Equals Rate per 100# Net 2000#	Gross 2240#	Rates Per Ton	Equals Rate per cu. ft.	Equals Rate per 100# Net 2000#	Gross 2240#
95.50	2.38750	4.77500	4.26339	97.75	2.44375	4.88750	4.36383
95.75	2.39375	4.78750	4.27455	98.00	2.45000	4.90000	4.37499
96.00	2.40000	4.80000	4.28571	98.25	2.45625	4.91250	4.38616
96.25	2.40625	4.81250	4.29687	98.50	2.46250	4.92500	4.39732
96.50	2.41250	4.82500	4.30803	98.75	2.46875	4.93750	4.40848
96.75	2.41875	4.83750	4.31919	99.00	2.47500	4.95000	4.41964
97.00	2.42500	4.85000	4.33035	99.25	2.48125	4.96250	4.43080
97.25	2.43125	4.86250	4.34151	99.50	2.48750	4.97500	4.44196
97.50	2.43750	4.87500	4.35267	99.75	2.49375	4.98750	4.45312
				100.00	2,50000	5.00000	4.46428

APPENDIX N

TABLE OF INSURANCE FACTORS

SCHEDULE OF MULTIPLICATION FACTORS COMPUTED TO INSURE CARGO SHIPMENTS AT 110% OF INVOICE VALUE INCLUDING INSURANCE CHARGES

Rate	Factor	Rate	Factor	Rate	Factor
0.10	1.1012	1.25	1.1154	2.40	1.1299
0.15	1.1018	1.30	1.1160	2.45	1.1306
0.20	1.1024	1.35	1.1166	2.50	1.1311
0.25	1.1030	1.40	1.1172	2.55	1.1318
0.30	1.1036	1.45	1.1179	2.60	1.1324
0.35	1.1043	1.50	1.1185	2.65	1.1332
0.40	1.1049	1.55	1.1191	2.70	1.1340
0.45	1.1055	1.60	1.1197	2.75	1.1345
0.50	1.1061	1.65	1.1204	2.80	1.1350
0.55	1.1067	1.70	1.1210	2.85	1.1357
0.60	1.1073	1.75	1.1216	2.90	1.1363
0.65	1.1079	1.80	1.1222	2.95	1.1369
0.70	1.1085	1.85	1.1229	3.00	1.1375
0.75	1.1092	1.90	1.1235	3.05	1.1382
0.80	1.1098	1.95	1.1241	3.10	1.1388
0.85	1.1104	2.00	1.1247	3.15	1.1395
0.90	1.1110	2.05	1.1254	3.20	1.1402
0.95	1.1116	2.10	1.1260	3.25	1.1409
1.00	1.1122	2.15	1.1267	3.30	1.1415
1.05	1.1129	2.20	1.1273	3.35	1.1422
1.10	1.1135	2.25	1.1280	3.40	1.1428
1.15	1.1141	2.30	1.1286	3.45	1.1435
1.20	1.1147	2.35	1.1293	3.50	1.1441

TABLE OF
CONVERSION FACTORS

UNIT	MEASURE	EQUALS UNIT		MEASURE
1	Barrel (Oil)	–	42	Gallons (oil)
1	Centimeter	–	0.3937	Inch
1	Centimeter	–	0.01	Meter
1	Centimeter	–	10	Millimeters
1	Cubic foot	–	28320	Cubic cms.
1	Cubic foot	–	1728	Cubic inches
1	Cubic foot	–	0.02832	Cubic meter
1	Cubic foot	–	0.03704	Cubic yard
1	Cubic foot	–	7.48052	Gallons
1	Cubic foot	–	28.32	Liters
1	Cubic foot	–	59.84	Pints (liq.)
1	Cubic foot	–	29.92	Quarts (liq.)
1	Cubic inch	–	16.39	Cubic centimeters
1	Cubic inch	–	0.000578	Cubic foot
1	Cubic inch	–	0.00001639	Cubic meter
1	Cubic inch	–	0.004329	Gallon
1	Cubic meter	–	1.000000	Cubic centimeters
1	Cubic meter	–	35.31	Cubic feet
1	Cubic meter	–	61.023	Cubic inches
1	Cubic meter	–	1.308	Cubic yards
1	Cubic meter	–	264.2	Gallons
1	Cubic meter	–	1000	Liters
1	Cubic meter	–	2113	Pints (liq.)
1	Cubic meter	–	1057	Quarts (liq.)
1	Decigram	–	0.1	Gram
1	Decimeter	–	0.1	Meter
1	Degree (Angle)	–	60	Minutes
1	Degree (Angle)	–	0.01745	Radian
1	Degree (Angle)	–	3600	Seconds
1	Dekagram	–	10	Grams
1	Dekaliter	–	10	Liters
1	Dekameter	–	10	Meters
1	Fathom	–	6	Feet
1	Foot	–	30.48	Centimeters
1	Foot	–	12	Inches
1	Foot	–	0.3048	Meter
1	Foot	–	1/3	Yard
1	Gallon	–	3785	Cubic centimeters
1	Gallon	–	0.1337	Cubic foot
1	Gallon	–	231	Cubic inches
1	Gallon	–	0.00378	Cubic meter
1	Gallon	–	4	Quarts (liq.)
1	Gallon, Imperial	–	1.20095	U. S. Gallons
1	Gallon, U. S.	–	0.83267	Imperial Gallon
1	Gallon, water	–	8.3453	Pounds of water
1	Gram	–	980.7	Dynes
1	Gram	–	15.43	Grains
1	Gram	–	0.001	Kilogram
1	Gram	–	1000	Milligrams

continued

UNIT	MEASURE		EQUALS UNIT	MEASURE
1	Gram	-	0.03527	Ounce
1	Gram	-	0.03215	Ounce (troy)
1	Gram	-	0.0002205	Pound
1	Hectoliter	-	100	Liters
1	Hectometer	-	100	Meters
1	Inch	-	2.540	Centimeters
1	Kilogram	-	980.665	Dynes
1	Kilogram	-	2.205	Lbs.
1	Kilogram	-	0.0011	Ton (short)
1	Kilogram	-	1000	Grams
1	Kiloliter	-	1000	Liters
1	Kilometer	-	100000	Centimeters
1	Kilometer	-	3281	Feet
1	Kilometer	-	1000	Meters
1	Kilometer	-	0.6214	Miles
1	Kilometer	-	1094	Yards
1	Liter	-	1000	Cubic centimeters
1	Liter	-	0.03531	Cubic foot
1	Liter	-	61.02	Cubic inches
1	Liter	-	0.2632	Gallon
1	Liter	-	2.113	Pints (liq.)
1	Liter	-	1.057	Quarts (liq.)
1	Meter	-	100	Centimeters
1	Meter	-	3.281	Feet
1	Meter	-	39.37	Inches
1	Meter	-	0.001	Kilometer
1	Meter	-	1000	Millimeters
1	Meter	-	1.094	Yards
1	Milligram	-	0.001	Gram

LUMBER :

Width (inches) times Thickness (inches) divided by
Twelve — Result to be multiplied by Length (feet)
equals Board Feet.

APPENDIX P

WEIGHT CONVERSION TABLES

Pounds Converted into Kilograms

Lbs.	Kilos	Lbs.	Kilos	Lbs.	Kilos	Lbs.	Kilos
1	.454	31	14.06	61	27.67	91	41.28
2	.907	32	14.51	62	28.12	92	41.73
3	1.361	33	14.97	63	28.58	93	42.18
4	1.814	34	15.42	64	29.03	94	42.64
5	2.268	35	15.88	65	29.48	95	43.09
6	2.722	36	16.33	66	29.94	96	43.54
7	3.175	37	16.78	67	30.39	97	44.00
8	3.629	38	17.24	68	30.84	98	44.45
9	4.082	39	17.69	69	31.30	99	44.91
10	4.536	40	18.14	70	31.75	100	45.36
11	4.990	41	18.60	71	32.21	200	90.72
12	5.443	42	19.05	72	32.66	300	136.08
13	5.897	43	19.50	73	33.11	400	181.44
14	6.350	44	19.96	74	33.57	500	226.80
15	6.804	45	20.41	75	34.02	600	272.16
16	7.257	46	20.87	76	34.47	700	317.51
17	7.711	47	21.32	77	34.93	800	362.87
18	8.165	48	21.77	78	35.38	900	408.23
19	8.618	49	22.23	79	35.83	1000	453.59
20	9.072	50	22.68	80	36.29	2000	907.18
21	9.525	51	23.13	81	36.74	3000	1360.78
22	9.979	52	23.59	82	37.19	4000	1814.37
23	10.430	53	24.04	83	37.65	5000	2267.96
24	10.890	54	24.49	84	38.10	6000	2721.55
25	11.340	55	24.95	85	38.56	7000	3175.15
26	11.790	56	25.40	86	39.01	8000	3628.74
27	12.250	57	25.85	87	39.46	9000	4082.33
28	12.700	58	26.31	88	39.92	10000	4535.92
29	13.150	59	26.76	89	40.37	15000	6803.89
30	13.610	60	27.22	90	40.82	20000	9071.85

Kilograms Converted into Pounds

Kilos	Lbs.	Kilos	Lbs.	Kilos	Lbs.	Kilos	Lbs.
1	2.2046	36	79.3664	71	156.5282	600	1,322.77
2	4.4092	37	81.5710	72	158.7328	700	1,543.24
3	6.6139	38	83.7756	73	160.9374	800	1,763.70
4	8.8185	39	85.9803	74	163.1421	900	1,984.16
5	11.0230	40	88.1850	75	165.3470	1,000	2,204.60
6	13.2277	41	90.3895	76	167.5513	1,100	2,425.08
7	15.4324	42	92.5941	77	169.7559	1,200	2,645.55
8	17.6370	43	94.7988	78	171.9605	1,300	2,866.00
9	19.8416	44	97.0034	79	174.1652	1,400	3,086.47
10	22.0460	45	99.2080	80	176.3700	1,500	3,306.90
11	24.2508	46	101.4126	81	178.5744	1,600	3,527.40
12	26.4555	47	103.6173	82	180.7790	1,700	3,747.86
13	28.6601	48	105.8219	83	182.9837	1,800	3,968.32
14	30.8647	49	108.0265	84	185.1883	1,900	4,188.78
15	33.0690	50	110.2300	85	187.3930	2,000	4,409.20
16	35.2740	51	112.4357	86	189.5975	3,000	6,613.90
17	37.4786	52	114.6404	87	191.8021	4,000	8,818.50
18	39.6832	53	116.8450	88	194.0068	5,000	11,023.10
19	41.8878	54	119.0496	89	196.2114	6,000	13,227.70
20	44.0920	55	121.2540	90	198.4160	7,000	15,432.40
21	46.2971	56	123.4589	91	200.6206	8,000	17,637.00
22	48.5017	57	125.6635	92	202.8253	9,000	19,841.60
23	50.7063	58	127.8681	93	205.0299	10,000	22,046.20
24	52.9109	59	130.0727	94	207.2345	11,000	24,250.80
25	55.1160	60	132.2770	95	209.4390	12,000	26,455.50
26	57.3202	61	134.4820	96	211.6437	13,000	28,660.00
27	59.5248	62	136.6866	97	213.8484	14,000	30,864.70
28	61.7294	63	138.8912	98	216.0530	15,000	33,069.30
29	63.9340	64	141.0958	99	218.2576	16,000	35,274.00
30	66.1390	65	143.3010	100	220.4620	17,000	37,478.60
31	68.3433	66	145.5051	200	440.9200	18,000	39,683.20
32	70.5479	67	147.7097	300	661.3900	19,000	41,887.80
33	72.7525	68	149.9143	400	881.8500	20,000	44,092.40
34	74.9572	69	152.1189	500	1102.3100		
35	77.1620	70	154.3240				

APPENDIX Q

DIGEST OF EXPORT REGULATIONS

U.S. DEPARTMENT OF COMMERCE - SESA, BUREAU OF THE CENSUS - DIBA, BUREAU OF EAST-WEST TRADE

Form Approved O.M.B. No. 41-R0397

SHIPPER'S EXPORT DECLARATION
OF SHIPMENTS FROM THE UNITED STATES
Export Shipments Are Subject To Inspection By U.S. Customs Service and or The Office of Export Control
READ CAREFULLY THE INSTRUCTIONS ON BACK TO AVOID DELAY AT SHIPPING POINT

CONFIDENTIAL – For use solely for official purposes authorized by the Secretary of Commerce. Use for unauthorized purposes is not permitted (Title 15, Sec. 30.91 (a) C.F.R. Sec. 7(c) Export Administration Act of 1969, as amended, P.L. 91-184).

Authentication (When required)

Declarations Should be Typewritten or Prepared in Ink

DO NOT USE THIS AREA	DISTRICT	PORT	COUNTRY (For Customs use only)

File No. (For Customs use only)

1. FROM (U.S. port of export)	2. METHOD OF TRANSPORTATION (Check one)
	☐ VESSEL (Incl. ferry) ☐ AIR ☐ OTHER (Specify)

2a. EXPORTING CARRIER (If vessel, give name of ship, flag and pier number. If air, give name of airline.)

3. EXPORTER (Principal or seller – licensee)   ADDRESS (Number, street, place, State)

4. AGENT OF EXPORTER (Forwarding agent)   ADDRESS (Number, street, place, State)

5. ULTIMATE CONSIGNEE   ADDRESS (Place, country)

6. INTERMEDIATE CONSIGNEE   ADDRESS (Place, country)

7. FOREIGN PORT OF UNLOADING (For vessel and air shipments only)   8. PLACE AND COUNTRY OF ULTIMATE DESTINATION (Not place of transshipment)

MARKS AND NOS. (9)	NUMBERS AND KIND OF PACKAGES DESCRIPTION OF COMMODITIES EXPORT LICENSE NUMBER OR GENERAL LICENSE SYMBOL (Describe commodities in sufficient detail to permit verification of the Schedule B commodity numbers assigned Do not use general terms) (10)	SHIPPING (Gross) WEIGHT IN POUNDS (REQUIRED FOR VESSEL AND AIR SHIPMENTS ONLY) (11)	SPECIFY D or R (12)	SCHEDULE B COMMODITY NO (Include Commodity Control List italicized digit, when required) (13)	NET QUANTITY SCHEDULE B UNITS (State unit) (14)	VALUE AT U.S. PORT OF EXPORT (Selling price or cost if not sold, including inland freight, insurance and other charges to U.S. port of export) (Nearest whole dollar, omit cents figures) (15)

VALIDATED LICENSE NO. _____ OR GENERAL LICENSE SYMBOL _____

16. BILL OF LADING OR AIR WAYBILL NUMBER   17. DATE OF EXPORTATION (Not required for shipments by vessel)

18. THE UNDERSIGNED HEREBY AUTHORIZES _____
TO ACT AS FORWARDING AGENT FOR EXPORT CONTROL AND CUSTOMS PURPOSES

(Name and address – Number, street, place, State)

EXPORTER _____ BY _____
(Duly authorized officer or employee) _____

▶ 19. I CERTIFY THAT ALL STATEMENTS MADE AND ALL INFORMATION CONTAINED IN THIS EXPORT DECLARATION ARE TRUE AND CORRECT. I AM AWARE OF THE PENALTIES PROVIDED FOR FALSE REPRESENTATION. (See paragraphs I (c) and (e) on reverse side.)

SIGNATURE _____ FOR _____
(Duly authorized officer or employee of exporter or named forwarding agent)

(Name of corporation or firm, and capacity of signer, e.g., secretary, export manager, etc.)

ADDRESS _____

▶ Declaration should be made by duly authorized officer or employee of exporter or of forwarding agent named by exporter.

aIf shipping weight is not available for each Schedule B item listed in column (13) included in one or more packages, insert the approximate gross weight for each Schedule B item. The total of these estimated weights should equal the actual weight of the entire package or packages.

bDesignate foreign merchandise (reexports) with an "F" and exports of domestic merchandise produced in the United States or changed in condition in the United States with a "D." (See instructions on reverse side.)

DO NOT USE THIS AREA

Form 7525-V (Unz Form 15-780) Export Forms, Hazardous Materials Labels, etc. can be purchased from Unz & Co., 190 Baldwin Ave., P.O. Box 308, Jersey City, N.J. 07303

FORM NO. 57525-V-ALT (Internal) (JAN. 1, 1971)

1. B/L NO.

U S DEPARTMENT OF COMMERCE - BUREAU OF THE CENSUS - BUREAU OF INTERNATIONAL COMMERCE

SHIPPER'S EXPORT DECLARATION

(See instructions on reverse side)

O M B. No. 41-R2544

DO NOT USE THIS AREA

2. EXPORTER (Principal or Seller-Invoicer and address)

5. DOCUMENT NO.

6. EXPORT REFERENCES

3. CONSIGNED TO

7. FORWARDING AGENT (Name and address — References)

8. POINT AND COUNTRY OF ORIGIN

4. NOTIFY PARTY/INTERMEDIATE CONSIGNEE (Name and address)

9. DOMESTIC ROUTING/EXPORT INSTRUCTIONS

10. PIER OR AIRPORT

11. EXPORT CARRIER (Vessel/airline, name and flag)

12. PORT OF LOADING

13. FOREIGN PORT OF UNLOADING (Vessel and air only)

14. FOR TRANSSHIPMENT TO

15. ONWARD INLAND ROUTING

DISTRICT | PORT | FLAG | COUNTRY

25. Customs Authorization (For customs use only.)

26. METHOD OF TRANSPORTATION (Check one)
☐ VESSEL ☐ OTHER (Specify)
☐ AIR

26. ULTIMATE CONSIGNEE (Give name and address if this party is not shown in item 3)

27. DATE OF EXPORTATION (not required for vessel shipments)

28. PLACE AND COUNTRY OF ULTIMATE DESTINATION

DECLARATION
should be made by authorized officer or employee of exporter or forwarding agent of exporter.

29. POWER OF ATTORNEY (see reverse side)

16. MARKS AND NUMBERS	17. NO. OF PKGS.	DESCRIPTION OF COMMODITIES in Schedule B detail, with export license number and expiration date (or General License symbol) below description of each item. See instructions IV on reverse side. (18)	GROSS WEIGHT (Pounds) (19)	MEASUREMENT (20)	NET QUANTITY (Schedule B unit) (21)	SCHEDULE B OR COMMODITY NO. (22)	NET QUANTITY (Schedule B unit) (23)	VALUE (Nearest whole dollar) (24)

CONFIDENTIAL — For use solely for official purposes authorized by the Secretary of Commerce. Use for unauthorized purposes is not permitted (Title 15, Sec. 301(a) C F R Export Administration Act of 1969, P.L. 91—184.

EXPORT SHIPMENTS ARE SUBJECT TO U S CUSTOMS INSPECTION

DO NOT USE THIS AREA

30. I certify that all statements and information contained in this export declaration are true and correct

_____ (Signature)

FOR _____ (Date)

WPBGE NO. 9881

Form 7525-V-Alt. Export Forms, Hazardous Materials Labels, etc. can be purchased from Unz & Co., 190 Baldwin Ave., P.O. Box 308, Jersey City, N.J. 07303

DO NOT DETACH THIS TOP PORTION FROM ORIGINAL, DUPLICATE, TRIPLICATE AND QUADRUPLICATE WHEN SUBMITTING APPLICATION

FORM DIB-622P (REV. 3-75)
(FORMERLY FC-419)
Form Approved: OMB No. 41-R 0735

CONFIDENTIAL — Information furnished herewith is deemed confidential and will not be published or disclosed except in accordance with provision of Section 7 (c) of the Export Administration Act of 1969, as amended.

U.S. DEPARTMENT OF COMMERCE
DOMESTIC AND INTERNATIONAL
BUSINESS ADMINISTRATION
BUREAU OF EAST-WEST TRADE
OFFICE OF EXPORT ADMINISTRATION
WASHINGTON, D.C. 20230

**APPLICATION FOR
EXPORT LICENSE**

DATE RECEIVED *(Leave Blank)*

CASE NO. *(Leave Blank)*

DATE OF APPLICATION

APPLICANT'S TELEPHONE NO.

1. APPLICANT'S NAME

STREET ADDRESS

CITY, STATE, ZIP CODE

3. ULTIMATE CONSIGNEE IN FOREIGN COUNTRY

NAME

STREET ADDRESS

CITY AND COUNTRY

5. COUNTRY OF ULTIMATE DESTINATION

2. PURCHASER IN FOREIGN COUNTRY
(If same as ultimate consignee, state "SAME AS ITEM 3"; if same as intermediate consignee, state "SAME AS ITEM 4.")

NAME

STREET ADDRESS

CITY AND COUNTRY

4. INTERMEDIATE CONSIGNEE IN FOREIGN COUNTRY.
(If none, state "NONE"; if unknown, state "UNKNOWN.")

NAME

STREET ADDRESS

CITY AND COUNTRY

6. APPLICANT'S REFERENCE NUMBER

7. (a) QUANTITY TO BE SHIPPED

(b) COMMODITY DESCRIPTION AS GIVEN IN COMMODITY CONTROL LIST *(Include characteristics such as basic ingredients, composition, type, size, gauge, grade, horsepower, etc.)*

(c) EXPORT CONTROL COMMODITY NUMBER AND PROCESSING NUMBER

(d) TOTAL SELLING PRICE AND POINT OF DELIVERY
(Indicate F.O.B., F.A.S., C.I.F., etc.)

UNIT PRICE	TOTAL PRICE
TOTAL	

Application for Export License—Form DIB-622P (front). Form DIB-623P accompanies this form (see page 620).

618

8 FILL IN IF PERSON OTHER THAN APPLICANT IS AUTHORIZED TO RECEIVE LICENSE

NAME

STREET
ADDRESS

CITY STATE
ZIP CODE

9 IF APPLICANT IS NOT THE PRODUCER OF COMMODITY TO BE EXPORTED GIVE NAME AND ADDRESS OF SUPPLIER
(If unknown, state "UNKNOWN.")

10 END USE OF COMMODITIES COVERED BY THIS APPLICATION
DESCRIBE FULLY

11 IF APPLICANT IS NOT EXPORTING FOR HIS OWN ACCOUNT GIVE NAME AND ADDRESS OF FOREIGN PRINCIPAL AND EXPLAIN FULLY

12 ADDITIONAL INFORMATION (Attach separate sheet if more space is needed)

13 APPLICANT'S CERTIFICATION. The undersigned applicant hereby makes application for a license to export and certifies as follows: That all statements herein, and in any documents or attachments submitted in support hereof, are true and correct to the best of his knowledge and belief, and that (a) he has read the instructions on the fifth copy of this application and is familiar with the U.S. Department of Commerce Export Administration Regulations; (b) this application conforms therewith and in any regulations; (c) under Item 14 (complete the purchaser) the ultimate consignee item 5 from the purchaser, ultimate consignee conforms or through his or their agents abroad; (d) all parties to the export transaction, the exact commodities and quantities, or the exact technical data, and all other terms of the order and other facts of the export transaction are fully and accurately reflected herein; (e) documents and records evidencing the order and other facts of the export transaction to which this application relates will be retained by him for 2 years from whichever is later, the time of (i) the export from the United States, or (ii) any known reexport, transshipment, or diversion, or (iii) any other termination of the transaction, whether formally in writing or by any other means, and made available to the Department of Commerce upon demand; (f) any material or substantive changes in the terms of the order or other facts of the export transaction as reflected in this application or any certification made in connection therewith, whether the application is still under consideration or after a license has been granted, will be reported promptly by him to the Department of Commerce; and (g) if the license is granted, he will be strictly accountable for its use in accordance with the Department of Commerce Export Administration Regulations and all terms and conditions specified on the face of the license.

Type
or
Print

SIGN
HERE
IN INK

(Applicant (Same as Item 1))   (Signature of person authorized to execute this application.)

Type
or
Print

(Name and title of person whose signature appears on the line to the left)

14 ORDER PARTY'S CERTIFICATION (See § 372.6 (c) of the Export Administration Regulations). The undersigned order party certifies to the truth and correctness of Item 13 (d) above, and that he has no information concerning the export transaction that is inconsistent with, or undisclosed by the application and agrees to comply with Items 13 (e) and 13 (f) above.

Type
or
Print

SIGN
HERE
IN INK

(Order Party)   (Signature of person authorized to sign for the Order Party)

Type
or
Print

(Name and title of person whose signature appears on the line to the left)

This license application and any license issued pursuant thereto are expressly subject to all rules and regulations of the Department of Commerce. Making any false statement or concealing any material fact in connection with this application or altering in any way the validated license issued, is punishable by imprisonment or fine, or both, and by denial of export privileges under the Export Administration Act of 1969, as amended, and any other Federal statutes.

FOR OFFICIAL USE ONLY

ACTION TAKEN	VALIDITY PERIOD	AUTHORITY	RATING	DV	RE EXPORT SUPPORT DOCUMENT	TECH DATA	TYPE OF LICENSE		
APPROVED									
REJECTED	MONTHS		END USE CHECK						
DOCUMENTATION							(Licensing officer)	(No.)	(Date)
							(Review officer)		(Date)

NOTE: Submit the first four copies of this application, Form DIB-622P (with top stub attached), to the Office of Export Administration, Room 1617M, Domestic and International Business Administration, U.S. Department of Commerce, Washington, D.C. 20230, retaining the quintuplicate copy of the form for your files. Remove the long carbon sheet from in front of the quintuplicate copy. Do not remove any other carbon sheets. See Special Instructions on back of quintuplicate. Reproduction of this form is permissable, providing that content, format, size, and color of paper and ink are the same.

ORIGINAL
OEA FILE COPY

Application for Export License—Form DIB-622P (front—continued)

INSTRUCTIONS¹ GOVERNING THE FILING AND USE OF
FORM DIB-622P, APPLICATION FOR EXPORT LICENSE

GENERAL INSTRUCTIONS

A. This form is to be used in applying to the U.S. Department of Commerce for a validated license where required, as authorization for the export of commodities or technical data. Applications must be submitted to the Office of Export Administration, Room 1617M, Domestic and International Business Administration, Bureau of East-West Trade, Department of Commerce, Washington, D.C. 20230. The under lined duplicate and the quintuplicate copies of this form must be submitted with the top stub attached. The quintuplicate copy should be retained by the applicant or agent.

B. An applicant shall not submit a duplicate application to cover any transaction for which an application for export license is still pending before the Department of Commerce.

C. Applications may be made only by a person, who, in fact, is the exporter. No application of any person not subject to the jurisdiction of the United States will be considered unless such application is made on his behalf by an authorized agent in the United States. The applicant to whom the license is issued becomes the licensee and will be held strictly accountable for the use of the license. Exports under a validated license may be made only for the account of the licensee.

D. Any attempt to export commodities or technical data other than as authorized on the license, or any alteration of a license except by a duly authorized officer of the Government, is punishable under appropriate acts of Congress.

E. There must be shown on each application the names of all parties participating on their own account in the proposed export transaction: the applicant who will be come the licensee as exporter; the ultimate consignee as the person in the country of ultimate destination who is to receive the export for his own account, and the intermediate consignee as the person who receives the export or documents for delivery to the purchaser or ultimate consignee. If the purchaser (the party to the transaction with the applicant) is not the same person as the ultimate consignee (the party actually to receive the commodities for the designated end use), the names and addresses of both persons must be given. ALL PARTIES IN INTEREST, AS KNOWN TO THE APPLICANT, MUST BE DISCLOSED, whether principals or agents, including order parties, brokers, financing parties, representatives, or other agents. Identify and describe the role of each such party in the transaction.

F. Except as otherwise provided by the Department of Commerce Export Administration Regulations, an application for an export license shall not be filed with the Department of Commerce unless and until the applicant or the party has documentary evidence of an existing order for export from the purchaser named therein for the stated commodities, quantities, and values, or for the stated technical data.

G. In submitting this application, the applicant should make certain that the provisions relating to individual or other validated licenses, and the special provisions relating to the particular commodities and technical data, or countries of destination set forth in the Export Administration Regulations have been complied with.

H. Complete and detailed instructions for filing out and filing an application for export license and other export control matters may be found in the Export Administration Regulations.

SPECIAL INSTRUCTIONS

(Answer all questions fully. If more space is needed, attach supplemental sheets.)

Enter the date the application is completed, and applicant's telephone number.

Item 1. The name and address of the applicant must be entered. The Postal Zip Code must be included as it is an integral part of the address. Failure to include ZIP Code on an application may result in delay in mailing of the export license. See General Instructions, paragraphs B, C, D, and E above.

Item 2. The person named as purchaser should be the person abroad who has entered into the transaction with the applicant or order party. If such person is not the same as the ultimate consignee, applicant should state "Same as Item 3"; if such person is the same as the intermediate consignee, applicant should state "Same as Item 4." If no entry is made in this item, the applicant represents that the ultimate consignee is the foreign purchaser.

alongside of Schedule C code number 484, or it may be "Crete" which is listed as a destination in the breakdown under "Greece." However, when "Crete" is designated, reexport may not be made to any other destination under "Greece," whereas, when "Greece" is designated, reexport may be made to any of the destinations listed under that number.

EXPORTERS ARE RESPONSIBLE FOR PLACING A STATEMENT OF ULTIMATE DESTINATION AND PROHIBITION AGAINST DIVERSION ON BILL OF LADING, OR AIR WAYBILL, AND COMMERCIAL INVOICE FOR VARIOUS EXPORT SHIPMENTS. OMISSION OF THE STATEMENT OR UNAUTHORIZED DIVERSION OF COMMODITIES FROM COUNTRY OF FINAL ULTIMATE DESTINATION, NOT IN ACCORDANCE WITH THE STATEMENT, ARE VIOLATIONS OF THE EXPORT ADMINISTRATION REGULATIONS SUBJECT TO DENIAL OF EXPORT PRIVILEGES AND TO CIVIL AND CRIMINAL PENALTIES.

Item 6. The applicant's reference number may be used for applicant's convenience.

Item 7. (a) Give the quantity to be shipped, using units specified in the Commodity Control List. If dots (. . .) are set forth in the unit column the application should show the unit of quantity commonly used in the trade (§ 399.1).

Item 7. (b) Commodities must be described in terms which correspond with the commodity descriptions in the Commodity Control List (Part 399). Additional details as prescribed by the Export Administration Regulations must be furnished to the extent necessary for identification of the specific items so classified. Include characteristics shown on the Commodity Control List such as basic ingredients, composition, type, size, gauge, grade, horsepower, etc. Where the Commodity Control List entry states "specify by name," all of the commodities to be included in the shipment must be listed by name on the application.

Item 7. (c) The Export Control Commodity Number and Processing Number must be shown in this column. All Commodities on a single application must have the same Processing Number, unless otherwise provided in the Export Administration Regulations.

Item 7. (d) Unit price should be shown except where a large variety of products within a single Export Control Commodity Number makes such a breakdown extremely difficult. In such cases only total price need be shown. The applicant must show total price in the customary form of quotation such as f.o.b. (factory), f.a.s. (named port), c.i.f. other form. The particular form of price quotation must be specified. The amounts entered in the total price column on the application shall be rounded to the nearest whole dollar, except where the actual total value is less than $1. For example, if the total price for a commodity listed on the application is $2,375.49, it should be listed as $2,375. $2,375.50 should be listed as $2,376. $0.78 should be listed as $1 and $0.38 should be listed, unchanged, as $0.38. Where the normal trade practice in a given commodity makes it impracticable to establish a firm contract price, the precise terms upon which the price is to be ascertained and from which the contract price may be objectively determined must be stated on the application. A mere statement by the exporter of "market price at the time of delivery of shipment" or other such general statement of price will not be acceptable.

Item 8. The name and address of the person, other than applicant, authorized by the applicant to receive the license, if issued, should be entered. The Postal ZIP Code must be included as it is an integral part of the address. Failure to include ZIP Code on an application may result in delay in mailing of the export license. The license will be transmitted only to the applicant or to the person designated on the license application as the person entitled to receive the license on behalf of the licensee.

Item 9. Leave blank if applicant is the producer of the commodities to be exported. Applicant so represents, where item is blank. If applicant is not the producer, give supplier's name and address, or state "Unknown," if unknown.

Item 10. End use of commodities or technical data covered by this application will be an important factor in determining issuance of license. Statement by ultimate consignee (end purchaser, if not same) as to ultimate destination and end use must be submitted for certain exports as required by the Export Administration Regulations. Applicant's reference to such statement does not relieve him of responsibility to fully disclose any additional or different information he may know. APPLICANT MUST INDICATE CLEARLY THE END USE INTENDED BY THE ULTIMATE CONSIGNEE.

Form DIB-622P (back). Application for Export License.

FILE THIS APPLICATION FORM DIB 622P
TO GET AN EXPORT LICENSE

Check the following before submitting the application

Did you fill in all required items on the form completely?

Did you follow instructions on the back of the form?

Did you furnish documents, when required, such as, import certificate, consignee/purchaser statements, etc.?

Did you sign the form? Did the Order Party sign, if required?

IF YOUR APPLICATION IS INCOMPLETE, IT WILL BE RETURNED TO YOU FOR
THE NECESSARY INFORMATION AND/OR DOCUMENTATION

(REMOVE THIS SHORT CHECK LIST SHEET AT PERFORATION)

Form DIB-622P (back, continued). Application for Export License.

621

THIS SPACE FOR OEA USE	APPLICANT'S NAME AND ADDRESS	
DATE OF APPLICATION		
COMMODITY DESCRIPTION	EXPORT CONTROL COMMODITY NO.	PROCESSING NO.
COUNTRY OF ULTIMATE DESTINATION		
APPLICANT'S REFERENCE NO.	**NOTE**: Complete every item on this form and attach with paper clip to upper left corner of application (Form DIB-622P).	

Form Approved; OMB No. 41-R1191.5

FORM **DIB-623P** (FORMERLY FC-420)　　　　　　　U.S. DEPARTMENT OF COMMERCE
(3-74)　　　　　　　　　　　DOMESTIC AND INTERNATIONAL BUSINESS ADMINISTRATION
USCOMM-DC　　　　　　　　　　　　　　　OFFICE OF EXPORT ADMINISTRATION
66376-P74　　**APPLICATION PROCESSING CARD**

Form DIB-623P—to accompany Form DIB-622P (see pages 618-621)

TABLE OF GENERAL LICENSES

General License Symbol	Definition or Purpose	Type of Commodities Covered [1]	Destinations	Specific Reference in Export Administration Regulations
G-DEST	Shipments of any commodity listed on the Commodity Control List to any destination for which a validated license is not required by the information in the Commodity Control List column titled "Validated License Required for Country Groups Shown Below."	Commodities indicated by information in Commodity Control List.	Destinations indicated by information in Commodity Control List.	§ 371.3
GIT	Intransit shipments	All commodities, except certain defined categories.	Country Groups Q, T, V, and Cuba.'	§ 371.4
GLV	Shipments of limited value..	Commodities valued within the GLV dollar value limits specified in Commodity Control List.	Country Groups Q, T, and V.	§ 371.5

General License Symbol	Definition or Purpose	Type of Commodities Covered [1]	Destinations	Specific Reference in Export Administration Regulations
BAGGAGE	Shipments of personal and household effects, certain vehicles, and personally-owned tools of trade.	Commodities within defined general categories not identified by the code letter "A," "B," "C," or "M" following the Export Control Commodity Number on Commodity Control List.	All destinations.	§ 371.6(a)
		Commodities within defined general categories identified by the code letter "A," "B," "C," or "M" following the Export Control Commodity Number on Commodity Control List.	Country Groups Q, T, and V.	§ 371.6(a)
GLD	Shipments of dunnage, in usual and reasonable quantities.	Types of commodities used for dunnage.	All destinations except Country Group Z (excluding Cuba).	§ 371.8
SHIP STORES ...	Shipments of ship stores for use on outgoing and immediate return voyage of vessels; necessary equipment and spare parts for proper operation of departing vessel.	Food, bunker fuel, and other commodities specified as ship stores, with stated exceptions.	All destinations except Country Group Z.[2]	§ 371.9
PLANE STORES..	Shipments of plane stores for use on outgoing and immediate return trip of aircraft; necessary equipment and spare parts for proper operation of departing plane.	Food, fuel, and other commodities specified as plane stores, with stated exceptions.	All destinations except Country Group Z (excluding Cuba).[2]	§ 371.10
CREW	Shipments by members of crew of usual and reasonable kinds and quantities of personal and household effects under prescribed conditions.	Clothes, adornments, medicines, toiletries, food, souvenirs, games, hand tools, and similar personal effects; furniture, household effects, and household furnishings; and their containers.	All destinations except Country Group Z.[3]	§ 371.11
RCS	Shipments to Canadian and U.S. vessels, planes, and airline installations or agents located abroad.	Food, fuel, and other commodities needed for use by or on such carriers.	Country Groups Q, S, T, V, W, and Cuba.	§ 371.12

[1] Except for exports made under the provisions of General License GTDA (see § 379.3), no export related to nuclear weapons, nuclear explosive devices, or nuclear testing, as described in § 378.1, regardless of type, and no export of any electronic, mechanical, or other devices primarily useful for surreptitious interception of wire or oral communications (see § 376.13), may be made under the provisions of any general license.

[2] Under specified circumstances, exports under this general license are not permitted for use on planes registered in or under control of certain Country Group Q, W or Y countries.

[3] Crews' effects may not be exported from the United States to any destination in Country Group Z or on a carrier registered in a Country Group Z country.

General License Symbol	Definition or Purpose	Type of Commodities Covered [1]	Destinations	Specific Reference in Export Administration Regulations
GUS	Shipments to members of U.S. Armed Services and civilian personnel of U.S. government for personal use. Shipments to U.S. government agencies for official use.	Commodities within defined categories.	All destinations.	§ 371.13
GLC	Shipments of commercial vehicles operated by private or common carriers or certain commercial airlines between the U.S. and other countries.	Civil aircraft.	Country Groups Q, T, V, W, and Cuba.	§ 371.14(b)
		Trucks, buses, trailers, railroad rolling stock and other commercial vehicles.	Country Groups Q, T, V, and W.	§ 371.14(c)
GTF-US	Shipments of commodities imported for display at exhibitions or trade fairs.	Commodities imported for display at exhibitions or trade fairs, under stated conditions.	All destinations except Country Groups S and Z.[2]	§ 371.15
GLR	Shipments of commodities returned to countries from which imported. Shipments of commodities returned to the country of manufacture or, the country from which imported for repair or overhaul. Shipment for replacement of defective or unacceptable commodities.	Specified types of commodities.	Country Groups Q, T, and V.[3]	§ 371.17
GIFT	Shipments of gift parcels from individual donors to or to religious, charitable, or educational organizations for use of donee or donee's immediate family.	Commodities not identified by the code letter "A," "B," "C," or "M" following the Export Control Commodity Number on Commodity Control List, up to a total of $100 in one parcel, ordinarily sent as gifts; such as food, clothing, medicines, toiletries, and drugs, with stated exceptions.	All destinations except Country Group Z (excluding Cuba).	§ 371.18
GATS	Authorizes departure from U.S. under its own power of civil aircraft on temporary sojourn.	Civil aircraft of foreign registry.	Country Groups Q, T, and V, and Cuba.	§ 371.19(a)
		Civil aircraft of U. S. registry.	Country Groups Q, T, and V.	§ 371.19(b)

[1] Except for exports made under the provisions of General License GTDA (see § 379.3), no export related to nuclear weapons, nuclear explosive devices, or nuclear testing, as described in § 378.1, regardless of type, and no export of any electronic, mechanical, or other devices primarily useful for surreptitious interception of wire or oral communications (see § 376.13), may be made under the provisions of any general license.

[2] Under specified circumstances, exports under this general license are not permitted to Country Group Q, W, or Y.

[3] Under specified circumstances, exports under this general license are permitted to Country Group W or Y.

General License Symbol	Definition or Purpose	Type of Commodities Covered [1]	Destinations	Specific Reference in Export Administration Regulations
GMS	Shipments of commodities sold by the U. S. Department of Defense to a foreign government under the provisions of the Mutual Security Act of 1954, P.L. 665, 83rd Congress.	All commodities.	Country Groups T and V.	§ 371.20
GTDA	Shipments of generally available technical data.	Technical data generally available to the public, scientific and educational data, and certain data contained in an application for foreign filing of a patent.	All destinations.	§ 379.3
GTDR	Shipments of restricted technical data.	Technical data not exportable under General License GTDA but exportable subject to specified restrictions.	Country Groups T and V.[2]	§ 379.4
GTE	Temporary exports for use abroad and return to United States of certain commodities.	Specified types of commodities.	Country Groups T and V.	§ 371.22(b)
		Specified types of commodities not identified by the code letter "A," "B," "C," or "M" following the Export Control Commodity Number on Commodity Control List.	Country Groups Q, W, and Y.	§ 371.22(c)

[1] Except for exports made under the provisions of General License GDTA (see § 379.3), no export related to nuclear weapons, nuclear explosive devices, or nuclear testing, as described in § 378.1, regardless of type, and no export of any electronic, mechanical, or other devices primarily useful for surreptitious interception of wire or oral communications (see § 376.13), may be made under the provisions of any general license.

[2] Under specified circumstances, exports under this general license are permitted to Country Group W or Y.

EXPEDITE SHIPMENTS BY COMPLETING THIS FORM CORRECTLY FOLLOW THESE SPECIFIC INSTRUCTIONS

1. Ultimate Consignee must be person abroad who is actually to receive the material for the disposition or use shown in Item 4. A bank, freight forwarder, forwarding agent, or other intermediary is not acceptable as an ultimate consignee.

2. Check box "a", if this is a single transaction, and give the name of person or firm in the U.S. with whom order was placed.
   Check box "b", if this is a continuing relationship that is likely to involve a series of orders for the same types of commodities for the same end-user and same end-use. Give the name of the person or firm in the U.S. with whom the orders will be placed.
   Show earlier but not later termination date than June 30 of the second year after the signing of this form, if desired.

3. Describe commodities in detail wherever possible, giving particulars such as name, basic ingredients, composition, type, size, gauge, grade, horsepower, etc. Descriptions should be broad enough, however, to include all commodities to which the statement applies.

4. Check "a", "b", "c", "d", and "e", as appropriate, and fill in the required information.

FORM DIB-629P
(Consolidation of DIB-626P and DIB-437P)

OMB No. 41-R2961 Approval Expires April, 1978

U.S. DEPARTMENT OF COMMERCE
DOMESTIC AND INTERNATIONAL BUSINESS ADMINISTRATION
OFFICE OF EXPORT ADMINISTRATION

STATEMENT BY ULTIMATE CONSIGNEE AND PURCHASER

GENERAL INSTRUCTIONS - This form must be submitted by the importer (ultimate consignee shown in Item 1) and by the overseas buyer or purchaser, to the U.S. exporter or seller with whom the order for the commodities described in Item 3 is placed. This completed statement will be used to support one or more export license applications to the U.S. Department of Commerce. All items on this form must be completed. Where the information required is unknown or the item does not apply, write in the appropriate word "UNKNOWN" or "NOT APPLICABLE." If more space is needed, attach an additional copy of this form or sheet of paper signed as in Item 8. Submit form within 180 days from latest date in Item 8.

1. Ultimate consignee name and address

Name

Street and number

City and Country

Reference (if desired)

2. Request (Check one)

a. ☐ We request that this statement be considered a part of the application for export license filed by
_____ U.S. exporter or U.S. person with whom we have placed our order (order party)
for export to us of the commodities described in Item 3.

b. ☐ We request that this statement be considered a part of every application for export license filed by
_____ U.S. exporter or U.S. person with whom we have placed or may place our order (order party)
for export to us of the type of commodities described in this statement, during the period ending June 10 of the second year after the signing of this form, or on _____

3. Commodities

We have placed or may place orders with the person or firm named in Item 2 for the commodities indicated below:

COMMODITY DESCRIPTION	QUANTITY	VALUE

4. Disposition or use of commodities by ultimate consignee named in Item 1 (Check and complete the appropriate box(es))

We certify that the commodity(ies) listed in Item 3:

a. ☐ Will be used by us (as capital equipment) in the form in which received in a manufacturing process in the country named in Item 1 and will not be reexported or incorporated into an end product.

b. ☐ Will be processed or incorporated by us into the following product(s) _____ (Specify)
   to be manufactured in the country named in Item 1 for distribution in _____ (Name)
   _____ of country or countries)

c. ☐ Will be resold by us in the form in which received in the country named in Item 1 for use or consumption therein.
   The specific end-user by my customer will be _____ (Specify, if known)

d. ☐ Will be reexported by us in the form in which received to _____ (Name of country(ies))

e. ☐ Other (Describe fully)

NOTE: If Item (d) is checked, acceptance of this form by the Office of Export Administration as a supporting document for license applications shall not be construed as an authorization to reexport the commodities to which the form applies unless specific approval has been obtained from the Office of Export Administration for such reexport.

(Reproduction of this form is permissible, providing that content, format, size and color of paper are the same)

Please continue form and sign certification on reverse side.

USCOMM-DC 46506-P78

Form DIB-629P (front)—Statement by Ultimate Consignee and Purchaser

5. Nature of business of ultimate consignee named in Item 1 and his relationship with U.S. exporter named in Item 2.

a. The nature of our usual business is — _____ (Broker, distributor, fabricator, manufacturer, wholesaler, retailer, etc.)

b. Our business relationship with the U.S. exporter is — _____ (Contractual, franchise, exclusive distributor, distributor,

wholesaler, continuing and regular individual transaction business, etc.)

and we have had this business relationship for _____ years.

6. Additional information (Any other material facts which will be of value in considering applications for licenses covered by this statement.)

7. Assistance in preparing statement/Names of persons other than employees of consignee or purchaser who assisted in the preparation of this statement.)

8. CERTIFICATION OF ULTIMATE CONSIGNEE AND PURCHASER (This item is to be signed by the ultimate consignee shown in Item 1 and by the purchaser where the latter is not the same as the ultimate consignee. Where the ultimate consignee is unknown, this item should be signed by the purchaser.)

We certify that all of the facts contained in this statement are true and correct to the best of our knowledge and belief and we do not know of any additional facts which are inconsistent with the above statement. We shall promptly send a supplemental statement to the person named in Item 2, disclosing any change of facts or intentions set forth in this statement which occurs after the statement has been prepared and forwarded. Except as specifically authorized by the U.S. Export Administration Regulations, or by prior written approval of the U.S. Department of Commerce, we will not reexport, resell, or otherwise dispose of any commodities listed in Item 3 above: (1) to any country not approved for export as brought to our attention by means of a bill of lading, commercial invoice, or any other means; or (2) to any person if there is reason to believe that it will result directly or indirectly, in disposition of the commodities contrary to the representations made in this statement or contrary to U.S. Export Administration Regulations.

Ultimate Consignee   Purchaser

Signature   Signature
in ink _____   in ink _____
      (Signature of official of ultimate consignee)   (Signature of official of purchaser firm)

Type or   Type or
print _____   print _____
      (Name and title of official of ultimate consignee)   (Name and title of official of purchaser firm)

Date _____   _____
                                                             (Name of purchaser firm)

                                               Type or
                                               print _____

                                               Date _____

9. CERTIFICATION FOR USE OF U.S. EXPORTER in certifying that any correction, addition, or alteration on this form was made prior to the signing by the ultimate consignee and purchaser in Item 8.

We certify that no correction, additions, or alterations were made on this form by us after the form was signed by the (ultimate consignee) (purchaser).

Type or   Sign here
print _____   in ink _____
      (Name of exporter firm)   (Signature of person authorized to certify for exporter)

                                               Type or
       _____   print _____
       (Date signed)   (Name and title of person signing this document)

The making of any false statement, the concealment of any material fact, or failure to file required information may result in denial of participation in U.S. exports. Notarial or Governmental certification is not required.

FORM DIB-629P
(REV. 11-70)   (Consolidation of DIB-629P and DIB-629TP)

Form DIB-629P (back)

5. Complete both "a." and "b.".

6. Supply any other information not appearing elsewhere on the form such as other parties to the transaction.

7. Name all persons, other than employees of consignee or purchaser, who assisted in the preparation of this form.

8. This item is to be signed by both the ultimate consignee and the purchaser if the purchaser is not the same as the ultimate consignee. Only an official of the ultimate consignee named in Item 1, and/or official of the purchaser should complete this item. These must be responsible officials who are authorized to bind the firms of the ultimate consignee and purchaser to the commitments in this statement. Be sure to sign in ink, and type or print the name and title of the person signing, as well as the name of the purchaser firm if the purchaser has signed the statement.

9. This item is reserved for use by U. S. exporter where additions, corrections, or alterations appear on the form.

THIS FLAP SHOULD BE DETACHED BEFORE SUBMITTING FORM.

627

Budget Bureau No. 41-R2493

FORM IA-543 (7-69)	U.S. DEPARTMENT OF COMMERCE BUREAU OF INTERNATIONAL COMMERCE OFFICE OF EXPORT CONTROL	1. Name and address of firm *(Street, City, State and Zip code)*

**SERVICE SUPPLY (SL) LICENSE
STATEMENT BY U.S. EXPORTER**

Instructions: All items on this form must be completed. The signature required in item 7 must be that of an official of the exporter's firm. If more space is needed, attach an additional copy of this form or add a page signed as in item 7.

Reference No. *(If desired)*

2. Request

I(We) request that this statement be considered a part of my(our) application (Reference No. as above) for export license submitted to the Office of Export Control covering exports of commodities described in Item 4 below to the destinations listed in Item 3d below for use solely in servicing U.S. equipment, as defined in Paragraph 373.7 of the Export Control Regulations.

3. Nature of Business

a. The nature of my(our) usual business is _____
(Specify as aircraft manufacturer, machine manufacturer, merchant exporter, etc.)

_____

b. Number of years in business: _____

c. Types of equipment to be serviced: _____
(Specify as computers, aircraft, radar, scientific Instruments, etc.)

_____

d. Destinations to be served: _____
(Specify by country)

4. Commodity Description - I(We) expect to export the following commodities as spare or replacement parts: (describe in general terms; e.g. electronic parts, communications parts and equipment, parts for scientific instruments and apparatus, etc.)

5. Comments (Add any additional pertinent facts relating to the servicing activities or nature of business.)

USCOMM-DC 20052-P69

Service Supply License Statement by U.S. Exporter

6. **Assistance in preparing statement** (Specify names and addresses of persons other than employees of the firm who assisted in the preparation of this statement.) If assistance has not been obtained, enter the word "None."

7. **Certification**

I(We) certify that:

a. I(We) will export the spare or replacement parts described in Item 4 for the sole purpose of servicing the equipment described in Item 3c in the destination(s) listed in Item 3d. Servicing this equipment is a normal function of my(our) firm and these commodities will not be resold or used for any other purpose.

b. The commodities described in Item 4 will not be exported to any person or firm listed on the Office of Export Control's Table of Denial and Probation Orders, or to Communist China, North Korea, the Communist-Controlled area of Vietnam, Cuba, or Southern Rhodesia. Further, these commodities will not be exported to any destination under the SL Procedure without the specific prior authorization of the Office of Export Control if such commodities will improve or change the basic design characteristics of the commodities to be serviced.

c. The equipment to be serviced was manufactured and/or exported by my(our) firm or by its subsidiary.

d. I(We) will export from the United States the commodities described in Item 4 to the USSR, or to any other country in Eastern Europe (including Poland and Rumania but excluding Yugoslavia), only if the commodities are for use as spare or replacement parts. Such commodities will not be shipped in a quantity in excess of immediate current requirements to service the equipment; and any commodities identified by the symbol "A" on the Commodity Control List published by the Office of Export Control will not be used on any equipment also identified by the symbol "A", and any shipment of such commodities will not exceed $2,000.00 in value.

e. No commodity excluded from the SL Procedure under the Export Control Regulations will be exported to any consignee in any destination under this procedure.

f. I(We) will maintain records of all exports of the commodities referred to in paragraph a of this certification in the detail set forth in the Export Control Regulations, for a period of three years from the date the commodities are exported. These records will be available for inspection upon demand, by the Office of Export Control or by any other U.S. Government agency. Further, I(we) agree to submit a monthly report on all exports to Eastern European countries of commodities as required by Paragraph 373.7(j) of the Export Control Regulations.

g. I(We) certify that all of the facts contained in this statement are true and correct to the best of my(our) knowledge and belief and I(we) do not know of any additional facts which are inconsistent with the above statement. A supplemental statement will be sent to the Office of Export Control disclosing any change of facts or intentions set forth in this statement which occurs after the statement has been prepared and forwarded.

_____   _____
(Signature of official of firm named in Item 1)   (Date of signing)

Type or print _____
(Name and title of person signing this document)

DO NOT WRITE BELOW THIS LINE - FOR OFFICIAL USE ONLY

Not approved unless the official validation stamp appears hereon.	Action taken by U.S. Department of Commerce:
	☐ Approved _____ (Expiration Date)
	☐ Not Approved _____ (SL License No.)
	U.S. Department of Commerce Bureau of International Commerce Office of Export Control Washington, D.C. 20230
	_____ (Date)

FORM IA-543 (7-69)   USCOMM-DC 20052-P69

Service Supply License Statement by U.S. Exporter (cont'd)

DISTRICT OFFICES OF THE U. S. DEPARTMENT OF COMMERCE

State	Address	Telephone Area Code & Number
ALABAMA	Birmingham (35205), Suite 200, 908 S. 20th St.	205-325-3327
ALASKA	Anchorage (99501), Rm. 412, Hill Bldg., 632 6th Ave.	907-272-6531
ARIZONA	Phoenix (85004), Rm. 508, Greater Arizona Savings Bldg., 112 N. Central Ave.	602-261-3285
CALIFORNIA	Los Angeles (90024), Rm. 11201, Federal Bldg., 11000 Wilshire Blvd.	213-824-7591
	San Francisco (94102), Federal Bldg., 450 Golden Gate Ave.	415-556-5864
COLORADO	Denver (80202), Rm. 161, New Customhouse, 19th & Stout Sts.	303-837-3246
CONNECTICUT	Hartford (06103), Rm. 610-B, Federal Office Bldg., 450 Main St.	203-244-3530
FLORIDA	Jacksonville (32207), Suite 119, Woodcock Dr.	904-791-2796
	Miami (33130), Rm. 821, City National Bank Bldg., 25 West Flagler St.	305-350-5267
GEORGIA	Atlanta (30303), Suite 523, 1401 Peachtree St., N.E.	404-526-6000
	Savannah (31402), Rm. 235, U.S. Courthouse & Post Office Bldg., 125-29 Bull St.	912-232-4321
HAWAII	Honolulu (96813), Rm. 286, Alexander Young Bldg., 1015 Bishop St.	808-546-8694
ILLINOIS	Chicago (60603), Rm. 1406, Mid-Continental Plaza Bldg., 55 E. Monroe St.	312-353-4400
IOWA	Des Moines (50309), Rm. 609, Federal Bldg., 210 Walnut St.	515-284-4222
LOUISIANA	New Orleans (70130), Rm. 909, Federal Office Bldg. (South), 610 South St.	504-527-6546
MARYLAND	Baltimore (21202), Rm. 415, U.S. Customhouse, Gay & Lombard Sts.	301-962-3560
MASSACHUSETTS	Boston (02116), 10th Floor, 441 Stuart St.	617-223-2312
MICHIGAN	Detroit (48226), Rm. 445, Federal Bldg.	313-226-6088
MINNESOTA	Minneapolis (55401), Rm. 306, Federal Bldg., 110 S. 4th St.	612-725-2133
MISSOURI	Kansas City (64106), Rm. 1840, 601 E. 12th St.	816-374-3141
	St. Louis (63103), Rm. 2511, Federal Bldg., 1520 Market St.	314-622-4243
NEVADA	Reno (89502), Rm. 2028, Federal Bldg., 300 Booth St.	702-784-5203
NEW JERSEY	Newark (07102), Suite 533, 24 Commerce St.	201-645-6214
NEW MEXICO	Albuquerque (87101), Rm. 316, U.S. Courthouse	505-843-2386
NEW YORK	Buffalo (14202), Rm. 910, Federal Bldg., 111 West Huron St.	716-842-3208
	New York (10007), 41st Floor, Federal Office Bldg., 26 Federal Plaza, Foley Square	212-264-0634
NORTH CAROLINA	Greensboro (27402), Rm. 258, Federal Bldg., West Market St.	919-275-9111
OHIO	Cincinnati (45202), Rm. 8028, Federal Office Bldg., 550 Main St.	513-684-2944
	Cleveland (44114), Rm. 600, 666 Euclid Ave.	216-522-4750
OREGON	Portland (97205), Suite 501, 921 S.W. Washington St.	503-221-3001
PENNSYLVANIA	Philadelphia (19107), Jefferson Bldg., 1015 Chestnut St.	215-597-2850
	Pittsburgh (15222), Rm. 431, Federal Bldg., 1000 Liberty Ave.	412-644-2850
PUERTO RICO	San Juan (00902), Rm. 100, Post Office Bldg.	... 723-4640
SOUTH CAROLINA	Charleston (29403), Rm. 631, Federal Bldg., 334 Meeting St.	803-577-4171
TENNESSEE	Memphis (38103), Rm. 710, Home Federal Bldg., 147 Jefferson Ave.	901-534-3214
TEXAS	Dallas (75202), Rm. 3E7, 1100 Commerce St.	214-749-3287
	Houston (77002), Rm. 1017, Old Federal Bldg., 201 Fannin St.	713-226-4231
UTAH	Salt Lake City (84111), Rm. 1201, Federal Bldg., 125 S. State St.	801-524-5116
VIRGINIA	Richmond (23240), Rm. 2105, Federal Bldg., 400 N. 8th St.	703-782-2246
WASHINGTON	Seattle (98109), Rm. 706, Lake Union Bldg., 1700 Westlake Ave, North	206-442-5615
WEST VIRGINIA	Charleston (25301), Rm. 3000, New Federal Office Bldg., 500 Quarrier St.	304-343-6181
WISCONSIN	Milwaukee (53203), Straus Bldg., 238 W. Wisconsin Ave.	414-224-3473
WYOMING	Cheyenne (82001), Rm. 6022, O'Mahoney Federal Ctr., 2120 Capitol Ave.	307-778-2220

APPENDIX R

CONTAINER TERMS AND DEFINITIONS
by
George D. Saunders

(Reprinted from January 2, 1967 Brandon's Shipper and Forwarder "Container World")

THE SUBJECT of container terminology and definitions does not have a high priority as to importance; either at the present time or in the foreseeable future. Any conclusions or possible courses of action agreed upon as a result of discussions on this subject, are more for the sake of convenience and efficient communications in the transportation industry, rather than compliance with mandatory regulations.

Possibly this relaxed criteria will create the proper background for objective discussions and sound evaluation; for unlike most container efforts, no financial considerations or far reaching hardware decisions are involved. Terms and definitions are strictly a matter of words and names but in everyday business communications they can be important.

Why do we need a specific set of terms and definitions? A fair question. The answer, rather simply is, so that the various facets of the transportation industry will have a common language when dealing with containers in domestic and international commerce. Therefore, every step should be taken to assure complete uniformity in the management of container systems, both afloat and ashore. Jointly agreed upon terms and definitions are a part of container management techniques.

United States of America Standards Institute.

This organization was formerly known as The American Standards Association. Its MH5 Project—**Standardization of Cargo Containers** is composed of several sub-committees each working on different projects, one of which is terms and definitions. The final product of this sub-committee is an excellent publication entitled: **Standard Terms And Definitions For Cargo Containers.**

In view of all that has been accomplished by The Terms and Definitions sub-committee it may seem a trifle pointless to propose that **still more** terms and definitions be taken into consideration. However, the writer feels there is good cause for so doing, and for the following reasons.

The above referenced publication serves a most useful purpose and should be in the library of any serious student of containerization. As seen by the writer, this booklet is most informative on all facets of container nomenclature, transportation equipment, and container handling devices, but is deficient in those terms and definitions that describe the commercial aspects of container operations from the standpoint of the shipper, the consignee, and the international freight forwarder; in other words, the people who actually use the containers.

Being primarily the product of the engineering disciplines, the MH5 Terms and Definitions publication has a degree of authority and excellence that cannot be challenged. And furthermore, no attempt is made to detract from this product of many splendid minds.

The terms and definitions found in this article are different in some respects because of the group for whom they were developed, the users of containers rather than the builders. It is for this reason that none of the MH5 Terms and Definitions is included in this paper; not that they are lacking in validation, but simply that they do not appear to be written with the needs of the shipping public in mind.

In developing the following expressions the writer has attempted to remain within the framework of the following four basic self imposed rules:—

1—At all times to draw upon existing terms and definitions from authoritative sources.

2—To keep the terms as simple, straightforward, and specific as possible.

3—To make the definitions as complete as necessary.

4—To avoid those terms and definitions that describe non-existing hardware, or theoretical operating practices.

No claim can be made for originality for any of the following material. Only the manner in which it is presented, the grouping by subject matter, is the authors. Some of the expressions will be familiar to the reader while others will not. It will depend 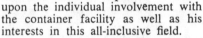 upon the individual involvement with the container facility as well as his interests in this all-inclusive field.

Terms and Definitions

For the sake of orderly reference, and to categorize the relationship as much as possible, six basic areas of terms and definitions have been established. They are:— General Terms, Containers, Container Services, Containerships, Railroads, Motor Carriers.

General Terms

During the past decade several new terms and expressions have been introduced into the world of transportation. Only four of the more important ones are included here.

UNITIZATION — The consolidation of a number of individual items into one large shipping unit for easier handling. It is also the securing or loading of one or more large items of cargo onto a single structure, such as a pallet.

CONTAINERIZATION — Is the act of using containers for the transportation of general commodities. In a narrower sense, it is the placing of the commodities in the container in a secure manner, and the eventual removal of said commodities in an orderly manner at destination.

PHYSICAL DISTRIBUTION — Goes under the dual title of **Distribution Logistics.** It is the coordination of the movement of goods from the raw material state to the finished product state.

It is the total movement of raw or semi-finished materials into the manufacturing plant, the intra-plant movement of such materials, the warehousing, shipping, and delivery of the finished product to the local distribution terminal, or the retailer's shelf.

INTERMODAL COORDINATED TRANSPORT—This is normally used to describe the capability of interchange of module van-container units among the various carriers. The fact that the containers are of the same size in height and width, and have common handling characteristics, permits them to be transferred from trucker, to railroad, to ocean carrier, in an origin-to-destination movement.

Containers

The subject of containers would easily constitute a lengthy article, just for a starter. Probably one of the best sources of container (hardware) information are the various manufacturer's brochures and descriptive literature.

CONTAINER (Basic Definition)— An inclosed, permanent, reusable, non-disposable, weathertight shipping conveyance. Fitted with at least one door, and capable of being handled and transported by existing carrier-owned equipment, both land and sea.

CARGO CONTAINERS—A group of non-module, non-standard, containers ranging between 140 and 400 cubic feet; meeting all the requirements in the definition of container (above. Such manufacturer's names as Champion, Dravo, Jeta, are frequently associated with the containers in this grouping. The CONEX containers of the Department of Defense are also in this group.

VAN-CONTAINER — A standard container so designed that it can be transported on carrier equipment. Standard containers are built in accordance with the dimension rules and corner fitting requirements of Task Committee 104 of the International Standards Organization. These standard dimensions for van-units are 8-ft. high, 8-ft. wide and in lengths of 5, 6²/₃, 10, 20, 30, and 40-ft.

DEMOUNTABLE CONTAINER— Almost without exception, the van-container is a demountable container that can be handled in transit as a unit. It can be mounted and secured in or on marine, rail, or highway carrier equipment, and thus become an integral part of that equipment for the duration of the movement.

MODULE UNIT— This expression applies only to van-containers in the 20-ft. and 40-ft. lengths at the present time. The smaller lengths exist in very limited numbers in actual practice, even though they are allowed for in the standards, described above.

SPECIAL PURPOSE CONTAINERS—These are most generally van-size units although a few special purpose cargo containers have been constructed in the past. This type of container is either for special cargoes, or has rapid loading unloading features, or both. Special containers, usually in the 20-ft. and 40-ft. sizes, are built as tank, refrigerated or insulated, platform, gondola, open top, car-haul, and livestock containers.

TRAILER/CONTAINER — This expression is sometimes found in the Container Rules Section of certain North Atlantic Conference Carrier freight tariffs. It is a dual purpose expression; meaning either van-containers **or** the smaller cargo container. It is **not** a specific item of container hardware.

Container Service

Containers are not an end in themselves but only a means to an end; the safe and economical transport of cargo from the point of shipment origin to final destination. The degree of container service provided or required will depend upon a great many things. The following six types or classes of container service are usually available.

PIER-TO-PIER — Ocean carrier containerizes shipper's cargo on the loading pier, and removes cargo from the container on the arriving pier.

PIER-TO-HOUSE—Cargo is containerized on the loading pier of the ocean carrier handling the shipment. Upon termination of the movement, the container is moved off the arriving pier and delivered directly to the consignees' factory or warehouse for removal of the shipment.

HOUSE-TO-PIER — Shipment is containerized at the shipper's factory or warehause, and then moved overland to the ocean carriers' pier for ship loading. Upon termination of the ocean movement, the shipment is removed from the container prior to its delivery to the consignee.

HOUSE-TO-HOUSE—Shipment is containerized at shippers' factory or warehouse and then moved overland to the ocean carriers' pier for ship loading. Upon termination of the ocean movement, the container is moved off the arriving pier and delivered to the consignee's factory or warehouse for removal of the shipment.

THROUGH BILL OF LADING (Also known as **Origin to Destination Service** and **Through Container Service**)—The shipper deals only with one carrier who handles the shipment from point of origin to final destination. This service is most frequently utilized in conjunction with containers which are supplied by the company offering the through service.

F.A.K. RATES—Freight All Kinds

rates are predicated on a specific rate for a certain size container between two ports, or ranges of ports. For example, there will be one rate for a 20-ft. van-container and another for a 40-ft. van-unit. This rate structure has only recently been introduced.

Containerships

The first containerships were conversions from general cargo ship types. At the present time there are several new containerships under construction in both North America and Europe.

CELLULAR CONSTRUCTION — Consists of vertical guides (similar to those in an elevator shaft) within which the container fits and is constrained at its four vertical posts. The containers are stacked one above the other and the bottom container takes the static and dynamic vertical loads resulting from those resting on it. These loads are transmitted through the corner posts of the containers to a reinforced doubling plate on the tank top, or bottom of the hold.

A L L - CONTAINERSHIP (Also known as a **Full Containership**)—All cargo spaces are fitted with vertical cells for van-container stowage. Additional van-containers are carried on deck. In some cases these may be twice the length of those carried in the cells. The ship has no capability to carry cargo in any manner except in van-containers.

SEMI-CONTAINERSHIP — (Also known as a **Partial Containership**)— A conventional general cargo ship with one or two holds fitted with vertical cells. In most configurations additional holds can be converted to cell stowage if van-container traffic demands. Non-standard cargo containers are carried in the conventional holds and 'tween decks.

COMBINATION CONTAINER-SHIPS—In addition to cell holds for the accommodations of van-containers, other distinctive means of handling cargo are present in the same

hull: roll-on roll-off, palletized cargo handling through side ports, or the capability for transporating bulk commodities in the lower holds.

TRAILER SHIPS (Also known as **Roll-On/Roll-Off** Ships)—The terms trailership and containership are sometimes used interchangeably when actually there is no similarity between the two types.

A trailership loads and discharges vehicles in the same manner as a ferry boat carrying automobiles and trucks. The term roll-on and roll-off, actually describes this very principal of loading and discharge; the vehicles rolling on and off. A trailership always carries its van-containers (as well as highway trailers and other vehicles) on their own wheels, while a containership carries only van-containers in vertical cells.

Railroads

The following definitions apply exclusively to the 20-ft. and 40-ft. intermodal van-containers. When the non-standard, non-moduls, cargo container moves in rail service, they usually do so at regular class or commodity tariff rates, utilizing box cars, flat cars, or open gondola cars.

PIGGYBACK—The point-to-point movement of one transportation vehicle upon another. A highway semi-trailer on a railroad flat car or trailer ferry, a van-container on board a ship, or new passenger automobiles on auto-rack cars are all forms of piggyback transportation.

TRAILER ON FLAT CAR (TOFC) —Probably the most common and best known form of piggyback. Highway truck trailers are either lifted on and off in side transfer, or else end loaded unloaded from a fixed ramp. When van-containers move in this type of service they are first mounted on a chassis or bogie, prior to loading on the piggyback rail car.

CONTAINER ON FLAT CAR (COFC)—Is the form of piggyback where the van-container is first demounted from the chassis or bogie, prior to being loaded and secured directly onto a railroad flat car. It is "piggyback" without wheels.

FLEXI-VAN CAR—The Mark III version can carry two 40-ft. or four 20-ft. intermodal van-containers. Two of the 20-ft. units are coupled together to form a 40-ft. container to facilitate unit loading.

Motor Carriers

Nearly all van-containers and their related equipment are produced by truck trailer manufacturers. Space does not permit a complete description of all the equipment types they collectively produce: only the more important are mentioned herein. It is strongly recommended that the reader obtain descriptive brochures from the various manufacturers. should the subject matter be of interest to him.

VAN-CONTAINERS CHASSIS—A semi-trailer chassis with tie-down corner fittings for receiving and securing a van-container of matching size. The 20-ft. chassis can be either a single or tandem axle. depending upon the load requirements. The 40-ft. chassis is a tandem axle unit and is usually equipped with sufficient tie down fittings to enable it to accommodate either two 20-ft or one 40-ft. van-container.

SPLIT-AWAY CHASSIS—A 40-ft. chassis is constructed so that it detaches at mid-point and becomes two 20-ft. chassis; each fitted with tie down corner fittings for receiving and securing a 20-ft. van-container. The two single axle bogies work in tandem when the chassis are joined together to form a 40-ft. unit. but separate (one under each chassis) when the unit is split into two 20-ft. chassis.

SINGLE AXLE BOGIE—An assembly consisting of two wheels, axle,, suspension system, and overhead mounting for securing and supporting one 20-ft. van-container. The bogie also carries rear lights, license plates, and mud guard flaps.

VAN-CONTAINER AND BOGIE(S)—This combination is the equivalent of a 20-ft. or 40-ft. semitrailer highway van. The recess for the tractor king pin is built into the bottom of the container in a reinforced area. Dollie wheels and antinosediving legs are also incorporated in the bottom structure of the container. When not in use they fold up into the recess areas.

CHASSIS FRAME — This unit serves as a chassis but without fixed wheels. It is the center of a three piece combination; the van-container, the chassis frame, and the bogie. The van-unit is secured to the top of the chassis frame by four corner tie down fittings. The bogie is secured to the bottom of the frame in the same manner as it would be secured to a van-unit were it a two piece combination.

VAN-CONTAINER — CHASSIS FRAME — BOGIE — This combination is the equivalent of a 20-ft. semitrailer highway van. For over the road or railroad piggyback (TOFC) service, all three sections or members are used. When carried on a Flexi-Van car the container is mounted on the frame. In container-on-flat-car (COFC) service, use of the frame depends upon the type of car and container handling equipment available. For overseas movement the bogie and frame remain ashore; on the van-unit goes aboard ship.

Manufacturers Hanover Trust Co.

International Division   Telephone
4 NEW YORK PLAZA   New York, N.Y. 10015   623-4485

No. 581   July 5, 1979

Rates good until receipt of next consecutively numbered card. You may apply these rates to drawings of drafts and transfers up to the limits specified in any one day. For amounts in excess or for currencies not listed please telephone or wire us collect.

COUNTRY	Limit Equiv. of	Currency	Rate
Argentina	$7,500	Pesos	.0010
Australia	$7,500	Aust. $	1.1300
Austria	$7,500	Schilling	.0760
Bahamas	$7,500	Bahama $	1.0300
Belgium*	$7,500	Francs	.0355
Brazil	$7,500	Cruzeiro	.0405
Canada	$7,500	Can. $	.8800
Colombia	$7,500	Pesos	.0330
Denmark	$7,500	Kroner	.1925
Finland	$7,500	Finmarks	.2625
France	$7,500	Francs	.2390
Germany (Western)	$7,500	Marks	.5600
Gr. Britain	$7,500	£ Sterl.	2.3000
Greece	$7,500	Drachma	.0315
Hong Kong	$7,500	Dollar	.1985
India	$7,500	Rupees	.1300
Ireland	$7,500	Pounds	2.0700
Israel	$7,500	Pounds	.0500
Italy	$7,500	Lire	.001300
Jamaica	$7,500	Jam. $	.5900
Japan	$7,500	Yen	.004750
Mexico	$7,500	Pesos	.0450
Netherlands	$7,500	Guilders	.4990
Norway	$7,500	Kroner	.2010
Pakistan	$7,500	Rupees	.1050
Philippines	$7,500	Pesos	.1400
Portugal	$7,500	Escudos	.0225
South Africa	$7,500	Rands	1.1925
Spain	$7,500	Pesetas	.0155
Sweden	$7,500	Kroner	.2390
Switzerland	$7,500	Francs	.6300
Uruguay	$7,500	Pesos	.1350
Venezuela	$7,500	Bolivars	.2340

Above rates do not apply to Foreign Banknotes or Coins.
*To be used for payment of Imports ONLY.

Public Law 95-52
95th Congress   An Act   91 STAT. 235

To amend the Export Administration Act of 1969 in order to extend the authori-   June 22, 1977
ties of that Act and improve the administration of export controls under that   [H.R. 5840]
Act, and to strengthen the antiboycott provisions of that Act.

Be it enacted by the Senate and House of Representatives of the
United States of America in Congress assembled,   Export
                                                                              Administration
SHORT TITLE   Amendments of
                                                                              1977.
SECTION 1. This Act may be cited as the "Export Administration   50 USC app.
Amendments of 1977".   2401 note.

TITLE I—EXPORT ADMINISTRATION IMPROVEMENTS
AND EXTENSION

EXTENSION OF EXPORT ADMINISTRATION ACT

SEC. 101. Section 14 of the Export Administration Act of 1969 is   50 USC app.
amended by striking out "September 30, 1976" and inserting in lieu   2413.
thereof "September 30, 1979".

AUTHORIZATION OF APPROPRIATIONS

SEC. 102. The Export Administration Act of 1969 is amended by   50 USC app.
inserting after section 12 the following new section 13 and redesignat-   2412, 2413.
ing existing sections 13 and 14 as sections 14 and 15, respectively:

"AUTHORIZATION OF APPROPRIATIONS

"SEC. 13. (a) Notwithstanding any other provision of law, no   50 USC app.
appropriation shall be made under any law to the Department of   2411a.
Commerce for expenses to carry out the purposes of this Act for any
fiscal year commencing on or after October 1, 1977, unless previously
and specifically authorized by legislation.
"(b) There is hereby authorized to be appropriated to the Department of Commerce $14,033,000 (and such additional amounts as may
be necessary for increases in salary, pay, retirement, other employee
benefits authorized by law, and other nondiscretionary costs) for fiscal
years 1978 and 1979 to carry out the purposes of this Act.".

CONTROL OF EXPORTS FOR NATIONAL SECURITY PURPOSES; FOREIGN
AVAILABILITY

SEC. 103. (a) Section 4(b) of the Export Administration Act of
1969 is amended—   50 USC app.
    (1) by striking out the third sentence of paragraph (1);   2403.
    (2) by striking out paragraphs (2) through (4); and
    (3) by inserting the following new paragraph (2) immediately
after paragraph (1):

91 STAT. 236   PUBLIC LAW 95-52—JUNE 22, 1977

50 USC app.
2402.

"(2)(A) In administering export controls for national security purposes as prescribed in section 3(2)(C) of this Act, United States policy toward individual countries shall not be determined exclusively on the basis of a country's Communist or non-Communist status but shall take into account such factors as the country's present and potential relationship to the United States, its present and potential relationship to countries friendly or hostile to the United States, its ability and willingness to control retransfers of United States exports in accordance with United States policy, and such other factors as the President may deem appropriate. The President shall periodically review United States policy toward individual countries to determine whether such policy is appropriate in light of the factors specified in the preceding sentence. The results of such review, together with the justification for United States policy in light of such factors, shall be reported to Congress not later than December 31, 1978, in the semiannual report of the Secretary of Commerce required by section 10 of this Act, and in every second such report thereafter.

Review by
President.

Report to
Congress.

Post, p. 241.
Rules and regu-
lations.

"(B) Rules and regulations under this subsection may provide for denial of any request or application for authority to export articles, materials, or supplies, including technical data or any other information, from the United States, its territories and possessions, to any nation or combination of nations threatening the national security of the United States if the President determines that their export would prove detrimental to the national security of the United States. The President shall not impose export controls for national security purposes on the export from the United States of articles, materials, or supplies, including technical data or other information, which he determines are available without restriction from sources outside the United States in significant quantities and comparable in quality to those produced in the United States, unless the President determines that adequate evidence has been presented to him demonstrating that the absence of such controls would prove detrimental to the national security of the United States. The nature of such evidence shall be included in the semiannual report required by section 10 of this Act. Where, in accordance with this paragraph, export controls are imposed for national security purposes notwithstanding foreign availability, the President shall take steps to initiate negotiations with the governments of the appropriate foreign countries for the purpose of eliminating such availability.".

50 USC app.
2403.

(b)(1) Section 4(h) of the Export Administration Act of 1969 is amended by striking out "controlled country" in the first sentence of paragraph (1) and in the second sentence of paragraph (2) and inserting in lieu thereof "country to which exports are restricted for national security purposes".

(2) Section 4(h)(2)(A) of such Act is amended by striking out "controlled" and inserting in lieu thereof "such"

(3) Section 4(h)(4) of such Act is amended—

(A) by inserting "and" at the end of subparagraph (A); and

(B) by striking out the semicolon at the end of subparagraph (B) thereof and all that follows the semicolon and inserting in lieu thereof a period.

Effective date.
50 USC app.
2403 note.

(4) The amendments made by this subsection shall become effective upon the expiration of ninety days after the receipt by the Congress of the first report required by the amendment made by subsection (a)(3) of this section.

(c) Section 4(h) of such Act is amended—

(1) in paragraph (1)—

(A) in the first sentence by striking out "significantly increase the military capability of such country" and inserting in lieu thereof "make a significant contribution to the military potential of such country"; and

(B) in the second sentence by striking out "significantly increase the military capability of such country" and inserting in lieu thereof "make a significant contribution, which would prove detrimental to the national security of the United States, to the military potential of any such country"; and

(2) in paragraph (2)(A) by striking out "significantly increase the military capability of such country" and inserting in lieu thereof "make a significant contribution, which would prove detrimental to the national security of the United States, to the military potential of such country or any other country".

(d) Section 6(b) of such Act is amended by striking out "Communist-dominated nation" and inserting in lieu thereof "country to which exports are restricted for national security or foreign policy purposes".

50 USC app. 2403.

50 USC app. 2405.

MONITORING OF COMMODITIES IN POTENTIAL SHORT SUPPLY

SEC. 104. Section 4(c)(1) of the Export Administration Act of 1969 is amended by inserting after the first sentence thereof the following: "Such monitoring shall commence at a time adequate to insure that data will be available which is sufficient to permit achievement of the policies of this Act.".

50 USC app. 2403.

EXEMPTION FOR CERTAIN AGRICULTURAL COMMODITIES FROM CERTAIN EXPORT LIMITATIONS

SEC. 105. Section 4(f) of the Export Administration Act of 1969 is amended—

(1) by redesignating such section as section 4(f)(1); and

(2) by adding at the end thereof the following new paragraph:

"(2) Upon approval of the Secretary of Commerce, in consultation with the Secretary of Agriculture, agricultural commodities purchased by or for use in a foreign country may remain in the United States for export at a later date free from any quantitative limitations on export which may be imposed pursuant to section 3(2)(A) of this Act subsequent to such approval. The Secretary of Commerce may not grant approval hereunder unless he receives adequate assurance and, in conjunction with the Secretary of Agriculture, finds that such commodities will eventually be exported, that neither the sale nor export thereof will result in an excessive drain of scarce materials and have a serious domestic inflationary impact, that storage of such commodities in the United States will not unduly limit the space available for storage of domestically owned commodities, and that the purpose of such storage is to establish a reserve of such commodities for later use, not including resale to or use by another country. The Secretary of Commerce is authorized to issue such rules and regulations as may be necessary to implement this paragraph.".

50 USC app. 2402.

Rules and regulations.

91 STAT. 238 PUBLIC LAW 95-52—JUNE 22, 1977

CONGRESSIONAL REVIEW OF EXPORT CONTROLS ON AGRICULTURAL
COMMODITIES

Report to
Congress.
Ante, p. 237.

50 USC app.
2402.

SEC. 106. Section 4(f) of the Export Administration Act of 1969, as amended by section 105 of this Act, is further amended by adding at the end thereof the following new paragraph:

"(3) If the authority conferred by this section is exercised to prohibit or curtail the exportation of any agricultural commodity in order to effectuate the policies set forth in clause (A) or (B) of paragraph (2) of section 3 of this Act, the President shall immediately report such prohibition or curtailment to the Congress, setting forth the reasons therefor in detail. If the Congress, within 30 days after the date of its receipt of such report, adopts a concurrent resolution disapproving such prohibition or curtailment, then such prohibition or curtailment shall cease to be effective with the adoption of such resolution. In the computation of such 30-day period, there shall be excluded the days on which either House is not in session because of an adjournment of more than 3 days to a day certain or because of an adjournment of the Congress sine die.".

PERIOD FOR ACTION ON EXPORT LICENSE APPLICATIONS

50 USC app.
2403.
Approval.

Notice.

SEC. 107. Section 4(g) of the Export Administration Act of 1969 is amended to read as follows:

"(g)(1) It is the intent of Congress that any export license application required under this Act shall be approved or disapproved within 90 days of its receipt. Upon the expiration of the 90-day period beginning on the date of its receipt, any export license application required under this Act which has not been approved or disapproved shall be deemed to be approved and the license shall be issued unless the Secretary of Commerce or other official exercising authority under this Act finds that additional time is required and notifies the applicant in writing of the specific circumstances requiring such additional time and the estimated date when the decision will be made.

"(2)(A) With respect to any export license application not finally approved or disapproved within 90 days of its receipt as provided in paragraph (1) of this subsection, the applicant shall, to the maximum extent consistent with the national security of the United States, be specifically informed in writing of questions raised and negative considerations or recommendations made by any agency or department of the Government with respect to such license application, and shall be accorded an opportunity to respond to such questions, considerations, or recommendations in writing prior to final approval or disapproval by the Secretary of Commerce or other official exercising authority under this Act. In making such final approval or disapproval, the Secretary of Commerce or other official exercising authority under this Act shall take fully into account the applicant's response.

Interagency
review.

"(B) Whenever the Secretary determines that it is necessary to refer an export license application to any interagency review process for approval, he shall first, if the applicant so requests, provide the applicant with an opportunity to review any documentation to be submitted to such process for the purpose of describing the export in question, in order to determine whether such documentation accurately describes the proposed export.

Denial.

"(3) In any denial of an export license application, the applicant shall be informed in writing of the specific statutory basis for such denial.".

PUBLIC LAW 95-52—JUNE 22, 1977   91 STAT. 239

CERTAIN PETROLEUM EXPORTS

Sec. 108. Section 4 of the Export Administration Act of 1969 is amended by adding at the end thereof the following new subsection:

"(j) Petroleum products refined in United States Foreign-Trade Zones, or in the United States Territory of Guam, from foreign crude oil shall be excluded from any quantitative restrictions imposed pursuant to section 3(2)(A) of this Act, except that, if the Secretary of Commerce finds that a product is in short supply, the Secretary of Commerce may issue such rules and regulations as may be necessary to limit exports.".

*Rules and regulations.
50 USC app. 2403.*

50 USC app. 2402.

EXPORT OF HORSES

Sec. 109. Section 4 of the Export Administration Act of 1969, as amended by section 108 of this Act, is further amended by adding at the end thereof the following new subsection:

"(k)(1) Notwithstanding any other provision of this Act, no horse may be exported by sea from the United States, its territories and possessions, unless such horse is part of a consignment of horses with respect to which a waiver has been granted under paragraph (2) of this subsection.

"(2) The Secretary of Commerce, in consultation with the Secretary of Agriculture, may issue rules and regulations providing for the granting of waivers permitting the export by sea of a specified consignment of horses, if the Secretary of Commerce, in consultation with the Secretary of Agriculture, determines that no horse in that consignment is being exported for purposes of slaughter.".

Waivers, rules and regulations.

PROHIBITION OF CERTAIN PETROLEUM EXPORTS

Sec. 110. Section 4 of the Export Administration Act of 1969, as amended by sections 108 and 109 of this Act, is further amended by adding at the end thereof the following new subsection:

"(l)(1) Notwithstanding any other provision of this Act and notwithstanding subsection (u) of section 28 of the Mineral Leasing Act of 1920, no domestically produced crude oil transported by pipeline over rights-of-way granted pursuant to such section 28 (except any such crude oil which (A) is exchanged in similar quantity for convenience or increased efficiency of transportation with persons or the government of an adjacent foreign state, or (B) is temporarily exported for convenience or increased efficiency of transportation across parts of an adjacent foreign state and reenters the United States) may be exported from the United States, its territories and possessions, during the 2-year period beginning on the date of enactment of this subsection unless the requirements of paragraph (2) of this subsection are met.

30 USC 185.

"(2) Crude oil subject to the prohibition contained in paragraph (1) may be exported only if—

"(A) the President makes and publishes an express finding that exports of such crude oil—

"(i) will not diminish the total quantity or quality of petroleum available to the United States,

"(ii) will have a positive effect on consumer oil prices by decreasing the average crude oil acquisition costs of refiners,

"(iii) will be made only pursuant to contracts which may be terminated if the petroleum supplies of the United States are interrupted or seriously threatened,

"(iv) are in the national interest, and

Presidential finding, publication.

"(v) are in accordance with the provisions of this Act; and

Report to
Congress.
42 USC 6421.
Congressional
review.

"(B) the President reports such finding to the Congress as an energy action (as defined in section 551 of the Energy Policy and Conservation Act).

The congressional review provisions of such section 551 shall apply to an energy action reported in accordance with this paragraph, except that for purposes of this paragraph, any reference in such section to a period of 15 calendar days of continuous session of Congress shall be deemed to be a reference to a period of 60 calendar days of continuous session of Congress and the period specified in subsection (f)(4)(A) of such section for committee action on a resolution shall be deemed to be 40 calendar days.".

TECHNICAL ADVISORY COMMITTEES

50 USC app.
2404.

SEC. 111. (a) Section 5(c)(1) of the Export Administration Act of 1969 is amended by striking out "two" in the last sentence thereof and inserting in lieu thereof "four".

(b) The second sentence of section 5(c)(2) of such Act is amended to read as follows: "Such committees, where they have expertise in such matters, shall be consulted with respect to questions involving (A) technical matters, (B) worldwide availability and actual utilization of production technology, (C) licensing procedures which affect the level of export controls applicable to any articles, materials, and supplies, including technical data or other information, and (D) exports subject to multilateral controls in which the United States participates including proposed revisions of any such multilateral controls.".

Report,
additional
information,
Post, p. 241.

(c) Section 5(c)(2) of such Act is further amended by striking out the third sentence and inserting in lieu thereof the following: "The Secretary shall include in each semiannual report required by section 10 of this Act an accounting of the consultations undertaken pursuant to this paragraph, the use made of the advice rendered by the technical advisory committees pursuant to this paragraph, and the contributions of the technical advisory committees to carrying out the policies of this Act.".

PENALTIES FOR VIOLATIONS

50 USC app.
2405.

SEC. 112. (a) Section 6(a) of the Export Administration Act of 1969 is amended—

(1) in the first sentence, by striking out "$10,000" and inserting in lieu thereof "$25,000"; and

(2) in the second sentence, by striking out "$20,000" and inserting in lieu thereof "$50,000".

Ante, p. 237.

(b) Section 6(b) of such Act is amended by striking out "$20,000" and inserting in lieu thereof "$50,000".

(c) Section 6(c) of such Act is amended by striking out "$1,000" and inserting in lieu thereof "$10,000".

Payment,
deferral or
suspension.

(d) Section 6(d) of such Act is amended by adding at the end thereof the following new sentence: "In addition, the payment of any penalty imposed under subsection (c) may be deferred or suspended in whole or in part for a period of time no longer than any probation period (which may exceed one year) that may be imposed upon such person. Such a deferral or suspension shall not operate as a bar to the collection of the penalty in the event that the conditions of the suspension, deferral, or probation are not fulfilled.".

AVAILABILITY OF INFORMATION TO CONGRESS

Sec. 113. (a) Section 7(c) of the Export Administration Act of 1969 is amended by adding at the end thereof the following new sentences: "Nothing in this Act shall be construed as authorizing the withholding of information from Congress, and any information obtained under this Act, including any report or license application required under section 4(b), shall be made available upon request to any committee or subcommittee of Congress of appropriate jurisdiction. No such committee or subcommittee shall disclose any information obtained under this Act which is submitted on a confidential basis unless the full committee determines that the withholding thereof is contrary to the national interest.".   *50 USC app. 2406.* *Ante,* p. 235. *Disclosure.*

(b) Section 4(c)(1) of such Act is amended by inserting immediately before the period at the end of the last sentence thereof "and in the last two sentences of section 7(c) of this Act".   *Ante,* p. 237.

SIMPLIFICATION OF EXPORT REGULATIONS AND LISTS

Sec. 114. Section 7 of the Export Administration Act of 1969 is amended by adding at the end thereof the following new subsection: *Review.*

"(e) The Secretary of Commerce, in consultation with appropriate United States Government departments and agencies and with appropriate technical advisory committees established under section 5(c), shall review the rules and regulations issued under this Act and the lists of articles, materials, and supplies which are subject to export controls in order to determine how compliance with the provisions of this Act can be facilitated by simplifying such rules and regulations, by simplifying or clarifying such lists, or by any other means. Not later than one year after the enactment of this subsection, the Secretary of Commerce shall report to Congress on the actions taken on the basis of such review to simplify such rules and regulations. Such report may be included in the semiannual report required by section 10 of this Act.".   *Ante,* p. 240. *Report to Congress.* *Infra.*

TERRORISM

Sec. 115. Section 3 of the Export Administration Act of 1969 is amended by adding at the end thereof the following new paragraph: *50 USC app. 2402.*

"(8) It is the policy of the United States to use export controls to encourage other countries to take immediate steps to prevent the use of their territory or resources to aid, encourage, or give sanctuary to those persons involved in directing, supporting, or participating in acts of international terrorism. To achieve this objective, the President shall make every reasonable effort to secure the removal or reduction of such assistance to international terrorists through international cooperation and agreement before resorting to the imposition of export controls.".

SEMIANNUAL REPORTS

Sec. 116. (a) Section 10 of the Export Administration Act of 1969 is amended by adding at the end thereof the following new subsection: *50 USC app. 2409.*

"(c) Each semiannual report shall include an accounting of—

"(1) any organizational and procedural changes instituted, any reviews undertaken, and any means used to keep the business sector of the Nation informed, pursuant to section 4(a) of this Act;

"(2) any changes in the exercise of the authorities of section 4(b) of this Act;   *50 USC app. 2403.* *Ante,* p. 235; *Post,* p. 246.

50 USC app.
2403.

Ante, p. 236,
238.

Ante, p. 240.

Ante, p. 240.

Post, p. 247.
50 USC app.
2409.

"(3) any delegations of authority under section 4(c) of this Act;

"(4) the disposition of export license applications pursuant to sections 4 (g) and (h) of this Act;

"(5) consultations undertaken with technical advisory committees pursuant to section 5(c) of this Act;

"(6) violations of the provisions of this Act and penalties imposed pursuant to section 6 of this Act; and

"(7) a description of actions taken by the President and the Secretary of Commerce to effect the policies set forth in section 3(5) of this Act.".

(b)(1) The section heading of such section 10 is amended by striking out "QUARTERLY".

(2) Subsection (b) of such section is amended—

(A) by striking out "quarterly" each time it appears; and

(B) by striking out "second" in the first sentence of paragraph (1).

SPECIAL REPORT ON MULTILATERAL EXPORT CONTROLS

Submittal to
Congress.
50 USC app.
2409 note.
50 USC app.
2401 note.
22 USC 1611
note.
Contents.

SEC. 117. Not later than 12 months after the enactment of this section, the President shall submit to the Congress a special report on multilateral export controls in which the United States participates pursuant to the Export Administration Act of 1969 and pursuant to the Mutual Defense Assistance Control Act of 1951. The purpose of such special report shall be to assess the effectiveness of such multilateral export controls and to formulate specific proposals for increasing the effectiveness of such controls. That special report shall include—

(1) the current list of commodities controlled for export by agreement of the group known as the coordinating Committee of the Consultative Group (hereafter in this section referred to as the "Committee") and an analysis of the process of reviewing such list and of the changes which result from such review;

(2) data on and analysis of requests for exceptions to such list;

(3) a description and an analysis of the process by which decisions are made by the Committee on whether or not to grant such requests;

(4) an analysis of the uniformity of interpretation and enforcement by the participating countries of the export controls agreed to by the Committee (including controls over the re-export of such commodities from countries not participating in the Committee), and information on each case where such participating countries have acted contrary to the United States interpretation of the policy of the Committee, including United States representations to such countries and the response of such countries;

(5) an analysis of the problem of exports of advanced technology by countries not participating in the Committee, including such exports by subsidiaries or affiliates of United States businesses in such countries;

(6) an analysis of the effectiveness of any procedures employed, in cases in which an exception for a listed commodity is granted by the Committee, to determine whether there has been compliance with any conditions on the use of the excepted commodity which were a basis for the exception; and

(7) detailed recommendations for improving, through formalization or other means, the effectiveness of multilateral export controls, including specific recommendations for the development of more precise criteria and procedures for collective export decisions and for the development of more detailed and formal enforcement mechanisms to assure more uniform interpretation of and compliance with such criteria, procedures, and decisions by all countries participating in such multilateral export controls.

REVIEW OF UNILATERAL AND MULTILATERAL EXPORT CONTROL LISTS

SEC. 118. The Secretary of Commerce, in cooperation with appropriate United States Government departments and agencies and the appropriate technical advisory committees established pursuant to the Export Administration Act of 1969, shall undertake an investigation to determine whether United States unilateral controls or multilateral controls in which the United States participates should be removed, modified, or added with respect to particular articles, materials, and supplies, including technical data and other information, in order to protect the national security of the United States. Such investigation shall take into account such factors as the availability of such articles, materials, and supplies from other nations and the degree to which the availability of the same from the United States or from any country with which the United States participates in multilateral controls would make a significant contribution to the military potential of any country threatening or potentially threatening the national security of the United States. The results of such investigation shall be reported to the Congress not later than December 31, 1978.

Investigation.
20 USC 2403 note.
50 USC app. 2401 note.

Report to Congress.

TECHNOLOGY EXPORT STUDY

SEC. 119. (a) The President, acting through the Secretary of Commerce, the Secretary of Labor, and the International Trade Commission, shall conduct a study of the domestic economic impact of exports from the United States of industrial technology whose export requires a license under the Export Administration Act of 1969. Such study shall include an evaluation of current exporting patterns on the international competitive position of the United States in advanced industrial technology fields and an evaluation of the present and future effect of these exports on domestic employment.

(b) The results of the study conducted pursuant to subsection (a) will be reported to the Congress within one year after the date of enactment of this Act.

Study.
50 USC app. 2403 note.

Report to Congress.

REPORT ON TECHNICAL DATA TRANSFERS

SEC. 120. The Secretary of Commerce shall conduct a study of the transfer of technical data and other information to any country to which exports are restricted for national security purposes and the problem of the export, by publications or any other means of public dissemination, of technical data or other information from the United States, the export of which might prove detrimental to the national security or foreign policy of the United States. Not later than 12 months after the enactment of this section, the Secretary shall report to the Congress his assessment of the impact of the export of such technical data or other information by such means on the national security and foreign policy of the United States and his recommendations for monitoring such exports without impairing freedom of speech, freedom of press, or the freedom of scientific exchange. Such report may be

Study.
50 USC app. 2403 note.

Report to Congress.

Ante, p. 241.

included in the semiannual report required by section 10 of the Export Administration Act of 1969.

TITLE II—FOREIGN BOYCOTTS

PROHIBITION ON COMPLIANCE WITH FOREIGN BOYCOTTS

50 USC app. 2403a.

SEC. 201. (a) The Export Administration Act of 1969 is amended by redesignating section 4A as section 4B and by inserting after section 4 the following new section:

"FOREIGN BOYCOTTS

Rules and regulations. 50 USC app. 2403-1a. *Post,* p. 247.

"SEC. 4A. (a)(1) For the purpose of implementing the policies set forth in section 3(5) (A) and (B), the President shall issue rules and regulations prohibiting any United States person, with respect to his activities in the interstate or foreign commerce of the United States, from taking or knowingly agreeing to take any of the following actions with intent to comply with, further, or support any boycott fostered or imposed by a foreign country against a country which is friendly to the United States and which is not itself the object of any form of boycott pursuant to United States law or regulation:

"(A) Refusing, or requiring any other person to refuse, to do business with or in the boycotted country, with any business concern organized under the laws of the boycotted country, with any national or resident of the boycotted country, or with any other person, pursuant to an agreement with, a requirement of, or a request from or on behalf of the boycotting country. The mere absence of a business relationship with or in the boycotted country, with any business concern organized under the laws of the boycotted country, with any national or resident of the boycotted country, or with any other person, does not indicate the existence of the intent required to establish a violation of rules and regulations issued to carry out this subparagraph.

"(B) Refusing, or requiring any other person to refuse, to employ or otherwise discriminating against any United States person on the basis of race, religion, sex, or national origin of that person or of any owner, officer, director, or employee of such person.

"(C) Furnishing information with respect to the race, religion, sex, or national origin of any United States person or of any owner, officer, director, or employee of such person.

"(D) Furnishing information about whether any person has, has had, or proposes to have any business relationship (including a relationship by way of sale, purchase, legal or commercial representation, shipping or other transport, insurance, investment, or supply) with or in the boycotted country, with any business concern organized under the laws of the boycotted country, with any national or resident of the boycotted country, or with any other person which is known or believed to be restricted from having any business relationship with or in the boycotting country. Nothing in this paragraph shall prohibit the furnishing of normal business information in a commercial context as defined by the Secretary of Commerce.

"(E) Furnishing information about whether any person is a member of, has made contributions to, or is otherwise associated with or involved in the activities of any charitable or fraternal organization which supports the boycotted country.

"(F) Paying, honoring, confirming, or otherwise implementing a letter of credit which contains any condition or requirement compliance with which is prohibited by rules and regulations issued pursuant to this paragraph, and no United States person shall, as a result of the application of this paragraph, be obligated to pay or otherwise honor or implement such letter of credit.

"(2) Rules and regulations issued pursuant to paragraph (1) shall provide exceptions for—

Exceptions.

"(A) complying or agreeing to comply with requirements (i) prohibiting the import of goods or services from the boycotted country or goods produced or services provided by any business concern organized under the laws of the boycotted country or by nationals or residents of the boycotted country, or (ii) prohibiting the shipment of goods to the boycotting country on a carrier of the boycotted country, or by a route other than that prescribed by the boycotting country or the recipient of the shipment;

"(B) complying or agreeing to comply with import and shipping document requirements with respect to the country of origin, the name of the carrier and route of shipment, the name of the supplier of the shipment or the name of the provider of other services, except that no information knowingly furnished or conveyed in response to such requirements may be stated in negative, blacklisting, or similar exclusionary terms after the expiration of 1 year following the date of enactment of the Export Administration Amendments of 1977 other than with respect to carriers or route of shipment as may be permitted by such rules and regulations in order to comply with precautionary requirements protecting against war risks and confiscation;

"(C) complying or agreeing to comply in the normal course of business with the unilateral and specific selection by a boycotting country, or national or resident thereof, of carriers, insurers, suppliers of services to be performed within the boycotting country or specific goods which, in the normal course of business, are identifiable by source when imported into the boycotting country;

"(D) complying or agreeing to comply with export requirements of the boycotting country relating to shipments or transshipments of exports to the boycotted country, to any business concern of or organized under the laws of the boycotted country, or to any national or resident of the boycotted country;

"(E) compliance by an individual or agreement by an individual to comply with the immigration or passport requirements of any country with respect to such individual or any member of such individual's family or with requests for information regarding requirements of employment of such individual within the boycotting country; and

"(F) compliance by a United States person resident in a foreign country or agreement by such person to comply with the laws of that country with respect to his activities exclusively therein, and such rules and regulations may contain exceptions for such resident complying with the laws or regulations of that foreign country governing imports into such country of trademarked, trade-named, or similarly specifically identifiable products or components of products for his own use, including the performance of contractual services within that country, as may be defined by such rules and regulations.

"(3) Rules and regulations issued pursuant to paragraphs (2) (C) and (2) (F) shall not provide exceptions from paragraphs (1) (B) and (1) (C).

"(4) Nothing in this subsection may be construed to supersede or limit the operation of the antitrust or civil rights laws of the United States.

Rules and regulations, issuance. Grace period.

"(5) Rules and regulations pursuant to this subsection shall be issued not later than 90 days after the date of enactment of this section and shall be issued in final form and become effective not later than 120 days after they are first issued, except that (A) rules and regulations prohibiting negative certification may take effect not later than 1 year after the date of enactment of this section, and (B) a grace period shall be provided for the application of the rules and regulations issued pursuant to this subsection to actions taken pursuant to a written contract or other agreement entered into on or before May 16, 1977. Such grace period shall end on December 31, 1978, except that the Secretary of Commerce may extend the grace period for not to exceed 1 additional year in any case in which the Secretary finds that good faith efforts are being made to renegotiate the contract or agreement in order to eliminate the provisions which are inconsistent with the rules and regulations issued pursuant to paragraph (1).

"(6) This Act shall apply to any transaction or activity undertaken, by or through a United States or other person, with intent to evade the provisions of this Act as implemented by the rules and regulations issued pursuant to this subsection, and such rules and regulations shall expressly provide that the exceptions set forth in paragraph (2) shall not permit activities or agreements (expressed or implied by a course of conduct, including a pattern of responses) otherwise prohibited, which are not within the intent of such exceptions.

"(b)(1) In addition to the rules and regulations issued pursuant to subsection (a) of this section, rules and regulations issued under section 4(b) of this Act shall implement the policies set forth in section 3(5).

Infra.
Post, p. 247.
Report to Secretary of Commerce.

"(2) Such rules and regulations shall require that any United States person receiving a request for the furnishing of information, the entering into or implementing of agreements, or the taking of any other action referred to in section 3(5) shall report that fact to the Secretary of Commerce, together with such other information concerning such request as the Secretary may require for such action as he may deem appropriate for carrying out the policies of that section. Such person shall also report to the Secretary of Commerce whether he intends to comply and whether he has complied with such request. Any report filed pursuant to this paragraph after the date of enactment of this section shall be made available promptly for public inspection and copying, except that information regarding the quantity, description, and value of any articles, materials, and supplies, including technical data and other information, to which such report relates may be kept confidential if the Secretary determines that disclosure thereof would place the United States person involved at a competitive disadvantage. The Secretary of Commerce shall periodically transmit summaries of the information contained in such reports to the Secretary of State for such action as the Secretary of State, in consultation with the Secretary of Commerce, may deem appropriate for carrying out the policies set forth in section 3(5) of this Act.".

Summaries, transmittal to Secretary of State.

Ante, p. 235.

(b) Section 4(b)(1) of such Act is amended by striking out the next to the last sentence.

50 USC app. 2406.
Ante, p. 244.
Post, p. 247.

(c) Section 7(c) of such Act is amended by striking out "No" and inserting in lieu thereof "Except as otherwise provided by the third sentence of section 4A(b)(2) and by section 6(c)(2)(C) of this Act, no".

STATEMENT OF POLICY

Sec. 202. (a) Section 3(5)(A) of the Export Administration Act of 1969 is amended by inserting immediately after "United States" the following: "or against any United States person".

50 USC app. 2402.

(b) Section 3(5)(B) of such Act is amended to read as follows: "(B) to encourage and, in specified cases, to require United States persons engaged in the export of articles, materials, supplies, or information to refuse to take actions, including furnishing information or entering into or implementing agreements, which have the effect of furthering or supporting the restrictive trade practices or boycotts fostered or imposed by any foreign country against a country friendly to the United States or against any United States person,".

ENFORCEMENT

Sec. 203. (a) Section 6(c) of the Export Administration Act of 1969 is amended—

Ante, p. 240.

(A) by redesignating such section as section 6(c)(1); and

(B) by adding at the end thereof the following new paragraph:

"(2)(A) The authority of this Act to suspend or revoke the authority of any United States person to export articles, materials, supplies, or technical data or other information, from the United States, its territories or possessions, may be used with respect to any violation of the rules and regulations issued pursuant to section 4A(a) of this Act.

Ante, p. 244.

"(B) Any administrative sanction (including any civil penalty or any suspension or revocation of authority to export) imposed under this Act for a violation of the rules and regulations issued pursuant to section 4A(a) of this Act may be imposed only after notice and opportunity for an agency hearing on the record in accordance with sections 554 through 557 of title 5, United States Code.

Notice and hearing.

"(C) Any charging letter or other document initiating administrative proceedings for the imposition of sanctions for violations of the rules and regulations issued pursuant to section 4A(a) of this Act shall be made available for public inspection and copying.".

Documents, public inspection.

(b) Section 8 of such Act is amended by striking out "The" and inserting in lieu thereof "Except as provided in section 6(c)(2), the".

50 USC app. 2407.
Supra.

DEFINITIONS

Sec. 204. Section 11 of the Export Administration Act of 1969 is amended to read as follows:

50 USC app. 2410.

"DEFINITIONS

"Sec. 11. As used in this Act—

"(1) the term 'person' includes the singular and the plural and any individual, partnership, corporation, or other form of association, including any government or agency thereof; and

"(2) the term 'United States person' means any United States resident or national (other than an individual resident outside the United States and employed by other than a United States person), any domestic concern (including any permanent domestic establishment of any foreign concern) and any foreign subsidiary or affiliate (including any permanent foreign establishment) of any domestic concern which is controlled in fact by such domestic concern, as determined under regulations of the President.".

91 STAT. 248   PUBLIC LAW 95–52—JUNE 22, 1977

PREEMPTION

Rules and
regulations.
50 USC app.
2403–1a note.

SEC. 205. The amendments made by this title and the rules and regulations issued pursuant thereto shall preempt any law, rule, or regulation of any of the several States or the District of Columbia, and any of the territories or possessions of the United States, or of any governmental subdivision thereof, which law, rule, or regulation pertains to participation in, compliance with, implementation of, or the furnishing of information regarding restrictive trade practices or boycotts fostered or imposed by foreign countries against other countries.

Approved June 22, 1977.

LEGISLATIVE HISTORY:

HOUSE REPORTS: No. 95–190 (Comm. on International Relations) and No. 95–354 (Comm. of Conference).
SENATE REPORT No. 95–104 accompanying S. 69 (Comm. on Banking, Housing, and Urban Affairs).
CONGRESSIONAL RECORD, Vol. 123 (1977):
    Apr. 20, considered and passed House.
    May 5, considered and passed Senate, amended, in lieu of S. 69.
    June 7, Senate agreed to conference report.
    June 10, House agreed to conference report.

WEEKLY COMPILATION OF PRESIDENTIAL DOCUMENTS, Vol. 13, No. 26:
    June 22, Presidential statement.

A SELECTED BIBLIOGRAPHY

Guidance can be obtained from study of the following source materials, which include documents, texts, and periodicals.

U.S. Department of Commerce Publications
Washington 25, D.C.

Comprehensive Export Schedule with amendments. (Export license requirements and restrictions.)

Export and Import Practice (A comprehensive handbook on foreign trade.)

Guides for New World Traders

Report No. FT-410--United States Exports of Domestic and Foreign Merchandise--Commodity by Country of Destination. Published annually. (Request that of the last calendar year.)

Report No. FT-420--United States Exports of Domestic and Foreign Merchandise--Country of Destination by Subgroup. Published annually. (Request that of the last calendar year.)

Schedule B--Statistical Classification of Domestic and Foreign Commodities Exported from the United States

Foreign Trade (Basic information Sources)

Foreign Commerce Yearbook

Foreign Commerce and Navigation of the U. S.

Modern Export Packing

Distribution Data Guide (Monthly Publication)

Books

Bross, Steward R. *Ocean Shipping.* Centreville, Md.; Cornell Maritime Press, 1956.

Cheng, P.C. *Financial Management in the Shipping Industry.* Centreville, Md.; Cornell Maritime Press, 1979.

Cooley, H.B. *Chartering and Charter Parties.* Centreville, Md.; Cornell Maritime Press, 1974.

Datz, I.M. *Planning Tools for Ocean Transportation.* Centreville, Md.; Cornell Maritime Press, 1971.

Dover, Victor. *Analysis of Marine and Other Insurance Clauses.* London, England; Witherby & Co., Ltd., 1956.

Fair, Marvin L. *Port Administration in the United States.* Centreville, Md.; Cornell Maritime Press, 1954.

Guaranty Trust Company of New York. *A Review of Export and Import Procedure.* New York, N.Y.; Guaranty Trust Company of New York.

Hazard, J.L. *Transportation: Management—Economics—Policy.* Centreville, Md.; Cornell Maritime Press, 1976.

Huebner, C.C., and Kramer, H.L. *Foreign Trade Principles and Practices.* New York, N.Y.; Appleton-Century-Crofts, Inc., 1952.

Kendall, L.C. *The Business of Shipping.* Centreville, Md.; Cornell Maritime Press, 3rd Edition 1979.

Knauth. *Ocean Bills of Lading.* Baltimore, Md.; American Maritime Cases, Inc., 1953.

McDowell, C.E., and Gibbs, Helen. *Ocean Transportation.* New York, N.Y.; McGraw Hill Book Co., Inc., 1954.

Moran, Charles J., *Handbook of Export Traffic.* New York, N.Y.; Duell, Sloane and Pearce, 1954.

Morgan Guaranty Trust Company of New York. *A Review of Export and Import Procedure.* New York, N.Y.; Morgan Guaranty Trust Company of New York.

Murr, Alfred. The Foreign Freight Forwarder. New York, N.Y.; New York University Press, 1947.

Nelson, J.R., Ed. *Criteria for Transport Pricing.* Centreville, Md.; Cornell Maritime Press, 1972.

Pratt, *Foreign Trade Handbook.* New York, N.Y.; Prentice Hall, Inc., 1952.

Rosenthal, Morris S. *Techniques of International Trade*. New York, N.Y.; McGraw Hill Book Co., Inc., 1950.

Stufflebeam, G.T. *Traffic Dictionary*. New York, N.Y.; Simmons-Boardman Books, 1950.

Turner, H.A. *Insurance of Exports*. London, England; Witherby and Company Ltd., 1952.

Unz & Co., *Foreign Consular and Customs Invoice Preparation Handbook*. 190 Baldwin Ave., P.O. Box 308, Jersey City, N.J. 07303

Winter, William D. *Marine Insurance: Its Principles and Practice*. New York, N.Y.; McGraw Hill Book Co., Inc., 1952.

Magazines—Annual Publications

Air Shippers' Manual. New York, N.Y.; Import Publications, Inc.
Air Transportation. New York, N.Y.
American Import and Export Bulletin. New York, N.Y.
Brandon's Shipper and Forwarder. New York, N.Y.
Business International. New York, N.Y.
The Customs House Guide. New York, N.Y.
Exporter's Digest and International Trade Review. New York, N.Y.
Exporter's Encyclopedia. New York, N.Y.; Thomas Ashwell & Co., Inc.
Export Trade and Shipper. New York, N.Y.; Thomas W. Ashwell & Co., Inc.
Shipping Digest Inc., New York, N.Y.

European Publications

Journal de la Marine Marchande. Paris, France.
Forwarders Index of the International Journal of Transportation. Basel, Switzerland.
Verkehr (Traffic) Transportation Journal. Vienna, Austria.
Transport-Dienst. Hamburg, Germany.
Holland Shipping and Trading. Rotterdam, Netherlands.
Transportation Kroniek. Antwerp, Belgium.

Index